Patricia Neal

Patricia Neal

AN UNQUIET LIFE

STEPHEN MICHAEL SHEARER

THE UNIVERSITY PRESS OF KENTUCKY

For more information about Stephen Michael Shearer, go to
www.smsmybooks.com.

Scholarly publisher for the Commonwealth,
serving Bellarmine University, Berea College, Centre
College of Kentucky, Eastern Kentucky University,
The Filson Historical Society, Georgetown College,
Kentucky Historical Society, Kentucky State University,
Morehead State University, Murray State University,
Northern Kentucky University, Transylvania University,
University of Kentucky, University of Louisville,
and Western Kentucky University.
All rights reserved.

Editorial and Sales Offices: The University Press of Kentucky
663 South Limestone Street, Lexington, Kentucky 40508-4008
www.kentuckypress.com

The Library of Congress has cataloged the hardcover edition as follows:

Shearer, Stephen Michael, 1951-
 Patricia Neal : an unquiet life / Stephen Michael Shearer.
  p. cm.
 Includes bibliographical references and index.
 ISBN-13: 978-0-8131-2391-2 (hardcover : alk. paper)
 ISBN-10: 0-8131-2391-7 (alk. paper)
 1. Neal, Patricia, 1926- 2. Actors—United States—Biography. I. Title.
PN2287.N33S54 2006
791.43'028'092—dc22
2005035533
ISBN 978-0-8131-2971-6 (pbk. : alk. paper)
ISBN 978-0-8131-7136-4 (ebook)

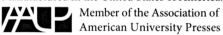

TO MY FATHER, ROBERT DEAN,
who showed me the value of books.

TO MY MOTHER, BILLIE MELBA,
who taught me how to read.

TO MY PARTNER AND COMPANION, MICHAEL,
who has supported and encouraged me.

TO MAXWELL AND MADELEINE,
who give me love and companionship.

AND TO MS. PATRICIA NEAL,
*whose friendship and gentle encouragement
I deeply appreciate.*

Contents

Part 3. Legend

Photo galleries follow pages 82, 178, and 274

A Note from Kirk Douglas

Patricia is a remarkable woman. She is extremely talented and of course very beautiful. I have known her for many years and my admiration for her courage grew with each year.

Of course, she is a very talented actress. That's a given. But as a person, her wisdom and character constantly grows.

She has faced many misfortunes in her life with extreme dignity. She has been an inspiration to me and to many, many other people. And with all that, she has retained that delicious sense of humor. Maybe by now you are getting the impression that I like and admire Patricia a lot. You are right!

Kirk Douglas

Preface to the Paperback Edition

After *Patricia Neal: An Unquiet Life* was published in 2006, Patricia Neal offered to endorse and promote the book at major book signings in New York, Washington, D.C., and California, as well as to attend various film festivals and other high-profile venues along with me. We taped several television interviews, including one on Martha's Vineyard that I was asked to host after another interviewer had been scheduled. Patricia asked me shortly before taping, "But darling, why you? You already know the answers." I explained that the station had asked me at the last minute. The resulting interview is the longest uninterrupted, filmed conversation Patricia Neal ever gave. Her comments and anecdotes were sharp and clear, and she never missed a beat. I am very proud of that experience.

During my book tour in June 2006, Patricia appeared live on the televised 60th Tony Awards ceremony. As she and Bill Irwin, actor and comedian, presented an award, Irwin interrupted the proceedings and handed Patricia a special Tony Award to replace the one that she had lost many years ago. She told me later how deeply moved she was to receive it, and she proudly displayed it next to her Oscar and Golden Globe awards in her Manhattan apartment.

On February 14, 2007, she was honored at the commonwealth of Kentucky's 2006 Governor's Awards in the Arts ceremony held in the Capitol Rotunda in Frankfort. Because Patricia was unable to attend, she sent me on her behalf to accept from Governor Ernie Fletcher a mixed-media glass art object, designed by Dan Neil Barnes. I brought it to her apartment in New York, where she proudly placed it in her living room, in front of the picture window overlooking the East River.

Early in 2007, independent film producer and director Jim Amatulli (*Artworks*) sent Patricia a script entitled "Encore." It was good, unlike many other scripts she had received over the years. I encouraged her to do it, Patricia agreed, and her people made the arrangements. It was her first film in ten years, and she adored Jim Amatulli, with whom she and I had once shared a limousine ride to the airport. The picture became *Flying By,* and it was filmed in late 2007 in San Diego. Patricia was well prepared and professional, and she gave an emotionally sincere performance. I was fortunate to have had a small role in a scene with her in the film.

Flying By, ARTE Films—Encore Partners, Lifetime, 90 minutes, April 18, 2009. Executive producers, Oscar Jarnicki and Jack E. Brown; producers, Jim Amatulli, Eric Abrahamson, and Jonathan McHugh; co-producer, Sanford Hampton; written and directed by Jim Amatulli; art director, Sharon Davis; set design, Charlie Brownell; original music, Geoff Levin; cinematography, Chris Chonym; costumes, Sherrie Jordan; costume supervisor, Tony Crawford; make-up, Lisa Ashley (for Ms. Locklear), Katie Kilkenny, Breanne McNally, and Gabby Suarez; editor, Howard Heard; unit production manager, Sanford Hampton. *Cast:* Billy Ray Cyrus (George Barron), Heather Locklear (Pamela Barron), Oleysa Rulin (Ellie Barron), Patricia Neal (Margie Barron), Mo Collins (Kate), Judith Hoag (Vicki), Ted Hutton (Freddy), Arabella Field (Beth), Robert Gossett (Michael), Eric Allan Kramer (Steve), Myk Watford (Willy), Stephen Michael Shearer (Doctor), David Zayas (Tony), Gene Rathwohl (Rick), Kevin Montgomery (Young George).

After the filming, Patricia accompanied me to La Jolla, the site of her 1951 stage performance in *The Cocktail Party* and of Gary Cooper's coyness with reporters. We did an important book signing at D.G. Wills Books. That night she was reunited with her former TV movie daughter, actress and author Mary McDonough, and she was able to meet her favorite leading man Victor Mature's daughter, Victoria. Both women had come down from Los Angeles to see her. Patricia loved that evening. A luncheon with her in Hollywood the next day was the last time I ever saw my friend Patricia Neal.

During the last three years of her life, I continued to speak with Patricia monthly on the telephone. Whether on the East Coast or West Coast, at Martha's Vineyard or in England, Patricia maintained an active schedule and was sometimes hard to reach. She was continuously on the move, constantly busy—travelling with the Theater Guild on their last cruises, appearing in a couple of documentaries, and being feted with numerous awards and tributes. During these years, Patricia's daughter, Ophelia, gave birth to a son, Luke, and she attended the weddings of her granddaughters, Sophie and Clover. As many of her costars and friends passed away, Patricia often spoke with me about the sadness she felt at their dying. And she sounded tired. She was especially grieved by the deaths of her longtime friend Helen Horton and Paul Newman, the last of her leading men.

Health issues continued to plague Patricia. She suffered another minor stroke but recovered surprisingly quickly. In February 2010, she fell and shattered her hip while visiting her daughter, Lucy, in California. Pneumonia set in, and X-rays taken at the hospital exposed a malignant spot on one lung. Friends were told that it had been dealt with and that Patricia was "taking it one day at a time." I knew of Patricia's illness. I knew she had bounced back so many times, and I truly expected her to recover from this difficulty; however, she was dying. On March 30, she converted to Catholicism and made her final arrangements with Mother Dolores Hart, prioress of the Abbey of Regina Laudis. Patricia returned to her Martha's Vineyard home and to her loyal housekeeper and companion, Ruth Parks. She surrounded herself with family and friends as she had done every summer on the Vineyard for nearly thirty years.

I last spoke with Patricia on July 26, 2010, and at the end of our conversation I told her she sounded healthy and strong. Her reply stunned me, "Well, that's what they say. But baby, some day I am just not going to wake up. I hope you will come to my funeral." I told her I loved her, and she told me the same. The evening of August 7, I am told, she held a dinner party at her home on the Vineyard. As guests were leaving, she remarked, "I've had a marvelous time." Patricia died the next day. After a family service on the Vineyard, she was buried in a handmade wooden coffin on the grounds of her beloved Abbey of Regina Laudis.

Patricia Neal had so many friends that it seemed everyone knew her. Like many stars and celebrities, she was constantly surrounded by what I call "limelight people," who basked in her attention and reflected glory. To me, Patricia was a close and dear friend for nearly twenty years. I asked nothing of her but to be her friend, and she allowed me that privilege and in addition encouraged me to write her definitive biography. When Patricia Neal passed away, I lost a very important person in my life. She was my muse, taking delight in my writing of *Patricia Neal;* she gave me credibility. She was happy when I wrote a short story entitled "September" for her because she wanted to work with Jack Nicholson. "Well, you'd better hurry, dear," she chuckled when I told her I had begun it. Perhaps she knew her time was coming to a close. When I finally read it to her, we laughed and cried together, and although she liked it, her death cut short the opportunity to see it produced with her.

Fortunately for us all, Patricia Neal left a remarkable legacy of film and television work. She was the last of America's great dramatic stage and screen actresses, and she died as she had lived—with great dignity and class. There will never be another like Patricia Neal. She was, and will always be, a star.

S. M. S.

May 2011

Preface

I met Patricia Neal many years ago in New York when I was performing in Luigi Jannuzzi's off-Broadway play *The Appointment*. It won the Samuel French Award that year. Ms. Neal, along with Philip and Marilyn Langner of the Theatre Guild, came to see the play one night, and we met afterward. At some point during our first conversation I told Ms. Neal of my interest in her career. I was of course familiar with her life and its struggles and triumphs. Her film output I only knew in parts. I did not know that she had produced such a large and important body of work.

One thing I discovered in my research for this book was how highly respected her career has been, revered by both contemporary critics and her professional colleagues. In studying her work and viewing rare television and film footage, I was pleasantly surprised to find so many truly strong performances by her. Her stage work in particular consistently garnered the highest praise, and her film performances, especially those of her middle career, received remarkable consideration.

Those whom I interviewed for this book love Patricia Neal and fondly recalled the pleasure of having worked with her. Without exception they gave generously of their time and memories in interviews. I count myself fortunate to have had for this, my first book, such a beloved and respected subject. The late Robert Stack told me, "Look, son, I don't write other people's books for them by giving interviews about people I worked with. But for you I will make an exception because it is Patricia, and she is still alive and well . . . and she is magnificent."

When I advised Ms. Neal that I was writing this book, she was forthright in telling me to be honest and to chronicle her life "warts and all." When the original manuscript was completed, I read it to her. Except for a couple of corrections for accuracy—no vanity issues were allowed—she asked for no specific changes. What I've taken from this is simple.

Patricia Neal is surely regarded as one of America's greatest living dramatic actresses. Neal's work has been abundant and varied; some have been masterpieces, some disasters. Her acting captured on film is a joy to behold. Her style of performance is natural and always rings true. And she brings to each of her projects her own unique qualities.

My greatest pleasure in seeing this work completed is to now share with the reader Patricia Neal's humor and sincere truth. I have had the pleasure of traveling with her to several festivals and events over the past few years, and I have witnessed her keen observations of her surroundings and her genuine interest in the people she meets.

Patricia Neal is first and foremost an actress. She is also a truly Southern woman, with solid, traditional values. Always warm and approachable, she's a formidable mother and grandmother and a decidedly wonderful audience for a good joke. She is a survivor and a role model, an advocate for research, education, and rehabilitation for stroke survivors and their families. And not surprising, Patricia Neal is a sincerely honest individual. (Her former husband once said she was the only truthful person he ever knew.) She is many things.

For me Patricia Neal has become a good friend. And for that reason, among so many other deeply appreciated qualities, I have written this book about her life and career with love and candor.

Acknowledgments

For a majority of the personal photographs and the use of letters, I must thank Patricia Neal and Reverend Mother Dolores Hart, as well as the kind sisters of the Abbey of Regina Laudis, for their staunch support and the generous gift of their time. At the start of this project, I contacted those friends in the publishing field whose knowledge and advice I deeply trust. I want to thank Leonard Maltin, John Fricke, David Stenn, Jean-Claude Baker, the late Doug McClelland, Lyle Stuart, Eve Golden, Sam Staggs, Richard Bojarski, Robert Osborne, William H. Miller, Alexander Genis, William J. Mann, and Ted Sennett. For their kind help in translating Italian and Spanish materials for me, I want to thank Cheryl Mitchell and José Deleon.

From the beginning Leila Salisbury, acquisitions editor, and the complete staff of the University Press of Kentucky in Lexington have understood my passion for this book and have allowed me to work closely with them. I would also like to extend a most sincere and appreciative thanks to my editor, Cheryl Hoffman, with whom I shared many an intense discussion and from whom I have learned a great deal about this industry.

In my research, I used several resource centers. I would like to thank the following for their uncompromisingly diligent assistance and time. In Los Angeles: Janet Lorenz and B. Caroline Sisneros (Louis B. Mayer Library) at the American Film Institute; Christine Kreuger, Tony Guzman, Barbara Hall, and the staff of the Margaret Herrick Library; Leith Adams and Ned Comstock at the Cinema-TV Library of the University of Southern California; Jennifer Prindiville, Randi Hokett, and the staff at the Warner Brothers Library archive at the University of Southern California; Mark Quigley and Robert Gitt at the University of California, Los Angeles Media Lab; Mike Hawks and staff of the Larry Edmunds Bookshop; Cinema Collectors; Johnny Grant and Anna Holler at the Hollywood Chamber of Commerce. In London: Simone Potter, José de Esteban, Melissa Bramley, Nina Harding, and Natasha Fairbaim at the British Film Institute; Richard Dacre at Flashback's Memorabilia; and Erin O'Neill of the BBC London. In Rome: Aurora Palandrani of the Archivio Audiovisivo del

Movimento Operaio e Democratico. In Madrid: Cristina Bernaldez Navarro of the Cooperative Department of the Filmoteca Española. In Washington, D.C.: Leslie C. Concha of the National Rehabilitation Hospital. In Atlanta: Robert Osborne and Shane Joiner at Turner Classic Movies. In New York and New Jersey: Charles Silver at the Museum of Modern Art, New York; the staff at the New York City Public Library of Performing Arts; the New York Museum of Television and Radio Broadcasting; Ronald Mandelbaum at Photofest; Jerry Ohlinger at Movie Memorabilia Store; Yuien Chin at ABC; Rita Ecke Altomara, Susan Kumar, reference librarian, and the staff at the Fort Lee, New Jersey, Public Library; and the librarians and staff at the Englewood, New Jersey, Public Library. In Connecticut: Patricia Blaufuss and Deborah A. Celia of the Westport Country Playhouse; Reverend Mother Dolores Hart of the Abbey of Regina Laudis in Bethlehem. In Virginia: Richard Rose, Debbie Addison, Callie Harrill, and Stacy N. Fine at the Barter Theatre in Abingdon.

As the manuscript for the book began to take shape, I relied heavily on the proofreading of DeNisha Kay Williams McCollum and Christine "Trudy" Collins. For use of their personal photographs and materials, I wish to extend my sincere thanks to Peter Douglas, John Buonomo, Valerie Eaton Griffith, Emily Mahan Faust, Film Star Randal Malone and Michael Schwibs, William Schallert, Paul Newman, Ian Miles, Anne Bell, Johnny Grant, Ophelia Dahl, Joseph L. Nicolosi, Jo Anne Sexton, Jean Alexander, and James N. Bullington (official co-photographer of the Southwest Vision Film Festival, Roanoke).

A special "thank you" to all those magnificent participants in Ms. Neal's life and career whom I interviewed for this project, particularly Patricia Neal's family and close friends. And especially those who are no longer with us: Marlon Brando, Dorothy Hart, Eddie Albert, Elia Kazan, Barbara Bel Geddes, Elmer Bernstein, Phyllis Jenkins, Anne Bancroft, Buddy Ebsen, Robert Wise, Tony Randall, Robert Stack, Fielder Cook, Virginia Mayo, Anne Meacham, Anthony Franciosa, Shelley Winters, Darren McGavin, and Dr. Edmund Goodman. How fortunate I was to have met and spoken with these treasured souls. I want to give my deepest appreciation for his support and encouragement to my childhood friend, Tony Morris; since we were boys, he has always believed in and encouraged me. I would also like to thank for their support and assistance throughout this journey Anthony Macchio, Irina Genis, Liz Renay, Bush James, Watson Bosler, Mrs. Elia Kazan, Jeanai Ratcliffe, Eric Stenshoel, Stephen "Deet" Reed, David Stevenson, Gregg Smith and Rosalind Rees, Dedra Tiger, Lena McNicholas, Robert Weisfeld, David and Sarah Huddleston, the Citigroup Corporation, and Pastors Amandus Derr and John Damm, the choir members, and my church family at Saint Peter's Lutheran Church in midtown Manhattan.

Part I

Actress

In the autumn of 1958, I underwent the most intense theatrical experience of my life to date. It came in the last ten minutes of the London production of Tennessee Williams's *Suddenly Last Summer*, when Patricia Neal . . . stood centre-stage with a single spotlight illuminating her pale, high-cheekboned features, gazed fixedly and hauntedly out across the footlights. . . .

Her long narrative speeches became declamations, incantations of virtuosity in breath-control and diction, always clear and coherent no matter what speed or urgency they were taken. At times, the urgency and speed of them made me quiver and stiffen in my seat. The pulsing "Run, run, run!" describing her reaction to the sight of the murdered poet Sebastian's corpse was followed by a huge, saw-edged, diminuendo scream torn from her depths, shattering and terrifying in impact. And the final numbed sentence, the last, still half-incredulous words, "White . . . wall," hung with paralyzing hollow slowness in the awed, electrified air of the auditorium. . . .

I heard once or twice the saliva rattle in my taut throat; and when she straightened, she appeared ten feet tall. As the curtain fell . . . there was a silence in the house which continued momentarily afterwards, before the engulfing thunder of applause. . . .

Why do I reprint those sensations at such length now? Because they reflect, in my view, the quintessence of what acting in the theatre may afford us.

—Douglas McVay, "The Art of the Actor," *Film and Filming*, 1973

1

Beginnings

A life is made up of a great number of small incidents and a small number of great ones.

—Roald Dahl, *Going Solo* (1986)

Patsy Louise Neal was born at 4:40 A.M. on January 20, 1926, in the small mining town of Packard, Kentucky. Packard, which at its peak had about four hundred residents, thrived for nearly fifty years, until its coal was depleted shortly after World War II. Founded as a mining camp soon after the turn of the last century by the Thomas B. Mahan family of Williamsburg, Kentucky, it took its name from a popular local schoolteacher, Brooklyn-born Mary Amelia Packard. It lay in a hollow lodged deep within the southernmost range of the Appalachian Mountains, in the lower southeast corner of Kentucky in what is today Whitley County.

The family houses in Packard were modest, their foundations camouflaged during warm months with scrub poplar, ash, and maple trees; pea vines; the white blooms of bloodroot; and bursts of purple Jack-in-the-pulpit. Front-yard gardens sported roses and chrysanthemums. Homes had no indoor plumbing and no electricity until the 1930s. Water had to be carried inside from outdoor wells for cooking, cleaning, and bathing, and oil lamps were used at night. Toilets usually were located in the garden. Packard families worshipped together at the only house of prayer in town, the Free Will Baptist Church. On warm, lazy afternoons, miners would gather outside of the commissary store to play checkers, chat, or strum guitars. There was even a hometown string band.

"The way of life in Packard had much to recommend it. It was a close-knit community whose citizens cared about one another," recalled Dr. Jo

Facing page: Patsy Neal at age twelve, 1938. From the Patricia Neal Collection.

Anne Sexton, who grew up there. "Former residents of Packard make no claim of objectivity regarding this little community. . . . [M]any harbor the irrational opinion that it was one of the finest settlements in all the history of the human race."[1]

Today Packard is gone. Just the crumbling foundations of a few buildings are left on what is now privately owned property. One must have permission even to visit the area.

The lone town doctor was Pascal Gennings Petrey, a friendly, rotund man. His wife, the former Flora Jane Siler—a descendant of one of the first families to settle in the area—was a rather distant and apparently none-too-affectionate woman. The Petreys had four daughters, Della Tople, Eura Mildred, Ima Victory, and Virginia Siler, who all adored their father and spoiled him with attention. Eura, their second child (born September 21, 1899) was an extremely tenacious, determined, and attractive young woman. Very well liked and quite popular around Packard, she had left boarding school at the age of sixteen when her beloved eighteen-month-old sister Virginia died. She returned to Packard in 1917 and soon after encountered the new transportation manager of the Mahan Jellico Coal Company (later known as the Southern Coal and Coke Company), William Burdette "Coot" Neal. The two met at a social gathering to play the popular card game Rook. The hostess was a local schoolteacher named Bertha Snyder, who had her sights set on the handsome Neal. Eura, however, made it firmly known that Neal was for her, and the couple began dating.

Coot Neal was the third child of W. D. (William David) "Willie" Neal and his wife, the former Mary Lucy Fitzgerald of Shockee, Virginia. Their marriage produced five sons and one daughter. Lucy Neal was a very loving, extremely attractive, and very large woman who "worked like a man and ate like a man."[2] In 1914, still young, she died of a heart attack while sitting at her kitchen table. Soon after, W. D. married Mollie Cox, a rather homely, good-hearted woman. "Miss Mollie" was the grandmother that the Neal children would remember. Coot was born in Shockee on January 29, 1895, and attended high school at the Hargrave Military Academy in Chatham, Virginia. He had beautiful brown eyes and as an adult stood six feet tall. He was heavy like his mother and eventually weighed almost 260 pounds. Blessed with a terrific sense of humor, Coot did have a temper, which would flare up on rare occasions. He was best known, however, for his kindness and compassion, traits acquired by his children.

His only sister, Maude, had attended Cumberland College in Williamsburg, where she met and married Packard coal company manager Will Mahan in 1911. Through this family connection Coot began working for the coal company in 1914 and remained employed with them for the next thirty years. He was considered a friendly fellow around Packard and was regarded as "the most popular man in town."[3] Coot Neal and Eura Petrey were married on November 5, 1918, the week before the end of World War I. They set up housekeeping down the road from the Petreys in a four-room wood-frame house with a coal-burning fireplace and a full front porch.

For a brief time Eura worked as the coal company's bookkeeper alongside her husband. Above his desk was a plaque (which his second daughter would eventually inherit) with a motto reading, "Organization is the art of getting men to respond like thoroughbreds. When you call upon a thoroughbred he gives you all the speed, strength of heart and sinew in him. When you call upon a jackass, he kicks." These were words Patsy liked and would live by her entire life.

On March 8, 1924, the Neals became the parents of a baby girl. They named her Margaret Ann. Two years later, Eura gave birth at home to a second daughter, who was named Patsy Louise at the suggestion of her aunt Ima. The eight-pound, twenty-two-inch infant was born with blue eyes, which would eventually turn hazel, and not a hair on her head. By all accounts she was a bubbly and happy baby. Margaret Ann was not the least bit impressed with this family intruder, however. Upon seeing baby Patsy for the first time, she simply remarked, "Well, if it isn't Bill," and toddled out of the room.[4] Patsy's family would call her "Bill" for years to come.

Late in 1928, Coot was offered a better-paying position as assistant traffic manager with the Southern Coal and Coke Company, as Mahan Jellico was now called, at its main offices in Knoxville, Tennessee. This meant uprooting the family, and he was reluctant to do so. But Eura wrote her husband a heartfelt letter encouraging him to accept the position.

In 1929, three-year-old Patsy Neal's rural and bucolic existence in the tranquility and security of Packard came to an end. "My family was always happy there," she would recall.[5]

Coot Neal began his new position with the coal company in early 1929, setting up his office on the fifteenth floor of the Hamilton Building on Gay Street, in the center-city area of Knoxville. The family moved into a small brick house on Parkview Avenue, along with Eura's unmarried sister Ima, who had come to live with them.

Knoxville was an industrial center in 1929, not at all the type of town the

Neals were accustomed to. Settled in 1791, it had had a long and turbulent past. During the Civil War, Knoxville was part of the Confederacy but was captured in 1863 by Union troops. During Reconstruction, it became the central location in the Southeast for the shipping of such products as marble, furniture, and cloth. Industrialization in the city boomed throughout the first part of the 1900s. With the onset of the Depression came a decline in industry and the first steps of the gradual deterioration of housing within the city center. Social standing within this industrial southern community was then, as it is even now, of supreme importance.

To escape the "citified ways" of Knoxville, the Neals made the ninety-mile, three-hour drive back to Packard two or three times a month. On these visits "Pappy" Petrey would give each Neal girl a nickel or a dime. The significance of the gesture was not lost on either child. From that first Easter in Knoxville, Patsy remembered wanting a new coat that her mother thought was too expensive. Insisting that she had the money to pay for it, Patsy offered up her few accumulated coins. Eura quietly provided the balance, and the coat was Patsy's. This was a decisive moment in the young girl's life. It was the very first time Patsy Neal found that she would have to pay for something she wanted. It would not be the last.

Patsy later recalled, "I didn't really get along with my sister. She was spoiled and she wanted her way all the time."[6] Both girls developed strong and independent personalities in competition for their parents' attention. "[Margaret Ann] was the librarian. I was the actress. She always wanted to play library and she'd have me check out a book, then two minutes later announce it was overdue. Me, I liked baseball," she once said.[7] They both slept in the same bed until they were eleven and thirteen years old, kicking and tussling with each other until they fell asleep.

When Patsy returned from the hospital after having her tonsils removed in 1935, Eura told the girls that a new baby was on the way. On December 22 of that year, William Petrey "Pete" Neal was born. When little Pete began to speak, he could not say his older sister Margaret Ann's name. He called her "NiNi," and the name stuck. Coot Neal was promoted to traffic controller for the coal company in 1935, and the family moved into a new house on the same block, at 2500 Parkview Avenue. Patsy would recall years later playing on the expansive front porch, giving little plays "on my stage."[8]

Patsy adored her father. In February 1936, both Coot Neal and his sister-in-law Della Tople were admitted to Johns Hopkins Hospital in Baltimore, and ten-year-old Patsy wrote him:

Dear Papa,

I hope you are feeling O.K. I am in the main show at the school carnival and so proud I could bust. I have to tap dance and of course say my part.

Pete is good in the day but mean in the night. I am a little bit jealous of him.

My birthday party was a success. I got stationary [sic], money and a whole lot of things. I doubt if you can read this because the stationary is so rough. I bet both of you are homesick.

Love, Patsy Lou

P.S. The reason I put Lou—I didn't think you would know my name if I didn't. Love again.[9]

This school carnival at her Knoxville grade school was perhaps one of Patsy's very first performances. Her desire to publicly "say my part," even at that age, was prophetic.

In 1936, Patsy's beloved grandfather "Pappy" Petrey died, and his loss affected Patsy deeply.

Late that year, the Neals moved once again, this time to 1415 Kenesaw Avenue, down the street from the Magnolia Avenue Methodist Church. Though they were Baptist, Patsy's parents allowed her to attend services at the Methodist church with her girlfriend Mary Emma Thompson. A turning point in Patsy's life occurred one evening soon after her grandfather's death when she and Mary Emma attended a revival meeting. "The most beautiful lady was standing at the altar. She was dressed in a pure white robe. She would have captured me by her looks alone, but when she spoke, her voice wrapped around me," Patricia later wrote. "She spread her hands and the shimmering robe opened wide in appeal."[10] Glorifying the love of God for all mankind, the woman so captivated Patsy that she attended the revival again the following two nights. When on the last evening the evangelist called, "Come," all of the drama and the emotions of the moment led Patsy to move forward in tears and receive the woman's blessings.

Soon after, a young classmate, Jane Hunter, died unexpectedly. The child's mother told Patsy that her daughter had told her just before her last breath that she had seen angels beckoning her. When no one could answer Patsy's profound questions about life, love, death, and angels, her concerned mother sought the help of neighbor Cornelia Avantini, who was Patsy's schoolteacher.

Miss Avantini told Patsy that Jane would rise from the dead on Judgment Day, and that not only did Patsy's parents and sister love her, but that she did as well. Sensing Patsy's fears regarding the briefness of life and the suddenness of death, Miss Avantini said, "There are so many things you want to do. Now do them!" Patricia later recalled, "Cornelia Avantini's influence on my life was to be more significant than either of us could have imagined."[11]

Answers and opportunities were soon in coming. In September 1936, the local paper announced that Miss Emily Mahan, daughter of Ed Mahan (brother of coal company manager Will Mahan), had graduated after two years' study at the New York School of the Theatre and was returning to Knoxville to begin teaching acting classes. That Christmas, Patsy placed in her stocking above the fireplace a brief message to Santa, written on the cardboard from one of her father's laundered shirts: "Dear Santa—What I want for Christmas is to study dramatics. *Please.*"

"It's not exactly an uncommon decision for an eleven-year-old girl," Patsy told a magazine writer many years later about her desire to be an actress. "Life in Knoxville wasn't too exciting."[12] And excitement was what Patsy craved.

Shortly after her eleventh birthday, she was accepted into the Emily Mahan School of Drama. Located over a tire company on C. Dean Block, the space was a former dance studio, a large loft with a potbellied stove. Miss Mahan offered "Courses in Acting," which included technique, "creation of roles," and scene study; "Special Lessons," which included voice technique and diction; and a "Regular Course," which included pantomime, improvisation, and "voice culture." For some time Emily Mahan had been performing readings and monologues at clubs and women's groups around Knoxville. Her Monday night classes and private lessons eventually produced several students of merit who began to appear at functions about town. Patsy was one of her first students, and perhaps her favorite. The girl caught a bus twice a week after school for a one-hour dramatics class. She always felt she got much more from her hours of study with Miss Mahan than from the time she spent at school. And Emily Mahan sensed and encouraged Patsy's budding talent.

"She had a gift," Emily would later say of Patsy Neal. "She definitely had talent. She wasn't self-conscious," although she was tall and somewhat of "a big overgrown girl," Emily said. "There wasn't much of a drama department at the school, and I gave her monologues that were humorous, and people would compliment her."[13] Starting in 1937 with Miss Mahan's Annual Spring Recital, a program of music and monologues, Patsy began speaking and performing monologues publicly, gaining confidence and ability. "Those appearances gave me a new sense of confidence that carried over at school," she later recalled.

In May of that year, Patsy appeared in her first play, *Twilight Alley*, portraying an elderly and crotchety tenement woman. Produced at her Knoxville grade school, featuring fifth and sixth graders, the play was an unusual concoction billed as "an operetta," even though fellow performer Elizabeth Marshall, writing in 1977, noted that "none of us could really sing."[14]

In school Patsy gained social recognition through her dramatics, participating in various acting activities and state speech tournaments. She was a Girl Scout briefly, "but not a very good one," she confessed years later.[15] Already having reached her adult height of five feet eight inches by the age of thirteen in 1939, the bubbly and attractive teenager developed a crush on a particular boy. Her childhood friend Gloria Lucas Young recalled, "We were both in love with a boy in our class at the same time. Bill Allen, I believe was his name . . . and we were both taller than him. She [Patsy] would stoop when she was around him. Patsy once directed us in an English class production of *Romeo and Juliet*. I was 'Juliet' and Bill Allen was 'Romeo.' When he kissed me, Patsy was heartsick."[16]

Gloria said that Patsy "would play anything just to have the opportunity to perform. A mother role was fine with her. When *Gone With the Wind* came out, we all went to see it, of course. Patsy probably saw it more than once. She had a quick memory and would do all the parts. She would do them in the girl's room, falling down on the tile and carrying on. She was marvelous—so good and so funny!"[17]

Patsy dreamed of becoming an actress. Wrote NiNi, "Mother and Dad were very helpful to her and gave her all the encouragement she needed. At recitals, Dad was always so proud of her. I shall never forget the one occasion when Dad took Mother and Pat to a movie one night and when they walked up to the front of the theatre, Pat looked up and said, 'Daddy, you are going to see my name up there in lights someday!'"[18]

In the fall of 1941, Patsy attended a play produced by the community little-theatre group, the Tennessee Valley Players (TVP). Attracted to the play's leading man, the dashing Wesley Davis, Patsy decided to join the group. The first time she spoke with Davis, he asked if he could call on her at dinner at home that same evening. Patsy ran home to get ready. To clear her conscience, and with strong insistence and encouragement from her mother, Patsy gathered up all the knives and forks that she had swiped from various eateries around town—Miller's Grill, the Blue Circle, Lane's Drug Store, Todd and Armstrong's—and returned them. Then she raced home, placed herself in front of her vanity mirror and anxiously waited for the handsome Wesley to come knocking at the door. Her heart swooned as he was invited into the Neal home that evening. But after supper, instead of concentrating on Patsy, the young Wesley spent the evening talking to Coot about insurance. Patsy's heart was broken.

Having assured her parents that joining the Tennessee Valley Players would not interfere with her schoolwork, Patsy auditioned for the group's first production of its ninth season, *Penny Wise*. After she read a few lines, she was given a substantial role in the production. Determined to prove herself worthy of Wesley's attention, she plunged into her part. Local critic Frank Friske wrote, "Outstanding honors for the feminine contingent go to . . . Miss Neal. . . . [S]he was exceptionally good. She seemed sure of herself throughout all three acts." But another local critic wrote that fifteen-year-old Patsy Neal "posed about the stage a great deal with a cigarette in her hand. It is doubtful that she knows anything about acting—or smoking either, for that matter."[19]

However, it was the powerful music and theatre critic Malcolm Miller of the *Knoxville Journal* who most strongly championed Patsy. His influence and interest in her budding career was essential. "Knoxville High School's Patsy Neal made her debut with the Tennessee Valley Players in the role of 'Martha,' and just about walked off with the show," he wrote in his review. "She had grace and poise; her reactions were well timed and natural; her reading was nicely pointed, and her voice projection was splendid."[20] From that moment on, Miller was enchanted with her.

The sudden attack on Pearl Harbor on Sunday, December 7, 1941, had a sobering effect on America's youth. Patsy's readings and monologues soon took on more serious and patriotic tones. After her performance in *Penny Wise*, invitations to speak in recitals started rolling in. With her Aunt Maude acting as her "manager," Patsy became quite a familiar personality around Knoxville and the surrounding communities. "When she got to high school, Patsy Neal made impressive arrivals each morning in her [family's] 1941 Fleetwood Cadillac," wrote Louisville *Courier-Journal* journalist Keith Runyon in 1973.[21] Another classmate, Louis Schneider, recalled, "She was always big in chapel, doing readings. The first time I knew I was in the presence of greatness was in 'small chapel' in the 10th grade. It was the first monologue, and I can't remember what she recited. But it was very sad, and she shed real tears. Remember this was a 16-year-old girl. She stopped reading and looked up, and everybody saw those tears roll down her cheeks all the way to the floor."[22]

Patsy also performed in local plays, such as the Masquers Dramatic Club's *One Wild Night* and the Knoxville Junior League's 1942 production *Nice Going America*, and worked backstage in two TVP productions, *The Shining Hour* and *The Philadelphia Story*. In the TVP's *Hay Fever*, she finally costarred opposite the raffish Wesley Davis, but her unrequited love for him had long been extinguished, as he had a girlfriend. As her interest in Wesley Davis declined, her popularity within the community continued to grow.

Patricia was becoming a young woman, with remarkably photogenic beauty. In February 1942, she was selected at the Ski Carnival Ball in Gatlinburg as an attendant in the court of the 1942 Queen of the First Annual Smoky Mountain Ski Club Carnival. A full-page photo layout in a local newspaper pictured the queen (who had been preselected) and her court, showcasing Patsy and the other contestants smiling cordially and modeling the latest in skiwear.

On Sunday, March 29, 1942, the *Knoxville Journal* featured Patsy in a lengthy article, probably written by Malcolm Miller, accompanied by a flattering photograph.

> There's a new personality rising to prominence in Knoxville—a sparkling, vivacious personality who, many are predicting, will rise right out of Knoxville and shine as a Broadway star some day. And who knows. . . . The object of all this speculation is 16-year-old Patsy Neal, KHS junior, who has entertained hundreds in the past few months with her brilliantly done monologues and dramatic presentations. Patsy isn't just another stage-struck school girl who recites a few lines and adds an awkward gesture. . . . [H]er disarming, professional style has left her audience breathless with admiration and clamoring for more. . . . Definite plans are being made for Patsy to continue studying for her chosen career after she completes high school next year. The school will probably be the American Academy of Dramatic Arts in New York.[23]

Patsy's ambitious plans were already in motion. If she was accepted into the nearby Barter Theatre acting colony in Abingdon, Virginia, she would be allowed to study and perform alongside professionals during the summer. After an exchange of letters, and a good word from Malcolm Miller, who was a friend of theater head Robert Porterfield and his wife, Patsy was accepted into the summer program. In June 1942 Miller himself drove Patsy and his daughter to Abingdon. By the end of the summer, she knew her calling for certain. Patsy Neal was going to become an actress.

2

Progress

What is the hardest thing for an actor to learn? . . . It's the fact that he has to act with his total self—and he has to discover that's more than saying lines emotionally, or memorizing lines, or becoming a star. To act with your total self means to act with . . . your humanity, with your humanness.

—Alvina Krause, *Class Notes*, 1976–1978

In Abingdon, Patsy was not so far away from home that Coot and Eura couldn't keep an eye, or more accurately, an ear, on their ambitious second daughter. Patsy knew that her acceptance into the prestigious Barter Theatre colony would prove to be a major turning point of her life. Carrying a new suitcase that was a gift from her parents, sixteen-year-old Patsy made her first trip away from home. She was one of the last Barter apprentices chosen that year.

Abingdon, Virginia, is one of the oldest towns west of the Blue Ridge Mountains. There the summer months, with their warm and sunny days, are ideal for recreation and other leisure activities. Established in 1933 on the site of what was once Martha Washington College, the Barter Theatre took its name from the practice of exchanging food or other goods for the price of admission—fifty cents in 1942. In an August 1935 *Commonwealth* article, Arthur T. S. Kent wrote, "At the Barter Theatre, Broadway casts present to Southern audiences the best plays of recent years and promising new scripts at the rate of thirty-five cents per ticket or the equivalent in produce. No theatre has ever tried this scheme before, but the Barter group has yet to find it a losing proposition. . . . [T]he opening night receipts this year included, besides (a) calf, several chickens, a well-bred cat, and (an) eighteen pound ham, vegetables of almost every variety, cakes and canned goods."

During its first two years of operation, the acting colony resided at the

---

Facing page: Patsy Neal at age fifteen, 1941. From the Patricia Neal Collection.

Martha Washington Inn. Its productions were given at the historic Abingdon Opera House, where legendary actor Edwin Booth had once performed. Bob Porterfield hired apprentices locally, allowing them to work, learn, and develop alongside professionals during the summer season. Successful plays and new productions in tryout, whose producers hoped for a Broadway opening, appeared annually. In 1935, the Barter colony moved to the campus of Stonewall Jackson College, a former seminary, and its theater members resided in the large student dormitories. During the summer, plays were rehearsed two or three weeks before being performed for one week, playing Friday and Saturday nights at the former Opera House. The other four nights the productions played on tour in such towns as Marion, Bristol, Wytheville, Saltville, Lebanon, Glade Spring, and Damascus in Virginia; Johnson City and Mountain City in Tennessee; and Lincoln, North Carolina, all within a seventy-mile radius. On the evenings that the productions played in Abingdon, Bob Porterfield would make a speech that concluded with, "If you like us, talk about us. If you don't, just keep your mouth shut!"[1]

The summer of 1942 marked the tenth season of the Barter Theatre's operation and was its last until 1946. Among other apprentices accepted with Patsy for their first summer were the Welsh-born Margaret "Maggie" Phillips and twenty-one-year-old Grand Rapids, Michigan, native Elizabeth Wilson. The three young actresses would become fast friends.

Beginning the first week of June and closing on Labor Day, the Barter Theatre staged twelve productions each summer. In his unpublished memoirs, Porterfield wrote:

> Most of the fine young actors whose development I had been watching had already enlisted or been drafted by the summer of 1942. The women we had that summer, on the other hand, were an exceptional group. [There were twenty-five women and thirty-five men, including Porterfield, at Barter that summer.] Among the apprentices were Jocelyn Brando (Marlon's sister) . . . and Patricia Neal, a beautiful teenager whom the drama critic on the Knoxville paper had spotted and recommended to me. . . . The award winner that year, chosen by Mildred Natwick, was a Welsh girl with lightness and grace and a captivating throaty voice—Margaret Phillips. To utilize their talents we gave a number of plays calling for strong feminine casts, among them *Letters to Lucerne*, and a backstage romp entitled *No Boys Allowed*. To match the mood of a public that wanted to forget the war

and laugh when it came through the doors, we gave *The Man Who Came to Dinner*, *There's Always Juliet*, and *French Without Tears*. [2]

There were no acting classes at the Barter Theatre at this time. Training was done hands on. "You worked backstage doing everything like handling props, painting scenery, sewing costumes and cooking alongside other apprentices," remembered Elizabeth Wilson. "The Barter Theatre taught discipline and dedication."[3]

Patsy was eventually rewarded with her first Barter role. Before being cast she wrote her aunt Maude, "As I said before I am completely nutty about this place. . . . I am eating my heart out for the play they are casting now."[4] The production was *Thunder Rock*, a surreal drama staged by Alexander Ivo. Originally produced by the Group Theatre in New York in 1939, *Thunder Rock* had been directed by Elia Kazan and starred Frances Farmer. The Barter production opened on July 16, 1942. Patsy was cast in the role of Melanie, her youth giving her characterization a new and fresh perspective. Cast as Miss Kirby the suffragette was Elizabeth Wilson, who recalled, "As usual I was a little old frumpy person. She [Patsy] was the most beautiful girl I had ever seen in my life. Her voice was low, but it really didn't get (as) low until about 1947, 'through drinking and cigarettes and staying up late' she told me."[5] In this production Patsy was billed as "Patricia" for the first time.

Taken on tour, *Thunder Rock* played Knoxville on July 24. Malcolm Miller met the cast members that afternoon and interviewed them on his 5:15 P.M. local radio show. After the Barter group erected the set for the play, Coot and Eura Neal entertained them at their home with a dinner before the evening performance. Though somewhat taken aback by the attire and rowdiness of the troupe, the Neals were proud of their second daughter just the same. Gloria Lucas Young recalled, "Coot Neal was very proud and very supportive of Patsy. And so was her mother, though she just wasn't as interested."[6]

In his *Knoxville Journal* review, Malcolm Miller, as always, praised his protégée. He wrote, "Naturally I looked forward to the Barter Theatre's presentation of 'Thunder Rock' last Thursday, because it marked the Barter Theatre debut of Knoxville's Patricia ('Patsy') Neal; . . . Patsy Neal made a real 'hit' in her debut as 'Melanie.' . . . She assumed a slight foreign accent, just enough to add piquancy to the part, and she depicted the petulance of an impatient girl, the understanding of budding womanhood, and one fleeting moment of sweet romance, with delicate appreciation of those varying moods."[7]

Elizabeth Wilson never forgot that evening in Knoxville. "I was standing backstage waiting for my cue. I remember hearing [Patsy] deliver her lines

and thinking, 'Oh my God! She's really got it!' You know, there's just sometimes the way someone breathes . . . or the way they clear their throat, or the
way a sentence comes out . . . you think, 'Hey, that girl!' I mean, I just knew
then. I didn't know what would *become* of her, but I knew that she was a very,
very talented person."[8] People took notice. Patsy was then featured in the role
of Diana Lake in the next Barter production, *French without Tears,* which
opened at the Abingdon Civic Auditorium on July 30. Portraying a sophisticated vamp, Patsy's comedic timing was well received. Also in the cast was
her friend Maggie Phillips.

Her next performance was in *No Boys Allowed,* an original play by Edith
Sommer, which had its world premiere in Abingdon on August 1. The cast
featured Margaret Phillips, Elizabeth Wilson, and Patsy Neal. Also with her
pals Wilson and Phillips, Patsy appeared in the drama *Letters to Lucerne,*
which opened on September 3.

Malcolm Miller, in his *Knoxville Journal* review of *Letters to Lucerne,*
wrote: "I saw 'Letters to Lucerne' on Thursday night. I had seen two previous
performances but wanted to see it again because Knoxville's Patsy Neal had
replaced Juin Whipple as 'Bingo Hill,' one of the important roles, on short
notice. Patsy gave the entire play quite a 'lift' with her enthusiasm, vitality
and splendid voice."[9]

To complete the season, Patsy appeared in the biblical production *Family
Portrait,* which had starred Judith Anderson on Broadway in 1939.

During that important summer Patsy corresponded with her first beau,
Frank Ball, whom she had met on vacation in the Great Smoky Mountains
the previous summer. He was a year older than Patsy, and as she later recalled, he "was a member of the ROTC, great fun, a little plump and perfectly
acceptable to mothers. He gave me my first sweet kiss. Later when he went to
the University of Tennessee, he gave me his Sigma Chi pin."[10]

Before she left for Abingdon, Patsy had agreed, at her parents' insistence, to
return to Knoxville in the fall of 1942 for her senior year in high school. Her
dream to train and perform in theatre had been realized in Abingdon. She
would not lose sight now of her ambition to eventually move to New York.
More than ever she was determined to achieve her goals, and her last year in
Knoxville proved to be anticlimactic.

Patsy's beau Frank Ball was now in the service. She dutifully wrote him
about her everyday activities in school and her continuing melodramatic crises. Once he wrote back, "Patsy, don't you know there's a war going on!"[11]
For Patsy, reality was soon to strike. Her homecoming was sadly underlined

by the death of the romantic and handsome Wesley Davis, of her Tennessee Valley Players days. He had suddenly taken ill and died of liver complications the day after he was admitted to the Fort Sanders Hospital. He had been employed by the Southern Coal Company before the war. He was just twenty-four years old. After his funeral at Weaver's Chapel, he was laid to rest at the Lynnhurst Cemetery. Patsy consoled herself through long talks with his bereaved mother.

Knuckling down to her scholastic responsibilities, Patsy renewed her relationships with her Knoxville friends. Beginning her senior year at Knoxville High School, she soon overcame her melancholy and became a member of the Junior Assembly, a "dance club of the young social set." Most important, she resumed her readings and appearances at benefits and patriotic pageants. "I entered speech contests and won awards for dramatic readings and even took on directing the High School Thespians in their big production of *Jane Eyre*," around Thanksgiving 1942.[12]

She desperately wanted to visit New York City during the spring break. After scheming for months with her Barter Theatre pal Phyllis Adams, whose wealthy family lived in Manhattan, Patsy was finally able, with the help of Emily Mahan, to convince her father to let her go. Miss Mahan told Coot that she thought it would be a great experience for Patsy. And besides, *she* had lived there.

Patsy was awed by the city, the theatre district, and the large and expansive Adams apartment, complete with servants. Appearing on Broadway were Helen Hayes in *Harriet*, Elizabeth Bergner in *The Two Mrs. Carrolls*, and Katharine Cornell in *The Three Sisters* at the Ethel Barrymore Theatre. Patsy would long remember the night she saw the great Cornell in the role of Masha.

Sneaking backstage after the performance, Patsy knocked on Cornell's second-floor dressing room door. The stagestruck teenager was greeted by the great actress herself. "Hello, I'm Patsy Neal from Tennessee, Miss Cornell. Everyone says I look like you," gushed Neal. "Well, perhaps a little younger," replied Cornell.[13] Sending her parents the required weekly letter, Patsy told them all about the play and meeting Cornell. She returned home determined that someday she would live and work in New York.

Patsy was a dutiful daughter, but her reckless nature sometimes landed her in trouble at Knoxville High School. She once skipped school with two of her friends. Several times during her last year in high school she was dismissed for some minor infraction of the rules. Each time, her father would have to speak with the principal. The last time she was expelled was for eating her lunch off campus. As NiNi would later recall, "I don't know why she did that. She always got caught. That evening at home, she pleaded, 'Daddy, you've just got to get me back into school!' And Daddy replied, 'I'm not about to. I'm more at home now in Dean Morton's office than I am here! NiNi will go with you tomorrow to talk to the principal and get you back in.' And I did. I'll never forget that."[14]

Patsy's talent was beginning to be taken seriously. Coot Neal and his Southern Coal and Coke Company associate Reid Ford were walking up Gay Street in Knoxville one afternoon when they passed the Tennessee Theatre. Reid said to Neal, "You know, Coot, I wouldn't be surprised to see Patsy's name on that marquee some day." To which Neal seriously replied, "And I wouldn't be surprised either."[15] Though sometimes lazy in her studies, Patsy was determined to make a success of her talent. In the Tennessee Interscholastic Literary League preliminaries, she won first prize for dramatic reading in the Sixth District High School Literary Contest competition. Finals were held at the University of Tennessee on Saturday, April 23, and Patsy again won first prize, this time for best humorous reading of the monologue "Open House" by Florence Ryerson and Colin Clements.

At Knoxville High, the senior class of play of 1943 was *And Came the Spring*. Patsy portrayed the character Virginia Hartman, "a lady of the world."[16] That same week, on Thursday, June 3, 1943, the graduation ceremonies for Patsy's class were held at the Knoxville High School Alumni Auditorium.

After graduation, Patsy chose to attend Northwestern University in Evanston, Illinois, and major in speech. Her other choice had been to study under the great theater actress Maude Adams, who since 1937 had been professor of dramatic arts at Stephens College in Columbia, Missouri. Patsy had also applied and been accepted to apprentice during the summer before her entry into college with the Priscilla Beach Theatre Group in Plymouth, Massachusetts.

On the way to Plymouth, she planned to visit her friend Gloria Lucas in New York for two weeks. Arriving in Manhattan on a strict budget, Patsy learned that the Priscilla Beach Theatre would use her mainly for backstage work and charge her $10 for a mailbox, $10 to rent a beach towel, etc. As she saw it, she had too much ambition and desire, and not enough funds, to waste time in Massachusetts. So she and Gloria decided to remain in New York for the summer and try to obtain work. Patsy called her parents and persuaded them to allow her to stay for six weeks in the city, on the condition that she and Gloria live with Gloria's uncle Albert in Queens. But the two girls instead rented a Bohemian apartment a block from the subway on Minetta Lane in New York's Greenwich Village.

Gloria landed a job on John Street while Patsy searched for work around Manhattan and on Long Island. Patsy told a magazine writer several years later, "I only bothered to see one agent and he told me I was a good 'type,' which is a remark I've heard a hundred times about this actor or that and I still don't know what it means. Probably that I was very young but I wasn't the standard ingénue model, too tall or something."[17]

After about six weeks, Patsy's sister NiNi unexpectedly came for a visit. Upon arriving at Grand Central, NiNi hailed a cab and gave the driver Patsy's street address. He said, "There are several streets with that name. There's one in the Village—" "Take me there," NiNi interrupted.[18] She knew that the Village would be where she would find Patsy. When she arrived, NiNi decided to stay a couple of days to determine if it was safe for her sister and her friend to remain in New York. The apartment the girls shared had a large bay window on the street level. One afternoon the three were hanging something in the living room when NiNi turned around to see a crowd of people on the street looking in at them. That scared NiNi enough to call her parents and let them know what the girls were up to. Patsy was unceremoniously summoned home to prepare for Northwestern.

"My family didn't want me to stay in New York that time," Patsy recalled in 1947. "But it was very good for me. . . . It takes people a year to get down to work. I remember I spent most of those months in drugstores talking to actors. That got the sitting stage out of my system."[19]

Patsy faithfully continued to study dramatics with Emily Mahan up until she left for college. Thirty years later, Emily recalled her advice to young Patsy, "'Your height will be a problem. You will miss parts. You can never play ingénue roles, Patsy, but you keep in the business till you are 30, and you will have no problems.' . . . The thing I'm proudest of is that I took her and didn't ruin her. I let her do her own broad comedy. I didn't try to tone down her wonderful big voice, and I didn't try to tame her great zest and enthusiasm. I had her do monologues and cuttings before audiences all over town and watched her gain confidence and poise."[20]

Northwestern University was noted for its speech department, headed by drama teacher Alvina Krause. But Patsy's first concern was which sorority would accept her. When rush week ended, she had been overlooked by her own choice, Kappa Kappa Gamma. All the other sororities *did* want her, however. She settled on Pi Beta Phi and was officially initiated into the sorority on April 22, 1944. Because the main dormitory was already full, Patsy lived with sixteen other girls at Pi Beta Phi's two-story McFarland House. One of her sorority sisters was Martha Hyer, future actress and wife of film producer Hal Wallis.

On December 1, 1943, Patsy (billed as Patricia) made her Northwestern University Theatre debut in *Beggar on Horseback*, a play by George S. Kaufman and Marc Connelly. The production starred Lydia Clarke, the future Mrs. Charlton Heston. Patricia's role was that of a juror—little more than stage dressing. Although speech majors were not permitted to perform until their sophomore year, an exception was made for Patsy.

Once during a long weekend, Patsy and a college girlfriend hitchhiked from Evanston to Sturgeon Bay, Wisconsin. Said Patsy many years later, "We were both big girls, wore blue jeans, and shamelessly thumbed rides. Not one good car picked us up. We rode a series of trucks and jalopies and had a marvelous time. One man and his woman had been married fourteen years and were expecting their first child. I remember tying my handkerchief into innumerable knots as they told the story of their hardships. For a time I took on their life. I learned then that the poor are generous and trusting because they have nothing to lose."[21]

On April 16, 1944, Coot Neal died suddenly of a heart attack. Though he was a heavy smoker as well as being a large man, his death at the age of forty-nine was unexpected. That very evening Patsy and her housemates were comforting a sorority sister who had just lost her mother. When the house telephone rang later in the middle of the night, Patsy was summoned from her second-story single bedroom. She knew as she entered the small house telephone booth that it was death calling. When her mother told her that her father had died, Patsy's heart pounded with a sense of unreality. The sorority housemother, Pearl Meilman, and two other girls delivered Patsy to the railroad station to return for the funeral. Arriving in Williamsburg the next morning, she was driven directly to her aunt Maude's home. There, she consoled her mother. Little Pete was not allowed to attend the funeral. Patricia remembered her grandfather, W. D. Neal, weeping uncontrollably after the funeral over the loss of his son.

Patsy continued corresponding with her beau, Frank Ball. When he finally was able to come home on leave, Patsy unburdened her sadness and woes and cried on his shoulder. She later wrote that she fell in love with him that summer of 1944. The loss of her father had a profound effect on Patsy. Frank's presence made the loss more endurable. Of Coot Neal, Patsy wrote her mother, "I will not believe that my Daddy died. Men like 'Coot' Neal do not die. They live on in every heart, in every place, in every thing that they have touched. He is my 'rock of ages,' the rock upon which anything good about me has been built. All I have ever known is 'do it for Daddy.'"[22]

During the summer of 1944 Patsy obtained a job as the dining room hostess at the Andrew Johnson Hotel in Knoxville. Always prepared for a real-life role, Patsy told a reporter several years later, "I wore black dresses with white collars and cuffs, and had my hair in a knot, and looked exactly like a dining room hostess."[23] Sister NiNi would take her back and forth to work, as Patsy didn't drive. When heartthrob film actor William Holden came through town on a war bond drive, he stayed at the Andrew Johnson Hotel. Patsy was determined to meet him. One day after driving her sister to work, NiNi, dressed in a crisp white dress, entered the hotel lobby with her. Immediately NiNi was approached by Holden's publicity people and asked to pose with him. NiNi recalls, "Patsy was livid that I was asked to meet him and have pictures made with him for the papers."[24]

When summer ended, Aunt Maude, who never failed to encourage and support her niece, offered to pay for Patsy's tuition at Northwestern. Now a sophomore, Patsy was finally allowed to study acting with the legendary Alvina Krause, known to her students as "A. K." Krause joined the faculty at Northwestern University in 1930 and taught there for thirty-four years. Among her students were Tony Randall, Cloris Leachman, Paula Prentiss, and Claude Akins.

In his autobiography *In the Arena*, Charlton Heston wrote that Krause "imposed a fierce discipline on an art generally regarded as having all the structure of a dish of Jell-O. Her reputation was formidable, so was her manner. She cared deeply about acting and was unforgiving with those pupils who fell short of her standards. She wasn't interested in teaching self-esteem."[25] Krause encouraged her students to purchase two books, *Acting, The First Six Lessons* by Richard Boleslavsky, and *An Actor Prepares* by Constantin Stanislavsky. Her lectures were mesmerizing, and a former student, actor-director Richard Benjamin, recalled, "She had steel blue eyes that looked into your skull. You couldn't hide. She (did) that magical thing that makes your imagination come alive."[26]

Patricia once gave Krause a reading from *The Hairy Ape* during a private half-hour lesson. "It was probably the first thing I ever did halfway decently, because I can remember Alvina getting so excited about it that she called in the next student who was waiting outside the door to listen to me doing it again."[27] That student was Chicago native Helen Virginia Horton. After their initial meeting, Helen and Patsy developed a lifelong friendship, though Horton later told Patsy, "It was the first time I thought to myself, I will have a hell of a lot of competition."[28]

Plunging into activities during her sophomore year at Northwestern, Patsy joined the Wildcat Council and the University Radio Playhouse and even modeled for the campus magazine, the *Purple Parrot*. She was crowned Syllabus Queen, was chosen by the student body as the Navy Ball Queen, and was named to the ranks of "Chicago's ten best-dressed women" by the Chicago Fashion Industries. There was a great deal of press focused on Patsy Neal as a result. Virginia Leimert in the *Chicago Daily News* wrote that Patsy's "American Look" in fashion, "is of importance to us, because the college girl of today means business in what she does, and she likes to look the part."[29]

Her new friend Helen Horton was considered "the queen of the drama department at NU" and was cast in the lead role of Viola in Northwestern University's two-hundredth major production, William Shakespeare's *Twelfth Night*, directed by Claudia Webster.[30] Patsy was cast as the beautiful Olivia. The school's publicity department sent Helen and Patsy to Chicago's Civic Theatre for pictures of them dressed in their *Twelfth Night* costumes with the actor Eddie Dowling, who was appearing in Chicago's tryout production of *The Glass Menagerie*, Tennessee Williams's first Broadway-bound play. Sadly, it was also the last play for its star, the brilliant and tragic Laurette Taylor. Of Taylor's historic performance Patsy later wrote, "It was, and is, the finest performance I have ever seen in my life. Absolutely inspiring . . . I prayed I could be that good."[31]

Twelfth Night played from February 26 to March 3, 1945. Patsy, now using the name Pat, continued giving recitals and monologues and appeared in recital on May 30 at Lutkin Hall in Evanston for the Alpha Chapter of Phi Beta. Then Patricia played Mother in the April 21, 1945, Northwestern University Radio Playshop broadcast of *Three Strikes You're Out*.

Patsy Neal's four-semester tenure at Northwestern came to an end at the start of the summer of 1945. Like many of her fellow students, she did not finish her degree, but chose to begin work professionally that fall.

During spring break that year, Alvina Krause and her longtime companion, Lucy McCammon, a physical education teacher at Bloomsburg State Teachers College, leased the small Forest Inn Playhouse, which was once run by Ethel Barrymore Colt. Its location in Eagles Mere, Pennsylvania, made it an ideal summer theatre. Krause drafted sixteen of her students from Northwestern to help produce and perform plays for the theatre's first season, beginning in June 1945. Patsy wanted desperately to be a part of the venture. After dedicated weeks of pleading her cause, she was finally told by A. K., "You come along, too."[32] Patsy was the youngest student chosen to participate.

Located just north of Bloomsburg, Pennsylvania, the Eagles Mere Playhouse would produce classic and contemporary plays, as well as musicals, to be directed or supervised by Krause. The first project at hand, however, was to clean the theatre, which had been in disrepair since the outbreak of the war. Efforts to eliminate bats and mice were never completely successful. The bats especially remained a problem (except during a production of *Macbeth*, when they coincidentally fit into the plot).

Patricia wrote, "I worked very hard at Eaglesmere helping cook for the company and going around literally knocking at people's doors trying to sell tickets. . . . I can tell you it was jolly hard work. But when you are young, nothing is too much trouble. The high point of my time at Eaglesmere was surely the end of World War II, when everyone cheered and yelled and we had tremendous celebrations."[33] As one of the three cooks, she oftentimes was found snapping "beans during rehearsals, or . . . across the road during breaks . . . (preparing) her specialty, tuna fish with noodles."[34] Patsy also sewed costumes and worked on sets. The colony members were lodged in one large house nearby. That first summer, nine plays were produced.

Patsy, billed as "Pat," appeared as Lucy in *Uncle Harry*, the second play of the season. A local reviewer wrote, "The parts of the quarrelling spinster sisters, as taken by Helen Wood and Pat Neal, show with what artistic ability these youthful actors portray difficult roles."[35]

Patsy also appeared in small roles in the productions *Squaring the Circle*, which opened July 19, and *Is Life Worth Living*, which opened in the next month. Late in July, in her largest role of the summer season, Patricia portrayed Ruth, the put-upon wife of Paul (Steven Meyer) who is taunted by the ghost of her husband's first wife in Noel Coward's *Blithe Spirit*.

During the twenty years she ran the Eagles Mere Playhouse, Alvina Krause produced 178 plays by Shakespeare, Shaw, Ibsen, Chekhov, Molière, and Edmond Rostand. Professional theatre and film scouts attended productions at Eagles Mere the summer of 1945. One girl in the colony was approached and asked to audition in New York for the role of "an Amazon" in Eugene O'Neill's *A Moon for the Misbegotten*. That actress declined the offer, but Patsy kept it in mind.

Before the summer season ended, Eura Neal sent her daughter a letter. Patsy's army lieutenant beau, Frank Ball, had been killed during the closing days of World War II. "It was not an unusual letter. Many families had received one just like it between 1942 and 1945," Patricia wrote in her autobiography. Indeed, her own cousin, the "incredibly handsome" air ace Thomas "Fitz" Neal, had been killed in Europe in 1944 when his plane crashed. "I always knew I couldn't keep from being hurt badly by the war. I thought my life was over. I cried for months."[36]

In September, Helen Horton asked Patsy if she would like to come to New York and share rent with her and three other young women. Patsy arrived by train with $300 in her pocket, and the girls quickly found an apartment at 303 West 105th Street at Riverside Drive on the Upper West Side of Manhattan. Though it was a small, top-floor apartment, it had a big sitting room, a bath, a kitchen, and four beds. Patsy was always the last one home at night, so she slept on the couch.

Two of the other girls were Natalie Brown, who worked as a proofreader at the *New Yorker*, and Irene "Petey" Petroff (who later became one of New York's first television camerawomen). They had attended Northwestern with Helen and Patsy. The fourth roommate was a rather strange girl named Sparkie, who had worked in a California defense plant during the war. Money was tight, and the girls pooled their resources, giving Petey control of the spending. They lived on tuna fish dishes, doughnuts, and popcorn. Every morning Natalie would wake Patsy up with a pleasant "Wake up, beauty!"[37] and for two months Patsy made the rounds, networking with other young actors at such hangouts as Horn & Hardart and Walgreen's Drugstore (located in Broadway's Astor Hotel) and looking for theatre work. She got a part-time job for 70 cents an hour working noontime in a Greenwich Village diner, cutting and serving pies and cakes.

The girls lost their apartment after they threw a keg party and invited boys who thought it would be fun to roll the empty barrels down the flights of wooden steps in the middle of the night. The young women were promptly evicted the next morning.

"When I first went to New York I was really ambitious," Patricia remembered many years later. "I was up and on those [casting audition] rounds always, even after I'd gotten my first [theatre] job. I was insulted—but I had to take it if I wanted a job."[38] That first theatre job was one that Patsy and Helen managed to get together, in a production of *Seven Mirrors* staged by Dennis Gurney and produced at the Blackfriars Theatre. Running from October 25 to November 18, 1945, the play also featured young actresses Geraldine Page and Peggy McCay. (Patricia remembered Geraldine Page being standoffish, seeming to resent Patricia being cast.) During the run of the show, Patricia asked for the night off to see a hit show in which she might have a chance to take over a part. As another cast member recalled, "Our director was annoyed. 'You're supposed to stick with us through this run. You'll never get anywhere being so will-of-the-wisp,' he stormed. He was wrong. Pat Neal started on her zooming career practically the next day."[39]

Patsy had scoped out *A Moon for the Misbegotten*, which she had heard about at Eagles Mere, but found that auditions for the O'Neill play would not take place for some time. She kept busy by attending acting classes, seeing as many plays as she could, and even assisting a young actor in a film test, for which she did not get paid. As it turned out, the test provided Patsy with her first agent, Maynard Morris of MCA, the man who had represented the young actor. One of the most powerful agents on Broadway, Morris had discovered the young Nebraskan Marlon Brando in 1944, recommending that he audition for Rodgers and Hammerstein's production of John Van Druten's *I Remember Mama*. Brando's career effectively began with that play. Morris's sudden decision to represent Patsy Neal proved most fortunate for them both.

The Voice of the Turtle, another Van Druten play, had opened at the Morosco Theatre on Broadway on December 8, 1943, starring Elliot Nugent, Margaret Sullavan, and Audrey Christie, and it quickly became a solid hit. After its second summer layoff, it reopened in September 1945. By October of that year the producers were looking for an understudy for the two new female leads, Vicki Cummings and Martha Scott. Of the many young hopefuls who auditioned for the understudy, it was Patsy Neal who was given the job by producer Alfred de Liagre Jr., after a stunning reading. Van Druten thought Patsy was too young for either of the roles, but de Liagre stood firm, saying, "I like her! And I'm gonna have her."[40] He thus emphatically became her next champion. Patsy accepted the understudy part in *Turtle* and received a new name, "Patricia Neal," de Liagre's choice.

"If someone turns you down you've got to get up and start again the next morning, no matter how rude that person was," Patricia once said. "I remember I just started weeping at one audition. But I stuck with it. After three months, I got a job."[41] As Patricia Neal, she had now become a professional actress. She was only nineteen years old.

3

Broadway

I mean, all of us . . . actors, and authors, too . . . we aren't really living in the real world at all. We're giving our whole lives to . . . make-believe.

—Sally, *The Voice of the Turtle*

John Van Druten's *The Voice of the Turtle* is a rather simple comedy performed in three acts by three characters: Sally Middleton, Olive Lashbrooke, and Bill Page. The story opens in Sally's apartment on New York's East Side one weekend in April during World War II. We are introduced to Sally, a rather young and naive actress in her early twenties, and her older actress friend, the more worldly Olive. As they discuss their various love affairs with men, Olive tells Sally that she has asked a visiting soldier on leave to meet her at Sally's apartment. Enter Bill, who is dumped by Olive as she leaves to meet another man. Because of the late hour and a raging thunderstorm outside, Bill is forced to spend the night on Sally's daybed. Over the course of the weekend, the two young people discover a mutual attraction, and by the end of the play they express their true feelings toward each other.

In 1943, when *The Voice of the Turtle* premiered, playwright Van Druten was enjoying immense popularity after having written such successful Broadway plays as *Leave Her to Heaven, Old Acquaintance, After All*, and *There's Always Juliet*. *Turtle* opened in tryout on November 4, 1943, at the Shubert Theatre in New Haven, Connecticut. It was directed by forty-one-year-old Alfred de Liagre Jr., a graduate of Yale University who had staged such Broadway hits as *Yes, My Darling Daughter* and *Mr. and Mrs. North*. *The Voice of the Turtle* proved to be an enormous success, in no small part because of its controversial—for its time—subject matter of promiscuity and its sharp dialogue.

Patricia signed to understudy for $150 a week. Now a professional ac-

Facing page: Patsy Neal at age eighteen, Northwestern University, 1944. From the Patricia Neal Collection.

29

tress, though an understudy, in a real Broadway hit, she must have felt that her hard work and determination were beginning to pay off. She was finally able to afford her own apartment on Morningside Drive and maintain a certain degree of independence while showing up at the theater diligently night after night in case one of the two female stars could not perform.

She also continued auditioning. Her friend Helen Horton told her, "Heavens, Patsy, you *have* a job!"[1] But she wasn't *acting* on the stage yet. In November her agent, Maynard Morris, told her that she would soon join the touring company of *The Voice of the Turtle* in Chicago and understudy the two leading actresses.

Shortly before she left for Chicago, Patricia heard that the Theatre Guild was finally planning to produce *A Moon for the Misbegotten*. She managed to get an audition with director Dudley Digges, but he found her completely inappropriate and too young for the role of Josie Hogan—"the Amazon" she had heard about at Eagles Mere. "In the end I didn't get the part. I think it was a case of trying too hard, of being too anxious and, as a result, I didn't have what was needed," Patricia recalled.[2]

But the effort wasn't wasted. As she was leaving the audition, Digges introduced her to the arriving heads of the Theatre Guild, Lawrence Langner and Theresa Helburn, and their party, the playwright Eugene O'Neill and his wife, Carlotta. Patricia could only stammer, "Oh!"[3] She knew who these people were and what their respected places were in the New York theater world. And she was sure she had not made a good impression.

However, O'Neill *was* impressed with the young Miss Neal and left a telephone message for her to meet with him before he allowed her a reading. He also had Theresa Helburn call Patricia. "I don't understand it," Helburn told the young actress, "but Mr. O'Neill wants to hear you read."[4] O'Neill felt that Patricia would be perfect for the role of Sara Melody in *A Touch of the Poet* and sent her the script.

"The Guild would phone that Mr. O'Neill wanted to see me," recalled Patricia years later, "and we'd meet in one of their offices and talk about the theatre, jazz, Hollywood, books we liked. He said he'd let me do any of his plays I wanted. I was thinking of accepting a movie offer, and he told me to go ahead; he said the theatre wasn't worth sacrificing for. For years I had a clause in all my Hollywood contracts that I could take a leave of absence if I was wanted for *A Touch of the Poet*."[5] The relationship that developed between O'Neill and Patricia was flirtatious, yet strictly platonic, and long-lasting. The problem was that O'Neill did not tell his wife about their meetings.

On a stormy Tuesday night just weeks into her understudy role, Patricia was advised by Morosco Theatre stage manager William Richardson that she was going on for Vicki Cummings, who was delayed by a blizzard in Connecticut, where she had gone that day to obtain a divorce. Dressed and made up for the role of Olive, Patricia stood in the wings reviewing her lines in her head as her adrenaline began to pump. Given her five-minute cue and feeling perspiration on her brow, she took her place for her entrance before the curtain went up.

Suddenly the stage door swung open, and there stood Vicki Cummings. "'Oh no, Vicki, it can't be you,' I cried," recalled Patricia. "'You break my heart kid. You want to go on? Go on!'" Vicki smiled back." Patricia, realizing she hadn't rehearsed with Martha Scott, asked, "What about the leading lady?" When Vicki told Martha Scott that Patricia was ready to go on, Patricia heard Scott reply, "No, Vicki darling, I want you to go on. We'll hold the curtain."[6] As Patricia removed her costume, she kicked herself for saying anything. She had come that close to finally appearing on Broadway that very night. She vowed it *would* happen someday soon.

In Chicago, the national touring production of *The Voice of the Turtle* had already run a year. It starred K. T. Stevens (daughter of film director Sam Wood), Hugh Marlowe, and Vivian Vance as Olive. Patricia arrived shortly before Christmas 1945. After dutifully reporting to the Selwyn Theatre for a week, her break finally came, quite unexpectedly, on New Year's Eve.

Vance, a moderately successful actress on Broadway in *Skylark* (1939), had made the role of Olive her own. Her reviews had been stunning. However, she had long been overly sensitive and insecure. She suffered a nervous breakdown during a performance in late December 1945 and froze in the middle of a scene. Both Stevens and Marlowe knew immediately that the understudy would have to replace her temporarily. On New Year's Eve, after a quick rehearsal with stage manager Arthur Hughes and a read-through with the nervous Marlowe and Stevens, Patricia went on.

Patricia performed the role of Olive for two and a half weeks; some performances were better than others. Eventually, Vance's replacement, who had a contract for the run of the play, arrived from New York, and Patricia returned to her understudy role.

While she was still standing in for Vance, Patricia received a letter from Zelma Brookov of Warner Brothers' New York talent department suggesting that Patricia meet with people from the movie studio. After seriously considering the Warners' offer, Patricia accepted the advice of cast member Stevens, who told her it was too soon to be thinking about a film career. She recalled the actress telling her, "Get yourself a name first. Make them really want you for your talent. You're pretty enough to get a small contract with anyone, but you will be miserable. Go out there under good conditions."[7]

Before *The Voice of the Turtle* moved on to Cincinnati, Patricia took a break and visited her family in Knoxville. While she was there, Maynard Morris told her that she'd been cast in the Broadway-bound play *Bigger than Barnum*. She was to receive fourth billing after Benny Baker, Chili Williams, and Sid Melton. When she returned to New York in mid-January, she handed in her notice to de Liagre.

Renewing her friendship with O'Neill, Patricia and the playwright met several times. On her twentieth birthday, January 20, 1946, recalled Patricia, after O'Neill "mentioned an ice cream parlor in New London that had the most wonderful sodas, I said they couldn't be any better than those at Hick's near Fifth Avenue, and persuaded him to go with me. His tremor wasn't too bad that day [O'Neill suffered from Parkinson's disease] and he looked so pleased with himself that he could manage the soda."[8] At Hick's, while nervously lighting her cigarette, he confessed, "You know if I were young, I would love you very much."[9]

At one of their meetings at the Theatre Guild offices, Patricia read for the part of Josie Hogan in *A Moon for the Misbegotten*. After the reading, Patricia didn't wait for comments. "Will I do?" she blurted.[10] She was told that she was too young for the role. But the fact that Carlotta O'Neill had learned of Patricia's friendship with the playwright might have had something do with it; Carlotta was furious and never forgave the young actress or her husband.

Patricia headed for Boston to begin rehearsals for *Bigger than Barnum,* a farce by Fred Rath and Lee Sands that depicted the misadventures of two optimistic carnival promoters. Patricia played the role of Claire Walker, the fiancée of Benny Baker. The production stumbled clumsily into Boston, opening at the Wilbur Theatre on April 22, 1946. The critics were ruthless. The *Variety* review that appeared on April 24 was typical: "As melancholy an entry as has come this way all year, 'Bigger Than Barnum' just hasn't got the stuff. Farce combines a not-too-happy idea with unamusing lines, silly situations and poor taste in general. It has no chance whatever of encountering anything but the severest notices anywhere."[11] The show closed in Boston on April 27.

Following the closing, Patricia received a telegram from her staunch supporter Alfred de Liagre : "Your job with the Turtle is still open."[12] She returned to New York, certain her luck would change.

Patricia still was earning only $150 a week as an understudy for the New

York production of *The Voice of the Turtle*. She found a cheap apartment one block from Helen Horton, who was now sharing an apartment with Petey. The communal bathroom down the hall was so filthy and cockroach ridden that she had to bathe in Helen and Petey's bathtub, which, with a board over it, doubled as a table.

Helen reintroduced Patricia to fellow Northwestern alumna and twenty-one-year-old actress Shirley Jean Verhagen, who had taken the fancy of Helen Hayes's husband, fifty-one-year-old writer Charles MacArthur. He had cast her as an understudy in *Swan Song* and advised her to change her last name to Hagen. She and Patricia hit it off immediately. Jean was funny and ambitious, and together the two found a fourth-floor walk-up on Third Avenue. There was only a single bed, but they would take turns sleeping on it. They had their own bathroom now with their own bathtub, which unfortunately had a drain that was always clogged, so they had to take sponge baths the entire time they lived there.

Patricia's agent next offered her a role in a two-week run of *Devil Take a Whittler*, to be produced by the Theatre Guild at the Westport Country Playhouse in Connecticut. Patricia once again handed in her notice to de Liagre.

Devil Take a Whittler was billed as an "authentic American folk fantasy" set in the Ozark Mountains of Arkansas and was presented as a Theatre Guild tryout.[13] With hopes for a Broadway run, *Devil Take a Whittler* opened on July 29, 1946. An original production based on four one-act plays by playwright Weldon Stone, it relates the struggle for the soul and body of a whittler, Lem Skaggs, involving a girl from the valley, Myra Thompson; a hillbilly renegade, Kat Skaggs ("a lusty mountain lass in a leopard skin"), played by Patricia; and the Devil.[14] *Devil Take a Whittler* is told in song, dance, and drama in two acts, each with three scenes.

The critics were generally enthusiastic. "Miss Neal . . . put fire into the role as the jealous girl from the mountain," wrote one.[15] Said another, "Patricia Neal as 'Kat Skaggs,' the mountain girl, primitive in her passions and ruthless in her endeavor to get 'Lem' away from 'Myra,' and abetted by the 'Devil,' turns in an excellent delineation of that character."[16]

Devil Take a Whittler closed on August 3, 1946, and Patricia returned to New York once again to resume her understudy job in *The Voice of the Turtle*, but this time not in defeat. It was during the run of *Whittler* that Herman Shumlin, a legendary agent and film director and later a Tony-winning stage director, noticed Patricia. He was impressed with her energetic and robust performance and emphatically recommended her to playwright Lillian Hellman, who was casting for a new show.

By now the production of *The Voice of the Turtle* featured veteran actor John Beal in the role of Bill and young actress Beatrice Pearson in the role of Sally. Patricia replaced the vacationing Vicki Cummings as Olive in New York for two weeks beginning August 12. No reviews exist of Patricia's performance, and the experience left her with unsettled memories. She recalled that Beatrice Pearson was definitely not happy to be working with her. Indeed, a friend of Pearson's sat in the balcony during each performance taking notes on Patricia's acting, something Patricia found particularly insulting.

During the rehearsals of *Devil Take a Whittler* two very important individuals, producer-playwright Richard Rodgers and Lillian Hellman, came into her life. They would have a profound impact on her future. Impressed with Patricia's lively and scene-stealing characterization of Kat Skaggs in *Devil Take a Whittler*, both Rodgers and Hellman vied for her services.

Patricia's agent soon advised her that she was being considered for the new Rodgers and Hammerstein production *Happy Birthday,* in one of the many ingénue female roles. She was not cast, but Rodgers asked Patricia to read for him again, this time for the lead in his and Oscar Hammerstein's other upcoming production, the nonmusical *William and Mary,* written by Norman Krasna and to be staged by Joshua Logan. Her reading went well and she was offered the role. News was leaked to the press. "Prospects seem favorable for Patricia Neal to receive the leading feminine role in *William and Mary*," wrote one columnist.[17] Meanwhile, O'Neill considered Patricia for the role of Margie in *The Iceman Cometh,* but again she didn't get the part.

Patricia assumed that *William and Mary* (later retitled *John Loves Mary*) would mark her Broadway debut. However, the night before the contract signing, Lillian Hellman's agent approached Patricia backstage at *Turtle* to offer her an audition for Hellman's newest production, *Another Part of the Forest.* "I never told her that I had read the role a few weeks before and had been turned down by somebody in the office who yawned through my reading," Patricia recalled. Patricia confidently told the stunned agent she already had a secure offer but agreed to read the following day for the playwright at the Fulton Theatre.[18]

Among the dozens of actresses auditioning for the part were Betsy Drake and Patricia's pal Helen Horton. The angry Horton exclaimed as Patricia entered the theater, "Oh no! No one will now stand a chance at this audition."[19] Escorted onto the stage, Patricia was handed a script and told to read for the key role of Regina Hubbard, a character portrayed as an older woman by Tallulah Bankhead in Hellman's 1939 production of *The Little Foxes*. Just before she started her reading, stage manager Richard Beckhard whispered in her ear, "Regina wouldn't do anything more underhanded than slice your throat."[20] At that moment, Patricia understood her character. With that, she began her reading.

"It was a rainy day, I remember, and you know how bedraggled one can look when coming in out of the wet. I didn't try too hard in my reading, either, and Miss Hellman took it for indifference," Patricia later recalled.[21] She assumed that Hellman herself was in the house that day, though she did not see her at first. Recalled Hellman in 1964, "I remember it very well. I let her read for about three minutes and then I stopped her. I knew she was right."[22] Approaching Patricia after the reading, producer Kermit Bloomgarden spoke simply and decisively: "We want you."[23] Wasting little time in notifying Richard Rodgers of her choice of roles, Patricia recalled in her autobiography, "I was stunned. Two Broadway offers in twenty-four hours! I knew immediately, instinctively, which part was the one for me. 'Regina,' sight unseen, had more range and potential. Besides, I wanted to be a dramatic actress and feared that once you got typed in comedy, it would be very hard to break away. And frankly, I didn't think I was very funny."[24]

At the same time, Patricia really wanted *William and Mary*, but Richard Rodgers wasn't offering her a substantial salary. When she asked for more money he flatly refused. She told him that Hellman had made an offer for her play. "And he told me to go ahead and take it," Patricia told a reporter several years later. "I love [Rodgers], but he was the stingiest man I ever met."[25]

Hellman, who had an immense hit with her 1939 play *The Little Foxes*, had chosen to write, cast, and direct *Another Part of the Forest*, which dealt with the earlier lives of the Hubbard family, the characters she had introduced in *The Little Foxes*. For Patricia the opportunity to star in a Hellman play was something she had strived for her whole life. She vowed to make the most of the moment. Writing home to Aunt Maude, Patricia gushed, "I am still so up in the clouds. I can't eat, sleep or think. You know that Lillian Hellman is just about the most wonderful American playwright. She and O'Neill and a couple of others. Following Bankhead is quite a task, too. . . . I am so glad that I signed with the [William Morris] agency after the play in Westport. They really took care of my business well."[26]

Indeed, Patricia would now receive $300 a week for the first year of *Another Part of the Forest*. She signed an exclusive two-year contract with the play's producer, Kermit Bloomgarden, guaranteeing her $460 a week should the play run a second year. *Another Part of the Forest* would first rehearse in New York and then tour briefly before its scheduled opening on Broadway at the Fulton Theatre on West Forty-sixth Street. Patricia was overjoyed that her roommate, Jean Hagen, after auditioning twice, had also been cast in the play as the Dixie trollop Laurette Sincee.

Another Part of the Forest concerns the Hubbard family of Snowden, Alabama, in 1880. In the first act, the characters Regina, Birdie, John Bagtry, Benjamin, and Oscar are introduced in their evil, selfish youth. The patriarchal family is controlled by the cerebral cruelty of their father Marcus (only spoken about in *Foxes*), who, through questionable actions during the Civil War, has achieved wealth and power within the community. Though he has total disregard and contempt for his two sons and his wife, he maintains an unnaturally deep love for his daughter Regina. Unbeknownst to him, Regina is as corrupt and deceitful as her brothers and uses her father's pathetic affection to her benefit. The characters, so successfully developed in *The Little Foxes*, are introduced and defined in *Another Part of the Forest*. The second act, with its musicale and introduction of other various characters, showcases Regina prominently. The third act, when Benjamin successfully takes charge of the family after blackmailing his father, completes a tale of darkness and deceit. It is pure Hellman.

The third act, however, was proving difficult for the playwright, not only dramatically, but also personally. Basically a tale of struggle for independence and the desire to take over one's destiny, the plot reflects Hellman's own relationship with her father. Hellman struggled with various versions of the action in the final scene between Regina and Marcus.

She also struggled as a director. Assistant stage manager Jose Vega remembered Hellman's inability to acknowledge her lack of stage technique while directing. "It was very strange. For a woman as talented as she was, she had absolutely no idea how to translate what she wrote to the stage. She did not know how to work with actors. For example, she had Bartlett Robinson [John Bagtry] and Patricia Neal [Regina Hubbard] play a love scene from opposite sides of the stage. These were very good actors and made what she made them do as good as possible."[27] In directing another scene with Patricia, Hellman told a friend, "Thank God you're here. How do I tell Pat to come from the back of the stage to the front?"[28] Hellman wouldn't listen to suggestions about her directing, although if approached aggressively about some particular staging, she would pay attention.

Hellman was not an easy individual to be around in stressful moments. In her autobiography, Patricia wrote, "It was clear from the very first moment that Lillian Hellman was going to dominate every aspect of this play. Although it was the first time she was directing, Lillian had the *air* of a great director." Hellman did not like many people; Patricia was an exception. The playwright sensed an extraordinary, raw talent in the young actress and was rarely at odds with her. Patricia continued, "Lillian's gentle, tender side was obvious to few. Most people only saw her impetuous temper and never the woman beneath the fire. Instinctively, I understood her and knew that when I got a swat, all I had to do was duck and wait it out. Being annoyed was her way of being Lillian Hellman."[29]

Hellman became very protective of Patricia. With Patricia in her dressing room, Hellman allowed herself to show a more feminine side. In her memoir, *Pentimento,* Hellman wrote, "It gives me pleasure that I found an unknown girl, Patricia Neal, and watched her develop into a good actress and woman."[30] The two would remain close friends for the rest of Hellman's life.

Writer Dashiell Hammett, Hellman's lover, frequently attended rehearsals, offering friendly and wise comments. However, he was usually completely drunk. He had noticed the young Patricia Neal and was becoming helplessly enamored of her. Patricia liked Hammett as well, and though Hellman was not blind to it, she trusted Patricia and knew that the young actress played straight. Besides, Patricia found the smitten Hammett to be too old.

Forest began tryouts in Provincetown, Massachusetts, on November 2, 1946. After playing Wilmington, Delaware, the play moved to Baltimore, opening at the Playhouse Theatre. Patricia's reviews were outstanding, with one critic remarking, "Much will be heard about Patricia Neal, the young and very beautiful and talented actress who plays the selfish, aristocratic daughter, 'Regina.' Hers is a rich voice, flexible and full of expression, and her playing is both subtle and vigorous."[31] Another said, "Throughout the play is felt the influence of 'Regina,' whose portrayal by Patricia Neal gives no indication that the youthful actress is playing her first major role. Miss Neal is beautiful but there is no softness in the beauty. She presented a character which is the worthy predecessor to the hard and avaricious woman portrayed by Tallulah Bankhead in *The Little Foxes*."[32] But Patricia's impact was best summarized by the critic who observed, "The revelation is Patricia Neal, practically a newcomer to the stage, whose behavior as the comely but deadly 'Regina' earmarks her for stellar eminence."[33]

In a letter she received while the play was in Baltimore, Patricia's agent Maynard Morris wrote, "You will be surprised to hear that I have had calls about you from Paramount, RKO, 20th Century and Samuel Goldwyn. I told them all your situation—that you are not available for two years. You will also be amused to hear that 20th wanted to know if I would give them the first option on you!"[34]

Throughout all this preopening adulation, Patricia did not forget her mentors, or her manners. She sent her dear Richard Rodgers a note of congratulations on the opening of his *Happy Birthday* on October 31. He in turn wrote her on November 3,

"I felt sort of silly to find that you had remembered my opening and I had neglected yours. Perhaps I didn't (or don't) have to tell you how much I hope for your success. I think you know that I feel I have a personal stake in you and I want you to be happy. Do write if you find time."[35]

After another successful tryout in Detroit, *Another Part of the Forest* was set to open at the Fulton in New York on November 20. When the cast returned to Manhattan on November 17, Patricia's mother, Eura, now the Pi Kappa Phi fraternity house mother at the University of Tennessee, and Patricia's brother, Pete, joined her for the opening. Aunt Maude and several Knoxville family friends had been invited to opening night as well. In the end they did not come because Grandpa Willie Neal was terminally ill. He died on November 19, the night before *Forest* opened.

Knowing how important opening night would be, Patricia found the presence of her mother and brother an additional strain. To relax she took them around the city showing them the sights, including the Empire State Building. Patricia wistfully regretted that her father Coot could not be with them.

Prior to the opening, Patricia had last-minute rehearsals, interviews, and appointments, and Eura's criticisms and remarks drove Patricia to distraction. Years later Eura would recall, "Two hours before the theatre and the curtain was to go up, I came back to the hotel and she (Patricia) was in the bathtub sitting there crying her heart out. . . . [S]he was just worn out and they had rehearsals until two o'clock in the morning . . . and [she was] nervous too, wondering too if it would go over."[36]

Patricia created a sensation in her first scene. Wrote Hector Arce, "She burst onto the stage, a tall, beautiful, and willful presence."[37] Patricia wrote, "Opening night was both the most frightening and most wonderful night of my life. I was the next thing to catatonic, but at the final curtain, when we were flooded with applause as only a New York audience can give, the Broadway opening was everything I had ever hoped it would be. I knew for certain that the reason I wanted to be an actress was for that moment. Applause was love. It was approval by everybody and I bathed in it."[38]

The cast awaited reviews at the opening-night party at Hellman's East Eighty-second Street apartment. When the papers arrived, the reviews of the play were mixed, but Patricia's personal reviews were exceptional. Robert Garland, in the *New York Journal-American,* raved, "Patricia Neal's 'Regina' is as beautiful as she is good, which is as good as it is beautiful."[39] Howard Barnes, of the *New York Herald Tribune,* exclaimed, "Miss Neal contributes an extraordinarily vital and memorable stage portrayal."[40] Brooks Atkinson in the *New York Times* called the play "a witches brew of blackmail, insanity, cruelty, theft, torture, insult, drunkenness, with a trace of incest thrown in for good measure and some chamber music in the background." He gave Patricia a glowing review, ending with, "As the old man's daughter, and ideal, Patricia Neal catches the bloom and greed of an amoral young woman determined to crush everyone around her."[41]

Heady with exhilaration, Patricia arrived at the Algonquin after the party. Eura told Patricia how very proud of her she was. She vowed to Patricia that she would never miss another of her openings. At last, Eura Neal was truly proud of her daughter.

On opening night, Eura collected eighty-six telegrams to Patricia wishing her well. Among them were messages from David O. Selznick, Charles MacArthur, and Tallulah Bankhead, as well as from family and longtime friends.

NiNi wrote, "Dad did not live to see that day but when I first saw her name in lights, I couldn't help but think about that evening. He would have been so proud of her."[42] For Patricia, that momentous night was hers. By the following morning she was a Broadway star.

4

Stock

Honestly, I don't want to get pushed ahead too fast. I am of the mind that one can't be a good actress until the middle 30s. Before, one is merely trying.

—Patricia Neal, 1948

Suddenly, Patricia Neal was news. *Another Part of the Forest* played to modest audiences throughout December. By January the talk around New York had focused on Patricia's performance. There were newspaper features about her and Jean Hagen's friendship dating back to their Northwestern days. Requests for publicity pictures and invitations to important functions kept the young actress busy. Upon seeing Patricia on the street around this time, one young actor recalled, "She was such an impressive person. This big, beautiful girl striding down the street, her chin out from Broadway to Shubert Alley. She was just so beautiful, so healthy, so had-it-all-made."[1]

But Patricia didn't see her height (five feet, eight inches) as an asset. Gloria Stroock, daughter of costumer James Stroock, recalls a heart-to-heart conversation they had after a double date. "Patricia's name was in lights by now in *Forest* on Broadway," Gloria recalled. "When our dates had left, Patricia said to me how lucky she thought I was. This really amazed me as she was so beautiful and successful and in demand. When I asked her why she would think that, Patricia remarked, 'Because you look so good sitting on the lap of a guy.'"[2]

Patricia soon found herself falling dangerously in love with a married man, forty-five-year-old Canadian-born film actor Victor Jory. She met Jory when she went backstage to congratulate him after a performance at an actors' benefit. Their attraction was immediate. Even though Jory was married and the father of two, he and Patricia were soon dating. Surprisingly, they were never an item in the New York papers.

Her relationship with Jory wasn't her first romantic entanglement in New

---

Facing page: Patricia Neal, 1947. Courtesy of the Barter Theatre, from the author's collection.

York. When Patricia was still an understudy in *The Voice of the Turtle*, she fell in love with a young medical intern. The affair came to an end when the young man disclosed that he had gotten married to a woman his family believed would help advance his career. Later Patricia was involved with a young actor, Bruce Hall (later Kim Stanley's first husband), another relationship that went nowhere.

One evening, Tallulah Bankhead attended a performance of *Another Part of the Forest*. As soon as the curtain came down, the legendary actress quickly forged backstage to congratulate Patricia. Exclaimed Bankhead to Patricia (and the waiting press), "You are as good as I am! And, *dahhling*, if I only called you half as good as I am, it would be a hell of a compliment!"[3]

With Tallulah Bankhead's blessing, Patricia Neal had arrived. In January 1947 *Look* magazine began an avalanche of accolades by picking Patricia as its Top Stage Newcomer of 1947. "A beauty who is also talented is unusual," said the article. "Patricia Neal is beautiful and an excellent actress. But more than this, she has an inner quality that can turn a play into an event." When the February 3 issue of *Life* magazine hit the stands, it carried a photograph of Patricia on its cover and the headline, "Three Broadway Actresses"; inside was a four-page photo layout featuring Patricia Kirkland, Susan Douglas, and Patricia Neal, along with other Broadway players. Of the group, only Patricia would enjoy sustained success.

After *Another Part of the Forest* played its hundredth performance in February, qualifying it as a bona fide hit, the spate of publicity continued. Write-ups quickly followed about Patricia and the play in *Harper's Bazaar, Charm, Junior Bazaar,* and *Redbook*. Photographs of Patricia soon appeared in such publications as *Newsweek* and *Click. Vogue* did a photo shoot with her and fellow cast member Leo Genn.

In quick succession she was awarded *Billboard's* fourth annual Donaldson Award for Best Debut Performance by an Actress of the 1946–1947 season, *Time* picked her as the Most Promising Actress of Last Year, and Daniel Blum gave her the 1947 Theatre World Award. The New York Drama Critics Circle gave Patricia its Most Promising Young Actress Award; she had also been nominated as Best Actress in a Straight Play.

And the best was yet to come. On Easter Sunday evening, April 6, 1947, the American Theatre Wing War Services presented the first annual Antoinette Perry Memorial Awards in the Grand Ballroom of the Waldorf-Astoria Hotel. The Tony Awards, as they soon came to be called, were given in memory of the late actress and director Antoinette Perry.

The first awards, given out to twenty recipients, consisted of a scroll for each winner and "useful articles": gold bill clips or cigarette lighters for the gentlemen and engraved silver compacts for the ladies. The very first award handed to a performer was to Patricia Neal for Debut Performance (later called Best Supporting Actress) in *Another Part of the Forest.*

Another Part of the Forest closed for the season on April 23, 1947. It was set to continue on the road in September. Her agents had signed Patricia for the fifty-sixth season at the Elitch Gardens Theatre in Denver, Colorado. But one more honor awaited her before she headed for Denver. At a ceremony at Club 21 on May 16, she received the Ward Morehouse *PIC* Magazine Award for "best young actress to make her debut during the 1946–1947 season."

Known as "America's Oldest Summer Theatre in Mile High Denver," the Elitch Gardens Theatre was part of a larger complex consisting of formal gardens and an amusement park. Founded in 1890 by San Francisco newlyweds John and Mary Elitch, the Elitch Gardens had originally been a sixteen-acre property called Chilcott Farms. Opening a restaurant and planting produce to supply the public, the couple soon transformed the property into a picnic grove and zoo. Construction on the theater began before John's unexpected death in 1891 and was completed in 1892.

Known formally as the Playhouse in the Gardens, the octagonal wooden structure with its two-story porch was built to offer quality entertainment for Denver audiences during the summer.

Patricia arrived in Denver as the female lead in nine out of that summer's ten productions. Her leading man was the handsome thirty-four-year-old Peter Cookson, recently seen in *Message for Margaret* on Broadway and considered among the most promising young actors.

Patricia originally stayed at the posh Brown Palace Hotel but soon took an apartment. She began an arduous routine, beginning rehearsals around 10:00 A.M., taking a break for lunch, and continuing rehearsals until dinner. While performing every evening in one play, Patricia rehearsed another play during the day and performed in two matinees weekly, on Wednesday and Saturday. Upon her first glimpse of Cookson, Patricia knew immediately that her affair with Victor Jory was over. Within days, Patricia contacted Jory in California and broke off their romance, her sights now firmly set on Cookson— who was married and had two children.

The opening production of the season was a light comedy, *Made in Heaven.* Written by Hagar Wilde, *Made in Heaven* was a marital comedy about the battle of the sexes, revolving around the mix-ups of a New York executive trying to decide if he and his young, bored wife can really get along. At the beginning of the play he cannot stand her; by the end of the last act he can't live without her.

Opening on Sunday, June 22, *Made In Heaven* featured Patricia as Elsa Meredith, with Cookson portraying her husband, Zachary. It was a hit with Denver's discerning audience.

The second production of the season, *Laura*, opened just four days after the play's Broadway premiere. Vera Caspary's novel on which the play was based had already been made into a successful movie in 1944 for 20th Century-Fox. The Denver production starred Cookson as Mark McPherson, with Patricia as Laura Hunt.

Laura was a murder mystery, adapted for the stage by its author and George Sklar. The body of a beautiful young woman is found in Laura Hunt's apartment, and detective Mark MacPherson is called in to solve the crime. Patricia once more garnered good reviews from the Denver critics. The *Denver Post*'s John Snyder called her "nothing short of majestic";[4] Richard Detwiler of the *Rocky Mountain News* was also complimentary, not just of her performance, but also of her appearance: "Patricia Neal as the ravishing, man-collecting Laura . . . handled the role beautifully, [and] appeared in the second act resplendent in lounging pajamas. Considering her generous endowment, this alone could have made the show."[5]

The Denver audiences were finding the 1947 theater season to be quite satisfying, hailing both Patricia and Peter as celebrities. Mrs. Mayfield's Advice to the Lovelorn column in the *Rocky Mountain News* that summer carried this letter and response:

Dear Mrs. Mayfield:

My husband is positively consumed with curiosity about Patricia Neal, leading lady at the Elitch's. We have second row seats and he wants me to change them for closer ones. He keeps talking about her well-developed personality and wonders if she is married.

While he's enjoying P. Neal, I, too, am having a good time. Peter Cookson suits me just fine, and I'm just as curious about his private life. Do you have the dope for a couple of FIRST NIGHTERS.

Dear First Nighters:

I'm delighted to hear you're having such fun. As long as Miss Neal is onstage, while hubby is two rows from the front, it all sounds perfectly safe, too. A usually reliable source informs me that the leading lady is MISS Neal. Mr. Cookson is married and has two children.[6]

But Cookson's marriage was on the rocks. He and his wife, Maureen, had separated that spring, and that summer they were attempting a reconciliation, taking a house along with their two children in Denver. That effort was doomed once Cookson met his young and beautiful leading lady. Patricia knew what she was doing. She found the actor handsome and appealing. She also knew he was married. "I was horrible, absolutely horrible," she said later.[7] Asked if she was in love with him, she candidly admitted that she wasn't. "But he was so attractive, and I wanted him."[8]

When Maureen found out about their affair, she left Cookson. Patricia recalled with shame that it was a horrible scene when Cookson's wife and children left Denver, about halfway through that summer season. "It was the only time in my life that I wrecked a marriage, but in those days I had no conscience," Patricia wrote.[9]

Patricia's most challenging and best-remembered role that summer was as Joan in Maxwell Anderson's *Joan of Lorraine*, a play that she was more than familiar with. A hit on Broadway the year before, it had starred Ingrid Bergman in her Tony Award–winning performance as Mary Gray/Joan. The modern-day story of *Joan of Lorraine* revolves around rehearsals of a play dealing with the historical story of Joan of Arc, done with minimal sets and partial costumes. The realism is heightened when the Director (played by Cookson) steps out from the audience to "direct" his cast. Conflict arises between Mary Gray and the Director over Joan's concept of the world.

It was in this play that, for the first time, Patricia forgot a line—perhaps because of the length of the speeches combined with the late hours spent with Cookson. Patricia recalled that Cookson, "true to his character [the Director] simply called out, 'Line!'"[10] Patricia never forgot that moment, and she never repeated the mistake again on any stage.

Denver audiences attending the opening on Sunday evening, August 3, were in for an astounding and amazingly dramatic theatrical experience. Immersing herself into the character, Patricia approached the role with deepest concentration, assuredness, and belief. The reviews were magnificent. Said John Snyder in the *Denver Post* the following day, "A jammed house made clear the expectancy of the play-goers, and they were far from disappointed as Patricia Neal, in the title role, turned in a brilliant performance. . . . The name of Patricia Neal was on the lips of nearly every first nighter as they left the theater. With exceptionally long stretches of dialog and without the benefit of an attractive setting, she received more comment than for any other performance she has given this season. Her sincerity was delightful."[11]

The following week's audiences saw Patricia as the sickly, bedridden Elizabeth Barrett in Rudolf Besier's drama *The Barretts of Wimpole Street*. Cookson costarred as Robert Browning. The three-act drama takes place in Elizabeth Barrett's bed-sitting room at 50 Wimpole Street, London, in 1845. Through a secret romance with Browning, Elizabeth is able to defy her domineering father and leave her sickly life.

Taking a brief respite the following week, Patricia did not appear in Elitch's ninth production, *Years Ago*, by Ruth Gordon. She finished the season with *The Two Mrs. Carrolls*, which opened on August 24. Written by Martin Vale, *The Two Mrs. Carrolls* tells the story of psychopathic Geoffrey Carroll (portrayed by guest film and theatre star Donald Woods), who paints his wives as angels, then kills them. As his next angel, Sally, Patricia was superb as a terrified victim.[12]

Returning to New York while Patricia was still acting in Denver, Cookson rented an economical one-room apartment at the Bristol Hotel on 129 West Forty-eighth Street for the few weeks they would be together before *Another Part of the Forest* began its tour. The two were often seen together about town. One evening they went to a fortune-teller, who told Cookson that he would one day marry a very wealthy woman and told Patricia that someday she would have "trouble in the head."[13]

Soon upon their return to New York both Patricia and Cookson were asked to join a new acting group, the Actors Studio, founded by director Elia Kazan, producer Cheryl Crawford, and producer-director-actor Robert Lewis. The three founders had been associated with the Group Theater, and the Actors Studio trained actors in the realistic style developed by the Group Theater in the 1930s, cultivating it into what is now known as the "Method." This approach stressed that actors must know and understand themselves and the selves of the characters they play. The Actors Studio began with a nucleus of some thirty young and talented stage newcomers; their work developed the foundation of film and stage acting for years to come.

At the outset, Lewis instructed the advanced players, and Kazan worked with the beginners. Kazan chose Julie Harris, Cloris Leachman, James Whitmore, Eli Wallach, Anne Jackson, Martin Balsam, E. G. Marshall, and Kim Hunter for his group. Lewis chose Mildred Dunnock, Marlon Brando, Peter Cookson, Beatrice Straight (who would later marry Cookson), Sidney Lumet, Tom Ewell, Montgomery Clift, Jerome Robbins (Clift's lover), Maureen Stapleton, and Patricia.

Patricia and Lewis did not get along. Lewis continually belittled Patricia and her craft. An instinctive and deeply sensitive artist, Patricia wasted little time bemoaning Lewis's psychological brutality. She had only a little time in New York before she left on tour with *Another Part of the Forest.*

Forest was set to play Philadelphia, Columbus, Indianapolis, and Chicago. Kansas City and St. Louis performances were scheduled later, followed by a tour of California and the West. Despite respectable reviews, *Another Part of the Forest* was not a hit on the road. Midwest audiences were not receptive to this prequel to *The Little Foxes*. The play closed in October, shortly after its Chicago opening. It had run a total of 182 performances.

Back in New York in late October, Patricia was offered a role in a revival of Marcel Pagnol's play *Topaz*, but she declined the offer.

Hollywood was very interested in Patricia Neal. One evening, Patricia was escorted about New York by film producer David O. Selznick. He promised her that if she signed with him, she would "win an Academy Award for her first part."[14] Patricia recalled that while out with Gregory Peck and his wife until the wee hours, probably at Club 21, Selznick "got very drunk, told me how much he loved Jennifer Jones, and tried to get me into bed."[15] Still believing that talent will out, she found his behavior appalling and refused to sign with him. Besides Selznick's proposal, Patricia was offered film contracts by Samuel Goldwyn, George Stevens, Paramount, and Metro-Goldwyn-Mayer. "It's dazzling to have all that money offered you," she remarked while visiting Knoxville prior to embarking for Denver for the summer.[16]

On November 24, Warner Brothers producer William T. Orr sent a telegram to Harry Mayer in Warner Brothers' New York office advising Mayer that a seven-year contract offer had been made for the services of "Pat Neale" with a guaranteed forty weeks a year at a starting salary of $750 a week, escalating to $1,250 a week the second year, $1,500 a week the third year, and climbing to $3,000 a week in the seventh year. Orr told Mayer that Patricia's agency, MCA, had said the offer was too low, "but you might be interested [in using] this offer as a basis for negotiations."[17]

Patricia and her agency insisted upon certain concessions. She still wanted to appear in the theatrical presentation of O'Neill's *A Touch of the Poet.* Most certainly she wanted to hold out for the option to return to the stage periodically. Thanks to the sage advice from K. T. Stevens, Patricia insisted upon featured or star-player billing and salary.

On December 18, Patricia received a two-page telegram from Lew Wasserman of MCA, stating that Warner Brothers had essentially agreed to her demands. The proposed seven-year contract would guarantee a minimum of forty weeks' salary beginning at $1,250 a week and rising in yearly increments to $3,750 in the final year. She would be permitted to return to the theater twice during the contract period and could take the role in *A Touch of the Poet*, but not before the third year of the contract. She wouldn't be allowed to stay away two successive years, but the two-year cap would permit her to be away for three full eight-month Broadway seasons.

She would, however, be permitted to act in only one play each season, so if a play closed early, she would have to return to the studio.

The telegram also said that "regarding billing the first picture will introduce Pat Neal the second third and fourth pictures will have special Pat Neal billing apart from other feature players in the cast starting with fifth picture you are to receive star or co-star billing naturally Warners reserves the right to star you immediately."[18] Her first part under the contract would be the female lead in *John Loves Mary*—and no screen test was involved.

Patricia accepted the offer and prepared to go to California to officially sign the contract.

Peter Cookson was committed to the run of a play and could not accompany her. Their affair had begun to wane already, as Cookson had grown melancholy over the separation from his children. Still, the farewell at Grand Central Station the second week of December 1947 was a tearful one. Patricia boarded a train to Knoxville and Williamsburg to spend the Christmas season with family and friends en route to California.

Patricia was gathered up at the station in Knoxville by Frank Ball's father, with whom she had kept in close contact. After she celebrated Christmas with her family at the home of friends—and after she agreed to send for her mother and brother, Pete, to join her in Hollywood after she settled in—Mr. Ball returned her to the train station. The two friends embraced, and in his quiet southern drawl the gentle old man gave Patricia some heartfelt advice: "Men will do you harm, Patsy. Do not succumb to them. Morals are very important. *They* will be with you always."[19] With tears in her eyes, she kissed Mr. Ball good-bye, and said good-bye as well to perhaps the last peaceful moments that she would experience for several years to come.

5

Warner Brothers

When I was 18 I thought I was so wise. I thought I was so smart dashing around Hollywood. Actually I was an ass. Wisdom comes from age and passing of the years, and usually from a few good, horrid experiences.

—Patricia Neal, 1979

After a three-day cross-country rail journey, Patricia Neal stepped off the train in Burbank, California, on Tuesday, December 30, 1947. Wearing a new Pilgrim bonnet and a suit her mother had given her, Patricia was met at the station by Warners publicist Eric Stacey. Her photograph was quickly taken, and she was whisked off to the Bel Air Hotel. When she was driven across the little bridge at the hotel and saw the swans gliding on the water, she literally swooned. "I thought, oh my God! I was in Paradise," she recalled.[1]

Warner Brothers wasted little time with formalities or even holiday cheers for their new investment. Delivered to the Warner Brothers Studio at 4000 Warner Boulevard, Patricia met with producer Jerry Wald and Warner Brothers legal executive Roy J. Obringer to sign her seven-year contract.

Later that afternoon, Stacey introduced the new contract actress to Perc Westmore and Margaret Donovan, of the studio's makeup department, and the studio's costume department head, designer Bill Travilla. The next morning, New Year's Eve, at 8:30 A.M., Stacey picked Patricia up at the hotel to have her hair fixed, and at 10:30 A.M. Travilla and Patricia traveled to downtown Los Angeles "to select on consignment suitable wardrobe for her part of 'Mary' in this picture" at Saks Fifth Avenue and I. Magnin.[2]

That evening, on a studio-arranged date, Patricia was introduced to several film stars at a New Year's Eve party, including her *John Loves Mary* leading man, Ronald Reagan. The star of such Warner Brothers films as *King's Row* (1942), *Knute Rockne: All American* (1940), and *This Is the Army* (1943),

---

Facing page: Patricia Neal at Warner Brothers, 1948. From the author's collection.

Reagan had just completed the filming of *The Voice of the Turtle* with the young starlet Eleanor Parker.

Approaching Patricia from across the crowded room, the thirty-six-year-old actor cheerfully extended his hand and introduced himself, saying, "I'm Ronnie Reagan. We're doing this *John Loves Mary* together. I'm very happy to meet you."[3] Patricia recalled that when next she saw him around midnight that evening, he was on the terrace with an older woman, weeping. Reagan had just separated from his first wife, Jane Wyman. Wyman had been offered and had accepted the role of Mary in *John Loves Mary*. But because of her marital difficulties, she pulled out of the agreement, and the role was offered almost immediately to Patricia. Within six months, Reagan and Wyman would divorce.

On New Year's Day 1948, preproduction for *John Loves Mary* began and Patricia stepped before the Hollywood motion picture cameras for the first time. *John Loves Mary* was adapted for the screen by Henry and Phoebe Ephron from Norman Krasna's play. Its plot concerns the return of U.S. Army Sergeant John Lawrence (Reagan) and his in-name-only war bride, Lilly Herbish (Virginia Field), after World War II. John has married Lilly as a favor to his less-than-scrupulous war buddy, Fred Taylor (Jack Carson), to secure her citizenship and entry into the United States. Lilly is supposed to divorce John and marry Fred, her true love, but Fred is already married and about to become a father. Stuck in the middle is Mary McKinley (Neal), the girl John left behind. After many complications, the humorous situations are resolved.

Primary rehearsals for *John Loves Mary* were called for the week of January 5 with Reagan, Neal, Carson, and Arnold, who were already under salary. Ronald Reagan would be paid $75,250, and Jack Carson would receive $74,000. Patricia would get $25,000 for her first role, less than Edward Arnold at $36,500 and Wayne Morris at $31,791. On January 8, Patricia was tested in her first change of wardrobe, designed by Warners fashion designer Milo Anderson. (The original wardrobe was returned to the stores.) Jerry Wald sent Patricia an interoffice memo that evening with an accompanying picture, stating, "Attached is the first still of your first picture in your first camp chair in your first studio. I know there'll be millions of other stills with other producers, other directors and other cameramen. However, since this is the first one—like the first apple and the first orange or the first bridge—it becomes important. Some day, when this picture is nice and yellow, all of us can look at it and say, 'We remember when—pleasantly,' I know."[4]

The first day of principal shooting on *John Loves Mary* was January 13, 1948, on Stage 3, the McKinley apartment, with Patricia's very first close-up—her character's opening telephone conversation with John. Wrote Patricia, "We did one scene that whole day. It took hours to fix every detail. . . . I was so impressed with the stars of the film, Ronald Reagan and Jack Carson. They knew what to do in front of a camera. In fact, everyone on the set was experienced but me. But I was too excited to be afraid."[5]

That evening, after viewing the first day's rushes (the takes of that day's scenes), producer Jerry Wald exulted in a memo to director David Butler, "I know that we have a winner!"[6] Recalled Patricia, "If the aim of the Hollywood movie of the forties was to re-create paradise, going to rushes was purgatory. Never before had I seen myself on the screen, and I was horrified. I thought I looked so bad. I was a caricature in false eyelashes and forties lips. My hair was pulled straight back on my head. I didn't know that on-screen one photographs a little heavier. I could see that I would have to keep a strict diet."[7]

In the first half of the twentieth century, the motion picture stars became America's royalty. Their pictures, clothes, actions, and lives were part of each studio's publicity mill, necessary to generate interest and sell movie tickets. The heads of the studios became dominant and wealthy figures in the film industry. Feted by politicians and royalty alike because of their fame, newly acquired wealth, and public following, many of the early film actors and studio executives wielded heavy corporate power. Motion picture studios became powerful marketeers whose commodities were physical beauty and some talent. Straddling the fine line between "the pursuit of art and the pursuit of profit," film studios churned out picture after picture—some profitable, some not, some good, some not.[8] In 1947, the two highest-grossing motion pictures in the United States and Canada, each grossing about $11 million, were *The Best Years of Our Lives* (Goldwyn), which won the Best Picture Oscar, and *Duel in the Sun* (Selznick), which was pure soap opera.

Patricia recalls that Jack L. Warner thought she would become the next Garbo, so pleased with himself that *he* had signed her over strong competition. Warner Brothers proudly welcomed Patricia with open arms. Ads in the trade papers announced, "Welcome! Patricia Neal—After your five award performances on Broadway, we are happy that you are now making your film debut in 'John Loves Mary' at our studios."[9] The Warners publicity machine began in earnest to promote the studio's new star. She was photographed on a shopping spree on Hollywood Boulevard and at the Farmer's Market that January, dressed in a becoming part-plaid outfit.

The papers paid attention. According to the *Hollywood Reporter*, when

Patricia arrived in town, she had "the distinction as being the tallest actress on screen."[10] In the *Los Angeles Times* on January 13, 1948, Edwin Schallert, in an article headlined "Young Stage Star Turns to Cinema," said about Patricia's quick rise to fame, "Patricia plans to organize a study group in Hollywood similar to the one with which she was identified in New York. Marlo[n] Brando, Karl Malden, Joan Chandler, who is a Selznick contractee, and Montgomery Clift were in this serious-minded ensemble. One reason Miss Neal is in Hollywood, in spite of her Broadway triumph, is that she believes pictures demand a more sincere expression from the actress. Her contract permits her to return to the stage if she desires. Films have an attraction for her which ultimately may prove irresistible."

In one magazine interview, Jack Carson and Ronald Reagan humorously commented on Patricia's low and mellow voice. Carson said it sounded "like a musically inclined dripping rain pipe playing the scales. Or a refined fog horn." Reagan commented a bit more delicately that her voice sounded like "an organ concert." To which Patricia added that it was "noisy, anyhow."[11]

Invitations began arriving frequently for her to attend various functions around Hollywood. The studio, of course, encouraged her participation, as the resulting press would give her and her upcoming films much necessary, and free, publicity.

Patricia soon became familiar with many of the stars at Warners. She was more than impressed with the queen of the lot, Bette Davis, who had her own studio car.

During the filming of *John Loves Mary*, Patricia's relationship with comedian Jack Carson (still married to his second wife) soon turned into casual friendship as they began taking lunch at the Golf Club near the studio, where Carson could drink. Sometimes they would end up at Carson's home at the end of the day. Their relationship remained strictly platonic; they simply enjoyed each other's company and laughs. The gossip columnists picked up on their relationship. Wrote one, "Jack Carson and Pat Neal seem to have discovered each other off the lot. They are working together in 'John Loves Mary.' And Jack is confiding to friends that he finds Pat 'different.' He means that she is intelligent."[12]

At the same time, Patricia and Peter Cookson's relationship was more than strained. It was only when he notified her that he was divorcing his wife that Patricia knew she couldn't put off the inevitable. She wrote a letter telling him, "I am so sorry, Peter, I really am, but it's not right and we're not right."[13] He never responded. In 1949, when the play he was appearing in, *The Heiress*, went on the road, Cookson met and married his leading lady, the thirty-four-year-old Beatrice Straight, a member of the wealthy Whitney-Vanderbilt family.

In February, Patricia's brother, Pete, and her mother, Eura, arrived in Hollywood, driven from Knoxville by her cousin Lenore McGimpsey, who left after a few days of sightseeing. The family took a three-bedroom apartment at 9925 Durant Drive. After enrolling her thirteen-year-old brother in public grade school in Beverly Hills, Patricia soon realized that her dream of providing for his education and making a home with her mother was a mistake. Pete was having problems at school, not fitting in because of his southern accent. Patricia had purchased a new Buick and learned to drive it, but Eura did not like the traffic in Los Angeles, so she stayed at home cooking foods Patricia needed to avoid. And the indomitable Mrs. Neal did not approve of the moral climate of Hollywood, forever making comments to Patricia about proper behavior. The arrangement became very uncomfortable.

Production wrapped on *John Loves Mary* on March 1, although retakes for a couple of scenes were called for with Reagan, Patricia, and Katharine Alexander on March 4. When filming ended, Patricia was immediately taken off salary. The suspension was rescinded by Warners executive Phil Friedman on March 8, but Patricia was again laid off on March 18.

After *John Loves Mary*, Patricia was immediately considered for other film roles. "Hollywood Is My Beat" columnist Sidney Skolsky announced, "Jimmy Stewart is being tempted to play 'Young Man With A Horn,' and if he does, the leading lady will be either Pat Neal of the Broadway stage, or Barbara Bel Geddes."[14] The picture was filmed and released in 1949, directed by Michael Curtiz and starring Kirk Douglas and Lauren Bacall.

Patricia soon developed a friendship with studio writer Harry Kurnitz, who squired her about the endless Hollywood events and parties. At a dinner one evening she met another writer, John Gunther, who also became a frequent escort. Her career was moving into high gear, and Patricia found little time to become romantically involved with another man so soon after the breakup with Peter.

While visiting her hairdresser soon after filming ended on *John Loves Mary*, Patricia discovered he was studying with acting coach George Shdanoff. She had recently received a "Dear John" letter from Robert Lewis of the Actors Studio in New York telling her and a handful of other students, including Sidney Lumet, not to come back. In search of study and training while working in Hollywood, she soon sought out the Russian-born Shdanoff, whose reputation was solidly established in Los Angeles.

Having written, directed, and acted in both theater and film in Germany, France, and England (most notably, he starred in the 1946 British film *Specter of the Rose*), Shdanoff had become quite popular within the film colony, in demand as a teacher. With his colleague Michael Chekhov (son of the great playwright Anton), Shdanoff soon developed a style of acting that was ideal for film, based on that which Constantin Stanislavsky and Lee Strasberg called "The Method." Shdanoff came to America during World War II, offering an alternative approach to creating and defining performance. Shdanoff and his wife, Elsa Schreiber, taught classes in their home at 9009 St. Ives Drive in Los Angeles to such Hollywood newcomers as Gregory Peck, Rex Harrison, Yul Brynner, Leslie Caron, Gene Kelly, and Robert Stack. (Shdanoff would continue to teach until his death at the age of ninety-two in 1998.)

Actor Robert Stack remembered these classes held at the Shdanoff home, "The class acts, Rex Harrison and Gregory Peck, were upstairs with Elsa Schreiber. We—Patricia and myself—not that we weren't good, were downstairs with George. He found ways [for us] even to play the most difficult scenes with the simplest motivation." Working on a scene study of *A Streetcar Named Desire* with Patricia as Blanche DuBois, Stack recalled, "I was the world's worst Brando. And she was perfectly wonderful with what she did. I was terrible. . . . And she has those wonderful eyes. . . . [Those with expressive faces] are the gifted ones, and she is, God love her."[15] When Shdanoff heard Patricia do the *Streetcar* scene with Stack, he quietly approached her and exclaimed in awe, "Who are you? Do you know that you are an exceptionally great talent?" Patricia proudly recalled, "He adored me."[16]

Soon, Warners would have *the* breakthrough role for Patricia, but it wouldn't be hers without a struggle.

In November 1943, Warner Brothers had acquired for $50,000 the rights to a best-selling novel by an idiosyncratic Russian émigré, Ayn Rand. *The Fountainhead*, a 754-page potboiler, deals with corporate corruption, sex, and the ultimate triumph of the individual over the masses.

The first draft of the screenplay was written by Rand herself, who was paid an additional $13,000 to write it, and was submitted to the studio in June 1944. The script went through several more drafts by other screenwriters and was finally submitted for production in June 1948. Rand rejected that version and rewrote the script, demanding that not one of her words be altered.

Well before the script was finalized, the movie was the subject of jealousy and controversy. Metro-Goldwyn-Mayer's top male star, Clark Gable, was upset with his studio for not purchasing for him the role of architect Howard Roark, the film's hero. (MGM gave Gable *The Hucksters* instead. It fizzled at the box office, and he never forgave them.) In January 1945, the *Hollywood Reporter* reported that Warners planned to film *The Fountainhead* with Humphrey Bogart and Barbara Stanwyck, who claimed to have brought the novel to the attention of the studio while the book was still climbing the best-seller lists.

Studio head Jack Warner had considered Jennifer Jones, Gene Tierney, Ida Lupino, and Eleanor Parker for the part of Dominique Francon, the female lead in *The Fountainhead.* In September 1945, the *Hollywood Reporter* announced that Warners wanted to borrow Alan Ladd from Paramount to star him opposite Lauren Bacall. The role of Howard Roark was eventually offered to Gary Cooper, whose wife, Rocky, had read the book. He was rightfully hesitant to take the part. Cooper's own attorney, I. H. Prinzmetal, had declined the offer, stating, "Cooper's audience was not intellectual, and if they heard him say such selfish things they'd hold it against him. It might change his reputation and career!"[17] Though she never interfered with Gary's decisions in choosing roles, this time Rocky strongly advised him to override his attorney's advice and accept the part. Said Rand about Cooper, "He is my choice for 'Roark.' His physical appearance is exactly right."[18] Cooper wired Jack Warner his acceptance on January 31.

Barbara Stanwyck fiercely coveted the role of Dominique. King Vidor simply found her too old for the part, especially after seeing her in Samuel Goldwyn's *Stella Dallas* (1937). He was also convinced that she could not play a lady.[19] Paramount player Veronica Lake, her stardom waning, told the press that Ayn Rand had written the part just for her because she wore her hair like Dominique. Even Joan Crawford, under contract with Warner Brothers and now forty years old, wanted the role; she hosted a dinner party for Rand, hoping to win her approval. That evening Crawford wore a white evening dress, designed by MGM's Adrian, and covered herself in aquamarine jewelry in a futile attempt to look the part. The author quickly set her sights elsewhere. Suddenly, Warners star Bette Davis wanted the part. But her temperament, combined with her age and failing box-office performance—and a veto by director King Vidor and producer Henry Blanke—did her in.

Rand favored Greta Garbo. According to Rand, after she received a copy of the script, Garbo quickly accepted the part, which would mark her return to motion pictures after six years. Then, just as suddenly, Garbo declined it the next day, saying she couldn't play love scenes with Gary Cooper. (In fact, Vidor had sent Garbo the script, and she did return it to him—in person, asking, "Do you really think I should come back in this part?" To which he candidly replied, "As a friend, I don't think you should.")[20]

With the question of the female lead still unsettled, Jack Warner invited Patricia to a luncheon in his office boardroom, along with other lovely young actresses to brighten the meeting. On this particular occasion in April, Patricia was introduced to Gary Cooper, who merely shook her hand and said a few kind words. Patricia recalled that studio stud Errol Flynn was also present, but her eyes were glued on Cooper after he politely greeted her and turned away. Shortly after that fateful meeting, Vidor rode by her on his bicycle on the lot and was stunned by her looks. He stopped and struck up about a fifteen-minute conversation with her. He asked her if she would like to test for the studio's hottest role, that of Dominique in *The Fountainhead*. "Well, Patricia Neal was tall, and she seemed to be right, opposite Gary," said Vidor. "I said [to Jack Warner] I'd talk to her. . . . She read the script and liked it. And I liked her. She had a lot of strength and vitality."[21] On May 18 Patricia officially met with Vidor to discuss the role. Grabbing her tattered copy of the sizzling novel off the shelf, Patricia diligently studied with George Shdanoff until she *knew* the character of Dominique.

Patricia stepped before the cameras on June 3 for sound and photographic tests. She recited her scenes with actors Harlan Ward and Lee Bowman. According to Ayn Rand, Cooper was there that day, both of them watching from off the set. "Her test was horrible," recalled Rand. "Her appearance was really good, but she had a terrible voice and she couldn't read lines. Cooper happened to come to the set during the test. He turned to me and said, 'What's *that*?' When I explained, he said he would stop this."[22] Of course, Cooper did not "stop this." And it's also possible Rand was never at the test. The truth was Patricia's first test was bad. However, the next day she was tested again before the sound cameras, this time with just Harlan Ward. And she passed with flying colors. On June 10, Jerry Wald sent Patricia the script with an attached note, "I know this is the first script of a long line of bigger ones to come."[23]

The Fountainhead tells the story of the fall and rise of Howard Roark (Gary Cooper), an aggressively idealistic architect. Says Roark in the film, "The form of a building must follow its function." His mentor Henry Cameron (Henry Hull) tells Roark, "You want to stand alone against the whole world." Roark is shunned by the architectural community and chooses to work as a driller in a stone quarry rather than sell out his ideals. While working in the quarry, he meets the sensual and emotionally charged newspaper columnist and heiress Dominique Francon (Patricia Neal). Her father, it seems, owns the quarry where Roark works. In a remarkably suggestive scene (which when filmed somehow passed the censors), Roark arouses Dominique's passion.

Roark returns to New York to accept an architectural commission. Dominique marries her boss, the wealthy newspaper magnate Gail Wynand (Raymond Massey), whose paper is running a smear campaign against Roark's architectural designs. Despite those tactics, Roark becomes successful and is reunited with Dominique at a party for the opening of a building that Roark has designed. Society architect Peter Keating (Kent Smith) asks Roark to design a proposed housing complex, Courtlandt Homes, which Roark agrees to do anonymously under the condition that none of his plans and ideas are changed.

Wynand and Roark become friends, with Dominique strangely completing the triangle. When the three return from a trip, Roark realizes that his design plans for the housing complex have been severely altered. With the help of Dominique, he literally dynamites the project. At his much-publicized trial, with public opinion strongly against him, he wins an acquittal by expressing his ideals and reasons for his destructive act. Wynand inexplicably commits suicide after commissioning Roark to build the world's tallest building in his name. Roark starts the new project, the Wynand Building, with Dominique by his side. As she ascends to the top of the largest building in the world in an open elevator lift, she spots Roark standing at the top, his legs straddling the skyscraper, which seems to expand from his lower body. Cut and print.

In a 2002 essay on *The Fountainhead*, Merrill Schleier says about Dominique's character, "She is passionate and repressed, but possesses too many masculine traits to be considered female. Rand renders her as a masochist and a defeatist, capable only of destructive acts, in contrast to Roark, who creates. . . . She is unable to respond sexually to men until she meets Roark, whose masculine creative agency ignites her passion, thereby completing her. Rand herself called Francon a masochist, 'like most women.' In the film, Francon's sexual dysfunction and gender confusion are demonstrated by her numerous changes in costumes, from masculine riding attire to lacy negligee. . . . (Her) mannish costumes were erotic, drawing attention to the femininity of the bodies they clothed, and a provocation, an example of gender ambiguity. Like other such female characters, Francon later casts aside her masculine attire to claim her true heterosexuality."[24]

Warners announced it officially on June 20: the role of Dominique was hers. Their faith in Patricia's talent was firmly established. Friends and family responded with joy.

But it appears that no one at the studio called Barbara Stanwyck to tell her the role of Dominique had been given to Patricia Neal. According to Stanwyck, it was Ayn Rand who broke the news in a telephone call. Furious and bitter about not landing the part, Stanwyck telegraphed Jack L. Warner on June 21: "A couple of years have gone by since I made a film for you and since then I am sure you will agree that the scripts submitted me have not compared with 'The Fountainhead.' I read in the morning papers today your official announcement that Miss Patricia Neal is going to play the role of 'Dominique' in 'The Fountainhead.' After all, Jack, it seems odd after I found the property, brought it to the attention of the studio, had the studio purchase the property, and during the preparation of the screenplay everyone assumed I would be in the picture, and now I find someone else is definitely playing the role. Naturally, Jack, I am bitterly disappointed. However, I can realistically see your problems, and certainly based on all of these circumstances, it would appear to be to our mutual advantage to terminate our present contractual relationship. I would appreciate hearing from you."[25]

Warner wrote back to Stanwyck, on June 22, "I have your telegram . . . and, while I know you brought *The Fountainhead* to Mr. Blanke's attention, I want to make it very clear to you that we have a huge Story Department here in the Studio as well as in New York that covers every book, periodical, etc.

The Fountainhead was called to the attention of our studio through regular channels. I personally knew about it long before you suggested it to Mr. Blanke, and we were considering it for purchase and subsequently closed for it. Naturally your interest in this property is well understood, but our studio does not confine its operations to cases where people bring in books or other stories and we buy them solely on their suggestion. It operates through regular channels, and did in this case as in most cases. However, since our actions have offended you and you desire to terminate your contract with us, it may be that under the circumstances this would be the best thing to do. It is with regret that I accede to your request and, if you will have your agent or attorney get in touch with our Legal Department here at the studio, the formalities of terminating your contract can be arranged."[26]

Stanwyck's contract was effectively terminated. In fact, her last two pictures for the studio, *The Two Mrs. Carrolls* (1947) and *Cry Wolf* (1947), both had only been moderately successful. Stanwyck would appear in just two more films for Warner Brothers, both in 1953—*The Moonlighter*, with Fred MacMurray, and *Blowing Wild*, with Gary Cooper.

As for Patricia, Warner Brothers was now committed to making her a star. Her future had never looked so promising.

6

Gary Cooper

Will you marry me? I want to stay with you. We'll take a house in some small town, and I'll keep it for you. Don't laugh, I can. I'll cook, I'll wash your clothes, I'll scrub the floors."

—Dominique, *The Fountainhead* (1949)

The filming of *The Fountainhead* began with the quarry scene, shot on location in Knowles, California, between Fresno and Yosemite National Park, in the state's largest and oldest quarry. Director King Vidor rode out to Knowles with Patricia and Cooper in a studio limousine, and the three had dinner together. "They went for each other right away," Vidor said of his two stars.[1]

Patricia and Cooper stayed at the California Hotel during the three-day location shoot, and Patricia recalls being aware of the dynamics of her and Gary's relationship from the beginning. She knew they shared a physical attraction.

The first scenes for the picture were shot in Knowles on July 12. The script called for Patricia's character, Dominique, to ride up to her father's stone quarry on horseback. Patricia didn't ride, and a stunt double, Audrey Scott, was hired for those scenes. However, just before shooting began, Scott pulled out because she felt that she could make more money at an upcoming horse show. So Patricia learned to ride. "The studio arranged lessons for me and I went faithfully," she recalled. "By the time we shot the first scene of the film, I could at least sit on the animal."[2] She told columnist Howard C. Heyn, "I'm a taxicab girl. This Los Angeles traffic has me licked. I'm afraid to drive in it. But horses are worse. I wouldn't cry if I never saw another horse."[3]

The quarry scene caused a bit of controversy because of its obvious sex-

---

Facing page: Patricia Neal and Gary Cooper in *The Fountainhead*, 1949. Patricia's favorite picture of the two of them together. From the author's collection.

ual overtones. Cooper, at forty-six, was still extremely attractive and fit. Surprisingly, the censors did not edit the Freudian symbolism of Dominique's encounter with Roark. The phallic imagery is unmistakable. Roark is seen in hard hat and snugly fitting pants, his shirt sleeves rolled up, sweat dripping down his keenly intelligent brow and drenching his clothing, holding his throbbing drill hammer at near crotch-position, relentlessly thrusting it into the tight hole in the unyielding rock. Dominique is consumed by the eroticism of the image. Filmed with Patricia's character looking down upon Cooper's, the meaning of the scene is obvious: she is dominant. At night, she is in agony as she visualizes that scene over and over in her head, and she returns day after day to watch him. Roark eventually mocks Dominique's behavior. As he walks along a dusty road, Dominique gallops up on horseback and slashes him across his face with her riding crop.

Problems with the film began as soon as the company returned to Los Angeles to resume shooting on the Warners lot. Between July 16 and 20, the two most important scenes between Cooper and Neal—the night scene in Dominique's bedroom and the love scene later in the picture at Roark's apartment after the Enright party—were shot. In the first scene, Roark realizes that Dominique desires him. He comes to her bedroom during a balmy night. "A sinister, phallic shadow above his head underscores his sado-erotic intentions," wrote Merrill Schleier in his 2002 essay on *The Fountainhead*.[4] Dominique is dressed in a revealing Chantilly lace negligee, Roark in his work clothes, his sleeves rolled up. Cooper is commanding and physically exciting. Without dialogue, he grabs Dominique and she wrestles violently with him. He throws her to the floor; she rises and attacks him, pounding his chest in a sexually charged struggle. This is followed by a long embrace and passionate kiss. Dominique breaks away, rushes to her balcony, stumbles and falls, Roark behind her. The camera moves in on him standing over her, a victorious smile forming on his face as the scene fades.

The censors found Dominique a little too sexually compliant, stating, "The action in Scene 66 is completely unacceptable. As presently written, this scene seems to suggest a sex affair. Moreover, this sex affair has about it a flavor suggestive of a not-too-strenuously resisted rape. . . . Here and elsewhere, the kissing should not be passionate, prolonged or *open-mouthed*."[5] In a July 19 memo from the censors, it is suggested, "After seeing first days' rushes, a couple of shots have to be made over—censorship. . . . Miss Neal's breasts were too clearly visible."[6] The provocative scene was reshot and toned down enough to pass the censors.

The second of the two scenes, shot on July 20, takes place after the Enright party. Following a beautifully tender scene in which Roark professes his love for Dominique, he picks her up in his arms and asks, "You won't leave me, will you?" He kisses her cheeks, her nose, her eyelids, and her hair. Dominique confesses her love for Roark, kneeling before him in a gentle and ironically sensitive moment—a symbolic reversal of roles. This one scene alone solidified the actual and very real moment when Patricia knew that she and Gary Cooper were in love. Patricia wrote, "Dominique sits at Roark's feet with her head in his lap. We were in that position for what seemed like hours. Actors usually leap to give their places to stand-ins while endless details of adjusting hot lights and camera angles are worked out. Ann [Urcan, whom Patricia would sometimes refer to as her understudy] and Slim [Talbot], our stand-ins, received their pay but did not work that day. We finished rehearsing and Mr. Vidor called for the crew. We didn't budge but stayed there, quite unable to leave each other's presence."[7]

Gary Cooper had begun his legendary Hollywood career as a $3-a-day stuntman, riding horses and taking falls at minor studios. At first he had only two things to offer the movies: his riding ability and his extraordinary good looks. His first break came in 1925, when he appeared in the two-reel westerns *Tricks* and *Three Pals*. His career began to take off the following year, when he worked for the first time for Samuel Goldwyn in *The Winning of Barbara Worth*. Hired as an extra, Cooper took over the featured male role when the original actor left the film.

After the release of *Morocco* (1930) with Marlene Dietrich, Cooper was established as one of Hollywood's most attractive and—most important—bankable stars. His films with Paramount Pictures and the Goldwyn Studios made millions. By 1947 he had starred with the likes of Joan Crawford, Tallulah Bankhead, Marion Davies, Claudette Colbert, Carole Lombard, Barbara Stanwyck, Ingrid Bergman, Jean Arthur, and Shirley Temple. His films included *The Virginian* (1929); *Design for Living* (1933); *Desire* (1936); *Mr. Deeds Goes to Town* (1936), for which he received his first Oscar nomination; DeMille's *The Plainsman* (1936); *The Westerner* (1940); *Meet John Doe* (1941); *The Pride of the Yankees* (1942), for which he received another Oscar nomination; *For Whom the Bell Tolls* (1943), where he was yet again nominated for an Oscar; and *Unconquered* (1947), again for DeMille. Cooper won Best Actor Oscars for his performances in *Sergeant York* in 1941 and *High Noon* in 1952.

Almost as famous as Cooper's pictures were his love affairs, beginning with his tempestuous 1927 romance with Paramount's top female star, Clara

Bow, the "It" girl. Her successors included Evelyn Brent, Carole Lombard, and Marlene Dietrich. There was also a stormy three-year affair with Lupe Velez, known later in films as "the Mexican spitfire," in a relationship that featured Velez chasing Cooper with a knife during one argument, and an interlude with the wealthy Countess Dorothy di Frasso, thirteen years older than Cooper. "Cooper was probably the greatest cocksman that ever lived," said director Stuart Heisler. "They fell all over themselves to get him to take them to bed. He couldn't stop screwing around. The women wouldn't let him. They'd go lay down for him in a portable dressing room by the soundstage. I guess he had the reputation of being a wonderful lay."[8]

Cooper also had a three-year affair with a man, the young Alabama-born Anderson Lawler, an aspiring film actor. Their letters indicate that they had a deep infatuation with one another; indeed, they lived together at Cooper's apartment for a time. Through Lawler, Cooper gained entrance into Hollywood society.[9]

In 1933, Cooper met the nineteen-year-old actress Sandra Shaw, whose real name was Veronica Balfe, better known as "Rocky." Very proper and still a virgin when she met him, she often used her sharp tongue to criticize the "ill-bred savages" of Hollywood.[10] A bit self-conscious, she was also very well informed, with a style and elegance that attracted Cooper. They wed on December 15, 1933; their only child, Maria, was born in 1937. Though faithful at the beginning of his marriage, Cooper eventually reverted to type and began an affair with costar Ingrid Bergman while filming *For Whom the Bell Tolls* in 1942. Because of that and other indiscretions, the Coopers' marriage was fraying at the edges by 1948, when Cooper met Patricia Neal.

By September 18, *The Fountainhead* was one day ahead of schedule. Ayn Rand seemed in control on the set. In such a hostile environment as Hollywood, Rand was insecure and overprotective of her work. Patricia recalled, "I rather liked her in spite of her loathing of Lillian Hellman. They were, of course, hemispheres apart politically, and Ayn lost no opportunity to run dear Lillian down. Lillian probably returned the attention in kind."[11]

Director Vidor was intimidated or overawed by Rand. Either way, he made remarkable concessions on her behalf. "When he was ready to film the scene in which Dominique goes to Roark's apartment after she learns who he is he told me he wasn't sure he could explain Dominique's psychology to Patricia Neal, and would I write it out for him. I did, and I also wrote out Roark's psychology for the scene. I think it's the best scene in the picture," Rand wrote.[12] Patricia told an interviewer many years later that Vidor was "one of the old-style directors who don't really expect to have to help actors. All he'd do when I had problems was say 'Come on baby, give it all you've got,' when really I was seriously wondering if I'd got anything to give in the first place."[13] Patricia recalled that as the filming progressed, she and Cooper began giving their lines meanings that reflected their blossoming relationship. "I looked forward to each scene we would play together with a new sense of expectation. Lines in the film became pregnant with meaning for us. Howard and Dominique said and did the things we could not yet express," Patricia said.[14]

The domineering Rand was particularly blind to the fact that she was so consumed with her efforts to expound her virtues of individualism, idealism, integrity, and power, both artistic and sexual, that she simply could not write for the common man. Basically, the film was a potboiler. Throughout the month of August, Warner's interoffice memos indicate that Roark's courtroom scene at the end of the film was much in question. The dialogue and the reality of the script just weren't working. Rand became incensed that the studio was considering trimming Roark's speech, but Cooper didn't understand it, and the studio thought it dramatically overlong and rambling. At one point, when Cooper found it almost impossible to speak an extraordinarily awkward passage, he complained. Director Vidor said, "If you're really sincere, we'll have to get Ayn Rand in. She's an hour away. It'll probably take another hour to get dressed." "Oh, to hell with it," Cooper said. "I'll read the line."[15]

On the set the day shooting commenced on the final courtroom scene, Rand was shocked to hear that Vidor had shortened Roark's speech. Infuriated, Rand told producer Henry Blanke that she would disassociate herself from the film if the final speech were cut. Wrote Michael Paxton in his biography of Rand, "Gary Cooper's lawyer and the Johnston office censors were concerned about the uncompromising principles of Roark's individualism. Neither was able to justify their objections, and their questions only prompted Ayn to lengthen the speech for clarity. Increased from four and a half to six and a half minutes, Cooper would now deliver the longest speech in the history of film. . . . It was truly unprecedented. The speech and her script were filmed without one single word changed."[16]

Eura and Patricia's brother Pete were living with her on Durant Drive during the filming of *The Fountainhead*. It was not possible for Patricia and Gary to meet secretly there. Wisely deciding to return home, Eura and Pete finally said their good-byes to Patricia in early fall.

Choosing not to stay in the Durant Drive apartment, Patricia moved temporarily into the Bel Air Hotel. She soon received a telephone call from Jean Valentino, first wife of silent film star Rudolph Valentino, who offered her a bungalow next to the one she shared with her companion, Chloe Carter, near the 20th Century-Fox studios. Located at 2146–2148 Fox Hills Drive, the secluded duplex was entered from a gate at the top of a series of steps leading up from the street. The apartment intended for Patricia (2148) featured an attractive living room with a high-beamed ceiling that opened to an area of lush, terraced gardens. Patricia fell in love with the house and moved in immediately.

The Fountainhead officially concluded on October 8, and a wrap party was held that evening to celebrate. As the guests were leaving, Gary asked Patricia if he could drive her home. According to Patricia, she told him he could follow her to Fox Hills Drive. Rocky was in New York, and Gary and Patricia were in love. Handing him the key to her apartment, she led him inside.

Both Patricia and Cooper participated in extensive promotion and interviews for *The Fountainhead*, before and after its release. Not once, relates Patricia, did the press ask questions about their possible relationship. Wrote Patricia, "Jean and Chloe were the only ones who knew the truth. They never questioned our relationship, and Gary and I never questioned theirs. We quietly cheered each other's team, knowing we were all in murky waters."[17]

Though nearly twenty-five years older than Patricia, Cooper was still a passionate, skilled, and consummate lover. Patricia had known other men, but none as deeply romantic and sensitive as Gary. And she was different from his other conquests. Not only was Patricia intelligent, talented, and beautiful, but she also possessed a joie de vivre and an ironic sense of humor. "Patricia, don't ever lose what you have now. Keep your enthusiasm. It's invaluable," Cooper told her during the filming.[18] Along with being sensuous, warm, and understanding, Patricia complimented Gary and encouraged him. She would always lovingly remember his clear blue eyes, his manner of speech, and the look and touch of his hand.

Patricia decorated her apartment in an Early American style. She was photographed dining on raspberries in her tiny kitchen–dining nook, where she had hung little Dutch curtains and papered the walls with farmhouses and animals. Patricia also began collecting art. A fan who visited Patricia remembered one painting in particular: "I just loved the Negro scene above the mantel in her living room."[19] (The painting was later sold to Mel Brooks and his wife, Anne Bancroft.) Another visiting fan recalled the apartment being like an English-style cottage, conservative, with simple furnishings and books and magazines scattered about. And of course, the fan mentioned Patricia's collection of paintings. Under Gary's tutelage, Patricia's tastes improved and developed. Eventually she would begin to acquire excellent pieces of art as investments.

By taking Jean and Chloe into her confidence, Patricia gave Gary the freedom to enter the gated building on Fox Hills Drive for leisurely and relaxing evenings and passionate nights. Late one evening, shortly after Gary and Patricia had started seeing each other, there was a fatal accident outside the apartment. Patricia immediately grabbed a robe and ran outside to investigate. A car had collided with a telephone pole, and a woman was trapped in the wreckage. The driver, a man, was sitting stunned on the ground beside the car. Two teenagers arrived on the scene. To avoid having Gary become involved, Patricia directed them to a nearby gas station to call an ambulance and the police. As the ambulance pulled away, Patricia heard a policeman say that the man was married, but not to the dying woman. The remark made Patricia shudder. To her horror, as she turned to go back into her bungalow, she saw Gary standing in the road in her dressing gown. No one had noticed him.

Patricia was wise not to question Gary when he left her apartment. She knew that their time together was special. When Patricia was working, Jean and Chloe would often prepare dinner for her and Gary. Patricia was a good cook herself, and oftentimes Gary would drive up to her bungalow with a sack of groceries in the back seat of his Cadillac. He wasn't a bad cook either, Patricia recalled. His specialties were shrimp cocktail and a delicious guacamole dip. After dinner, if they didn't spend the evenings with Jean and Chloe having drinks in the garden, they would simply talk and relax together while listening to music. Sometimes they walked the quiet beaches of Santa Monica, drove to downtown Los Angeles for Mexican food, or visited with intimate mutual friends like Hugh Marlowe and K. T. Stevens, who had a young son who loved to play with Gary. They shared intimacies with each other, grabbing these memories and savoring their pleasures. Wrote Patricia, "I knew I had no rights with him. I did not allow myself then to consider the possibility of a permanent relationship. We were not building a future together. We were seizing moments. He came into my life as he wanted."[20]

Until they were long into their relationship, neither Gary's forceful mother, Alice, nor Rocky herself suspected they were having an affair. At studio functions and other social settings, the two did not publicly display their affection. But Gary's eyes were forever focused on Patricia. At times his hand would quietly slip beneath a table, briefly, to hold hers. And she was reassured of his love. He bought her gifts—the first was a sapphire and ruby pin in the design of a Civil War woman in a hoopskirt and bonnet, an homage to Patricia's southern roots. Patricia gave Gary a gold tie pin, which he kept for years afterward. He also bought her a red polka-dot dress. When Patricia rushed to try it on, she was surprised to find it was too large and cumbersome. Thanking him later and telling him it fit perfectly, she had it altered. For a movie magazine piece a couple of years later, Patricia wore that dress in a photo shoot on a beach with a little boy named Christopher, the son of her good friend Mimi Tellis. Cooper also brought her a fur rug made from an animal he shot while he was in Africa.

Eleanor Parker was slated to play the female lead of *The Hasty Heart*, a film version of the John Patrick play, but when preproduction on the film began, Parker had to drop out because she was pregnant. The picture was scheduled to be filmed in England during the winter months, and Parker was reluctant to travel in her condition. Offered the role, Patricia signed to play opposite her *John Loves Mary* costar Ronald Reagan and film newcomer Richard Todd.

Gary wanted to prolong his hours with Patricia by encouraging the studio to sign her opposite him in his upcoming film *Task Force*, to be directed by Delmar Daves. Warners wisely saw that the female lead in *Task Force* (1949) was a minor role, not fitting the status they had prepared for the star of the still unreleased *John Loves Mary* and *The Fountainhead*. The rather thankless role was eventually given to Jane Wyatt.

Patricia had seen the pre-Broadway production of *The Hasty Heart* in Chicago and realized not only that her role was the only female part in the cast, but also that the script was dramatically challenging. Gary vowed to write her every day during the couple of months she would be gone. Patricia told Gary she would use Jean and Chloe as go-betweens and send her letters to him to Fox Hills Drive, where he would pick them up.

Patricia boarded the train in Los Angeles, along with film star Alan Ladd and his wife, former actress Sue Carol, the first week in November 1948. Patricia said later, "As to fans, I learned a lot about them when I crossed the country with Alan Ladd. . . . He'd get off the train and walk among thousands of fans and he never lost a button off his suit or had a necktie pulled awry. I learned then that you set the tempo for the crowd; if you love them and let them see it, they are the same with you."[21]

Because of a dock strike in New York, the travelers were detoured to Halifax, Nova Scotia, where they boarded their ship to England. After arriving by train in Halifax, where they were greeted by throngs of admiring fans, the

Ladds and Patricia boarded the Cunard–White Star liner RMS *Mauretania* (the second ship of that name). Patricia was not lonely on the voyage. Also on board were Warners actress Virginia Mayo and her husband, actor Michael O'Shea, comic character actor Billy De Wolfe, and young actress Joan Caulfield, who confided to Patricia during the voyage that she, too, was conducting an affair, with the married entertainer Bing Crosby.

Patricia stuck to her cabin during most of the voyage in a futile attempt to avoid Caulfield's bossy mother. Patricia, Caulfield, and De Wolfe invented names for each other—Patricia was "Lady Sybil" to De Wolfe, and the women called him Lord Reginald. Wrote Patricia to Malcolm Miller, the Knoxville drama critic who had championed her cause, "We sleep, eat, sit in deck chairs and talk, walk around a bit, then eat again, and sleep."[22] The voyage went smoothly for the most part, with beautiful weather and a full moon.

Arriving in Southampton on Thursday morning, November 25, the celebrities enjoyed an early breakfast prior to the formalities of immigration that accompanied disembarkation. Naturally the American and the British press took advantage of the opportunity to photograph the stars. After locating Patricia in a lounge talking to fashion reporters, the photographers had the stars pose lining up along the railing on deck. In the cold, Patricia and Virginia Mayo both sported full-length mink coats. Patricia looked smartly attractive and genuinely happy, despite being separated from Gary.

After boarding the boat train for Waterloo Station in London, Patricia was impressed by the "quaint English trains, divided into compartments," as she wrote Miller. Ensconced at the posh Savoy Hotel for the duration of the filming were Patricia, Ronald Reagan, and the film's director, Vincent Sherman. At a reception at the Savoy that Thursday evening, British columnists met and interviewed Patricia, Virginia Mayo, and Michael O'Shea. Patricia remembered that it was a fabulous party and that the handsome British star Robert Donat approached her and said, "You are the most beautiful woman I have ever seen in my life!" Patricia called that "Extraordinary!"[23]

Before filming began, Patricia attended a royal command performance of John Mills's recently completed *Scott of the Antarctic.* Asked to give a message of sympathy from the American people to the royal family and the war-ravaged Brits, Patricia was introduced to the audience by Vivien Leigh, wife of British star Laurence Olivier. Her reading went well. "At the conclusion of a stage show," wrote the *Daily Telegraph,* "in which British and American stars took part, Miss Patricia Neal, as the junior member of the American party, expressed regret at the illness of the King [George VI]."[24] Afterward, Olivier read a message from the king, who sent his regrets at missing the event. (Patricia recalled that when Olivier was handed the message backstage, she asked him if there was something she could do. "It has nothing to do with you," Olivier said in brusque dismissal.)[25] Patricia was thrilled to meet such other luminaries as Sid Field and Anna Neagle. All in all, the event raised $140,000 for the benefit of the Cinematograph Trade Benevolent Fund.

Presented formally to Queen Elizabeth (mother of the future Queen Elizabeth II, who was then pregnant), Princess Margaret, and Prince Philip after the performance, Patricia, wearing a green velvet presentation gown, was indeed enthralled with the pomp and circumstance of the event. Patricia remembered that the queen politely greeted her and then moved on. Suddenly she stopped, came back to Patricia, and said, "I will give the King your message." She then stepped away.[26]

Along with costar Ronald Reagan and Joan Caulfield, Patricia made a personal appearance, followed by a dinner and a ball where she was the official speaker, in Cardiff, Wales. After having coffee with Cardiff's lord mayor, the visiting celebrities toured Cardiff Castle. Traveling on to Paris, Patricia did some sightseeing, including visits to the Eiffel Tower and the Arc de Triomphe, and a performance at the Folies Bergères. "But the city cannot be seen in four days," she wrote Jean and Chloe.[27] She vowed to return one day to see Versailles and tour the Louvre.

On December 8, Patricia and Ronald Reagan appeared at a Catholic Actors benefit show in Dublin. She was introduced to the man who later became the Irish president, Eamon De Valera, and became reacquainted with her idol Katharine Cornell. In a letter to Jean and Chloe dated December 12, Patricia sent "a very special thanks for taking care of my boy."[28]

In night letters (telegrams sent at night for a reduced rate) sent to Patricia throughout her trip abroad, Jean, Chloe, and Gary addressed her as Reginapat. Cooper soon began signing his messages as Reg. On December 16 his message read:

Reginapat, London England

Darling better make me very happy we all had medicinal drink for celebration. Please do not wait so long again.

Love—Love, Reg[29]

7

London

"It's a Great Feeling. . . . If you're in love you're feeling great!"

—*It's a Great Feeling* (1949)

"I went to England for the first time in 1948 to make *The Hasty Heart*," Patricia told a reporter in 1955. "And I hated it. Just hated it. Everything went wrong. The picture just went on forever—a modest picture in black and white, but it took four months. I didn't get to know the British people at all. I was living at the Savoy, very chic, but who wants to live in a hotel room for four months? Then I had an American friend who put a damper on things. We were at the Tower of London one day and he said in a loud voice, addressing the local tourists, 'You ought to see the Empire State Building.' When I went out to functions, I never met any Englishmen; I might as well have stayed in Hollywood. I met Elizabeth Taylor and Robert Taylor and Barbara Stanwyck and David Niven. When I did see Englishmen I thought their coats were too short and their haircuts atrocious. There seemed to be a singular lack of romance between couples; men called their wives 'old girl' or even 'old sausage.' I was frankly bored and homesick."[1]

Filming of *The Hasty Heart* began shortly before Christmas 1948, during Britain's worst winter in more than twenty years. Production was at Associated British Pictures Corporation (ABPC) studios at Elstree, a forty-five-minute drive outside London. *The Hasty Heart* would be the first postwar film shot in its entirety at the facility since its rebuilding; the studio had been a camouflage headquarters during the conflict. Warners decided to make the film in England because of postwar rules that money earned by American pictures could not be taken out of England but could be used in productions filmed there. The picture was a coproduction with the British studio (40 percent owned by Warner Brothers), to be financed by both for $1.2 million.

Facing page: Patricia Neal, 1950. From the author's collection.

Warners supplied the script, the director, and some of the stars; ABPC supplied the studio and production facilities.

With the capable Vincent Sherman set to direct, Warners wisely assigned the script to screenwriter Ranald MacDougall. Fresh from his director's chores on *Adventures of Don Juan* with Errol Flynn and *Backfire* with Virginia Mayo, Sherman was prepared and eager to begin the production. Seeing *The Hasty Heart* not as a war picture per se but as a very human story set against the background of battle-torn Burma, Sherman set about to direct it with restrained good taste. It tells the story of several wounded soldiers: an Englishman named Tommy (Howard Marion-Crawford), a New Zealander named Kini (Ralph Michael), an Aussie named Digger (John Sherman), an American called Yank (Ronald Reagan), and a Basuto African called Blossom (Orlando Martins), watched over by a Canadian nurse, Sister Margaret Parker (Neal). The men are told by Lieutenant Colonel Dunn (Anthony Nicholls) that a recently wounded soldier (Richard Todd), a young Scot, is being assigned to their ward. Dunn advises the men in the ward that the fellow has lost a kidney and will not likely live much longer with only the one remaining. The colonel feels that the men in this ward are sympathetic, and that is why he has assigned the dying young man to them. The young Scot has no one to go home to and has not been told his fate. He is naturally upset that he can't be released to return home.

The soldiers try to befriend the fellow, but he rejects them at every turn. The nurse pleads with the other men to be patient and understanding to Lachie, as they call him. Eventually he comes round. He even falls in love with the nurse and asks her to marry him, and she accepts. But when he finally does find out the truth about his condition, he becomes angry and hostile once again, fearing that the men in the ward have been giving him sympathy, and he tells them off. He also feels that the nurse was just showing him pity when she agreed to marry him. She explains to him "that there is pity in every woman's love" and that if he leaves, he faces dying alone. In the end, love and friendship prevail over anger and bitterness.

The Hasty Heart, seen today, packs an emotional punch. The characters are finely drawn, the script is superb in its rhythm and pace, and the original music by Jack Beaver is memorable. The viewer empathizes with each of the characters. Even though Patricia is dressed in plain and simple costumes, designed by Peggy Henderson, the remarkable cinematography by Wilkie Cooper accentuates her unconventional beauty.

In 2003, Vincent Sherman wrote of his lead actors in the film, "The relationship between Pat and Todd and Reagan could not have been better." He said, "We all loved and respected each other and stood up to the bitter cold of that winter."[2] Sherman recalled that Patricia became upset with him over a particular scene. Sherman's impression of a British war nurse was that of someone who could joke and laugh with the men but who was a bit more reserved than an American nurse. "After several scenes, during which I had cautioned her and repeated a few takes, she broke down and began to cry, saying she could not give me what I wanted, and that I should find an English girl to do the part and let her go back to Hollywood. We stopped shooting for an hour while I tried to assure her that she was doing a fine job and that perhaps I was overemphasizing the importance of the matter. She calmed down, and I discovered she was highly sensitive and a little insecure."[3] (In the film, Patricia's character says she is Canadian, perhaps a compromise on the character's demeanor.)

Jack M. Warner, son of the studio chief, was in England with his wife, Barbara, during the filming of *The Hasty Heart* and corresponded frequently with his father. In a letter dated January 11, he told Jack L. of the heavy snows that had blanketed the area. By January 14, filming was already five days behind schedule. Complaining to his father about the Labor government in power, he mentioned the breaks the British crew took throughout the day, which the American crew found disruptive, costly, and time consuming. When the studio doors would open to allow the tea and food wagons in, the cold air would quickly freeze up the sets. No one asked the director if the breaks could be taken. Reagan in particular thought this custom "rude and inexcusable."[4] There was a palpable tension throughout the shooting between the newly organized British unions and the American union members.

Shooting scenes at the studio in what was supposed to be a hot and humid climate, with many of the characters wearing shorts, director Sherman had to resort to spraying the actors with water to resemble perspiration. Wrote Todd, "The weather in England during our shooting of 'The Hasty Heart' was absolutely filthy, but that did not affect us, since the entire film was confined to a large soundstage at Elstree Studios. Most of the action takes place in a large 'basha,' or bamboo hut brilliantly designed and devised by Terence Verity, our scenic designer, and mounted on a turntable so that the entire set could be revolved for each scene without the lighting plot having to be significantly altered."[5]

The wardrobe supervisor, Peggy Henderson, had the unusual job of scheduling a series of washdays in order to have the costumes look old and worn from wear in the jungle. Live plants were brought in to the studio for the set and were watered with precision to combat the harsh British winter weather. A technical advance used for the first time on the set of *The Hasty Heart* was the unidirectional microphone developed at Warners Brothers in Burbank. Officially known as RCA's M.I. 10,001, it was capable of shutting out noise from all angles except the angle from which it was aimed. (This was especially beneficial when the bamboo started popping on the set because of the heat of the studio lights.)

After the first week's shooting, the rushes were sent to Hollywood for the studio chiefs to view. Jack L. Warner was so pleased and confident that the picture would go well that he wrote that no more rushes were necessary.

During production, a studio car arrived at 7:00 A.M. and picked up Reagan and Neal at the Savoy Hotel and sometimes Todd at his home, then drove to director Sherman's rented flat; all arrived at the Elstree Studio before dawn. With one tea break at 10:00 A.M. and another around 4:00 P.M., shooting proceeded slowly, but without major delays. The cast was given a long vacation over the Christmas holidays; the studio closed at 1:00 P.M. on Friday and remained closed until the following Wednesday. On Christmas Day, Sherman threw a party attended by the principal cast members. Robert Clark sent over a case of Mumm's champagne, which made up for the English food, which most of the Americans, Patricia included, found almost inedible. Britain was still under rationing. Ronald Reagan had steaks from New York's Club 21 sent over to the Savoy Hotel's kitchen. When they arrived, several "disappeared," so he sent for more. As it turned out, many had "turned bad" (or so they were told), and this infuriated Reagan. However, the British people had suffered considerably during and after the war, unlike the well-fed Americans.[6]

In England, the movie studios did not operate on Saturdays, so the cast was able to relax and prepare over the weekends. When they weren't being used at the studio, Reagan and Neal were "good copy." Wrote Patricia of this time, "Fortunately, we got along well enough to choose each other's company even when we were not working. We would have dinner and even go dancing at some of the local dance halls. People may have been shabbily dressed and their food rationed, but at night they sang and danced with all their hearts. They were so happy that the war was over. Ronnie was a delightful and interesting companion."[7] While Patricia was in England, her friend Helen Horton entrusted her English beau, Hamish Thomson, to her. On an outing with Patricia and Ronald Reagan, Thomson asked Reagan what he would like to be more than anything else in the world, to which Reagan laughingly replied, "The president of the United States."[8]

On December 17, Patricia wrote Jean and Chloe, "As to Christmas, I have done nothing about it. I thought that we could celebrate when I got home. I trust that is alright with you. But I do wish you the merriest of times. What does one do about Coop? Just what can I get for him? I have thought and thought—there seems to be no answer. . . . I am quite settled now and content, I think. This has really been a great opportunity. I am becoming more and more pro-British."[9]

Patricia also kept in touch with her acting coach, George Shdanoff. In a fascinating letter to Patricia dated Christmas Day, Shdanoff advised his favorite pupil about what to remember while performing before the cameras in England. Shdanoff wrote, "Think of your character as we planned—she is composed, collected, inwardly strong, poised, sure, efficient, has authority, therefore efficient, knows her job, warm-hearted and good-hearted but *never* sentimental. Therefore: watch that you are always—truthful, simple, concentrate on your partners, away from yourself, never 'not' feeling, never outward, never 'theatrical or mannered,' justify everything—every bit of dialogue and every movement—think what is behind that line etc.—Be careful to leave your voice and throat relaxed."[10]

On New Year's Eve, Reg sent a night letter: "Worlds of happiness for New Year and years to come. God bless you and hurry home to us—Chloe, Jean and Reg."[11]

Jack M. Warner wrote his father, Jack L., on February 8, "Yesterday was a real banner day for us. Vince shot six minutes of a wonderful sequence and I just saw it on the screen. Really, it was fine. . . . [I]t is the scene where the boys and Sister Margaret give Lachie his birthday gifts . . . the kilt, jacket, shoes, etc. It moved along beautifully and held everyone tense watching it. It is the most difficult and moody scene as it is the point where Lachie's character turns . . . and it came off fine. I think you are going to like Richard Todd in the Lachie part."[12]

On February 19, Jack L. Warner cabled his son to advise him that Warners was contemplating using Patricia with Ronald Reagan for another picture right away, so impressed was he with the raw footage of *The Hasty Heart*. Unfortunately, there was to be no other film that the two would do together.

On March 5, Jack M. wrote his father, "About Reagan and Neal. I know they also want a week to see Paris and comb some of this damn London out of their scalps. I previously wrote you of my conversation with Reagan when he told me he would refuse to go into another picture until he had at least six weeks rest. Believe me, anybody who has worked here requires a rest before being put on anything else—and that goes for me too."[13]

Filming of *The Hasty Heart* wrapped the end of the first week in March 1949. British union laborers continued to delay production up until the last day and the last shot of the film. They felt put upon when asked to stay one additional hour and promptly left their positions on the set at the assigned times. At the farewell dinner for studio executives Robert Clark, Vaughn Dean, and Alex Boyd and the cast and crew, host Vincent Sherman and his stars, Neal, Reagan, and Todd, all gave eloquent speeches following the meal.

On March 21, Jack M. wrote his father in Hollywood that two days' work had been "overcooked" at the film developers, Humphries Laboratory; much of it needed to be reshot.[14] Reagan was summoned from Monte Carlo and Neal from Paris, and both were on the set by the following Wednesday. Retakes were completed on March 23. After viewing a rough cut of the film later, Sherman made few changes. In Hollywood, Jack L. Warner, after running the film, made some minor editing changes and ordered a new musical score (by Jack Beaver, under the direction of Louis Levy).

Returning from England near the end of March 1949 on the R.M.S. *Queen Mary*, Patricia was more than eager to arrive home. In particular, she was eager to see Gary. Writing ahead to him, she advised that she would spend a few days in New York before continuing on to California by train. After her ship docked in New York, Patricia stayed with Jean Hagen and her husband, agent Tom Seidel. When she arrived at the Seidel apartment, Patricia was thrilled to see the old gang gathered to greet her—Helen Horton, Petey Petroff, Natalie Brown, and Nancy Hoadley. The doorbell rang, and Jean insisted that Patricia answer it. When she did, there stood Gary. In New York with Rocky, he had secretly arranged with Jean and Tom to stop by and surprise Patricia. After the group disbanded, Tom and Jean graciously left their flat to Patricia and Gary so that they could have the afternoon together. Because of Rocky's presence in New York, Patricia wasn't able to see Gary in New York after that afternoon. Before returning to California, Patricia made a side trip to Knoxville to visit her family.

Back in Hollywood, Patricia and Gary resumed their affair. He began to shower her with gifts, including a new Cadillac, a mink stole, and a pair of diamond-drop earrings from Harry Winston's. Patricia was temporarily at peace and happy. Her first film, *John Loves Mary*, was about to open, and her career and personal life were soaring.

John Loves Mary premiered at the Strand Theatre in New York on February 4, 1949, with general release February 19. Reviews were mixed. Hollywood reporter W. E. Oliver wrote, "Romantic treatment is practically left all to Patricia Neal, a reserved beauty . . . as the girl."[15] Los Angeles critic Lowell E. Redelings commented, "Miss Neal has some commendable moments. Her delivery of dialogue is faultless, but her facial expressions leave much to be desired."[16] The *Time* magazine reviewer liked Patricia and wrote, "The picture's chief blunder is the miscasting of Patricia Neal, an able young Broadway actress whose throaty, stagy intensity in this featherweight role suggests a tigress in a cat show."[17]

Bosley Crowther, in his *New York Times* review, wrote, "In the role of the American fiancée, Patricia Neal, a brand-new Warner girl, shows little to recommend her to further comedy jobs. Her looks are far more arresting, her manners are slightly gauche and her way with a gag line is painful. She has a long way to go and a lot to learn. And we must say that 'John Loves Mary' is a weak perch from which to be launched."

Despite respectable box-office returns, *John Loves Mary* was not the success Warner Brothers had hoped for. *John Loves Mary* cost $1,346,000. By 1957 it had grossed more than $2 million in total domestic and foreign rentals.[18]

Years later, Patricia recalled seeing herself in the movie for the first time. "I was rather appalled," she said. "I had good reason to be, because I discovered later that everything they did to me was wrong. My hair, my makeup, even my clothes were unbecoming. I wanted so much to make a success of this, but the harder I tried the worse it was. As I watched myself, I realized the necessity of learning to relax."[19]

In a letter dated February 21, Patricia's aunt Maude, still her biggest fan, wrote,

"I've seen you twice [in *John Loves Mary*], and just love you—your hairdo isn't flattering but your acting is superb. I'm going to see you again this afternoon and maybe tonight—It thrills me [to] . . . look at Patricia Neal . . . surrounded by all those beautiful, bright lights. You told your Daddy you'd do it, didn't you?"[20]

In an interview at Henri, the popular Hollywood restaurant, over a luncheon of oysters, eggs, and asparagus, Patricia commented to Eileen Creelman on her work in films, saying of drama, "That's the sort of thing I ought to do. I'm no ingénue. I just don't look like an ingénue, and I don't think I play one very well." About *Another Part of the Forest*, she said, "Now I know it wasn't a great play. When we were playing in it we were all sure it was great [Hellman took great offense at this remark.]. . . . I look well in costumes, a costume picture should be fun to do." Candidly stating that she hadn't any idea what she was doing during the filming of *John Loves Mary*, Patricia remarked, "Your first picture is easy. You don't know what to do anyway, so you just do what you're told—it's all marked out for you anyway—and enjoy yourself." Of *The Fountainhead*, Patricia explained, "It was the kind of part I do best, the kind that interests me anyway. The girl had something a little different, a character of her own. She is a newspaper woman, terribly idealistic. The story is really a conflict between the forces of good and evil."[21]

On June 30, Warners allowed Patricia to take part in a televised charity art exhibition, where she sat in a roundtable discussion with art critics. This broadcast marked Patricia's television debut. Later that summer, Patricia appeared on NBC's *Hollywood Calling* with Milton Berle. On the air they discussed their upcoming films, Neal's *The Fountainhead* and Berle's *Always Leave Them Laughing*.

The premiere of *The Fountainhead* was approaching, and Patricia brought her mother, Eura, and her brother, Pete, to Hollywood to join her for it. After obtaining additional tickets for them for the event, held June 23 at Warners Beverly Theatre, Patricia immediately set out to find the perfect gown to wear.

Patricia's date for the evening was Kirk Douglas, and this was to be his first Hollywood premiere. Wrote Douglas, "Patricia was elegant, intelligent, beautiful. I liked her a lot. She liked me. But she was madly in love with Gary Cooper. . . . We attended the premiere of *The Fountainhead* together. Poor Patricia. She couldn't go with Gary."[22] Before the screening of the 114-minute film, Patricia received good wishes, and she and Kirk signed autographs. However as the film unfolded, Patricia had the uncanny feeling she was not going to survive the hype and buildup. After the closing credits, Douglas and Patricia adjourned to the Warner Theatre lobby, where she noticed people avoiding her, turning their faces away (except for fellow trans-Atlantic shipmate Virginia Mayo, who approached Patricia and exclaimed, "My, weren't you *bad*!").[23] Douglas and Patricia quickly made an exit to the Mocambo nightclub, where Jack L. Warner was throwing a party. Cooper joined them at their table for photographers. Then Patricia and Kirk drank champagne and danced.

The Fountainhead was panned by nearly everyone. Said Brog in *Variety* the following morning, "'The Fountainhead' is a film with an idea and it clings to it with such complete tenacity that the end result is a cold, unemotional, loquacious feature. . . . As Cooper's co-star, Patricia Neal makes a moody heroine, afraid of love or any other honest feeling."[24] After its July 8 premiere in New York, the *New York Times* film critic Bosley Crowther was ruthless:

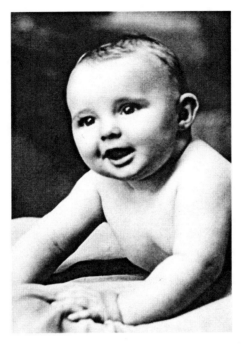

Patsy Louise Neal, 1926. From the Patricia
Neal Collection.

Above left, William "Coot" Neal, Patricia Neal in his reflection. From the Patricia Neal Collection. *Above right,* Eura Petrey Neal. From the Patricia Neal Collection.

Margaret Ann "NiNi" and Patsy
Neal, circa 1931. From the Patricia
Neal Collection.

Patsy and Margaret Ann
Neal, circa 1939. From
the Patricia Neal
Collection.

Above left, Patsy Neal in her first acting role in *Twilight Alley,* Knoxville, Tennessee, 1937. From the Patricia Neal Collection. *Above right,* Wesley Davis. From the Patricia Neal Collection.

Left to right: Steven Scheuer, Patricia Neal, and Elizabeth Wilson in Barter Theatre's production of *Thunder Rock*, 1942. From the Patricia Neal Collection.

Patsy Neal's Knoxville High School graduation photograph, 1943. From the Patricia Neal Collection.

Patsy Neal, Northwestern University's 1946 Syllabus Queen. From the Patricia Neal Collection.

Right (left to right): Patsy Neal, Steven Meyer, and Priscilla Weaver in Alvina Krause's *Blithe Spirit*, Eagles Mere, 1945. From the Patricia Neal Collection. *Below,* Benny Baker and Patricia Neal in the disastrous *Bigger Than Barnum,* 1946. From the Billy Rose Collection, NYPL for the Performing Arts. Astor, Lenox, and Tilden Foundations.

Patricia Neal as Regina Hubbard in *Another Part of the Forest*, 1947. From the Patricia Neal Collection.

Lillian Hellman, circa late 1930s. From the author's collection.

Tallulah Bankhead congratulating Patricia Neal backstage during the run of *Another Part of the Forest*, 1947. From the Patricia Neal Collection.

The touring company of *Another Part of the Forest*, 1947. *Seated (left to right)*: Mildred Dunnock, Percy Waram, Wesley Addy. *Standing*: Scott McKay and Patricia Neal. From the Patricia Neal Collection.

Patricia Neal as Joan in Elitch Gardens Theatre's production of *Joan of Lorraine*, Denver 1947. From the Patricia Neal Collection.

The fifty-sixth Elitch Gardens Theatre stock company. Seated third from left, Patricia Neal, with Peter Cookson on her left, 1947. From the Patricia Neal Collection.

Patricia Neal arriving in Los Angeles, December 1947, sporting her "pilgrim bonnet" and the outfit that her mother purchased for her. From the Patricia Neal Collection.

Peter Cookson, 1947. Courtesy of Photofest.

Above, Patricia Neal with her leading man, Ronald Reagan, in her first scene on the set of *John Loves Mary.* From the author's collection. *Below,* The cast and crew of *John Loves Mary,* 1949. *Left to right (seated on sofa):* Jack Carson, Patricia Neal, Katharine Alexander, and Ronald Reagan. *Left to right (standing behind sofa):* cinematographer Peverell Marley, Edward Arnold, Wayne Morris, and director David Butler. From the author's collection.

Patricia Neal and Gary Cooper in King Vidor's The *Fountainhead*, 1949. From the author's collection.

Above, on the set of *The Fountainhead. Standing (left to right)*: Robert Douglas, Kent Smith, Patricia Neal, Gary Cooper, and Raymond Massey. *Seated (left to right)*: Producer Henry Blanke, Ayn Rand, and director King Vidor. From the Patricia Neal Collection. *Below,* on the set of *The Fountainhead. Left to right*: King Vidor, Patricia Neal, and Gary Cooper. From the Patricia Neal Collection.

2146-2148 Fox Hills Drive, circa 2005. From the author's collection.

Patricia Neal rehearsing in her living room on Fox Hills Drive, 1949. (The painting over her left shoulder was eventually sold to Mel Brooks and his wife, Anne Bancroft.) From the Patricia Neal Collection.

Above left, Patricia Neal, 1949. From the author's collection. *Above right,* Painting of Patricia Neal by artist Anne Bell, 2005. Courtesy of Anne Bell, from the author's collection. *Below, (left to right),* Kirk Douglas, Patricia Neal, and Gary Cooper, at the Mocambo following the premiere of *The Fountainhead*, 1949. From the Patricia Neal Collection.

Above, arriving in England aboard the R.M.S. *Mauretania* for the filming of *The Hasty Heart,* 1948. *Left to right:* Joan Caulfield, Billy De Wolfe, Patricia Neal, Jack M. Warner, Michael O'Shea, Virginia Mayo, Sue Carol, and Alan Ladd. From the Patricia Neal Collection. *Below,* cocktail party reception at the Savoy Hotel, London, 1948. *Left to right:* Virginia Mayo, John Mills, and Patricia Neal. From the Patricia Neal Collection.

Right (right to left), Ralph Michael and John Sherman (*standing*) and Ronald Reagan and Patricia Neal (*seated*) in *The Hasty Heart*. From the author's collection. *Below*, Patricia Neal and Richard Todd in *The Hasty Heart*. From the author's collection.

"A long-winded, complicated preachment on the rights of the individual in society; and also upon the privilege of a lady to change her mind. . . . And a more curious lot of high priced twaddle we haven't seen for a long, long time. . . . Patricia Neal is almost funny, so affected is she as the girl, and a half dozen other actors do no better in minor roles. 'The Fountainhead' is a picture which you don't have to see to disbelieve."

The film did win praise back home in Knoxville, however. After its opening at the Tennessee Theatre on August 7, Patricia's old mentor Malcolm Miller wrote, "Our own Patricia Neal achieved motion picture stardom opposite Gary Cooper in a lush production of 'The Fountainhead.' Her performance thrilled me to no end, because she is the girl that I took to the Barter Theatre in Abingdon, Va., when she was barely 16 years of age and a junior at Knoxville High School. I said to Robert Porterfield, 'Bob, I've brought you an actress!' And now she has burst upon us as a dramatic actress in 'The Fountainhead.' She gives a thrilling characterization . . . gloriously, entrancingly beautiful . . . statuesque . . . aristocratic . . . cold, until she found her man. Then passionately determined, almost deadly in her tumultuous, tigerish amorality. 'The Fountainhead' . . . is sometimes wordy, and it is burdened with some clichés, but it is one of the worthwhile pictures of the year."[25]

Wrote the ever-pragmatic Eura Neal after the film's Knoxville premiere, "Emily thinks the picture too talkey—didn't like it but thought Pat did well. She hopes Pat will soon get something in New York."[26]

In the final analysis, *The Fountainhead* did not bring in the profits that Warners had expected. Ayn Rand's control of the production and her long-winded script, which audiences of the day simply could not relate to or understand, plus the added expense of Cooper's exorbitant salary, all helped make the film one of the year's most notable failures.

And Patricia's participation in *The Fountainhead* lost her much professional ground. After the disastrous reviews, Warners felt that its latest "sure bet" was just not going to pay off, and they began to lose interest in promoting Patricia. It also affected Cooper's career, which took a sharp decline. In an attempt to find a vehicle in which to costar again with Patricia, he bought the rights to the novel *The Girl on the Via Flaminia* by Alfred Hayes and pitched it to Warners, but the studio was not interested. (He later sold the rights, and United Artists made the novel into the 1953 film *Act of Love,* starring Kirk Douglas.)

For publicity purposes, Patricia continued to be seen about Hollywood in the company of eligible bachelors, notably Robert Stack and Kirk Douglas.

Though there was never anything physical between her and Douglas, one evening Patricia invited Douglas up to her apartment for a nightcap. She had had a few too many drinks, she later wrote in her autobiography, "and, let's face it, Kirk was very attractive."[27] As they passionately kissed, Patricia suddenly withdrew—she knew she loved only Gary. And, taking the cue, Kirk retreated. Cooper, however, had been watching them from outside. After Douglas left, Cooper knocked on Patricia's door. After she opened it, Gary told her he had seen what had gone on—though nothing really had. But the realization that he might be jealous caused her to smile. Angered, he slapped her across the face, drawing blood. Furiously, she told him he would never do that to her again. His gentle apology smoothed the matter over for the moment. "As strange as it seems," she wrote, "we did not speak about the incident again. It was as if he had lowered a curtain. But he never hit me again."[28]

On July 18, Warner Brothers was notified that the producer of KHJ Radio's *Family Theatre* had requested Patricia's services as hostess for an upcoming episode of the early evening Catholic radio show. The Rev. Raymond E. Finan, the producer of the show, sent Patricia her script and four complimentary tickets that same day. Airing over the Mutual Network on July 20 and originating in Studio One on Vine Street in Los Angeles, the *Family Theatre* broadcast of "My Terminal Moraine," based on a novelette by Frank Stockton, told the humorous tale of a young man, Walter (Alan Young), and his girlfriend, Agnes (Mala Powers), who set their sights on happiness by discovering an "ice mine."

Patricia introduced the show and followed the broadcast with an inspirational message:

> Lots of people do found their married life on things almost as unsubstantial as ice. On money, for instance, or the infatuation of a quick romance, or the wild gamble that things will turn out all right, that this time, somehow, love and happiness will be found.
>
> We of *Family Theatre* believe that a marriage needs a much stronger foundation. Yes, we really believe that marriages are made in heaven. We believe that a man and woman, who vow to love, honor and obey one another, need God's constant help if they are to be faithful to their promises.

8

Hollywood

They say that sorrow is born in the hasty heart.

—Sister Margaret, *The Hasty Heart*

On a lazy Sunday afternoon in the spring of 1949, Patricia met publicist Harvey Orkin at the home of Gene Kelly and his wife, actress Betsy Blair. The Kellys' place was a very informal weekend retreat for the Hollywood crowd, where the Kellys hosted Sunday cookouts with volleyball and swimming. Orkin was Gary Cooper's close friend and publicist, and Patricia had signed with his agency as well. Orkin became one of Patricia's dearest friends.

On a later Sunday at the beach, Orkin suggested that Patricia and her mother, Eura, who was visiting from her home in Florida, accompany him and his girlfriend, Helen, to Aspen, Colorado. Albert Schweitzer was scheduled to give a speech in Aspen, and the Coopers were building a new home there. Harvey, who was not aware of Gary and Patricia's relationship, called the Cooper home in Hollywood and suggested that they all get together and go to Aspen for the event. Gary suggested that they all come over that very afternoon to discuss the idea.

It must have been titillating for Gary to have Patricia and Rocky under the same roof, and he was noticeably awkward and nervous. "What is wrong with you, Gary, anyhow?"[1] Rocky said to him when he started nervously stumbling around. Gary suggested that they all travel to Colorado with Harvey and Helen and Patricia and her mother. Rocky and their daughter, Maria, agreed to fly into Aspen beforehand and meet Gary there.

The remainder of the party drove to Colorado in two cars, Patricia riding with Gary, her mother with Harvey and Helen. Leaving early in the afternoon of June 30, Patricia and Gary agreed to meet the other three at a motel

Facing page: Patricia Neal from *The Breaking Point*, 1950. Photograph by Bert Six, from the author's collection.

midway to Aspen for the evening. Patricia recalled that on the way she and Gary held hands in silence. After dinner, the rest of the party retired early, and Patricia and Gary drove out into the desert as the sun was setting and made love.

Arriving in Aspen on July 1, the group met up with Rocky and Maria and toured the construction site of the Coopers' new home. Patricia noticed that Gary was very quiet, and the atmosphere was strained. The next morning Harvey drove Patricia to the Jerome Hotel, where Gary met her. While getting into Gary's pickup truck, Patricia was concerned by the look on his face. At that very moment Rocky and Maria walked by, and Patricia saw that the little girl had been crying. When she spotted Patricia, Maria spat hatefully on the ground in front of her. Breaking the silence as they drove, Gary said to Patricia, "Last night Rocky asked me if I was having an affair with you. I said yes. She wanted to know if I was in love with you. I said yes."[2] He told Patricia that just as he finished confessing to Rocky, Maria had come into their bedroom. Rocky told Maria everything, saying, "Your father thinks he's in love with her."[3] Patricia was shocked—not only because she and Gary had been found out, but also because Rocky had told her child about the affair.

Sensing Patricia was troubled, but not knowing why, Eura wisely took the train back to Los Angeles. Patricia's drive back with Harvey, and Helen was extremely tense. Patricia feared that her affair with Gary would soon be in the open, and all of Hollywood and the public would know the truth. She would be labeled "the other woman."

Rocky told Gary she would blow "the lid off his sexual life. It was a declaration of war." In private, Rocky referred to Patricia as a "southern cow who eats cornbread and black-eyed peas."[4] But in public, she maintained a different demeanor. "I knew them all and felt sorry for all of them," said Jack Warner's wife, Ann. "Rocky was very smart. During that period, she wasn't nasty, she looked good, and she made her own life. She went out with a few boys. And she acted cleverly. She was fighting a woman like Pat Neal, who happened to be a decent woman . . . a truly lovely girl."[5]

Cooper was concerned now because Maria had been told the truth, and having been taught by Rocky never to fault her father, Maria blamed Patricia. Gary did not want to see his daughter, or Rocky, humiliated by his actions. On the surface, life proceeded much as before. The Cooper family was pictured in the newspapers, and Rocky even allowed their Brentwood home to be photographed. As late as the fall of 1950, nothing was being written about Gary and Patricia. All of Gary's public appearances were in Rocky's company, yet it was commonly understood that they had "an arrangement." Though he was living at home, Gary was seen coming and going from Patricia's apartment.

This situation took its toll on Patricia. "Before I met Gary Cooper I had been attracted to other women's husbands, but I had not been in love with them," she later wrote. "I played my cards straight. It was pure competition, and if a woman wasn't strong enough to hold her man, it wasn't my problem. But love stripped away the old attitudes." With Cooper it was different. "I was Gary's woman. Yes I was, and my double life was becoming hellish. I wanted to be with Gary always. Always. Never parted, not even briefly. I began to allow myself to feel it was a matter of time before the truth of our love would have to be known and accepted."[6]

Ann Warner said, "If Pat were conniving, she might have been able to break up the marriage. Pat was so in love with him, and Gary with her. She satisfied him a great deal. There was an intellectual quality to her, and she was a real woman."[7] But Patricia's respectable and staunch upbringing conflicted with her deep love of Cooper. She was tortured with shame. At a large dinner party one evening at Jack and Ann Warner's home, Patricia was seated opposite Rocky at the table. Thinking that the large number of guests and the conversation would make it impossible for direct communication, Patricia was shaken when she looked across the table and saw Rocky staring at her with anger and disgust written on her face.

Regardless of what was happening in her private life, Patricia's professional life continued. Besides her film work, this life included interviews and ads designed to keep her, and her films, in the public eye to maintain her value to the studio. Harvey Orkin's agency was initially uncertain that the twenty-three-year-old lacked the career background to be a valuable client. Her agency biography touted her "star quality" and her association with such notables as Eugene O'Neill and Lillian Hellman. A Lucky Strike smoker, Patricia was in a series of ads for Chesterfield cigarettes that also plugged her current films. Yet another vehicle for boosting value to the studio was the fan club. Film magazines sponsored the clubs, which were eagerly supported by both studios and actors. "The Official Patricia Neal Fan Club" was registered by *Movie Stars Parade* magazine in July 1949. Patricia was designated the club's honorary president and communicated to her fans through a quarterly publication called *Patricia Readings*.

Her main business, of course, was making movies. In her next film, *Three Secrets,* made in the fall of 1949, Patricia played a hard-boiled newspaperwoman, Phyllis Horn. Phyllis, a journalist reporting from the site of a plane crash in the California mountains, suspects that she may be the mother of the sole survivor, a five-year-old boy whose adoptive parents were killed in the crash. Phyllis had learned she was pregnant shortly after divorcing her husband; when she called to tell him the news, he had already remarried.

After news reports about the attempted rescue broadcast the child's birthdate, two other women, played by Eleanor Parker and Ruth Roman, come to the site, each convinced that the child is the son she gave up for adoption. Susan Chase (Eleanor Parker) has never told her husband of the child she bore out of wedlock. Ann Lawrence (Ruth Roman) is a convicted murderer who gave up her child while she was in prison. As they await news from the rescue team—now stranded in a landslide, with all communication cut off—the women gather in a mountain cabin and share their life stories. At the end, the true mother is identified.

Three Secrets was the first of three films Patricia would make under the direction of Robert Wise. Wise later said of the film, "I realized *Three Secrets* was a soap opera, but I liked the idea. I hadn't done a woman's picture and was intrigued by working with three actresses who were already cast for it, particularly Patricia Neal."[8]

Although social mores have changed since the film was made, *Three Secrets* is timeless in its emotional sincerity, the plotlines still relevant though dated. The script is tight, and the direction moves briskly, supported by David Buttolph's dramatically sweeping music and attractive photography by Sidney Hickox. Costuming, too, had a role to play: it clearly reflects the types the three women represent. The good girl (Eleanor Parker) is always dressed girlishly and yet in a womanly style; the bad girl (Ruth Roman) wears starkly sophisticated, dramatic outfits; and Patricia, the career girl, is dressed entirely in tailored, almost masculine clothing, except for one scene with her (former) husband, played by Frank Lovejoy.

The movie gave Patricia powerful moments to shine, and it is her favorite of her early film period.

Filming of *Three Secrets* concluded in mid-November. On November 18, Warner Brothers picked up Patricia's option, assuring that she would stay with the studio.

Perhaps because of the developing gossip around town, or because Warner Brothers simply needed to generate more interest in *The Fountainhead*, currently in release, Patricia and Gary were assigned their next production, *Bright Leaf*. The film would costar Lauren Bacall, who was finishing out her original Warners contract with this picture. Warner Brothers' top director, Hungarian-born Michael Curtiz, was assigned to direct. The novel by Foster Fitz-Simons had been a best seller the year before. Bought by Warners for $10,000, with a screenplay adaptation by Ranald MacDougall, *Bright Leaf* was set to begin shooting in November.

A historical melodrama, *Bright Leaf* tells the story of tenant farmer Brant Royle, who returns to his hometown of Kingsmont, North Carolina, in 1894, several years after his family was run out of town by tobacco and cigar baron Major James Singleton. Royle meets Singleton's willful and beautiful daughter Margaret, "the loveliest belle of the South," and lets her know that he is interested in seeing her again. Royle adopts a new technology, an automatic cigarette-making machine, spurned by Singleton. To finance his venture, Royle seeks aid from boarding house/bordello owner Sonia Kovac, with whom he has a relationship.

The cigarette machine is such a success that it drives Singleton out of business. To save her father from ruin, Margaret agrees to marry Royle, but the major commits suicide. Royle and Margaret marry and rename the old Singleton house Bright Leaf. But Margaret is consumed with hatred and a desire for revenge. She sells her stock in the company and leaks information to the attorney general who is investigating Royle's business. On New Year's Eve 1900, Margaret tells Royle she wants a divorce. He accidentally burns down Bright Leaf and returns to Sonia, hoping to renew their relationship. But she tells Royle he is a few years too late. He leaves town alone, the way he rode in, with nothing.

For once, Patricia *really* wanted a part—that of Sonia. And she wanted it desperately. As originally written, the role of Sonia had more depth and character than that of Margaret. Patricia wanted to play Sonia for a change of pace, because she felt she had played "the bitch" too many times. Patricia cried and pleaded with studio executives for the part, but they would not budge. She even asked Gary to demand that the role be given to her. But he wouldn't fight for her. "Not because he thought I should fight my own battles and not because he was unwilling to raise suspicion about our relationship," she wrote later. "He simply did not want to get involved in any conflict. Conflict was something Gary Cooper was a master at avoiding."[9] Michael Curtiz remembered Patricia wanting the part and was surprised that Gary did not intervene. "Cooper could have suggested the reversal of roles. She [Patricia] had wanted a chance to talk about it. He did nothing. He didn't want to become involved. I waited, but . . . he did nothing."[10] On November 11, Lauren Bacall was officially signed to the role of Sonia, and Patricia was given the role of Margaret. Patricia loved Gary, but she never forgave him for not going to bat for her.

By the time the final script was written, the role of Sonia had been greatly weakened, and Bacall did not have a lot to work with—nor was she very good in the film.

Patricia enjoyed working with her costars, but from the beginning of the picture, she and director Michael Curtiz clashed. Her stormy bouts with such a renowned and respected professional were uncommon for her, but others also found him difficult. Bacall wrote in her autobiography, "Coop . . . was a pro, but not always on time. One morning he was late and Mike [Curtiz] was livid—so much so that he screamed at me. He wouldn't dare let go at Coop, knowing he'd just walk off the set. . . . Finally Coop arrived, not all that late, and Mike was all over him: 'Gary, dahling, how are you—how do you feel?' Coop knew that Mike was full of it, but played the game."[11]

One particularly difficult day on the set, Patricia's character, Margaret, was required to battle with Royle in a tense and dramatic scene to be shot in the morning. Then that afternoon Curtiz was going to shoot the wedding scene. "How can I fight with a husband before I marry him?" Patricia balked. She asked that they film the wedding scene first, saying that she would fuss with her husband that afternoon. Curtiz refused. "You will do the fussing and fighting, and then you must make love for the wedding," he said. "But I tell you one thing: you must not eat any lunch. Because you cannot make love on a full stomach. You will be gay, lovely and charming if you pass up the tray at noontime. Ditch diggers can eat lunch, yes; actors no. I have no use for any of them who eat."[12] Patricia played her scenes hungry.

The actors' experiences in *Bright Leaf* were affirmed in later films. Bradford Dillman, who worked with Curtiz years later, toward the end of the director's life, wrote, "Curtiz was a sadistic man who despised actors. It was his belief no actor was capable of expressing pain without actually experiencing it."[13]

Production on *Bright Leaf* began the third week of November, and Patricia found the professional time spent with Gary nearly as satisfying as their personal time together. Their scenes sparkled—sometimes literally: in one scene, Patricia wore a stunning antique pearl drop necklace, which Cooper later had copied for her.

One bright spot in the fall of 1949 was the reception accorded *The Hasty Heart*. From its sneak previews in Hollywood in September and October, the film was considered a winner, and Patricia garnered her share of praise. After one preview, producer Jerry Wald wrote Patricia, "Nothing pleased me more . . . than to see 'The Hasty Heart,' and watch you give a superb performance of which I always knew you were capable, if given half a chance."[14] Warners seemed pleased with the film's reception.

When *The Hasty Heart* premiered in England, shortly before its American release on December 2, 1949, the first-night audience stood and cheered. Patricia was voted one of Britain's top ten film favorites for her performance, and Richard Todd was acclaimed a new star (indeed, he was eventually awarded the coveted gold medal of Britain's *Picturegoer* magazine).

At its premiere in Los Angeles on December 14, 1949, *The Hasty Heart* was again extremely well received. At the premiere, the Highland Pipers Band and Drum Corps, accompanied by bagpipes, led a parade of Hollywood stars and civic notables to the theater. The critics fell over themselves praising the film. Louella Parsons, writing in the *Los Angeles Examiner* the following day, said, "Until I saw 'Hasty Heart' I was never a Patricia Neal fan. Now she has completely converted me to the Neal cause, and if she continues to be as good she is as the nurse in 'Hasty Heart' she'll have me on her side. Moreover, Warner Brothers will have a new star. . . . She brings warmth, humor, and personal strength" to the role.

The favorable reviews continued after the film's New York opening in January, and the *New York Times* in March 1950 saluted it as "one of the best of the year."[15] Richard Todd won a Golden Globe as Most Promising Newcomer–Male and was nominated for a Golden Globe as Best Motion Picture Actor. He was also nominated for an Academy Award as Best Actor in a Leading Role (as was Kirk Douglas, for *Champion*), but the Oscar went to Broderick Crawford for *All the King's Men*. Ranald MacDougall's screenplay was nominated for the Writers Guild of America award as Best Written American Drama.

But the critics are not always right. By the time Marjorie Turner wrote in the March 12 *New York Times* that "Miss Neal is boosted to a little higher niche in the Warner Brothers world," Patricia's stock at the studio had already tumbled.[16]

Although her reviews for her role in *The Hasty Heart* were the best she had received to date, and she had undeniably proved that she could brilliantly underplay, Warners offered her a Western for her next film project. Patricia was advised the third week of January 1950, by casting director Solly Baiano, that she was to report to work sometime in early February for the role of Reva Cairn in the upcoming Western, *Sugarfoot*, based on a story by Clarence Budington Kelland. Patricia emphatically, and officially, declined the part on January 25. Under the terms of her contract, Patricia was suspended, and would remain so until *Sugarfoot* completed filming.

Louella Parsons admonished Patricia in a January 28 piece:

> Patricia Neal is on suspension today at Warner Brothers. Pat wasn't cooperative about doing a western, "Sugarfoot," with Randy Scott.
>
> I know the glamour girls don't like to go into westerns, but at the same time, I always feel it is a mistake for a young actress to quarrel with a studio when things are going good.
>
> After all, Pat wasn't exactly a riot at Warners until 'Hasty Heart,' and, of course, she's getting another good break in 'Bright Leaf.'
>
> But she still has a long way to go in her career—and as a rule, studios, like mother, usually know best.[17]

Writing about her refusal to do *Sugarfoot,* Patricia said, "I was suspended for refusing a part with Randy Scott in a western called 'Sugarfoot.' Actually I have nothing against western pictures or stories . . . as a matter of fact I like them . . . but, this particular part was just a 'part' and not a role. I felt I would gain nothing by being in it, especially since I didn't believe in the part. . . . I know when or if any of you see the film, you'll agree with me."[18]

Patricia was placed back on payroll on March 11, the day after Adele Jergens, who had replaced Patricia in the film, finished *Sugarfoot*.

This episode marked a crossroads in Patricia's career, especially affecting her relationship with Warner Brothers. It was a decisive moment that lowered her standing in Hollywood. Still, once the suspension was over, Warners was anxious to get her back to work. Her salary had now escalated to more than $1,300 a week, and for her next project, Warners was planning to remake Ernest Hemingway's *To Have and Have Not,* which the studio had filmed successfully in 1944 with Humphrey Bogart. That film had introduced eighteen-year-old Lauren Bacall to the screen, and she became a sizzling new star. The screenplay adaptation, by Jules Furthman and William Faulkner, was nothing like Hemingway's storyline: the locale had been changed from Key West to Martinique; the Chinese being smuggled from Cuba changed to Free French leaders being smuggled from Vichy, France, and so on. Needless to say, Hemingway was not pleased.

For the remake, the new film was given a somewhat more faithful adaptation by Ranald MacDougall, and the title was changed to *The Breaking Point.* A grim tale about smuggling, gangsters, and murder, *The Breaking Point* concerns the efforts of boat owner Harry Morgan to keep himself, his wife Lucy, and their two young daughters financially afloat in Newport Beach, California. He rents out his boat, the *Sea Queen*, to fishing parties. One party, consisting of a Mr. Hannagan and his pretty blonde girlfriend, Leona Charles, charters the boat for fishing off the Mexican coast. Once they land in Mexico, Hannagan deserts Leona and takes off without paying Morgan. Desperate to return to Newport, Harry strikes a deal with a disreputable lawyer, Duncan, and agrees to smuggle illegal Chinese workers into California. Harry's efforts to keep his mate Wesley from getting involved fail, and both Leona and Wesley stow away on the *Sea Queen*. When Harry docks the boat in a secluded cove that night to take aboard the Chinese laborers, a Mr. Sing shorts Harry the money. In a scuffle, Sing is accidentally shot and killed. Harry dumps his body overboard and sets the laborers ashore. Leona and Wesley witness the whole episode. The Chinese are picked up by the border patrol and tell the officers the name of the boat, and the *Sea Queen* is confiscated in San Diego.

Without a boat to earn a living, Harry is more financially desperate than ever and again asks Duncan for money. Harry gets the *Sea Queen* back and agrees to smuggle two gangsters to another boat offshore, planning to double-cross them. His wife, Lucy, unhappy with the whole situation and also aware that Harry is attracted to Leona, tells him in desperation that she will leave him if he walks out the door. He leaves, and she knows the marriage is over. At sea, the gangsters kill Wesley, who once again is a stowaway, and dump his body overboard. In a shootout with the gangsters, Harry is nearly killed, but the Coast Guard finds the *Sea Queen* drifting and brings him back. The doctor finds Lucy and tells her that Henry's arm must be amputated if he is to live. The couple reunite. As the crowd at the dock clears, Leona sighs heavily and says, "I hate mornings. It's the worst part of the day," and walks away.

The film starred John Garfield as Harry Morgan and Phyllis Thaxter as his wife, Lucy. Patricia won the role of Leona, who was much earthier in this version than in the 1944 *To Have and Have Not*. Patricia jokingly told the press, "I play a girl with no inhibitions worth mentioning. I have plenty of inhibitions myself, but while the picture is shooting I can lose them—and get paid for doing it."[19] But comments by others about her character weren't always so gentle. In an episode that Patricia recalled as "tacky," Garfield approached her at a party before shooting commenced and took her aside, telling her, "I want to talk to you. You know you're a whore, you know what I'm saying? In the picture, I mean, you know? You're *all whore,* you know what I'm saying?"[20]

Viewed today, *The Breaking Point* is not a typical run-of-the-mill studio picture. What stands out about the film is its production values and its faithfulness to Hemingway's story. Hemingway himself said that this was the best film adaptation of any of his works, with its faithful direction and style and, most importantly, its acting. With excellent set design by Edward Carrere, script by Ranald MacDougall, and the sweeping music of Ray Heindorf, the viewer is transported to a place of grim reality and intense drama.

Michael Curtiz was the director of *The Breaking Point,* and it is arguably his masterpiece. His direction is brilliant. What perhaps makes the film a classic is its final scene: as the drama is resolved, the camera pulls back slowly to reveal Wesley's little boy standing alone on the dock desperately searching for his father.

Although Patricia was chagrined to be working with the irascible Curtiz again, their relationship this time was more congenial, and Patricia's performance was more controlled. Filming proceeded briskly. Patricia's first scene was shot on March 24, and her last was filmed on May 10. On May 13, Patricia was once again placed on suspension.

In an interview that Patricia gave to Philip K. Scheuer of the *Los Angeles Times,* which ran on May 28, she said, "All my parts have sort of been neurotic. What I'd like now is a good lusty one, somebody with a tremendous life—and nothing on her mind. . . . Ever since I came to Hollywood, two and a half years ago, I've had a tendency to start panicking. I hadn't had a great deal of experience previously, but I had been used to—and approved of—rehearsals. 'Just be effortless,' they told me—but that takes effort first! And I can't 'walk through' a scene. How can a part be yours unless it is complete, a finished thing? Yet here I found that even your movements are worked out with a stand-in. Then it's your turn. You are still trying to adjust—and suddenly it's your performance! I think it's terribly important that all actors and directors reach some form of agreement as to what they're trying to do in a scene. This is not done now. For myself, I have managed to get a little bit of knowledge and a little bit of courage, enough to trust myself. But I still have a lot to learn." But her opportunities to learn in Hollywood were becoming more limited.

Bright Leaf premiered on June 16 at the Strand Theatre in New York. The reviewers were ruthless in their comments on Patricia's performance, and the reviews jarred Patricia badly.

The typically acerbic Bosley Crowther in his *New York Times* review the following day said that the 110-minute film "runs too much to the conventional and is too insufferably long." His criticism of Patricia's performance was particularly harsh: "Patricia Neal plays [Royle's] female tormentor as though she were some sort of vagrant lunatic. Her eyes pop and gleam in

crazy fashion, her face wreathes in idiotic grins and she drawls with a Southern accent that sounds like a dimwit travesty. It is hard to perceive how this
lady could fascinate anyone." Crowther even sniped at Bacall, "As the sporting house friend of Mr. Royle, Lauren Bacall is torpid and dull—not much
more of a charmer, indeed, than the aberrant Miss Neal."[21]

Louella Parsons took Crowther to task in her *Cosmopolitan* magazine
monthly Movie Citations column. Wrote the columnist, "'Bright Leaf' . . .
makes me salute Patricia Neal as an important star—something I never expected to do. I've heard again and again from Warners how completely they
believe in her . . . I simply didn't feel her impact. This month in 'Bright Leaf,'
I distinctly do. But without taking one thing away from Pat's magnetism, I
think the credit for her triumph . . . must go to Michael Curtiz." Patricia's
character, Parsons wrote, was "described as being 'poised, graceful, charming, and beautiful, every inch a lady—until she's otherwise.' It's the 'otherwise'
that Mike lets Pat project with power. . . . I'm going to give Mike the Cosmopolitan Citation for the Best Direction of the Month, nonetheless, chiefly
for the devilish incandescence he drew from Patricia Neal."[22] But even the
influential Parsons could not counterbalance the bad reviews.

Although it fared badly at the time, *Bright Leaf* in retrospect is a compelling film to watch. It is beautifully filmed by Karl Freund, who lit close-
ups of Bacall and Neal with shadow and light, in stark contrast to the flat
shots of Cooper, which make him look surprisingly haggard. About Patricia's
much maligned performance in *Bright Leaf*, Bacall film biographer Lawrence
Quirk wrote, "Neal gives a mannered, often-overwrought, but rather vivid
and distinctive performance . . . in retrospect more credible than was then
conceded. Neal's problems—like Bacall's—stemmed from the turgid, over-
lengthy script, which was short on character analysis and long on superficial
melodramatics and sometimes pointless action."[23] Seen today, Patricia's performance in *Bright Leaf* is remarkably ahead of its time.

But at the time, the picture signaled the beginning of the end of Patricia's
early film career. Warner Brothers began giving her bad scripts to finish out
her contract. As a testament to her talent, Patricia took these mediocre roles,
creating characters the public found hard to forget.

9

Tinseltown

Maybe I envy your wife a little. You know now, I didn't believe it when you told me you were in love with her. Usually when a man tells me he loves his wife, it ends up with, "but . . ."

—Leona, *The Breaking Point* (1950)

Patricia, decidedly stunned by the poor reviews of *Bright Leaf,* continued working. On June 19 she appeared with Ronald Reagan on CBS radio's *Lux Radio Theatre* presentation of *John Loves Mary*. Patricia was granted approval to appear again on *The Family Theatre*—"The family that prays together stays together"—to introduce the radio play *The Triumphant Exile,* about Robert Louis Stevenson. The episode was taped on June 28 and aired on the Mutual Network July 12. Patricia was paid the standard AFTRA fee of $70.

In the June 20 edition of the *Los Angeles Times,* in an article headlined "Warners Buys Original to Star Patricia Neal," Hedda Hopper wrote: "Patricia Neal, who's gone places at Warners since 'Bright Leaf' and 'Three Secrets,' has a special story bought for her. Titled 'Mary's Lam,' it deals with a society girl who gets tied up with a gang of hoodlums and takes it on the lam. The story, an original by Howard Leete, will be produced by Everett Freeman. Jerry Wald recently told me that he thought Pat had the greatest natural talent of any girl in Hollywood. Those are strong words from anybody." Warners apparently had second thoughts about the project, and it was never filmed with Patricia.

On July 22, Patricia appeared on the popular *Stars over Hollywood* radio broadcast. That same day, a Warners interoffice memo announced that William Orr was holding salary conferences regarding the upcoming shooting of the Western *White Face*. Eleanor Parker had declined to star as the leading

Facing page: Patricia Neal wearing the copy of the antique necklace Gary Cooper had made for her from *Bright Leaf,* 1950. From the author's collection.

lady, Ann Challon, and Patricia, her value to the studio lower than ever before, was suggested for the part. There was, however, a brief, possibly brilliant moment when Patricia's studio value would have risen considerably.

Patricia went to a dinner party that Gary had arranged at a Chinese restaurant to welcome Laurence Olivier and Vivien Leigh to Hollywood. There was a discussion of the filming of Tennessee Williams' play *A Streetcar Named Desire*. Leigh had recently portrayed the fragile Blanche on the London stage and was the hands-down favorite for the role in the film, Olivia de Havilland having declined the part. Patricia casually remarked to Leigh that when the play went on the road, "My good friend Helen Horton took over for you in *Streetcar*." Leigh caustically replied, "No one takes over for me, dear. When I leave a play, it's over." Patricia recalled years later, "It was really a ghastly supper and on the way home I began weeping and I cried, 'Oh, I want to be old, I want to be old.' I needed a lot to make me grow up."[1]

Shortly after that dinner, word came that Elia Kazan was considering Patricia for the role of Stella. In a telegram dated July 11 to Warners executive Steve Trilling, Harry Mayer inquired: "Kazan here. Looking at films. Very impressed Pat Neal. Please wire immediately exact height Neal in stocking feet."[2] The reply that Patricia was five feet, seven inches tall was unsatisfactory: Patricia was much taller than Leigh, and audiences wouldn't consider it realistic if they were cast as sisters. Kim Hunter would after all be given the role she had created on Broadway, and win a Best Supporting Actress Oscar for it.

Instead of what gloriously could have been, Patricia was thrown into what carelessly was: *White Face,* which was finally released as *Raton Pass,* taking its name from Thomas W. Blackburn's novel on which it was based. Patricia was cast as Ann Challon opposite the tenor Dennis Morgan.

The eighty-four-minute feature had little to recommend it other than a weak film score by Max Steiner, the rugged good looks of Steve Cochran, and, in the final analysis, the astute acting of its leading lady. Initial photography began on July 19.

Filmed in black and white, *Raton Pass* is a convoluted tale about the struggle for control of the Challon Ranch in Raton, New Mexico. Ann (Neal) marries Marc Challon (Morgan), and each owns 50 percent of the ranch. Marc brings in a Chicago railroad owner, Prentice (Scott Forbes), to help with the banking. Soon Prentice has designs on the ranch as well; he and Ann become lovers and later wrest control of the ranch from Marc. When Ann betrays Prentice, he declares, "A half million acres won't make a man out of me and it can't make a lady out of you." Ann is eventually—after many a plot twist—shot by her former partner, Cy Van Cleave (Steve Cochran), and dies in Marc's arms.

Given the mediocre material, Patricia made the best of it, developing an unforgettable character and marvelously underplaying the death scene. Many years later, in 1984, Patricia proudly said of *Raton Pass*, "I played a rotten woman but it was the best dying I ever did in my life."[3]

About portraying such a "rotten woman," Patricia wrote in *Patricia Readings:* "Nice girls aren't as colorful as the wicked ones. And there are many nuances in the playing of a sweet little thing. You can't make her too nice, you know. . . . Even the nicest of girls is still a woman, if you know what I mean. She's still got to be played like a human being. Playing the part of a sultry female, you can call on many strictly feminine tricks; a lift of the eyebrow, a gleam in the eye, a gentle sneer, a ladylike pout or even an all-out female display of temper. When you play a good girl you're more restricted. A little fluttering of the eyelids, the way you carry yourself, maybe a tear or two. . . . [B]eing nice is a lot harder work on the screen. When you play a good girl and play her well, you can go home with the feeling you've really accomplished something. On the screen, as in real life, virtue is its own reward."[4]

Filming of *Raton Pass* was completed the third week of August at a film negative cost of $768,000. By the end of 1957, it had grossed over $1.7 million.

Word of mouth and preview reports indicated that Patricia's performances in the as-yet-unreleased *Three Secrets* and *The Breaking Point* were very strong. Warners first previewed *Three Secrets* on June 27 and *The Breaking Point* on August 29.

Patricia attended the preview of *Three Secrets* dressed in an extremely unattractive print dress with a large, open collar, and she was coiffed with the unbecoming bleached-blonde hairdo she had sported in *The Breaking Point*. She also wore the copy of the antique necklace Gary had made for her from *Bright Leaf*.

After this and other pre-release showings of *Three Secrets*, critics were generous with their praise. In the *Variety* preview review, Brog wrote, "Miss Parker's footage is longer than her co-stars', and she scores decisively. The same can be said for Miss Neal, who appears to decided advantage, and for Miss Roman, very colorful as the girl who meted out her own revenge for a wrong." Dorothy Manners praised Patricia's performance as "her best and most vital . . . to date. As the brittle, cynical newspaper woman who has sacrificed her marital happiness to her career, Pat is vividly effective. . . . 'Three Secrets' [is] one of the best of the season's melodramas."

The Breaking Point previewed at the end of August at the Warners Beverly Theatre in Los Angeles. At the preview Patricia was escorted by Steve Cochran. In the audience that night were Gary Cooper and Rocky. In the crowded lobby after the screening, Gary's and Patricia's eyes met. As Rocky looked away briefly, Cooper mouthed to Patricia, "You were good." To which she mouthed in reply, "Thank you."[5]

The ninety-seven-minute-long film received glowing notices. Said one reviewer, "'The Breaking Point' is a fast moving melodrama. . . . Garfield delivers strongly in this role, and Patricia Neal . . . shines brilliantly in every scene as the easy-virtued beauty who has a yen for Garfield. . . . Miss Neal's career is certain to be helped by the easy way in which she handles herself."[6]

The Breaking Point was the first of the two movies to be officially released. It premiered on September 30 and opened nationally on October 6. Said Kay Proctor in her Hollywood column, "In the acting department it's a toss-up for first honors between Patricia Neal, doing a brilliant job as the amoral and yet strangely sympathetic Leona, and Phyllis Thaxter, who creates a courageous and unforgettable portrait of Lucy, the wife."[7]

In his *New York Times* review Bosley Crowther, quite uncharacteristically, wrote, "Warner Brothers . . . finally has got hold of that fable [*To Have and Have Not*] and socked it for a four-base hit. . . . All of the character, color and cynicism of Mr. Hemingway's lean and hungry tale are wrapped up in this realistic picture." For once, the bristly critic got it right.[8]

The Breaking Point opened overseas to similar praise. Leonard Mosley of the London *Daily Express* gave the film four stars, saying, "All the acting is on a high level. . . . Miss Neal gives the impression that she looks on life as an apple specially made for her teeth to bite on—and in this film she munches her way right down to the core."[9] Reg Whitley, of the London *Daily Mirror*, agreed, writing that Patricia "[put] up an amazingly good performance as a seductive but tough character. . . . John Garfield is excellent as a man without real guts, and Phyllis Thaxter is first rate as his loyal wife, but this is Pat Neal's picture!"[10]

Three Secrets was officially released on October 14 to favorable reviews. The Reel Dope columnist in *Family Circle* magazine said, "Miss Neal scor[es] in a tight little showdown with a fellow reporter . . . that is the most convincing scene of the bunch. The blonde Patricia's episode is keyed to the surest popular response, and her role fits that almost masculine personality of hers better than she's taken before."[11] *Photoplay* that month was most succinct:

"Bring out the handkerchiefs." By the fall of 1950, however, the Hollywood film studio system was crumbling, and there were few moneymaking pictures that year. Despite good reviews, *The Breaking Point* died at the box office, and *Three Secrets* barely made back its costs. (By 1957, *Three Secrets* had grossed over $2 million in domestic and foreign rentals.)

Much of the film industry's woes stemmed from the competition introduced by television. People were staying home and enjoying the novelty of the small screen. Studios began turning to larger screen processes like Cinemascope and Cinerama, which television could not duplicate. More adult themes were sought and were being presented in gritty, hard-hitting pictures. Studios were no longer able to make profits through their own theaters, and high-priced stars who did not produce profitable films were let go. Patricia realized that she fit this mold: she had produced no hits for Warners, yet under her contract her salary was increasing.

The good reviews for *The Breaking Point* and *Three Secrets* were too little, too late. Warners had already assigned her to her last project under her contract: a part in *Operation Pacific,* starring John Wayne, then the number one box-office draw in the nation but not the acting equal of Gary Cooper or John Garfield. This was Wayne's first picture under a nonexclusive deal with Warner Brothers, and he would earn nearly $300,000.

On August 29—the date of the sneak preview of *The Breaking Point*—Patricia was tested for the role of Mary Stuart, John Wayne's former wife in the film. (Janice Rule was also tested for the same part that day). The role was a very secondary, walk-through part, and Patricia knew it. Filming officially began the very next day. Parts of *Operation Pacific,* but none of Patricia's scenes, were shot in Hawaii, with the cooperation of the U.S. Navy.

Operation Pacific, set in World War II, tells the story of Duke E. Gifford (Wayne), lieutenant commander of the submarine USS *Thunderfish,* skippered by "Pop" Perry (Ward Bond). On a mission patrol off an enemy island, Duke and his companions rescue from Japanese control several young children and a couple of nuns. In typical heroic John Wayne fashion, Duke carries a baby in his arms—a baby his friends and crew members know reminds him of the child he lost while married to Mary. The *Thunderfish* returns to port at Pearl Harbor, where Duke encounters Mary, now a nurse with the rank of lieutenant, currently dating the skipper's younger brother, Lieutenant Bob Perry (Philip Carey).

On the *Thunderfish*'s next mission, Pop Perry is wounded in battle. To save the rest of the crew, Duke orders the sub to dive, leaving the dying skipper behind. When they return to port, Bob Perry blames Duke for Pop's death. Mary, still in love with Duke, tries to convince Bob otherwise. On yet another dangerous mission, Duke, in command of the *Thunderfish*, rescues seven downed pilots, one of them, coincidentally, Bob Perry, whom Duke personally saves. When the sub returns to port, Duke is finally hailed as a hero. He finds Mary waiting for him.

Patricia did not like working with the forty-three-year-old John Wayne. In an article years later, she said, "Wayne was having marital problems [his second marriage, to Mexican film actress Esperanza Baur, was unraveling], which kept him in a bad mood. He fought with the director and he was a big bully, especially to the film's publicist, who was a homosexual. Wayne would grab the poor guy by the neck. It was awful!"[12] (Years later, she enjoyed working with a much mellower John Wayne.)

George Waggner, the film's fifty-six-year-old director and author of the story on which the movie was based, was a "perfect gentleman and a nice man," Paul Picerni recalled, but an ineffective director. His task was certainly not made easier by Wayne's bullying.[13]

During the filming of *Operation Pacific*, Patricia appeared bloated and was not photographed attractively. Of course, her costumes (consisting entirely of nurse's uniforms) and her short, dark hairstyle were simply not appealing. She looked heavier, her face strained with fatigue. In late October, studio executives were told that Patricia would be laid off until the thirtieth of the month. She had called in ill.

Her contract was ending. Her personal life appeared to be going nowhere. And now her toughest crisis appeared: Patricia was pregnant.

10

20th Century-Fox

I must be out of my mind. I've got my life all tangled up in yours and now . . . well look at me. I can't stop.

—Joan Ross, *Diplomatic Courier* (1952)

The timing could not have been worse. Patricia and Gary's relationship was coasting; a sameness of their lives together had set in, and neither one wanted to alter it for fear of what might happen. Neither could address their situation. Patricia admittedly felt guilt and displeasure as Gary was not making any attempts to change his relationship with Rocky, and Cooper was racked with worry about the effect on Maria if he did change it. He would not make a commitment. Patricia briefly saw a psychiatrist and told him that she wanted children, a home, and a husband. These things were clear to her.

Weighing on Patricia's mind was the question of what would happen to her career if she had the child. Earlier in the year, actress Ingrid Bergman had given birth to an out-of-wedlock child, the fruit of her affair with director Roberto Rossellini, and a great scandal had ensued. Not only Bergman's marriage (to Dr. Petter Lindstrom) but also her career had been destroyed. She was branded a home wrecker and a loose woman and could no longer get work in the United States, for a period that was to last several years.

Jean Valentino's doctor called with the confirmation that Patricia was indeed pregnant. At first Patricia was happy about the news. Gary was as emotionally touched as she. This child represented the culmination of their love. Yet they were both walking on thin ice. For several days they continued to work at the studio as if nothing had changed. They simply went about their normal routines. Finally, the situation had to be addressed. Patricia knew that Eura Neal would die if she found out.

Gary was in the midst of filming *Dallas* with Ruth Roman and Barbara

---

Facing page: Patricia Neal, 1952. From the author's collection.

Payton, an attractive blonde with a sometimes debatable talent and a no-
toriously questionable reputation. Rumor had it that Cooper and Payton
were more than just friends. Whether Patricia heard those stories or not, she
nonetheless feared what Gary might do if she pressed him about their situation. Cooper finally acted. He contacted a friend, then called Patricia and
told her he had set up an appointment with a doctor for the following afternoon. She realized no other outcome was possible. On a bright October day,
Gary, Patricia, and Chloe drove to an unfamiliar neighborhood in downtown
Los Angeles, parked the car, and, alone, Patricia walked up to the door of a
small office. She handed over cash, supplied by Gary, to the dispassionate
young doctor.

Patricia's abortion was completed within hours. After it was over, she
somehow managed to return to the car where Gary, soaked in perspiration,
and Chloe waited. The three returned to Fox Hills Drive, where she and Gary
spent the rest of the afternoon weeping together on the floor, Jean and Chloe
bringing in a pillow and blanket for them to rest on. Patricia continued to
bleed from the abortion for five months, and the emotional repercussions
lasted long beyond that. "For over thirty years, alone, in the night, I cried.
For years and years I cried over that baby," Patricia wrote. "And whenever
I had too much to drink, I would remember that I had not allowed him to
exist. I admired Ingrid Bergman for having her son. She had guts. I did not.
And I regret it with all my heart. If I had only one thing to do over in my life,
I would have that baby."[1]

Patricia finished filming her last scene for *Operation Pacific* on November
16, the final day of her contract. On December 1, she walked out of the Warner
Brothers gates—alone. This time there was no studio car to drive her home.
There was no press, and no representative from the studio to bid her farewell.
She recalled simply, "I said goodbye to the cop and drove out the gate."[2]

Before Patricia returned to Knoxville for the holidays, a couple of potential projects presented themselves. She met with MGM director Richard
Thorpe to discuss a role in *Ivanhoe,* but the part eventually went to Joan
Fontaine. And her New York agent, Maynard Morris, let her know that the
script for *Blue Light* was being sent to her. But the project never got off the
ground.

However, her California agents secured for her a nonexclusive, three-
picture, seven-year deal at 20th Century-Fox. She would earn less money
than she had at Warners, but she would at least be able to choose better pictures than the final two she had been forced to endure.

In explaining the change to her fan club, Patricia somewhat sugarcoated the situation: "I am no longer with Warner Brothers. It seemed the new production schedule held not a single picture I was interested in doing or that was right for me; so, being a little weary of suspensions, I decided a release from my contract was best. Warner Brothers agreed; it was settled amicably.

"Now I have signed with Twentieth Century Fox—it's a one picture a year deal with option of two! This way I'm allowed to do outside pictures and don't feel tied down to one studio. Also, there'll be more of a challenge for variations of roles. I feel extremely lucky the way things turned out. But, I will always be grateful to Warners for having given me my first film chance."[3]

Warners rushed *Operation Pacific* into theaters to cash in on Wayne's popularity at the box office. From its opening on January 9, 1951, it was a tremendous success. *Variety* commented, "Wayne, occasionally called upon to be over-heroic, still turns in a topnotch performance and has strong support right down the line. Miss Neal is pretty and able. . . . [C]amera work by Bert Glennon is first-class. Max Steiner's musical score is atmospheric."[4]

Patricia's performance drew somewhat mixed reviews. The *Fortnight* critic wrote, "Miss Neal, in fact, often seems as unemotional and disinterested as a mere spectator, although her dialogue indicates she's quite worked up about it all."[5] The *New York Times*'s Bosley Crowther said that "the performance of Patricia Neal in this thankless role of this lady does not help matters in the least. Our old friend John Wayne as the hero does a good, square-jawed, iron-man, ship-shape job, but Miss Neal with her airiness and sashays is a walking jeremiad against dames."[6] The *Hollywood Reporter* critic was kinder: "Patricia Neal is splendid in the big dramatic moments but the role generally is too kittenish for her commanding talents."[7] And Ruth Waterbury, in her *Los Angeles Examiner* review, wrote, "I don't think it's so good for that excellent character performer, Patricia Neal. . . . Given a superb part, she would be superb in it. Any pretty girl could have played her Navy nurse role."[8]

Operation Pacific is perfect drive-in fare. Today it's terribly outdated and only passably compelling, but it proved to be a real moneymaker because of Wayne's box-office draw. By 1957 it had grossed almost $3.9 million in domestic and foreign rentals. There are a few gloriously photographed air sequences in the film, and one particularly visually stunning scene on a moonlit night at sea aboard the submarine. One scene is especially touching, if one knows the circumstances of Patricia's life: in the hospital nursery, Mary Stuart briefly holds an infant's tiny head to her cheek (apparently to indicate the compassion she feels toward her own deceased child by Duke). The

Max Steiner score is unfortunately not memorable, and the editing by Alan Crosland Jr. is sometimes abrupt and choppy.

Raton Pass finally crept into theaters the second week of February. The *New York Times* review (thankfully not by the acerbic Bosley Crowther) was the most generous: "The last fifteen minutes or so are charged with sound and fury. . . . This is good old-fashioned Western action stuff, right down to the amazing recovery Mr. Morgan makes after being shot in the back. Miss Neal has a fat role in this picture and plays it commendably. . . . With a little more dramatic punch 'Raton Pass' could have amounted to something."[9] Perhaps more typical was the reviewer who said, "Principals try hard, but dialog and contrived situations are beyond them. . . . Miss Neal is obviously miscast."[10]

Essentially, *Raton Pass* is not a very good picture. With its startling brutality, it is more of an adult film. But, except for Patricia, Cochran, and Forbes, not one actor in the film reacts to any of the violence or action in the film: they all just say their lines and clear out of the shot. *Raton Pass* eventually was placed on the lower bill of double features and died a quick death at the box office. Its total grosses by 1957 amounted to approximately $1.4 million.

The State Department offered Patricia an opportunity to participate in a publicity junket to South America in late February and March 1951. Along with Ricardo Montalban, Joan Fontaine, June Haver, and other stars, Patricia was invited to attend the First Annual Montevideo International Film Festival beginning in Punta del Este, Uruguay. Overcoming her fear of flying, Patricia and her colleagues boarded a Pan American Airways Clipper, complete with sleepers, on Thursday, February 22, bound for Montevideo on the first leg of their tour.

For three weeks, in each participating major city, the stars toured and were feted, and in return they promoted their respective studios' product, posed for pictures, and signed autographs. In Buenos Aires, the group was granted a rare interview with President Juan Peron and his wife, the legendary Eva Peron.

Throughout the tour, Patricia and June Haver (who, Patricia noticed, read a religious book on the flight to Buenos Aires) would visit churches and participate in masses. They dined with nuns and priests, and Patricia noticed the peace and serenity that Haver received from these visits. Years later, she would recall this trip as an introduction to faith, which June Haver treasured and shared with her. Wrote Patricia of the experience, "I felt wholesome. It made me forget I was sleeping with a married man."[11]

But it was impossible to avoid all associations with Gary. At a party one evening in Buenos Aires, Patricia was approached by an impressive and obviously wealthy matron, who asked her if she knew Gary Cooper. It was Cooper's former lover Countess Dorothy di Frasso. The two women met three times during the tour, and the countess shared her memories of Gary. At their last party in Montevideo, the countess advised Patricia, "Fight for him, he's worth it."[12] Patricia replied that she'd met Cooper's wife, and that Rocky was tough. The countess said that Rocky had once held a tea for her and two of Cooper's other former lovers. Unashamedly Rocky returned the gifts the three women had given her husband. "You're going to need all the spunk you've got, my dear," the countess told Patricia.[13]

Patricia and the Countess di Frasso were invited to stay overnight at the home of the very elderly bon vivant Albert Dodero, one of the richest men in the world. The old man was ill during the day and stayed in his room. That evening he came downstairs to meet the group and see that all their needs were met. He then returned to his room and promptly died—which the countess thought was "spunky."[14] The next morning, the countess called Joan Fontaine, who had stayed at the American embassy. As Fontaine recounts, di Frasso asked, "'What should Pat and I do? Ask the ambassador.' As my host was not up yet, I suggested that they eat a hearty breakfast, tip the servants, pack and leave . . . a thank-you note would not be expected!"[15]

Patricia flew to Florida at the end of the first week in March and was astonished to be met at the airport by both Gary and her mother. Gary wanted to take Patricia to Cuba to meet novelist Ernest Hemingway and his wife, Mary Welsh. When Cooper arrived in Florida, he had called on Eura and asked her if she would ride with him in his limo to the airport to pick up Patricia. Cooper had confided to Mrs. Neal that he loved Patricia. Eura told Patricia, "He told me he had never known a love for anyone the way he did you, Patsy. There was no reason for him to fib to me. Still . . . still, I told him that my family was not accustomed to anything like that."[16]

After a short stay in Florida, Gary and Patricia flew to Cuba to visit Hemingway, whom Gary had met when he starred in the 1932 film adaptation of *A Farewell to Arms*. They arrived in time for cocktails at the Hemingway hilltop retreat, Finca Vigia, near Havana. Patricia knew that Gary was searching for Hemingway's approval of their relationship. She was reassured by Hemingway's overtly masculine charm. But at dinner Patricia knew without a doubt that Mrs. Hemingway disapproved of her—Mary was a friend of Rocky's. That evening, however, Gary and Patricia were escorted to their room in another building to discover a double bed prepared for them.

Cooper and Hemingway had several serious and quiet talks that weekend, to which Patricia was not privy. Hemingway gave Patricia every indication that he liked her and was demonstrative and gracious. Later, she was told he did not approve of the relationship after all. At the end of the weekend, Gary put Patricia on a plane to California. He stayed an additional day in Cuba before continuing on to New York for a radio broadcast. On the flight back to California, Patricia was alternately confident and worried and anxious, wondering if Hemingway had told Gary to divorce Rocky; or if Gary needed approval from more of his friends; or if Gary would ever be able to decide on his own.

Home at Fox Hills Drive, Patricia tuned in on the evening of Gary's radio broadcast with Jean and Chloe. Afterward, impressed with his performance, Patricia wired Gary a note of congratulations. A telegram was quickly sent back to her: "I have had just about enough of you. You had better stop now or you will be sorry.—Mrs. Gary Cooper."[17]

Patricia froze in horror. Now she questioned herself and her motives. And the answers frightened her. A showdown at some time between her and Rocky was inevitable.

The situation was becoming more and more public. In mid-March Louella Parsons reported that the Cooper marriage was in deep trouble. The previous Christmas, Rocky and Maria had gone to New York for the holidays, while Gary remained in Los Angeles, though he was not filming at the time. Rumors began to circulate.

Patricia's first film with 20th Century-Fox was something completely different from anything she had done before: a science fiction movie. She was less than thrilled with the assignment. For one thing, the leading man was the relatively unknown Michael Rennie. And in fact, the six-foot, four-inch, angularly handsome Rennie was ideally cast in this, his first U.S. picture. But the director was Robert Wise, with whom Patricia had worked in *Three Secrets,* and she trusted his judgment.

The movie was based on the 1940 novelette "Farewell to the Master," by Harry Bates, who sold the rights to 20th Century-Fox producer Julian Blaustein for about $500. Blaustein then sold the story to the studio for $1,000. When Edmund H. North submitted his screenplay to studio chief Darryl F. Zanuck in the summer of 1950, Zanuck did not much like the title, which was eventually changed to *The Day the Earth Stood Still.* He also objected to the opening scene, which took place onboard a spacecraft. "When you open a picture on something that does not 'exist,' you have great trouble in capturing your audience," he commented in an August 10 memo.[18]

The film opens with the sighting and tracking of a flying saucer, which lands on the Ellipse in Washington, D.C. The military is called out and surrounds the craft, weapons at the ready. Suddenly a door appears on the spacecraft and a humanlike figure, Klaatu (Rennie) emerges, bearing a strange object in his hand. A soldier shoots the device from the alien's hand, injuring Klaatu. Suddenly a huge robot appears at the door, and with a brilliant flash of light from its eye, it disintegrates the soldiers' weapons. Klaatu stops the robot, Gort (Lock Martin), from further destruction. In English he explains that the destroyed object had been intended as a gift to the president and it would have given him knowledge of life on other planets. Taken to Walter Reed Hospital for examination, Klaatu escapes and mingles among the Washingtonians. Fear is rampant in the city: Is the alien hostile? Is he good or evil? Is he a Communist?

Assuming the name "Carpenter," Klaatu takes a room at a boarding house where he befriends Helen Benson (Neal) and her son Bobby (Billy Gray). Leaving the impenetrable robot Gort to guard the equally impenetrable spacecraft, Klaatu sets about his mission to contact world leaders and give them the message he has been sent to Earth to deliver. He enlists in his cause a renowned scientist, Professor Barnhardt (Sam Jaffe), who lives in Washington. Barnhardt tells Klaatu that humans are fearful of the unknown, and that world leaders would never unite for a common cause. He suggests that some kind of supernatural display might grab their attention. Klaatu decides on the nondestructive course of interrupting all electrical power on the planet, except for that needed in planes in flight and in hospitals, thereby bringing the world's activity to a sudden halt (hence the name of the movie).

Bobby follows Klaatu when he goes to the spacecraft to set his plan in motion, then tells his disbelieving mother and her boyfriend, Tom Stevens (Hugh Marlowe), what he has seen. Tom senses he can make a name for himself if he can turn the alien in. Trapped in an elevator with Klaatu during the electrical outage, Helen finally believes Bobby's story and warns Klaatu of Tom's plans. Klaatu tells Helen that if anything should happen to him, Gort would destroy all of mankind. The government soldiers shoot Klaatu down in the street, and Helen escapes to the spacecraft. She gives Gort the message given to her by the mortally wounded Klaatu—"Gort! Klaatu Barada Nikto"—and he takes her inside the saucer. Gort then rescues Klaatu from the morgue, takes him to the spaceship, and resurrects him.

As the world leaders gather around the spacecraft, Klaatu appears with Helen and Gort. Klaatu tells them that alien nations have united and have created a race of robots with absolute and irrevocable power that act automatically against any aggressor. "The result is that we live in peace. Your choice is simple: Join us and live in peace—or pursue your present course and face obliteration. We shall be waiting to hear from you." Acknowledging Helen with a nod, Klaatu and Gort reenter the spacecraft and depart.

The film, budgeted at $960,000, utilized stock footage and actors' doubles for scenes shot in Washington, D.C., and Arlington Cemetery. Journalists Drew Pearson, Gabriel Heater, H. V. Katlenborn, and Elmer Davis supplied an unsettling realism to the film. (Too vain to show his bald head, Pearson wears a hat in his scenes inside a television studio.)

No one involved in the making of *The Day the Earth Stood Still* realized that it would become *the* hallmark science fiction film. Its themes resonated with the public because of the cold war and the very real fear of atomic warfare, and because of the atmosphere of distrust generated by the hunt for Communists under every rock. In fact, Sam Jaffe was almost dismissed from the film, having been listed in the infamous right-wing pamphlet *Red Channels: The Report of Communist Influence in Radio and Television*. Inclusion in the report essentially resulted in blacklisting, pending a satisfactory appearance before the House Un-American Activities Committee. Jaffe's scenes were quickly completed; he didn't work in pictures again for five years.

Two days before *The Day the Earth Stood Still* wrapped production on May 18, 1951, Rocky's attorney, Graham Sterling, announced that the Coopers were separating after seventeen years of marriage and that negotiations for a property settlement were under way. Gary had already moved out of the Brentwood house and taken up residence in the Bel Air Hotel. At the time of the announcement, he was in Naples, Florida, filming *Distant Drums*. That night he returned to Hollywood and took thirteen-year-old Maria to a quiet dinner.

While she was finishing work on *The Day the Earth Stood Still,* Patricia was asked for a statement about the Cooper breakup and if she was in love with the actor. Her only comment was, "Could be, maybe, but I'd be silly to advertise it, wouldn't I? After all he's a married man. Where does that leave me?"[19]

Rocky's only comment to the press at that time was, "I'm Catholic and under no circumstances would I ever consider a divorce."[20]

The columnists quickly began speculating about what had led to the separation. Wrote one journalist, "Always when Gary gets a romantic gleam in his eye he sees his tailor. Back in the 'Thirties when Gary was first a star he used to wear the most awful clothes with a heavy watch-chain strung across his middle. Then he met Countess Dorothy di Frasso. And how he did spruce up. During the Lupe Velez era he wore, and you might guess, gayer socks and ties and tweeds. Later, with the advent of Rocky, he went Brooks Brotherish. And now his grooming, having picked up again, is more casual in tone."[21]

Soon Gary and Patricia were seen in public together. Cooper had warned the owners of the various establishments and restaurants that he and Patricia were not to be photographed while they were there, or he would sue.

Helen Horton came to Hollywood for a visit with Patricia. She met Gary Cooper and was charmed by him. Years later, Helen told Patricia that Jean Hagen, their mutual friend from Northwestern days, had confided to her during the visit, "Pat thinks Gary is going to marry her. But he is not. Everybody in town knows it but her. And Pat is not going to accept it."[22] During Helen's stay, she accompanied Patricia to a party at David O. Selznick's home. Gary was also there. When Gary and Patricia walked into the room, the tension was palpable, and the other women attending grew cold and disdainful. The only woman who was civil to her the whole evening was Tyrone Power's wife, Annabella.

Patricia continued to be evasive in interviews. *Photoplay* correspondent Aline Mosby asked her if she was in love with Cooper. "Oh this is such a touchy subject," Patricia responded. "I'm very fond of him. He's quite wonderful and I've known him for three years, ever since we acted in 'The Fountainhead.' But I had absolutely nothing to do with the breaking up of their marriage. We're very good friends. He's a wonderful guy and I love working with him. But I had nothing to do with his marriage trouble. . . . I'm sure most intelligent people agree with me that no such thing could happen—that no one could break up a happy marriage."[23] Discussing the onslaught of adverse publicity, Patricia said, "Yes, I was upset. I'm from a pretty conventional family background and I don't like this kind of thing at all. Actually only one columnist has been unkind to me. I hope this talk will die down, and that people will find something else to talk about. I wish everyone would just ignore this."[24] But her evasiveness created hostility among the press.

Friends such as Arlene Dahl and Michael Rennie tried to protect Patricia. Rennie felt that "the most powerful gossip columnists were killing Pat's career with hostility when they should at least be giving her professional support and allowing people to lead their own private lives. It wasn't in lurid colors, but Pat Neal was being painted as a home-wrecker."[25]

As for Gary's friends, they "claim[ed] Pat could take care of herself—that she had more guts and determination than Gary did. But the fact is she didn't know the right people and never took advantage of her relationship with Gary to further her career. . . . Since most moviegoers were women Pat Neal was doomed. Hollywood insiders were divided, but the majority scorned her. Her name was taken off the guest lists at dinner parties and other social gatherings on and off the set. She was left to fend for herself."[26]

Patricia appeared to agree with Gary's friends. In an interview Hedda Hopper, who liked Patricia, said, "On the screen you are often aloof, or seem remote . . . you give a very independent effect, more so than most players." To which Patricia replied, "Perhaps I give that impression because I am rather like that myself. I always feel that I can take care of myself."[27]

That proposition would be tested in the coming months.

11

Purgatory

But even when I find my way out of the forest
I shall be left with the inconsolable memory
Of the treasure I went into the forest to find
And never found, and which was not there
And perhaps is not anywhere? But if not anywhere,
Why do I feel guilty at not having found it?

—Celia, *The Cocktail Party* (1951)

After *The Day the Earth Stood Still* was completed, Patricia started work on a picture for Universal-International—a comedy produced by Ted Richmond called *Week-End with Father*, with Van Heflin. Based on a story by George W. George and George F. Slavin, it was directed by the competent Douglas Sirk. *Week-End with Father* would be Patricia's second comedy, excluding two brief scenes in *It's a Great Feeling*. She had signed with Universal for this one film on the day the Coopers announced their separation, May 16. Again she would portray a mother, this time of two young boys. *Week-End with Father* would also be the first comedy in ten years for Van Heflin. British actress Virginia Field, with whom Patricia had worked in *John Loves Mary*, and thirty-five-year-old Richard Denning were also in the cast. (One of the young Universal contract actors tested for Denning's part was twenty-five-year-old Rock Hudson, who had actually been assigned the role on May 18. For whatever reason, ten days later, Denning took over the role.)

In his book *Sirk on Sirk*, author Jon Halliday wrote that Douglas Sirk was "the best read man I ever met in my life," and that he was considered the most literate director in Hollywood during his heyday in the 1950s.[1] "There is a very short distance between high art and trash," Sirk was credited as saying.[2]

Facing page: Patricia Neal wearing the Helen Rose designed dress she would take with her to Korea, 1952. Courtesy of Photofest.

The plot of the screenplay of *Week-End with Father* by Joseph Hoffman concerned New York advertising agency vice president and widower Brad Stubbs (Heflin) and his two daughters, Anne and Patty (portrayed by actual sisters Gigi and Janine Perreau), who are going to Camp Minnishwaka in Maine for the summer. Brad literally runs into a young widow, Jean Bowen (Patricia), mother of two boys, Gary and David (Jimmy Hunt and Tommy Rettig). The boys are spending the summer in Maine at Camp Hiashwaka, brother camp to Minnishwaka. Meeting again in Central Park, Jean and Brad talk about their children and become attracted to each other. Brad is being pursued by TV personality Phyllis Reynolds (Field), who thinks Brad is going to marry her. Jean and Brad decide to marry, and they drive up to Maine to surprise their children. Phyllis decides to drive up to Maine as well.

At the camp, Brad and Jean meet health instructor Don Adams (Denning), who takes a shine to Jean. The weekend becomes a disaster when Anne, at her eleventh birthday party, tells her friends she doesn't want her father to marry Jean. Jean overhears the conversation and breaks the engagement, assuming Brad wants to marry Phyllis. The children change their minds and decide they want to see their parents happy, so they devise a scheme to reunite them. At the fadeout, everything is resolved, and Brad and Jean marry.

Hunt, probably best remembered today for his role as David in *Invaders From Mars* (1953), recalls Patricia lovingly: "She treated Tommy and I as if we were her own boys. . . . She was so good to us, and so professional. It was just a very good time we had making the movie."[3] Denning and Field, Hunt remembered, were very kind people as well. On his home office wall today, Jim Hunt still keeps a picture of Patricia Neal.

Principal photography for *Week-End with Father* was completed July 13. After seeing Patricia walking across the Universal lot, producer Ted Richmond realized the film did not have one "cheesecake" shot in it, and he felt that Patricia merited at least one. Patricia always had maintained a splendid figure, one that she was very proud of. Thus an extremely brief beach scene was hastily prepared and shot so Patricia could be seen in a bathing suit. This would be her only cheesecake film appearance.

At the invitation of either Mel Ferrer or Gregory Peck, two of the theater's founders, Patricia was invited to play the role of Celia Coplestone in T. S. Eliot's *The Cocktail Party* at the La Jolla Playhouse. Eliot called his verse play a "sophisticated comedy of marital misunderstanding." Actually, *The Cocktail Party* tells the story of infidelity and convoluted relationships in a highbrow manner and style that is definitely not everyone's cup of tea. Patricia's character recites long and esoterically dreamy speeches throughout the first two acts. The relationship in the play between Celia and Edward, with whom Celia is having an affair, seemed to parallel Patricia's personal situation. Celia has several speeches dealing with being alone. In one passage in the first act, Celia says to another character, "Surely you don't hold to that silly convention that the husband must always be the one to be divorced?"

The Cocktail Party opened August 14 for eight performances, playing to sold-out audiences in its first presentation outside of New York. Director Norman Lloyd recalled a trick he pulled on the cast the afternoon of the opening. "Patricia was lacking in confidence and intimidated by the play, as was everyone at the time," Lloyd said. Cast member Vincent Price had received a telegram from a playwright of his acquaintance who said he would be coming to the opening performance. Calling the cast onto the stage, Lloyd recalled, "I read the telegram to them as if it were from T. S. Eliot. And when I finished reading it, Patricia Neal jumped up and ran to the ladies' room. She may have thrown up. Whatever she did, it absolutely galvanized her and her performance was absolutely, oh—beautiful, absolutely marvelous!"[4]

The reviews of *The Cocktail Party* were mixed, but Patricia's performance won praise. Wrote Robert MacDonald in his August 15 review in the *San Diego Union*, "Wafting one of the most entrancing voices we've ever heard over the footlights, Miss Neal turns in an altogether pleasing performance in a demanding and exacting role, which needs all the talent she pours into it."

The noted *Los Angeles Times* critic Edwin Schallert, father of cast member William Schallert, said in his August 16 review, "There is something very special to be said about the excellent playing by Price and Miss Neal of their very crucial scene together in the second act. It is beautifully accomplished."

Lloyd's final analysis of Patricia and her performance is telling. "I felt at the time that Pat Neal, . . . had she stayed in the theatre, . . . would have been a great star. In the theatre she would have been the successor to Katharine Cornell."[5]

Gary Cooper was admitted to the St. John's Hospital in Santa Monica for a hernia operation the first week in August. Within a few days he was able to leave the hospital and drive down to San Diego to attend a performance of *The Cocktail Party*. Promised there would be no photographers present, Gary agreed to be interviewed by reporters after the performance. Asked what he thought of the production, Cooper said breezily, "Oh, I liked it very much. I had already seen it in New York with Alec Guinness, and I thought it was awful. I've never been able to get with T. S. Eliot anyway. I called it 'The Yakking Party' and didn't understand the yakking. But after I saw it I read the play, and then I knew what it was about. Hey, Pat's great, isn't she?"[6] End of interview. Patricia recalled that Gary came to other performances as well. To the press Cooper would never, until the day he died, discuss his relationship with Patricia.

When Gary's most recent picture, *Dallas*, was released, people noticed that he looked drawn and weary. Said Bosley Crowther in the *New York Times*, "There is something about the sadness that appears in Mr. Cooper's eyes, something about the slowness and the weariness of his walk, something about the manner that is not necessarily in the script, which reminds the middle-aged observer that Mr. Cooper had been at it a long time."[7]

Gary was able to talk about the play, but not his personal life. The strain was starting to show. Though still in close contact with his daughter, Cooper was feeling pressure and guilt. Said Hector Arce in his book on Cooper, "He wanted to marry Pat, but not if it sacrificed the respect of an adolescent daughter who worshiped him. Rocky had yet to agree to a divorce. Pat was caught in the middle of the impasse, bearing the brunt of outraged opinion. The American public was at its most sanctimonious at this time."[8]

Gary's weakening health may have been related in part to the stress he was experiencing during the filming of *High Noon*, his latest film. As well as being depressed over his breakup with Rocky and the knowledge that Maria knew of his infidelities, Cooper was suffering from a declining career and ill health. He was literally a mess. Besides the hernia, he had an ulcer and suffered from a painful hip. He also knew that he had been fourth choice for the role of the over-the-hill sheriff Will Kane in *High Noon* (the other candidates were John Wayne, Charlton Heston, and Marlon Brando, all of whom turned down the role). He had to have felt discouraged.

Cooper faced another issue that simply would not go away—the House Un-American Activities Committee. *High Noon*'s screenwriter and coproducer, Carl Foreman, was blacklisted in Hollywood for alleged Communist sympathies, and he eventually moved to England, where he worked under a pseudonym. At one point prior to filming *High Noon*, Foreman and Cooper had been in partnership, but that had ended. The influential columnist Hedda Hopper was insistent that Gary renounce his relationship with Foreman, but Cooper, who had himself appeared before the committee in 1947, would not. Hopper then proceeded to blast Cooper in print at every opportunity. Patricia said Gary "didn't have the fight in him that I had in me, and I think he admired it in me. He was always very secure and avoided fights, but I think his doing *High Noon* in spite of the House Un-American pressure on

Carl Foreman had something to do with me. This time he had the courage to go out and say, 'I'll stick with him.'"[9]

Film hero Wayne, with a severe dose of bitter grapes after seeing Cooper's performance in *High Noon*, railed against it and the film: "It's the most un-American thing I've ever seen in my whole life! The last thing in the picture is ol' Coop putting the U.S. marshal's badge under his foot and stepping on it! I'll never regret having run Foreman out of this country!"[10] The fact is, the final shot in the film is *not* as Wayne suggested, nor was it ever written that way by Foreman. Will Kane simply removes his badge, resigning his position as marshal, and tosses it to the ground.

Grace Kelly, Cooper's cool, Philadelphia-born, blonde costar in *High Noon*, was an up-and-coming young film actress. *High Noon* was her second picture. Kelly's moral reputation was questionable. She allegedly had affairs with almost all her leading men—in particular Ray Milland, William Holden, Bing Crosby, and Clark Gable. Gary Cooper was no exception. According to observers on the *High Noon* set, Kelly made absolutely no attempt to hide her flirtation with Gary. Their conversation often bordered on the intimate. Patricia recalls that Gary did not want her to visit the set in Sonora, California. But she did for a few days, having dinner one night with Gary, director Fred Zinnemann, and Kelly. Patricia recalled, "I realized she [Kelly] was neither looking at me nor talking to me. I was used to being snubbed in public, but this I couldn't figure out. Unless she felt I was competition. When I was alone with Gary I asked a question I never had before. But I did it in a roundabout way. 'Is Grace interested in you?' He wasn't totally convincing. 'Nope, I think she's set her cap on Freddie [Zinnemann].' Whatever I may have thought, I did not ask him about Grace again."[11]

In an interview in the early 1950s, Clara Bow, Cooper's lover of years before, told columnist Louella Parsons, "Gary called me about *High Noon* and asked if I had ever heard of Grace Kelly, but the name did not ring a bell. . . . Grace Kelly was not the angel she appeared to be. . . . I'd heard he was serious about Pat Neal and it's a crazy thing because Gary never mentioned her. I figured he had his reasons so I wasn't going to pry. One of my friends thought it was terrible that he was cheating on that girl . . . Neal. I said, 'What's new?'" Bow spoke openly with Parsons about her relationship with Cooper when they were both with Paramount, and concluded with her feeling about Gary's mother, "I read in the gossip columns she (Cooper's mother) isn't so chummy with Gary's wife, either. If he married the Queen of England, she wouldn't be good enough for him. She poisons his mind. She's the biggest phony of them all."[12] Patricia would soon be able to testify to that.

The Day the Earth Stood Still opened in Los Angeles on September 18 and in New York on September 28. Bosley Crowther, in his *New York Times* review, as usual missed the point. His tongue-in-cheek panning of *The Day the Earth Still* appears ridiculous today in light of the reverence in which the film is now held. He wrote, "Michael Rennie, who plays this genteel soul, while charmingly suave and cosmopolitan, is likely to cause unguarded yawns. His manners are strangely punctilious for a fellow just off a space boat, and his command of an earthly language must have been acquired from listening entirely to the B.B.C. Nice chap, Mr. Rennie, but a bit on the soft side, don'tcha know. . . . It is comforting, of course, to have it made plain that our planetary neighbors are much wiser and more peaceful than are we, but this makes for a tepid entertainment in what is anomalously labeled the science-fiction field."[13]

Reams and reams of words have been printed about this film masterpiece since its release in 1951. Suffice it to say, it is perhaps the best science fiction film of all time. Since its release, every picture of its genre has been compared to it. Elements of the film's design are still influential today. According to the American Film Institute "Gort is regarded by science-fiction aficionados as one of the most beloved and well-known of motion picture robots, and the command [issued by Patricia's character], 'Gort! *Klaatu Barada Nikto!*' has become part of the American film lexicon."[14]

The first release of *The Day the Earth Stood Still* grossed $1.8 million on worldwide rentals. The film was nominated for two Golden Globe Awards in 1951, winning for Best Film Promoting International Understanding. In 1995 the film was placed on the National Film Registry for film preservation. The picture still draws admirers annually at science-fiction conventions and film festivals (in 2004 it was presented on the big screen to a packed house at the Stony Brook Film Festival in New York).

What truly secures the position of *The Day the Earth Stood Still* as a classic are the performances of its stars. Professionals every one, they make even the most ridiculous dialogue sound sincere. Patricia's earnest performance struck fear into the hearts of many a mother and child in its time—her vulnerability and belief in Klaatu's dedicated purpose are pure. *The Day the Earth Stood Still* will undoubtedly be the one motion picture for which Patricia Neal will always be remembered.

Early in October, 20th Century-Fox, pleased with the returns of *The Day the Earth Stood Still* and with Patricia's performance and personal reviews, signed her for two more pictures. The first, *Diplomatic Courier*, would costar her with Tyrone Power. (The second was not announced at that time; it turned out to be *Something for the Birds*.)

Based on a 1945 espionage thriller by Peter Cheyney, *Diplomatic Courier* tells a tale of adventure and deceit among cold war spies in Europe. Power plays a secret agent who must retrieve a vital document containing details of the Russian invasion of Yugoslavia after a diplomatic courier is murdered by two Russian agents. Patricia plays an American widow who turns out to be a Soviet spy.

Location shooting was done in Paris, Salzburg, and Trieste, using doubles. In one scene for the picture, Patricia was required to lie in bed for the two days it took to shoot the scene. In between takes she would pace the sound stage for exercise. "Lying down on the job in this instance," she joked, "is tough work!"[15] The picture was economically shot on an extremely tight schedule, with filming completed on November 30, 1951.

Week-End with Father premiered on November 22, 1951, with national release on December 1. It received respectable reviews. Said Kay Proctor in the *Los Angeles Examiner*, "Lovely-to-look-at Patricia Neal, playing the widow, comes off somewhat the better of the two, possibly because she is not called upon to fall into a bucket of whitewash, get dunked in a lake, or hop about in a gunny sack."[16] In the *Hollywood Citizen-News* the reviewer commented that the film "is a bright and breezy family comedy that should please even the most particular filmgoers. . . . Patricia Neal and Van Heflin play a widow and widower with a nice understanding of the roles."[17]

Today, *Week-End with Father* still holds up as a delightful family romp. Rarely seen on television, it is a gem of a little movie. Both Patricia and Van Heflin, best known for their quality dramatic performances, come across capably, though a bit uncomfortably. The children fare better, especially Gigi Perreau, who was a top child actor of the day.

Though Patricia and Gary did not socialize a great deal, they were photographed together by Nat Dallinger at a dinner party hosted by Cobina Wright. This was one of their first public appearances since the breakup of the Coopers' marriage. Another guest was Joan Fontaine, and she and Patricia were photographed together in deep conversation. Patricia appears particularly stunning in a lovely strapless gown and elbow-length gloves, her dark hair pulled back. Gary, on the other hand, looks rather lost and uncomfortable.

Sadly, Patricia had begun to notice a change in Gary. He obviously was declining physically, but as usual he covered it up. Gloom seemed to accompany them everywhere. As for Rocky, she was often seen on the arm of screen actor and playboy Peter Lawford, the two adopting what many believed to be the same lifestyle that Gary and Patricia were enjoying.[18]

On October 15, Gary and Patricia attended a dinner dance hosted by Mike and Gloria Romanoff in honor of socialite Dolly Tree, one of Clark Gable's many ex-loves. Gossip columnist Hedda Hopper was also there and recounted the following events. Patricia wore "an awful dress," her hair unflatteringly adorned with flowers. When they arrived, Cooper and Patricia went directly to the bar. Shortly thereafter, Rocky entered the party on Lawford's arm. Rocky looked stunningly attractive, and every eye in the room was on her, including Gary's. Said Hopper, "I was sorry Pat didn't look prettier that night. She wore flowers in her hair, like an ingénue. They didn't become her. Rocky, in contrast, being a sophisticated woman of the world and having all the cards in her hand, was very gay, danced every dance, and never took the smile off her face. At about midnight—when Pat was dancing—Coop got up and, for a few minutes, visited Rocky's table. Everyone held his breath. I would not be surprised if it was then and there that Pat accepted the fact that things would not work out."[19]

Recalled Patricia, "When Gary returned to our table, we sat quietly, avoiding the curious eyes that followed him back. He finally turned to me and said, 'Let's go, Pat. I don't feel so good.'" He took her directly home but did not stay the night.[20]

Cooper boarded an early flight to New York the day after the party. When next Patricia heard about him, it was from Harvey Orkin, who called to tell her that Gary had been admitted to Roosevelt Hospital in New York with a duodenal ulcer. Cooper did not want Patricia to come to New York, and he begged her not to worry. She spent the rest of the day crying as she walked the beach in Malibu. Days later she called Gary's mother. "What is it you want?" Alice bluntly asked Patricia. "I-I-I just want to take you to tea," Patricia replied. "Oh, no," said Mrs. Cooper. "I'm a snob, my dear." Ruthlessly, the pragmatic and overprotective Alice Cooper rebuffed Patricia, saying, "Why should I see you after what you've done to my son? He is sick because of you. Do you know what you are?"[21] Stunned, Patricia hung up. She knew in her heart that she could not see Gary again. She knew she would always be "the other woman," and Gary would never commit himself to her. And she felt, perhaps, that she was indeed a bad woman.

Her heart breaking, she called Gary, who was in Colorado with Rocky and Maria. Patricia wrote in her autobiography,

"Gary," I cried. "It is over. I really mean it, Gary; I can never see you again. Your mother—I called her. She insulted me. No, she told me the truth. It is over."

Silence.

"Do you hear me? Are you there?" I felt that curtain.

"You want it that way?" he asked. "All right . . . if that's what you want."

"Yes," I said quietly into the receiver. "Yes, that is what I want." And I hung up on him.[22]

Fox asked Patricia to take part in a Mexican goodwill junket and she traveled to Acapulco with such celebrities as Groucho Marx; Alexis Smith and her husband; Craig Stevens; Lex Barker; Ricardo Montalban and his wife, Georgiana; Arcady Boyther; Don Taylor; and Sofia Alvarez, among others. The local press photographed Patricia, elegantly dressed in a strapless gown, as she addressed a radio audience. Before returning to the United States, Patricia finished her Christmas shopping for Gary, adding to what she had already purchased for him in California. She bought knitted sweaters and socks, handmade silk shirts, and miniature antique guns, wrapping them all individually and sending them to Gary at the Bel Air Hotel, where just weeks before Cooper had told friends he wanted to marry Patricia and find a house together. Cholly Knickerbocker reported in his column that Cooper and Patricia were still an item. On December 20, Hedda Hopper set the record straight by telling her readers that Cooper was hospitalized while Patricia was in Mexico.

Patricia's emotional life had shifted into neutral. She couldn't control her shattered emotions. Her every thought was on Gary. She could not talk with anyone openly about her feelings. And frighteningly, she later admitted that she could not remember parts of her life during this bleak period. Her survival instincts led her to make a dedicated effort to start over. She knew she could not continue living in her Fox Hills apartment; there were simply too many memories of Gary. Though she would stay close to Jean and Chloe, she knew she had to separate herself from the home she had often shared with her lover.

She soon found an apartment on Levering Drive in Westwood, in a complex of round bungalows. Everything about the place was round—the complex, the buildings, the rooms, the swimming pool. Patricia ordered new furniture, much of it round, including many heavy pieces of fine wood, and decorated the apartment in a crisp, clean modern style.

Her secret life with Gary—her real life—was over. Now, little made sense to her. Her Fox Hills apartment was rented by Lex Barker. Barker told Patricia that Rocky, whom he knew, had asked to see the bungalow. "I hope you don't mind," he said.[23] She didn't. Patricia knew she had done the place up well.

The Sunday before Christmas, Patricia received a holiday gift from Gary—a mink jacket. He left the package outside the door on her step. (When Van Johnson's wife, Evie, heard how thrilled Patricia was to receive it, she thought, "Oh-oh, this is the kiss-off.") Patricia read the attached note, "I love you, baby. Gary." Shortly before New Year's, Patricia heard that Gary was at the Sun Valley Lodge in Idaho. She called him and somehow she was able to get through. But the conversation was not exactly what she had expected. She asked if he had received his presents, and he said he had not. He did tell her that he was *not* coming to California. She suddenly began "shaming myself and I knew it." She told him she loved him, asked him why he was doing this to her, and what was he going to do? He told her that he might go to Paris. She slammed the phone down, and died a thousand deaths. She couldn't think, couldn't talk with anyone, couldn't eat, and couldn't stop hurting.[24]

In late December, Patricia began filming *Washington Story*, costarring Van Johnson. This was her first picture for Metro-Goldwyn-Mayer. Metro had originally wanted Nancy Olson for the role of Alice. When she became unavailable, Patricia stepped in. Nervous about this assignment because Johnson was a good friend of Rocky's, Patricia nonetheless approached the film with professional preparedness. Sent for location work in Washington, D.C., to achieve as much realism as possible, Patricia was shooting there over New Year's. An all-out effort was made to film as much as possible outside as well as inside the Capitol building—the film was given more access to the building than any previous picture—and there was a rush to complete work while Congress was in adjournment.

Washington Story is a clear attempt to show the public, in the wake of the anticommunist witch hunt of the 1940s and 1950s, that the political system still worked. Journalist Alice Kingsley (Patricia) is allowed to follow around a young House member, Massachusetts Democrat Joseph T. Gresham (Johnson), for a week. Gresham is accused of changing his vote on a shipbuilding bill because of a payoff from a wealthy shipbuilder and lobbyist, but Alice learns Gresham's change of heart has nothing to do with a payoff. Alice, who is secretly working for a muckraker who hopes to bring Gresham down, quits her job and falls in love with the congressman.

Primary cast members remained in Washington until January 8, 1952.

Filming resumed in Hollywood on January 21, the day after Patricia's twenty-sixth birthday, and was completed on February 20.

Patricia's mother, Eura, who was living in Atlanta with NiNi and her husband, George, came to California to visit Patricia during the first week of February 1952. When she saw the painfully thin and despondent Patricia, she offered to take her daughter back with her to Atlanta when *Washington Story* was completed; Patricia agreed. On the train trip to Georgia, they made a short stop in New Orleans, where, coincidentally, Gary was in the hospital for an ulcer; Patricia had no idea he was there. When Gary was released, he went to Europe and Mexico for two years to make films.

Cooper had been spotted dating Annabella Power, as well as Kay Spreckels, who would become Clark Gable's last wife. According to Jeffrey Meyers, "Cooper played around with many obscure women between breaking with Neal in December 1951 and meeting . . . Lorraine Chanel exactly one year later."[25] The Chanel-Cooper relationship would last a year. He would not return to Rocky until 1953.

In January 1952, Rocky, who knew that Patricia had ended the affair with her husband, was quoted as saying, "I told Gary last July I would get a divorce if he wanted it."[26] This was not a completely truthful statement, and it proved painful to both Patricia and Gary. No doubt it was Rocky herself, her dignity perhaps slipping a little, who helped spread the rumors that Patricia was "cold," a characterization that was beginning to appear in the press, now that the affair was out in the open.

The relentless press wanted a last word from Patricia about the breakup. She could only say, "My feelings are still the same as they were. I don't say this will last for ten years, but that's the way it is now."[27]

To suggest that Patricia was "drummed out" of Hollywood would not be a false statement. The fact is, there *was* a "Hollywood wives' club" of sorts that existed as long as the studio system did. Despite her vehement denials, Ann Warner wielded considerable influence over her husband, Jack, in deciding who would and who would not be accepted and advanced within the Hollywood community. It was Olivia de Havilland's close friendship with Ann that persuaded Jack Warner to finally lend de Havilland to Metro-Goldwyn-Mayer and David O. Selznick for the role of Melanie in *Gone With the Wind*.

Hollywood wives accepted the affairs that were so common in the movie community, as long the marriage of one of their own was not threatened. Maria Cooper once remarked that her mother was fully aware of Gary's extramarital relationships and that even as a young girl she knew what was going on. However, Patricia was a definite and powerful danger to the Cooper marriage, as Gary loved her deeply, and Rocky Cooper was a most powerful member of the wives' club. Thus Patricia's film future, not to mention her social acceptance in Hollywood, was in severe jeopardy. Years after the studio system had failed and Gary was long dead, Rocky was advised by insiders that she no longer held social clout in Hollywood. She wisely returned to her society roots in New York.

Like so many times before, Patricia returned home to her family. In the past she had always returned in triumph. Now her life was in turmoil, her career and her heart shattered. She needed time to heal. Before Hollywood, almost everything had come so easily for her. In a relatively brief amount of time, she had become a successful star on Broadway. Brought to Hollywood, she had sold her talent to the treadmill, where the bottom line was not art and personal fulfillment but money and profits. Her films were not impressive, but her performances were. Patricia had made a common human error—she had fallen in love with a married man. In Hollywood, she made many enemies. She had to find out what had gone wrong. She had to find out what to do next.

In Atlanta, secure in the embrace of her beloved family, Patricia would regain her footing.

Part 2

Survivor

Don't make me out to be a Saint, baby. I suppose I have lived many lives, but please remember that I am, after all, *first*–an actress."

—Patricia Neal to SMS, June 2005

12

New York

Again . . . This couldn't happen again. . . .
For when this doesn't happen again,
We'll have this moment forever.

. . . .

But never, never again.

—Again (1948)

Within the bosom of her family in Atlanta, Patricia sought refuge and salvation. Her sister, NiNi (Margaret Ann), and NiNi's husband, George Vande Noord, were enjoying a successful and prosperous marriage. Their first child, George John, nicknamed Dutch, had been born the previous September, and their life together was good. In an interview a few years before her Atlanta stay, Patricia said of her sister, "As children we didn't seem to have too much in common; we were very different from one another and, oh, the arguments! We like to think of ourselves as adults now and I can and do appreciate all her wonderful qualities. She's utterly lacking in ambition, and since she's awfully loyal to family, she is also lacking in the jealousy that so often exists between sisters. She's a really good girl, a good daughter, and a good wife. She's terribly affectionate and generous. I think what I love most in Margaret Ann is her unselfishness."[1] Eura Neal was living with NiNi and George in their apartment. Without hesitation, Patricia was welcomed into the fold.

Patricia was physically and emotionally devastated; she could barely speak from exhaustion. Quickly realizing that her younger sister needed professional help, NiNi contacted her family physician, Henry Stelling, to examine Patricia. Recognizing that she needed rest and sleep first, he administered a sedative, which induced the first deep, solid sleep Patricia had

---

Facing page: Patricia Neal in *The Children's Hour*, 1952. Courtesy of Photofest.

experienced in some time. She slept for a day and a half, straight through. For the next three months, Stelling would see Patricia three times a week at the apartment, primarily to let her talk and talk. A stout and rotund middle-aged family man, Stelling reminded Patricia of her father, Coot. She recalls that she couldn't stop talking, and she told him everything—her dreams and ambitions shattered by her love for Gary and heartbreak over their parting. She realized through the good doctor's patience and understanding that Hollywood had damaged her considerably. But she was not completely broken.

In March 1952, there appeared in the press a flurry of misinformation, possibly geared to keep Patricia's name in the public eye. Reports were released in February that Patricia was headed for Europe for a long-deserved rest (or possibly to reunite with Cooper). Louella Parsons wrote that Patricia had fled to Palm Springs to gain pounds she had lost from dieting. The *Hollywood Reporter* erroneously told its readers that Patricia had gone to Palm Springs to sweat off twenty pounds. Sheilah Graham, obviously not concerned with the actress's weight, wrote in her *Variety* column that Patricia was "heading into another romance with complications."[2] Walter Winchell hit it accurately: "The Gary Cooper–Pat Neal finale has left her in tatters, her closest friends report."[3]

At the end of April, Patricia returned to Hollywood for a third 20th Century-Fox film, *Old Sailors Never Die*. Columnist Hedda Hopper, predatory as ever, contacted Patricia before her return, inquiring about the shattered affair with Cooper. Gary hadn't yet returned to Rocky, and Hopper was hoping for an exclusive. Would Patricia consider resuming her affair with Coop? "I will not see him when I return to Hollywood," Patricia said convincingly. "I have been very much in love with him. And I am sure he has loved me. But I saw that it wouldn't work. So I've stepped out. I have a lot of life ahead of me. And I want to live it with someone who is fun and untangled, someone with whom I can have a relationship that will be good—and permanent. Coop is wonderful. I never knew anyone like him. But he's a very complex person, as you well know. . . . It is, I assure you, over and ended forever." Still digging, Hopper asked, "How many times have you been in love, Pat?" Her reply was succinct, "Only once."[4]

Patricia knew that when the time came to leave Atlanta, she couldn't repay her dear Dr. Stelling enough in terms of money. She instead graciously gave him a small white speedboat. In her way of thinking, he had given her something that she hadn't received in years: he cared. Patricia never forgot his kindness.

Director Robert Wise was assigned to helm *Old Sailors Never Die* as his first comedy film venture. Wise was thrilled to have the opportunity to direct Patricia, one of his favorite actresses, once again. He was, however, startled at her appearance when she arrived in California for the shooting. She was painfully thin, but her nervous demeanor did not betray her frayed nerves. She was professional and prepared. Wise, the consummate director, wisely saw to it that the film was shot in just four weeks.

The *Hollywood Reporter* said in July 1951 that the stars of the film would be Anne Baxter, Dana Andrews, and Victor Moore. By the time filming commenced on May 8, 1952, the picture, retitled *Something for the Birds*, starred Patricia with Victor Mature and Edmund Gwenn, who had enjoyed great success the year before in *Mister 880*. Scenes were shot at Exposition Park and Los Angeles City College in California, as well as exteriors in Washington, D.C., using doubles.

The plot of *Something for the Birds* concerns the loveable Johnnie Adams (Edmund Gwenn), a printer for over thirty years in Washington. He has been a part of the social circle of the nation's capital for years because he prints his own invitations granting him admission to functions around town. Johnnie, known affectionately as the Admiral, meets Anne Richards (Neal), who represents the Society for the Preservation of the California Condor. She is in Washington to lobby against plans to drill for gas on a condor sanctuary.

Anne asks for his assistance. Johnnie introduces her to lawyer Steve Bennett (Victor Mature), a professional lobbyist. Bennett agrees to help Anne until he finds that his firm represents Continental Gas Company—the company that wants to drill on the sanctuary. Columnist Roy Patterson (Larry Keating) unmasks Johnnie, and a Senate investigation is launched. Johnnie wins over the investigating committee with his story of how and why he became a party crasher. Steve manages to get Continental to drop its drilling plans. Johnnie returns to his old job, where he proudly engraves Steve and Anne's wedding announcement.

The shooting of *Something for the Birds* progressed quickly and smoothly. Because of the generous and friendly cast and crew, both Wise and Patricia fondly remember *Something for the Birds*. Patricia particularly enjoyed working with the gentlemanly Victor Mature. The film's production values were sumptuous. Dressed in costumes and gowns designed by Eloise Jensson, Patricia looked stunning despite her dramatic weight loss. Perhaps the best of Patricia's handful of comedies, *Something for the Birds* deserved better than "its fate seemed to decree," Wise said. "That's one Fox film I did not try to get out of."[5]

In a magazine article, Patricia commented about her role in *Something for the Birds*: "I was delighted to get this part. It is the first picture I've ever done that is written around the girl. All the others have been written around a man and the girl was incidental."[6]

When she was in Hollywood during the filming of *Something for the Birds*, Patricia stayed at Hotel Bel-Air. She had let her round apartment go when she left Hollywood in February, storing her furniture and belongings. For the few weeks of filming of the comedy, she felt like a transient. She did not attend Hollywood functions and tried to stay out of the limelight as much as possible.

While on the set of *Something for the Birds*, Patricia received a phone call from comedian Johnny Grant, who had interviewed her at the premiere of *Bright Victory* the year before. He asked if she would accompany him and his troupe on a USO tour of Korea later in the year. She advised him she would consider the offer and notify him at a later date. That same afternoon, guests arrived on the set, and Patricia caught the eye of one young man in particular. He introduced himself as Lewis William Douglas III, better known as Peter. Patricia was surprised by her attraction to the good-looking, strapping Douglas. Patricia unhesitatingly exchanged her telephone number with him. He called her that very night, and the two dined out with guests at a Hawaiian restaurant.

The son of the United States ambassador to England, Peter came into Patricia's life at a time when she was particularly vulnerable. His gentle nature and attractiveness, in addition to his financial and social position as an ambassador's son, were a balm for her low self-esteem and insecurities. With Douglas, Patricia regained her self-confidence. He was boyishly fun and unspoiled, and just a year or two older than Patricia. Like her, he was thin, yet vitally attractive. The two made a good-looking couple. They dated frequently and were photographed together at such nightspots in Hollywood as Ciro's and the Crescendo. Eventually, Douglas invited Patricia to accompany him on a visit to his brother's home in Arizona. While there, the two became lovers.

At a gathering one night, Patricia encountered Gary Cooper. As he came through the door with another man and two women, Patricia glanced up and their eyes met ever so briefly. Patricia's first thought was, did the hostess set this up? Gary walked over to Patricia as she stood with Peter. Introductions were made. Taking his cue, Douglas excused himself to refresh his drink, leaving Pat and Gary alone together.

Patricia later recalled that the first words were from Gary,

"Baby, how are you? You look good."

"I'm perfect!" I loathed the phony ring in my voice.

I was shocked at his appearance. He looked as if he'd been drinking for a long time. He was very thin and he needed a shave. I never knew Gary to go without shaving except when he was out with his dogs in the country. His tie was spotted and his coat rumpled. I spoke into the saddest face I'd ever seen. "How are you?"

"Great! What are you doing with yourself?"

"I'm working at Fox," I answered. "Everything is sensational." We were both going to pieces and stupidly trying to hide it from each other.

He just kept saying, "Are you all right, baby?" and I kept lying.

There was a silence that the hushed chatter in the room barely covered. I looked at him searchingly. There were tears in his eyes. I thought my heart would break.[7]

Shortly after Gary left the party, Peter and Patricia did, too. Patricia did not thank her hostess.

Patricia could not escape mention in the gossip columns, even now, a year after the Coopers' separation. In June, the *Hollywood Reporter* asked, "Didn't Rocky's alimony demands wreck the marriage plans of Pat and Gary?"[8] According to Cooper biographer Jane Ellen Wayne, a friend of Gary's claimed, "Coop never asked for a divorce. Rocky knew him better than anyone else and he didn't have the fight in him. He rarely mentioned Pat Neal by name after they parted. It was 'she' or 'her.' I don't think he had the heart to say, 'Pat.' He was shattered when she left him for good. He never got over it."[9]

The filming of *Something for the Birds* was completed in early June 1952. Johnny Grant was persistent in urging Patricia to join him and his troupe on the upcoming tour of Korea for the USO, and with some reluctance, Patricia finally agreed. In an interview with Louella Parsons shortly before departing on the junket, Patricia spoke for several hours about her broken romance with Cooper, the filming of *Something for the Birds*, and the upcoming tour. Said Pat of her seventeen-pound weight loss, "Yes, I've lost a lot of weight but before you feel sorry for me, or I feel sorry for myself, my boss Darryl Zanuck says I look much better on the screen this way."[10] When the interview ended, Patricia told Parsons that she'd just had a wisdom tooth removed that morning. She had been in pain throughout the interview. Parsons wrote, "Patricia

Neal . . . has great courage and fine principles. She'll always do what she knows is right and the big emotional crisis through which she has just gone has made her a finer person."[11]

20th Century-Fox premiered *Diplomatic Courier* on June 7 at the Roxy Theatre in New York and in Los Angeles on July 25. Patricia's notices were good, and Fox signed her for another picture. Much was made in print about *Diplomatic Courier* being Tyrone Power's first modern-dress film since 1948. It was also the last collaboration between the star and director Henry Hathaway. Patricia looked marvelous in the film, costumed in outfits by Charles LeMaire and Eloise Jensson, including a stunning pleated black cocktail dress (which actress Debbie Reynolds eventually purchased for her collection of historical Hollywood costumes). The reviews for the film and its stars were decent. Wrote the critic in *Variety*, "Miss Neal, playing an American who is actually an undercover Communist agent, supplies plenty of sparkle as she pursues Power romantically."[12] In his *New York Herald Tribune* review Otis L. Guernsey Jr. wrote, "Miss Neal, as always, cuts a most attractive figure on the screen as a well heeled playgirl, and there is nothing half-hearted about her approaches to Tyrone Power."[13] Ruth Waterbury of the *Los Angeles Examiner* praised Patricia's performance: "She is simply devastating here, this tall, thin Miss Neal. She has double entendre lines that she reads with sexy humor in a manner that gives them even a third meaning."[14]

Viewed today, *Diplomatic Courier* seems dated, although the direction by Henry Hathaway is compelling and the performances of the cast are sincere, particularly Patricia's interpretation of her role. For Tyrone Power fans, *Diplomatic Courier* was a pleasant enough return for their favorite back to modern dress. But it was not the huge success Fox had planned. Whether Fox took notice of Patricia's next film release (for Metro-Goldwyn-Mayer) just two weeks later is unknown.

The premiere of *Washington Story* was held at the Lowe's Palace Theatre in Washington, D.C., on June 27. It received mixed reviews. Said Brog in *Variety*, "Johnson and Miss Neal make a pleasant team, and there are a number of other good performances to help carry the picture. . . . Technical assists are well valued including John Alton's lensing of the Washington scene and players."[15] Another reviewer found, "Performances are all good, with Miss Neal delivering a splendid job as an alert, intelligent and decidedly pretty news hawk. Johnson makes a convincingly sincere congressman, and Louis Calhern stands out as a wise, tolerant House member."[16]

But Bosley Crowther wrote in his *New York Times* review, "In its new film . . . the studio has waxed almost lyric over the unsung heroes and patriots on

Capitol Hill. . . . But they also have got Mr. Johnson playing a Congressman's role in the manner of a solemn movie idol, and they have got the angular Miss Neal pretending to be a newswoman as though she were a slumming Hollywood star."[17]

All in all, *Washington Story* was an oddity even when it was released. Today, it is an interesting historical piece, a scenic tour of the nation's capital as it was over fifty years ago. Van Johnson, his career in definite decline at MGM, was attractive enough, but not convincingly sincere enough to carry his role.

Patricia made a quick trip home to her family at the end of June, returning just days before the USO tour was to begin. On July 12, the Johnny Grant Galaxy, consisting of Grant, Patricia, television singer Ginny Jackson, comedian Pat Moran, handsome young accordionist Tony Lovello, and actress Joy Windsor, left Los Angeles for Korea. Bidding farewell to Peter Douglas, who told her he would be waiting for her upon her return, Patricia made sure to pack a selection of the gorgeous dresses she had worn in *Washington Story*. She knew that a stylish appearance would impress the boys stationed overseas. (The army provided GI uniforms, broad belts, and bright-colored scarves for the troupe.) Before leaving, she told Louella Parsons, "There isn't much I can do, I can't sing or dance, but I feel it might help the boys if there is someone from home to laugh with them, tell jokes, play cards and if necessary, just sympathize."[18]

Patricia's reluctance to take the tour was understandable. She feared she was pregnant with Douglas's child. She never told Douglas. On the flight over, Patricia was seated behind the slumbering eighteen-year-old Lovello. When jarred awake by Johnny Grant, the youth suddenly stood up and froze as if in some kind of a kind of trance. A doctor spoke slowly and soothingly to the young fellow until he eventually came out of it, smiled, and sat back down. When Patricia asked Lovello what had happened, he told her, "It's happened before, and I love it when it does. It takes me right out of this world. I feel such peace."[19] Patricia envied him that feeling.

On a stopover in Japan, the troupe performed at army bases, where it was reported that Patricia was a hit with the tour. She was invited to be a guest of General and Mrs. Mark Clark while in Tokyo. In Seoul, Korea, Patricia was given the second-floor quarters of an officer. When she went to bed, she left the bathroom light on. As she was falling asleep, a soldier crept into the room, turned off the bathroom light, and started to get into bed with her. "You had better get right out of here now or you will be in big trouble," Patricia said calmly. "I'll leave in five minutes, Miss Pat," he told her in a southern accent.[20] Screaming loudly, she fled the room as Johnny Grant and others rushed in. The soldier apologized, and officers promised it would not happen again. A lieutenant agreed to spend the rest of the night safeguarding Patricia in the room. "The bastard made such a pass at me," Patricia recalled.[21] She slept with the other women on the floor of their tents for the rest of the tour. "The boys would rub up against me, and touch my breasts," Patricia said years later. "Oh, it was terrible."[22]

Patricia told Johnny Grant, "If the soldiers can sit in this pouring rain, we can perform for them."[23] She performed blackout routines with Johnny Grant and did a slow-motion boxing skit with former acrobat and vaudeville entertainer Pat Moran. In footage of the USO show shot by servicemen, as well as by a Warners Pathé newsreel cameraman, one sees the thin Patricia in her satin designer dress with her wet hair streaming down to her shoulders gamely performing a slow motion skit with Moran. Wrote one soldier to Patricia over fifty years later, "You will never know how much it meant to us to be able to come and see your show and forget what was going on around us for that length of time."[24]

Two other servicemen, David C. Bass and Richard L. Salhany, composed a nifty song dedicated to Patricia entitled "Pat Is Our Girl." The tune is a heartfelt tribute by a couple of soldiers to their favorite screen star. Wrote the two to Patricia:

> To our gal, Pat,
>
> These are our feelings set to words and a familiar old tune. Thanks for making *one* day in Korea enjoyable beyond compare!
> From a couple of guys who will always remember and consider you as their "#1 Gal" both on and off the screen—
>
> Dave and Dick[25]

The humidity and heat, coupled with continual rain, made for continual discomfort. Traveling mostly by plane, the entertainers also maneuvered the usual half-hour jaunts from base to base by jeep. Patricia recalled that she could never keep her hair fixed, and she and the other two women in the troupe were always wet and dirty. The U.S. troops had not seen American women in Korea since December 1951. Their appreciation and joy at seeing the familiar faces of film and TV stars on the stage was overwhelming, despite occasionally bad behavior and rude remarks from the boys ("Hey, Patsy! Where's Gary?"),[26] in hindsight, Patricia was glad she made the tour. Her anxieties about possibly being pregnant were resolved about midway through the trip.

Back in Hollywood in August, Patricia found she was still persona non grata at many social functions. Though her affair with Gary Cooper was long over, most people still thought they were an item. And strangely enough, those who still pandered to Rocky Cooper were also jealous of Patricia's very public affair with the handsome and affluent Peter Douglas.

There was other bad news as well. Sensing that the upcoming release of *Something for the Birds* would not be very profitable, Fox executives cancelled Patricia's next film agreement. It may have been a sign of the times. Hollywood in 1952 was suffering huge financial losses. World War II had changed the tastes and expectations of the average American family, and television had cut into movie attendance.

Patricia resumed her romance with Douglas. Unfortunately, it didn't progress very far. Though he had always enjoyed Patricia's delicious sense of humor, her honesty, and her gorgeous appearance, Douglas simply wasn't ready for a commitment. She truly liked him and seriously considered marrying him—if he asked. Things finally came to a head on a night when Peter was to pick up Patricia at 6:00 P.M. for a dinner engagement. By 7:30, she later wrote, she was beginning to suspect he had stood her up. Her anger built and her humiliation grew. Douglas never showed. At midnight she prepared for bed. "It was the last straw," Patricia wrote. From her suite at the Bel-Air Hotel, she said, "I looked down on those swans and the perfectly groomed gardens. There was no real life for me here now. I was finished with Hollywood and its disappointments and its heartaches. I wanted a career I could be proud of. I wanted a home and family. I wanted my self-respect."[27]

That night, disheartened, disillusioned, and disgusted with Hollywood, Patricia vowed to return to New York.

Within days, she bade farewell to Jean and Chloe, Mimi Tellis and her family, K. T. and Hugh, and the Seidels.

In a film magazine article entitled "This Is the Real Me," Patricia stated, "What do I want of the future as an actress? A lot! [What] I have always wanted and will always want to be is a fine stage actress. . . . However, both the theatre and screen are important to me. Actually I find the theatre more satisfying. . . . The year 1952 would reach its zenith for me if I could feel again that excitement I felt when, some years ago, I was able to choose between three parts in three different plays."[28] Her direction was clear. She would return to New York and the Broadway stage. "I've never liked to visit New York," she told a New York newspaper. "I like to live here. And the longer I live here the better I like it."[29]

Leaving Hollywood on August 21, Patricia, as always, stopped off in Atlanta to see her family. Arriving in New York in early September 1952, Patricia contacted Marian and Ed Goodman, new friends whom she had met through Peter Douglas. At their first dinner, Patricia brought Marian, pregnant with her first child, Wendy, a lovely bouquet of flowers.

In Manhattan, Patricia felt refreshed and rejuvenated. She had never been good with money, and with the little she had remaining from her film work, she checked into an eleventh floor suite at the Plaza Hotel until she could find an apartment. Her first was a rather cheap one, and she moved out. She quickly found a suitable place at 903 Park Avenue and sent for her furniture from Hollywood.

Something for the Birds, which premiered on October 10, received mixed notices. The *Hollywood Reporter* reviewer found the film, "a warm, mirthful comedy, rich in satire, that lands several devastating swipes at the Washington scene. . . . Miss Neal is a delight as the fanatical bird lover, playing her role with amusing earnestness."[30] The *New York Herald-Tribune* found the film enjoyable but lacking in humor. "Both Mr. Mature and Miss Neal turn in neat performances, and it is hard to imagine a likelier sample of the public relations grin than Mr. Mature's," the review commented.[31]

20th Century-Fox had quickly thrown *Something for the Birds* into release with little imagination in its promotion, and it sank at the box office. But viewed today, *Something for the Birds* is a very entertaining film. Elements of the script are still relevant, and it is acted with subtlety by all concerned. Patricia's performance is a joy to watch, though comedy was never her strong suit. The scene in which Patricia and the handsome Victor Mature converse as the lovely tune "Again" is heard in the background is stunningly romantic.

Reading in the *New York Times* that a revival of Lillian Hellman's play *The Children's Hour* was to be produced by Kermit Bloomgarden, Patricia wasted little time in calling him and asking to read for one of the leads. "Yeah, O.K., come on," he replied lackadaisically.[32] Patricia needed the work, and she knew that a reading would not diminish her once-prominent position on Broadway. Entering the Coronet Theatre on a crisp September morning, Patricia was greeted by the familiar voice of playwright Lillian Hellman, "Hello, Patsy Neal! Glad you're back in New York where you belong!"[33] The key scene between Karen and Martha, the two teachers who are the play's main characters, was chosen for the audition piece. Patricia was asked to read either role.

She gave it her all. "Five years of frustration and a broken heart exploded on the stage," wrote Patricia in her memoirs. Bloomgarden came onto the stage, and said, "We want you!"[34] She was given her choice of either role. "I knew immediately which one I wanted," she continued. "I chose Martha. I was still ragged from the bitterness I had endured from personal rejection and public censure. I could really get my teeth into her [Martha's] problems."[35] Patricia felt back on course at last. She was back in New York, starring in a major Broadway production. And Lillian Hellman was there to support and bolster her wounded confidence.

Patricia focused on her career now, especially her acting. She reenrolled at the Actors' Studio, determined to reestablish her stage career. "She came back humble and judging herself very harshly," said fellow actress Anne Jackson. "She had to begin all over again, and that is a hard and rare thing to do. She was incredible. I've never seen anybody develop the way Pat did. It was a beautiful thing to watch—this slow, steady progress."[36] About Hollywood and its effect on her career, Patricia told Howard Thompson of the *New York Times,* "I don't know how anybody gets ahead in Hollywood. The place has so many stone walls. No one gets in. They say knowing the right people is so important. But those walls!" Wrote Thompson, "Miss Neal is a person of surprisingly youthful mien and has an unstudied directness that suggests a good deal of coiled introspection." [37]

Before rehearsals for *The Children's Hour* started, Lillian Hellman threw a dinner party and invited Patricia, who dressed simply, expecting Lillian's party to be casual. It turned out to be a formal, black-tie affair. When she arrived Patricia noticed a distinguished-looking gentleman across the room. Quietly turning to Hellman, she whispered in her ear, "Who is that tall man?" Relishing the moment, the devilish Hellman replied in a very exaggerated stage whisper, "Roald Dahl!"[38] At supper, Hellman sat Patricia beside the writer Dahl and across the table from Leonard Bernstein. Patricia remembered that throughout the meal that evening, Dahl directed his conversation to Bernstein, discussing writers and writing and completely ignoring the beautiful Miss Neal. Patricia found this act deliberate and appallingly rude. She was used to being the center of attention, especially when surrounded by handsome, creative, and intellectually stimulating men. Dahl did not speak a word to her, and Patricia surmised that he was terribly arrogant.

"When Pat and I met in 1952," Dahl said years later, "we were both eager to get married, but in the abstract. My being thirty-six, and Pat about ten years younger, it was time for us to get married, and we felt that. So Lillian Hellmann, knowing this and wanting us to meet, invited us to a dinner party, where I behaved badly, I suppose. I was getting into one of those arguments with Lennie Bernstein, and there was no backing off from it. Pat thought I was rude and decided I was 'someone not to know,' as she says."[39]

Obtaining her telephone number from Lillian Hellman, Roald called Patricia to arrange for a date, which she refused. Enticed, and certainly not used to being rebuffed, Dahl called once again; this time, Patricia accepted. Dining at a fashionable Italian restaurant in Manhattan, Dahl cautiously opened up to her. Patricia told a reporter in an interview, "At one point in the evening he called me 'old girl,' and it suddenly sounded affectionate . . . he almost got around to calling me 'old sausage,' but I guess he saw the look in my eye." Dahl also spoke with her about "paintings and antique furniture and the joys of the English countryside."[40] His charm and intelligence flooded over her like a comfortable, warm blanket. Before the evening was over, Dahl took her to the apartment of his good friend, the newspaperman and resort owner Charles Marsh. Wrote Patricia, "Before we left, Marsh told Roald, 'Drop the other baggage. I like this one!'"[41]

13

Roald Dahl

And I am sure I was a fool to marry you—an old dangling bachelor who was single at fifty, only because he could never meet anyone who would have him.

—Lady Teazle, *The School for Scandal*

Roald (pronounced *Roo-ahl*, silent *d*) Dahl was born to Norwegian-born parents on September 13, 1916, in Llandaff, Wales. He was given no middle name at birth. His father, Harald, was a co-owner of a ship-brokering business near Cardiff. Harald's first wife, Marie, had died at the age of twenty-nine in 1907, and for four years Harald was a widower with two small children, Ellen (born in 1903) and Louis (born in 1904). He met his second wife, Sofie Magdelene Hesselberg (born in 1885), on a vacation in Norway.

Besides Roald, Sofie and Harald had four other children, all girls: Astri (born in 1912), Alfhild (born in 1914), Else (born in 1917), and Asta (born in 1920). In February 1920, seven-year-old Astri died of appendicitis; Harald died of pneumonia shortly afterward, on April 11. Sofie, pregnant again, sold the family home in Ty Mynydd and moved her two stepchildren, now teenagers, and her own children back to Llandaff. That fall, she gave birth to her last child, Asta.

His mother's only son, Roald was nicknamed "the Apple" (of his mother's eye).[1] Sofie seldom showed physical warmth toward her children, though they knew she loved them. Perhaps Roald felt himself something of a loner, which may explain the many single-child experiences he would later write about in his children's books. But he had a fertile imagination and was encouraged and spoiled by his mother, a nurse who adored him, and his large family.

Roald graduated from Repton Public School in Derby in 1934 and went

---

Facing page: Patricia Neal and Roald Dahl in front of Gipsy House, circa 1962. Patricia's favorite picture of the two of them together. From the Patricia Neal Collection.

to work for the Shell Oil Company in London, transferring to the East Africa branch office in 1938. When Britain entered World War II, Dahl became a fighter pilot with the 80 Squadron for the Royal Air Force, training in Nairobi, Kenya. On September 19, 1940, Dahl's Gloster Gladiator, a plane he had never flown before, ran low on fuel over Libya. Dahl crash landed the plane in the desert near Mersa Matruh and struck a boulder. The impact smashed his nose back into his head and fractured his skull. He subsequently spent several months in Alexandria, Egypt, recovering from his injuries.

Dahl returned to England in July 1941. While in London that fall he sought out the artist Matthew Smith. The two became friends, and Smith became the first of many artists whom Dahl befriended over the course of the next several decades. Ordered to Glasgow to board a ship for Canada, Dahl met another RAF pilot, Douglas Bisgood, during the crossing. Dahl and Bisgood exchanged stories about gremlins—elves with unnatural powers—who were frequently blamed for aircraft mishaps during flight missions.

Upon arrival in North America, Dahl traveled to Washington, D.C., as an assistant air attaché with the British Embassy. There he met author C. S. Forester, who became his mentor; Forester encouraged Dahl to become a writer. Sharing a house in Georgetown with future advertising giant David Ogilvy, Dahl also befriended Eton graduate Ivar Bryce, who was a good friend of British writer Ian Fleming. Dahl, Bryce, and Ogilvy became associated with such important figures as columnist Drew Pearson, reporter Ralph Ingersoll, and Vice President Henry Wallace's close friend, newspaper owner Charles Marsh.

Dahl was considered by his friend Creekmore Fath as "one of the biggest cocksmen in Washington."[2] The arrogantly handsome Dahl was very appealing to the opposite sex. Both Claire Boothe Luce, the playwright wife of *Time* magazine publisher Henry Luce, and Standard Oil heiress Millicent Rogers bestowed expensive gifts on Dahl from such jewelers as Tiffany's. But some acquaintances believed Dahl, raised in a household of doting females, actually hated women.

Invited to Hollywood because of his reputation in the nation's capital as a teller of tall tales, Dahl was pressed to create a story about the gremlins he had talked about so engagingly. The first draft of his book on the subject impressed Walt Disney enough to proceed with plans to make a feature-length film of the work. Those plans were eventually shelved, but Disney published the picture book *Walt Disney: The Gremlins (A Royal Air Force Story by Flight Lieutenant Roald Dahl)* in 1943. Now a published writer, Dahl's short stories began to appear in such publications as *Harper's*, *Atlantic Monthly*, and *Ladies' Home Journal*.

In 1946 Dahl's first adult novel, actually a collection of his fictionalized war stories, *Over to You*, dedicated to Charles Marsh, was published in the United States and England. By 1949, Dahl had a deal with the British Broadcasting Company and, in April, sold his first short story, "The Sound Machine," to the *New Yorker*.

Soon after meeting Patricia at Lillian Hellman's party, Dahl began aggressively pursuing her. Indeed she was truly a "catch," and Marsh's approval more or less sealed Dahl's commitment to her. Regarding Patricia's emotional equilibrium when they met, Dahl recalled, "She was in a depressed state when I met her. She was not gay. She was reserved, holding herself in; obviously pretty shaken all around. . . . I think she planned to work hard as an antidote against her personal misfortunes. So it wasn't a happy girl I was seeing."[3]

When Patricia visited Dahl's apartment soon after they met, she saw photographs of his nephew and his two nieces, daughters of his sister Elsa. They were stunningly attractive children, and Patricia's initial take was that perhaps Dahl would give her beautiful babies. Shortly thereafter, she began telling her friends that she and Dahl would wed.

The original production of *The Children's Hour* had more or less established Lillian Hellman as a major American playwright. Opening on November 20, 1934 (exactly twelve years to the day before *Another Part of the Forest*), the original production of *The Children's Hour* ran 691 performances. By the time *Another Part of the Forest* opened in 1946, Hellman was well established and enjoying her success. But in the years since the run of *Another Part of the Forest*, Hellman had not had an easy time of it. Her relationship with the alcoholic Dashiell Hammett had emotionally and financially drained her. Called before the House Un-American Activities Committee in July 1951, Hammett took the Fifth Amendment and was promptly arrested for contempt of Congress. (Sentenced to ten years in federal prison, Hammett served only six months. Upon his release, in poor health, he was taken in and nursed by Hellman until his death in 1961.)

Attempting to raise Hammett's bail, Hellman went so far as to sell her jewelry. Then the Internal Revenue Service ordered her to pay more than $100,000 in back taxes. Meanwhile, she faced her own scrutiny from the Communist hunters. Blacklisted from Hollywood because of her past involvement with the Communist Party, Hellman had her date with HUAC in February 1952. After testifying for a little more than one hour before the committee, refusing to name names, Hellman was excused. Unlike Hammett, she was not charged with contempt of Congress.

A revival of *The Children's Hour* was crucial for Hellman. She felt the restaging of *The Children's Hour,* a proven success with its theme of a lie and the destruction it causes, would vindicate her and her beliefs. She would direct it herself. To ensure that she would be understood as a director, early in rehearsals she told each of the cast members, "If I say anything during rehearsals you don't understand, if I am not making myself clear, please come to me and let's talk about it."[4]

The Children's Hour takes place at the Wright-Dobie School for Girls and focuses on teachers and friends Martha Dobie (Neal) and Karen Wright (Kim Hunter), and two of their students, Mary Tilford (Iris Mann), a spoiled, willful, and manipulative liar, and Rosalie Wells (Janet Parker), Mary's gullible and bullied friend. Mary is reprimanded for an infraction and fakes a heart attack. Both Martha and Karen see through Mary's behavior, as does physician Joseph Cardin (Robert Pastene), Karen's beau. Mary in turn uses lies to get her way.

Other girls overhear Martha and Martha's aunt Lily Mortar (Mary Finney) argue over the relationship between Karen and Dr. Cardin. Lily tells Martha that it is unnatural for Martha to be so fond of Karen. The girls tell Mary, and she proceeds to tell her grandmother, Amelia Tilford (Katherine Emmett), a major benefactor of the school, that the two teachers are unnatural. Mary blackmails Rosalie into backing her up, and the horrified Amelia Tilford believes the lie. When confronted about their behavior, the two teachers react in shock and anger. They reevaluate their relationship, with Martha finally admitting to Karen that perhaps the lie is true—at least in her heart. The play concludes with the truth becoming known, but by this time lives have been destroyed.

Kim Hunter, cast as Karen Wright, had won the Best Supporting Actress Oscar that year for her portrayal of Stella in *A Streetcar Named Desire.* When rehearsals began, noticing the rapport the director had with Neal, Hunter advised Hellman that she needed time, "to mush into the play, the situation, the relationships, the character—everything." To which Hellman replied, "Good to know, good to know." Hunter considered Hellman to be "a bloody good director," and she also stated, "You knew where you stood with her. She didn't mince words."[5] However, from the start of rehearsals, Hellman began to clash with Hunter.

There was a point during rehearsals when Hellman felt that Neal was unconsciously dominating a particular scene with Hunter, performing like a leading lady. Recalled the producer's wife Virginia Bloomgarden, who was visiting rehearsals, Hellman screamed at Hunter, "You're not playing Stella!"[6] Hellman was attempting to relay to Hunter that Karen was actually stronger than Martha, but the director simply couldn't articulate that. In her dressing room, Hunter was in tears. The assistant stage manager of the production, Jose Vega, recalls that Hellman at one point even considered replacing the actress. "Oh she's never going to do it!" exclaimed the exasperated Hellman. [7]

Hunter found that it was difficult to withhold tears at the end of the play when Martha takes over her destiny. Hellman pleaded with Hunter not to cry, as it would distract the audience, and they would not think about what was happening. "Of course, she was right. And I knew it," recalled Hunter.[8]

Impressed from the start with thirteen-year-old Iris Mann, who was cast as Mary, Hellman talked with the girl about her role as if she were an adult. "I think she liked me personally," recalled Mann. "She would say to me after I did something she liked, 'I like that—do it again.' She would tell me things like, 'Be sly.' But I don't believe she knew the actor's process, though her suggestions were always strong."[9]

The thirty-four-year-old Bostonian Robert Pastene played Dr. Joseph Cardin in *The Children's Hour*. Though he was well liked, Iris Mann found Pastene not to be a strong actor. Apparently Hellman felt the same way. According to witnesses, Hellman lashed out at Pastene during a rehearsal, causing the actor to affect a permanent debilitating muscular disorder. Neal wrote that Hellman used her usual bark-and-bite method of directing rehearsals. Neal was used to it and recalls that both Hunter and Mann adjusted to Hellman's style quickly. However, it was difficult for Pastene to take the verbal assaults from Hellman. Wrote Neal, "Poor Robert Pastene, who played Karen's fiancé, fell victim to Lillian's blunt and sometimes brutal method. It was frightening to watch her paralyze him, and to feel the hatred of her for doing it."[10]

Mann recalled that during the run of the play Neal invited the young girls in the cast to chat with her in her dressing room, and Sandee Preston, who played Leslie and was making her Broadway debut, spent "every night during the run" with Neal. Neal would reminisce with the girls about her experiences in Hollywood and working for the studios. Iris Mann remembered Neal having been "a strong influence" on her.[11]

The Children's Hour opened on December 18. The reviews were mixed. Said William Hawkins, in the *New York World-Telegram and Sun*, "The performances seem to be exactly what is demanded by the play. Patricia Neal lets her character's faint neurosis lead her into deep terror. Kim Hunter moves from warm realism to chilly unbelief as the survivor. Iris Mann, a fledgling Lady Macbeth, handles the intricate complexities of the villainous child with incredible aplomb."[12] Richard Watts Jr., in his *New York Post* review, praised the play but not the acting, stating, "I thought Miss Neal, as the girl who discovers that there is really abnormality in her, rather gave the secret away in an early scene, but she plays the final episode admirably."[13]

Brooks Atkinson, of the *New York Times*, wrote, "Kim Hunter and Patricia Neal play the parts of the schoolteachers with great skill—Miss Hunter soft and grave in her responses to the situation, and Miss Neal tall, gaunt, wild and incredulous. . . . Iris Mann gives a marvelous performance. . . . 'The Children's Hour' is still taut and pertinent."[14]

Patricia's mother, Eura, and her brother, Pete, came to New York for a performance of *The Children's Hour*, and Roald Dahl was frequently at the theater to fetch Patricia. After rehearsals and late performances, Patricia and Dahl would dine together. Her southern roots on display, Patricia would charmingly refer to Roald as her "beau." Said Roald, "I had a book that was just coming out, so that left me plenty of time to sit around in an empty theatre during rehearsals, and of course nip back to her dressing room as soon as it was over. When the play opened it was pretty much the same routine, my attending a good many performances and clapping wildly, you know, and then afterward we'd go out for supper or to a party with her friends."[15]

Patricia's personal relationship with Kim Hunter was solid, and the two kept in touch until Hunter's death in 2004. Hunter was pregnant during the play's run. Patricia was into numerology at the time and insisted that the baby would arrive on her birthday, January 20. Hunter, who lovingly called Patricia "Patty," told friends throughout her pregnancy that the child would come on that date. Though it was actually just a joke between the two friends, Hunter's baby, Sean Robert Emmett, was born on January 20, 1954.

Gloria Lucas Young recalled that she and her husband visited Patricia and attended a performance of *The Children's Hour*. They thought she was "brilliant" in the play. After the show, along with Roald Dahl, the four "whipped in a nearby coffee shop so that Patricia could get four slices of bread, which the shop was reluctant to sell her. It just never occurred to Patricia, standing there in a full-length mink, dripping in jewels, to buy a full loaf of bread. My husband was so embarrassed."[16] Eventually the coffee shop reluctantly relinquished four slices of bread, and the four proceeded to Patricia's apartment, where she prepared a real southern snack of salty Kentucky ham with eggs fried in butter within the cut-out centers of the bread slices.

The Children's Hour proved to be a modest success, providing Hellman for a while a substantial income as playwright and director. "It got lovely reviews and then no business," said Hunter. "It was very tight as to whether we could make it at all."[17] Kermit Bloomgarden eventually addressed the backers and the cast, telling them that there was an audience waiting to see the play, but that they simply could not afford it. Apparently the older playgoers had seen the play and weren't coming back, and the younger generation was just not able to afford tickets. The cast took cuts in pay and even gave two performances on Sundays. Despite these extreme measures, according to Richard Maney in *Fanfare*, the play never recovered its costs. *The Children's Hour* played 189 performances in total, ending its run on May 30, 1953. Though a revival, the play was eligible for Tony Award consideration. When the Seventh Annual Antoinette Perry Awards were handed out, *The Children's Hour* did not receive a one.

Lillian Hellman invited the cast of *The Children's Hour* to her country estate, and Patricia renewed her friendship with Dashiell Hammett, who had recently been released from prison. The two enjoyed many hours of quiet talks at all of Hellman's homes as well as at restaurants in the city. Hellman knew and trusted Patricia's feelings toward the elderly and ill Hammett.

Patricia's romance with Dahl flourished. The first columnist to get it *almost* right was Louella Parsons. She reported, "Good news from New York is that Patricia Neal . . . is a very happy girl these days. Her constant escort is Ronald [sic] Dahl, a fighter pilot on the last war and currently on the staff of the *New Yorker* magazine. He's with Pat everywhere, and she is again sparkling as she did when she first came to Hollywood."[18]

Dahl pursued Patricia with as much charm as he could muster. A name dropper for sure, he fascinated her with stories of his war exploits and the people he had met and befriended, including Eleanor Roosevelt, who had invited Dahl to the White House, and Harry S Truman, with whom Dahl played poker. He boasted of his passing acquaintance with Ernest Hemingway and the fact that he had dated Annabella Power, the wife of Tyrone Power, whom Patricia had worked with. Neither was Dahl hesitant to tell Patricia that his friend Ivar Bryce had married the former Josephine Hartford, whose family owned the A & P grocery store chain.

Roald's latest pal was a bon vivant from England, the handsome Colin Leslie Fox, who had made something of a name for himself by sailing single-handedly across the Atlantic from England to the Bahamas. A smuggler during the war, he'd made and lost a fortune and was now a model. (He was the man with a patch over his eye in the Hathaway shirt ads.) Fox later told Jeremy Treglown that he and Dahl would demean their mutual friends in private, calling "this one a jerk, that one a show business Jew, the women all gushing sycophants . . . and philanthropic Rhode Island senator Claibourne Pell . . . a prick who gave out food parcels to the reindeer keepers in Finland."[19]

How much of that dual personality rubbed off on Patricia is subject to speculation. One friend told Treglown, "She adopted Roald's values, and one of them was a prodigious amount of name-dropping, and a prodigious amount of gossiping about the people they were name-dropping about. And also, a tremendous [amount of] attention to money. Who was rich and famous and important."[20] But others insisted that Patricia never behaved like this.

In a chatty letter to Jean Valentino and Chloe Carter, who were both in retirement and appearing as film extras, Patricia wrote on March 3 that she might visit California in May. If that was possible, she said, she would "like to borrow your couch for a couple of days."[21] She would also stay at her friend Lex Barker's place while he was gone, and possibly see various other pals while there. She mentioned some minor physical problems she was experiencing, for which she would need hormone shots for a few weeks. And carefully she told them of her "beau": "I am becoming more and more fond of Roald Dahl. So who knows. Might work . . . He is cautious too. And I think—stable. You would like him—I think. Very British."[22]

At a meeting with television director Fielder Cook, who was attempting to woo Patricia into doing an episode of his television series, *Lux Video Theater*, Patricia told him, "I can't take a job right now. Roald and I are getting married."[23] Eliza Schallert announced in the *Los Angeles Times* that Patricia "May Be Writer's Bride." Referring to the prospective bridegroom as "Ronald" Dahl, Schallert wrote, "He's an exceptionally gifted writer, has done touchy and satirical pieces for the *New Yorker* magazine and loves the theatre. . . . Miss Neal . . . plans to go abroad this summer. It is hinted their marriage will take place there."[24]

After performances in *The Children's Hour*, Dahl would come to Patricia's dressing room and wait for her, often simply sitting on her chaise, watching her remove her makeup. As she prepared tea on her hot plate one night, Patricia spoke of the small "broom closets" she and Jean Hagen called dressing rooms during the tour of *Another Part of the Forest*. She mentioned to Dahl that Jean and her husband, Tom, were always on the telephone, repeating in their conversations, "kiss-kiss." Eventually, Dahl very slowly asked, "I would like to know how you think it would work if we got married?" Taken off guard, Patricia replied, "Oh no!"[25] Realizing that she did not love him, she told him she thought they should just continue their relationship as it was. She wanted marriage eventually, and certainly children. But not right now with him. Taken aback, Dahl never mentioned it again.

Patricia heard from Peter Douglas shortly after the proposal from Dahl. In New York briefly, Douglas wanted to meet for dinner, and Patricia wanted to know why he had stood her up in California. He said he had been drinking with buddies in Texas and had been too drunk to board the plane to fly to the West Coast. He asked Patricia to marry him. Patricia wrote, "Then the most surprising thing happened. I heard myself say, 'I'm going to marry Roald Dahl.'"[26]

Charles and Claudia Marsh were happy about the prospect of Dahl marrying Patricia. It was Marsh who gave Dahl a large marquise diamond ring, expecting Dahl to eventually pay for it. Roald and Patricia planned to wed privately on July 2. This would be after Patricia appeared in *The Scarecrow* and *School for Scandal*, to be produced by Terese Hayden at the newly restored Theatre de Lys. (Hayden and Patricia had become friends during the run of *The Children's Hour*.) After a honeymoon in Europe, Roald and Patricia would need to be back in the States by fall, as Patricia was committed to the tour of *The Children's Hour*.

Not everyone, however, was overjoyed about the coming nuptials. Patricia's dear friend Mildred Dunnock admitted that Dahl was definitely "not a man I could love."[27] His irascible nature and arrogance had turned off many of Patricia's friends. After learning about the engagement, Leonard Bernstein pulled Patricia aside at a party at Lillian Hellman's one evening and told her, "I really think you're making the biggest mistake in your life."[28]

Patricia discovered Dahl was jealous of many of her friends. At a party in their apartment held for some friends from the Actors Studio, Dahl boldly told Patricia's friend and future agent Harvey Orkin that there was something about him that he didn't like.

At another dinner, held at the Cusicks, Roald became very verbose and arrogant at the dinner table. Alone in the kitchen with Edla Cusick, Patricia voiced her doubts about the marriage. "Well nobody's holding a gun in your back. Why don't you break it off with him?" asked Edla.[29]

One of the most vocal objectors to the marriage was Dashiell Hammett, who had quarreled with Dahl the night they met at Lillian Hellman's and hadn't spoken to him since. "Don't marry him, Patsy, he's a horror," pleaded the writer. "I can't understand why you're doing this."[30] Patricia told him that she wanted children, and that they would name their firstborn in honor of him.

On May 26, Dahl wrote to Eura Neal:

Dear Mrs. Neal,

I know Pat has told you that she and I are now hoping to get married some time around the end of June, before we go to Europe, but I just wanted to write you myself and let you know how happy we are about it all, and how fortunate I think I am to be getting such a fine girl. It's going to be a bit strange to have a wife who earns more money than me, but that really isn't a problem and I'm confident that I'll always be able to support her myself with my own work whether she earns anything or not. After we return from Europe, and she goes on the road with the play, I'll start looking around for a slightly cheaper, but also a larger, apartment and I hope you'll come and see us often when we're finally settled in.

Pat naturally wants to get married in a church, so we'll do that. But I would not like it to develop into a large affair with press photographers and all that, so maybe we can manage to be a bit secret about it when the time comes, and just slip in somewhere quietly with four or five friends at most. It will also help to avoid publicity if we can do it just before leaving for Europe, preferably the day before—which would be July 2nd—but at the moment, nothing is decided.

All my sisters (4 of them) and my brother have been happily married for a long time now, so I'm hoping I can manage things as successfully as they. Pat seems happy and excited, and I certainly am.

With love
Roald[31]

14
Marriage

Marriage isn't a career—it's an incident.

—Fanny, *The Royal Family* (1927)

With her wedding plans set, Patricia turned her attention to the plays in which she had agreed to perform at the Theatre de Lys. Terese Hayden and her associate Liska March had scheduled four play revivals for production beginning in June at the Off-Broadway theater, located at 121 Christopher Street in Greenwich Village. With a budget of only $5,000, the plays—*Maya*, *The Scarecrow*, *The School for Scandal*, and *The Little Clay Cart*—would star such dedicated actors as Eli Wallach, Anne Jackson, Douglas Watson, Susan Strasberg, and Patricia.

The actors would all be paid a special Equity contract waiver salary of $5 a week for rehearsals and $25 a week during the run. The unions insisted that stagehands and the people who built the sets be paid scale, however. The sets were ingeniously designed for the small stage by husband-and-wife team William and Jean Eckart. Each production would run just one week, with Saturday and Sunday matinees and the possibility of return performances later in the year.

"There was no air conditioning in the big Broadway theatres during the late 1940s and early 1950s," recalled Eli Wallach. "Those theatres would close during the summer. Summer stock theatres in such states as New Jersey, Pennsylvania, Connecticut, and rural New York were very active during the warm months because they offered cooler weather. The idea of the Theatre de Lys was to present summer theatre productions within the city of New York, starring known and new actors honing their craft."[1] Wallach starred with Helen Craig, Martin Ritt, and Susan Strasberg in the premiere production of the summer season, *Maya*, which opened on June 9.

Facing page: Patricia Neal, circa 1956. From the Patricia Neal Collection.

Terese Hayden had developed a close friendship with Neal upon her return to New York and recalled that Neal was extremely supportive of the summer project. For the next production Hayden suggested that they stage Strindberg's *Miss Julie*. But, according to Hayden, it was Neal who brought *The Scarecrow* to her attention. Hayden recalled Neal's enthusiasm for the project, and the two went shopping together for costumes for all four productions. Hayden had not been impressed with Neal's performance in *The Children's Hour* but thought this venture would be an excellent challenge for the actress.

First produced in 1908, *The Scarecrow* was written by Percy MacKaye, son of the nineteenth-century director-producer-playwright Steele MacKaye, the man who invented the folding theater seat. *The Scarecrow* premiered on Broadway at the Garrick Theatre on January 17, 1911. For the new Theatre de Lys production, staged by Frank Corsaro, the cast would include Patricia as Goody Rickby, Eli Wallach as Dickon, Anne Jackson as Rachel Merton, Douglas Watson as The Scarecrow/Lord Ravensbane, young Bradford Dillman as Richard Talbot, Albert Salmi as Captain Bugby, and, in the nonspeaking role of the Scarecrow's reflection, stage novice James Dean.[2]

The Scarecrow, based on a story by Nathaniel Hawthorne, is set in seventeenth-century Massachusetts. It tells the tale of female blacksmith and witch Goody Rickby, who seeks revenge for being spurned by Justice Gilead Merton. She makes a pact with Dickon, also called "the Evil One," and casts a spell that brings to life a Scarecrow to woo Merton's daughter, Rachel. As a human, now called Lord Ravensbane, the Scarecrow falls in love with the young girl and breaks his pact with Dickon. This dramatic act brings about his death, but not before he has experienced, ever so briefly, the joys of life and love.

This was Bradford Dillman's professional acting debut. Naturally he was in awe of such actors as Wallach, Jackson, and Neal, finding them "thrilling and daunting." Dillman remembers Patricia "as a warm, vivacious woman with that enchanting voice and throaty laugh; a woman kind and understanding to a novice."[3]

In a 2004 interview, director Corsaro remembered his cast as a "very lovely unit" and that "Patricia was surrounded by people she liked, and managed to be very persuasive. She held her own [on stage]," and she "seemed to find great enjoyment [in portraying her character]. Particularly she relished playing an older woman—a witch."[4]

The Scarecrow opened on June 16, in the midst of one of New York's hottest and rainiest summers. "Everybody in the business was there," recalled

Hayden. The critics were much more pleased with *The Scarecrow* than they were with *Maya*. Walter Kerr said in his *New York Herald Tribune* review, "Patricia Neal is a garishly colorful, and very nearly convincing figure as the brawny, gray-haired, curt-spoken crone who acts as smith to a colonial village."[5] Brooks Atkinson in the *New York Times* said the play "represents the romantic theatre of pure imagination. And it gives actors accustomed to realistic theatre an opportunity to act with gusto and latitude. . . . Patricia Neal's acting as the witch is the best thing she has done here this season; it is hearty and relaxed."[6]

While *The Scarecrow* was running at night, rehearsals began for the third production of the summer, Richard Brinsley Sheridan's *School for Scandal*. A comedy of manners set in eighteenth-century London society, *School for Scandal* was originally produced in 1777. Wealthy bachelor Sir Peter Teazle (John Heldabrand) has married the much younger daughter of a country squire. As Lady Teazle (Neal), the girl has entered a malicious circle headed by vicious Lady Sneerwell (Sara Seegar). Lady Sneerwell wants Charles Surface (Leo Penn) for herself. She joins forces with Charles's unscrupulous young brother Joseph (David J. Stewart). Unfortunately, Charles is deceived by Joseph. Sir Oliver Surface (Howard Caine) arrives after hearing reports of the behavior of his nephews and heirs. He disguises himself, only to discover that Charles truly cares for the less fortunate. When he approaches Joseph as a poor relation, Joseph shows his true character. Sir Peter confronts Joseph in his apartment. Lady Teazle hides behind a screen. When Charles suddenly appears, Sir Peter hides in a closet. After Charles reveals Lady Teazle, Sir Peter comes out of the closet with a new understanding of the situation. Lady Teazle begs Sir Peter's mercy, saying she truly loves her husband.

Terese Hayden took over the directorial reins for the production. Her estimation of Patricia as an actress had increased considerably since the beginning of their friendship. "In the 1940s she wasn't really taken very seriously," said Hayden. "When she went to Hollywood, as so many young actors who had enjoyed minimal success on Broadway would do—oh, we were just terrible to them. We didn't think too much of them. But she had a wonderful part in *The School for Scandal*. And as her career continued, one saw the beginning of a more serious commitment for the theatre."[7]

In a *New York Post* article by Vernon Rice entitled "Pat Has That Extra Tension," Patricia spoke about her character in *The School for Scandal* and mentioned that in preparation for the role she had begun studying dance with Anna Sokolow. "The whole thing in a play of this kind is learning how to move," she told Rice. "I had no idea how difficult the movement could be.

One should train for this for years." She said she was excited about working with other actors at the Theatre de Lys, adding, "The whole project is much more personal. It is not 'my career' sort of thing. You care about all the others concerned. You are all working together."[8]

The School for Scandal opened on Tuesday, June 23, to poor reviews. Brooks Atkinson's *New York Times* notices put it succinctly: "The styles of acting are mixed, and the accents range from Brooklyn to the Bronx. Under the impromptu conditions that govern Dame Terese Hayden's summer project, those imperfections could be practically guaranteed. . . . Patricia Neal is cursed with vigorous personal health and a forthright nature. Miss Neal lacks wiles. There is nothing depraved or insidious about her characterization. . . . As works of art, this performance and this production are uneven and rather shiftless."[9]

Though her emotional equilibrium and confidence were now somewhat restored, Patricia suffered doubts the night before her marriage. She had arranged everything herself—picking out her trousseau, sending out invitations, ordering baskets of flowers for the church. She forgot only one thing: the music.

On Thursday, July 2, 1953, at New York's Trinity Episcopal Church, Patsy Louise Neal wed Roald Dahl. The day was unbearably hot and humid, reaching 105 degrees by midafternoon. Patricia wore a pink chiffon evening gown with a form-fitting bodice, which she had specially cut down for the wedding. She also wore a hat with tiny flowers that matched the wedding bouquet Roald had given her. Dahl wore a tailored suit, from which he had ripped out the silk lining because of the day's heat. In photographs, the two look radiantly happy.

The wedding ceremony was conducted by the Rev. Ernest Nicholson. Mildred Dunnock stood up with Patricia, and Charles March was Dahl's best man. There were no family members present, something that was agreed upon due to the fact that Dahl's relatives could not come because the British government had placed restrictions on the amount of money citizens could take out of the country. When the wedding party threw rice inside the church, Patricia remembered the clergyman becoming upset about the mess. Afterwards a small reception was held at the Marshes' apartment. Guests included Harvey and Gisella Orkin; Ivar and Josephine Bryce; Maureen Stapleton and her husband, Max Allentuck; Peter and Edla Cusick; and Edmund and Marian Goodman.

Former Chicago gossip columnist Radie Harris claimed she broke the news of Patricia's marriage to Gary Cooper in Madrid, where he, Rocky, and Maria were attending a publicity junket for the opening of the Madrid Hilton Hotel. She wrote that Gary seemed happy again with Rocky, possibly because of his recent conversion to Catholicism. According to Harris, "At the first opportunity I took him aside and said, 'Gary, I want to tell you something before you read about it or hear it on the radio. Pat married the English writer, Roald Dahl, today.' Gary's face whitened and suddenly there was no light in his eyes as if a switch had been turned off. Then very quietly he said, 'I hope he's a helluva guy. She deserves nothing but the best.'"[10]

On July 3, Roald and Patricia boarded an Air France flight for Europe. As far back as May the couple had planned to visit Roald's family while in England. They agreed to visit the Neal family during Christmas holidays. Dahl had planned the honeymoon down to the minute. Said Patricia, wryly, "He had an enormous appreciation for anything he generated."[11]

They arrived in Naples, where they picked up a secondhand Jaguar and drove up Amalfi Drive to their first stop in Positano. From Positano the couple motored up the Italian coast to Rome, where they stayed at a small hotel at the foot of the Spanish Steps. Touring the city, they visited museums, dined at out-of-the-way restaurants, and shopped. The couple was photographed touring the ruins of the ancient Coliseum in Rome. Patricia fell in love with Italy.

They continued on to Switzerland, where they bought each other Patek Philippe watches as wedding gifts. (Patricia still wore hers in 2005.) In France, Patricia and Roald visited for about two weeks with Mimi Tellis, who was living in the south of France with her two young boys. "They had this marvelous, huge touring car, I remember. And at night Roald would tell stories to my two young children," said Tellis. With adults, Dahl wasn't as endearing. "He was a difficult man who could wither you with a remark. You had to be tough. He was cocky because his short stories were selling and he was beginning to make money."[12]

Taking the ferry at Calais over the English Channel to Britain in August, the Dahls arrived in Great Missenden, between London and Oxford, a village of about two thousand people where the Dahl family resided. They stayed with Roald's sister Else and her husband, John Logsdail. Patricia recalled that Dahl's nephew Nicky and niece Astri were sitting on the fence waving hello as she and Roald drove up to the house. Patricia met Dahl's sister Alfhild and her husband, Leslie Hansen. And she finally met Dahl's arthritic mother, whom they called Mormor, the Scandinavian word for "grandmother."

The Dahl family was not especially demonstrative, and no kisses or hugs were exchanged. However, Mormor told Patricia she would have many babies—two girls, a son, and two more girls. Before leaving England, Patricia was introduced to Dahl's half-sister, Ellen, and half-brother, Louie, as well as his youngest sister, Asta, and her husband, Alex. And Patricia finally met Roald's friend the elderly Sir Matthew Smith, who would one day paint her portrait.

Recalling her first meal with the Dahl family, Patricia told John McLain in 1955, "We all sat down together to have our first meal; nine sets of eyes were leveled at me. I tremble to think what might have happened if they'd hated me. As it was, it was very funny—my accent made the kids laugh and when I ate with a fork, instead of using the knife to pile a dozen vegetables on the back of the fork they thought I'd lost the use of one hand. It was cozy."[13]

After their two-month honeymoon, Patricia and Roald returned to New York. They took a ground-floor apartment on the West Side, at 44 West Seventy-seventh Street, off Central Park. It was a small apartment with two bedrooms in a huge, Gothic-looking building. The rent was cheap, and Roald was able to use the second bedroom as a writing studio. When he first met Patricia, Roald thought she had no taste in furnishings or paintings. Her apartment was full of large, "deplorable, Hollywood-type" furniture,[14] including a beige sofa "that cost a thousand dollars and eventually grew so tatty they tried to peddle it to a radio giveaway show, where no one would accept it, even as a prize."[15] (Patricia soon learned about good furniture and woods and grew to know and appreciate antiques as well.)

As they downsized, Roald insisted that Patricia sell a few of her paintings that he had never liked and suggested she also liquidate the diamond earrings Gary had given her. She told him she would think about it. Patricia freely admitted that she wasn't much of a housewife and simply never thought of getting up early and making Roald coffee. She was a decent cook and would spend hours preparing meals when they entertained. But she spent little time in the kitchen when she and Roald were home alone. Roald apparently did not make comments about her homemaking skills immediately after they wed. Even this early in their marriage, sometimes he wouldn't speak to her for days at a time.

The Children's Hour was scheduled to tour beginning September 17 in Wilmington, Delaware, continuing to Baltimore, Pittsburgh, and Chicago. Changes in the cast had Janet Parker assuming the role of Mary Tilford, Fay Bainter as Amelia Tilford, Theodore Newton as Dr. Joseph Cardin, and Priscilla Gillette replacing Kim Hunter as Karen Wright, since Hunter's pregnancy prevented her participation. Patricia's was the only star name in the cast.

Shortly before *The Children's Hour*'s October 13 opening in Pittsburgh, reporter Kasper Monahan interviewed Patricia. Asked if she found the highly emotional role of Martha exhausting, she replied, "No, exhilarating—if we feel we are pleasing the audiences." Was Hollywood beckoning? "Nothing like that," she said. "But I would like to do a movie now and then—but not mediocre ones. I've had my fill of them."[16] She told Monahan that *The Breaking Point* and *Three Secrets* were her favorites among her films and that playing the role of Regina in *Another Part of the Forest* was her toughest acting experience.

The out-of-town reviews were generally good. Harold V. Cohen wrote in the *Pittsburgh Post-Gazette*, "Miss Patricia Neal's performance as one of the teachers has improved immeasurably since this 'Children's Hour' was encountered several months ago in New York. Miss Neal has harnessed the role, and it has the quality now of a wild, caged animal fighting for its very life."[17]

Chicago critic Sidney J. Harris wrote, "Miss Neal, especially, achieves an intensity through restraint that is agonizingly realistic. And when, in the final scene, she breaks down and begins to believe the lie about herself, her dramatic impact is everything the playwright could have wished."[18] But the play was not successful on the road, and it closed soon after its opening in Chicago.

While the play ran in Chicago, a young man named Michael stopped by Patricia's hotel suite to ask if she would consent to recording a work of Roald Dahl's for his theater group, something she agreed to do. Explaining to her that he wanted to become an actor, Patricia carefully and tactfully attempted to dissuade him. She felt he had no future in theater. Several years later, during rehearsals in New York for *The Miracle Worker*, Patricia saw a couple in the audience. The man kept waving at her. When she approached them afterward, the man asked her if she didn't recognize him from Chicago. "I'm the fellow you told not to go into show business," Mike Nichols reminded her.[19] The woman he was with was Elaine May, and their comedy team was perched on the brink of stardom.

While Patricia was on tour with *The Children's Hour*, her husband was conducting a strange and intricately choreographed friendship with society heiress Gloria Vanderbilt. Patricia wanted to believe Roald when he told her that after he and Gloria had met at a party and, according to Roald, she had fallen in love with him, nothing happened between them.

Vanderbilt's account in her 2004 autobiography is rather different. She said that "baby Dahl," as he was called when the "six-foot-four-something" was in the RAF, asked to meet her in Central Park shortly after they met. When Dahl went on a book tour soon after meeting Vanderbilt, he wrote letters to her, which she diligently kept (and later offered to Patricia during her divorce hearings), describing his fantasies of what their relationship could be. Upon his return to New York, and shortly before Patricia's return from Chicago, he invited the infatuated heiress to the West Side apartment. He led her into the bedroom, wrote Vanderbilt. "Eerie seeing their bed (king size) with the flowered sheets, but it was even more eerie when he tried to pull me into it, even though he knew I wasn't going to comply," she wrote.[20]

Roald didn't take rejection easily. He reached over to a drawer and removed a black leather jewelry box, taking out a "plump little enameled Victorian pin, purple and yellow as could be with a twinkly diamond in the center," which he had purchased at James Robinson's. Roald presented it to her, and Vanderbilt could only say, "Oh, Roald, I, I . . ." His next remark stung like a bee: "Do you think Pat will like it?" (Years later, when the Dahls were divorcing, Vanderbilt wrote, she invited Patricia to Southampton. At the dinner that Saturday evening, Patricia wore the pin, and Vanderbilt discreetly said nothing.)[21]

Back in the city in December after the tour, Patricia glanced at a newsstand and saw a picture of the newly reconciled Gary and Rocky Cooper at Paris's Orly Airport. Seeing that they were happy in the photo, she decided to sell Cooper's diamond earrings, which Roald had asked her to purge. She wrote that when she returned them to Harry Winston, the jeweler was not interested in buying such low-quality stones. Patricia explained where they had come from, and after checking their history, the jeweler told Patricia that they had indeed been purchased by Cooper. They were one of three pairs he bought at the same time. Winston offered her a very low price, and, numbly, she accepted.

The Christmas holidays were spent with Patricia's family in Atlanta. It was to be the opportunity for Patricia's family to meet and approve of her husband. But Dahl made no effort to tolerate his new in-laws and was rude and arrogant. His condescending attitude barely disguised his impatience with their thoughts and their talk. Patricia's family was not happy. Patricia's mother, now living in Brook Haven, Georgia, felt particularly insulted; her feelings toward Roald would never be favorable. Patricia could not understand why his behavior was so rude.

Upon their return to New York, the Dahls realized their marriage was in severe trouble. One night shortly after their return, Dahl told Patricia that he wanted a divorce. Spending a sleepless night walking the streets of Manhattan, Patricia picked up the scarf she had knitted for Roald during the play tour at a store where she had left it to be blocked. Returning to the apartment, she handed it over to her husband, and he was moved by the gift. Dahl's brother-in-law Leslie Hansen had come to visit and burst into tears when they told him of their problems. The two men left for Texas so Leslie could have his teeth fixed. Patricia flew to Ocho Rios, Jamaica, to visit with Charles and Claudia Marsh. She was determined to save her marriage.

For weeks Patricia listened to the advice Charles Marsh freely doled out. She came to the realization that she had not done her best to please her complicated husband. At the heart of all their troubles was Dahl's expressed need to handle the bank account. A man's libido could be directly affected if he were not allowed control, Patricia was told. She vowed to begin cooking for him regularly, to clean for him, not to lie around in bed. She agreed to do more to support his needs and career. When Dahl and Hansen arrived in Ocho Rios, Roald and Patricia began their marriage in earnest.

Though Roald's short-story collection *Someone Like You* was successfully published in the fall of 1953, he suggested Patricia take a few television offers, as they could use the money. By 1954, television had evolved from its infancy after the war, from the grainy images and sometimes uneven live performances featuring former vaudevillians in variety acts to slicker, more polished productions, often filmed, with literate teleplays featuring respected and gifted actors guided by intelligent direction. Patricia had appeared on local television in Los Angeles on talk and interview shows as far back as 1949. In 1953, she had been a guest on DuMont Television's panel show, *Twenty Questions*. Now she would have the opportunity to act in a new medium, under much tighter and shorter production schedules than she was used to. Said Patricia, "I rather liked television and don't recall ever feeling frazzled by the hectic pace or pressured by performing live. I loved the challenge of learning lines quickly and working in a whirlwind of changes."[22]

In early April, Patricia began rehearsals at the NBC Studios at Rockefeller Center in New York for a dramatic turn on the *Goodyear TV Playhouse*. Airing Sunday, April 11, the hour-long episode entitled "Spring Reunion" was produced by Fred Coe and written by Robert Alan Aurthur. "Spring Reunion" starred Patricia with Kevin McCarthy and Kathleen Maguire. It told a tale about a woman, Maggie Hackett (Neal), who had been voted the prettiest girl in her senior class but for some reason has never married. Maggie works for her father's real estate office and lives at home. She attends her class reunion and meets a drifter (Kevin McCarthy) who interests her. They begin an affair and run off together to San Francisco.

Patricia appeared next in another hour-long dramatic series, *Studio One*, for CBS. In the episode "A Handful of Diamonds," she costarred with Lorne Greene and William Harrigan. *Studio One* was one of the more prestigious anthology shows of the time, introducing such talented young writers as Rod Serling, Gore Vidal, and Reginald Rose.

"A Handful of Diamonds," set in the 1870s and 1880s, tells the story of Mrs. Frank Leslie (Neal), wife of the publisher (Lorne Greene) of *Leslie's Illustrated Weekly*. She is torn between "the salons of fashion and a bent for journalism."[23] This show established Patricia as a strong talent in dramatic anthology series.

Patricia also hosted an episode of *Your Show of Shows*, a comedy series starring Sid Caesar, Imogene Coca, and Carl Reiner that was a giant hit for NBC; it had just won the 1953 Emmy for Best Variety Show. All Patricia did was introduce the stars and the show. It was great fun, she remembered, though she didn't appear in any of the skits. Carl Reiner recalled that Patricia was a good sport, and that particular night's show went splendidly. (Patricia recalled that she hadn't been paid at the time for her work on the show, which had been done for scale. Many years later, in an accounting cleanup, NBC realized their error and sent Patricia a check for her work plus interest, which amounted to thousands of dollars.)

By February 1954, *Someone Like You* was in its fourth U.S. printing. It had been selected by the Book-of-the-Month Club, and in April it won the Mystery Writers of America Edgar Allan Poe Award. There was talk about adapting parts of it for a play and an opera. Dahl's career was firmly established.

An independent film company in England sent Patricia a screenplay, *Stranger from Venus*, and Roald encouraged her to accept the offer. After all, they had already decided to spend their summers in England. However, Patricia's mind wasn't on her career at the moment. Her monthly periods had been erratic, and she had become concerned about not being able to conceive a child. She thus consulted her physician, Dr. Rubin, at Mount Sinai Hospital in New York. Rubin did a medical procedure that opened up Patricia's blocked fallopian tubes. Reassured that nature would take its course, Patricia and Roald were told to simply relax. She later wrote that when she had her next period, she was overjoyed.

From England, one of Roald's sisters sent news that a three-bedroom, two-story Georgian farmhouse situated on five acres of land outside of London in the village of Great Missenden was up for auction. The Dahls made a successful bid of 4,500 pounds (half paid by Dahl's mother and the other half by Patricia's earnings) for the property and thus obtained Little Whitefield. The Dahls left the United States the first week in June. Upon seeing their new property for the first time, Roald and Patricia realized it would take a lot of work to fix up. But they had the whole summer of 1954 to begin. And Patricia was working.

15

England

You are very quiet and very warm. It's that your eyes are soft and sensitive, and that your character is deep and filled with meaning.

—The Stranger to Susan North, *Stranger from Venus* (1954)

Within weeks after arriving in England, Patricia was whisked off by producer-director Burt Balaban to the English countryside to start work on *Stranger from Venus*. Produced by Princess Pictures and filmed at Britain's MGM Studios, *Stranger from Venus* was shot on a tight schedule and on a cheap budget. The story of *Stranger from Venus*, by screenwriters Hans Jacoby and Desmond Leslie, is very similar to that of *The Day the Earth Stood Still*. This was not a good sign for Patricia's career.

A spacecraft is heard flying over the English countryside. When the aircraft lands, its lights blind Susan North (Neal) as she is driving in her car, and she crashes into a tree on a deserted road. As she lies motionless at the wheel, one sees only the legs and feet of a strangely dressed man approach the vehicle. The Stranger (Helmut Dantine) suddenly appears at a pub. Announcing to the owner, his daughter, and inn resident Dr. Meinard (Cyril Luckman) that he is an alien from the planet Venus, the Stranger tells them he was sent to Earth as a preliminary emissary before the arrival of a larger delegation.

The police and Susan's fiancé, scientist Arthur Walker (Derek Bond) discover Susan's wrecked car. After they arrive at the inn, Susan dramatically appears, her clothes torn. Though she surely was killed in the crash, she somehow is still alive and suffering from amnesia. The Stranger tells the spectators that a large delegation will be coming to land in a highly magnetically charged field in four days with an important message for all the nations on Earth.

Facing page: Patricia Neal at Great Missenden, 1957. Photograph by Dave Preston, from the Patricia Neal Collection.

After meeting with five British dignitaries, the Stranger explains the reason for the visit of the Venusian delegation. The British officials plan to capture the spacecraft by magnetizing it when it lands. By preventing the spacecraft from landing in the trap, the Stranger seals his doom on Earth.

Patricia wore five dresses in the film, all of the same style. None was particularly modish, and her hair was done equally unattractively in a short, side-parted fashion. Her love scenes with Dantine were dull and unconvincing ("You read my mind," says Susan to the Stranger. "It isn't fair, especially for a woman.") No matter how much she tried, Patricia could not bring life to her character.

The poster art for *Stranger from Venus*, with its multiple and menacing flying saucers and exploding airliners, promised a lot more visually than the audiences would ever see. There are virtually no special effects. The writing, cinematography, music, and direction are dreadful. The script generates no suspense. Lines in the film are delivered with great pathos, followed by a "ta-ta-ta-TA" horn effect to emphasize their relevance. By 1954, several big-budget American science fiction pictures, like *When Worlds Collide* (Paramount, 1951), *War of the Worlds* (Paramount, 1953), and *Invaders from Mars* (20th Century-Fox, 1953) had proved worthy successors to *The Day the Earth Stood Still*. Discerning film audiences had come to expect excellent production values and intelligent scripts. *Stranger from Venus* was a failure on all levels.[1]

Shortly after its completion, it was shown first on American television, not in the theater, under the title *Immediate Disaster*. It proved to be just that, though the music was by Eric Spear, who achieved acclaim years later for *Coronation Street*. Entitled *The Venusian* in some markets, it was not extensively seen in theaters in the United States. *Stranger from Venus* was released in Europe in the fall of 1954 and did poor business. The picture proved to be a huge setback for Patricia's film career.

Roald's friend Wally Saunders assisted with the remodeling of the farmhouse in Great Missenden, a service for the Dahls he continued for the next twenty-five years. Roald ordered costly eighteenth-century English furniture, of which he was very fond. On the walls he would eventually hang paintings and watercolors by Francis Bacon, Rodchenko, Moholy-Nagy, Klee, Bomberg, Cezanne, Renoir, Soutine, Matthew Smith, and Winston Churchill. While the house was under renovation, the Dahls stayed with Roald's mother. This was a good period in their marriage. On a beautiful, sunny afternoon in the fields around Great Missenden, Patricia wrote, she became pregnant with Roald's first child.

Roald had begun writing a play called *The Honeys*, to be produced under the direction of Frank Corsaro and starring Jessica Tandy and her husband, Hume Cronyn, and he needed to be in the United States. Meanwhile, Patricia had agreed to appear in an Italian film, *La tua donna* (Your Woman). Thrilled at the prospect of having a baby in the spring, Patricia was reluctant to leave for Italy to make the film.

But when she arrived in Rome in October, Patricia instantly fell in love again with Italy. During the filming, she stayed at the magnificent Hassler Hotel, which was at the top of the Spanish Steps, overlooking the Dahls' honeymoon hotel. She appeared radiantly happy and more beautiful than she had in some time. Patricia had chosen not to tell the production company, Deneb Films, that she was pregnant; she knew the shooting schedule would be brief. Hollywood friend Marta Toren and her husband, Leonardo Bercovici, lived in Italy, and the three spent many hours touring and dining together when Patricia was not shooting.

Her costars in *La tua donna* were Italian heartthrob Massimo Girotti and film favorite Lea Padovani. Patricia was the only English-speaking player in the picture; her voice was dubbed in Italian. *La tua donna* tells the story of a young man, Sandro Ademari (Girotti), who takes refuge from the Germans during World War II in the farmhouse of a farmer whose daughter Luisa (Padovani) he falls in love with. After the war, Sandro and Luisa marry and settle in Perugia, where he becomes a successful lawyer. Elected as a political representative, he is sent to Rome, leaving his wife and young son at home. In Rome, he falls under the spell of the rich and beautiful countess Germana de Torri (Neal). As his patron, as well as his lover, she encourages him to forget his wife and young son and concentrate on her and his political ambitions.

Realizing that he cannot dismiss his wife and son, with his love and longing for his young family destroying him, Sandro returns to Perugia and confesses to Luisa. After an emotionally violent reaction from Luisa, Sandro leaves, vowing to marry the countess. In Rome, he seeks an annulment of his marriage, but Luisa refuses. She goes to the countess and pleads with her to give up Sandro. Luisa is accidentally shot and dies. Sandro is accused of the murder. On the witness stand he does not defend himself. He is acquitted, however, leaves the countess, and, penitent, starts a new life with his little boy.[2]

The 105-minute-long *La tua donna* premiered in Italy on December 28, 1954, with a continental European release in early 1955. It was never shown in the United States.

Patricia kept in touch with Roald by letters and transatlantic phone calls during the filming. Dahl's play *The Honeys* was having a difficult tryout tour. Director Frank Corsaro was let go in New Haven, and the play's star, Hume Cronyn, took over direction. Cronyn brought in some new writers, which displeased Roald. He and Cronyn fought bitterly. Roald incorporated several of his short stories, including the classic "Lamb to the Slaughter," into the plot of the play. But it was just not coming together. *The Honeys* was similar to *Arsenic and Old Lace*, but the characters in Roald's play were not lovable, and the plot was not easy to follow.

During the filming in Rome, Patricia began seeing a local physician for regular checkups. Still keeping her pregnancy concealed from the Italian filmmakers, she had noticed a bump in her growing belly, which she surmised was just a limb, possibly a foot, of her unborn child. The Italian doctor told her that it might also be a tumor and that she could lose the baby. When she called her friend Dr. Edmund Goodman in New York, he notified Roald, and Patricia flew to New York the minute shooting was completed. The bump turned out to be nothing. Now in the United States and comfortable with her surroundings, Patricia relaxed, and the baby within her continued to grow.

It was announced in the *New York Times,* in November, that Patricia would star with Karl Malden and Douglas Watson in the American National Theatre and Academy revival of Eugene O'Neill's *Desire under the Elms*, to be staged by Harold Clurman. Set to open January 16, 1955, this was a play Patricia wanted to do. But shortly before Patricia signed for the role of Abbie Putnam, Carlotta O'Neill heard about her involvement with the project, and negotiations were quickly broken off without explanation. In any event, Patricia's pregnancy forbade her participation.

She continued her work with the Actors Studio, however. There Patricia met the young actor Paul Newman, who had "the most penetrating blue eyes," she remembered.[3] Patricia performed a scene from Tennessee Williams's *Cat on a Hot Tin Roof* at the studio with Pat Hingle. When word of Patricia's performance reached Elia Kazan, he suggested that she consider "cutting a tooth on Tennessee Williams" someday.[4]

Walter Winchell reported in his November 16 column that the Dahls were expecting, and on December 6, Hedda Hopper advised her readers that Patricia's baby would arrive "in five months."[5] This time the venerable reporter got her story right, almost to the day. Roald was with his play in Boston the evening of April 19, when Patricia went into labor. She gave birth at New York's Doctors Hospital on April 20 to her first child, a baby girl weighing five and one-half pounds. Roald and Patricia named her Olivia Twenty, her first name for Patricia's character in *Twelfth Night* and her middle name given by Roald because of the date she was born. (Roald was receiving $20 a day expense money from the play, and in an interview shortly after the baby's birth, Patricia suggested that the child would "get a $20 bill on her birthdays.")[6] Patricia's first visitors at the hospital were members of the Actors Studio; Anne Jackson and Eli Wallach told Patricia that Olivia was the best production she had ever done.

Roald and Patricia were overjoyed at the birth of their first child. The baby was breathtakingly beautiful from the start, with fair skin, blonde hair, cornflower blue eyes, lovely arched eyebrows, and possessing, as she grew and developed, a brilliant mind and clever disposition. Patricia and Olivia developed a tender and emotional bond immediately.

Dahl's play *The Honeys* opened at the Longacre Theatre on April 28, 1955, to terrible reviews. It ran just thirty-six performances, closing on May 26. Dahl had little time to bemoan the play's failure. As head of his household, which Patricia generously allowed him to be, he oversaw the hiring and firing of nannies as well as the running of the everyday functions of the household. Eura Neal was actively involved with her daughter and grandchild whenever she was in New York, which was frequently. Dahl's sister Else handled much of the young baby's care while Patricia and Roald were back in England. Indeed, little Olivia would spend a large part of her early life traveling back and forth across the Atlantic.

Just days after returning home with Olivia, Patricia was offered the lead in a new play, *A Roomful of Roses*, by Edith Sommer, who had been heralded by the Barter Theatre shortly before Patricia's summer of 1942. (This would be Sommer's only Broadway play.) It was produced and staged by Guthrie McClintic, husband of Katharine Cornell. Both Patricia and Roald liked the script and decided she would do it when they returned from England after the summer. The second week in June, the Dahls boarded a jetliner to England to introduce their new baby to the Dahl family. That summer Roald's sister Else came over to Little Whitefield every evening for a drink and a visit. Patricia, with Olivia, left for the United States on July 29 so she could begin rehearsals for *A Roomful of Roses*. Roald would remain in Great Missenden and work until the play opened.

Patricia enjoyed rehearsals of *A Roomful of Roses*. She was back doing her craft, and she had great hopes for the success of the production. *A Roomful of Roses* tells the story of Nancy Fallon (Neal), who had abandoned her first husband, Carl MacGowan (David White), and her young daughter Bridget

(Betty Lou Keim) eight years earlier. Now fifteen, Bridget is coming to visit her mother. Nancy, who lives in Illinois with her second husband, Jay Fallon (Russ Conway) and their small son, Larry (Darryl Richard), is anxious about the reunion. Bridget is guarded, bitter, and in steely control of her emotions. Nancy wants desperately to regain her daughter's love and trust. Bridget finds out that her father is remarrying and that he allowed her to visit her mother only to keep her out of the way. When she finally sees her father for the man he truly is, she reconsiders her mother's love.

Patricia was playing a mother for the first time on the Broadway stage. Thrilled to be working with the incomparable director Guthrie McClintic, she felt that *A Roomful of Roses* might prove the best experience of her career. Betty Lou Keim would later say, "Pat was so very generous with me. When I was on the stage with her, Patricia was my mother. I always felt that she had taken me under her wing, that she nurtured me. Our scenes together were believable."[7]

A Roomful of Roses opened in tryout at the McCarter Theatre in Princeton, New Jersey, on September 19, and at the Shubert Theatre in Washington on September 26. Roald joined Patricia for performances in the nation's capital. The early reviews were good.

Considered a comedy despite its serious subject matter, *A Roomful of Roses* opened at the Playhouse Theatre on Broadway on October 17. Shortly after 11:00 P.M. that evening, when the final applause died down, NBC reporter Leon Pearson announced live from the lobby of the Playhouse Theatre, "What a beautiful actress is this Patricia Neal. 'A Roomful of Roses' should be full-blown for a long time."[8]

Robert Coleman in his *New York Daily Mirror* review wrote, "Patricia Neal, too long absent from Broadway, brings a glowing warmth to the mother who succeeds in re-claiming her daughter from arrogant despair."[9] Walter Kerr of the *New York Herald Tribune* gave Patricia a rave, "Patricia Neal would grace the cover of any magazine you care to name. 'I suppose it's the large bones,' muses a friend of the family in an effort to describe the 'splendid innocence' that clings to this earnest mother. Miss Neal's bones are indeed magnificent, her resonant voice is a pleasure to listen to, and the performance itself is impeccably wrought."[10] And Brooks Atkinson in his *New York Times* review states, "Miss Neal gives her best performance to date as the troubled mother. It is relaxed in style without losing emotional force, and it puts a solid foundation under the drama."[11] Despite the decent reviews, *A Roomful of Roses* was not marked for a long run. It closed on December 31. McClintic allowed Patricia to keep her wardrobe, specially designed by Christian Dior, when the play closed.

At home with her husband, Patricia maintained a rigorous and disciplined schedule. "I rose early to bathe and feed my now six-month-old, walked her in the park and did the shopping," she wrote. "I made breakfast and lunch for my husband, conferred with the nurse, cleaned the apartment, prepared supper, did the dishes and made it to the theatre for an 8:30 curtain."[12] In a newspaper interview shortly after *A Roomful of Roses* closed, she said, "I'd come home from the matinee, cook supper, wash the dishes, then dash back to the theatre for the evening performance. But then I love to cook. I'm famous for my sauces, and Southern country cooking. But I'm not as good on baking."[13] She also told the press, "I may go back to Hollywood to act in movies, but I have given up all ideas of being a movie star. You have to be dedicated for that."[14] Indeed, baby Olivia, with her eyes "an odd shade of grayish-blue, very much like Dior blue," whom Patricia would set in her little pink high chair every morning while she was fed, was her first priority and love.[15]

While walking down Fifth Avenue one afternoon in October after the play closed, Patricia ran into Gary Cooper, who was staring into the window of a store across the street from the St. Regis Hotel. Patricia recalled she was wearing the Christian Dior suit she had been given from the play, and she knew she looked good. But Gary did not. She greeted him, "Hello, Gary." Startled, he looked at her for possibly thirty to forty-five seconds with a perplexed, cold look on his face. He then realized it was Patricia, and exclaimed, "Oh, my baby!"

Patricia and Gary went to tea at the St. Regis Hotel, and after small talk, she told him about her marriage and baby Olivia. Unexpectedly, she confided to him, "You broke my heart, Gary. You really did."

"You know baby, I couldn't have hurt Maria for the world."

"I know," Patricia said. "I loved you so much."

"I still do," replied Gary.

Patricia wrote that she thought to herself, "And I always will." The two sat and simply looked at each other, their thoughts private. A chapter must have ended that afternoon, for after tea, Gary hailed a taxi for Patricia, and she went home to her husband.[16]

Patricia continued her study at the Actors Studio. Wrote Dorothy Kilgallen in her syndicated column, "Patricia Neal isn't letting star billing go to her head. Although she's being applauded for one of the season's finest performances in 'Roomful of Roses,' she checks in at the Actors Studio twice weekly for practice sessions in the drama."[17] This study was vital for her work as well as for her self-esteem and confidence. Marriage and motherhood held their rewards, but acting was her life's blood. Patricia kept active with her studies as well as her social commitments.

She also continued her work in television, appearing as Herodias in a production of Oscar Wilde's *Salome* on the prestigious CBS series *Omnibus*. Hosted by Alistair Cook, the award-winning ninety-minute series offered such diverse programming as ballet, opera, dance, and real-life dramas, as well as documentary films. Such important actors and entertainers as Rex Harrison, Yul Brynner, Kim Stanley, Anne Bancroft, Carol Channing, and Claude Rains appeared in dramas on the series.

The hour-long presentation of *Salome*, with teleplay by Ellen Violett and incidental music by Leonard Bernstein, was preceded by a short concert by singer Anna Russell and followed by a short film, *The Towers*, about Italian artist Sabato "Sam" Rodia, who spent from 1921 until 1955 building the famous Watts Towers in South Central Los Angeles.

Variety critic Chan wrote, "'Salome' . . . brought out all the lechery of the piece in a hell-'n-brimstone style that made for fascinating if somewhat offbeat viewing. . . . Miss Neal, as the sinful Herodias, was a fortunate choice, lending the role all the bitter callousness it required and more. It was a change of pace for Miss Neal, but a very welcome one."[18]

Roald was proud of Patricia's *Omnibus* appearance. Though it didn't pay as much as the film *Stranger from Venus*, her participation in the broadcast was certainly much more dignified. So important now was Patricia's standing in New York's social and theatrical circles that she was invited to perform at the First Night Ball on December 30 in honor of Helen Hayes's fiftieth year in the theater. Patricia was asked to perform passages from Michael Arlen's 1925 play *The Green Hat* in the persona of Katharine Cornell as part of an all-star cast of theater and entertainment luminaries.

Patricia's two-minute performance in *The Green Hat* also featured Douglas Watson. Costumed in a 1920s long-sleeved, waistless, knee-length, dark chemise, wearing low heels and a green vintage 1920s hat, Patricia performed the dialogue with Watson with humor, and the audience was overwhelmingly responsive. (In the early 1970s, Patricia and Phyllis Jenkins attended a lunch with Katharine Cornell and her companion Nancy Hamilton. Patricia wore the green hat, and Cornell loved it.)

Life in New York was good. The year 1955 was ending on a high. Patricia had no work prospects lined up in the immediate future, but she had every reason to count her blessings. She was happily married to a rising, successful writer, she was the young and healthy mother of an equally healthy and beautiful baby girl whom she adored, and her career was strongly back on track.

Gary Cooper and Patricia
Neal in *Bright Leaf*, 1950.
From the author's collection.

Patricia Neal with director
Michael Curtiz on the set
of *Bright Leaf*. From the
author's collection.

Patricia Neal costume test for *Bright Leaf*. From the author's collection.

Patricia Neal with Leah Rhodes, costume designer for *Bright Leaf*. From the author's collection.

Above, Frank Lovejoy and Patricia Neal in *Three Secrets*. From the author's collection. *Below,* arriving home for a visit. *Left to right*: sister Margaret Ann "NiNi," Eura Neal, Patricia Neal, and Pete Neal, circa 1949. From the Patricia Neal Collection.

John Garfield, Ralph Dumke, and Patricia Neal in *The Breaking Point*, 1950. From the author's collection.

Patricia Neal hair test for *The Breaking Point*. From the author's collection.

Patricia Neal, Eva Peron, and June Haver in Buenos Aires,
1950. From the Patricia Neal Collection.

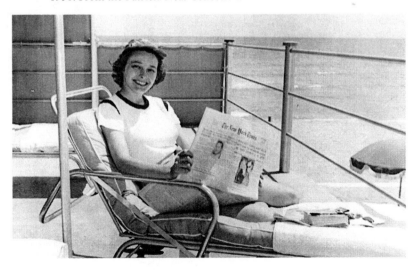

Patricia Neal, photographed by Gary Cooper in Florida, 1950. From the Patricia
Neal Collection.

Above, Dennis Morgan and Patricia Neal in *Raton Pass,* 1950. From the author's collection. *Right,* Patricia Neal costume test for *Raton Pass.* From the author's collection.

John Wayne and Patricia Neal
in *Operation Pacific*, 1950.
From the author's collection.

Patricia Neal leaving her doctor's office,
September 1950. Courtesy of John Buonomo, from the author's collection.

Patricia Neal and Michael Rennie in the film classic *The Day the Earth Stood Still*, 1951. From the author's collection.

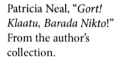

Patricia Neal, "*Gort! Klaatu, Barada Nikto!*" From the author's collection.

Above, Harry Ellerbe (standing), Patricia Neal, and William Schallert in the La Jolla Playhouse production of *The Cocktail Party,* 1951. Courtesy of William Schallert, from the author's collection. *Left,* John Buonomo and Patricia Neal on closing night of *The Cocktail Party.* Courtesy of John Buonomo, from the author's collection.

Tyrone Power and Patricia Neal in *Diplomatic Courier*, 1952. From the author's collection.

Victor Mature and Patricia Neal in *Something for the Birds*, 1952. From the author's collection.

The elegantly handsome Peter Douglas, circa 1950s. Courtesy of Peter Douglas, from the author's collection.

Tony Lovello, Johnny Grant, and Patricia Neal on the 1952 Korean USO Tour. Courtesy of Johnny Grant, from the author's collection.

Above left, Patricia Neal and Kim Hunter in Lillian Hellman's Broadway revival of *The Children's Hour,* 1952. From the Patricia Neal Collection. *Above right,* Patricia Neal in the Theatre de Lys production of *The Scarecrow,* June 1953. From the Patricia Neal Collection. *Right,* John Heldabrand and Patricia Neal in the Theatre de Lys production of *The School for Scandal,* June 1953. From the Patricia Neal Collection.

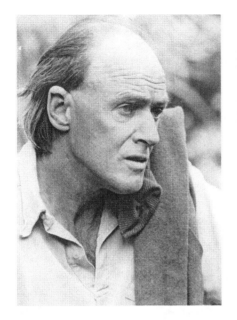

Left, Roald Dahl, circa 1950s. Courtesy of
Ophelia Dahl, from the author's collection.
Above, newspaper wedding photograph of
Roald Dahl and Patricia Neal, July 2, 1953.
From the Patricia Neal Collection.

Patricia Neal and Roald Dahl on their honeymoon in
Rome, July 1953. From the Patricia Neal Collection.

Massimo Girotti and Patricia Neal in the Italian-made picture *La tua donna*, 1954. From the Patricia Neal Collection.

Warren Berlinger, Patricia Neal, and Betty Lou Keim in *A Roomful of Roses*, 1955. From the Patricia Neal Collection.

Patricia Neal, Elia Kazan, and Anthony Franciosa in Arkansas in the summer of 1956 for *A Face In the Crowd*. Courtesy of Photofest.

Patricia Neal and Andy Griffth in *A Face In the Crowd*. From the author's collection.

Home in Great Missenden, England. Patricia is pregnant with Tessa and Roald is holding Olivia, 1957. From the Patricia Neal Collection.

Above left, Olivia Twenty Dahl, circa 1959. From the Patricia Neal Collection. *Above right,* Chantal Sophie "Tessa" Dahl, circa 1962. From the Patricia Neal Collection.

Things were coming easily for her again. And because they were, and because her life seemed fulfilled, Patricia worried. For her there were still demons.

Running into Gary on Fifth Avenue that October proved to be cathartic yet bittersweet to her; she couldn't stop thinking about the encounter. Something had ended that day at the St. Regis, and Patricia realized much had been lost of her years in Hollywood. She had not written a long, newsy letter to Jean Valentino and Chloe Carter, the two women whom she had long ago befriended, confided in, and experienced some of her darkest moments with, since she had left Hollywood. Shortly before the First Night Ball, Patricia sat down in her kitchen, after Roald and the baby were in bed, and wrote Jean and Chloe:

> Thank you for your Christmas cards. . . . Christmas night I had people to dinner for the first time since we returned from England. Olivia thought she was Portland Mason and I had dinner with her on my lap. Very much present was the center of the universe—else our ear drums would have been split. . . . She is, however, divine. . . . She is 8 months old now and not a tooth—which pleases me as they are supposed to be better teeth when they arrive late. She has great humor and vitality. Loves music. And is so loud mouth. Da-da-da all day long. . . .
>
> I loved pregnancy and I loved birth. I only have one horrible shame on my soul. That is my lack of guts five years ago. I still think I might have had that baby if there had been one voice telling me that knew that I should. Even today it is my great regret and I'm afraid I hold the four of us responsible. (And my middle class morality.) Which is, I'm sure, unfair—but it is probably why I haven't written all these years. Things tried to be forgotten. . . .
>
> I am really quite happy. I much prefer the theatre to movies and I go to the Actors Studio, which is stimulating. I have many good friends here. And they were so scarce in Hollywood.
>
> I have a beautiful husband and child. And we now have a nice place to live. We want at least two more babies.
>
> I am sure that—naturally—none of this would be if everything that happened hadn't caused each thing to fall into place.
>
> Yet you must understand how painful that period was for me and how closely—unfortunately—you were connected in my memory. All this is in way of explanation of my long silence.
>
> I just wanted to forget those years.

But I have two regrets now—firstly I mentioned—the baby. Secondly—I wish I had saved my money. . . .

Maybe I will be invited out by the film industry again one day and if so my husband and child just must come with me.

A Happy 1956!

Love, Pat[19]

Patricia and Jean and Chloe would keep in touch for the rest of their lives. They would share much happiness, and much sadness as well.

16

Career

I always should have been an equal partner. Well I'm gonna be an equal partner. And I want it on paper!

> —Marcia to Lonesome, *A Face in the Crowd* (1957)

Patricia and Roald spent part of the spring and summer of 1956 restoring their Georgian house, Little Whitefield. They added a small guesthouse, which Roald quickly turned into a workshop for restoration of antique mirrors. Roald's sister Alfhild gave them an old gypsy caravan, which they made into a playhouse for Olivia and the other children they were planning.

Before heading for England that year, Patricia had two acting jobs. The most significant one was replacing Barbara Bel Geddes in the demanding role of Maggie for three weeks during the spring, in Tennessee Williams's *Cat on a Hot Tin Roof* while Bel Geddes was vacationing in Spain. Patricia was the choice of director Elia Kazan, who had been impressed with her work at the Actors Studio. She took over the very long role on short notice, memorizing her lines on just six days' notice. There are no reviews of Patricia's portrayal of Maggie. Her performance is well remembered, however, by those who happened to see it. Said Eli Wallach many years later, "Patricia's performance in 'Cat' was stunning. She gave a much more honest performance of the desperate 'Maggie,' with more depth and understanding of the role than, in all respects, did Barbara Bel Geddes. Perhaps because she *is* a true southern woman."[1]

The play had opened March 24, 1955, starring Bel Geddes and Ben Gazzara. It went on to win the Pulitzer Prize for Best Play of 1955 for Williams.

Patricia also filmed an episode of the *Matinee Theatre* for NBC, "The Good-Time Boys," that finally aired on June 4, 1956. Adapted by Nicholas Baehr from a short story by Ira Avery, it told the story of the conflict between

---

Facing page: Patricia Neal in *A Face In the Crowd*, 1957. Courtesy of Photofest.

an established and well-respected publisher and his son. It was hosted by John Conte and costarred Addison Richards.

At Little Whitefield, soon to be called Gipsy House, Roald and Wally Saunders began remodeling a garden shed into a work space for Roald's writing. Roald wrote his friend Charles Marsh, "It's marvelous, isolated, and quiet."[2] After he completed the renovation, he told an interviewer, "It's a lovely place to work. It's small and tight and dark and the curtains are always drawn and it's kind of a womb—you go up here and you disappear and get lost."[3] Surrounded by his childhood trinkets and family pictures and mementos, this became Dahl's refuge from the world, a place where he would write and think—and also find momentary and precious solace during the bleak times to come.

His hut became his sanctuary, where he could be alone and create. Wrote Barry Farrell in his dual biography *Pat and Roald*, "Equipped with a thermos jug of hot coffee, he would stride the fifty paces from the house, light the Aladdin Blue Flame heater against the permanent chill of his hut, sharpen a half-dozen Dixon Ticonderogas to an accountant's taste and settle down into his chair."[4] All Dahl's writing was done in longhand on legal-size yellow writing pads. With steady concentration he would produce about three short stories, going through a gross of pencils, each year. Also in the hut was a lamp connected to the house. When it flashed once, it meant that someone at the house was asking for him. If it flashed twice, there was an emergency.

Over the years, Roald planted hundreds of varieties of roses on the property, as well as a vegetable garden with plenty of his favorite varieties of onions. He also renovated an outdoor teahouse into an aviary in an attempt to imitate the one at Moynes Park, the Elizabethan mansion of his friend Ivar Bryce, complete with several varieties of brilliantly colored budgerigars. "This was Olivia's special place," wrote Patricia in her memoirs. "She loved to come with me to feed the birds and help me clean. Her favorites were the rare, pure white and yellow parakeets that somehow were always disappearing. . . . For Olivia these vanishing beauties were like tiny angels who could evaporate at will."[5]

While at Little Whitefield, Patricia received a call from Elia Kazan asking if she could meet Budd Schulberg in Florida to discuss her possible return to pictures as the feminine lead in his upcoming film *A Face in the Crowd*. Cutting their stay in England short, Patricia and Olivia boarded a flight from Heathrow Airport to the States on July 22. When they arrived, they joined

Eura, Patricia's sister, NiNi, and her brother-in-law, George, at their home in Knoxville. Leaving Olivia with her relatives, the next day Patricia flew to Florida for two days to talk with Schulberg about the film.

"He liked my reading and me very much," said Patricia.[6] Kazan was hoping that the role in *A Face in the Crowd* would secure her place in the film industry again, and he told her, "It's a great part, Pat."[7] She accepted the role.

Schulberg and Kazan developed the script for *A Face in the Crowd* together, basing it on Schulberg's short story "Your Arkansas Traveler." Though he did not write a word of the dialogue, Kazan contributed the language of the film (the basic movement of the story and camera blocking). The character Lonesome Rhodes is loosely based on the bucolic humor of Bob Burns and the true-to-life behavior of Arthur Godfrey, a popular television and radio personality who was loved and revered by the nation's viewers and listeners but was secretly feared and hated by those who knew him within the industry.

Schulberg worked with Kazan on *On the Waterfront* (Columbia, 1954), and the two had agreed to work on another project. Kazan's concept of *A Face in the Crowd* was for a black comedy that made a political statement about the "hypnotic, terrible force" of television and personalities in mid-twentieth-century America.[8]

Marcia Jeffries (Neal) interviews jailhouse detainee Larry Rhodes (Andy Griffith) in Pickett, Arkansas, for her radio show, *A Face in the Crowd*. Nicknaming him "Lonesome" Rhodes, she recognizes his talents as a storyteller and singer and decides to develop him as a radio personality. As his popularity grows, so do Marcia's feelings for him. Rhodes signs with a local Memphis television station. His homeboy good looks, flirtatious charm, and unconventional humor catch on immediately. The viewing public loves his goodhearted jabs at his sponsor and his comments on politics and society in general.

When Lonesome is fired by his sponsor, his fans picket. Joey de Palma (Anthony Franciosa) gets him a job with another sponsor, Vitajex energy tablets, in New York. Lonesome Rhodes becomes a national television star. Marcia and Lonesome are now lovers. Marcia confides in Mel Miller (Walter Matthau), one of Lonesome's writers. Lonesome's on-air charm hides his ambition and cynicism from his adoring viewers. Lonesome turns into a corrupt megalomaniac, bullying his coworkers, drinking, and womanizing. Marcia accepts his faults and is unaware of his real self. He promises to marry her but takes up with teenage baton-twirler Betty Lou Fleckum (Lee Remick, in her film debut).

Marcia decides she must attempt to stop him. After a broadcast of his show, when the onstage microphones are turned off, Lonesome starts to belittle his viewing public with sarcastically cruel remarks. He is mumbling under his breath to others on the set as the credits roll over his smiling face. In the control booth, Marcia throws the sound levers up to full volume, and Lonesome's disparaging remarks about the public are broadcast coast to coast, destroying his career.

Patricia was determined to give an outstanding performance in the film. She felt that Kazan offered her a second chance in an industry that had snubbed her, and she was going to show the critics and the studios that she could deliver. Filming began on *A Face in the Crowd* on location in Piggott, Arkansas (called "Pickett" in the film), on August 13. Patricia learned that the filming would take only three months. And she was excited about what she had learned during wardrobe fittings: she was once again pregnant. She wired the news to Roald in England.

It was sweltering in Arkansas during the ten days the company filmed there, shooting interior and exterior scenes. On the first day on the set, the stars—Patricia and film newcomers Griffith and Franciosa—met for the first time to read through the script. After the read-through, Kazan worked with Griffith on Lonesome's final scenes. On the last day of shooting in Arkansas, August 23, a catwalk Patricia was on collapsed over a cattle pen during the filming of a scene (not used in the film) where Marcia runs through cattle to catch a train. Filming came to a tense halt. "Even while I was still lying there in the mud it occurred to me that I had probably scared the heck out of the whole crew," she told a reporter that evening. "I knew they could just see all that investment gone to pot and men having to start over with a new girl in my role."[9] She suffered scratches on her leg and hands and a bruise on her face, as another woman in the scene had fallen on top of her. Patricia was quickly checked out by a doctor and given the a-okay. Filming resumed, and that evening the company moved on to Memphis for a few days of shooting at such locations as the exterior automobile entrance of the Hotel Peabody, the Magnolia Roof of the Hotel Claridge, Beale Street, and Handy Park.

In New York, at the newly refurbished D. W. Griffith Biograph Studios on East 175th Street in the Bronx, the company continued filming. (There were some additional scenes shot on location at the Iverson Ranch in Chatsworth, California.) Filming was completed on Tuesday, November 20, 1956, at a film negative cost of $1.75 million.

Griffith recalled, "Every scene, everything I did with Patricia, brought me up. Everything! I'll always love her for doing that."[10] One scene in particular with Patricia, Griffith remembers, was hard for him to do. He recalls that she was pregnant while they filmed the realization scene, when Marcia sees Lonesome for the despicable character he truly is. Dressed only in a dark slip, she frantically grabs a coat and rushes out into the rain. Griffith remembered he felt bad that he had to yell at her like he did in the scene.

Patricia recalled she had to slap Franciosa in one scene. Slaps are usually choreographed so the actor receiving the slap will pull back as if actually hit, with sound added later, but Kazan told Patricia to really haul off and hit the actor. Patricia gave it everything she had. Franciosa, stunned by the force of the slap, began to cry. Patricia recalled, "He was utterly fantastic. But when the camera stopped, he kept on crying and cried all through lunch. I felt terrible. I wanted to tell him what a great job he'd done, but he wouldn't come near me. I'm sure he thought I was a number one bitch."[11] Unfortunately, the scene was not used in the film.

Franciosa remembered that Kazan wanted a close-up reaction shot of shock on Patricia's face for a particular scene. After telling cinematographer Harry Stradling exactly what he wanted, Kazan told Franciosa to do the scene with an unscripted curse word to get a reaction from Patricia. "Patricia stayed in complete control, with only a flicker in her eye," Franciosa recalled. "She was so professional."[12]

Patricia worked hard for Kazan in *A Face in the Crowd*. Her character is rich, fully developed, and convincing from the start. In several scenes, the actual heat on the set added to the film's realism, and Patricia's character sweated and fussed, as did everyone else. Patricia had two very well-played scenes with Walter Matthau as well as two telling scenes with Griffith. As both are played with her character dressed in nightgowns, the devastating sensuality of her character is evident. When Lonesome comes to Marcia at the hotel late at night after being fired, Patricia, dressed in a light-colored nightgown, her hair messed and stringy, is photographed beautifully. "Don't play with me. Don't hurt me. . . . Don't hurt me," she pleads.

Patricia's best scene, when Marcia pulls the sound levers to reveal Lonesome's loathsome comments to the viewing public, was also a very physically strenuous one. As Marcia hears his vile remarks about the viewing audience, she senses her opportunity. As she pulls the levers, the script called for two soundmen to pull her away. "The scene began, and when I grabbed the handles on the board, I felt the pulling at my back, my arms, my shoulders. Those two guys were strong, all right. I hung on with all the determination of an animal holding fiercely to its kill. Finally, the terrifying weight from behind succeeded in pulling me off and I burst into tears, certain that I had let Kazan down," Patricia recalled in her memoir.[13]

Patricia's performance was heralded in the press even before the film was released. Said director Kazan about Patricia in an interview with Edwin Schallert of the *Los Angeles Times*, "She is actually a very warm, very human person. The prevailing estimate when she previously appeared in pictures, namely that she was a cold individual, is totally wrong." Wrote Radie Harris in her column for the *Hollywood Reporter*, "Pat Neal isn't a new face to Hollywood but will have a new lease on her career."[14]

Settled back in Gipsy House, the Dahls waited for their next baby, whom they thought just might arrive on Olivia's second birthday. That was not to be, however, and on April 11, Chantal Sophie was born at the Radcliffe Hospital in Oxford. When she was christened shortly after, Patricia's dear friend Betsy Drake was made her godmother. Patricia talked to the press about guests she and her husband were entertaining, "I seldom go into London, I am so happy in the country, but we always have houseguests. Last week, Betsy Drake visited us and the week before we had Julie Harris."[15]

Three months after the baby's christening, having discovered that "Chantal Dahl" rhymed, the family started calling the infant Tessa. Patricia's mother came over to England shortly after the baby's birth, and friction between Eura and Roald was soon evident. Eura chastised him for his apparent obsession with the wealthy, and he complained about her rich southern cooking. Patricia recalls that Eura and Mormor hit it off, however, and would remain friends until their deaths. For his part, Roald was always happy to see Eura leave. When the summer came, the family traveled to Norway on the first of what became annual visits—to fish, swim, and visit Roald's family.

Late summers in England included family gatherings; visits with Roald's mother, Sofie, at her home in a wing of Whitefield; the home of Roald's sister Else and her husband, John; picnics by the Thames with all of Roald's sisters' children; and trips to the Cotswolds, where Roald could often be found playing snooker with men from the village. There were also greyhound races at White City. The girls were sometimes left with their nanny so that Roald and Patricia could drive down to London for dinner and the theater. One evening, while dining with Sir Matthew Smith at the exclusive restaurant Prunier's, Patricia remarked that she adored the silver sugar tongs at their table. Roald pocketed them, and after a waiter unsuccessfully approached Sir Matthew, not Roald, about the theft, they left.

Roald and Patricia also spent time at the Moyns Park estate of his good friend Ivar Bryce and his heiress wife, Josephine. The two couples would stay up late at night enjoying each other's company and playing cards. The next morning, they were served large English country breakfasts in bed by the Bryce servants. The Dahls also befriended Richard Kirwan, his wife, Patricia, and their two children; the son was close to the same age as Olivia and Tessa. The Kirwans farmed on the other side of the hill from Gipsy House. Patricia remembers calling out to Richard when they first became friends, "Would you care for tea, Brigadier?"[16] The title "Brigadier" stuck.

The world premiere of *A Face in the Crowd* was held in New York at the Globe Theatre on May 28. At the closing of *A Roomful of Roses,* Patricia wrote, "It should have had a better run but this season is so crazily crowded with hits there is no room for a medium success."[17] The same could be said of *A Face in the Crowd.* By 1957, though television had indeed taken its toll on the motion picture industry and fewer films were being produced, the quality of many of the releases was very high. Big blockbusters that year were *The Bridge on the River Kwai, The Three Faces of Eve, Peyton Place, Sayonara, Twelve Angry Men, A Hatful of Rain, A Farewell to Arms, Love in the Afternoon* (with Gary Cooper), and *Heaven Knows Mr. Allison.* The reviews for *A Face in the Crowd* were mixed, and the film did not do the business Warners had projected.

Said David Bongard in his *New York Mirror* review, "Patricia Neal is the best we've ever seen her as the woman to whom Griffith runs whenever he is in trouble."[18] William K. Zinsser of the *New York Herald Tribune* wrote, "Patricia Neal is excellent as the girl who launched, loved and lost the hillbilly, and she covers many moods from the girlish exhilaration of the first months to the bleak despair of the last."[19] In his *New York Daily Mirror* review, Justin Gilbert wrote, "Patricia Neal, too, is brilliantly triumphant in her role of the well-educated small-town girl."[20]

The picture opened in Los Angeles in May at the Downtown Paramount, the Egyptian, the Wiltern, the Pasadena Academy, the Westwood Village, and the Westchester Paradise theaters, as well as at seven drive-ins (on a double bill with the Warner Brothers Randolph Scott oater *Shoot-Out at Medicine Bend*). It was obvious that *A Face in the Crowd,* though widely distributed, was simply not going to be promoted or given an important push by Warner Brothers. Said Edwin Schallert in his *Los Angeles Times* review, "Far and away outstanding in their stellar performances are Griffith, Miss Neal and Matthau, with Franciosa also very capable. They are nearly all at their peaks in their interpretations, even though the actual reading of lines is not too easy to understand at times. Schulberg has, however, written a splendid screen-play, and the picture is by far one of Kazan's most penetrating and inciden-tally ironic."[21]

Today, the story line of *A Face in the Crowd* is dated. Television audi-ences, now having had their fill of discredited televangelists, are far more adept at sniffing out sham than those of the 1950s. But for its time, *A Face in the Crowd* was groundbreaking. From the opening shot of Lonesome in the jailhouse, drunkenly asleep while hugging his guitar, until the last shot of the taxi pulling away from his New York penthouse, the film is raw, unnerv-ing, and completely compelling. Selecting his unconventional actors from the ranks of the best performers available, Kazan also struck gold with his uncanny ability to bring out performances so real and gritty that, even today, they jar one's sensibilities and judgment. When Lonesome is kicked awake in the opening shot, Griffith reacts as if he were a cat on its back, ready to fight.

Considered today a flawed masterpiece, by 1960 *A Face in the Crowd* had only earned back $1.3 million. The picture completely lost out in the Oscar race, without a single nomination. Elia Kazan, though, was nominated for Outstanding Directorial Achievement in 1958 by the Directors Guild of America.

Before leaving England for the States in September, Patricia attended the Eu-ropean premiere of *A Face in the Crowd* held at the Regal Cinema in Edin-burgh, Scotland. Roald did not attend the event with her, preferring to play the dogs at White City. When asked if she and Roald were planning any more children, Patricia replied, "Another one, but we couldn't keep crossing the Atlantic with half a dozen. It is so much less expensive living in England." Asked if she ever thought of retiring, she replied, "The idea of never work-ing again does not appeal to me. It is a terrible thing for an actress—you can never quit happily."[22]

By 1957 the Dahls had taken an apartment that was being vacated by Pa-tricia's friend Mildred Dunnock at 26 East Eighty-second Street in the third-oldest apartment building in Manhattan. The eight-story, fifteen-unit build-ing, with two apartments on each floor, was situated on Madison Avenue across from the Campbell Funeral Chapel and just down the street from the American Museum of Natural History and Central Park. The Dahls, whose apartment was on the fourth floor, found it a perfect space for their grow-ing family. Their rent was approximately $182 a month and never exceeded $250. Their apartment had high ceilings and huge rooms, including three bedrooms, a maid's room, and a large living room with doors opening into the dining room. Patricia once hosted a party for more than a hundred guests and had space to spare. This was their home in the United States for nearly ten years.

17

Triumph

[Acting is] everything! They'll tell you it isn't—your fancy friends—but it's a lie! And they know it's a lie! They'd give their ears to be in your place! Don't make any mistake about that!

—Fanny, *The Royal Family* (1927)

Roald Dahl submitted a total of seven stories to the *New Yorker* between February 1957 and March 1959. All were rejected. Wrote Jeremy Treglown, "Dahl was being pressed by Alfred Knopf to put together a new collection [of short stories] but told the publisher that he found ideas harder and harder to come by and was beginning to fear that they would run out altogether."[1] The salary Patricia had earned for her role in *A Face in the Crowd* would only go so far, especially now that the Dahls' lifestyle was so expensive to maintain.

Patricia had to work. Much of her acting was in television, and much of it was done in California, so she spent a fair amount of time flying between New York and Hollywood.

In the fall of 1957, she flew to California for a role in the excellent television anthology *Playhouse 90*. In an episode entitled "The Playroom," Patricia played Margaret Flood, an Oscar-winning actress, who, along with her brothers, Kenneth (Tony Randall) and George Rutherford (Charles Drake), returns to her childhood home, where her mother (Mildred Dunnock) is receiving a Mother of the Year award from a national magazine. In their former playroom, the three siblings confront issues that have haunted them since their youth. Margaret and her mother have issues that are irreparable. "You're so perfect I could strangle you," Margaret tells her mother. Kenneth, the youngest and the most obviously spoiled of the three, has ruined his successful criminal law career by having an affair with a notorious woman. After

---

Facing page: Patricia Neal in *Breakfast At Tiffany's*, 1961. From the author's collection.

a confrontation with his mother, Kenneth runs off with the woman, and the two are killed in a car wreck. Margaret must deliver the news right before the award ceremony at the house, where the press has already gathered. The mother, knowing that she is not worthy of the award, must accept it just the same.

The episode was directed by Franklin Schaffner and produced by Martin Margulis. The teleplay, specially written for the broadcast, was by Tad Mosel, whose Broadway play *All The Way Home* won the 1961 Pulitzer Prize for Drama.

The episode, which aired October 10, was recorded live, a practice not without its hazards. During the first part of the performance, the three children all refer to Mildred Dunnock's character as "Mother." Perhaps because of their close friendship, in one particularly tense scene between the two women, Patricia turns to Dunnock and calls her "Millie." The other actors quickly picked up on what appears to have been a mistake, and throughout the rest of the play, they all call Dunnock's character "Millie," as if it were very normal to address their mother by her first name.

In 2003 Tony Randall remembered Patricia as "a big, bouncy girl, absolutely full of fun. She was much given to play and laughter—just full of laughter and fun and mischief."[2]

Returning to New York in mid-October, Patricia busied herself with the day-to-day lives of her children and her husband, who was now writing for television.

Soon after the holidays, Patricia flew back to the West Coast to guest star in "Someone Is After Me" on the short-lived drama series *Suspicion*, broadcast from the NBC Studios in Hollywood. In "Someone Is After Me," written by Robert Soderberg and directed by David Greene, Patricia played Paula Elgin, a housewife who starts receiving anonymous telephone calls threatening her life. These calls only happen when she is alone. She then begins to believe that they are from either her family, including her husband Guy Elgin (Lee Bowman), or her neighbors. Also in the cast was Joanne Linville as Lois. The episode aired on Monday, January 6, 1958.

Just one week after returning home, Patricia was back in Hollywood for her second *Playhouse 90* episode, "The Gentleman from Seventh Avenue," directed by Alan Reisner. Successful dress manufacturer Mr. Golden (Walter Slezak) finds his attractive designer, Rena Menken (Neal), in tears. She has fallen for the firm's Lothario salesman, Morris Kogen (Robert Alda). Mr. Golden innocently takes Rena out for dinner and a few drinks to comfort her. But the news that they were seen together in public is misinterpreted by

Mr. Golden's family—his wife (Sylvia Sidney); his son, Elbaum (Lawrence Dobkin); and daughter, Jenny (Judy Nugent). Even Kogen is shocked by his boss's "escapade." Eventually, the facts are sorted out.

Patricia's hair was styled very short and curly and was not becoming, and her wardrobe was rather plain. But her face told the story, and her acting was natural and instinctive.

Written by Elick Moll and produced by Martin Manulis, the comedy was introduced by actress Dana Wynter. The episode aired January 30 and, with its superb cast and well-written script, was favorably reviewed. Said Raus in *Variety*, "Elick Moll, who fashioned 'The Gentleman From Seventh Avenue' . . . had excellent support in all departments, acting, directing, and production. . . . Walter Slezak . . . played it superbly well. In fact, the entire cast . . . turned 'The Gentleman from Seventh Avenue' into a high-grade piece of dramatic goods. . . . [Among the] standout scenes were the underplayed drunk bit by Miss Neal; the bedroom conversation between husband and wife, and the crisp cracks of the salesman on the make. This offering humanized the garment industry. It was indeed hand-tailoring by scriptwriter Moll."[3]

Critic Marie Torre wrote, "'Playhouse 90' spun a warm-mannered sometimes delightful presentation out of Elick Moll's 'The Gentleman from Seventh Avenue.' . . . As the designer, Patricia Neal embodied the lonely girl in the big city with a measure of conviction."[4]

Hedda Hopper announced in her column that Patricia told her that the broadcast was so successful that there was talk of expanding it into a Broadway play, but the idea never progressed beyond that stage.

In February Patricia was once more before the television cameras, this time in New York, for an episode on CBS's *Studio One*, "Tide of Corruption," about crooked politicians. In mid-March CBS announced that Patricia would appear in an episode, "So Deadly My Love," of its hit series *Climax!* but at the last minute Kim Hunter was given the role. Written by Marc Brendel, the episode aired Monday, February 17. In mid-April, Roald's teleplay of "Lamb to the Slaughter" (based on his short story first published in 1953 in *Harper's*) aired on *Alfred Hitchcock Presents,* starring Barbara Bel Geddes. The episode earned both Roald and director Hitchcock Emmy Award nominations for 1958.

Patricia and Roald departed in April for their usual six months abroad. While in England, Patricia was scheduled to make a picture and appear in several BBC television productions. The family settled back into the summer routine at their Great Missenden home, Gipsy House.

Patricia made her British television acting debut in the BBC production of S. N. Behrman's delightful adaptation of his 1932 Broadway comedy *Biography*. Produced by John Jacobs for the popular *Sunday-Night Theatre*, *Biography* is about Marion Froude (Neal), a renowned young portrait artist who has traveled the world and is now living in New York. A national magazine wants to interest her in publishing a serialized version of her life story. However, there are several important and prominent men in her life, including Richard Kurt (Vivian Matalon) and Leander Nolan (Gordon Sterne), who would likely feel compromised by her revelations.

For this television adaptation, Patricia was fashionably dressed in several scenes. The sets were lush and the production stylish and expensively presented. It drew a huge audience when it aired on June 22; everyone wanted to get a look at the American wife of Britain's famous short-story writer Roald Dahl.

Later that summer, Patricia appeared in another *Sunday-Night Theatre* production, *The Royal Family of Broadway,* an adaptation of the stage play by Edna Ferber and George S. Kaufman. *The Royal Family,* a comedy loosely based on the lives and peccadilloes of the Barrymore family, had been a great hit on Broadway, running for 345 performances after its opening at the Selwyn Theatre on December 28, 1927. The 1930 film, directed by George Cukor and Cyril Gardner, was a major box-office hit.

In the live BBC production, Patricia was Julia Cavendish, a daughter in a famed theatrical family. The family's matriarch, stage actress Fanny Cavendish (Fay Compton), has been unable to perform for two years and walks with a cane. Julia and her daughter, Gwen (Eira Heath), are about to star in a play together, but Gwen is engaged to a young stockbroker, Perry Stewart (Michael Sands), and is having doubts about her career. Perry wants her to leave the stage. Julia's suitor, the bon vivant Gilbert Marshall (Jon Farrell), likewise wants Julia to quit the stage and marry him. And Julia's flamboyant younger brother, the film matinee idol Tony (Peter Wyngarde), has recently caused a great scandal and is being sued for breach of promise. By the third act, Tony has left for India to avoid his problems, Julia continues with her career, Gwen decides whether she should marry her young stockbroker fiancé, and Fanny returns to the stage.

Patricia loved the grand old actress, Fay Compton, who played Fanny. The sixty-three-year-old Compton could be very haughty to anyone she didn't like. But she and Patricia got along "fantastically."[5] During rehearsals, Patricia told Fay about a very expensive turquoise necklace Roald had given her after he'd made a killing at the dog tracks. Patricia proudly wore the necklace to a very swanky party, where another actress made a big fuss over the new jewels. Patricia lent them to her to wear the rest of the evening. A jeweler approached the actress and asked to take a closer look at the necklace. As if he'd placed his hands on a hot stove, he withdrew them quickly. The actress told Patricia and Roald about it when she returned the necklace. When Roald stuck a pin into one of the stones, it went right through. He was furious he'd been taken, although the jeweler tried to make amends. Compton found the story hilarious, and at the end of the filming of *The Royal Family of Broadway,* she presented Patricia with an exquisite turquoise necklace.

In return, Patricia, who knew that Compton loved small dogs with large floppy ears, gave her a puppy at the wrap party. "How dare you give me that thing!" exclaimed Compton to the shocked Patricia. "What am I going to do with that!"[6] Compton kept the dog and loved it dearly until it died some seventeen years later.

The Royal Family of Broadway was broadcast on August 3. Reviews were favorable. Wrote one British television critic, "The pace was brisk yet the sentimental scenes were given their due, and the many domestic rows in the temperamental family were unusually spontaneous. Further, [producer and director] Mr. [Eric] Fawcett had obviously realized that in Patricia Neal he had an exciting actress in very fine form. He saw to it that she was, as part and performance demanded, admirably caught by the cameras, some close-ups being especially effective. Not only did Miss Neal look radiantly the successful actress she was portraying; she also sounded like one, making her lines seem a good deal more natural than others in the cast. This no doubt was largely because she is an American, whereas other parts were mostly in the hands of English actors, struggling with the accent."[7]

By the end of August, Patricia was deeply involved in stage rehearsals of *Garden District,* a new work by American playwright Tennessee Williams, first presented on the American stage earlier in the year in New York. *Garden District* consisted of two one-act plays, *Something Unspoken* and *Suddenly Last Summer.* She had been asked by director Herbert Machiz to appear in *Suddenly Last Summer* and was eager to make her British stage debut. *Garden District* opened at the Arts Theatre Club on Great Newport Street in London on Tuesday, September 16, 1958.

Suddenly Last Summer opens in the tropical, lush garden of the home of wealthy Mrs. Violet Venable (Beatrix Lehmann). She has asked Dr. Cukrowicz (David Cameron) to her home to talk about her niece, Catharine Holly (Neal). Mrs. Venable wants Catharine to submit to a lobotomy to rid her of her delusions about the death of Venable's son, Sebastian, a poet. Catharine had accompanied Sebastian to the small island of Cabeza de Lobos during the last summer of his life. She says his death is too terrible to imagine. Her suggestions about what happened to him are too vile to believe.

Catharine has been released from an asylum and arrives at her aunt Violet's home, where she is joined by her mother (Beryl Measor) and her brother, George (Philip Bond). George tells Catharine that Aunt Violet will give them $50,000 if Catharine agrees to be admitted to the asylum and submit to a lobotomy. Dr. Cukrowitz administers a truth serum to Catharine, and the horrific story emerges.

Catharine's memory gives up the horror she has witnessed: Sebastian used her, and possibly his own mother, to procure young boys for his sexual appetite during annual summer excursions. At Cabeza de Lobo the young boys lived naked and hungry on the beach. Suddenly last summer, Catharine witnessed those hungry youths turn on Sebastian, chase him through the white-hot streets of the town, and eventually catch him. His naked body is discovered, parts of it devoured by the hungry young men. The young doctor believes Catharine and realizes it is Mrs. Venable who is deranged.

"How I wanted to do that role," Patricia wrote. "If for no other reason than the last scene, which is in fact a fifteen-minute monologue. I was back to my roots. Herbert staged the scene very simply, with only a single spotlight on my face. I remember I acted my heart out to that single beam of light shining down on me.

"On opening night, the curtain went down slowly and there was what seemed an eternity of silence. Then the applause came, rolling over us like thunder. It was the crowning moment of what was, for me, the most thrilling acting experience of my life."[8]

Garden District, especially *Suddenly Last Summer,* did indeed create a sensation. London's West End sported more than forty active theaters, compared to New York's twenty-odd. Tickets in London were still around $3, and audiences were hungry for new and exciting productions, which were scarce—so scarce that theater critic Kenneth Tynan had told *Holiday* magazine a couple of years before, "There is nothing wrong with the London theatre that a couple of masterpieces couldn't cure."[9] *Garden District* was one such production, and it stunned London audiences, although its combination of homosexuality, cannibalism, and insanity was not for everyone.

Patricia received the strongest reviews of her career. One critic wrote, "British theatre critics squirmed . . . [and] termed the play 'squalid,' 'slimy,' and 'lurid.' But they praised the dramatic power of the work and raved about the performance of Hollywood actress Patricia Neal, who made her London debut in the role of Catharine Holly."[10] Said Cecil Wilson in his *London Daily Mail* review, "One thing to be said at once for *Suddenly Last Summer*, the longer, grimmer and better of these two new plays in one, is that it introduces Patricia Neal to the London stage. We have suffered with this American actress in films like *The Hasty Heart* and *A Face in the Crowd*. We have admired her intelligent beauty on TV. And last night we saw her playing, quite brilliantly, one of the most tortured women Tennessee Williams ever created. . . . The strength of Patricia Neal's performance last night lay in her agonized—and agonizing—picture of a maligned person protesting her sanity to the very edge of sanity."[11]

Other reviews were in much the same vein. Milton Shulman in the *London Evening Standard* said, "Patricia Neal brings a quivering intensity to the role of the niece that haunts like a high-pitched scream in the night."[12] John Barber, the *Daily Express:* "An unscripted cry of 'Help!' tore from the throat of actress Patricia Neal last night to climax the latest melodrama by Tennessee Williams. She seemed to have terrified herself with the horror of what she was saying." *Suddenly Last Summer,* Barber wrote, "is the most insane, the most lurid, and the most shock-creating [play] that even this author has achieved. It held the audience frozen stiff in the black sorcery of explosive words, most of them spoken by . . . Miss Neal."[13]

And Harold Conroy, of the *London Daily Sketch*, said of the concluding monologue, "Brilliantly spoken and acted, it was the most horrible, loathsome speech I have heard in any theatre."[14]

In the *London Tribune*, reviewer Weyland Young wrote, "Sometimes in a torrent of velocity which reminded me of the records of Sarah Bernhardt, sometimes convulsed, gurgling after the loaded word, sometime dispersing her whole personality among the characters whose words she was repeating, so that she *had* for a moment in her throat an angry man or a frightened little girl, and sometimes laying out across us like a bell tolling the life-slow, death-simple monosyllables which crown this awful vision, she brought a range and a control to the job which we do not often see on the London stage."[15]

It was left to *London Observer* critic Kenneth Tynan to place Patricia among the demigods of the theater: "I must pause here to salute Patricia Neal, the American Method actress who plays the girl. The power and variety of her dark brown voice, on which she plays like a master on the cello, enable her to separate the cadenza from its context and make of it a plangent cry from the depths of memory. Rhetoric and realism, in this harrowing performance, not only fuse but fertilize each other. . . . Mr. Williams, whose specialty is hysteria precariously held in check by formal habits of speech, has given Miss Neal some of his richest prose—a *symphonie en blanc majeur,* in which image after image of blazing pallor evokes the climate of Sebastian's death."[16]

During the six-week run of the play, the audiences, too, were mesmerized by Patricia's performance. Wrote one admirer:

> When I read the criticisms of 'Suddenly Last Summer,' I had no idea that I was going to see a performance I should always remember.
>
> Whatever were the difficulties of writing the part of Catharine Holly they could hardly compare with the arduous task of acting it. That you accomplished it goes without saying, but what needs to be said is that you did it magnificently.
>
> From the moment you came on the stage you imprisoned everybody's attention, and it is no exaggeration to say that when the other characters spoke they appeared as impertinent interrupters.
>
> One can only thank you for what must be described as a soul-stirring performance and a great revelation.[17]

So impressed by Patricia's performance in *Suddenly Last Summer* was film producer Sam Speigel that he purchased the movie rights, with the idea of filming Patricia in the role for Columbia Pictures in London in 1959. He sent people over from the States to watch Patricia in every performance, and Gore Vidal was assigned to write the screenplay. So it was with great shock that Patricia read on the flight home to the United States that the part had been given to Elizabeth Taylor. "Losing that film was the hardest professional blow of my life," she wrote.[18]

Back in New York in the autumn, the Dahls settled into their Manhattan apartment routine. Whatever the critical acclaim for her work on the London stage, the monetary awards were small, and the play had generated no great demand for her services. Theatrical producer Terese Hayden commented in 2003, "Patricia's work in *Suddenly Last Summer* was superb. But the British stage for some reason just never translates to American audiences."[19] According to Patricia's memoirs, she was considered for a role in a Broadway play that did not pan out. However, CBS called for her services, and, needing the work, she immediately flew to California to tape an episode of the anthology *Pursuit,* "The Silent Night," directed by Buzz Kulik and produced by Charles Russell.

The hour-long drama starred Patricia with Lew Ayres and two of her previous leading men: Frank Lovejoy, from the movies, and Victor Jory, from real life. The teleplay by Paul Monash told of John Conrad (Ayres), a patient in a mental asylum who has applied for a permit to return home for the holidays to be with his wife (Neal), who is being wooed by a suitor (Eduard Franz). The request is denied, and Conrad escapes, dressed like Santa Claus to avoid authorities. He is pursued by a police sergeant (Jory) who irrationally hates mental patients and considers Conrad a killer, and a doctor (Lovejoy), who is trying to locate Conrad before the cop does.

The episode aired on Christmas Eve 1958. *Variety* found the story line itself weak but generally praised the actors' performances, noting that "Kulik and the cast couldn't plug enough script holes quickly enough to bring this one off."[20]

At their fourth-floor apartment, the Dahls soon discovered they had new neighbors, Geoffrey and Sonia Austrian and their daughters. Shortly after the Austrians moved in, Roald and Tessa met Sonia waiting at the elevator with her daughter Susie. "How old is *that*?" Roald asked Sonia. "*That* is two," replied the mother. "So is *that*," said Roald, pointing to Tessa. "They must play together."[21] The two families became close friends, and their children were inseparable. Patricia and Sonia became New York mothers, taking their girls to the movies, to the circus on early Saturday mornings, and to Central Park, where the girls loved to climb all over the Alice in Wonderland statue.

"Tessa would arrive at our apartment every Saturday morning," recalled Sonia. "I would say to her, 'Tessa, did you have breakfast yet?,' and she would always say 'Oh, no!' and she'd be fed another. The children were very good to be with."[22] On one circus outing at Madison Square Garden, Olivia just had to have a pet chameleon as a souvenir. It quickly became lost in the taxicab on the ride back uptown. "There was mass hysteria," laughed Sonia years later, "until we found the creature under the cabdriver's seat."[23] Patricia added, "The driver of course left the meter running until we found the animal. It was the most expensive chameleon ever bought!"[24]

Roald could really talk to the children, in a dry and knowing manner, Sonia recalled, sometimes telling them stories. He was working at the time on his first children's book, *James and the Giant Peach*, based on some of those stories.

In early March, the family returned to England, and Patricia went back to work. Roald's own career and finances were slowly improving, but not as quickly as he would have liked. The couple began to have frequent arguments around this time, especially when they had had a few too many drinks.

The arguments were mainly about Patricia's continuous work schedule and Roald's frustration that he was not earning as much as she did.

Patricia's first project in England in 1959 was an appearance on the popular joint American-British television series *Rendezvous,* which had debuted on Britain's ITV network in 1958. The thirty-minute weekly dramatic anthology starred American actor Charles Drake as John Burden, an American writer living in the south of France whose experiences are the plots of each story. The first thirteen episodes of the series had been filmed in the United States; the following twenty-five episodes were shot in 1959 for MGM at Elstree Studios in England.

Patricia appeared in the thirty-sixth episode, "London–New York," starring as Kate Merlin. The cast also featured a young, up-and-coming actor named Peter O'Toole, who had just made a name for himself on stage in London's West End, in *The Long and the Short and the Tall.*

"London–New York" takes place at a London airport, where a flight has been delayed for fifteen hours by fog. When the passengers are finally allowed to board the plane, attractive Kate Merlin (Neal) is seated next to a charming, debonair young fellow named John (O'Toole), whose flirtatious manner catches her attention. Once airborne, the flight runs into trouble, and the passengers are faced with impending disaster. The gripping episode, produced by Edwin K. Knopf and directed by Fletcher Markle, employed a quasi–Eugene O'Neill *Strange Interlude* style, with voice-overs revealing the thoughts of the distressed passengers; before the fade-out, John and Kate declare their love for each other aloud.

Because of major television actors strikes in the United Kingdom, "London–New York" did not air until 1961. By that time O'Toole was on the road to stardom; his breakthrough film, *Lawrence of Arabia,* was released the next year.

Shortly before filming commenced on "London–New York," Patricia was contacted by the American stage director Arthur Penn and asked to audition for a role in the new production of *The Miracle Worker,* set to debut on Broadway in the fall. Patricia was surprised that she wasn't offered the role of Annie Sullivan, which went to Anne Bancroft, but was instead asked to play Helen's mother, Kate Keller. She hadn't done a film in three years, and it had been five years since she'd performed on stage in the United States. On May 27 she signed with producer Fred Coe to costar in *The Miracle Worker.*

While filming "London–New York" at Elstree Studios, Patricia learned that Gary Cooper was shooting *The Wreck of the Mary Deare* on another set and went to see him. Shown to a chair, Patricia waited for Charlton Heston and Gary to finish a scene. Heston said to Cooper, "Patricia Neal is here."[25] Gary left the set and sat down beside her. The two were courteous to each other, Patricia recalled. He held her hand, and she told him she had just wanted to see him once more. As he showed her to her car, Patricia realized that he was a part of her life before, but now he wasn't. There were no second thoughts. She never saw him again.

Before leaving for the States to start rehearsing *The Miracle Worker*, Patricia filmed Clifford Odets's *Clash by Night* for BBC television. The production was directed by John Jacobs, and Odets had done the adaptation of his failed 1941 Broadway play. In the teleplay, Patricia portrayed Mae Wilenski, who is unhappily married to the older, none-too-smart Jerry Wilenski (Nehemiah Persoff). Settled into poverty and domesticity on Staten Island in 1941, during the hot summer nights Mae can find relief only through a couple of bottles of beer or a night at the movies. She is sexually discontent and wants more than Jerry's doggedly dull devotion. Jerry's best friend, smooth, smart-talking movie theater projectionist Earl Pfeiffer (Sam Wanamaker), moves in with Jerry and Mae and proceeds to seduce her. Jerry finds out and becomes enraged but eventually finds it in himself to forgive Earl. But when he seeks Earl out to explain this, he is met with such hostility that he is forced once more into wrath—and murder.

When it aired on July 7, the ninety-minute play was exceptionally well received. The ensemble work of Patricia, Persoff, and Wanamaker was heralded as "quality stuff that would have swept the board if an Oscar were given for trios."[26] Said A. V. Coton in the *Daily Telegraph*, "Miss Neal and Mr. Persoff played the tortured and torturing married pair with a seething intensity that never veered into exaggeration for a moment. Their performances, and most of the play itself, ought to make a morsel of television history."[27]

Patricia returned to the United States at the end of July. While waiting for rehearsals of *The Miracle Worker* to begin, she attended some of the new shows in town, including Elia Kazan's recent hit play *Sweet Bird of Youth*, starring Paul Newman and Geraldine Page.

Backstage at *Sweet Bird of Youth*, Patricia ran into actress Elizabeth Wilson. As Wilson related the incident, "We were glad to see each other. . . . I was nowhere . . . just nowhere. And [Patricia] said, 'You're still going back to Barter? How do you do that?' or something like that, and I thought, 'Oh, God—yeah, it's true. I ain't anyplace.'" As Wilson was walking over to Fifth Avenue to take a bus home, "A taxi came by . . . and it was Patricia. And she said, 'Bye, Eleanor.' At the time there was a well-known older actress named

Eleanor Wilson. And I thought, 'Oh, shit!' I mean, she doesn't even remember my name!" continued Wilson. "Well, about ten minutes later she had that taxi driver . . . drive back around and [she] found me in the middle of a block and said, 'I know you're Elizabeth. I know you're Liz. I just got mixed up with Eleanor. I'm sorry baby.'" That story, Wilson said, "is quintessential Patricia Neal."[28]

Rehearsals for *The Miracle Worker* were scheduled to start August 17. *The Miracle Worker* was based on the teleplay of the same name written by William Gibson and presented on CBS's *Playhouse 90* in 1957. Expanded into a three-act drama for the stage, the play tells the well-known story of Helen Keller (Patty Duke), and her teacher, Annie Sullivan (Anne Bancroft), who leads Helen out of her dark, wordless world. Torin Thatcher played Helen's father, Captain Keller, and Neal her mother, Kate.

Director Arthur Penn and Anne Bancroft asked Patricia out for a drink shortly after rehearsals began and asked her frankly if she was miffed at being cast in a secondary role. She told them candidly that she was but that she realized this was an opportunity to work steadily in a play that seemed destined to be a hit. And she truly liked Bancroft. Both darkly attractive, the two were not dissimilar in appearance (Bancroft was a couple of inches shorter than Patricia), and they shared the same sense of ironic humor and dramatic intensity.

Patricia did the most she could with what few lines she had. She had a bit of trouble with one particularly demanding scene, an argument between Kate and Captain Keller. Throughout the rehearsal period in New York and on into the road tour, Patricia found it difficult to do the scene. Then one night, Bancroft recalled, Patricia finally got angry. "That night Patricia found the moment," Bancroft said. "I was backstage with director Arthur Penn, who turned to me and said, 'She's pretty damned powerful when she opens up.'"[29]

The production was in the hands of the team responsible for the success of *Two for the Seesaw* the year before. The scenery and lighting design were by George Jenkins. (Jenkins had married Patricia's Barter Theatre pal Phyllis Adams, and the two women renewed their friendship during the play.) Jenkins's ingenious set design with a rotating double-level cutaway of the Keller Victorian house, which had a scrim lower corner for essential scene changes, was masterfully executed. The period costumes were designed by Ruth Morley.

The production was scheduled for a four-week road tour, two weeks in Philadelphia and two weeks in Boston. *The Miracle Worker* premiered at Philadelphia's Locust Theatre on September 12, 1959. In spite of high hopes that the play would be a hit, there were doubts about whether the Philadelphia public would pay over $9.50 a ticket to see a play about a deaf, blind girl. And in fact ticket sales for *The Miracle Worker* were very slow. As it turned out, the unbearably hot weather the city was experiencing was a boon for *The Miracle Worker*. The out-of-town tryout of *The Gang's All Here*, starring Melvyn Douglas, was running in a nearby theater. Douglas collapsed from the heat on *Miracle Worker*'s opening night, and when Douglas's audience showed up that night, they were given tickets to the new show down the street.

When the final curtain came down on that first performance, the less-than-full house rose and gave it a standing ovation. Patty Duke counted eighteen curtain calls (more likely there were fewer), and as she and the actress Kathleen Comegys, who played Aunt Ev, climbed the endless iron stairs to their dressing rooms, the old actress said to Duke, "Well, my little dear, I want you to take a moment and really remember this, because it doesn't happen very often." They were in a hit.[30]

The *Philadelphia Inquirer* critic Henry T. Murdock wrote, "It has been many years since an ovation the like of that which followed the final curtain of 'The Miracle Worker' at the Locust Saturday night has been heard in a Philadelphia theatre. And it has been a long time since such an ovation (there were eight curtain calls and there could have been more) has been so honestly earned. . . . Anne Bancroft . . . little Patty Duke . . . Torin Thatcher and Patricia Neal give sensitive and eloquent performances."[31]

The play's run in Boston, at the Wilbur Theatre where *Bigger than Barnum* had laid its mammoth egg, was also a success. Very little rewriting was needed. Someone asked Bancroft if she didn't think the play was sad, with all the action revolving around a deaf, dumb, and blind child. "Yeah," replied Bancroft. "Sad like Christmas."[32]

Roald brought the girls to a performance in Boston. Patricia, as was usual in preopenings, was more high-strung than normal, and she and Roald argued. Roald didn't like the play and told the playwright as much. Coming backstage after the performance to Patricia's dressing room, Arthur Penn let her know what Dahl had said and done. "We'd appreciate it if you'd see that he doesn't come again," said the angry director. Humiliated, Patricia told Dahl, "Keep your fucking nose out of my business and let me make my own enemies!"[33]

Dahl continued to resent Patricia's continuous work, and he was jealous of her success. While he freely admitted that Patricia herself was not "movie star-ish," he did not like her actor friends. Years later, he complained to writer Barry Farrell, "Actors congregate together, you know. They're not like writers. They huddle and get strength from each other. They were in our apartment all the time, pushing and swarming around, trying to persuade her to keep working, get into some new show. They were all—well, *actors*, and it was me against the lot of them."[34]

The Miracle Worker opened at the Playhouse Theatre on Monday, October 19, after four previews. Advance ticket sales were estimated at around $500,000, and the theater lobby was crowded with ticket buyers the day before the opening.

On opening night, during a scene in which there is a food battle between Annie and Helen, Patty Duke was to toss a pitcher of water on Bancroft. In her zeal, Duke overshot Bancroft and drenched Rosalind Russell, who was sitting in the first row. Russell refused to let anyone assist her as she sat there dripping, as she didn't want to interrupt the action on the stage. When Helen threw spoons at Annie, some landed on Russell. Fearing that Duke would not have enough to throw throughout the rest of the scene, Russell quietly placed one back on the stage.

That night the play received thirteen curtain calls. The cast retired across the street to the Absinthe House to await reviews. By the time they arrived, *The Miracle Worker* was the talk of the town.

Variety's Hobe raved over the production and its stars. "It should make an excellent picture. . . . Patricia Neal and Torin Thatcher are excellent as the anguished and sometimes difficult parents."[35] These remarks were echoed by other critics. Walter Kerr in his *New York Herald Tribune* review said, "Patricia Neal is handsome, yearning, yet realistic," a rare remark from a man who never cared for her.[36] *New York Times* critic Brooks Atkinson wrote, "Under Arthur Penn's perceptive direction, Patricia Neal gives an excellent performance as Helen's anxious, loving mother whose heart is torn between pity and fortitude."[37] And Ward Morehouse wrote of Patricia's definitive moment, "Her scream early in the play, when she discovers that little Helen is blind and deaf, provides one of the most harrowing moments in current New York theatre."[38]

Settling in for a long, successful run of a hit play, Patricia was ready to enjoy her success.

18

Tempest

She learns, she learns, do you know she began talking when she was six months old? . . . I never saw a child so bright, or outgoing. . . . You should have seen her before her illness, such a good-tempered child.

—Kate Keller, *The Miracle Worker* (1959)

For Patricia, however, the run of the play was not to be long. "I got pregnant on opening night," she said.[1] She managed to stay in the cast until March, when her pregnancy forced her to withdraw and allow her understudy, Clarice Blackburn, to step into the role of Kate Keller. But Patricia made the most of her time on the stage.

In one performance about three months into the run, Torin Thatcher went up on his lines during a key dramatic moment with a stage full of actors. Thatcher had never had a problem with lines before; his mind simply drifted off. Recalled Duke, who was only twelve at the time and playing a deaf, blind, and speechless child, the actor whispered loudly to her, "What do I say child? What do I say?" instead of turning to one of the sighted, hearing adult characters. Patricia later told him off in front of the complete cast, "Of all the people to ask, Torin!"[2] The stunned Thatcher later gave her a large box of chocolates for the advice.

To critic Ward Morehouse, Patricia said, "I'm not terribly ambitious anymore. I feel I could have been a big star, but I've found out how useless the whole thing is. I think you have to be a good actress or a good mother. I get up in the morning with my children. I see them more than most working mothers do and I certainly think my marriage is permanent. When you have children you don't want to hurt them. I don't know really what it would take to want a divorce at this point."[3]

Patty Duke, who often visited Patricia during the run of *The Miracle*

Facing page: Patricia Neal in *Hud*, 1963. From the author's collection.

Worker and played with Tessa and Olivia, recalled that Neal, whom she "worshipped," had "an earth-mother aura about her"—and that "she had a great command of four-letter words, but they sounded like poetry coming from her."[4]

Neither the play nor domestic duties occupied all of Patricia's time. She attended morning sessions at the Actors Studio, where she met a new young actor named George Peppard, whom she found handsome and sexy. And she worked on other projects. In January 1960, Patricia agreed to appear on a broadcast of a *Play of the Week*, "Strindberg on Love," which was aired on January 25. She played Miss Y (Amelia) in Strindberg's one-act play—a monologue really—*The Stronger*.

It is a simple story of two actresses circa 1912 who meet in a restaurant around the cocktail hour. Mrs. X (Nancy Wickwire), a former stage actress, has been out Christmas shopping for her husband and their two young children. Encountering her friend and fellow actress Miss Y, she begins to boast about her life. Miss Y never says a word, and gradually Mrs. X realizes that Miss Y and her husband have had an affair. Her suspicions build, then subside when she rationalizes that she still has her husband and that Miss Y doesn't.

The Stronger, only about fifteen minutes long, was the second part of the two-part program, the first being the two-act play *Miss Julie.*

Patricia conveniently hid her pregnancy by remaining seated. Wearing a period outfit and a large hat, drenched in jewels, her hair up, and wielding a lorgnette, she looked stunning. Her character never utters a word, yet one cannot take one's eyes off her face as actress Nancy Wickwire delivers the monologue. Said *Variety* critic Art, "Patricia Neal, who plays the other woman, speaks no lines, but she subtly mimes her troubled lady and makes as much of her hands and eyes and mouth as many actors do with their voices. It was an interesting study, and it's a shame that it didn't comprise the major work of the night."[5]

Roald's career was looking up. In early February, his latest collection of short stories, *Kiss Kiss,* was published by Alfred A. Knopf. Among the eleven stories, the standouts were "William and Mary," "The Way Up to Heaven," and "Parson's Pleasure." The collection did very well, and Dahl received his second Edgar Allan Poe Award and his second Mystery Writers of America Award.

In March Patricia left *The Miracle Worker,* telling a reporter just before she announced her departure, "If I left the cast it wouldn't hurt the play at all, not at all. Nobody really matters except the characters played by Anne

Bancroft and Patty Duke."[6] And indeed, the cast and the play went on to win numerous awards. Patty Duke was given the Theatre World Award, and Anne Bancroft picked up a Tony for Best Actress—one of four Tonys for the play, the others being Best Play, Best Direction (Arthur Penn), and Best Stage Technician (John Walters).

In mid-March the Dahls left for their annual trip to England, this time sailing on the R.M.S *Queen Elizabeth*. Patricia spent the spring and early summer awaiting the arrival of her next child, who was born on July 30, weighing in at seven pounds, three ounces. Patricia was overjoyed. The baby was christened Theo Matthew Roald. Ivar Bryce, Roald's longtime friend, was made Theo's godfather, and Susan Denson, the children's young nanny, was his godmother.

At the end of the summer, Patricia was asked to appear in *Breakfast at Tiffany's,* to be filmed in Technicolor for Paramount. Patricia was not the first actress considered for the role, that of an older woman who vies with the young Holly Golightly for the affections of a young man. Virginia Mayo was among several other actresses of "a certain age" who read for the part. "I just wasn't good enough," Mayo said in 2003. While she wasn't glad that Patricia got the role, "it was right for her. She gave something to the role, and was better than I would have been," Mayo said.[7] What probably cinched the deal for Patricia was the recommendation of her friend Judy Shepherd, wife of coproducer Richard Shepherd. Patricia signed her contract on September 28. She was to receive a substantial fee for her services and living expenses not to exceed $350 a week for the duration of the filming. Shooting was to begin on location in New York and be completed in Los Angeles. It would be Patricia's first Hollywood film in nearly ten years.

The movie was based on Truman Capote's short novel *Breakfast at Tiffany's*, adapted for the screen by George Axelrod. Paramount Pictures wanted to star Audrey Hepburn in the role of Holly Golightly. John Frankenheimer, who had directed television dramas, was originally assigned to direct, but Hepburn had never heard of him, and he was let go. He was replaced by Blake Edwards, who had directed the hit 1959 film *Operation Petticoat* (Paramount) with Cary Grant. By the time he was brought onto the scene, the major casting for the film was completed. "I was with Patricia from the beginning," said Edwards. "As far as I was concerned she was the only actress [who could have done the role]."[8]

Breakfast at Tiffany's is the story of a young, attractive madcap named Holly Golightly (Hepburn), who lives in a pricey brownstone on Manhattan's East Side. She earns her living by accepting money from gentleman escorts.

She also pays weekly visits to mobster Sally Tomato (Alan Reed Sr.) in Sing Sing and, apparently unwittingly, transmits his orders to his underlings. She hopes to marry a wealthy man, but when aspiring young writer Paul Varjak (George Peppard) moves into her building, she is attracted to him. He is supported by a wealthy New York socialite, Mrs. Falenson (Neal), called simply by her apartment number, 2E, who is not going to give him up without a struggle. In spite of her feelings for Paul, Holly plans to marry South American millionaire playboy José da Silva Pereira (José Luis de Villalonga), but when the papers run a story accusing Holly of having smuggled narcotics to Sally Tomato, José leaves her, and Paul steps in.

Hepburn's costumes, by Givenchy, for *Breakfast at Tiffany's* started an enduring fashion trend: the little black dress, accessorized depending on the engagement. For most of the film, Hepburn wore her long, dark hair, which was streaked, piled high on her head. Director Edwards asked Patricia to dye her hair red, to contrast with Hepburn's hair color. Patricia's wardrobe, by Pauline Trigere, featured fashionable outfits of capes and turbans of rich materials. (Other costumes were designed by Edith Head.)

The location scenes in New York were completed quickly, and the film moved on to Hollywood. On the Paramount soundstages, problems soon developed with George Peppard. According to Patricia, Peppard had become a boorish egotist. He was being groomed for stardom, and it seemed to have gone to his head. "He was going to be the next big thing!" she said.[9] Peppard felt that Patricia's character was coming across as too strong and domineering and that he should be the dominant one in the "kept man" role. One day he almost came to fisticuffs with Edwards. Surprisingly, Edwards allowed Peppard to play the role the way he chose, and his performance truly suffered.

Said Edwards, "I do remember a certain tension between [Patricia and Peppard], which wasn't bad for their characters—her being a strong woman, and him a kept man. Patricia had suggested in one scene that George sit on her lap. He was horrified. He said he would never do anything like that. To which she replied, 'Maybe you wouldn't, but would Paul?' She really cut him down to size. As for their dislike of each other, I just didn't want to touch it."[10] Edwards said about the casting of Peppard, "We went to New York . . . and . . . the producers [Martin Jurow and Richard Shepherd] and I went to a theatre to see George in a film, and after coming out of the film I dropped to my knees on the sidewalk to the producers (Jurow and Shepherd) and begged them not to not to cast him. I liked George; he was such a ham, so vulnerable really. He was an ex-Marine and all that stuff, and I'd tease him unmercifully. And he'd try and tease me back but didn't have the wit for it. As a consequence, I always thought he was a piss-poor actor. And a great deal of fun, and someone who was *very* tortured. And I had a love for him."[11]

Toward the end of filming in Los Angeles, Judy and Richard Shepherd invited Patricia to a cocktail party . There she met the young and handsome Dr. Charles Carton, Richard's brother-in-law. In her memoirs, Patricia recounted their introduction:

> "I am very glad to know you then," I smiled. "What is it you fix?"
> "Heads," he answered. "I'm a neurosurgeon."
> "Well," I laughed, "I hope you never have to operate on me."[12]

The two-week filming in Hollywood wound up in early November, and Patricia flew back to New York and her family.

Life was good for the Dahls that fall of 1960. Roald's career was gaining momentum, and *Breakfast at Tiffany's* promised to be a smash hit. The children were thriving. Five-year-old Olivia was charmingly articulate and intelligent, and three-year-old Tessa was equally intelligent and active—and fractious at times. Both girls were enrolled in nursery school. Four-month-old Theo, who, Patricia remembered, had the most beautiful fingers and the longest eyelashes she'd ever seen, was a sweet and chubby baby. As the family prepared for the holidays, Manhattan settled into its seasonal hustle and bustle.

On December 5, as the day began to warm up, Patricia and the children's nanny, Susan Benson, wrapped Theo up in his pram. Susan was going to pick up Tessa from the nursery school at noon, while Patricia went to the grocery store.

On the way back from the school, Susan reached the curb at East Eighty-second Street on the west side of Madison Avenue, Tessa just a step or two behind her. The streets were full of children let off for the lunch hour from nearby P.S. 6. Just as Susan stepped off the curb, pushing the baby carriage, a taxicab jumped the green light and rammed into the pram, tossing it some thirty feet across the street and into the rear wheel casing of a bus just starting off. The street erupted into chaos.

As soon as the activity on the street came to a halt, Susan ran across to where the carriage lay mangled, leaving Tessa standing at the corner. Within minutes, the police and an ambulance were on the scene. (Patricia, still in the grocery store, heard the wail of an approaching ambulance and said a silent prayer for whoever was in distress.) Paramedics treated Theo on the scene, and a policeman placed him in the ambulance. Susan and Tessa were seated in the back of a police car and whisked off to the hospital.

The Dahls' daily cleaning woman met Patricia on the street and cried, "Oh, Mrs. Dahl, Theo has been hit by a taxi."[13] Patricia immediately called upstairs to the Odets' apartment, where Roald used a spare room as a study, and told him about the baby and that they needed to rush to Lenox Hill Hospital. Before Dahl could gather his thoughts, the telephone rang again. It was Susan, pleading with him to "hurry, hurry, *hurry!*"[14]

When Patricia and Roald arrived at the hospital, the doctor on duty in the emergency room told them they were doing everything they could. Theo's tiny body had been smashed, and there had been "tremendous neurological deficit," and he had suffered several cranial fractures.[15] "He will die," the doctor told them.[16] Roald's immediate reaction was typical: he took charge and contacted anyone he knew who could help. He called their good friend Dr. Ed Goodman. Their own pediatrician, Dr. Milton Singer, had the child X-rayed, and the severity of the case was evaluated. It was some comfort to them that Dr. Goodman did not tell Patricia and Roald that Theo would die. Patricia followed Roald and the doctors down the hallway to intensive care and looked down at her wounded baby. "He was unconscious and his tiny head was swathed in bandages," Patricia wrote. "I did not have to see through the layers of white. I knew the head was shattered. My precious doll was shattered."[17]

During the coming hours, a nurse approached Dahl with a newspaper clipping and told him how excited she was to be assigned the case. She then gave the baby Dilantin, an anticonvulsant. Dahl questioned her on it, and the nurse brushed him off. When he was left in the room, he saw the nurse dash out of the room and summon help. Within moments the doctors were pumping the drug out of the child's stomach. Horrified by these actions and what he felt was the apparent ineptitude of the hospital's staff, Dahl told Patricia he was going to have to do something radical. During the three days Theo was at Lenox Hill Hospital, Patricia sat with him, taking brief breaks to visit her old friend Dashiell Hammett, who was also in the hospital, dying of lung cancer. (Hammett passed away on January 10, 1961.)

When a Lenox Hill Hospital neurosurgeon informed the Dahls that they could not allow so many doctors in, Roald saw his opportunity. That night as a heavy snow fell, with help from Dr. William Watson, Dr. Goodman's friend, Roald simply wrapped the baby in blankets and, with Patricia by his side, fought his way through an army of protesting nurses and left the hospital. Waiting in a running car was Patricia's agent, Harvey Orkin, who rushed them uptown to Columbia Presbyterian Hospital, where Dr. Goodman practiced. Theo remained there for ten days.

Within hours of bringing Theo home, Patricia and Roald realized the baby was blind. They rushed him back to the hospital, where the doctors drained fluid from his brain to reduce the pressure that was causing the blindness. After a battery of tests, surgeons inserted a tube from the head to a vein to allow the fluid to disperse in the blood. This procedure was the best treatment available at the time, but it had its problems. The tube contained a one-way valve that would clog up periodically, allowing the fluid to build up again. Theo had to undergo a second operation in early January, and by the end of the month, his condition had stabilized enough to permit him to go home. However, over the next two and a half years he required several more surgeries.

Patricia and Roald were close during this trying period—they were "the most married" they would ever be, Patricia recalled—as they took shifts sitting at the hospital with Theo. The girls were looked after most of the day by Sonia Austrian, and other friends pitched in to answer phone calls, cook meals, and care for the children. Sonia recalled that Olivia, Tessa, and her daughter Susie were "like triplets," always together, and that at night Roald would read to them from *James and the Giant Peach*.[18] Patricia, "was always very good in a crisis. . . . She was in control, not hysterical," Sonia said.[19] "Pat was remarkable," commented Dahl. "She had a kind of strength you could only step back from and admire."[20] Patricia collapsed only once at the hospital, according to Dahl, when they were told that Theo would have to have a new shunt. Roald's response to the crisis was to attempt to see that everything was being taken care of.[21]

The repeated crises did take a toll on Patricia, of course, and when she needed to unburden herself, she sought out Dr. Watson, a friend and psychiatrist who lived in their apartment building. She felt it would be unfair to share all her feelings with Roald, who was holding it together as well as he could. Patricia was having negative feelings toward Susan, who she felt was in some way responsible for Theo's accident—although both she and Roald had assured Susan (who herself felt guilty) that she was not at fault and had allowed her to stay. Theo's medical expenses were mounting rapidly, and the Dahls' insurance was not sufficient to cover them. Both Patricia and Roald found it necessary to return to work as soon as possible.

In February, Patricia signed to do another *Play of the Week* in New York, for *The Magic and the Loss*, adapted from the play by Julian Funt.

Theo was doing well at home, so Patricia went to California briefly to tape an episode ("Mother and Daughter") of the *Purex Special of the Week*, an NBC daytime show with Arthur Hill and Lynn Loring.

While she was in Hollywood, Patricia visited with Jean and Chloe, who asked if she was going to contact Gary. Patricia wrote him a brief note, which Chloe passed on to him; he never replied. Chloe said Gary had recently converted to Catholicism and attended her church. She also told Patricia that Gary had recently fallen, which sounded strange to Patricia. While visiting with Judy Shepherd, Patricia mentioned that she was having problems dealing with Theo's accident. Judy recommended a psychiatrist in Beverly Hills, and Patricia talked with him and was able to come to terms with the accident and to forgive Susan.

Roald had begun hosting his own television anthology for CBS, *Way Out*. The half-hour series, which debuted March 31, dealt with strange and macabre subject matter, along the lines of *The Twilight Zone*. The first episode was "William and Mary," adapted by Dahl from his short story about a quarreling couple. The series lasted only three and a half months, but it provided needed income for the family.

In any event, Roald had decided New York City was simply too dangerous an environment for his children. He wanted the family to return to England and live there permanently. Not only would Roald be near his family, but England offered free nationalized health care. While Patricia had reservations about the move—she would have to leave her support system of friends and family—by mid-April the decision was made.

Walter Winchell announced in his April 21 column, "Patricia Neal turned down the co-starring role in the film version of 'The Miracle Worker' because it would have delayed her return to London where she and her husband, playwright Roald Dahl, dwell six months a year. And when they want to go home, they go home."[22] Dahl advised his publisher, Knopf, that the family would return to England until further notice.

The Dahls sublet their apartment, asking the Austrians to watch over it.

Returning to the safety of Great Missenden in May, the Dahls quickly settled into a casual and relatively pleasant lifestyle. The girls were enrolled in school, Olivia in Godstowe, a short way away in High Wycombe, and Tessa at Gateway School, a nursery school in the village.

On May 13 Gary Cooper died after a long bout with cancer. Patricia slipped into a Catholic church and said a prayer of relief for him and for herself. Now she would never have to look twice when she saw a man of that particular height, nor would she ever have to consider and remember Gary's beauty and grace again. An era in her life was finally over, she thought.[23]

After the past few difficult months, the family was adjusting to the slower pace of the country lifestyle and its apparent security. To keep the girls busy,

Dahl took them on outings to a hillside in Amersham, where he had once flown model gliders. While there, he met another glider enthusiast, Stanley Wade, a hydraulic engineer who liked to make toy airplane engines. Roald and Patricia were able to become more involved in the community now that they were permanently in residence at Gipsy House. The local residents were not impressed by the fame of either of the Dahls and accepted them as equals, for who they were, not what they had done.

The same bucolic existence which Patricia had in Packard was hers once again. But circumstances were different. She had two healthy older girls to attend to, and an infant who needed her constant care. And she was anxious still about her career, as the family needed her income.

Dahl's major concern that spring and summer of 1961 was Theo's condition. The valve to treat the hydrocephalus continued to clog up from time to time, and the boy had already had to undergo further operations and treatments at Great Ormond Street Children's Hospital in London. When Theo was home, the tube had to be monitored three times a day. The senior specialist at the Children's Hospital was unimpressed with the new methods of treating hydrocephalus and handed the case over to a younger colleague, Kenneth Till, a neurosurgical consultant whose patients were primarily children.

Patricia was concerned about Theo's growth and muscular development. Her worries were returning. "The whole thing is a terrible crime," she wrote at the time. "He was such a strong and confident baby by nature. I have been deeply depressed by it all lately. Until recently I truly believed in my heart of hearts that Theo would one day be quite all right. Now I am not so sure. To think that one careless second could cause so much agony. . . . It is very hard."[24]

As summer turned into fall, Theo's condition had not improved. The valve would clog, and the blindness would return. He was nauseated and couldn't keep food down; at the age of one he only weighed twenty-four pounds. Yet Theo was a happy and sweet baby.

Dahl searched for ways to improve the simple one-way valve system being used on his son—and thousands of others—so that major surgery would not be needed when it became clogged. Discussing these matters with Dr. Till and Stanley Wade, Dahl encouraged them to help design and develop a workable new apparatus. Within a month after the three men pooled their knowledge and resources, they had developed a prototype. The new device was a small cylinder with two stainless steel shutters inside that would allow fluid and solid matter to flow in both directions. Wade also devised a better way of inserting the tube into the brain. He had connections with engineering firms that made it possible to conduct their experiments at no cost. The men agreed that should the new valve prove medically viable, they would only charge patients the amount it cost to make.

After working months at High Wycomb, the three eventually sent the device, called the Wade-Dahl-Till Valve, off for patent in the late spring of 1962. By June that year, the first valve had been implanted into a patient at the Great Ormond Street Children's Hospital. Within eighteen months, the valve was improved upon and marketed at an even lower price. It was used all over the world. Before it became obsolete, some three thousand to four thousand children were treated with it. As it turned out, Theo would not need his father's lifesaving valve by the time the device was available; he had improved on his own.

Breakfast at Tiffany's premiered on October 5, 1961, at Radio City Music Hall in New York. With its lovely Henry Mancini score and haunting theme song, "Moon River," the film was an unqualified hit. Critics praised Hepburn's performance and singled out Peppard, Martin Balsam, director Edwards, and screenplay writer George Axelrod. A. H. Weiler of the *New York Times* wrote, "Patricia Neal is simply cool and brisk in her few appearances as Mr. Peppard's sponsor."[25] Judith Crist said in *TV Guide*, "George Peppard and a sleek Henry Mancini score lend fine support; and, during repeated viewing, you might take special pleasure in Martin Balsam's portrait of a brash Hollywood agent and Patricia Neal's sophisticated lady."[26] Hepburn was nominated for an Academy Award for Best Actress, Axelrod for Best Writing Adaptation, and the film was singled out for a nomination for Best Art Direction–Set Decoration, Color. But it was the music that garnered the Oscars: Henry Mancini and Johnny Mercer won for "Moon River," and Mancini won an individual statuette for the score.

Patricia made a brief trip to the States, returning to England well before the holidays. Roald was deep in his development of the valve. *James and the Giant Peach* had not yet been published in England, and the family's debts were mounting. In early November, Patricia was offered a television role on Britain's ATV *Drama '62*, in an episode entitled "The Days and Nights of Beebee." William Hartwell Snyder Jr. wrote the adaptation from his play *The Days and Nights of Beebee Fenstermaker*, which is essentially a long monologue. Beebee (Neal) is a stenographer in America's Deep South who is so overeager to meet new friends that she literally sabotages her close relationships. "She tries too hard," Patricia said about her character. "Her compulsive talking is usually fatal to a new friendship, but when it is not, she seems hell-bent on destroying all her chances of happiness. Beebee is a sloppy creature in mind and habits. But she's full of humour and the play is wonderfully warm and touching."[27]

"The Days and Nights of Beebee" aired on January 14, 1962, and was well received. The *London Times* reviewer wrote, "Mr. Philip Wiseman had the good sense to engage Miss Patricia Neal for the impossibly demanding part of Beebee, and her performance was undeniably glorious, especially in so far as the adjective carries an overtone of heroism in adversity. . . . The emotional range is small and the part has to be played full out all the time. But Miss Neal's technical resources were more than equal to its difficulties, and her performance, always a pleasure to watch, was never in the slightest monotonous."[28] A viewer wrote to the *TV Times*, "*The Days and Nights of Beebee* was one of the best TV dramas I have seen in quite a while. Patricia Neal gave a fine performance, and the director and the designer [Vic Symonds] were superb. If future plays are anything like this, it will be well worth staying home every Sunday evening."[29] "The Days and Nights of Beebee" remains one of Patricia's favorite dramatic performances on television.

With Theo's health improving, Patricia accepted a television role in the United States. She flew to Los Angeles immediately after "Beebee" to appear on the popular CBS mystery drama *Checkmate,* starring Anthony George, Doug McClure, and Sebastian Cabot. For "The Yacht Club Gang," Patricia was cast as Fran Davis, the hostess of Caleb's Beach Yacht Club, who is having an affair with one of her late husband's friends. Suspicious that someone is trying to kill her lover, Fran contacts the Checkmate Agency to investigate. After plot complications typical of the genre—cars that have been tampered with, suspicious characters—the real culprit is revealed.

"The Yacht Club Gang" was hardly a dramatic challenge for Patricia, but it did give her one brief moment to shine, in the scene in which she confronts her lover's wife, Martha. Patricia added dimension to Fran as she nervously comes to terms with her futile relationship with Kane. "Don't ever underestimate him again," Fran tells Martha. "Idiot—go back to your husband."

In a lukewarm review of the show, *Variety*'s television critic remarked that "Patricia Neal lorded it over the regulars, yet only suggested rather than fulfilled the role of a woman buffeted by men and scorned by women."[30]

Returning to England, Patricia wasted little time in accepting yet another U.S. television role. She would have almost two months with her family before flying back to California in mid-March to appear on *The Untouchables,* one of the best crime drama shows in the history of television. It made a household name out of film actor Robert Stack and his character, FBI agent Elliot Ness. In "The Maggie Storm Story," Patricia, in the title role, plays nightclub owner and chanteuse Maggie Storm, who is being investigated by Ness in connection with narcotics smuggling. By the end of the episode, Maggie has lost her nightclub and been stabbed in the back.

Robert Stack remembered Patricia as a consummate actress. "You judge people by the way they handle themselves in adversity," said Stack in 2003, and Patricia was "a class act."[31]

Paul Picerni, Stack's "second banana" in the crime series, recalling "The Maggie Storm Story," said that Patricia "had a seductive look, with those beautiful soulful wide-spaced eyes and that great smile—long before Julia Roberts. And she had that voice that went right through you. I am sure that every leading man who ever worked with her fell in love with her."[32]

When the episode aired on March 29, it caught the eye of film director Martin Ritt, who knew Patricia from the Actors Studio. He saw something in her performance that touched his heart, a depth, a sincerity and vulnerability in her work. He knew she would be perfect for a role in his upcoming film, *Hud Bannon*.[33]

Patricia flew home to England with the script of *Hud Bannon*. Roald liked it. Theo was progressing better than expected, and somewhat reassured, Patricia returned to New York to appear in a *Westinghouse Presents* special, "That's Where the Town Is Going," a story by playwright Tad Mosel about two sisters in a small midwestern town. (Also in the cast were Kim Stanley, Jason Robards Jr., and Buddy Ebsen.) While Patricia was there, she signed the contract for *Hud Bannon*, agreeing to a fee of less than $30,000.

The movie, its title shortened to *Hud,* was based on Larry McMurtry's first novel, *Horseman, Pass By.* Paramount had purchased the rights to the book to showcase Paul Newman. While the original story focuses on the young teenager Lonnie Bannon, it is Lonnie's uncle Hud who is the main character in the film adaptation by screenwriters Irving Ravetch and Harriet Frank Jr.—a character made up from only a few lines in McMurtry's novel.

Hud (Newman) is the hard-drinking, womanizing, self-centered, difficult son of Homer Bannon (Melvyn Douglas), the owner of a West Texas cattle ranch. Among the many women Hud is attracted to is Alma (Neal), the Bannons' sensual and world-weary housekeeper. Hud's teenaged nephew, Lonnie (Brandon De Wilde), is also attracted to Alma. Initially, Lonnie idolizes Hud and wants to be like him—until he sees Hud attempt to rape Alma. When hoof-and-mouth disease hits the ranch and the livestock begin to die, Homer begins to crumble, and family matters come to a head.

In presenting the "hero" of the film as immoral and corrupt, *Hud* set a new standard in the demythologizing of the American West—a trend that had begun to take hold under the influence of early 1960s European film realism.[34]

Ritt's one concern in offering Patricia the role of Alma had been that she would find it too small. Indeed she did, but she also found that it was a strong role, the only woman of consequence in the script, and she wanted desperately to do it.

"She was an earthy, shopworn gal who had been handled badly by life, which made her wise and tough but not vulnerable," wrote Patricia. "Alma had no real highs, no dramatic monologues, and she played mostly in the background to the other characters. But I knew her in my bones."[35]

Martin Ritt told a magazine writer, "[Alma] was a very tough part to cast. This woman had to be believable as a housekeeper, and still be sexy. It called for a special combination of warmth and toughness, while still being very feminine. Pat Neal was it. She's a first-class actress, free, unafraid. . . . She is stylish in the best way a woman can be stylish. That is, very womanly."[36]

Patricia was also attracted to the project because of her fellow cast members. She knew Paul Newman from the Actors Studio and Melvyn Douglas from his long film career. She also knew of Brandon De Wilde, then a handsome twenty-year-old, from his role in the Broadway production of *The Member of the Wedding*, when he was just nine, and from the film *Shane*, which had won him an Oscar nomination just two years later.

Because Patricia was concerned about leaving her family—especially Theo, who had just undergone his seventh operation—for an extended period, Ritt agreed to let her do the four-week location shoot in Claude, Texas, then return to England for three weeks before rejoining the picture for another four weeks of interior shooting at the Paramount Studios in Hollywood. "When they'll do that, you know they want you," said Patricia's friend Mildred Dunnock.[37]

In early May Patricia reported to Paramount in Hollywood for rehearsals before the company moved to the Texas Panhandle. "We just sat around reading the script for two weeks before we began shooting—rehearsing, we called it—and really worked ourselves into it," Patricia told an interviewer. "And not only the actors benefited; doing this we found one or two flaws in the original script in plenty of time for the writers to put them right. . . . [T]he scene where Paul Newman sees me off at the bus station originally ended with a great passionate kiss. I grumbled and grumbled about it, and finally persuaded Martin that he would shoot it both ways, with and without; then

. . . everybody realized that the kiss was wrong, and in the end it was shot only the one way."[38]

Principal photography in Texas began on May 21, after a couple of extra days of rehearsals. Patricia relished working with Ritt. For the first time since filming with Elia Kazan, she felt she could do anything the director asked. As the rushes came through, Ritt knew Patricia *was* her character.

The second week in June, with the four weeks of location shooting in Texas completed, Patricia returned to England. She would return to the United States, this time to Hollywood, the first week in July.

Most of the interiors for *Hud* were filmed on the Paramount soundstages in Hollywood. Martin Ritt was "extraordinary for actors to work with," Paul Newman recalled.[39] "Films were fun in those days. Production companies left you alone to do your work. Marty always had a great set. The technicians would come in and do their work, then the actors took over. It was the best of all climates."[40] During filming Newman found Patricia to be "a real pro and no prima donna. . . . She was willing to try anything to get a good performance."[41] Newman said, "Patricia was very specifically responsive to the way [Ritt] worked. Actors always responded well with him. Patricia's character suited her. She is really gifted, with a patient quietness. She was not competitive, but was concerned with the faithfulness to the script, I think. Every scene I had with her was a delight. She was very generous to me."[42]

Filming on *Hud* was completed on August 1, and Patricia flew home to England, exhilarated at having worked in a feature film with a dependable director and a top-notch cast. Besides, film work paid a lot more than television, and the Dahls needed money.

The family traveled to Norway for their annual holiday in mid-August, but the weather there was horrid, and they were all glad to get back to Gipsy House and the British early autumn.

Patricia wrote Jean and Chloe on September 25 to let them know all was well. Roald had finished his "4th and last" draft of his second children's book, *Charlie and the Chocolate Factory,* and his work on the new shunt was very successful. Theo was thriving—walking, running, and climbing, and he was so proud that he could blow out a match. Olivia had had a tonsillectomy, and the operation went very well. "Tessa is a terror. She is always so busy trying to outsmart us," Patricia wrote. "I really don't know when to believe her—as she is a fine and cunning actress."[43]

On September 27, Patricia began rehearsals for *The Country Girl,* which was to air on BBC as *Winter Journey.*

The Country Girl tells the story of once-famous Broadway actor Frank Elgin (Eddie Albert), now an alcoholic and reduced to working as an understudy. Stage director Bernie Dodd (Sam Wanamaker) remembers Elgin when he was a star and believes he can still give a performance if given a chance. The chance comes when the leading actor in Dodd's new play suddenly quits. Elgin doubts that he can stay sober and do the part, and so does his wife Georgie (Neal). Dodd suspects she is trying to undermine her husband's attempt to make a comeback. A dramatic confrontation comes in tryouts in Boston as the actor tries to keep from taking a drink.

Aired on October 19, the production was well received. Wrote C. Hardy in the October 26 *London Spectator,* "I adore Patricia Neal. If I ever get to [play] a drunk actor, I hope she will be around to suffer for me."[44]

The second week in October, Olivia came home from school with a note from her teacher, which she handed over to her mother. "This is to notify all parents that measles are in the school."[45] Patricia crumpled it up and put it in her pocket, as a strange feeling came over her, she remembered.

Concerned because Olivia was always susceptible to colds, Patricia asked Sir Ashley Miles, the head of the Lister Institute (and husband of Roald's half-sister Ellen), if he could possibly obtain gamma globulin for the children, hoping that if they did get the measles, the cases would be mild. He told Patricia to let the girls get the measles, saying, "It will be good for them."[46] Miles did, however, get gamma globulin for Theo.

By mid-November, Olivia was sick. Not wanting Olivia's illness to spread to Tessa, Patricia and Roald separated the two girls by bringing Olivia into their bedroom. They immediately sensed the child's energy was spent.

Olivia slept all day long on November 14. The children's physician came to the house the next day and told them not to worry, that she simply had "sleeping sickness," which was common in children after having the measles. November 16 brought no improvement. Roald tried reading and playing with the little girl, but she did not respond. The doctor was called again, and he still insisted that Olivia was recovering.

On November 17 Patricia went upstairs to check on Olivia around 5:15 P.M. The child's eyes were open, and she was having seizures. Patricia intuitively knew, she recalled years later, that her child was dying. She frantically buzzed Roald in his work shed. He rushed inside. An ambulance was summoned and sped them to the Stoke Mandeville Hospital in Aylesbury, about six miles away. Else stayed behind with Tessa and Theo. After being told that there was nothing they could do, Roald and Patricia anxiously remained at the hospital for another five hours. Olivia did not regain consciousness.

Roald called in Dr. Philip Evans, who had attended Theo. Patricia agreed to return home to be with the other children. Frankie Conquy came by to sit with Patricia, but only briefly, as she had to return to her home to attend her Sarah, who also had the measles. Within minutes, the telephone rang.

"Mrs. Dahl," the voice on the other end said. "Olivia is dead."[47]

19

Tragedy

Her life was like a great wave
Breaking in the lonely sea:
Oh, the wonder, the magic and the loss.

—Thomas Wolfe

Patricia and Roald grieved deeply for their first child. Roald cried continually after he returned from the hospital. The loss of Olivia was something from which he would never recover. That night at Gipsy House, Patricia sat by the window until dawn, quietly staring into the dark. Her memoirs describe the struggle the family endured those first days, weeks, and months after losing Olivia. Eura Neal said that she would come right over, but Patricia told her it was unnecessary, that things would be all right. Sonia Austrian remembered that she and her husband were hosting a dinner party late at night when actress Mary Fickett, at Patricia's request, called with the news of Olivia's death. Fickett also contacted Harvey and Gisella Orkin and Ed and Marian Goodman. Austrian was prepared to fly over with her girls. Susie and Tessa were the best of friends, and Tessa had never even spent a night alone in a room in her short life. However, Susie, too, came down with the measles and plans were put on hold.

Dahl's sisters handled the funeral arrangements—the music, the flowers, the casket. They refused to allow Patricia to see her child in death. The funeral was held midday the following Tuesday at the Little Missenden Church, a short drive from Great Missenden. This was the same church where Olivia had been baptized. The coffin was closed, and for years Patricia regretted not having been able to see Olivia's face just once more. The Rev. S. F. C. Roberts led the service, which was attended by family and such friends as Frankie Conquy, Helen Horton and her husband Hamish, Leslie O'Malley, and Wally Saunders.

Facing page: Patricia Neal, circa 1962. From the author's collection.

"The service was peaceful and short," wrote Roald's sister Alfhild from her home, Old Farm in Aylesbury, to Patricia's mother, Eura, on November 28. "And no-one went to the gravesite (later) . . . but Pat and Roald went down to the churchyard in the late afternoon. . . . Roald and Pat have been quite wonderful—they try to carry on quite normally—seeing friends, telephoning and playing with the children. . . . Pat is able to cry and talk about Olivia, which helps her."[1]

Frankie Conquy recalled the day in 1960 when she first met Patricia, who had appeared at the Godstowe schoolyard at High Wycomb to pick up Olivia. Conquy's daughter Sarah also attended the school, and Conquy always remembered how beautiful Patricia was that day and how good she was with the five-year-old Olivia. "Olivia was so talented. She would make up rhymes, and songs. And she would draw little pictures," Conquy said.[2]

Within days of Olivia's death, Roald called Conquy, insisting, "Now look, you've got to get your child gamma globulin."

Frankie replied, "I don't think it's possible."

"Of course it's possible!" said Dahl.

"I'll ring my doctor to see if I can get any," she responded.

"I'll ring your doctor and I'll get it!" concluded Roald.[3] And he did, though Roald never told his friend how.

The family pulled together remarkably during those first few difficult days. Patricia put Olivia's belongings away in an African trunk Roald had brought home from his travels, and Patricia's mother-in-law, Mormor, comforted her by telling her that she would survive this. The older woman had lost her own firstborn to appendicitis, and Harald Dahl had died just six weeks later, possibly from a broken heart over the loss of his child.

The swiftness of Olivia's death shattered Roald, and his mourning took on a grand scale. To help him cope with his grief, he tended Olivia's grave. Around the site, Roald and Valerie Finnis planted an extensive garden with rare and exotic species. He and Patricia selected literally hundreds of plants, the names of some of which Olivia had known. Dahl would spend months collecting rocks and porcelain animals, which Patricia helped him place. Patricia purchased the headstone for the child's grave. Engraved on it were the words, "She stands before us a living child." Roald couldn't handle looking at it and had it stored away.[4]

Years later Roald would say, "Pat was better able to cope with the period right after Olivia than I was, I suppose. She never broke down completely and she was always able to talk very freely about it. I think that talking worked for her to help her strengthen herself against the fact of it. Her Southern Protestant upbringing also came to the fore and she became deeply religious—gloom and doom, crime and punishment. She had a very immediate religious feeling that was in many ways like superstition."[5]

But Patricia wrote Jean and Chloe that she was finding it hard to talk about Olivia's death. "Roald, who truly wanted to die, is much, much better," she wrote. "I have been oddly in control most of the time. . . . I now struggle with myself. I long, ache to let her go—let her be free. . . . Pray—*please*—for Olivia's soul. Pray more, because I am less than perfect, for me that I can overcome my many terrors. Pray for Roald that he may find peace. And pray that Tessa and Theo will not have to endure any more pain."[6]

In her novel, *Working for Love*, Tessa named Olivia "Mary" and wrote of the family during this time: "My father built a rock garden on Mary's grave. The grave consisted of two plots instead of one and every day he was down there planting and tending. A gravestone arrived. No one could bear even to look at it, so they covered it and put it in the garage, where it has been ever since. Mary's paintings were framed and hung in the house. Her poems were too. The local church was given two twelfth-century wood carvings in her memory. My parents donated a silver cup to my school. It was called 'The Mary Cup.' It sat in a case and was to be awarded to the best high-jumper each year. . . . My mother became the stronger member of the couple. My father could not function, and my mother, realizing the need for solidarity, rallied herself. For about a year she held our family together."[7]

Dahl contacted his friend Annabella to come and visit, and he took her to Olivia's gravesite. He didn't shed a tear or discuss his feelings with her. His drinking increased, as did his barbiturate intake, either for his bad back or to relieve his emotional misery. Patricia felt, at that time, that Olivia was now gone. Roald believed otherwise. Having arranged an appointment for himself and Patricia with the former archbishop of Canterbury, Geoffrey Fisher, who had been the headmaster at Roald's boyhood school, Roald challenged Fisher's assertion that there were no animals in heaven. He said this wasn't possible, because Olivia had loved them so. Patricia felt Roald had lost his mind with grief.

Her own release, and possible salvation, was work. Patricia also realized that the family had to be held together. After reviewing their funds, she knew that she needed to go back to work. Dahl's children's book, *James and the Giant Peach*, dedicated to Theo, had just been released in October, and they had not seen any profits yet. They needed the income. Acting would also allow Patricia to meet new people and have the distraction of thinking through the mind of her characters. Thankfully, a television offer popped up almost immediately after Olivia's death. At that time Patricia would have taken almost anything.

She was offered a part in the BBC television series *Zero One*, "call sign of International Air Security," which starred the popular actor Nigel Patrick, voted one of England's ten best-dressed men in 1961.[8] In an episode titled "Return Trip," directed by George Pollack, Patrick's character, Alan Garnett, encounters a woman named Margo (Neal) who is suffering from amnesia in Chicago. Somehow he must prove her connection with a murder in Detroit. The one-hour drama aired on November 28, 1962.

Tessa was finding life without Olivia difficult. Sonia Austrian and her daughter, Susie, flew over to England the day after Christmas 1962 and stayed for about ten days. Sonia recalls that their first evening at Gipsy House was Tessa's first full night's sleep since Olivia's death. The two little girls cuddled close in their sleep. Sonia and Patricia stayed up late that evening, talking. Roald was "catatonic" and difficult to deal with, Sonia recalled.[9] When he couldn't sleep, he drank wine. Neighbor and friend Frankie Conquy said, "It was all so sad. Patricia felt if she could talk about it that she'd better be able to cope with Olivia's death. Roald just wouldn't mention Olivia's name."[10]

Jean and Chloe in California sent Roald and Patricia a cross and a St. Christopher medal for the holidays. Patricia wrote to thank them and let them know the family was trying to heal. She told them that they had given the old church in Great Missenden a wooden statue of St. Catherine that they had acquired in France on their honeymoon. (The statue later disappeared, and the Dahls replaced it with a replica, which also vanished.) Half of Olivia's trust fund, about $6,000, was given to build a home in Bethlehem for blind girls. "Tessa is very well in the daytime. Very social," she wrote. "But night is difficult."[11] She let them know Theo was doing well and that they were hoping that the cold and the snow would go away so they could begin the rock garden they were planning to construct around Olivia's grave.

The family flew to California in early February. Patricia had agreed to appear in an episode of ABC's *Ben Casey*, a popular medical series starring Vincent Edwards and Sam Jaffe. Titled "My Enemy Is a Bright Green Sparrow," the episode was written by Barry Oringer and directed by Robert Butler. It tells the story of hospital staff psychiatrist Louise Chappelle (Neal), who has skid-row patient Richard Anderson (John Larch) transferred to her care. Dr. Ben Casey (Edwards) disagrees with Chappelle about her methods of treatment, and Dr. David Zorba (Jaffe) agrees with him. Anderson's revelations under narcosynthesis deeply disturb Chappelle, and she shares with Casey her own revelations.

Later Patricia told a reporter who had asked why she accepted a television role, "I did . . . 'Ben Casey' simply to pay the expenses for five of us to come to California."[12] Regarding the tragedies that had befallen her family, when Patricia arrived in Hollywood for the filming of the episode, she told Louella Parsons, "We feel like we have been living the book of Job. Tragedy has welded us still closer together. We don't want to be apart even for a short time."[13]

The Dahls returned to England in March. Theo was developing into a physically normal three-year-old. His speech was limited, but it would improve. Patricia wrote friends on March 29 that she was going to have tests done, "as I am a glutton for punishment and would like two more babies in *rapid* succession." She wrote in closing, "It is a pity we weren't healthier, happier and livelier."[14]

Hud opened in New York on May 29, 1963, to critical acclaim. "Paul Newman's new film *Hud* is the best American picture since Newman's *The Hustler*," raved Stanley Kaufman of the *New Republic*. "Its distinctions are his and Patricia Neal's performances, Martin Ritt's direction, James Wong Howe's camera work, and the swift, sharp knife-play in the dialogue. . . . Miss Neal, with her lovely mezzo voice and, one might say, lovely mezzo eyes, gives a performance of wit, womanliness, and reticent dignity."[15]

Justin Gilbert of *Newsday* wrote, "Patricia Neal, as Alma, gives the best performance of her career."[16] Richard L. Coe wrote in the *Washington Post*, "Brilliantly played by Patricia Neal (surely our most undervalued major actress), the hired girl is the ideal Wise Woman, attracted and repelled, able to stand to one side and to hold her own battered values."[17] New York critic Thomas Wiseman wrote, "Patricia Neal, as the one woman immune to Hud's malignant charm (having been inoculated against his type by past experience), manages very well the tricky business of being stand-offish, recalcitrant without being priggish, and enticing without being a tease. One must lament the fact that she is so rarely in films."[18]

In his *New York Times* review, Bosley Crowther wrote, "Patricia Neal is brilliant as the lonely housekeeper for these men. She is a rangy, hard-bitten slattern with a heart and a dignity of her own. There is also much else that is excellent: the camerawork of James Wong Howe, the poignant musical score of Elmer Bernstein, the insinuating use of natural sounds. They merge in an achievement that should be honored as a whole."[19]

Hud was one of the decade's first truly adult motion pictures, and its emotional intensity and quality of performances have made it a modern-day Western classic. Some contemporary critics faulted the structure of the script, and several cited flaws in some performances, but the assessments of Patricia's portrayal of Alma were almost unanimously favorable.

In 2003, Newman said, "*Hud* kind of backfired on me. It was a chance for me to play a real bastard, void of any external graces—great with women, tough and masculine." Asked about the impact of *Hud* on his career, Newman commented, "I don't think it made much difference in my career—it certainly didn't hinder it."[20]

But *Hud* had a profound effect on Patricia's life and career. Though billed third after Newman and Douglas, she had only twenty-five minutes of screen time; she made the most of each second. In ten brief scenes, she made an indelible impact. Her most memorable sequence is probably the porch scene when Hud makes an unsuccessful pass at Alma as she is making cheese. Patricia, improvising, swats a moth on the porch screen. She succinctly lets Hud know she is not interested.

For 1962 audiences, the brutal rape attempt depicted in the film was fairly raw. Though not visually explicit, as it was filmed in shadows, it is enacted with dangerous violence. The emotional and tender farewell scene between Lonnie and Alma at the bus stop is touchingly and carefully played. The searching look in Patricia's eyes as she lovingly clutches young Brandon De Wilde to her trembling body is heartbreaking. Patricia recalls one scene she loved that didn't make it to the final print. In it, young Lonnie asks Alma what life is all about. Alma replies, "Honey, you'll just have to ask someone else." Noted film critic Pauline Kael wrote that Patricia's Alma is "perhaps the first female equivalent of the 'white Negro' in our films."[21]

Edith Head was given credit as costume designer for *Hud*, but one has only to look at the off-the-rack skirts and dresses Alma wears, plus the denim pants and simple shirts the men are dressed in, to see it wasn't really much of a stretch for the costumer. (One of the dresses Patricia wore in the film was purported to have cost $3.95.)

In England, Patricia was asked by director Lindsay Anderson to test for the role of Mrs. Hammond in *This Sporting Life*, based on the novel by David Storey about life in the early 1960s in northern England. Patricia worked for two weeks on the necessary northern England accent with a neighbor in Great Missenden. However, the role was given to Rachel Roberts, and it made her a star, netting her a Best Actress Oscar nomination for 1963.

Because of *Hud*, film offers started to roll in. By July, Patricia had been offered leading roles in two pictures, both scheduled to begin shooting immediately in England. The first was *The Pumpkin Eater,* for Romulus Films, costarring Peter Finch. The second film was *Psyche '59,* for Royal Films, to be directed by Alexander Singer. Patricia recalled that the producers of *The Pumpkin Eater* could not come up with a definite offer for the picture or a definite start date. For *Psyche '59,* both were guaranteed, and Patricia, again pregnant, agreed to take it.

Filming went smoothly and briskly. The plot of the adult melodrama involves beautiful Alison Crawford (Neal), wife of industrialist Eric Crawford (Curt Jurgens). She has been blind for five years; doctors believe that Alison's condition is psychosomatic, due to some traumatic event of her past. Alison's younger sister Robin (Samantha Eggar) comes to London for a visit, and Alison senses a certain tension between her sister and Eric. Family friend Paul (Ian Bannen) arrives, and Robin and he are attracted to each other. Eric discloses to Paul that he seduced Robin when she was a schoolgirl. Alison begins to regain her sight after a fall in the garden, but she does not tell anyone, not even her annoyingly odd grandmother (Beatrix Lehmann). After Robin announces her engagement to Paul, Alison finds Robin and Eric in bed together. She suddenly realizes her blindness was caused by her having witnessed a similar scene between them years before. Paul leaves Robin, and Alison leaves Eric. Off with the glasses, bright sunny sky, and "The End."

During the filming of *Psyche '59* Patricia found Eggar "cold and distant" at first.[22] But later the two became good friends. Patricia recalled she truly liked the Scottish-born actor Bannen, finding him masculine and handsome, as well as enjoyable to work with. In an interview, Patricia was asked why she hadn't done more British films, especially after her brilliant stage role in *Suddenly Last Summer.* She replied, "Because nobody has offered me a part before; they just say there aren't enough parts for American women in British films, and that's that."[23]

An American newspaper writer asked, "What about Patricia Neal? She deserved an Academy Award for her performance in 'A Face In the Crowd' a few years back, but the film was not a hit so it was ignored. Europe recognizes Pat as one of the greatest living actresses—do we? Okay, she's in Paramount's new film, 'Hud,'—but will somebody else have the taste to give her another one? It seems pretty hit or miss to me."[24]

In mid-September Patricia began filming a cameo role in *The Third Secret* for 20th Century-Fox. It starred Stephen Boyd, best remembered as Marsala in the 1959 classic remake of *Ben-Hur* (MGM). "There are about six of us in two-day bits—Jack Hawkins, Richard Attenborough, Diane Cilento.

I've forgotten the others," Patricia told columnist Sheilah Graham.[25] Patricia rationalized her participation to another reporter, "One of the wonderful things about films today is the fact that you don't have to worry about the size of the part. The spirit today is better than it ever was."[26] *The Third Secret* marked the screen debut of twenty-nine-year-old Judi Dench, whose role as Miss Humphries was severely edited in the final print. Patricia's scenes were cut entirely.

The picture suffered, and in hindsight, it may well have been a success had Patricia's scenes remained intact. Dench wrote in 2003 that she had no idea that Patricia had even been in the picture, "You say her role was cut—mine was severely damaged!"[27] Also landing on the cutting room floor was a cameo appearance by Margaret Leighton.

On September 8, while Patricia was filming *Psyche '59*, the steel tube inside Theo's head was removed. As his health improved, Patricia grew in girth with her fourth child. She was truly experiencing a renewed happiness with the life inside of her, and certainly she was pleased with the way things were going with her career. Since Olivia's death, she had sometimes felt that perhaps God had punished her for aborting Gary's and her child. She was also haunted by remorse over the times Roald had spanked Olivia when she misbehaved. So Patricia kept busy. Roald was still not coping with the death of his firstborn child. His drinking had increased, and he was more disagreeable than ever before. Family arguments within the home were commonplace. Patricia wrote friends in early September, "Poor, dear Roald still thinks about Olivia all the time. It gets worse rather than better. I want him to get a job that will force him to see people and work with others."[28]

And through this difficult period, Tessa's life was in turmoil. Always willful and determined, yet deeply sensitive, she was becoming more and more difficult. Tessa was less than seven years old. Her wounds then were still fresh. And sadly, her emotional scars would never heal. After her sister's death, Tessa tried desperately to please her father and gain his love and trust. Decades later, she wrote in her semiautobiographical novel, *Working for Love*, "There I was, watching those people I loved so dearly suffer. Their suffering was all-consuming. My father was beyond help. He could not speak for grief. I remember vividly seeing his beautiful blue eyes fill with tears. I saw him weep in his bedroom, and then when he noticed me he asked me to leave. . . . These people were inconsolable. They could not help each other, either. So my beautiful mother threw herself into her work, relentlessly, not stopping for a minute, not allowing herself four seconds to think her thoughts for fear that they would engulf her—and she would be drowned in her sorrow."[29]

In one scene in Tessa's novel, the father is driving the protagonist, Molly (Tessa), to school. He asks her to sing the songs that her dead sister once sang for him. Tessa wrote:

> And I tried. I desperately wanted to do it well. I spent nights afterwards thinking about what I should have sung. But it was pathetic. I can see it now. I even know exactly where we were. Turning right by the *Plough* pub.
> "Oh, the fields and the trees and the grass and the cows . . ."
> "No, no, no," he shouted. Exhausted, at last he let go.
> "Why can't you be more like her? Why can't you sing like her? The woods, the walks, the spark, you haven't got it, have you? Why can't you be like her?"[30]

Patricia was rehearsing for the cameras yet again. On October 2 she filmed an episode of the television thriller series *Espionage* called "The Weakling." Directed by Stuart Rosenberg, who directed Patricia in *The Untouchables* episode, "The Weakling" tells the story of Joe Ferno (Dennis Hopper), who was drafted by Allied Intelligence during World War II for one of the war's most dangerous missions—to infiltrate the enemy and give false information that would lead to a victorious invasion of Fortress Europe. He is captured and tortured by Nazi agents, including collaborator Dr. Jeanne Termoille (Neal). She tells Ferno, "It could be so easy if you'd acted like a human being and told me what I wanted. You couldn't even blame yourself—you were drugged. Who are you trying to impress? Tell them what they want to know. In one minute it can be all over and we can be together." He gives his information, not knowing it is all lies. In the process, Ferno loses his mind. And Colonel Trevor Ballin (John Gregson) must make peace with himself for betraying Ferno to save the lives of countless others.

Espionage was filmed on location for Plautus Productions; it was aired on NBC in America and over the ITC network in Great Britain. "The Weakling" was only the second episode in the series. Patricia, her pregnancy cleverly disguised by lighting and a laboratory smock, played a villain for a change. In one scene Dennis Hopper had to slap Patricia. Hopper remembered asking director Rosenberg if the slap was necessary. Rosenberg told Hopper that reality was important, and Hopper followed through, although, he recalled, Patricia was taken aback by the blow.[31]

Patricia told British columnist Sylmar Welder, if not completely candidly, "It's strange to find myself suddenly in demand again. . . . I'm not an ambitious woman, and had been very happy just living with my family in the country, perhaps making a film every couple of years or so."[32]

Patricia told *Parade*'s Lloyd Shearer in London, "What I want most of all is good health for my family and peace of mind. When I started out in the business I was exceedingly ambitious, but life has tempered my drive and has taught me what is truly important. I don't want money or fame. I just want—and now I'm speaking for myself as an actress—a continued sense of duty to my work. When people say I did a fine job in *Hud*, that makes me feel wonderful, but it's even better if I know in my heart I've done my best." About wedded life she said, "The secret of a happy marriage lies in choosing a partner of quality. That's what I'm going to tell my children. It's not so much what you do as whom you do it with. If a girl gets a good man, a man with character and a sense of duty and responsibility, then not very much can go wrong. I really don't think you can tell children very much. You can show by example. I want Tessa to want to give something to life and this world. And I want her to have a nice person to do it with. I have, and that's why I am a happy and fulfilled woman."[33]

The coming year of 1964 was promising to be spectacular. Patricia was riding the crest of her career, and at the same time she was praying that she and her family would experience a new beginning. Both personally and professionally, it would be the last successful period she would have for several years to come.

20

Stardom

Twelve years ago, Pat Neal left Hollywood with both her professional and personal life a shambles. Today, she's married to a brilliant writer, her career is at its pinnacle, and once again she is able to say: "I'm a happy woman."

—John Keating, "The Second Life of Patricia Neal,"
Cosmopolitan, May 1964

Hud seemed a sure bet to capture a share of the 1964 Academy Awards, and Patricia was considered a favorite for the Best Actress Oscar. After all, she had already received numerous pre-Oscar accolades, including Best Actress awards from the National Board of Review and the New York Film Critics Circle, Best Supporting Actress from the Cleveland Critics Circle, and Best Foreign Actress from the British Academy of Film and Television Arts.

There had been some speculation about whether Patricia would be nominated as Best Actress or Best Supporting Actress, but the Academy of Motion Picture Arts and Sciences, recognizing the dramatic importance of her role in *Hud*, placed her in the more prestigious Best Actress category, along with Rachel Roberts for *This Sporting Life*, Natalie Wood for *Love with the Proper Stranger*, Leslie Caron for *The L-Shaped Room*, and Shirley MacLaine for *Irma La Douce*.

Hud was passed over in the Best Picture category, but it received six nominations other than Patricia's: Best Actor (Paul Newman), Best Supporting Actor (Melvyn Douglas), Best Director (Martin Ritt), Best Cinematography for Black and White (James Wong Howe), Best Art Direction for Black and White (Hal Pereira and Tambi Larsen), and Best Screenplay Based on Material from Another Medium (Irving Ravetch and Harriet Frank Jr.).

Patricia, awaiting the birth of her fourth child in England, would not be

Facing page: Patricia Neal, 1963. From the Patricia Neal Collection.

able to attend the April 13 Academy Award ceremony in Hollywood. Hedda Hopper wrote in a column published March 11, "Pat Neal writes me from her home in Buckinghamshire, England: 'I have been basking in glory! Glory that I never dared hope since "Hud" was released. I knew it was a lovely part in a splendid film but never dreamed of any further honor than the joy of doing it. Thank you for your part in my success of the moment.'"[1] Not to be outdone, Louella Parsons reported March 18 that Patricia "sounded great when we talked via phone between Beverly Hills and London. I told Pat she may well be an Oscar winner as well as a new mother by June. 'I hope so,' she said, adding, 'It would make me very happy.'"[2]

When Gregory Peck stepped up to the podium at the Santa Monica Civic Auditorium to announce the Best Actress winner, *Hud* had already received two Oscars, for Douglas and Howe. When he read Patricia's name, Annabella Power rushed to the stage to accepted the Oscar on Patricia's behalf. "I chose Annabella Power to accept my award for me because she is so lively," Patricia told the press.[3] Hedda Hopper said Annabella "seemed jet-propelled when she raced to the stage to receive Pat Neal's Oscar."[4]

Patricia got the news in a 5:00 A.M. phone call from her high-school friend Charlcey Adcock. "Patsy, you won! *You won!*" she screamed. Then she heard from her agent Harvey Orkin. "We knew we would be awakened by the telephone if I'd won," Patricia told the press. "But if we woke up without hearing it, then I'd lost."[5] Throughout the morning the telephone continued to ring. "I didn't realize I had so many friends who wanted to congratulate me," she told the reporters.[6] "I couldn't be more excited. These things happen once in a lifetime. But I've got to keep a cool head. I'm expecting a baby in six weeks and if I get too worked up over this award, who knows—I might bring on baby in the middle of tonight's celebrations."[7]

Annabella sent Patricia's Oscar statuette to London, and on her last outing before the birth of her baby, Patricia took the train to London to fetch the package. Stepping onto the platform at Marylebone Station, Patricia was blinded by flashbulbs. "Good heavens, I feel just like Elizabeth Taylor!" she exclaimed.[8] Wearing Gary's mink and sporting a huge smile, Patricia was asked by the newsreel press how it felt to have won the Oscar. "Well, it's something I do think every actor dreams about always. You have fantasies about it your whole life, and then when it really happens it is quite unbelievable." Was she expecting to win? "No. No. I loved the role and I thought it was beautifully written, and I knew I was being wonderfully directed. But I didn't even think of it that way. I just loved doing it."[9]

When asked if the events of the past three years had in any way influenced her acting, Patricia candidly replied, "I really don't know. It is not pleasant to think that you are better at your profession—one simply wouldn't want to be better—because of such things happening to those who are so near and dear to you. I think I am probably a better actress than I was—but not for that reason."[10]

By honoring a mature woman for her role as an integral character in a dramatic film, the Academy of Motion Picture Arts and Sciences turned the spotlight on a performance that helped change the view of modern woman in American film—from melodramatic victim to survivor. Millions of filmgoers recognized Alma as a very real human being, someone they could empathize with, be comforted by, and, most important, care about. The sound of Patricia's voice, the depth, warmth, and suffering found in her eyes, the maturity earned through experience—all these qualities characterized a different type of actress: a victorious survivor with whom audiences could identify.

Although Patricia insisted, "I can't think of a thing I want that I don't have except more children," her Oscar fueled much speculation about the direction her career would now take.[11] Louella Parsons reported, "Patricia Neal's getting everything. First, she got the 'Oscar.' Now she gets Cary Grant—and that's good getting. It is Jack L. Warner's very good idea to co-star Pat (the year's 'best actress' in 'Hud') and Cary, the perennial charmer, in 'My Blood Runs Cold,' a chiller-thriller set to roll on the Warner lot this fall."[12]

Patricia's next exposure to the public after the Oscars was in *Psyche '59*, which crept into the country's movie houses for its American premiere on April 29. The film was a major disappointment. Howard Thompson in the *New York Times* said, "Oscar or no Oscar, Patricia Neal has brightened many a blighted movie. But she is an actress, not a miracle woman, and even her restrained, unstudied characterization of a blind wife can't save 'Psyche '59.' This dismal bundle from Britain, an exercise in sexual psychology, really takes the cake for turgid, listless movie-making. . . . Miss Neal handles herself and those dark glasses gracefully, no mean feat considering the tightrope demands of Julian Halevy's script. Her three colleagues are in there pitching in a strange film that strikes out almost triumphantly."[13]

Edward Lipton, of *Film Daily*, considered the film "too obvious for art house tastes and too torrid for the general audience. But the performance of Patricia Neal . . . [provides] this film with very strong art house possibilities. . . . What raises this film to a worth-seeing, and therefore worth-booking level, is both the quality of the performances and the sensuousness of the directing. Miss Neal is magnificent. As the blind woman, she 'sees' with her hands, her mouth, her ears, and one can marvel at the sheer artistry of her performance."[14]

Psyche '59 is rarely seen today. It's a strange, haunting melodrama that was rather ahead of its time with its adult themes. There is a brief nude scene of Eggar and Jurgens in bed. Neal did a scene in a revealing negligee, which is actually more erotic in what it does not reveal. It is worth noting that in one scene, Neal and Eggar are having tea in a restaurant. Eggar asks Neal what is wrong with her eyes. Her character replies, tapping the left side of her forehead, "There's nothing wrong with my eyes. It's in my head—pressure on the brain center, from a brain hemorrhage."

On May 12, Patricia gave birth to her fourth child, naming her Ophelia Magdelena Dahl. Born at the Radcliffe Infirmary in Oxford, about twenty-five miles from Great Missenden, Ophelia had four godparents: Roald's twin nieces, Anna and Louise Logsdail, Harvey Orkin, and Colin Leslie Fox. The proud father told the press, "Patricia is simply overjoyed. She never said whether she wanted a boy or a girl, but I knew she secretly longed for a daughter to replace the one we lost."[15] Theo called the new baby "Don-Mini," and the nickname would remain. A beautifully healthy, chubby little girl, "Ophelia was a blessing on the Dahl household and we all felt it," Patricia later wrote.[16]

Life was stable and good for a change. Patricia wrote friends, "Miss Ophelia Dahl is radiantly beautiful. She weighed in at 6 pounds 11 ounces. And it was the easiest, nicest birth imaginable. . . . She looks just as a little girl should. Very tidy features. Absolutely rosebud. Her eyes are big and wide apart. . . . Her mouth is exactly like Olivia's."[17] She wrote that Theo was going to school now, from 9:15 to 11:30 A.M., every morning, and that Tessa adored her baby sister. "I now have my Oscar in my possession and he is mighty handsome," she concluded.[18]

By July, Patricia had recovered sufficiently, and Ophelia was now big enough, for the whole family to travel to Hawaii for the ten-week filming of *In Harm's Way*, a film she had agreed to do for director Otto Preminger. She had originally turned it down, but Preminger told her, "We will wait for you."[19] (At the same time, Patricia was offered the Broadway role of Nettie Cleary in *The Subject Was Roses*, by Frank D. Gilroy. This was one role she truly wanted to play, but again her condition prevented her taking it.) Arriving in Honolulu on July 10, the Dahl family, their nanny Sheena Burt, and friend Nesta Powell were quickly settled into the new Ilikai Hotel at Waikiki on Oahu. "Past tragedy has welded us close together," she told a movie magazine writer. "We don't want to be apart, even for a short time."[20]

Based on the 1962 best-selling novel *Harm's Way* by James Bassett, the film *In Harm's Way* was the first motion picture to deal with the attack on Pearl Harbor. Preminger planned a sweeping war epic depicting the immediate aftermath of the attack and the lives of its survivors. With John Wayne, Kirk Douglas, and Neal as its stars, the picture also featured Tom Tryon, star of Preminger's *The Cardinal*, as well as the newlywed Brandon De Wilde, Jill Haworth, and Burgess Meredith. Henry Fonda was given guest-star billing. Also in small roles were Larry Hagman and George Kennedy.

Preminger wanted to produce and direct *In Harm's Way* with as much realism as possible. He told the Defense Department, "If you won't give me what I want, I'm prepared to use the Brazilian Navy."[21] The Defense Department gave him permission to film aboard actual American warships. *In Harm's Way* would prove to be one of the last of the big-budget war movies, and the Defense Department had no problem being cooperative with Preminger. "After all these anti-war films which have been more defeatist than pacifist, the Navy needs a film like this!" said the director.[22]

"What good troopers John Wayne and Kirk Douglas are," the Austrian-born Preminger enthusiastically told a reporter. "I do not even show them the script, just told them the story, and they came."[23] Preminger later told journalist Stanley Frank, "When I read the script of *In Harm's Way*, I knew Pat was ideal for the role of Maggie, the fortyish, divorced Navy nurse who makes a deliberate play for John Wayne. Deborah Kerr and two or three other actresses could have done the part very well, but Pat was my first choice because of the special, believable quality she would bring it. This was several months before she won the Oscar. I was so anxious to have Pat in the picture that I held up production until she had her baby and was ready to work. The delay was well worthwhile. Pat did a beautiful job in her key scenes. She gave it such a warm feeling of feminine sensitivity that it was shot almost without direction."[24]

Patricia recalls that the director treated his stars with the utmost care, but the lesser actors were subjected to his yelling and typically rude behavior. "I don't welcome advice from actors," Preminger said. "They are here to act."[25] Preminger had made life hell for actor Tom Tryon the previous year in *The Cardinal*, as he had in 1954 with Dorothy Dandridge in *Carmen Jones* and in 1957 with eighteen-year-old Jean Seberg in *Saint Joan*. He continued with his abuse of Tryon in *In Harm's Way*. "I hate to see him torture other people," Patricia told an interviewer. "It's so humiliating to an actor to see another actor being really tortured, you know."[26]

In Harm's Way opens on the evening of December 6 in Honolulu. At a party are Lieutenant William "Mac" McConnell (Tryon) and his wife Bev (Paula Prentiss), as well as an Air Force major (Hugh O'Brien) who dances with the drunken Liz Eddington (Barbara Bouchet), the young wife of Commander Paul Eddington (Douglas). Eddington is on active duty somewhere in the Pacific. On December 7, Japanese airplanes attack Pearl Harbor, and chaos engulfs Honolulu. Captain Rockwell Torrey (Wayne) is ordered to lead the U.S. Navy in its battle against the enemy. When his mission becomes a disaster, Torrey is ordered back and given a desk job. He meets the nurse Lieutenant Maggie Hayes (Neal). She tells him that his son, Ensign Jeremiah "Jere" Torrey (De Wilde), who was raised by his mother and never really knew his father, is on the island.

Jere is a callow and unscrupulous lad who holds ill feelings toward his father. Torrey's hotheaded executive officer Eddington learns that his unfaithful wife has been killed in a car wreck. Meanwhile, Torrey's true merits are reevaluated, and he is made a rear admiral. On the island of Gavabutu, where Maggie and Jere are also stationed, Torrey launches successful attacks against the enemy and earns the respect of his son, Jere, who volunteers for PT boat assignment. At a late-night beach party, the tormented Eddington drunkenly rapes Jere's young girlfriend, Ensign Annalee Dorne (Haworth), who is also Maggie's bivouac mate. In shame Annalee commits suicide. To redeem himself, Eddington volunteers for a certain-death reconnaissance mission to find the Japanese fleet. He finds the fleet and reports in detail before he is shot down. Torrey tells his son that Annalee is dead, and the two reunite. A huge sea battle ensues, and Jere is killed. The American fleet is largely destroyed, but the enemy retreats in confusion. Torrey is severely wounded, losing his leg. When he returns to port, he finds Maggie there waiting for him.

The final sea battle in the film, which lasts less than five minutes in the picture, cost more than $1 million to shoot. Principal photography was completed in early September; the film was actually completed ten days ahead of schedule. At the wrap, the governor of Hawaii gave a party for the cast. Additional scenes were shot in San Diego, San Francisco, and aboard the U.S.S. *Braine*, the U.S.S. *Capitaine*, the U.S.S. *O'Bannon*, the U.S.S. *Renshaw*, and the U.S.S. *Walker*.

While Patricia acted before the cameras, Dahl spent his time searching for rare orchids to take back to England. Patricia's work on *In Harm's Way* was completed in seventeen days. The Dahls stayed in Honolulu a few additional vacation days. Roald had been approached that summer in Hawaii by former child actor Jackie Cooper and a little-known young director named

Robert Altman with a property they wanted him to develop into a screenplay called *Oh Death, Where Is Thy Sting-a-ling-a-ling?* During that additional week in Hawaii, Dahl worked on the screenplay. (Dahl completed the work, which was to star Gregory Peck. It was "cashiered as unproducible after six disastrous weeks of mayhem in the Swiss Alps, where the action was set.")[27] On August 15, Patricia wrote her mother in St. Petersburg, Florida, "'Don-Mini' is still gorgeous, Theo so brown and well looking. Tessa wildly active and everyone had a good time. I groan at the idea of packing."[28]

While she was in Hawaii, Patricia was approached by director John Ford with an offer to star in his upcoming film *Chinese Finale*, to be filmed in Hollywood at MGM some time the following year. Patricia was offered $125,000 to do the role. Though it was lower than her usual salary (she was paid $130,000 for her part in *In Harm's Way*), she wanted to work with Ford and signed to do the film.

Returning to California the following Monday, the Dahls spent a week in Los Angeles, then flew to New York for another week to visit friends. Patricia told Hedda Hopper that she had to turn down a film project that would have given her more money than she had ever earned for a picture. Patricia's agents, it was reported, were now asking $200,000 per film for her services.

There were reports that Patricia would take the coveted lead role in the movie version of Edward Albee's *Who's Afraid of Virginia Woolf?* over Bette Davis and Rosalind Russell. Patricia's stalwart supporter, seventy-four-year-old columnist Louella O. Parsons, reported, "Already I can hear the 'howls' set by actresses of Hollywood and Broadway who thought they had the inside track for the movie version of the play which shocked jaded theatre-goers for two years. . . . [N]ow [Patricia's] even money to cash in with 'Virginia' at Warner Bros."[29] But columnist Louis Sobol wrote in his *New York Journal-American* column, "Pat Neal, mentioned by Hollywood columnists as likely to get the prized role in 'Who's Afraid of Virginia Woolf?' was not so confident as she discussed it at Gallagher's. But [she] did say that Kermit Bloomgarden wants her to star in his forthcoming play 'Things That Go Bump in the Night' which starts casting shortly and that the offer appeals to her."[30] Patricia did not do the play, and the film role went to Elizabeth Taylor, who won a Best Actress Oscar in 1967 for her portrayal of Martha.

In September, the Dahls returned to England. While Patricia looked over scripts, the children thrived, and Roald's second children's book, *Charlie and the Chocolate Factory*, was published in the United States to much acclaim. Within the first month, the first printing of 10,000 copies had sold out. Said

Dahl at the time, in reference to his children's books, "For one who is used to writing for adults only, it is . . . an uneconomic diversion."[31]

Patricia told *Parade* magazine writer Arno Johansen that her career was now on a level keel. "I never expected to win an Academy Award for *Hud*. But it certainly made a difference," said Patricia. "I'm getting so much money on *[In] Harm's Way*, it's almost ridiculous, but I'm certainly not going to turn it down. Roald and I never had much money, and there's a steady income from his royalties, but I never hit it really big in Hollywood. I never got large sums. What we're going to do with all this money is put it into a trust fund for the children. One advantage of living in England is that money lasts longer there and goes farther. I've been offered several other parts—*Who's Afraid of Virginia Woolf?* is one—and I guess I'll never be hotter or perhaps more in demand, but none of that is going to change our way of life."[32]

Roald made some very telling remarks in the same interview regarding Patricia's role in his life. "Pat is an actress. Pat is an unusual woman because she doesn't act or behave as most actresses do. She's not obsessed by her career. She's far more interested in her home and her children. And that's why she's content to live tucked away in a village in England. . . . Most American girls are proudly independent and rebellious and when I first married Pat I thought it would be difficult to train her, but it hasn't been. In England, you know, a family is lost if a woman is allowed to take charge of everything, and I think the American wife is very much inclined to do this. It makes her miserable. She would much prefer not to, but she can't help it, because so many American husbands abrogate their rights and duties. I do not. Pat does all the cooking, and we have a nanny to help with the children when Pat's filming. We both have now reached a point where we are no longer looking for pleasures—only serenity."[33]

During the rest of 1964 the Dahls relaxed, spending a great deal of time with their friends Brigadier and Patricia Kirwan. The Kirwans' daughter Angela was in her early twenties and bored with her job in Great Missenden. Dahl often played tennis with Angela on the Kirwans' tennis court, and Patricia would slyly joke with her, asking if she was not just a little in love with her husband. Angela came around Gipsy House frequently, and eventually she was asked to accompany the family to California during the filming of *Chinese Finale*, as they would need help for the several weeks they would be in Los Angeles. Angela would be the secretary and cook and help Sheena with the children.

On November 10, Patricia wrote friends in Los Angeles, "We are pretty certain to be in California in January for 10 or 12 weeks. I am meant to do

'Chinese Finale' for John Ford. We will all be coming, of course." In addition to asking whether she should bring a mink coat, she told her friends, "This is the sad anniversary of the day that Olivia came down with the measles. The point of no return."[34] Martin Ritt called that same day and offered to rent the Dahls his Pacific Palisades home, complete with kidney-shaped swimming pool, during the shooting of Ford's film. Ritt and his wife Adele would be in Ireland for that period while he was directing a film. The Dahls gladly accepted.

Louella Parsons, in her November 16 column, announced, "Oscar-winning Patricia Neal arrives here bag, baggage, husband and children in January, to star in 'Chinese Finale' which John Ford will direct and Bernard Smith will produce for MGM. Making this picture with John Ford is enough to make up to Pat her keen disappointment in losing 'Who's Afraid of Virginia Woolf?' to Elizabeth Taylor. There's not an actor, actress or four-footed animal in the business who doesn't jump with joy over working with Ford."

The Dahl entourage arrived in Los Angeles on January 23 after a difficult flight from England—the leg from London to New York was delayed by a storm in Labrador—and settled into the Ritt home. Unpretentious by Hollywood standards, the house featured limestone floors and a large stone pillar with a wooden base in the middle of the living room. Dahl went to work immediately padding the sharp and rough edges around the house to prevent Theo, who was still suffering from balancing problems, from hurting himself. Patricia was called to the studio, where she began costume fittings, rehearsals, and visits with countless friends.

Chinese Finale was going to be a departure for action director Ford.[35] Based on Norah Lofts's novel *I Met A Gypsy*, *Chinese Finale*, later retitled *7 Women*, tells the story of a 1935 mission in China headed by Agatha Andrews (Margaret Leighton), who is assisted by Jane Argent (Mildred Dunnock), the young Emma Clark (Sue Lyon), and the weak-willed Charles Pether (Eddie Albert) and his middle-aged and pregnant wife Florrie (Betty Field). The Chinese border is being terrorized by the Mongol Tunga Khan (Mike Mazurki), and rumors are rampant about the cruelty the barbarian and his forces are inflicting.

Florrie is close to delivery, and Dr. Cartwright (Patricia) is sent for. She is a cynical and worldly individual whom Florrie is disturbed to find is a woman. Miss Binns (Flora Robson) arrives at the mission with cholera patients she has brought from her nearby and now-ravaged British mission. Agatha refuses to spend the money to send the nervous Florrie to a hospital so she can have a male doctor. After the Chinese soldiers who were protecting the mission depart, Pether builds up his courage to seek help and is killed. Tunga Khan and his soldiers attack the mission just as Florrie goes into labor. Cartwright realizes that she must give herself to the warlord so she will be allowed to deliver the baby. With her newfound power over the Mongol, Cartwright demands that he let the women and children leave the mission. While Agatha calls Cartwright a "wanton and lustful woman," the others understand her sacrifice. Cartwright eventually secures Tunga Khan's permission to let the women and children leave. After they have gone, Cartwright poisons the wine that she and the warlord drink in a toast.

The film was scheduled to be shot in forty days at a budget of $2.1 million. (It ended up costing nearly $2.3 million.) Shortly before New Year's 1965, Patricia discovered she was pregnant again. Discussing it with Roald, she decided to keep her condition a secret from the studio, as the filming would start the first of January. She was to begin her scenes at the end of the month. But the filming was continually delayed.

By February 13, Patricia still hadn't been called to appear before the cameras. She told Roald if the call did not come for her to begin that day she would tell Metro and Ford of her condition; it would probably mean she would have to leave the film. That evening her first call, for filming the next day, came through.

On February 17, Ford required Patricia to do rather strenuous work on her very first scene in the film (shot out of sequence), riding into the mission's courtyard on a donkey. Over and over again she had to repeat that scene. First there were technical difficulties, then in one shot the camera picked up the animal trainer and additional crew standing off the set. Then there were lighting and sound problems. Ford had Patricia do the scene a half dozen times, with her jumping down off the donkey at the end of each take. By the end of the day she was exhausted and feeling a bit weak. Costume shots that day show Patricia looking very thin and tired.

When she returned to the Ritts' house late that afternoon, Patricia had a slight headache.[36] The children wanted to hear about what had happened at the studio that day, and she told them all about the donkey. "How exciting! A donkey! What was it like? Tell us again, Mummy! Are you sure you didn't fall off just once?" they asked. "What's a donkey?" inquired Theo.

By 6:00 P.M. it was time for the older children's baths. Sheena took Theo upstairs first for his. "Please, Mummy, bathe me in your bathroom," pleaded Tessa. Roald remained downstairs to prepare the evening cocktails and visit with Sheena's new beau.

Kneeling on the floor beside the bathtub, Patricia began soaping her daughter's shoulders with the warm bathwater. Within seconds she felt a sharp pain from the lower back of her neck that shot up to the top left of her head. Perhaps she had overdone it that day and should not be bending over. Suddenly she felt queasy and disoriented. Standing up, she reached her hand to her left temple. Like a bolt of lightning the pain struck.

"Mummy! Mummy, what's wrong?" Tessa cried out. The little girl knew in the pit of her stomach that something was wrong. Roald started climbing the stairs with their drinks. He knew Patricia always looked forward to a martini after work. Tessa by now had jumped out of the bathtub and was crying to him, "Daddy, something is wrong with Mummy!" Roald bolted to the bedroom where his stricken wife stood swaying in the bathroom doorway.

"What is it? Are you all right?" he called to her.

"I've got the most awful pain right here," she said slowly, putting her hand on her temple. "I think something is wrong. I've been seeing things, too."

"What sort of things?" he asked.

"I don't know. I can't remember," she replied with ever-growing fear in her voice.

"Are you seeing things now?" he asked.

"No, not now. But I feel ill. I feel rotten." Carefully lying down on the bed, Patricia placed her head back on the pillow. For half a minute Roald observed her. What was happening? Suddenly her eyes opened and she cried,

"The pain is terrible."

"Is it only in one place?" he asked quietly.

"Yes . . . it's here . . . right here."

The pain struck again. Her head suddenly jerked forward, then back, as she lost consciousness.

Roald rushed to the adjoining study, located an unlisted telephone number thumbtacked to the wall, reached for the telephone, and called Dr. Charles Carton, who he had recently met at a party. Fortunately, Dr. Carton, one of Los Angeles's leading neurosurgeons, was home.

"Can you come right over?" Roald pleaded. Carton assumed something was wrong with Theo. When told the patient was Patricia, the stunned doctor advised Roald that he would send an ambulance to rush her to the UCLA Medical Center emergency room. He would meet them there.

Turning back to Patricia, Roald saw that she was covered in vomit. Nausea had overcome her while she was unconscious. Briefly regaining consciousness, Patricia cried, "Who is in this house? What are the names of the people in this house, please? Who are they all? You must tell me the names!"

"You mean the children's names?" he asked.

"Yes! Yes! The children's names." This could not be happening. She had children to raise. She had a new life inside of her. She had to work the next morning. The pounding echo of her heart drummed and amplified inside her head as she lapsed into coma.

Part 3

Legend

In terms of what has happened in my life, I don't quite understand it. I don't know why some people are picked on and some people aren't. But you just can't be a sissy. You can't give up.

There were times when I was so indignant, so furious about all this. Somehow, I don't know when it happened, I came to believe that we do live in a fabulous world. Sometimes, when I think about all the amazing countries and the oceans we have on Earth, I become so happy to know that I'm here.

I really adore life now. I even adore the fact that you never know what's going to happen in life from one minute to the next. Now, I'm just going to continue to do the best in this life. I don't conk easy.

—Patricia Neal to Mary Alice Williams, *Quiet Triumphs,* 1999

21

Illness

There are many things which give me pleasure now. Simple things like waking up in the morning and finding out I'm alive.

—Patricia Neal, May 1965

As he waited for the ambulance, Roald sat still, breathing heavily, holding Patricia's hand while intently watching her. Even with her body in distress, her face was still beautiful, he thought. The room was deathly quiet.

Sheena tried to calm Tessa and Theo by reading to them in Tessa's room. The children heard the ambulance's siren.

"What's that?" Theo asked.

Sheena told them, "It's a cat."

"No, it's not," Tessa said quietly. She'd heard that sound before. "It's an ambulance coming for Mummy."

As the sound of the siren grew louder, Angela's boyfriend rushed outside to flag down the ambulance. Two paramedics rushed up the pink marble steps to the bedroom. They immediately began resuscitation on Patricia, attaching an oxygen machine. Strapping Patricia to a chair and covering her with a blanket, they carried their charge down the steps as Patricia mumbled and passed in and out of consciousness. The time was 6:20 P.M. Roald climbed into the ambulance behind the stretcher. He asked the driver not to turn the siren on until after they had cleared the house; he did not wish to frighten the children. Neighbors stood watching as the ambulance sped off toward the hospital.

Dr. Charles Carton, the neurosurgeon, met the ambulance at the emergency entrance of UCLA Hospital. Patricia was awake and aware upon arrival, but quickly slipped into unconsciousness. Immediately they wheeled her into the emergency room and conducted a spinal tap that disclosed blood

Facing page: Patricia Neal in *7 Women*, February 1965. From the author's collection.

253

in her fluid, indicating she had suffered a hemorrhagic stroke. To find exactly where the hemorrhage had struck, they brought her into X-ray. Roald told them Patricia was pregnant, and a lead apron was placed over her abdomen to protect the unborn baby. Apparently there had been two hemorrhages by the time Carton began his examination, and as they studied the X-ray angiography, Patricia suffered a third—the most massive of all.

After examining the radiographs, Carton sought Dahl's permission to operate. "Her condition is very critical," he told Roald.

"Are you going to operate?" asked Roald.

"I doubt she would be able to survive an operation."

"What will happen if you don't?"

"If I don't, she is certain to die."

Dahl was indecisive, and asked the neurosurgeon if he would operate if Patricia was his wife. "I would operate," Carton replied, but added, "Please don't be too hopeful." Roald gave his consent.

Without wasting another minute, Carton and two resident surgeons began to prepare for surgery. Patricia's head was shaved, and Carton, heading the surgical team, sawed open her left temple bone, making a four-by-six-inch "trapdoor" with which to gain access to the brain. There Carton began removing blood clots that had formed and, guided by X-rays, found that the original break had been in the left carotid artery, caused by the ballooning and eventual bursting of an aneurysm in the artery wall. After he removed the clot between the brain and its dura mater, the parchmentlike covering of the brain, Carton cut into the left temporal lobe, the area of the brain that controls speech, and carefully removed another clot. He then painstakingly lifted the left temporal lobe, attached a tendon-like clip across the base of the aneurysm, and, to reinforce the artery wall, sprayed a plastic coating on it before completing the surgery, which lasted over seven hours.

Claire Carton, the neurologist's wife, arrived at the UCLA Medical Center while the surgery was still in progress. Her anxiety and concern were genuine. Patricia had visited Claire when she had given birth to the Cartons' second child just the year before. The doctor's wife found Roald pacing the floor. He had called Millie Dunnock at the Chateau Marmont, where she was staying during the filming of *7 Women*, and asked her to tell the children what had happened.

Even in 1965, surgeries on the brain, especially those dealing with aneurysms, were not uncommon. But these operations were still intricate and tricky, and Patricia's damage was severe. Said Dr. Carton in 2003, "Technically we did what we had to do." After surgery, Dahl thanked the neurosurgeon.

Candidly, considering Patricia's condition, Carton told Dahl, "I'm not sure if I've done you a favor." Patricia was listed in severely critical condition.

During Roald's vigil that night, Betsy Drake arrived at the hospital. She commented later that after the surgery, Patricia "looked as though she was in a storm at sea."[1] Dahl had the presence of mind to see that the children were taken care of. When not on the *7 Women* set, Mildred Dunnock assisted at the Ritt home daily, making telephone calls and caring for the children, as did other friends of the couple. By dawn the morning of Thursday, February 18, the news media had caught wind of the operation. Telephone calls started coming in, and they never stopped. Wires and letters arrived at the Ritt home from Robert and Rosemarie Stack, Robert Porterfield, Ann Sheridan and Scott McKay, screenwriter Harry Kurnitz, Katharine Cornell, Elsa and George Shdanoff, Annabella Power, and Judy Garland. Anne Bancroft wired as soon as the story hit the news, "Absolutely thunderstruck. Please call me if I can be of help."[2]

Notified of Patricia's condition the evening of February 18, George and NiNi boarded a plane to fly to the coast. Eura Neal was ill with an ear disorder in St. Petersburg, Florida, and could not immediately come to her daughter's side; her doctor simply forbade it. "I just talked to my son-in-law," Mrs. Neal told the press the morning of February 19. "He said that Pat is holding on and that if she makes it through the critical period, there's a chance."[3] K. T. Stevens sat by the telephone at the hospital fielding calls. Roald himself did not return to the Ritt home until the morning of February 19, exhausted.

Family friend Alex March told the *New York Journal-American*, "Her life is up for grabs. Her husband is with her night and day. . . . He has done a remarkable job all through this thing. He seems to be made of steel."[4] It was much too early to tell if Patricia had permanent brain damage, but the papers speculated just the same. "Patricia Neal's Condition Grave," said one headline.[5] "Patricia Neal May Survive Two Strokes," reported another.[6]

The head of UCLA Medical Center's intensive care unit, registered nurse Jean Alexander, reported to work on February 19 to discover that actress Patricia Neal, admitted into the hospital under the name Mrs. Pat Dahl, was now in her post-op charge. A reporter had attempted to sneak in and snap a picture of Patricia and was caught. The ICU sign was quickly taken down to deter another attempt.

"Dr. Carton is a very special kind of physician," Alexander later said. "He's the neurosurgeon, so he got a specialist to deal with the other aspects of Patricia's care. He had a gastroenterologist looking after her stomach, he had an ob/gyn looking after her pregnancy. He had all the bases covered and they [the specialists] would come in every day and check *every*thing."[7]

The newspapers continued their vigil. The *Los Angeles Herald-Examiner* headlined its February 20 report, "Little Hope For Actress." *Variety* reported on February 22, "Film Actress Patricia Neal Dies at 39." Needless to say, *Variety* spoke too soon, and later news reports quickly corrected the error.

A week after the stroke, Roald's sister Else wrote Eura Neal, "Poor, poor Roald, how much more can he take? But I spoke to him the night before last and he said that he is being well looked after and the children, too. . . . Our house has been like a telephone exchange for the past week and I go out just to get away from it, even the village shopkeepers ring me up. Pat is so much loved and so much needed that she's got to get better and there are so many people to help her on what is bound to be a long, hard road back, that that will make it all easier. You must be very proud to have a daughter who is so much loved."[8]

Roald was continually by Patricia's bedside, talking to her, coaxing her to respond. When he was just too exhausted to continue, he would catch a few hours of sleep in a waiting room chair. "I was nearly as worried about Roald as I was about Pat," said Dr. Edmund Goodman, who left his Manhattan practice the week after Patricia's stroke to join Roald in California. Goodman continued, "Pat was a pitiful sight. She was unconscious and made no voluntary movements. It was a frightening thing to see her. But Roald was there just all the time. He would get up at six to be at the hospital for the morning rounds. He almost supervised the care that was given her. He was so aware of everything—what helped her and what didn't, how she was turned, what she was fed and whether it was too little or too much. He was constantly bending over her, shouting into her ear, 'Hello, Pat. This is Roald. This is Roald. Tessa says hello. Theo says hello. Don Mini says hello.' He was *giving* her life."[9]

But Mildred Dunnock, who visited Patricia nearly every day, was sometimes taken aback by Roald's actions. She couldn't abide Roald's shouting into Patricia's ear and raising her eyelids in hopes of getting a response. He even slapped Patricia's face in Millie's presence.

Roald angered NiNi considerably by throwing away religious get-well messages and cards. NiNi reported this to Eura, who, though her own health prevented her from coming to California, would always believe that Roald had told her not to come. This was unfair, but Eura began to search for and exaggerate things to discredit her son-in-law. For example, she claimed, inaccurately, that Roald prevented Chloe Carter, a devout Catholic, from seeing Patricia. Arthur and Mary Kennedy frequently came to the hospital. Devoted friends expressed their compassion in different ways, and Dahl found great support through these individuals.

On March 10, Patricia slowly regained consciousness. As she wrote in her autobiography, "Everyone has said the first thing I saw was Roald's face looking down at me. It may have been so. He said I opened one eye and looked at him for five seconds and shut it again. He said my hand was squeezing his. I hope so. . . . I don't remember."[10] She did recall that when she came out of the coma, she realized she could not talk, she suffered from double vision, and her right side was paralyzed. She was frightened and angry; these were perhaps her bleakest moments. Patricia recalled that when alone in the darkness of her room, the only sounds she could hear inside her head were "wubble-wubble-wubble-wubble." She wanted to die.[11]

On March 11, Roald's sister Elsa wrote Eura that Roald "rang the other evening to tell us that Pat was now out of danger and conscious. That was indeed music to our ears too, and poor Mama [Mormor] burst into tears when she was trying to tell someone about it—it was such a relief. Roald tells us that there seems to be considerable damage, but of course there will be improvement. Otto Preminger rang me last night and said that he had just spoken to his wife, who had seen Pat, and that there were very encouraging signs—recognizing everyone and trying to speak. That was wonderful news and good of him to ring me. . . . We have had lovely letters from Sheena and are so relieved to hear that the children are bearing everything so well. It must be so very hard for Tessa and Theo too."[12]

Dahl's mother sent Eura a touching letter four days later. She told Eura that when she heard the news about Patricia's strokes, she lost the hearing in one ear. "My doctor thought it was due to shock," she wrote. "Last night we telephoned Roald and the news was very cheerful. Pat was sitting up in a wheelchair, and Tessa and Theo had been allowed to see her. This I am very pleased about, especially for Tessa's sake as she has had so many tragedies in her life. Luckily Sheena is there and Angela Kirwin [sic] and Roald says that Sheena is doing a marvelous job with the children. . . . I can well understand that you would like to go there, but I understand that they have everything well organized, and are hoping to take Pat home this week with a nurse, I expect, and to fly here in 4–6 weeks time, where we hope to have the alterations to their house finished. Let us hope that Pat's paralysis is only a temporary one."[13]

Physical therapy was begun immediately. Jean Alexander assisted with the daily lumbar puncture, in which a needle was inserted into Patricia's back to draw spinal fluid to check how the cleansing of blood was progressing. When

Dr. Carton repeated his remark to Roald about not being sure whether he had done Patricia and Roald a favor by saving Patricia, Jean recalled saying, "Don't you worry, doctor. She is going to walk and talk and act again."[14] To keep Patricia's upper and lower limbs flexible, the therapists exercised them for ten to fifteen minutes with passive and resistant pressure three times a day. Patricia's right arm had been clutched close to her body. Once the right arm was forced open, the skin of the inner elbow, finally exposed to the air, began to slough off. Tests were begun to determine what lasting effects the strokes had inflicted on Patricia. She was given an eye patch to alleviate the double vision, a brace was placed on her right leg, and her feet were placed in sensible oxfords and she was forced to stand and walk.

As Jean Alexander was washing Patricia's feet one day, the nurse started quietly singing "I Could Have Danced All Night," which was playing on the radio. "Then came this deep voice into the song," recalled Jean. "It was Pat. She sang at least a whole sentence. She was grinning at me. Then she turned herself off."[15] After fourteen days of silence, Patricia had regained her ability to communicate, but only through song. For the next ten days, Jean and Patricia would cheerfully sing together the few songs they both knew, like "Down in the Valley," "My Darling Clementine," and "Bluetail Fly."

During Patricia's recovery, nurse Gloria Carugati began assisting Jean Alexander. "[Patricia] would be limping in a slovenly fashion," Alexander recalled. "Then we'd sing 'A Pretty Girl is Like a Melody,' and up would come that hammy face and she would straighten her shoulders. And when we got a camera, Miss Neal just sat right up."[16] At first Patricia's vocabulary was impaired, and she would make up words for objects. An "oblogon" was her word for cigarette, for example. Roald would insist that she think and form the proper words.

On the evening of March 17, exactly one month after her strokes, Patricia was released from the hospital to recuperate for a few weeks at the Ritt home before returning to Gipsy House in Great Missenden. The same two ambulance attendants who had carried her out of the Ritt home to the UCLA Medical Center came to take her back. "She has been talking some," someone from the hospital told the press. "She is quite a bit better." Hedda Hopper told her readers on March 17, "Pat Neal, before leaving the hospital, was visited by John Ford, who got a daily bulletin about her condition on the set of 'Seven Women.' As he stood looking down at her, she opened her eyes and smiled at him, then put out her hand which he took and held. She can now move and bend her right leg. The doctors didn't believe she had a chance. It's possible that she may have a full recovery."[17]

There had already been a report in the press that Patricia was pregnant. As he and Patricia left the hospital, Roald told reporters that Patricia was indeed four months along, but, "We don't know whether or not she'll be able to have the baby. We'll have to evaluate the effect of the medication and the x-ray treatment she's received. . . . But she is responding well to rehabilitation treatment. She is fully conscious and her thought processes are perfect. She can sit up in bed and feed herself with her left hand. And her speech is beginning to come back very well. Seeing our children has done her a lot of good. She had the youngest, Ophelia, 19 months, in her bed with her. She has been exceedingly cheerful since she became conscious after two and a half weeks in the hospital. She smiles. She is a tremendous fighter. Will she act again? All one could say is possibly."[18]

Roald also told the reporters that within the coming two weeks doctors would be able to tell if Patricia would be well enough to travel. He concluded the press interview with his comment: "I am overwhelmed by the magnificent treatment that Pat has received at the UCLA Medical Center during the four weeks she was there. The standard of nursing in the intensive care unit of Ward 2–East is superb."[19]

Anne Bancroft was hired to replace Patricia in *7 Women*. "My feelings are very complicated, and I have mixed emotions about doing this part," said Bancroft between scenes to reporter Vernon Scott. "I really couldn't say 'No' to accepting the part—for Pat's sake. I think she would rather have me replace her than anyone else."[20]

The film's producer, Bernard Smith, told Army Archerd of *Variety* that the cost incurred by Patricia's illness, $50,000, was not recoverable as it fell under a deductible insurance clause. Nevertheless, Ford-Smith Productions issued a check for $20,000 to Roald as part of Patricia's salary. Smith told another writer, "Things started to go wrong with *7 Women* when Patricia Neal had her stroke. We got the wrong girl, Anne Bancroft, the wrong girl. She was a wonderful actress, but she once described herself as a guinea from Brooklyn, and what we wanted was an austere lady. The story was much more of a tragic leap that way. And Ford shot it carelessly; he lost interest."[21] Ford said of Bancroft, "I couldn't get her to expand."[22]

The picture proved to be a mess, but Bancroft was not the only reason for its failure. As entertainment, *7 Women* is stunningly bad. It is stagy and badly acted, with perhaps the worst performance being that of the highly paid Sue Lyon. Seriously missing from the picture is the spark that Ford could have added. When *7 Women* opened in general release in January 1966, it bombed both critically and financially. Metro placed it on a double bill, always a bad sign, with the equally poor *The Money Trap*. Its gross worldwide was only $1 million upon its first release, putting it in the red by $2.3 million.

Roald believed that Patricia's mind should receive constant stimulation. At the Ritt house, Alexander and Carugati continuously questioned and tested Patricia, keeping her mind active and her interest focused. She was not an easy patient. "To get Pat to do a few exercises, unless I was a director from MGM, was like pulling teeth," Alexander recalled.[23] Games were made of finding the right names for things Patricia wanted; she would be rewarded when she got the words correct. Said Dr. Carton in 2003, "She was aphasic. Aphasia is the problem when people develop an inability to communicate either in understanding what is said or trying to express what they want to say. It was fortunate that the amount of damage she had from the spurting blood from the aneurysm could be obviated to some degree by the time and practice [of] people who knew how to handle speech therapy."[24]

Louella Parsons wrote in her Hollywood Snapshots column, "Ann [Rutherford] and Bill Dozier literally dragged Roald Dahl from Patricia Neal's side long enough to have his first dinner out in two months. But he bolted his meal at La Scala and hurried back to Pat."[25] Said Claire Carton, "I think he was extraordinarily instrumental in the amount of recovery she was able to do."[26]

Within a week after Patricia's release from the hospital, Mel Brooks and his wife, Anne Bancroft, invited Patricia and Roald over to their house. Brooks told reporter Louella Parsons, "We expected Pat to arrive in a wheel chair, but Pat was walking and got around unaided all over the house. The paralysis in her [right] side seems to be leaving. Her speech is much improved—she was laughing and joking!" Patricia wrote in her memoirs, "Annie had come by the house often. She was another with whom I felt totally at ease. Annie knew when to talk and when to shut up. . . . It was a fine evening. I couldn't follow a word of conversation, but in my heart I knew I was with good friends, and that was a joy."[27]

Roald's relentless focus on Patricia's recovery and well-being alienated some people, not the least of whom was Patricia's own mother, who was unable to fly to California because of her health. There were also friends and colleagues who deeply resented Roald's imperiousness. Selected people were allowed to visit with Patricia in and out of the hospital for short periods of time—friends such as Mel Brooks and Anne Bancroft, Mildred Dunnock, Lillian Hellman, Cary Grant, John Ford, K. T. Stevens and Hugh Marlowe, and Hope Preminger. Out of necessity, others were excluded, and there were hurt feelings.

Eura felt shut out and expressed herself in letters to Roald's sister Else, who on March 22 wrote Mrs. Neal, "I can fully appreciate your hurt and distress, and understand everything you feel. I can easily put myself in your place. Recently we have all felt that Roald's and Pat's understanding of each other has been to the exclusion of everyone else and this is a wonderful thing. They have been through so much together that it has strengthened their love and trust of each other to a degree not experienced by many people. I feel that anything Roald is now doing is with only one thought in his mind—what will be best for Pat. We all feel that outsiders are the best for them both as any strong emotional element could be damaging. . . . So I think that you should try not to feel hurt and be patient until they are ready to see you. It will be of more value for you and Pat to see each other when she is better, and of course, she will know and be told how much you all care."[28]

In Harm's Way premiered on March 31, 1965, with a huge publicity campaign. The 165-minute film received fairly favorable reviews, with praise for the magnificent black-and-white photography, musical score, and sound effects. The film is long and ponderous at times, but the special effects are superb. Paramount spent a lot of money on this picture, and it shows.

In Harm's Way blends fact with fiction. Period artifacts like automobiles and military equipment, and the use of real naval vessels, add to the realism. However, no attempt was made to dress the female cast members in period dress or alter their 1960s hairstyles. These blatant oversights are prevalent in every scene. At the opening party sequence, the extras are so amateurish that some actually look at the camera. Viewed today these errors are glaring and detract from the picture's realism.

Patricia's few scenes are placed strategically throughout the film, making her scenes with Wayne, which add necessary dramatic credibility to his character, convincing. She enjoyed working with Wayne this time, and the few scenes she shared with Brandon De Wilde were poignant. Patricia had a wonderful time filming the one encounter she had with Kirk Douglas's character.

Said *Variety*, "Miss Neal brings to her role a beautifully proportioned, gutsy strength and sensitivity, heightened by nuances of a woman desperately hoping to have and hold her dream man. But on its own terms 'In Harm's Way' is a compelling action-drama-romance. This is an accomplished work of picture making which should be gratifying to Preminger—just as it seems destined to please audiences generally."[29]

The critic in the *Hollywood Reporter* said John Wayne was "the best he has ever been in his career" in the film. He continued, "Patricia Neal, as a rather big, comfortable woman who returns him to the human race, is absolutely unique. Miss Neal, scorning most artifice, has such depths of integrity, and such ways of projecting them. She also has an aura of sex appeal that the little girls with the empty heads and bulging bras will never understand or never, never approximate."[30]

On April 5, 1965, the Dahl family watched the Thirty-seventh Annual Academy Awards presentation on television. Normally the preceding year's winner of the Best Actress Oscar presented the Best Actor Oscar. Replacing Patricia as presenter in 1965 was Audrey Hepburn, who did not receive a nomination for her work in *My Fair Lady*.

"There! There!" exclaimed Patricia as she saw the cool and serenely elegant Hepburn float out onto the stage of the Santa Monica Civic Auditorium to present the Best Actor Oscar to the equally slick and elegant Rex Harrison. Hepburn did not mention Patricia's name. (Emcee Bob Hope had acknowledged briefly on the telecast that Patricia Neal could not be there that night.) "God! God! Me! Not me!" cried Patricia.[31] Asked later if she was annoyed that Hepburn had not mentioned her name, Patricia recalled, "I bloody well was!"[32] Dahl knew that the outburst was encouraging. Normally there would not have been a response so soon from someone recovering after a stroke. But Roald knew she was healing, and her illness was not necessarily her sole priority.

The telephone rang, and a reporter asked Roald how Patricia liked the broadcast. He said, "She thought it bloody well stunk."[33] Roald told the press later, "She and Audrey have known each other for a long time. And Audrey didn't even call until the day after the ceremonies—and that was after I think someone told her Pat was hurt. Audrey had to leave on a one o'clock plane so she didn't have time to see Pat either. Had we not sent the telegram to Bob Hope from Pat at the awards, there probably would have been no mention of her at all."[34]

Friends became important in the lives of the family during their remaining weeks in Hollywood. Millie's husband, Keith Urmy, took the children to Disneyland. Jean Hagen, Peter Douglas and his wife Virginia, and Eddie and Margo Albert came to visit. Robert and Kathryn Altman and Carolyn and Alex March cooked meals for the family. Therapy was improvised. Even Theo's flash cards—DOG, CAT, GOAT, HOUSE—were used to stimulate Patricia's healing mind. Dahl was most impressed with the two nurses, Jean and Gloria, and he asked them if they would consider traveling back to England with the family.

Eura Neal was finally able to fly to Los Angeles during the last month the Dahls were in the Ritt home. She was given the guest bungalow in back of the main house. Eura still blamed Roald for her inability to visit earlier, and she was shocked that Patricia would allow Roald to make all the decisions. She said to Patricia, "Your daddy would never have treated me like that. George would never treat Margaret Ann like that."[35] The tension mounted. When the Dahls found that Marjorie Clipstone was in the States, they asked Eura to move upstairs into Ritt's small office so that Marjorie could have the guest house. One of the nurses had to leave temporarily, and Roald expected Eura to stand in for her until the family left for England. Eura had had enough, and she left before her scheduled departure date. Between Roald and the unyielding Mrs. Neal there would never be peace.

Patricia's improvement was encouraging. Every morning she would arise at 7:30 and dress herself. If she needed to go to the bathroom during the night, she would quietly creep out of bed so as not to disturb her sleeping husband, and often she would literally crawl to the bathroom. On May 12 the family celebrated Ophelia's first birthday with a cake, and afterward the doctors examined Patricia and concluded that she was well enough to travel by air. Their return to England was set for the following week. Dahl told the press that a fifteen-minute press conference would be held at the airport prior to their May 14 departure. "She is going to walk on the plane and she won't need help," Roald said.[36]

Cary Grant offered to drive the family to the airport. Leaving the Ritt home wearing a turban, an eye patch, and a brace on her right leg, Patricia proudly displayed her bulging stomach. At the airport, she told the waiting reporters, "The doctor's prediction is fine."[37] (Roald was impressed when Patricia said the word "prediction"; it was not a word she had practiced.) Carefully choosing her words, Patricia continued, "I don't do it [speak] right, you know." When asked how her baby was doing, she simply replied, "Fine." In conclusion, she told the reporters, "You've made me strong—and happy."[38] The press had found her to be in a cheerful mood, holding her own with the rapid-fire questioning. Hugh Marlowe and K. T. Stevens and John Ford arrived at the airport to see them off. Ford brought Patricia an orchid.

The Dahls stopped over in Washington for two days, staying with their friend Claudia Haines Marsh. For reasons Patricia couldn't understand, Robert and Ethel Kennedy invited the Dahls to visit their home, Hickory Hill. The Dahls' former nanny Susan had a friend who took care of the Kennedy children, and Patricia believed that Ethel Kennedy must have been roped into hosting the party. On the contrary, Ethel Kennedy was thrilled to have them. Dignitaries and well-wishers lined up to greet the Dahls, and they had a good time. While in Washington, Patricia told the press, "I haven't forgotten anything. It's simply that particular words escape me."[39] Of Roald she said, "He insists on making games out of everything and the children play it too, especially five-year-old Theo, who seems to think mummy's just playing another part."[40] Dahl told the reporters the *Ladies' Home Journal* had commissioned him to write an article about Patricia's battle for recovery. "It will help pay the bills," he said candidly.[41]

The family arrived at London's Heathrow Airport on May 17 and were met by a barrage of press questions and flashbulbs. When asked if she would return to acting anytime soon, Patricia cautiously told them, "I would like to, but I may not be able to. If I can't, I suppose I will settle down to being just a wife."[42] Most of the Dahl family was there to welcome them back, and after hugs and kisses, Patricia found herself crying from happiness for the first time since before her stroke. Back in Great Missenden Roald and Patricia were welcomed like returning heroes. When asked what was making her happy now, Patricia replied, "having my children around."[43]

The local village chemist had sent a bottle of vintage champagne to Gipsy House to welcome the family back. When Dahl proposed a toast and Patricia took her first sip, she removed her eye patch. "It's gone!" she exclaimed. "The double eyes."[44] Her double vision had vanished. The house was filled with flowers from every garden in the village, and the villagers had brought over all sorts of food.

Gipsy House had undergone renovation while the family was in America. When they entered their home, both Roald and Patricia were appalled. The Dahls had intended for a British home interior magazine, which had offered to do the modification of the cottage, to spend approximately $3,000. The workmen became overzealous, however, and the modifications now totaled over $14,000. Three of Roald's sisters had been left to oversee the project, but for some reason they simply allowed the crew free reign. (Roald could not be bothered with the details of the house while Patricia was in the hospital.)

The workmen had ripped out the old wooden doors and antique floor tiles and replaced them with new ones. Impractical bookshelves with imitation books were installed between windows; the Dahls' magnificent antique furniture was replaced with new pieces of bamboo. And worst of all, the living room had been painted a ghastly dark brown, and the carpet was the same color—the color of "elephant turds," said Dahl.[45] "For the next few weeks the house was a jungle of ladders and tool boxes," wrote Barry Farrell in a *Life* magazine article. (Roald had agreed that Farrell could travel to Great Missenden and cover the last stages of Patricia's pregnancy.) "The living room was painted white again and Roald restored the paintings and furniture he lovingly and expertly collects—the Sheraton sofa table in faded rosewood (circa 1795), the little Charles I cricket table in wychelm, the vast Francis Bacon landscape, the Delacroix, the Tiepolo. It became a warm and lovely room to sit [in] again."[46]

The family was finding it hard to adjust. Tessa mentioned to Sonia Austrian at one point that she wanted to leave the house because "there are too many children here," referring to her siblings and her mother.[47] Theo was forever trying to get his mother to respond to his needs. Together they were learning to read, often using his flash cards. Patricia wrote in her memoirs of trying, sometimes futilely, to feed Ophelia. Yet she persisted. At one point Sheena became so frustrated with Patricia's determination to care for her child that the girl actually struck Patricia across the face. This infuriated Patricia, and she insisted Roald fire Sheena immediately. Roald calmed his wife, and Sheena left her position with the Dahls shortly afterward.

Friends of the Dahls in the village were at the family's disposal. Roald organized a meeting to lay out his program for Patricia's rehabilitation, and schedules were immediately set up to accommodate the volunteers. He insisted that Patricia experience stimulation and activity for eight hours between 7:00 A.M. and 6:00 P.M., with breaks for lunch and tea. Roald's sister Else was to teach Patricia to cook again, and the Kirwans, their daughter Angela, and Frankie Conquy would each spend an hour every day playing board games to encourage Patricia to spell. Actor Kenneth Haigh and English actress Joan Maynell read plays to Patricia. A Mrs. Newland, who was Mormor's companion-nurse, would come in some afternoons and do an hour of reading and writing with Patricia. And Helen Horton assisted Patricia with her mail and letters when she visited. Betsy Drake and Patricia had agreed to communicate through the use of audio tapes, but Patricia still needed written cards from which to read her responses.

Patricia's daily schedule also included a drive to the local Royal Air Force hospital near Halton, about ten miles from Great Missenden, for exercise for her right hand and ankle with therapist Hugh MacDougall. She was also learning to walk unaided. All the same, Patricia had grown tired of waiting for the birth of her child and was slipping into depression. She had lost interest in keeping her slow-growing hair combed, and because she was hugely pregnant, she now only had three brightly printed Mexican sack dresses she could wear. Eventually Patricia became too large to continue physiotherapy.

Dahl decided that her other lessons were to be suspended as well until after the baby's birth.

Patricia had begun to question God. She had been reared in a Southern Baptist family and had chosen at an early age to become a Methodist. Patricia was confirmed in the Anglican Church after her move to England. Her life circumstances began to reshape her faith. She once said, "I simply think there are so many things that happen, and I just don't think they can all be explained. I don't have any more definite idea of God or afterlife than anyone else does, but I simply do believe that there's something other than what we think we can control and figure out."[48] As her depression worsened, she spoke of deepening concern over her condition and especially her fear that she would never act again. "It's sad not to believe," she told Barry Farrell. "I can't help it—I just don't. When I woke up in the hospital, the first thing I thought of was that I didn't . . . I didn't believe anymore." Of suicide, she remarked sadly, "I'd like to—but I don't know how."[49]

Patricia started to scribble notes for the first time since her stroke. Columnist Radie Harris had made an error that particularly irked Patricia, and on July 14 she wrote in scratchy yet legible penmanship to Jean and Chloe, "I got your letter today. Thank you. Aren't I a great girl replying so soon? Yes, I am fed up waiting for the baby. We have no names for it yet. Radie Harris was wrong. I do have friends and visitors."[50] She was quite aware of what was being written about her, and this and the approaching delivery of her fifth child helped move Patricia toward emotional and physical recovery.

On August 2, Patricia and Roald left for Oxford's Radcliffe Hospital for the delivery. Patricia, wearing a heavy yellow coat and pink headscarf, posed for over ten minutes for photographers. "I love anyone who will take my picture," Patricia told the press.[51] Dahl had checked himself in at the Randolph Hotel in Oxford but spent virtually no time there. At the hospital, Dr. Hawksworth, whom everyone called "The Hawk," agreed, with Roald's consent, to induce birth two weeks earlier than expected. Patricia spent the next day pacing the floor to help induce the birth, and eventually nature took its course.

Inside the delivery room on August 4 were the medical delivery staff, Roald, Barry Farrell, and *Life* magazine photographer Leonard McCombe, who was there to photograph the mother and child. After less than four hours of labor, at 8:23 A.M., Patricia delivered a six-pound, eight-ounce girl whom the Dahls named Lucy Neal, after Patricia's grandmother. In spite of the whole ordeal of Patricia's strokes and medications, the child had endured and was pronounced unaffected and healthy. When close friend and senior clinic nurse Nesta Powell placed the newborn in her mother's arms, Patricia was heard to coo, "Oooo, Lucy, you're my last baby. You're good and you're fine and you're my last baby."[52]

Within six hours, Patricia was sitting up in bed, drinking beer and playing dominoes. Six weeks before, Roald had bid on and won at Sotheby's a fourth-century B.C. ring to give Patricia as a baby gift. The ring had an engraving of Persephone on the oval bezel. This beautiful gift compelled Patricia to apply some lipstick and to brush her hair, a display of vanity she had not shown in some time.

Later that fall, little Lucy was christened in the chapel of St. John the Baptist in Little Missenden, the same church where her older sister Ophelia had been christened. Roald began renovation of the kitchen at Gipsy House, removing a wall to "give the nursery some character,"[53] and a new wing of the house was begun. The Dahls also had a new au pair they called Klara (her real name was Klari Szalay), an attractive twenty-two-year-old brunette from Budapest, Hungary, to look after the children.

Patricia's lessons resumed on a daily basis. She was now physically lighter and feeling more and more self-confident each day. She also expressed a desire to start going out again. Roald took her to see the Beatles' second feature film, *Help!* but she didn't understand a thing about it.

By the fall of 1965 Patricia was receiving great amounts of mail. Letters from most well-wishers and fans were answered at random, but all personal friends were sent handwritten cards and notes. Eura Neal still believed that Roald was too controlling of her daughter's life, perhaps because she didn't realize the full extent of the therapy Patricia needed. Eura seemed to think that because she was alert, talking, and had given birth again, Patricia was fully rehabilitated. Eura also complained that she wasn't receiving enough letters from Patricia and Roald.

Patricia wrote her mother on August 17, "I have my good baby. I had no pain when she was born. Because I had an injection in my spine so that I felt nothing."[54] Roald's accompanying letter was tolerant: "I am afraid that life is almost too hectic here right now for much letter writing and certainly for me. I have the house to run, and all my own and Pat's affairs to deal with as well, not to mention the business of trying to work so as to earn a living for this large family. You must therefore excuse the lack of letters. But Pat is extremely well, and so is the baby. She has quite wisely been advised against trying to feed it herself so that she can concentrate entirely upon her rehabilitation. She has already began again her strict routine of physical therapy and speech therapy, and among other things, she has around 20 pounds to lose in weight."[55]

Roald's article for the September 1965 issue of the *Ladies' Home Journal* was entitled "My Wife, Patricia Neal." It gave the family some needed income. For one thing, Patricia's insurance through Actors Equity and the Screen Actors Guild would be depleted by the end of the year.

Farrell's *Life* magazine article, which was later expanded into the book *Pat and Roald*, hit the stands shortly afterward. *Life* hosted a party at Patricia's favorite restaurant, the seventeenth-century Bell Inn in Aston Clinton, famous for its duck dishes. Patricia's short hair was cut and styled by an assistant sent from Vidal Sassoon's in London, and she looked lovely. British actor Stanley Holloway sang a song to her, and Harvey Orkin brought Patricia's director Marty Ritt to the party, who told the press while raising his glass in a toast, "She's a first-class actress, free, unafraid. She'll try anything. She's stylish in the best way a woman can be stylish."[56] Patricia wrote later that she needed to hear that remark at that particular moment in her life. The party marked the end of worries for many regarding Patricia's recovery.

Eura Neal wrote Patricia that she didn't like the magazine pieces or much else that had been going on. Roald had stood enough. In an uncharacteristically pleading letter to his indignant mother-in-law, Dahl asked her to explain her rude comments and criticism of him, especially regarding the magazine articles. Eura was apparently outraged because there was no mention in the article in *Ladies' Home Journal* of the Neal family. "I admit I didn't mention you," he wrote her. "But I didn't mention *my own mother* either." She was also dissatisfied with the choice of pictures of Patricia large with child. Dahl stated,

"I had no choice . . . of the picture. So please don't blame me for that. But remember that Pat was 8/9 months pregnant when those pictures were taken, so you can hardly expect her to be wearing a glamourous suit. She *had* to wear a maternity dress. And if you want to know, she *still* has to wear a maternity dress because she is 14 pounds overweight."

Continued Dahl, "The only one I wrote was the L.H.J. piece. Personally I thought it was a fine article. So did thousands of others. I must have received *ten thousand letters* of appreciation from America for it. . . . So, *please*, what is it that bothers you? How have I offended you? . . . In a case like this, Pat's family has only one duty—to support the husband who is trying desperately to cure her. Any letters that contain criticisms or demands or requests to her serve no purpose. So for heaven's sake stop them. I will not concede that I have wronged you in any way in the magazines. . . . But I shall write no more unless you explain the reasons of your hostility and send nicer letters."[57]

In the second week of September, Dahl flew Jean Alexander and Gloria Carugati to England to work for six months. Through his influence with Dr. Till, he was able to secure permits for them to work at the Atkinson Morely Hospital, a neurological center in Wimbledon. On their days off, they would be able to take the train down to Great Missenden to visit and work with Patricia. "I am not a physical therapist," Jean advised Dahl. "And I am not a speech therapist. So I'll do anything else that might help her."[58] Dahl knew that the love and humor the two women shared with Patricia would be invaluable.

A brief crisis occurred one afternoon when Patricia accidentally walked into a door jamb, suffering a minor cut on the left side of her head. When she screamed, Roald rushed into the room to see her holding her hand to her left forehead, which was oozing blood. He called out for Jean and Gloria. While the four were driving to the hospital, the car ran out of gasoline and Roald and Gloria went off to find the nearest station. Jean and Patricia sought refuge in a small farmhouse, where Patricia charmed the farm couple who lived there, sharing her life and asking questions about theirs. Jean knew then that the "new" Patricia would be fine.

22

Comeback

I was an idiot, a complete idiot. Like an enormous pink cabbage.

—Patricia Neal, New York (1967)

As 1965 drew to a close, Patricia still could not communicate clearly, and she continued to wear the metal brace and occasionally the eye patch. But her path to recovery took a new and encouraging turn when she met Valerie Eaton Griffith, who lived about a mile from Gipsy House.

Griffith was born in 1924 and had enlisted in the Auxiliary Territorial Service, the women's branch of the British army, at the age of seventeen. She was a tennis player and worked as manager of an Elizabeth Arden salon in London before a thyroid operation left her with a limp in her right leg. She had returned to her father's home and was not working when Patricia Kirwan suggested that it might be of benefit to both Patricia and Valerie to work together.[1]

Valerie met the Dahls at their home shortly after Lucy's birth. When Valerie first walked through their door at Gipsy House, Patricia thought, "She is the one."[2] Valerie recalled, "When I first went to work with Pat we had a joke—Pat couldn't talk and I couldn't walk."[3] Valerie remembered that one of the first things Patricia ever told her was, "My mind is gone."[4] Valerie knew that was not true.

Roald dropped Patricia off at Grimm's Hill, the Griffith home, as he took the children to school each day. Together the two women devised methods of rehabilitation that helped them both. Sometimes Valerie's father, Eaton, and sister Daphne would join Valerie, and the three would play card games and do puzzles with Patricia, being careful not to overlap their conversation so that she could follow what was being said and join in. Valerie's methods of

---

Facing page: Patricia Neal, 1967. From the author's collection.

rehabilitation were truly improvised, yet they seemed to work. Both Patricia and Roald were impressed by her dedication and application, and she and Patricia soon became good friends.

Valerie said Dahl told her, "She has got to be stimulated a lot each day and every day. And that is the only way, if there is any." She added, "I recall Patricia's enormous interest in other people—she was genuinely interested." Regarding her initial work with Patricia, Valerie concluded that the hardest thing she had to do was "getting her sad eyes to focus."[5]

The villagers of Great Missenden gave occasional interviews to the press regarding Patricia's improving condition. Mrs. Wilkin, owner of the village's Fabella Boutique, said, "She began to make fantastic progress. She became— as she is now—amazingly cheerful, quite chatty, and smiling. She began to come into the shop once in a while to buy things for her girls—her maids."[6] The press was told that Patricia developed a habit of picking up trash she found along the streets of the town, and that the villagers called her the "town sweeper" and told her it wasn't really necessary she do that.[7]

In January 1966, BBC television broadcast an interview with Roald and Patricia from their home. Roald wanted Patricia to face the camera and regain her confidence. This would be the first time both would talk about Patricia's stroke and recovery to the world together via television. Speaking slowly and hesitantly, Patricia said, "It is very good to be alive, I think. But I am not sure. But I am alive, and I must just wait for things to happen to me, and I hope they will happen."[8] Recapping their years of tragedy, the two spoke candidly. Dahl mentioned his work with the development of the Wade-Dahl-Till shunt. They talked about Patricia's illness and recovery, and as she walked away from the camera in the final shot, the camera lingered on her until she was out of sight. "It was an honest interview with a woman who doesn't know how to be anything but honest," wrote one magazine writer.[9] Within hours of the broadcast, flowers and cards started arriving at Gipsy House, and the telephone rang continuously as friends, fellow actors, and well-wishers sent their love.

One of the many thousands of cards that Patricia received was from Gary Cooper's daughter, now Maria Cooper Janis. "I cannot describe the feeling its short but generous greeting imparted," wrote Patricia in her autobiography. "I will never forget its three most important words: *I forgive you.*"[10]

In late January, director Mike Nichols, who had once been advised by Patricia to leave show business, entered her life again. After the success of his comedy act with Elaine May, he had turned to film directing. He wanted Patricia to play the role of Mrs. Robinson in his second picture, *The Graduate.*

Lee Israel wrote in *Movie Life* magazine, "She reminded him that she still limped; he reminded her that Herbert Marshall had a wooden leg and the movie audiences never even noticed. She feared that she could not remember the lines; he told her that actors often forget their lines and that, if she wished, a blackboard could be used with the lines written on it."[11] However, Patricia wasn't ready for it, and she knew it. Anne Bancroft was eventually cast in the iconic role. Nichols told Patricia, "When you feel you are ready to return to work, I want the first call on your services."[12]

In Hollywood to finalize a deal with the Mirisch Brothers for his script of *Oh, Death Where Is Thy Sting-A-Ling?* as it was now called, Roald was more optimistic than Patricia, telling reporters he was sure she would be ready to act in September, when Nichols wanted to begin his film. "Pat's speech is virtually normal except for a slight hesitancy," he told *Los Angeles Mirror-News* reporter Bob Thomas. "Her face is 100 per cent normal. She still has a slight but obstinate limp caused by a weak right ankle. Her right hand is a little weak as yet, so that her handwriting is a bit wobbly, although she can write and spell perfectly. Her memory is good, except for names. . . . She may have to work at memorizing lines when she returns to work. . . . We can't tell now when she will be able to work again. But she wants to very badly. . . . Pat realizes she must rise to the challenge I have set for her and she is doing it."[13]

On February 24, Patricia visited the set of Peter Sellers's new picture, *Casino Royale*. Sellers said he would like her to star with him in an upcoming picture. That morning, Patricia sat off the set with Sellers's wife, Britt Ekland, and watched him do a scene. Her agent Harvey Orkin told London's *Daily Express*, "I knew the offer was in the air when Peter asked her to have lunch at the studio with him and Britt. I just knew when I took her to the studio it would stimulate her, you know, get her excited about work again. Listen, she's still the greatest. She's money from home, baby. There's not another actress with her range anywhere today."[14] When he brought her home that evening, she told Orkin, "I want to work again. Oh, yes. But it won't be for six months. I'm just hoping everything will be all right." To which he replied, "Baby, everything's going to be just fine."[15]

On March 23, Patricia attended the British Film Academy's BAFTA award ceremony, which was held at London's posh Grosvenor Hotel and broadcast throughout the British Isles. Patricia had been nominated for Best Foreign Actress for her role in *In Harm's Way*, along with Jane Fonda (*Cat Ballou*), Lila Kedrova (*Zorba the Greek*), and Simone Signoret (*Ship of Fools*). Perhaps the most emotionally touching moment of the ceremony was when Leslie

Caron announced that Patricia had won. Wearing a sleeveless evening gown, Patricia slowly rose and climbed the eight steps to the rostrum to receive her Wedgwood plaque. Patricia was sobbing. Gathering her composure, she addressed the eight hundred–odd "mink-and-diamond customers"[16] in the audience with a simple, "Thank you, but I didn't deserve this."[17] Wrote *Time* magazine later, "The audience exuberantly disagreed."[18]

In the United States, the broadcast of the Thirty-eighth Annual Academy Awards ceremony on April 18 included a special segment that had been filmed in England featuring Patricia talking about her 1963 Oscar win. Also that April, Patricia and Roald appeared on the syndicated *Merv Griffin Show*. In a twelve-minute interview filmed at Gipsy House, Griffin talked to Patricia about her life and recovery. He asked whether she thought she would be able to return to work within the year. She told him frankly she hadn't talked to her doctors about that. Dahl was then asked about his children's books and his wife's recovery. He answered that he was determined Patricia would get better and that she would return to work.

At home in Gipsy House, Patricia faced two usurpers of her position within the family. Tessa had taken it upon herself to become the hostess and conversationalist when company called. Roald was domineering and decisive in his actions. He began to add onto Gipsy House to make room for the ever-growing staff. He discussed menus with the cook and attended to the children and their education, social activities, and health care. Patricia by her own admission was often lethargic, sitting around eating candies, incessantly smoking, and gaining weight. She couldn't make sense of a simple children's book until Valerie appeared.

Patricia told Roald Dahl biographer Jeremy Treglown, "Everything was changed now. It was sad because our marriage, it had been really good, it really *was* good. I did the cooking; I did the children, keeping the house, the garden, the weeds—and then when I got ill, everything changed in the end. He was the only person who really could control the children, and it was 'Daddy! Daddy!' You know, they looked up to him and it was just so irritating to me. Everything was turned upside down. We'd been through so much, and [before] we did it equally, really."[19]

When Patricia became ill, she needed to protect herself and could not physically open herself up to her children; their energy was too much for her. Naturally, they gravitated to their father. "I would cry, 'Talk to me . . . talk to me!'" Patricia once recalled. "He would never support me. He just took them. That was difficult. My children turned against me. And he was not clever enough, or he must have liked the fact that he was the sole center."[20]

"Suddenly Last Summer," *Garden District*, 1958. *Left to right*: Beatrix Lehmann, Margo Johns, Gwen Nelson, Patricia Neal, Beryl Measor, and Philip Bond. London. From the Patricia Neal Collection.

Patricia Neal and Peter O'Toole in the British television episode "London—New York," for *Rendezvous*, 1959. From the author's collection.

Above left, Patricia Neal in *The Miracle Worker,* 1959. From the Patricia Neal Collection. *Above right,* Olivia, Tessa, and Susie Austrian under Patricia's dress in New York, 1960. Photograph by Roald Dahl, courtesy of Valerie Eaton Griffith

George Peppard and Patricia Neal in Blake Edwards's *Breakfast At Tiffany's,* 1961. From the author's collection.

Gipsy House, Great Missenden, England, 1961. From the Patricia Neal Collection.

Above left, Tessa, Olivia, and Theo at Gipsy House, 1961. Photograph by Roald Dahl, from the Patricia Neal Collection. *Above right,* Olivia with a pet bunny, England 1962. From the Patricia Neal Collection.

Patricia Neal in "The Days and Nights of Bee-bee" on Britain's *Drama '62*, 1962. From the author's collection.

Kim Stanley and Patricia Neal in "That's Where the Town Is Going" on *Westinghouse Presents*, 1962. Courtesy of Photofest.

Above left, Patricia Neal as Alma in *Hud,* 1963. From the author's collection. *Above right,* Patricia Neal and Paul Newman in *Hud,* 1963. From the author's collection.

Patricia Neal and Paul Newman in *Hud,* 1963. From the author's collection.

Patricia Neal and Curt Jergens in *Psyche 59*, 1964. From the author's collection.

Patricia Neal and Stephen Boyd in a scene cut from *The Third Secret*, 1964. Courtesy of Doug McClelland, from the author's collection.

John Wayne and Patricia Neal in Otto Preminger's *In Harm's Way*, 1965. From the author's collection.

Kirk Douglas and Patricia Neal in their only acting scene together. *In Harm's Way*. From the Patricia Neal Collection.

The Dahl family arriving in Los Angeles for the filming of the ill-fated *7 Women*, January 1965. From the Patricia Neal Collection.

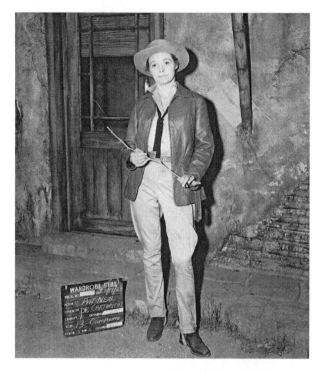

Patricia Neal costume test on the set of *7 Women*, February 17, 1965. From the Patricia Neal Collection.

Patricia Neal filming her arrival in *7 Women* on MGM's stage 15, February 17, 1965. (Notice crew members off the set.) From the Patricia Neal Collection.

Margaret Leighton and Patricia Neal in a rare scene still from *7 Women*, February 1965. From the author's collection.

The same scene re-shot with Leighton and Anne Bancroft, March 1965. From the author's collection.

Ophelia Magdelena and Lucy Neal Dahl, 1966. Photograph by Roald Dahl, from the Patricia Neal Collection.

Producer Edgar Lansbury and Lee Strasberg watching Patricia Neal greet Joan Crawford at the Evening with Patricia Neal ceremony at the Waldorf Astoria Hotel in New York, March 1967. From the Patricia Neal Collection.

Patricia Neal as Nettie Cleary in her film comeback, *The Subject Was Roses*, 1968. From the author's collection.

Patricia Neal and Dr. Charles Carton at Club John after the Los Angeles premiere of *The Subject Was Roses*, 1968. From the Patricia Neal Collection.

Richard Thomas and Patricia Neal in the television classic *The Homecoming*, 1971. From the author's collection.

Patricia Neal as the deranged Lupe in *Widow's Nest*, 1976. From the Patricia Neal Collection.

Patricia Neal, Roald Dahl, and Valerie Eaton Griffith, circa 1970s. From the Patricia Neal Collection.

Patricia Neal as Cookie in Robert Altman's black comedy *Cookie's Fortune*, 1999. From the author's collection.

Patricia's seventieth birthday celebration in New York. *Standing (left to right)*: Madeleine Dahl (Theo's wife), Sophie Dahl, Tessa Dahl, Ophelia Dahl, and Lucy Dahl. *Seated*: Theo Dahl and Patricia Neal, January 1996. From the Patricia Neal Collection.

Left, Patricia Neal and President Ronald Reagan, circa 1980s. From the Patricia Neal Collection. *Above,* Patricia Neal and Paul Newman at the closing of *Our Town,* in New York on Newman's birthday, January 26, 2003. From the Patricia Neal Collection.

The seventy-fifth Academy Awards rehearsal luncheon, Los Angeles, March 22, 2003. *Left to right:* Olivia de Havilland, Celeste Holm, Luise Rainer, Margaret O'Brien, Randal Malone, and Patricia Neal. Courtesy of Michael Schwibs, from the author's collection.

Patricia Neal, January 2004. Courtesy of Turner Classic Movies. All rights reserved.

Author Stephen Michael Shearer and Patricia Neal, Roanoke, Virginia, April 2005. Courtesy of James N. Bullington, from the author's collection.

In mid-August, Patricia flew to Tokyo to join Roald, who was in Japan for the filming of his screenplay of Ian Fleming's novel *You Only Live Twice*. Patricia only stayed for two weeks before returning to England by herself. She told a magazine writer, "It was just marvelous—Roald and I alone. Usually Roald likes to take the children everywhere with us."[21] A friend who was with them in Japan recalled, "She had terrible trouble with thought and speech associations. Well, she talked rubbish. Her memory was uneven. Maybe I was good for her, because we talked a lot about Hollywood and mutual friends. Roald would walk away and leave her alone at the damnedest times. He would send her out shopping alone, and she couldn't speak English, let alone Japanese. But he never let her develop self-pity. Every little thing she did accomplished something; she began to rally, and this led to her pride in self-accomplishment. So Roald was *not* cruel."[22]

Back in England, Patricia resumed her work with Valerie Eaton Griffith three times a week. Dahl returned to England around September 13, his birthday. Geoffrey and Sonia Austrian flew over to visit, and Sonia made a telling comment to Patricia, "Well, Tennessee hillbillies just don't conk that easy, do they?" Roald picked up on that remark, and as Patricia said, he "filed it away for future use."[23]

Roald had struck upon the idea of booking Patricia to give a speech in New York on behalf of the Association for Brain Injured Children that coming March. With that purpose in mind, he left for New York the first week in November to make arrangements. He continued to Hollywood for talks with United Artists regarding his next screenplay, to be based on another Ian Fleming story, *Chitty Chitty Bang Bang*.

While he was in the United States, he met with producer Edgar Lansbury (brother of actress Angela Lansbury), director Ulu Grosbard, and playwright Frank D. Gilroy. They had approached Dahl about whether Patricia was capable of performing the role of Nettie Cleary in the projected film version of their stage success *The Subject Was Roses*, which had won a Tony Award for Best Play and a Pulitzer Prize for best drama in 1965. Roald told them that Patricia would be delighted to do the film.

In November, Lansbury, Grosbard, and Gilroy flew to England to get a look at Patricia, and she did not let them down. Dahl made certain she wore makeup, and Patricia looked every inch the glamorous movie star. She also made a splendid lunch for them—"a delicious coq au vin, if I recall right," said Lansbury—and they spent the entire day at Gipsy House discussing the project.[24] Valerie encouraged Patricia to do the picture, though Patricia at first balked at the idea. Apparently the three men liked what they saw, and after agreeing to allow her several months to memorize and rehearse her lines before filming began in early 1968, they departed.

Just before Christmas, columnist Sheilah Graham broke the news that Patricia would return to films in *The Subject Was Roses*. It was a star part. Harvey Orkin told the press, "We had to be careful about the choice of film, but this is it. It's a great part. I've known for some time that Pat was going to be all right. Eight months ago a director offered her a cameo role in his film—the kind that Peter Sellers did in *What's New Pussycat?* after his heart attack. It was a good part, though not the star part, and when I told Pat about it she said, 'No, I want to be the star.' I knew then she'd be just fine. The old competitive spirit was still there."[25]

The Association for Brain Injured Children event was called "An Evening with Patricia Neal" and was held at the Waldorf Astoria Hotel on Park Avenue the evening of March 12, 1968. Sol Harrison, a comic magazine art director who had been a volunteer for the New York Association for Brain Injured Children ever since his own son had been born brain damaged twenty-one years before, told *Good Housekeeping* magazine, "We never had been able to get a celebrity to spearhead a fund-raising affair. But when I read of Pat's recovery I wrote her a letter outlining our objectives and asked her for her help." He had flown to England for a day, met with the Dahls and Valerie, and told them all about his own son, Billy. He told of his and his wife's trials gaining support, financially and therapeutically, through the years, until his son was tested and found to be artistic and intelligent. Billy was now holding a job and preparing to marry. When Harrison finished his story, Patricia, with tears in her eyes, told him, "I'll come. What's the date?"[26]

Leaving the children in England with their father, Patricia and Valerie arrived in New York on March 8, 1967, and settled into a suite at the Waldorf Astoria. With Valerie's help, Patricia had rehearsed her speech, written by Roald, for an entire month. In a press conference at the hotel, city public events commissioner John S. Palmer presented Patricia, dressed in a blue-and-white tweed suit and blue boots, with a proclamation from Mayor John Lindsey designating the following week as Brain-Injured Children's Week in New York.

"I feel so much better now," Patricia told the reporters who flooded the room. "For a year and a half I did not feel like living. Last November I started to want to live again, and now I like living."[27] As for her speech, she told the *New York Times*, "I hope it will be good—I'll probably be nervous. My husband's making me do it. No, I have no enthusiasm. I don't care. My husband is making a living and I'm spending it."[28] Regarding the filming of *The Subject Was Roses*, Patricia candidly remarked, "I hope I can memorize the lines. I'm going to try this summer."[29]

An Evening with Patricia Neal, which was preceded by a cocktail party at the apartment of theatrical attorney Arnold Weissberger, the benefit chairman, began at 8:00 P.M. in the Waldorf's Grand Ballroom with dinner for two thousand people. At the end of the meal the ballroom darkened, and host Rock Hudson introduced Michael Maitland, who dramatically read "Sometimes I Cry," a lament by a brain-injured child. Next on the program was Valerie Eaton Griffith, who introduced Patricia. Valerie recapped the story of their meeting, their work, and their accomplishments toward rehabilitation. In conclusion Valerie said, "Finally, I would like to tell you—as Americans, as friends of Pat—I would like to tell you about Great Missenden, our village. It is very small and old-English with a twelfth-century church and eight pubs in three hundred yards of High Street. A pleasant place to live in, obviously. It is not an important place on anybody's map. But Pat and Roald are a part of this village. I want you to know this because it is important to me that we have had this wonderful chance to help this most extraordinary woman. We are proud of her and we love her—Patricia Neal."[30]

The audience rose as Patricia, dressed in a sleeveless green blouse and a long violet skirt separated by a wide purple sash and accessorized with a string of pearls, was brought up to the rostrum by Rock Hudson. She acknowledged the ovation, which lasted a full minute, and then began, "I thank you. I thank you. I hope what happened to me never happens to any of you." She talked about her stroke and spoke lovingly of Dr. Carton and the staff at the UCLA Medical Hospital. With humor she said, "I know very well that Dr. Carton thought I would conk out in the middle of it. But Tennessee hillbillies don't conk that easy." Roald loved that expression.

She described coming out of her coma and experiencing double vision and being unable to associate words to objects. She told the audience about her schedule of rehabilitation and of the villagers and friends who all pitched in to aid her, and she spoke about her children and family. She then told them about her introduction to Valerie and their work together and stressed Roald's support and determination. "My husband is a great man and I love him," she said. Finally she spoke about why she was there that evening: "And now I want to say something about brain-injured children. I can only speak for our son Theo." Here, for the only time, her voice broke. She spoke about his accident, his recovery, and his life, concluding with, "He's the most cheerful person I know. Theo's courage has been a real inspiration to me—and I needed it. So you can see why I feel so close to the aims of this society. And I want to thank all of you for coming here tonight—some of you from far away." The audience stood again in applause as Hudson presented her with the official gold medallion of the City of New York, followed by a presentation by Albert Hans of the statue "The First Step."[31]

Patricia told the press, "It was beautiful. Oh, it was just beautiful. I did it. I really did it. It was good, wasn't it?" She later told Barry Farrell, "Do you know I loved it when they all stood up and clapped. I don't think I've ever had anything like that before. I loved that. I loved it."[32] The fund-raiser brought in more than $90,000 for the Brain-Injured Children Association, for which Patricia was very proud. Valerie and Patricia returned to England the following week.

In England, Patricia prepared for her appearance in April on the Thirty-ninth Annual Academy Awards to present the award for Best Foreign Film. She selected a colorful sleeveless gown off the rack at Charlotte's on High Street in Great Missenden, paying only $36.40 for it. Patricia flew to Hollywood on April 7 with ten-year-old Tessa, who stayed with Patricia's friend K. T. Stevens Marlowe during the ceremonies.

Patricia's appearance at the Santa Monica Civic Auditorium April 10 was her first public appearance in Hollywood since the stroke. She looked wonderful in a mink coat over her bargain gown. Emcee Bob Hope introduced Patricia: "We're pleased to welcome a former winner whose talent speaks an international language, and whose courage has been saluted in every tongue. All of us are grateful for the return to our community of Miss Patricia Neal." Acknowledging the standing ovation, Patricia said, "I'm sorry I've been away so long. It really is wonderful, wonderfully wonderful, to be back with you tonight."

Columnist Sidney Skolsky wrote, "The biggest prize of the night was won by Patricia Neal, and the entire audience at the Santa Monica Civic Auditorium, some 2,800, gave her a standing ovation for what she had accomplished. And because they were happy to see Patricia Neal as Patricia Neal."[33] Patricia told the press, "Life is beginning for me again. Now I believe there's only sunshine ahead."[34]

Flying to Atlanta before their return to England, Patricia and Tessa visited with Eura Neal; her aunt Maude; Patricia's brother, Pete, and his new bride, Charlcie (they were married in 1964); NiNi and her husband, George, and their two children, sixteen-year-old George Jr. and thirteen-year-old Ann.

Just weeks after returning to England, Patricia found she was not yet ready to begin *The Subject Was Roses*. Filming was originally set to commence at the end of the summer, but Patricia told the press she didn't want to leave England at that time. The start date was pushed to December, but Patricia asked Roald to tell them to wait until after the holidays. The film was then set to begin shooting in New York in February 1968. Patricia was clearly trying to avoid studying the script for the film, and this was somewhat maddening to Roald. He knew she needed to get back to work. After a month-long family holiday in France late that summer, Roald finally told Patricia, "You are an actress. You were born to be an actress. You will never be completely recovered until you face working again."[35] Patricia and Valerie began to study the script of *The Subject Was Roses* in earnest.

On November 17, Roald was in Oxford's Radcliffe Hospital recovering from major back surgery when his mother Mormor passed away. She had been ill for some time, and her death was not unexpected. Patricia wired her mother the news and noted that it was the fifth anniversary of Olivia's death. Sofie Dahl's funeral was held on the same day, five years later, as Olivia's. Patricia attended, although she was suffering from the flu, but Roald could not. Mormor had always been at Roald's side when he was ill in the hospital, and Patricia wrote that she tried to take Mormor's place this time, but Roald would close his eyes "and suffer in silence."[36] Nesta Powell was on the nursing staff at the hospital, and with her aid and friendship Roald improved considerably.

As 1967 concluded, film critic Gene Shalit penned a lengthy and rhyming magazine poem that included the lines, "Holiday bells triumphantly peal, for Roald Dahl's Patricia Neal."[37] Indeed, the coming year would prove to be one of the most successful and rewarding of Patricia's life.

After the holidays, Patricia flew to New York for the filming of *The Subject Was Roses*. Roald did not intend to travel to New York with his wife. Valerie, however, was going to join Patricia in a few days' time to help her with the film. "It's wonderful to be back to work again," Patricia told the press when she arrived at John F. Kennedy Airport in New York. "I haven't worked for so long, but I feel sure that everyone will now see I can do it. I feel fine now, and happy, although I shall miss my family while I'm away."[38]

Before she started filming, however, Patricia had to fly to Washington, D.C., with Barry Farrell and publicist Lars McSorley to accept the American Heart Association's Heart of the Year Award from President Lyndon Johnson. Shortly before landing in Washington, the plane's landing gear malfunctioned. When the captain announced that the flight was returning to New York as "they had better fire-fighting equipment," Farrell and McSorley started to panic.[39] But Patricia noticed she felt strangely calm. She loudly told the stewardess, "I think we all deserve a free martini. I'd like to propose a toast to you and you and you, and to all the people we are going to leave behind."[40] As they approached New York, the crew prepared the passengers for an emergency landing. They removed their shoes and loosened their clothing. The plane landed safely.

Patricia and her party finally arrived in Washington on a different flight that evening. The following morning, wearing a new deep-blue suit and kelly-green boots, Patricia was introduced to President Johnson at the White House. They had a lively, animated talk. "I guess you're as grateful as I am for the science that made it possible for you and me to be here together," said Johnson, who had received the award in 1959 following his heart attack.[41] "They're also improving the appearance of the recipient."[42]

"I had never met President Johnson before," Patricia told columnist Cindy Adams. "Nor did I have anything to do with the Heart of the Year Award which he gave me. It's just that a friend knew about this annual citation which is supposedly given to people who have shown great heart or courage and are supposed to be an inspiration to others everywhere. Well, she sent my story to the White House and I knew nothing about it at all until I received an invitation from the President. I was terribly thrilled about meeting him. I even went out specially and bought a new, navy blue suit to wear. I hope he liked it."[43]

Back in New York, rehearsals began on February 5 for *The Subject Was Roses*, with principal photography to commence on February 19 at the Production Center in Manhattan. *The Subject Was Roses* tells the story of World War II veteran Timmy Cleary (Martin Sheen), who returns to his parents' Bronx home only to find that their marriage is falling apart. His salesman father John (Jack Albertson) and housewife mother Nettie (Neal) quarrel constantly. Timmy, a mother's boy as a child, tries to bond with his father; he doesn't want to take sides in his parents' problems. When John finds out that Timmy no longer attends the Catholic Church, a fight ensues, and John leaves. Timmy accuses his mother of trying to make him take her side, and she leaves for the day. When she returns, she finds John berating their half-drunken son. Timmy realizes that each of his parents is responsible for the problems in the family, and he decides to leave the house. Both John and Nettie feel he is making the right choice; when Timmy changes his mind, his father tells him he must go. The three sit down for a final breakfast together.

Director Ulu Grosbard and producer Edgar Lansbury were thrilled to finally have Patricia in the picture. *The Subject Was Roses* would be Patricia's comeback film, and one of her greatest accomplishments.

23

Roses

TIMMY: What was it that drew you to Pop?
NETTIE: I think it was his energy . . . a certain wildness. He was not like my father at all. . . . I was attracted . . . and I was afraid. I've always been a little afraid of him. . . . And then he was clearly a young man who was going places . . . and his prospects were unlimited. . . . Strangers thought he was magnificent. And he *was* . . . as long as the situation was impersonal. . . . At his best in an impersonal situation. . . . But that doesn't include the home, the family. . . ."

—Frank D. Gilroy, *The Subject Was Roses* (1968)

When filming began on *The Subject Was Roses* in February 1968, Roald was in England writing the screenplay of *Chitty Chitty Bang Bang*, which, like his previous screenplay, was based on an Ian Fleming book. The film, starring Dick Van Dyke, was scheduled to start shooting at Pinewood Studios in England later that year.

For *Roses*, there would be a full week of read-through and rehearsals before the cameras rolled. The first day of rehearsals was unbearable. The second day, Patricia was still questioning whether she could even do the part. On the third day something clicked, and she began to relax and enjoy the work. Jack Albertson and Martin Sheen were very fond of Patricia and extremely patient with her. She sensed they were willing to work with her in ensemble.

Albertson, who had starred in the Broadway production, had quite a wit and was forever telling jokes throughout the filming. When they toured with the play in the Mormon regions, where drinking was frowned upon, he told Patricia, his character was changed from "an alcoholic" to a "root-beer fiend."[1] This was the second film for twenty-seven-year-old Martin Sheen, who had starred in the Broadway production of *Roses* with Albertson.

Facing page: Patricia Neal in *The Subject Was Roses*, 1968. From the author's collection.

Interior scenes were filmed at the CBS Studios. Location shooting was done in Greenwich Village, on the New Jersey shoreline, and in Queens. The rushes were stunning, and talk was beginning to spread even before the film was completed that all three of the actors were turning in Oscar-worthy performances.

On March 3, Patricia wrote friends, "I am so happy to be able to tell you that the film I'm doing is going well indeed. I love all the people that I'm working with: the director Ulu Grosbard is wonderful, and I love Jack Albertson and Martin Sheen and the producer, all of them in fact. And I'm so happy to be working again. But I do have to work very hard. Up at 6 A.M., back from the studio at 6:30 P.M.—it's a long day."[2]

In England, Dahl told an interviewer, "I kicked Pat into doing this film because I wanted her back to 100 per cent health. It was a challenge. Now she is acting better than ever. . . . Pat's not ambitious. But I am ambitious for her contentment. If she didn't act she would be 80 per cent happy. But for her I want that 100 per cent. Acting for Pat makes up the measure. I really did bully her into making another film. She didn't want to do it."[3]

Because this was Patricia's first movie role since her illness, the film project attracted a good deal of media attention. Director Ulu Grosbard, making his directorial debut in *Roses*, spoke about Patricia in an interview with Joan Crosby, "We were all jumping into the unknown. But at the first reading of the script, I knew it was right. . . . We found her with a full range of emotions and access to memory. She's fantastic and you can quote me without reservations. She is an extraordinary actress with such a marvelous range of emotions from humor to the depth of sorrow. She is so subtle she can play from a subdued note to a wild and open anger. . . . I would rather do six extra takes with her and get what she gives than use someone else who couldn't approach her range in 72 takes."[4]

For her part, Patricia told Crosby, "I don't memorize lines as well as I did but I think I act as well as I did." To another reporter she said, "I am learning [my lines] much better than I could have immediately after the strokes, and I'm happy to be back to work!"[5]

The *Roses* company moved to the New Jersey shore in mid-March for two days of location shooting with a caravan of two buses—one a vintage 1946 bus painted blue—three truckloads of film equipment, two station wagons, and a camper dressing room. For one scene, the blue bus pulled up in front of the sixty-four-year-old Monmouth Hotel to drop Patricia off as her character tries to re-create her honeymoon there. Each take Patricia would climb the steps of the hotel, both in long shot and close-up, and the shooting went on well into the afternoon. Later Patricia was required to walk along the seashore in solitude. It was a blustery, cold afternoon, with hundreds of bystanders watching as Patricia went through her paces before the camera. She told newspaper reporter Nancy Razan, "Even the makeup man can't do anything about my nose running. But he doesn't like me to blow it because it will ruin my makeup."[6]

Later in March, the company was in a small nightclub in Greenwich Village, where John Cleary takes Nettie and Timmy to celebrate their son's return from the war. Filming of the sequence began at 10:00 A.M., with the three stars and ninety-three extras. Reporter Carol Kramer wrote in the *Chicago Tribune*, "In the scene they are rehearsing, Cleary . . . says he frequents [the bar] only on 'special occasions.' Then, a master of ceremonies calls Cleary, a 'faithful patron,' up to the bandstand, where he is asked to sing 'Bluebonnet Sue.' As he sings, Miss Neal, his long-suffering wife, registers love, embarrassment, pride, and reticence. They all flicker across her face as she bites her lip or glances at the audience nervously."[7]

The most important scene in the picture for Patricia was with Martin Sheen, a ten-minute near monologue that was filmed late at night on a rooftop in Queens. "It was a closed set," remembered Valerie Eaton Griffith, who was there that night. "I sat only about two yards from Pat during the shooting. There were street urchins down in the street making a hell of a din. They could see that we were filming on the roof. Someone actually went down there and paid them to be quiet."[8] For over a year Patricia and Valerie had practiced the five-page monologue, which was written in such a manner that it built in momentum. However, the script kept getting rewritten, and by the night of the filming Patricia was truly nervous. As the two stars and Valerie sat wrapped in blankets waiting to shoot, teleprompters were set up off camera so that Patricia could read her lines if she needed to. Patricia recalled that she may have glanced at a monitor a couple of times, but for the most part she did not need it. The scene was shot a couple more times at different angles. Patricia's energy was pumping, and she completed each one in a single, long take. By dawn they were finished.

Grosbard called it a wrap, and the crew broke into spontaneous applause. The stars and the director hugged, and Patricia felt she was a working actor again. Filming concluded the first week in April. The picture had cost $875,000. A ten-minute promotional short, *Pat Neal Is Back*, produced and directed by Edward Beyer, was made during the filming of *The Subject Is Roses* and was shown prior to the release of the film.

Patricia was busy in New York throughout the making of *The Subject Was*

Roses. Accompanied by Valerie, she spent weekends at the home of Mildred Dunnock or Richard Rodgers and took in plays whenever she could. When she attended a performance of *Hello Dolly!* the audience stood in applause for five minutes. "It was fantastic," Jack Albertson recalled. "I've never seen anything like it in thirty-five years of show business."[9] After the performance, its star, Pearl Bailey, invited Patricia onto the stage.

Roald flew to the United States the second week in March to join Patricia for the Gala for the Association of Brain-Damaged Children. Patricia cochaired the event with Sharman Douglas. Among the luminaries on the guest list were England's Princess Margaret and her husband, Lord Anthony Snowdon, Douglas Fairbanks Jr., and Paul Newman and his wife, Joanne Woodward. Entertainment was provided by Arlene Francis, Richard Harris, Kitty Carlisle, Tammy Grimes, and Burt Bacharach.

Early in April, Patricia appeared at the New York Drama Critics Award ceremony, afterward attending a party held at Sardi's. On April 9, Patricia was among those honored by the National Women's Division of the Albert Einstein College of Medicine of Yeshiva University in New York as one of 1968's Spirit of Achievement Honorees, which also included Rebekah Harkness and Estee Lauder.

The day after filming wrapped, Patricia flew home to London on a TWA Boeing 707. The flight almost ended in disaster. As the plane touched down, the control tower at the London airport noticed smoke coming from the engine. The captain shut the engine down immediately as fire engines raced to the plane. No one was injured.

Resuming her life at Gipsy House was not easy for Patricia. She had proved to herself and Roald that she could still work, and now she was itching to do so again, this time in a Hollywood film. Still, there were family issues to be attended to, such as placing the children in school for the coming year. When school started up that fall, Tessa, who never really liked her school, Roedean, was to attend Downe House, "which has a fantastic art department and acting one," Patricia wrote to Jean and Chloe. "I am delighted that she is changing." Theo would only be allowed one more year at Godstowe; they were hoping to enroll him in Redelis. Patricia hoped that Ophelia and Lucy would go to Downe House, saying, "I adore that school."[10]

Patricia received encouraging news in July about the rough cut of *The Subject Was Roses.* Harvey Orkin wired her that, although he had not seen the rough cut, he had heard that Patricia was "absolutely marvelous, and it [was] a most brilliant performance."[11] This was immediately followed by a telegram from MGM: "All of the executives at MGM consider Roses an excellent film screening first roughcut today. Stop. Your performance along with Martin and Jack was superb."

In August, the Dahls traveled to Norway for their family holiday, their first in six years. Roald's eighty-one-year-old, blind aunt was in a hospital there, and he wanted to see her. Three weeks before the New York premiere of *Roses*, while vacationing in Norway, where the weather was "glorious," Dahl's nose began to bleed profusely, and he had to undergo a corrective nose operation.[12] Patricia recalled sleeping on the floor of his room at night and visiting him twice daily. One day she brought him grapes; he flung them out the window. She wrote that she felt then that he was perhaps tiring of her. But she turned her attention to preparing for the opening of *The Subject Was Roses*.

The trade papers were enthusiastic after the film was previewed in Los Angeles on September 15. John E. Fitzgerald said it was "like a breath of fresh air."[13] Critic John Mahoney wrote, "Miss Neal gently projects the longing, the sweet manipulation, the stubborn ideals and the treasured memory of her character, willing at least momentarily to sacrifice her son to the compound of her disappointments. The scene in which she recalls for Sheen her courtship by Albertson and the others is one of the most beautiful assessments of expectation measured against fact, the parting of a dream, an acknowledgment of the crippling each has afflicted on the other, a recalling of merits, accepting the score. Her journey to Monmouth on coins she has saved is heightened not alone by its facial studies of her but by the poetic and poignant investment of the Lee Pockriss song which underscores it, 'Albatross,' and its plaintive performance by Judy Collins."[14]

At the end of September, Patricia and Roald flew to the United States to attend the New York premiere of *The Subject Was Roses*. The film—and Patricia—was generating a good deal of media coverage.

The October 5 issue of the *Saturday Evening Post* featured a six-page article, "Patricia Neal: A Star is Reborn," by Richard Lemon. Interviewed during the making of *The Subject Was Roses*, Patricia had spoken candidly with the writer about her illness, her career, and her life. The article was very well received and did much to promote Patricia's rehabilitation, outlook on life, and, of course, her new film.[15]

Patricia was interviewed on several national network television shows in conjunction with the release of *The Subject Was Roses*, appearing on the *Today Show*, the *Dick Cavett Show*, and the *Merv Griffin Show*, as well as Chicago's *Irv Kupcinet Show*. Producer Don Silverman said many years later,

"When I was producing *The Dick Cavett Show,* Pat came on to talk about . . . her first movie after the stroke. We could engineer standing ovations, but this time we didn't. She was still shaky on her pins and we were being very careful with her. But when she walked out, the audience rose as one person with a spontaneous ovation."[16]

In Washington, D.C., Patricia told *Washington Post* On the Aisle columnist Richard L. Coe what it felt like to be considered a "living legend": "People tell me that and it seems unreal, but I can't deny that total strangers seem to know my story and it seems to do something to them just to see me. It's wonderful, amazing, isn't it? I can't think of my life as extraordinary yet surviving three strokes makes me exceptional. No cases seem to have made such a recovery as mine. I still limp and some names don't shake loose from my brain's filing compartment." When asked about her plans, Patricia told Coe, "I'd like to do another film but first we have to see how this is received."[17]

Drama critic Harry MacArthur, in the October 9 edition of the *Washington Evening-Star,* wrote a love letter of sorts after having met Patricia: "If you have to know the blunt truth, I am sitting here trying to think of a way to get into this column without coming out and flatly declaring that I am in love with Patricia Neal," he wrote following a luncheon with her at the Madison Hotel. "Besides, being in love with Patricia Neal is no distinction these days. If you read newspapers and magazines you are well aware that men who write pieces for them are falling in love with her all over the place. In fact, you don't have to be a writer. Non-fiction writers are falling in love with her all over the place, too. All that is required is brief exposure to her sunny approach to a life that has dealt her more tragedy than most people have to face in twice her years. . . . Lunch with Miss Neal becomes a memorable lunch among a lifetime of them. Her laugh is always near the surface and bubbles forth frequently. She is less in awe of herself than almost any movie star you can think of. The honesty that marks her acting . . . appears to be a permanent part of her nature. She is not one to dodge any question by dissembling. . . . Miss Neal also has a disarming habit of turning a conversation around. The interviewer suddenly finds himself the interviewee. 'How old are you?' she wants to know. 'Are you married? Do you have children? How many? How old are they and what do they do? Do you have a dog?'. . . If you let her go on, she'll find out more about you than you know yourself. It isn't that she'd rather ask questions than answer them. It's just that she likes people and wants to know all about them. Maybe that's why people like Pat."[18]

Roald escorted Patricia to the New York premiere of *Roses* on Sunday, October 13, 1968, at the Plaza Theatre. The audience included Henry Fonda,

Robert Ryan, Rod Steiger and Claire Bloom, Chester Morris, Zoë Caldwell, Teresa Wright, Maureen Stapleton, Angela Lansbury, Gloria Vanderbilt Cooper, Anne Jackson, Tallulah Bankhead, and Hope and Otto Preminger (who was dressed in a Nehru jacket and beads). In unison the crowd rose in applause as the Dahls entered the auditorium. Patricia and Roald received another standing ovation at the postpremiere party at Sardi's.

The film was heralded. *New York* magazine critic Judith Crist wrote, "'The Subject Was Roses' has sent us groping for superlatives to surpass all the superlatives we had applied in the past to the performance of Patricia Neal."[19] Earl Wilson in the *New York Post* said, "There's a new candidate in the 1969 Oscar sweepstakes—an older girl named Patricia Neal. . . . There was Academy Award fever hovering over Pat Neal's premiere of 'The Subject Was Roses' at the Plaza Theatre . . . because the word's been out for some time that Pat is the gal to watch."[20] Vincent Canby wrote in the *New York Times*, "Miss Neal's presence—after her long illness—gives the movie an emotional impact it wouldn't otherwise have. She has a slight limp, but nothing has impaired the husky voice, the large, magnificent eyes that listen as well as see, or the over-all screen intelligence."[21]

The *Time* magazine critic best defined Patricia's return to film: "As the mother, Patricia Neal makes her first appearance in films since her paralytic stroke in 1965. It would be worth waiting a decade for. She retains her vast resources of energy and intelligence. Yet she has altered in appearance and style. Her face is still lovely, but it has assumed a melancholy dignity, no longer fresh, but not quite old, like a fine tablecloth preserved for special occasions. Her acting is neither shrewd underplaying nor is it larger than life; it is exactly life-sized. She no longer indicates suffering, she defines it."[22]

After the New York opening, Roald returned to England, and Patricia flew to Los Angeles for the West Coast invitational premiere on October 17, at the Pacific's Beverly Hills Theatre. Patricia was honored with a pre-premiere banquet at the Beverly Wilshire Hotel.

For the Hollywood premiere, Edgar Lansbury escorted Patricia on his arm. Afterward, Patricia, author Gilroy, producer Lansbury, and director Grosbard all went to Club John, a discothèque co-managed by twenty-seven-year-old Michael Walker, son of Jennifer Jones and Robert Walker. Blasted by throbbing music and overwhelmed by the "flowing pants and minis of the girls and jabots and bellbottoms for boys," Patricia ordered a hamburger and a beer. The next day she told the press, "I *loathe* those places, because those people are so *young*, so I *really* adore them."[23]

The West Coast reviews were as magnificent as those in New York. Dale

Munroe of the *Los Angeles Herald-Examiner* wrote, "Patricia Neal, Jack Albertson, and Martin Sheen. All three actors are scene stealers to a point where the critic is helpless to do anything but declare a draw. Each delivers a performance worthy of an Academy Award. In her first appearance since a serious illness temporarily manacled her career, Miss Neal has made a remarkable recovery comeback as a lonely woman yearning for understanding from her son and for the rekindling of a spark of love she once had for her husband. She gives a performance that may very well prove to be the crowning achievement of a fine career."[24] More succinctly, Los Angeles entertainment editor Charles Champlin wrote in his *Los Angeles Times* review, "Patricia Neal's return to the movies . . . is triumphant. . . . It is no news that Pat Neal has been one of the finest of all screen actresses. It is a pleasure to know that she still is."[25]

When the film opened in Patricia's hometown later that month, *Knoxville News-Sentinel* reporter John Torzilli commented, "Miss Neal's cold, passive characterization is given full depth and meaning in the monolog where she tells her son of her dreams for marriage and life with her husband. In this scene, Miss Neal's face, voice and timing set definitive examples for students of acting."[26]

While she was in California, Patricia was introduced to Barbara Stanwyck, who summoned Patricia to her table in the bar of the Beverly Wilshire Hotel. "You're gorgeous," Stanwyck said to her.

Patricia laughed, "Oh, you finally saw *The Fountainhead.*"

The legendary Stanwyck did not catch the humor, and staring into Patricia's eyes, said, "I admire you very much."[27]

After the West Coast premiere, Patricia visited the Van Dykes at their Encino home. They had become good friends during the filming of *Chitty Chitty Bang Bang* in England, and Dick Van Dyke built an aviary copied after the Dahls' in Great Missenden.

Patricia then embarked on a tour for MGM, promoting *The Subject Was Roses* in such cities as Chicago, Boston, Washington, D.C., and Atlanta, with a stop in Dallas to visit her brother, Pete, and Charlsie, who lived there and were expecting their first baby. *Look* magazine was along to capture the tour for a magazine piece. Patricia's agent, Irving Lazar, sent her good news: *Variety* had reported that as a result of the success of *The Subject Was Roses*, Patricia had received film offers from 20th Century-Fox, Paramount, Universal, and Warner Brothers.

While in Chicago, Patricia was invited to spend an afternoon at the Chicago Rehabilitation Institute. There she talked with patients young and old, cheer-

ing them on. Patricia told them, "Work, work, work is the only way to rehabilitation. I went through exercises and spent long hours in swimming pools.
My husband worked long hours with me. I am, even though I limp a little and
my memory sometimes fails and my vocabulary isn't so large, rehabilitated."[28]
She talked freely and shook hands with the patients. Dr. Henry B. Betts of the
institute told the *Chicago Daily News* that Patricia's visit was "Phenomenal! It
was one of the most inspirational things I've seen. Her approach was unique.
She was able to establish immediate warmth, understanding and rapport."[29]
This was the first of many appearances Patricia would make at rehabilitation
hospitals for stroke victims to generate interest and raise money.

In Texas, Patricia was able to visit with her brother, Pete, who was now
a teacher there, and his wife and their new baby, Celia Ann. Traveling on to
Atlanta, Patricia was reunited with her mother and her sister NiNi's family.

Patricia told a reporter for the *Hartford (Conn.) Times*, "Well, there's a
book written about Roald and me now by Barry Farrell. I don't know what
it's going to be called—maybe 'Pat and Roald.' Oh, God, I hope not."[30] She
wished in vain, and Farrell's book, indeed titled *Pat and Roald*, was published in the United States by Random House in late 1969. (Before publication, Farrell and Roald, who were to share the profits, had a falling-out over
changes proposed by Roald. Patricia always regretted that she was unable to
make amends before Farrell's untimely death.) The book, which became a
best seller, perpetuated the somewhat exaggerated story of Roald's control
over Patricia's rehabilitation and his effort to restore her life.

The February 18, 1969, issue of *Look* carried an article titled "Does Everybody Love Patricia Neal? O, Yes!" by senior editor Gereon Zimmermann.
The piece followed Patricia through the final days of shooting *Roses*, its pre-
mieres, and her trip to Texas. Zimmermann interviewed Patricia's Northwestern instructor Alvina Krause, who said, "There is a deep truth inside
her. I see integrity. Patricia left school in a crisis. She had flopped in *Twelfth
Night*. She wanted to give up. I told her to be in my room one morning at
eight o'clock. She didn't try to brazen it out. She said, 'How would you like it
if you're a head taller than anyone else?' I told her, 'Your body is your instrument, Pat.' You know she is fearless. In her work, there is never a moment of
showing off. When I saw *Hud*, I forgot that I was watching Pat."[31]

In Hollywood on February 24, 1969, the Academy of Motion Picture Arts
& Sciences announced the nominees for the Forty-first Annual Academy
Awards. Nominees for Best Actress were Katharine Hepburn, her eleventh
nomination (*The Lion in Winter*); Barbra Streisand, in her film debut (*Funny Girl*, Columbia); Joanne Woodward (*Rachel Rachel*); Vanessa Redgrave

(*Isadora*)—and Patricia Neal for *The Subject Was Roses*. Jack Albertson also received a nomination, for Best Supporting Actor. And while Martin Sheen was shut out of the Oscar running, he was nominated for the Golden Globe's Best Supporting Actor. Roald's work, too, made it into the nominations: the title song from *Chitty Chitty Bang Bang* was up for Best Song.

In April, Patricia and Roald flew to Los Angeles for the Academy Awards ceremony on the fourteenth. Patricia did not take home the Oscar that year. It was the only time in the academy's history that the Best Actress Oscar was split—a tie between Hepburn and Streisand. Jack Albertson won the Best Supporting Oscar, though.

The Dahls stopped in New York for a couple of days before their return to England. Sonia Austrian wanted to stop by, but Roald insisted she make an appointment first. She told Patricia later she thought that was a bit much. Roald was becoming more and more dominant, and his behavior cost them friends. In another case, their friendship with the Dulantys came to an end after Roald and Brian Dulanty had an intense argument and Brian threw Roald out of the house.

Charlie and the Chocolate Factory was sold to Paramount Pictures in 1969, and Dahl was able to add more art, collectibles, and furniture to Gipsy House. "Our furniture bore the names of Chippendale and Gibbons," Patricia wrote.[32]

Early in November 1969, Roald, Patricia, and Valerie Eaton Griffith flew to Los Angeles. Roald and Valerie had persuaded Patricia to participate in a half-hour film, *Stroke Counter Stroke*, to educate brain-damaged individuals and their families about rehabilitation. Both Valerie and Roald were called upon to do a bit of acting. Patricia opined, "He's a wonderful writer but, I must say, one terrible actor."[33] Roald and Valerie returned to England, and Patricia went to visit her aunt Maude in Williamsburg, Kentucky.

It had been an eventful year for Patricia. She was back in the spotlight, and people not even familiar with her acting were beginning to recognize her because of her fortitude and courage. In December, *Good Housekeeping* magazine announced its first annual "Ten Most Admired Women" of the year. Patricia was listed as number one by the readers. She was followed in ranking by Pearl S. Buck, Mrs. Dwight D. Eisenhower, Mrs. Richard M. Nixon, Mrs. Martin Luther King Jr., Queen Elizabeth II, Indira Ghandi, and Golda Meir. Patricia would continue to place on the *Good Housekeeping* magazine survey until 1975.

The year 1970, however, was very quiet. Film offers were not plentiful after Patricia's success in *The Subject Was Roses*. Producers were apparently hesitant to hire her. At home in England, Patricia was beginning to feel like an outsider within her family. The children were becoming independent of her, relying more and more emotionally on Roald, who, Patricia noticed, was also withdrawing from her. She was beginning to pick up on things Roald did and did not do. Their future together was not looking bright.

Dahl could not abide Patricia's inactivity, emotionally or financially. She had been asked in late 1969 to star in a proposed film made from Joy Cowley's novel *Nest in a Falling Tree*, but that deal had fallen through. Roald took on the task of adapting the novel, whose heroine is a stroke survivor. At the end of June, he flew to the States and was there for most of July, securing backing for the film, which he proposed to begin shooting at the end of September. Now called *The Road Builder*, it would be the first production of Yongestreet Film Productions.

Filmed on the Thames at Bray in an old, crumbling mansion near Windsor, *The Road Builder* tells the story of Maura Prince (Patricia), a woman who has survived a stroke and must now take care of her mother (Pamela Brown), an old, blind woman, an invalid, who had paid for Maura's medical treatments years before. Maura's life is miserable, as the old woman is cruel and demanding. Into their lives comes a young man on a motorcycle, Billy Jarvis (Nicholas Clay), who begins to work for the women as a handyman. Maura finds herself drawn to the young Jarvis, and eventually he begins to woo her. However, Jarvis has a secret. He is actually a homicidal maniac who rapes young women, straps them onto his motorcycle, and late at night buries them at road construction sites. Maura, now transformed by love into an attractive woman, not knowing Jarvis may kill her, runs off with him. Their relationship is doomed, and her love for him ends in tragedy.

Patricia recalled the filming of the picture as unpleasant. Valerie was with her off the set throughout most of the shooting, and Patricia sensed that the cast and crew were against her. Some actors and the director himself made unkind remarks about Patricia behind her back. "Stroke survivors develop their senses, and I could hear their talk," she would say later.[34] After filming of *The Road Builder* ended, Patricia told American celebrity writer Rex Reed, "I don't really care about making films now. I was so ambitious once. But I don't really want to work. I would not care a lot if I don't do another film. I'm just pleased I am married to the man who is my husband."[35] She was not paid for this project.

Roald quickly became involved in another project for Patricia called *The Lightning Bug*, based on the 1970 bestseller by Donald Harington. To be filmed in America's Deep South the following year, the story took place in the Arkansas Ozarks. "It's a honey of a book," Patricia told the press. "And it's something nice to look forward to."[36] She never made the film.

In November 1970, Valerie Eaton Griffith's book *A Stroke in the Family* was published by Penguin Handbooks. Roald had encouraged Valerie to write about her experiences working with Patricia. The book was a handbook for stroke survivors and their families, based on the principles and procedures used in Patricia's rehabilitation. Patricia and Roald helped promote the book, which was eventually published worldwide. Through the publication of *A Stroke in the Family*, Valerie was able to establish the Chest, Heart and Stroke Association in England.

The film version of Roald Dahl's book *Charlie and the Chocolate Factory* commenced shooting as *Willy Wonka and the Chocolate Factory* in Munich, starring Gene Wilder and Patricia's *Roses* costar Jack Albertson. It became a smash hit upon its release the following year, producing the hit song "The Candy Man," written by Anthony Newley and made popular by Sammy Davis Jr. By the end of 1970 Roald was busy writing his next children's book, *The Fantastic Mr. Fox.*

On March 4, 1971, Patricia appeared on the BBC broadcast of *The British Screen Awards: A Gala Night for Television and Film.* Hosted by Richard Attenborough, the ceremony featured filmed segments by such celebrities as Dustin Hoffman, Mia Farrow, Peter Sellers, and John Mills. Presenting the awards was Britain's Princess Anne.

Patricia flew to New York with Roald and Valerie in late April to attend the awards ceremony for the annual Speech Rehabilitation Institute held at the Plaza Hotel. Patricia presented awards to Roald and Valerie for their work in helping her develop a rehabilitation program used on both sides of the Atlantic. "Val made the first speech and Roald the second," Patricia wrote later. "Val's was very, very fine and Roald's was uproariously funny."[37] During this visit, Peter Cookson and his second wife, Beatrice Straight, had supper with Patricia and Valerie. Years before, Patricia had run into Peter and Beatrice pushing a baby carriage with their baby son Tony in it, and Straight had been very rude and cold to her. Now they were great friends. At one point during the evening Valerie and Beatrice left Patricia and Peter alone so they could talk.

Patricia reestablished contact with another old friend during her time in New York. She read in the newspaper that Peter Douglas's wife, Virginia, had died of cancer. Patricia sent Douglas a sympathy letter, renewing their friendship.

After the ceremonies, Roald and Valerie flew back to England, and Patricia flew to St. Petersburg, Florida, to visit her mother. NiNi surprised Patricia by coming down.

After she returned to England, Patricia was interviewed in London by Raymond Villwock for the *National Enquirer.* She told her interviewer, "Life is good. It's really beautiful—even though the producers aren't chasing me anymore. . . . Things have changed a great deal for me since I had my stroke. Before this I was a temperamental woman. I don't know how my husband stood me. Of course I don't like it that the producers fight shy of me. I want to act because I know I can. But they must think I can't, or that I would forget my lines and make harder work for everyone. I don't know. All I know is they don't come around like they used to."[38] Patricia said, "I used to believe in God, completely. But I don't believe now, not completely anyway, not since Olivia's death and my stroke. I believe in life, but I'm not sure about God."[39]

When Patricia and Roald saw the final cut of *The Road Builder,* released in mid-May 1971 as *The Night Digger,* they were disgusted. "It's pornographic," said the disgruntled Patricia.[40] The critics were decidedly lukewarm about the film. *Variety* critic Gold wrote, "The exercise is only moderately successful. . . . Patricia Neal . . . gives a fine, sensitive performance. But her character is essentially colorless, and she is outshone by both Pamela Brown . . . and by Nicholas Clay."[41] Ann Gurino in the *New York Daily News* found the picture "a strange tale that builds slowly to a tragic climax. . . . [T]he tale is strictly for those with a taste for the perverse."[42] And A. H. Weiler wrote in the *New York Times*: "It begs for sympathy for its tortured principals, but despite the clearly dedicated contributions of Patricia Neal, Roald Dahl, her scenarist-husband, Pamela Brown and a young newcomer, Nicholas Clay, the strain on credibility is a good deal more notable than the impact on the emotions. . . . Miss Neal, cast as an intelligent, sensitive spinster enslaved to the demanding, blind mother who adopted her at an early age, does not appear to be the type who would fall for a strange, shifty young man who has insinuated himself into the household."[43]

Today the film holds up, minimally. The photography by Anthony Pratt captures the gothic atmosphere, and the musical score by Bernard Herrmann, who had written the score for *The Day the Earth Stood Still,* is magnificent. Critic Judith Crist eventually wrote a favorable review of *The Night Digger,* long after the film had closed up and left town.

After the family's annual vacation in Norway, Patricia began preparation for a role in a made-for-television film *The Homecoming.* She flew to Los Angeles the first week in October to begin rehearsing and shooting interior scenes. Filming would take only about a month: three weeks in Los Angeles and a week of location shooting near Jackson Hole, Wyoming. While she was in Hollywood, Patricia visited her friends Jean Valentino and Chloe Carter, as well as Jean Hagen, now divorced and suffering the effects of alcoholism, who resided at the Motion Picture Country House and Hospital. Patricia then spent two days in Wyoming filming an outdoor snow scene—for which she was not paid. "Lee Rich [the executive producer] was a tight son-of-a-bitch," said the wife of one of the cast members.[44] When shooting completed on the scene, director Fielder Cook gave Patricia a long and loving hug.

Produced for CBS by Robert L. Jacks, with Lee Rich as executive producer, *The Homecoming: A Christmas Story* is an autobiographical story by Earl Hamner Jr., who adapted his novel for the picture. It tells of Christmas Eve 1933, during the Great Depression, from the perspective of John-Boy Walton (Richard Thomas), oldest son of the Walton family. John-Boy lives with his parents, grandparents (Edgar Bergen and Ellen Corby), and six younger siblings in poverty in the Appalachian Mountains of Virginia, at the foot of Walton Mountain. The family is preparing for the holiday, but the father, John (Andrew Duggan), has been delayed, and his wife, Olivia (Neal), must cope with growing worry as the radio announces there was a bus wreck on the highway he was traveling on. Before she sends John-Boy out into the night to look for his father, Olivia discovers that her son wants to be a writer. Eventually John makes it home, and his gift to John-Boy is several Big Chief writing tablets. When the family is reunited at the end of the story, their Christmas is complete.

Basically a brilliantly written coming-of-age story, the project was almost not produced. The original idea was the brainchild of Fred Silverman the year before, when he was reorganizing CBS programming. Silverman wanted the network to produce family TV movies and place them opposite NBC's *Walt Disney* anthology series on Sunday nights at 7:30 P.M. But that project was cost prohibitive, and the network opted instead to air old family feature films. But Silverman liked Hamner's story of the Walton family, and he eventually prevailed.

Patricia was Hamner's first choice for the role of Olivia, and director Fielder Cook also wanted Patricia to accept the role. "Outside of the fact that she's rather perfect for it, " he told *TV Guide* reporter Dick Adler, "Pat Neal is in that very small group of people that the world owes it to me to work with. If you're going to be in as rough a business as this, and work as hard and try to do as well as you can, you should not die before you've used Olivier and

Gielgud and Richardson and George C. Scott and Pat Neal and a few others. That's where I have my fun. I tried hard to get Pat once before; I sent her the only original script William Faulkner ever did for television, for the old *Lux Video Theater* ["The Brooch," broadcast April 2, 1953]. But she was too busy making movies then."[45]

Patricia told writer Phil Strassberg, "When the part came up and they called me at my home in England, they wanted to know precisely how well I would memorize lines. . . . Fielder Cook, the director, very much liked the idea of my portraying the leading role in this special but . . . they wanted to be certain."[46]

Patricia had one nonnegotiable demand: In the first draft of the script, the mother's name was Dorrie; Patricia insisted it be changed to Olivia, in honor of her daughter. But when Patricia arrived in Los Angeles, she was advised that the name of Dorrie would stick. Not only were the storyline, locale, and characters similar to those in Hamner's earlier *Spencer's Mountain*, but the mother's name in that film had been Olivia. Patricia stood firm and was prepared to return to England if the name was not changed. She won that battle.

Like Patricia, Richard Thomas was Hamner's first choice for the role of John-Boy. Hamner had seen Thomas in *Red Sky at Morning* (Universal, 1971) and liked his type: the sensitive and emotional adolescent, not the stereotypical teen idol, the rebellious, misunderstood male youth. Thomas's performance in *The Homecoming* made him a major film and television star during the 1970s.

Thomas had worked in theater and on the small screen with such actresses as Geraldine Page and Julie Harris, and he maintained that "child actor" sense of wanting to please when he approached a project. He met Patricia for the first time on the soundstage at CBS, he said, and found her to be "a mixture of grandness and down-to-earth. I quickly picked up on her sense of humor, and she was capable of saying anything. She would not stand on ceremony. There was a quality of playing with her—she was very generous, strong, she had a sense of self which allowed her to be giving. Anytime you work with someone of her stature the bar is raised, and your game goes up. She inspires emotional devotion. In her acting her intensity was broadcast— moving outward intensely as it moved away from her. She simply lets go of it during performance. Her vocal instrument is so rich, intense, it's almost impossible for her to hide her emotions. The other actor in a scene with her becomes awash in the sea of that intensity. You then play a duet." Patricia was, he said, "a force of nature."[47]

When *The Homecoming: A Christmas Story* aired over the CBS network on Sunday night, December 19, it won high praise. *Variety* reviewer Tone wrote, "The performances are first-rate. Patricia Neal, the mother, patient and hopeful, watchful and commanding, speaks with her eyes as fervently as with her rich voice."[48] Writer Morton Moss commented, "The Homecoming— A Christmas Story . . . is suffused with a great warmth. Patricia Neal, as Olivia Walton, and Richard Thomas, her oldest child, paint portraits rich in feeling. And they're only the best of a generally accomplished cast."[49] In the country's heartland, Bill Barrett of the *Cleveland Press* praised Patricia's performance: "Patricia Neal held it all together with her strength of presence and that magnificent voice. She was everything she should have been as the mother of the big brood whose husband may not get home for Christmas—brave and loving and loved."[50] Such praise was echoed throughout the nation's newspapers. The *Houston Chronicle* reviewer wrote, "The performance of star Patricia Neal was almost a Christmas story in itself."[51]

And Alan Bunce, writing in the *Christian Science Monitor,* said, "Most of all, perhaps, you saw the perfect Appalachian face of Patricia Neal, who played the lanky mother waiting for her husband to get home. Her role was the kind she could have made anything of. The lines tended to be short and straight, with room for invention. And Miss Neal poured in a tired but expansive humanity that seemed a bit threadbare—like the old clothes worn by the family—yet enough to infuse the household with its only real grace. Her croaking baritone echoed the creaking woodwork of the home."[52] Cecil Smith, in the *Los Angeles Times,* gave a special nod to Patricia's performance:

"Most of all . . . you cherish Pat Neal and the quiet strength of her, holding the family together, her husband lost out there in the storm, no money, no presents, wrapping herself in a worn black coat and dragging the tired body down to the store to buy a bit of sugar for a Christmas cake. Oh, you remember the twisting smile of her and the haunted despair of her waiting, waiting for 'The Homecoming' of her man on that long-ago Christmas."[53]

The Homecoming is today a classic, shown annually at Christmas. It has become a tribute to the directorial work of Fielder Cook. It represents what television filmmaking could be. The actors remember their work with fondness and pride. The film's musical score was by the Oscar-winning composer Jerry Goldsmith, its photography beautifully executed by Earl Rath. The film is timeless.

When NBC expanded *The Homecoming* into a weekly television series for the fall 1972 lineup, they retitled it *The Waltons.* They kept the original cast, with the exceptions of Edgar Bergen, Andrew Duggan, and Patricia, who was replaced by Michael Learned. Patricia said she was simply not asked to do the series. And not one episode was directed by Fielder Cook. *The Waltons* debuted on NBC on Thursday, September 14, 1972, and enjoyed a long and prosperous run, ending August 20, 1981.

Patricia's career should have taken off after her performance in *The Homecoming,* and she did in fact participate in several television films and dramas during the 1970s. But none equaled the quality of Hamner's *The Homecoming.*

24

Television

When you are real you don't mind being hurt.

—Margery Williams, *The Velveteen Rabbit* (1922)

Patricia's performance in *The Homecoming* received deserved recognition on January 11, 1972, when she was awarded the Golden Globe for Best TV Actress in a Drama Series or Television Movie. (She was also nominated for an Outstanding Actress–Single Performance Emmy, but lost to Glenda Jackson when those awards where given out in May.)

Also in January, Patricia finished work at the Elstree Studios on the film *The Boy* for Anglo-EMI. Directed by Lionel Jeffries and costarring Scott Jacoby, Jean-Pierre Cassel, Britt Ekland, and Lynn Carlin, *The Boy* tells the story of a lonely twelve-year-old American boy named Roger Baxter (Jacoby), who has a speech defect. Left on his own most of the time by his wealthy, divorced parents, he eventually comes under the care of a speech therapist, Dr. Roberta Clemm (Neal), who tries not only to help him with his speech, but also with his loneliness. Valerie Eaton Griffith was on the set with Patricia throughout the shooting of *The Boy*. Late one afternoon she was asked to play a nurse and was given a couple of lines in a brief sequence of the picture. The film was completed in just a few weeks. On the set, director Jeffries said of Patricia, "She's like all the great actresses. She *listens* to what the other actor is saying."[1]

During the filming, Patricia and Lynn Carlin became friends. Carlin was very close to Peter Cookson's first wife, Maureen, and Patricia asked Carlin if she would give a message to Maureen asking her for forgiveness for her affair with Peter. Carlin later told Patricia she had delivered the message and that Maureen had forgiven her. Maureen Cookson died of cancer shortly afterward.

Facing page: Patricia Neal in *The Homecoming*, 1971. From the author's collection.

It was for both Maureen Cookson and Virginia Douglas, wives of two men she had loved, that Patricia took on her next project. In January she flew to Los Angeles to narrate and film a few on-camera scenes for an upcoming television special, *Life, Death and the American Woman*, for ABC. The one-hour program was the second of three specials on health. The program explored the uncertainties of breast and cervical cancer, sickle cell anemia, heart disease, pregnancies and births, and psychological problems resulting from menopause. While in California, Patricia gave an interview to reporter Dick Kleiner, saying, "I don't get many offers any more. But I get enough. I do one or two things a year and that keeps me happy. But I'm always busy with something or other. I can't cook anymore—and I was a lovely cook—but I do the shopping."[2]

Patricia was back in Los Angeles in mid-September to appear in an episode of the short-lived NBC anthology *Ghost Story*. In the last episode of the series, "Time of Terror," Patricia portrays Ellen Alexander, who, after an unusual keno game at a nightmarish casino, is escorted by Brett, the assistant manager (Craig Stevens), into oblivion, where she and other guests await their fate.

Later in the month, Patricia and Tessa flew to Nova Scotia to film *Happy Mother's Day, Love George*, directed by actor-turned-producer Darren McGavin. The script was sent to Patricia by McGavin's wife, Kathie. For the part of her character's daughter, Patricia suggested fifteen-year-old Tessa. Roald was definitely not keen on the idea, as it would mean Tessa would have to miss school. McGavin flew to London to hear Tessa read, and she was given the part. Patricia was quite impressed by Tessa's natural acting ability, and would always say that Tessa was better in the film than she was.

The plot concerns mysterious murders that take place in a small fishing town. An overprotective mother, Cara Perry (Neal), has a daughter Celia (Tessa Dahl), who is emotionally disturbed. Cara attempts to hide the truth about the girl's father's death and to shield her from reality. Into the eerie town comes a young stranger, Johnny Hanson (Ron Howard, in his first adult film role), who is searching for his mother. Terror builds as the town's secrets are revealed and bodies are discovered.

Happy Mother's Day, Love George was budgeted at $1 million and was completed in five weeks. The cast included Cloris Leachman, fresh from her Best Supporting Actress Oscar win for *The Last Picture Show*, and actor-singer Bobby Darin in his last screen appearance.

McGavin told Earl Wilson, "Pat Neal is a love. . . . There's something very youthful about her and this caused a very interesting situation between Pat

and her daughter Tessa Dahl. . . . In a sense it was like two little girls squab-
bling—a female kind of competitiveness between them, not professional.
They had only one scene together. Pat said to her daughter, 'You're going
to be an actress; you do your own damn scene.' Her daughter said, 'So all
right, I won't help you learn your lines.'"[3] McGavin's wife Kathie Browne was
also in the cast, and she predicted that Tessa was "going to take the town by
storm."[4] Tessa told the press about appearing with her mother, "We only had
one scene together. We didn't see each other too much, so we got on fantastically when we did."[5]

Patricia had signed with Oglivy & Mather Advertising in late 1972 to appear
in a series of thirty-second television commercials for Maxim freeze-dried
instant coffee. There were also print ads. (Because of new laws governing the
endorsement of products, Patricia was required to test Maxim at home with
her husband over a certain period of time. Fortunately, both she and Roald
liked the coffee.) One commercial was with daughter Tessa, who hands her
mother a cup of Maxim. Patricia says to the camera, "It's delicious. This is my
daughter Tessa. She's a pretty good cook." "When people come for dinner,"
Tessa says, "I sometimes make dessert."

These coffee commercials were very popular when they were televised
in 1973, making Patricia Neal a household name. One fan wrote, "Patricia
Neal on the Maxim commercial is absolutely *the most*! Beautiful, lovely and
enchanting. Her voice is great, without a doubt the best commercial for anything I have ever seen. I would buy whatever she advertised even if it was
poison."[6] Asked if she had any qualms about doing commercials, Patricia told
Hollywood reporter Bob Thomas, "Not at all. Everybody's doing them, even
Henry Fonda and Laurence Olivier."[7] She later told columnist Archer Winston that she had discovered she was paid about half the amount others were
receiving for pitching similar products on TV. "I'll get a lot more next time,"
she told him.[8]

The Boy, renamed *Baxter!* opened in New York on March 3, 1973, to
decent reviews. *Variety* said, "'Miss Neal's dancing voice and eyes are as magnificent as ever."[9] Vincent Canby of the *New York Times* wrote, "'Baxter!' is a
sincere, quite solemn film about the breakdown of a teen-age boy who has
a speech defect. . . . Patricia Neal, especially, seems wasted in the very small
role of a speech therapist who will probably be the one eventually to rescue
Baxter."[10]

In mid-April, Patricia flew to Madrid to begin shooting her brief role in
Hay que matar a "B" (B Must Die) for Darren McGavin's Taurean Films. Di-

rected by José Luis Borau, who also cowrote the screenplay, the picture tells the story of Pal Kovak (McGavin), a U.S. exile adrift in a South American country. He seduces Susana (Stephane Audran), the wife of an industrialist. Too late, he realizes that he is being set up to take the fall for the political assassination of "B," an exiled leader of a country torn apart by political chaos. Patricia's character, Julia, aids Pal in his attempt to escape the country, but by the end of the film there is no escape, only death. Also in the cast is Burgess Meredith. His voice, along with McGavin's and Patricia's, was dubbed into Spanish when the picture was finally released in 1975.

The picture quickly disappeared, but one film buff who saw it on American television in 2000 wrote, "This film can surprise you. And it can really stick with you. It's one of those films that you keep trying to find out if anyone else has ever seen. What looks like a typical low-budget, off-the-cuff 1970's attempt at a slick intrigue picture . . . actually shows forethought, consideration, and carefulness despite its modest production values."[11] In 1975, *Hay que matar a "B"* won the Cinema Writers Circle Award for Best Film.

On May 16, 1973, Patricia attended the thirtieth reunion of her Knoxville High School graduating class. During a stopover in Atlanta, she learned from Pete and Charlsie that NiNi's son Dutch, just out of the service and a student at St. Petersburg Junior College, had drowned while cave diving in Florida. She felt obligated, however, to attend the reunion, though her heart went out to her sister and her family. After the event, Patricia flew to Atlanta to be with NiNi and George.

Now sixteen years old, Tessa had decided to quit school, and she told the New York press about the decision when she flew to New York to photograph some Maxim print ads with her mother. "In England you don't graduate as you do here. You take exams at 15 or 16 and only the very clever go on to university. But there was no point in staying on. I wasn't doing anything, any studying. I did read a lot of books, " she said.[12] From New York, Patricia flew on to England, and Tessa flew down to Virginia to begin her one season as an apprentice at the Barter Theatre.

After the Dahl family's annual Norwegian vacation ("Daddy's Norwegian," Tessa told columnist Eve Sharbutt. "We just lie on the beach and do nothing."),[13] Patricia and Tessa flew to the United States to promote *Happy Mother's Day, Love George*. In an article that appeared in the *New York Post,* on July 28, Patricia and Tessa commented on their relationship: "We get along, but we certainly shout at each other," Patricia said. "Not shout," Tessa corrected. "Well, I am very. . . . I continue to make you angry and you shout," continued Patricia. Tessa explained, "When my mother gets excited, I say 'Calm *down*' and she says, 'I CAN'T CALM DOWN' and *then* I shout." Patricia said, "I love Maxim, and I like money."[14]

Happy Mother's Day, Love George opened in New York on August 17. Wrote Robe in *Variety*, "Leachman and Neal are excellent as the warring sisters, Howard is impressive whenever he settles down (which isn't often), but the big impression is the debut of young Tessa Dahl (daughter of Miss Neal and writer Roald Dahl) as the strange daughter of Neal whose interest in the opposite sex leads to some strange happenings. She's a very pretty girl, at this stage a bit awkward and hampered by being a rather large girl, but suggesting a talent worthy of her lineage. . . . A flawed but generally entertaining suspense item."[15]

Roger Greenspun in the *New York Times* said the film "makes use of several distinguished performers. Cloris Leachman was seen to better advantage in 'Last Picture Show.' Ron Howard is currently seen to better advantage in 'American Graffitti.' And Patricia Neal may be seen to better advantage in Maxim Coffee television commercials. . . . The locations, actually in Nova Scotia, are predictably lovely."[16] The film failed to generate much interest. It worked as a melodrama, but not as a psycho-thriller. The title of the picture was eventually changed to *Run Stranger, Run*, and it quickly disappeared.

In January 1974, Patricia and Roald took a vacation together in Tobago. On this trip, Patricia felt closer to Roald than she had in years. Afterward they referred to that trip as their second honeymoon. The Dahls also traveled to Switzerland to visit Theo, who was in boarding school there. "In school he's last in his class, but he's with his own age group," Patricia told *Chicago Tribune* reporter Nancy Mills. "His difficulty is what he's going to do when he grows up. . . . He plays very good chess. . . . He's a lovely boy. Already he's my height—5 foot 8—and he's just turning 13. I think he's going to be as tall as Roald."[17]

While in Switzerland, Patricia and Roald rented a car and picked up Theo and his friend Billy from school one evening for dinner and a ride. At dinner Patricia and Roald drank vodka martinis and a couple of bottles of wine. On the way back to the school, Roald crashed into a bridge. Patricia and her husband never wore seatbelts, and Patricia woke up on the floor of the car. The boys pulled her out. She suffered a concussion and needed twelve stitches to repair her mouth where she smashed into the windshield. Roald, who screamed that he was dying, had merely split the caps on his teeth.

The Maxim ads, originally filmed in London, were now produced in New York, requiring that Patricia travel to the United States every three months.

On one trip, Patricia met with Maria Cooper, with whom she had corresponded after her stroke. Maria came up to Patricia's suite at the hotel, and the two had breakfast sent up. They discussed Gary and the abortion. Before their conversation ended, Maria handed Patricia her mother's address and made Patricia promise to write her. Patricia said she wouldn't know what to say, but Maria told her she would when the time was right.

Patricia flew to Los Angeles that spring to film an episode of the ABC television series *Kung Fu*, starring David Carradine. She also flew to Chicago to help dedicate the new $26 million Chicago's Rehabilitation Institute. She gave a speech, written by Roald, to commemorate the event.

That June, Patricia had a facelift in New York, as her face had begun to sag as a result of the strokes. While in the hospital, she developed a smoker's cough and coughed so hard she broke her stitches, requiring another surgery. Helen Horton and Jean Hagen rushed over to see her. Hagen was no longer drinking, but now she suffered from throat cancer and was on her way to Germany to obtain the drug laetrile, unavailable in the United States.

Another important event of this period was the entry of Felicity Ann Crosland into the Dahls' lives. A Welsh-born woman in her mid-thirties, Felicity was a descendant of a lady in waiting to Queen Elizabeth I. Her young daughters lived mostly with her ex-husband, Charles Reginald Hugh Crosland. Felicity had a Battersea flat near the Albert Bridge in London and worked for Scenery Ltd., with which Ogilvy & Mather had contracted to supply Patricia's costumes for her London-produced Maxim commercials. Felicity had been warned that the job might be difficult because both Patricia and Roald were drinking heavily.

The two women quickly became good friends, and Felicity was soon a frequent visitor to the Dahl home. She often bought the Dahl children gifts, and the Dahls occasionally invited Felicity to dine with them at Curzon's. She liked to gamble as well, and found a gambling companion in Roald. Felicity, Patricia discovered, usually won.

In the summer of 1974, Roald suggested that instead of vacationing in Norway they all go to Minorca and bring along Felicity and her daughters, as well as Felicity's friend Phoebe Berens and her daughters. They shared lazy days on the beach, with outdoor barbeques. The Dahl family and the two women and their daughters stayed in separate houses, and as Patricia visited with Phoebe one afternoon she mentioned that she and Roald were enjoying themselves as they had done in Tobago. The woman rolled her eyes, and something about that gesture shook Patricia's confidence.

Back in England, at Felicity's home, Patricia noticed an expensive man's dressing gown hanging on the bathroom door. When Patricia asked Felicity leading questions about its owner, including if he was married and how many children he had, Felicity answered bluntly, "He adores his children but not his wife." Patricia then asked, "Will he get a divorce?" Felicity abruptly ended the conversation.[18]

Patricia was entering a period in which her scripts tended to feature fatal illnesses. CBS wanted her for *Things in Their Season*, to be broadcast after Thanksgiving. When she received the script that summer, she gave it to a friend to read. The friend told her, "Don't read it, it's too depressing."[19] Another friend told her the same thing, so Patricia set the script aside. When a CBS executive called and asked, "Will you do it?"[20] Patricia said no, though she confessed she hadn't read it. "Promise me you will read it," the executive said. When she did, she signed. "It's very touching and theatrical," Patricia told *New York Sunday News* reporter Kay Gardella. "And I think it's a great drama."[21]

Things in Their Season is a sentimental tale of a Wisconsin dairy farm family, Carl and Peg Gerlach (Ed Flanders and Patricia Neal) and their son Andy (Marc Singer). Andy wants to marry Judy Pines (Meg Foster) and leave the farm. It turns out, though, that Peg is dying from leukemia. Patricia told Gardella that one of things she liked most about the end of the film is when Carl learns about Peg's illness and gently says to her, "I love you, Peg." Said Patricia of Roald, "I've never heard it in all these married years. My husband just never says things like that."[22]

Critics praised the show, which was aired on November 27, 1974. Reviewer Tom Donnelly wrote, "The quiet intensity of Patricia Neal's performance . . . is a lovely and affecting thing to see. . . . Ed Flanders and Marc Singer give solid performances as father and son, but Patricia Neal makes this a real occasion. She was always a powerful presence, even in her beginning years as an actress, though neither she nor Hollywood (certainly not Hollywood) could seem to figure out a rational career for her. Now, with all mannerisms and excess burned away, she is strong and true and moving; she shows us how eloquent simplicity can be."[23]

In May she began filming a *Hallmark Hall of Fame* production, *Eric*, for NBC. The screenplay by Nigel and Carol Evan McKeand was based on a book by Doris Lund about the life and death of her son. Eric Swenson (John Savage) is a seventeen-year-old who is diagnosed with leukemia and told he will die soon. His parents, Stanley and Lois (Claude Akins and Neal), his brother Paul (twenty-four-year-old Mark Hamill), and his sister Linda (Eileen Mc-

Donough) experience his illness and remissions with him. Dr. Duchesnes (Nehemiah Persoff) and Marilyn Porter (Sian Barbara Allen), who becomes his girlfriend, enter the picture as the story draws to its conclusion.

Patricia told the press, "This is the first time I've worked this year and I love it. . . . I love to leave home from time to time when I get nervous. And coming to work in Hollywood really is like a holiday for me. . . . Hollywood producers haven't been offering me roles. And I haven't worked in England for years. Maybe it's because I'm still an American citizen, even though I've lived in Britain for more than 21 years. I wouldn't think of moving back to the United States permanently. Not even for a television series. I couldn't drag Roald away from England." When asked if she was happy, Patricia thought for a moment and replied, "Who's really happy? Let's just say it is enough not to be unhappy and let it go at that."[24]

While in Los Angeles, Patricia met with Peter Douglas. Patricia had been a faithful wife throughout her marriage to Dahl, and her meeting with Douglas did not alter that. Douglas recalled in a recent interview, "Patricia and I had so much fun when we visited then. We could never remember the names of the hosts of parties we went to, and we laughed so much about that."[25] It was good for them both to rekindle their friendship. He was a good listener and recommended a psychiatrist friend in Newport to her. Patricia saw the woman, who told her the reasons for her anger were valid, but that she was allowing the anger to change her at times into a guilty and hopeless human being. The woman sent Patricia a copy of *Angry Book* when she arrived back in England.

Patricia's activities and work kept her away from Gipsy House a great deal of the time. She knew that her children were growing away from her, but there was nothing she could do to change that situation. Her work became her salvation. Roald, having recently published two children's books and a short story collection, was content to stay home and play billiards. He began to act sometimes as if Patricia annoyed him. She sensed that something was wrong in their marriage, but she couldn't figure out what it was. When she was away, of course, Roald was seeing Felicity.

When she returned to England after filming *Eric*, Patricia learned that Felicity had undergone a tonsillectomy. Felicity was invited to recover for a week at Gipsy House. Patricia remembered bringing trays to Felicity in her room and noticing little notes that Roald had written her. Once she even saw Felicity giving Roald affectionate little kisses, and his embracing her, while he and their friends played billiards at home.

The signs were becoming obvious. Once, when Felicity was staying at

Gipsy House, Roald left his and Patricia's bed in the middle of the night. At a dinner at Curzon's, Felicity took over the ordering. When they were together in the ladies' room, Felicity gave Patricia what she interpreted as a look of victory. The following day at a lunch with Tessa before a fashion show, Patricia asked her daughter if her father and Felicity were having an affair. Tessa did not want to talk about it. Patricia pressed the issue for almost thirty minutes until Tessa finally said, "Yes. Yes, they are."[26]

When Patricia confronted Roald, he admitted it was true. And when she confronted Felicity at a luncheon with Marjorie Clipstone, she did not deny it either. This was not Roald's first affair during his marriage to Patricia, according to Annabella Power. "Roald didn't make passes at women; the women ran after him," she said.[27] Patricia was aware that her children had known what was happening all along, and her sense of betrayal must have been overwhelming. Of course, Roald's siblings did not want them to divorce; that had never happened in their family before. Infidelity was accepted; divorce was not. Roald was ruthless with his verbal abuse and cruel behavior toward Patricia during this time, and she held nothing back in expressing her bitterness and pain. In her autobiography, Patricia admits that this period of their lives together was a nightmare.

That spring, Patricia flew to the United States to be with Harvey Orkin, who lay dying of a brain tumor in a New York hospital. Known in Hollywood and New York as "the Mighty Ork," he was just fifty-seven years old. (He died in November.) When Patricia returned to England, she discovered that Felicity had gone off to France to think over her and Dahl's affair.

The two-week family vacation to Norway that year was an absolute disaster. The pent-up anger and bitterness Patricia felt toward Roald exploded one evening while they were dining at a restaurant on a lake. It was a horrid scene. It was the last vacation that the family ever took together.

As soon as they returned to Great Missenden, Patricia was off to Hollywood to begin the filming of a two-part *Little House on the Prairie* episode entitled "Remember Me," written by Michael Landon, who was also the show's producer and star. The series, based on the books by Laura Ingalls Wilder, had become a monster hit. Of "Remember Me," Landon told Hollywood reporter Bob Thomas, "I got the idea for the show from a news article about a woman who was dying and was searching for a home for her three children. When I was writing it, I realized that Patricia Neal was the actress who had to play it. So I sent her the script."[28]

Widow Julia Sanderson (Neal) is told she will die soon, and she sets about trying to find a family who will take care of her three children, the teenager John Jr. (Radames Pera), his younger brother Carl (Brian Part), and his little sister Alicia (Kyle Richards). At the end of part one, Julia dies and her children are left homeless. In part two the children are adopted by Isaiah Edwards (Victor French) and his fiancée, Grace Snider (Bonnie Bartlett). For the funeral scene, Landon wrote a four-line poem entitled "Remember Me" that, in the script, Julia has written and given to the Rev. Robert Alden (Dabbs Greer) to recite at her graveside. Actress Melissa Gilbert and Landon's daughter read the poem at Landon's own graveside after his death from pancreatic cancer in 1991.

When Patricia was in Hollywood, she received a lengthy letter from Roald giving his views about their marriage. He told Patricia, for only the third time in their married life, that he loved her. But he also pointed out that he cared for Felicity. In Patricia's estimation she would simply have to accept Felicity as part of Roald's life if the marriage was to continue.

In mid-August, Patricia and Tessa flew to Los Angeles to film an episode of NBC's *Movin' On* entitled "Prosperity One." The series, aimed at capitalizing on the CB radio–trucker convoy fad that was sweeping the country at that time, told of two truckers, the middle-aged veteran Sonny Pruitt (Claude Akins) and his companion, the ruggedly good-looking and well-educated Will Chandler (Frank Converse), who together own a big rig and cross the country "in search of adventure and freight to haul." In "Prosperity One," Patricia portrays Mady Staton, the owner of a coal mine. The two truckers deliver freight to her mine, where the workers are on strike. Sonny and Will are divided in their loyalties. Trouble erupts when Mady hires scabs, and the mine collapses with Sonny trapped inside. Gary Merrill plays Sampson Eubanks, who is caught between the miners and his concern for Mady, and Tessa plays his daughter Haley.

Patricia looked particularly haggard and tired during this time. Her work on this show was erratic, unbalanced, and not at all convincing. But considering what was happening in her personal life, it is a wonder she was able to give a performance at all. Tessa's scenes in the Eubanks home were mercifully brief. Her English accent was jarring, and she didn't photograph well at all.

All Patricia's television work of 1975 was shown in quick succession in November: "Remember Me" on November 5 and 12, *Eric* on November 10, and "Prosperity One" on November 18. Of *Eric*, Joan Hanauer of United Press International said, "Patricia Neal plays his mother, and the sorrow of the world is reflected in her brown eyes and her tentative smile that is almost a grimace of hope."[29]

Back in England, life with Roald was unbearable. He decided she should keep busy, so Patricia was featured in a made-for-daytime television ninety-minute special titled *The American Woman: Portraits of Courage*, that aired on May 20, 1976, on ABC. The show depicts through newsreels and reenactments the lives of ten American women who struggled to establish equal rights for women. Patricia narrates the special, which features Celeste Holm, Helen Gallagher, Hal Holden, Melba Moore, Lois Nettleton, Frank Langella, Kate Mulgrew, and Claudia McNeil, among others. The show won three daytime Emmy Awards, plus the Clarion Award for Human Rights. It was the only Patricia Neal performance that aired in 1976.

25

Independence

We must all find open doors and make our lives as beautiful as God intended. I never think of my limitations because my life has been happy.

—Helen Keller

When Tessa asked Felicity if she was having an affair with her father, at first Felicity denied it. Tessa then asked her aunt Else about it, and she suggested Tessa ignore it. Tessa recalled that while the Dahl family "loved to discuss drama, they didn't like to discuss the effect on people's emotions."[1] One night she overheard her father talking on the telephone to Felicity, and the next morning she asked him directly about his relationship with Felicity. According to Tessa, he denied everything and then turned on her, saying, "You've always been trouble, you've always been a nosy little bitch. I want you to get out of this fucking house now."[2] Roald had Felicity apologize to Tessa the following day, and Tessa decided to keep quiet about the issue. She did, however, spend a few evenings with Felicity and sometimes stayed the night on her couch, in effect allying herself with her father and Felicity.

When Tessa was in her late teens, she fought her own demons. Roald bought her a London apartment. She had tested for John Huston's *The Man Who Would Be King*, starring Sean Connery and Michael Caine, and was offered the female lead on the condition she lose twenty pounds. When Roald sent her to Champney's outside of London to fast, Patricia wrote friends, "Her figure looks great now. Tomorrow she is having her two ghastly canine teeth capped, which will make a big difference in her looks."[3] Tessa starved herself thin for the Huston film only to learn that Caine's wife, Shakira, had been given the part.

Tessa, who had grown into a beautiful young woman, embarked on a series of unsuccessful affairs, including a liaison with the fifty-year-old Peter

---

Facing page: Patricia Neal, circa 1980s. From the Patricia Neal Collection.

Sellers, with whom she lived briefly. She told the press, "He was a very, very lovely man. My mother was horrified, but I think she knew it would run its course. I know it would never have worked."[4] She next began an intense relationship with thirty-year-old David Hemmings, moving in with him as well.

By 1976 she was living with the thirty-two-year-old actor Julian Holloway, son of British entertainer Stanley Holloway. By the time she was nineteen, she was pregnant with his child. On September 15, 1977, Patricia and Roald became grandparents for the first time with the birth of Sophie Dahl, who would later be immortalized by her grandfather in his book *The BFG* as Sophie, the little girl the giant befriended. Tessa and Holloway chose not to marry.

By late fall of 1976, Patricia was back in the United States filming *Tail Gunner Joe* for NBC. A true story, told in flashbacks, *Tail Gunner Joe* was based on events of the 1950s, when Wisconsin Republican Senator Joseph McCarthy (Peter Boyle) exploited the fears of the nation by going after high-profile citizens suspected of being Communist sympathizers. His ruthless campaign helped flame the Red Scare across the nation. He ruined the reputations of many people but met his match when he took on the U.S. Army, accusing it of harboring subversives. His attacks provoked attorney Joseph Welch (Burgess Meredith) to say during a televised hearing, "Have you no decency, sir?" He is exposed as a demagogue after a blistering ten-minute speech by Maine Senator Margaret Chase Smith (Neal). McCarthy quickly plunged into obscurity and acute alcoholism, dying in 1957 while still in his forties. Hal Erickson in his *All Movie Guide* said, "this made-for-TV movie works as a brisk, entertaining recollection of an era in which 'guilt by association' was a byword. As Joe McCarthy, Peter Boyle's performance is so convincing that it borders on the supernatural."[5]

The real Margaret Chase Smith responded on September 25 to a note Patricia had sent her: "I did not know about the film on Senator McCarthy. I am delighted that you portray me, as I have long admired your acting. Because of your beauty, dignity, and intelligence, there is no one I would rather have preferred more than yourself in portraying me. . . . I not only admire your superb acting but as well your inspiring courage on your tremendous comeback from the stroke. We have something in common as in 1968 I was faced with the prospect of being confined to a wheel chair because of crippling arthritis."[6]

On December 1, Patricia and Roald flew to Chicago for one night to see the Organic Theater Company's stage production of *Switch Bitch*, an adaptation of three short stories from Roald's collection of the same title. In an interview with Sandra Pesman of the *Los Angeles Times*, Patricia said, "I was better known during our early years. But he's a much greater success than I am now. But it never really mattered to us. We met and married when Roald was 36 and I was 27. Neither of us had been married before, so we were serious about it. We moved into our house in England and had children, and that became the focus of our life." Roald said, "That's very true. And that was always lovely for me. No one had ever taken the slightest interest in me at all and I never wanted it any other way. In fact, it made my life ever so much easier. Old Pat was out there, able to make enough money to keep me going. So I was free to be true to my art, and write serious short stories, which I did for 30 years. And it was lovely to have someone making the money, which allowed me to do my work."[7] Dahl referred to Patricia later in the interview as "my weathered beauty."[8]

Tail Gunner Joe, which aired over NBC television on February 6, 1977, earned an Emmy award nomination for Patricia in the Outstanding Supporting Actress–Comedy or Drama Special, along with Susan Oliver, Rosemary Murphy, Diana Hyland, and Ruth Gordon. Hyland, who had died of cancer on March 17, was given the honor posthumously.

That spring in England, Patricia was interviewed for a BBC series called *The Hollywood Greats,* in an episode on Gary Cooper. Also interviewed were Maria Cooper Janis, Helen Hayes, Henry Hathaway, Delmar Daves, Joe Hyams, Princess Grace of Monaco, Howard Hawks, and Stanley Kramer.

In August, Patricia was in Spain filming *Nido de viudas* (Widow's Nest), produced, written, and directed by Tony Navarro, once a Warner Brothers publicist. "Oh, God!" she said of the film in 2003. "It was revolting! Have you ever seen anything so revolting in your whole life?"[9] Patricia recalled there were two reasons she agreed to do the film. First, she had been charmed by Navarro into doing it; and second, it was supposed to be filmed in Mexico. The location was changed to Spain, and when Navarro ran out of money, the actors were notified that they would not be paid.

Navarro somehow gathered a rather impressive cast—Valentina Cortese, Gina Lollobrigida, Yvonne Mitchell, Jadwiga Baranska, Jerzy Zelnik, and Lila Kedrova. Also in the cast was Patricia's friend from Northwestern days, Helen Horton. (Horton had etched a rather successful career in television and stage in England, and later achieved cult TV status as a regular on Britain's *Benny Hill Show.*)

Nido de viudas tells the grim story of three sisters, Dona Dolores (Cortese), Dona Elvira (Mitchell), and Dona Carmen (Baranska), who have locked themselves away in a dingy mansion in Las Vallalas, Cuba, for over twenty years, existing in a world of their own. Their only contact with the outside is through their servant Lupe (Neal), a one-eyed witch who wanders the street purchasing food and necessities for the women. Enter their dead brother's wife Isabel Sotomayer (Susan Oliver) and her brother Carlos (Zelnik), who had been Isabel's husband's lover. Secrets are disclosed, curses are made, and insanity runs rampant. At the climax of the film, the three sisters are left praying furiously for the forgiveness of their sins. Grim stuff, indeed.

The $1.25 million picture was set to film in Mexico on July 19, but the Mexican backers didn't come through. Then the U.S. backers withdrew and the producers hastily accepted a deal with Cadeo Villalba's Alexandra Films and Victor Zapata of Fotofilm. Navarro then relocated the filming to Spain. When the money ran out after only eighteen days of shooting, about halfway through the film, Navarro scrambled to find new backing, directing during the day and working the phones at night.

Patricia was one of the first cast members to arrive in Madrid. She told Navarro, "I know you have no money. You must have a meeting with us to tell us you have no money." She recalled, "He broke down crying. We all agreed to work for nothing." They all stuck except the fiery and beautiful Gina Lollobrigida. When she discovered she would not be paid, she quit the film and was replaced by Oliver. Some members of the cast and crew vividly recalled Lollobrigida's outburst as she exited the hotel at 2:00 A.M. The cast, crew, and director were gathered in the lobby. In burst Lollobrigida, cursing a blue streak, "Fuck you! You horse's ass! Fuck you up your ass!" she screamed at Navarro. "Shit on you, too, Gina!" yelled Navarro back. Noticing Patricia sitting there in shock with Horton, the Italian actress leaned over and said, "Oh, not you, not you. . . . I admire you so much. You are a lady. . . . I love you." Spinning on her heels as she exited, Lollobrigida screamed to the director, "Fuck you! Up your ass!" Navarro had the last word, "I spit on your mother's grave, Gina!"[10]

Patricia next narrated a PBS documentary called *Including Me*, broadcast on September 11. It focused on a new federal law, the Education for All Handicapped Children Act, which went into effect that fall. It guaranteed the nation's physically, emotionally, and mentally handicapped children the same rights as other children. Patricia told Associated Press reporter Mike Silverberg, "Naturally I feel very strongly about the subject. It's my problem—but it's everybody's problem, really. I'm not Joan of Arc, and I sure as hell don't want anyone to think I'm a martyr. . . . I consider it an honor when they think of me for something like this show. I'm always willing to make speeches about strokes." Patricia mentioned that she was headed to Knoxville the following month. "I'm going there to dedicate a hospital," she said. "Believe it or not, they're going to name it after me."[11]

In Los Angeles, Patricia filmed a very brief role in *A Love Affair: The Eleanor and Lou Gehrig Story* for NBC, playing the part of Gehrig's German-speaking mother. That production marked the last time Patricia would work with director Fielder Cook. The Patricia Neal Rehabilitation Center, "A Place for Miracles," in Knoxville, Tennessee, would become a major part of Patricia's life. From October 27 through November 3, she participated in numerous opening events, including an awards banquet attended by more than two hundred prominent citizens and entertainment figures, including Kim Hunter and Maureen Stapleton. Patricia was given the Fort Sanders Hospital Foundation Award for inspiring courage and the Hyatt Regency Hall of Humanitarians Award for her inspiration and philanthropic interest in rehabilitation. "Cocktails with Patricia Neal" at the Cherokee Country Club, with more than a thousand guests, kicked off the dedication of the center, which was an $8.5 million wing of Fort Sanders Hospital.

The medical center was designed to provide the latest medical and rehabilitation procedures to survivors of strokes and debilitating physical diseases. Patients live in apartments with living areas, bedroom, bath, and kitchen so their rehabilitation can be carried out in a home-like environment. Pictures of Patricia placed around the facility remind patients that recovery is possible. The wing also houses an emergency department with thirty-two beds, an intensive care unit, and a coronary observation unit.

The Patricia Neal Rehabilitation Center has remained the project to which Patricia's is most dedicated. She visits numerous times each year and sponsors the annual Patricia Neal Golf Classic, which raises funds for the hospital's operation.

The Widow's Nest opened in December to generally horrible reviews. Jeff Freedman in the *Hollywood Reporter*, said, "Masturbation, incest, lesbianism and virginity abound, with lust and greed leading to torture and murder. The plot—vague and vicious—comes in second best to the performers' insanity—it's not so much that it is hard to follow what's happening, just that such sins are better left in the closet. . . . Every echo, every whisper is emphasized in 'Widows' Nest,' a tale of murder and madness which should appeal only to those predominantly interested in the seamier side of life."[12]

Los Angeles Times arts editor Charles Champlin, said, "In its banality, the dialogue is unwittingly funny, at the level of 'The Drunkard' revisited: 'Get out, get out, I say!' 'Why are you telling me all this?'. . . They all go out and Miss Neal, chewing a cigar and murmuring incantations over ritual chicken claws, her eye blazing, is, for want of a better word, spectacular. . . . The ambition is admirable but self-defeating, I'm afraid."[13] Bridget Byrne, of the *Los Angeles Herald-Tribune*, said, "'Widow's Nest' needs a strong dose of smelling salts to bring it to its senses. Overwrought to the point of lunacy, Tony Navarro's film displays several fine actresses making spectacles of themselves, scene-stealing pathetically from each other through a nonsensical plot, overlaid with absurd dialogue. 'Let me tell you, not only do I look like a witch. I am one,' rasps Patricia Neal as the drooling, one-eyed hag who caretakes for the three Spanish widows in pre–World War II Cuba. . . . It is hard to tell which performance is the most preposterous. . . . The film, in the absolute sense of the word, is laughably bad."[14]

In January 1978, Patricia played a small role in the syndicated television mini-series *The Bastard*, based on the best-selling novel by John Jakes. While she was filming *The Bastard*, Roald dutifully sent her long letters with newsy bits from home—Theo's friends keeping him out until midnight and Roald not liking it, Wally finishing the corking of the kitchen floor. He also told her, "I've just got your tax for 1977. You'll be pleased to hear that your expenditure was greater than your income, so there can't possibly be anything to pay, even over here."[15]

Roald had Patricia sign with Robert Keedick of the Keedick Lecture Bureau to represent her on speaking engagements. This would provide her a substantial income. Keedick immediately sent her on a speaking tour of twenty-five engagements in the United States.

In the spring of 1979 Patricia flew to France to act in the United Artists film *The Passage*. Based on the novel *Perilous Passage* by Bruce Nicolaysen, who adapted it for the screen, *The Passage* tells the sinister tale of a peasant simply called the Basque (Anthony Quinn) who is coerced into leading an American scientist, Professor Bergson (James Mason), his wife Ariel (Neal), and their two children, Leah (Kay Lenz) and Paul (Eleanor Parker's twenty-one-year-old son Paul Clemens), through the Pyrenees from occupied France to Spain and freedom during the darkest days of World War II. Throughout their escape, they are pursued by Von Berkow (Malcolm McDowell), a milk-drinking SS captain who likes fine food, enjoys killing gypsies, and wears a swastika on his jockstrap.

The ninety-nine-minute picture, directed by J. Lee Thompson, was shot partly on location and partly at the Victorine Studios in Nice, France. While Patricia was on location, Tessa and Julian Holloway arrived from Cannes for a few days. Patricia told the French press, "Tessa's changed. She's a fantastic mother, a lot better than I was! She loves her baby, and so do I."[16] While she was in Nice, Roald came over to spend some time with her on his way to Switzerland.

In the lobby of the Negresco Hotel in Nice, Patricia encountered Maria Cooper Janis, who was accompanying her husband on a concert tour. They met several times, but Patricia never told Maria about her problems with Roald. She did reveal that she had questioned her belief in God since her stroke, and Maria told her, "I know an abbey you would love. You should go sometime."[17]

After filming *The Passage*, Patricia returned to Great Missenden, where on July 2, she and Roald celebrated their twenty-fifth wedding anniversary with a party held at Gipsy House for more than a hundred guests. Patricia gave Roald a mynah bird who talked nonstop, and a game of boules that she had bought in Nice. He gave her two rings, a third-century silver Roman ring and a gold ring of the same era from the Egyptian delta.

On August 16, 1978, Jean Valentino died at the age of eighty-four. Jean and Chloe had continued to live at Fox Hill Drive, renting out the other half of the duplex. They had appeared in numerous pictures as extras throughout the 1950s and into the 1960s. Patricia was in the States shortly after Jean's death and stopped to visit with Chloe. She told Chloe in a letter written later that month, "Jean was a great lady with a marvelous sense of humor. I am sure you are very lonely without her but time makes things easier. Believe me—I know."[18]

On August 29, Roald was rushed by ambulance to the hospital to have an operation to remove a loose disc that was causing pain in his back. He had already had several back surgeries and was also awaiting a hip replacement. When he returned from the hospital, the sixty-two-year-old Roald apparently felt his mortality, as he wrote a lengthy letter to Eura Neal detailing his and Patricia's financial assets. He told Mrs. Neal about the trusts they had set up for the children and about his projected royalties. He even mentioned the worth of several pieces of their collected art.

Patricia flew to Lexington, Kentucky, for a couple of weeks in October to shoot on-camera narration for the three-part documentary *This Other Eden* for Kentucky Educational Television. The five-hour series, based on the book *Kentucky, A History* by Steven A. Channing, traces the lives and stories of the men, women, and events that shaped Kentucky's history, from Daniel Boone's days to the present. Patricia continued on to Knoxville, where her Knoxville Alumni Club had chosen the establishment of the Pi Beta Phi Patricia Neal Endowment Fund for the Patricia Neal Rehabilitation Center as its project of the year. At the Patricia Neal Rehabilitation Hospital were displayed the autographs of many celebrities on the "Friends of Patricia Neal" wall. In a glass case in the lobby of the hospital was a newly sculpted bronze bust of Patricia by sculptor Jerry Hester.

In London the night of November 22, Roald and Patricia attended a cocktail party at the London Park Lane home of Sir John Woolf, who was producing Roald's new British television series, *Tales of the Unexpected.* At the soiree were several of the shows' stars: Dame Wendy Hiller, Kenneth Haigh, Richard Greene, Elaine Stritch, Patricia Medina and her husband Joseph Cotten, and Marius Goring. Then television personality Eamonn Andrews, host of Thames television's *This Is Your Life,* joined the party, and to no one's surprise but Patricia's, the night became hers. She was the show's subject.

Taken to the television studio, Patricia found that many people from her life had been flown in for the occasion. She was delighted to see her mother, Eura; sister, NiNi, and her husband, George; her brother, Pete; Helen Horton; and Valerie Eaton Griffith. Emily Mahan Faust had flown from Knoxville with Eura Neal; also present were such family members and close friends as Alfhild Hansen, Else Logsdail, Asta Anderson, Margery Clipstone, Brigadier Richard and Patricia Kirwan, Audrey Ray-Smith, Angela Hogg, Jane Figg, Pam Lowndes, Frankie Conquy, and Wally Saunders, who talked about "the house that Wally built." Of course Tessa, Theo, Ophelia, and Lucy, as well as a film clip of little Sophie, were included in the program. Also featured were filmed messages from Dr. Charles Carton and Patricia's former leading men John Wayne and Kirk Douglas.

Throughout the show, Dahl looked bored and distracted. What viewers didn't see was a shocking gesture on Roald's part. Since her stroke, Patricia had developed a habit while she was seated of taking the hand of someone standing near her and, when she was at a loss for words, kissing the person's hand. At the end of the broadcast, as the credits for *This Is Your Life—Patricia Neal* were rolling, Patricia reached for Roald. He yanked his hand away from her and shoved it in his pocket. (*This Is Your Life—Patricia Neal* aired on December 13, 1978.)

Patricia recalled that the evening was an emotionally moving experience. After the taping, though, tensions flared. There were not enough rooms at Gipsy House to house the entire family because the children were home for the holidays. Eura was disappointed with these arrangements, and when she arrived back home in the States, she wasted little time in sending Patricia a letter deploring what had happened. Roald exploded and sent Eura a scathing reply telling her they never wanted to see her again.

On February 21, 1979, Patricia was the keynote speaker at Rockford (Illinois) College's Charter Day Convocation forum "Against the Odds." She spoke about her recovery from her strokes and received an honorary doctorate of humane letters from the college, the first of several she would receive.[19]

The Passage opened in March 1979. *Variety* said, "This is Neal's first pic in some years, and she's suitably self-serving as the wife whose ill health prevents her passage through the mountains. The character kills herself off early in the pic, but it's not clear just how. One morning she turns up frozen on a wintry slope."[20] David Ansen wrote in *Newsweek*, "James Mason, Anthony Quinn and Patricia Neal are given dialogue that could have been written by a pretentious second-grader."[21]

Vincent Canby in his *New York Times* review said, "'The Passage' is so awful you must suspect it was designed to be someone's tax write-off. As such it should be a smashing success. . . . The performances are very, very bad, and the mountains boring."[22] Canby couldn't have been more perceptive. Interviewed in 2003, Malcolm McDowell said, "I barely remember it. All it was was a tax write-off for most of us. I just remember it was an awful picture."[23]

The film failed on all levels and did nothing for anyone's career. It is unbearable to watch today; the photography is dark and grainy, the editing sloppy, and the music loud and intrusive. What's more, the acting of Lenz and Clemens is pedestrian, to be kind.

The spring of 1979 saw Patricia on the lecture circuit once again. In March she was in Minneapolis to draw awareness to AASK (Aid to Adoption of Special Kids), which she became interested in sponsoring after reading the book *Nineteen Steps Up the Mountain*, about the DeBolt family. The DeBolts, who had six children of their own, adopted thirteen more children of different nationalities who had varying degrees of physical limitations. (Later they would adopt one more child, an abused Mexican boy.) Patricia wrote the publisher of the book and received a letter from Dorothy DeBolt asking her to help find homes for handicapped children. Mimi Tellis took Patricia to meet the DeBolts. Continuing with the tour on behalf of AASK and the DeBolts, Patricia spoke to an audience in Chicago the first week of May, asking for financial support.

Back in New York, Patricia asked her driver to take her to the Abbey of Regina Laudis, in Bethlehem, Connecticut, a contemplative Benedictine community founded in 1947. The abbess was former actress Dolores Hart, whose credits included two films with Elvis Presley, *Loving You* (Paramount, 1957) and *King Creole* (Paramount, 1958), directed by Michael Curtiz. She left pictures to join the order in 1963. Maria Cooper Janis had contacted Reverend Mother Dolores Hart about Patricia. In May 1979 the abbess wrote Patricia, welcoming her to visit. She also sent Patricia a copy of her final vows and a prayer book made from a special redwood that Maria Cooper Janis had given the abbey. Patricia was now accepting that invitation.

Knowing that she would be denied alcohol at the abbey, she had the driver stop at a liquor store so she could get a bottle of wine, a bottle of vodka, and a mixer, which she placed in her luggage. "The abbey was an unpretentious place in the New England countryside," Patricia wrote in her memoirs, "almost hidden in a valley of pine and maple and surrounded by flowers. I was glad it was spring."[24] Patricia wrote about her three-day visit, meeting the kindly sisters, following the simple rules of conduct and the schedules for meals and worship, all the while keeping her liquor securely tucked in a drawer in her humble room. She found the courage to talk about her life and her failing marriage with a sister she met when she first arrived, and on the third day she was taken by the abbess into her garden, where she spoke about her life, her love for Gary Cooper, the death of Olivia, and the crumbling of her marriage to Roald.

The abbess chose a special flower from the greenhouse to place in the chapel in remembrance of Patricia's daughter Olivia, and when Patricia attended vespers, she saw that the flower had been placed in front of the altar. When she returned to her room, alone, she cried. At the end of her visit, when she was packing, she realized that she had completely forgotten about the liquor.

Patricia flew back to England briefly, and then on to Czechoslovakia for a small role in a three-hour CBS television remake of Erich Maria Remarque's classic antiwar novel *All Quiet on the Western Front*. Patricia portrayed the mother of the young soldier Paul Baumer, played by Richard Thomas. Thomas recalled his brief scenes with Patricia as heartbreakingly emotional. "Patricia and I had already established a relationship, a mutual respect," said Thomas. "We had the perennial mother-son bond there." Regarding the final scene with Patricia, in which her character lies dying, Thomas commented, "I knew it was going to be heavy . . . intense. I knew it was going to be the real thing." Thomas said he was overwhelmed by the contrast between her character in *The Homecoming*—"that gut country strength and stoicism"—with the vulnerability she portrayed in *All Quiet.* "The sickness, the illness in the end, the fragility . . . it's just devastating to me," Thomas said.[25]

That summer, Patricia visited Martha's Vineyard for the first time. With her were Ophelia and Lucy; the three stayed for ten days with Millie Dunnock and her husband Keith Urmy. Patricia fell in love with the island on that trip. Continuing on to California, she and the girls met up with Theo, and with Jean Alexander and Gloria Carugati, they all spent a glorious holiday driving up the California coast in a camper trailer. Patricia's children were beginning to understand and develop a new relationship with their mother.

At the end of August, Patricia surprised her Northwestern University and Eagles Mere director Alvina Krause, now director of the Bloomsburg Theatre Company, by visiting her at her home in Bloomsburg, Pennsylvania. Patricia then attended the Eagles Mere Friends of the Arts presentation of *Under Milkwood* at the Eagles Mere Community Hall. "She taught me timing. She taught me imagination," Patricia said of Krause to the press. "Nonsense," replied Krause. "I taught her to stand up straight!"[26]

CBS broadcast *All Quiet on the Western Front* on November 14. Wrote one television reviewer, "The supporting players are uniformly outstanding . . . especially Patricia Neal. . . . This new version of the classic novel measures up to the original movie in every way. In fact, its powerful anti-war message has even more impact on the small screen. It's destined to become a TV classic."[27] Patricia received a Best Supporting Actress Emmy nomination, along with Eileen Heckart, Carrie Nye, and Mare Winningham. Winningham won.

That November Patricia was back in the United States for a month, her fifth trip to America that year, to visit her ailing aunt Maude, who was in a hospital in Williamsburg. Patricia attended a performance in Louisville, Kentucky, of a new play, *Packard*, by Nancy Niles Sexton and Robert Sexton. Robert Sexton's father had taken Coot Neal's job with the mining company when the Neals moved to Knoxville in 1929, and Robert was born in the Neals' Packard home. The play tells the story of Packard and its residents in folklore and music. At a reception before the play, Patricia ran into her old beau Victor Jory, who was in town visiting his son Jon, producer-director of Louisville's Long Wharf Theatre. The two sat side by side, Jory gently holding Patricia's hand throughout the performance.

Back in England, Tessa gave up her London apartment, and Patricia took it over. She furnished it as her place in the city, a retreat away from Roald, whose behavior was becoming intolerable. At a supper at the Curzon House Club in early 1979, Roald, Patricia, and Tessa were treating George and Phyllis Jenkins to an evening out. Roald decided that the dinner and the decor of the newly redecorated club were not to his liking. He drunkenly stood up and told the other diners what he thought about the food, as well as throwing out choice comments about the club's decor. According to Tessa, who was with a wealthy Greek suitor then, her father then started to complain about the number of Jews in the club. People nearby simply told him to shut up. "Go home if you don't like it," said one.[28] Dahl then weaved his way to the gambling tables, after which the management effectively kicked them all out of the club, permanently revoking the Dahls' membership. The messy scene made the papers.

Patricia's lecture career also kept her away from Roald. A new speech, "An Unquiet Life," was proving to be very popular with audiences in the United States. Her trips to America were more frequent now, and she began to look for a home in her native country. Patricia rented Katharine Cornell's house on Martha's Vineyard for the summer of 1980. That spring James Kelly, Tessa's current beau, told Patricia about a house in Edgartown, which she bought sight unseen for $400,000. Once owned by the whaling boat captain on whom Herman Melville based his character Captain Ahab in *Moby Dick*, the seventeenth-century, three-story clapboard structure faced the sea, directly across from Chappaquiddick.

When Patricia finally toured the place, it was with her friends Sue Conrad and Phyllis Jenkins. The house had a picket fence and roses growing in back. Patricia summoned Warren Langton from California to help paint the house, and along with her friend Anne Fonde Walter, she shopped the stores in Knoxville for inexpensive yet tasteful furnishings. Langton renamed the place "Moby Neal." Roald only visited the house once, in the summer of 1981.

That fall, in the midst of her latest lecture tour, Patricia participated in a benefit to raise funds for a new speech building at Northwestern University. The two-hour event, *The Way We Were*, filmed for television, featured illustrious Northwestern alumni such as Charlton Heston, Cloris Leachman, Ann-Margret, Jerry Orbach, Carol Lawrence, Garry Marshall, McLean Stevenson, Paula Prentiss, and Patricia. Heston eloquently introduced Patricia, gallantly kissing her hand when she reached the podium.

After touring the country as far as Tacoma, Washington, Patricia started winding her tour down. She traveled to Knoxville after the intensive lecture series and took part in a fund-raiser for the Patricia Neal Rehabilitation Center on November 14. She read a selection from Helen Keller, and President-elect Ronald Reagan sent a wire: "Both our lives have changed drastically in the past 30 years. . . . You're a pro, a real performer, both on and off the stage."[29]

Around this time Patricia was asked why she wasn't working more in films. She said, "You will start squaring off with Barbara Stanwyck. . . . That is where most aging actresses are in Hollywood. . . . Every old actress comes back squaring off in *The Love Boat*. . . . What does that mean? They have no idea what the purpose of that was. . . . Let's just say if you're an actor . . . you love to act. That is what my purpose was."[30]

By the start of 1981 Patricia was preparing for a new film role, as Fred Astaire's wife Stella in *Ghost Story*, based on Peter Straub's best seller. *Ghost Story*, told in flashbacks, focuses on four wealthy New England school friends: John Jaffrey (Mark Chamberlin as a youth, Melvyn Douglas as an old man), Edward Charles Wanderley (Kurt Johnson/Douglas Fairbanks Jr.), Ricky Hawthorne (Tim Choate/ Fred Astaire) and Sears James (Ken Olin/ John Houseman). When they were young in the 1920s, they were responsible for the death of a girl named Alma (Alice Krige). For the next fifty years they meet every two weeks as members of the Chowder Society to tell ghost stories and reminisce. A series of murders occur, including the horrible death of one of Wanderley's twin boys, both played by Craig Wasson. The one who died was seeing a mysterious young woman named Eva (Krige again). The old men are worried that their ghost stories are coming true. Indeed, one by one they themselves experience gruesome deaths.

Patricia recalled that she was originally going to turn down the role, but Ophelia insisted she do the part if for no other reason than that it would get her in front of the cameras again. Her role was filmed quickly and her screen time is brief, even though she appears in several scenes. Patricia had the opportunity to work again with Douglas in his last film role; he died on August 4, 1981. *Ghost Story* was also Fred Astaire's last film. Patricia's scenes with Astaire included several in which they were in bed together. In one, Astaire awakes in terror as visions of the boys' crime haunt him. Patricia Neal holds the dubious honor of being the only actress ever to go to bed with the debonair Astaire on-screen.

26

Divorce

I done my time with one cold-blooded bastard. I'm not looking for another.

—Alma, *Hud* (1963)

The filming of *Ghost Story* not only got Patricia in front of the camera again; it also put an ocean between her and her husband. In England, Roald told newspaper writer Nancy Mills, "When Pat's away, I love to stay here and mind my own business," which consisted of taking care of Ophelia and Lucy. Roald also spent time in London's gambling casinos. "I go more often when Pat's away. I love it. Pat doesn't like gambling, so I can't enjoy myself when she's at my elbow," Roald said.[1]

Her relationship with Roald was very shaky, but Patricia was finally able to effect a reconciliation on another front. While she was in New England filming *Ghost Story,* Patricia read in the papers about the death of Dr. John Converse, husband of Veronica Cooper Converse. Patricia sent a letter of condolence, which read in part:

Dear Rocky,

Time passes so quickly and we endure many crises—life, death, and great, great pain.

I have for many years wanted to write you and to express my deepest regret for your loss of Gary. . . .

Do, please do, accept my sympathy and know that I have respected you. . . .

Again, my compassion and my sincere love,
As I am, Patricia Neal[2]

Facing page: Patricia Neal, circa 1990s. Photograph by Bill Donovan, from the Patricia Neal Collection.

Within a few weeks, Patricia received a reply:

Pat Dear,

   . . . [Y]ou surely have carried your cross as I have. A priest here told me that that act lets us bypass Purgatory. Let's hope he's right. Do, dear Pat, let me know when next you are in this city. The three of us [Rocky, Patricia, and Maria] can have lunch up here and perhaps you can buck me up if anyone can. Life is surely full of surprises. . . .

Affectionately,
Rocky[3]

Tessa and James Kelly married on February 28, 1981, at the Little Missenden church, the same church where the Dahl children were baptized, and where Olivia was buried. The Kellys took up residence in Boston. Tessa was still a surrogate mother–figure for her younger siblings, and according to Dahl biographer Jeremy Treglown, Lucy was a troubled teenager. With Theo's help, Tessa found an excellent school for the sixteen-year-old, the Cambridge School at Weston, Massachusetts, a progressive academy. Said Tessa, "If all goes well, Lucy will stay there until she's 18."[4]

During his brief visit to the States that summer, Roald told *Boston Globe* writer Susan Slavetin, "People get tired of being with each other for years—day in, day out. They need some time away from each other." After he'd wandered off, Patricia shrugged off his comment by telling the reporter, "'Men are such conceited asses. But I love being here on the Vineyard. Tomorrow we'll have a gorgeous party. Cagney will be here. Hellman, too.' She smiles broadly. Somehow, the smile does not synch with what seems to be a great well of sadness in her eyes." The Dahls' marriage had become a charade.[5]

On June 7, 1981, Patricia was a presenter at the Thirty-Fifth Annual Tony Awards, held at the Mark Hellinger Theatre in New York and broadcast over CBS. She then returned to her Edgartown home on the Vineyard for the summer, leaving from time to time to go on the lecture circuit.

In July, while at the Vineyard, she received word that NiNi had suffered a stroke that paralyzed her left side. Eura Neal went to her older daughter's side in Atlanta, and Patricia stayed in constant touch by telephone. Fortunately, NiNi's recovery was quicker than Patricia's had been.

Shortly after that crisis, Patricia once more journeyed to the Abbey of Regina Laudis in Connecticut. While there, she announced that she was going to become a Catholic. Roald declined to take instruction with Patricia, and she began her instruction alone.

In October Patricia traveled to Dallas, where she was honored at the USA Film Festival's Great Actress/Actor retrospective—the first woman to receive the retrospective. Past honorees were Kirk Douglas, Gregory Peck, and Charlton Heston. The event was cosponsored by the Visiting Nurses Association of Dallas and Southern Methodist University's Division of Communication Disorders. The two-day Patricia Neal Retrospective was conducted at the Bob Hope Theatre, on the campus of SMU. Patricia also participated in a daylong seminar on aphasia management.

On December 10, *The Patricia Neal Story* aired on CBS television. Called *An Act of Love* in Britain, the hundred-minute television film was produced by Lawrence Schiller, directed in the United States by Anthony Harvey and in England by Anthony Page. The television film dramatized Patricia's and Roald's life immediately prior to her strokes in 1965, continuing through her recovery, and concluding with the premiere of *The Subject Was Roses*. Based on the book *Pat and Roald* by Barry Farrell, with teleplay by Robert Anderson, *The Patricia Neal Story* starred two-time Oscar-winning actress Glenda Jackson as Patricia and Dirk Bogarde as Roald. Also in the cast were *Dallas* television star Ken Kercheval as Dr. Carton, Jane Merrow as Valerie Eaton Griffith, and as themselves Mildred Dunnock, Gloria Stroock Stern, and Rock Hudson.

Patricia and Roald had not wanted the picture made, until they realized that telling their story could benefit stroke victims and their families. Tessa, speaking out to the press, said, "We're very unhappy about the whole thing. My parents won't get a penny out of it. And as for the casting, they've got an oversensitive Englishman as my father and a Northern shop-girl playing my mother!"[6]

But Patricia was pleased with the outcome. The Dahls were allowed to view a rough cut of the film before it was broadcast, and Patricia told a *New York Times* reporter, "I couldn't have played myself, but Miss Jackson, whom I've never met, did a lovely job. I think I owe her lunch, at least."[7]

Eura Neal, however, was not impressed. Interviewed by a local television critic at her home in Florida after the broadcast, the indomitable Mrs. Neal said that "the girl [Glenda Jackson] did a marvelous job as Pat," but she thought the character of Roald in the film was a bit embellished. She felt Bogarde played Roald as a saint, concluding, "He's far from it. I think it showed Mr. Dahl a little kinder and more patient than I think I remember him to be."[8]

The press reviews for *The Patricia Neal Story* were excellent. *New York Times* critic John J. O'Connor called it "a genuinely inspiring story" that was "handled with restraint, sensitivity and marvelous acting."[9] Said *Dallas Morning News* writer Ed Bark, "*The Patricia Neal Story* joins . . . movies that upgrade the definition of 'made-for-TV.' They're the best films so far this season."[10]

Time magazine called *The Patricia Neal Story* one of the best shows on television for 1981. The film went on to win several award nominations. The 1982 Golden Globe Awards nominated Glenda Jackson for Best Performance by an Actress in a Mini-Series or Motion Picture and Dirk Bogarde for Best Performance by an Actor in the same category. When the Thirty-fourth Annual Emmy Awards for 1981–1982 were announced, Glenda Jackson was nominated for Outstanding Actress–Limited Series or Special for her portrayal of Patricia.

Ghost Story, which premiered December 16 at New York's Rivoli Theatre, did not fare quite so well. The R-rated picture did decent business but received only lukewarm reviews. It was, however, nominated for the Saturn Award by the Academy of Science Fiction, Fantasy & Horror Films, USA, as Best Horror Film in 1982.

Shortly before the holidays, Patricia received a letter from Roald telling her it wouldn't be necessary for her to come home for Christmas. She couldn't understand why Roald would suggest such a thing. She flew back just the same, to a strained holiday.

Even her children were more distant than usual. Late on the evening of December 27 she walked into the family television room, and Ophelia and Roald exchanged quick glances. Patricia sensed something was up. Ophelia told her that her father was seeing Felicity once again. Roald did not deny it. Patricia flew into a rage. Ophelia insisted that her mother telephone someone—anyone—in America who could help her. Patricia called Sonia Austrian, who told her to get out of England right away. She could stay with the Austrians in New York until she could figure out what to do. That night as he lay sleeping, Patricia whispered in Roald's ear, "I wish you were dead. I wish something would kill you."[11] The next morning, the family took Patricia to London's Heathrow Airport. Roald had arranged the flight—one way. She kissed her weeping children goodbye as if she were off on another film assignment. When the airline began boarding the flight, Patricia turned around one last time to see her family. Roald had his head back laughing. "He looked like Satan," she wrote. "I did not turn back again."[12]

Sonia and Geoff Austrian allowed Patricia to stay with them for several months during the first part of 1982. She then stayed briefly with her friend Carolyn March. Patricia talked on the telephone for hours, ranting and raving to friends about Roald. A friend recommended a psychologist, and Patricia saw him a few times.

Playwright John Pielmeier offered her the role of Mother Miriam Ruth in his play *Agnes of God,* directed by Michael Lindsey-Hogg. Patricia attended a performance and slipped backstage to congratulate the play's three stars. But she realized that she was in no state of mind to attempt a stage role, and the part went to Geraldine Page.

Patricia began her first speaking tour of the year in March, and her work took her mind off the separation from Dahl, at least temporarily. Back in New York, she was seen about town with forty-nine-year-old Gotham Book Store owner Andreas Brown. But contrary to press accounts, they were just friends. Patricia wrote a friend, "My lawyers are working on the separation of Roald and me. I don't know how long it will be before a formal separation is underway. I know that Roald and Felicity are going on holiday about the last week in June—I think to France. Hope they have a glorious time," she wrote sarcastically, her anger evident.[13]

Patricia withdrew once more to the abbey in Connecticut. The sisters advised her to "Stop chewing on Felicity."[14] But try as she might, Patricia couldn't shake the bitterness.

The same week that Roald filed for divorce in England (she had already filed in America), Patricia bought an apartment on Manhattan's East Side, overlooking the East River. It was perfect for her. It had two bedrooms—she used one for a study—two baths, a small kitchen, a large living room and dining area, and a balcony.

Patricia spent most of the summer of 1982 at her home on Martha's Vineyard, watching television. Her friends Millie Dunnock and Lillian Hellman resided there year-round, but she did not see them much. Lillian was very ill most of the time. And Patricia suspected that many of her friends were beginning to avoid her because she was frequently unbearable to be around. At a charity auction that summer, she was one of the prizes—a dinner with Patricia Neal. She had such low self-esteem that she was afraid no one would bid on the dinner, or that if they did, it would be an embarrassingly low bid. It wasn't. But Patricia's life was an emotional roller coaster.

By the time she embarked on another speaking tour that fall, the legal separation had gone through, and the London tabloids were having a field day. Patricia's sister-in-law Alfhild wrote, "The horrible 'Daily Express' has told all and made it quite horrible—Roald I am glad to say was polite and reserved and sad—as are all of us. I do hope . . . you will find happiness and that you especially will come to see us all in England."[15]

After spending Thanksgiving with her family in Atlanta, Patricia headed once more for the abbey in Connecticut. She dreaded the idea of Christmas away from Gipsy House. The nuns invited her to stay with them for the month of December, not just as a guest, but as a pre-postulant, even though she was not planning to join the order.

After smoking her last cigarette, Patricia entered the confines of the abbey, exchanged her clothes for a black outfit and headscarf, removed her makeup, and accepted blessings from a priest. For the rest of December, she lived as much like the postulants as she could. She did chores, baked bread, kept silence at meals, and attended services. Her heart, however, still burned with hatred for Roald and Felicity. Patricia talked with Reverend Mother Dolores, venting her anger, fears, and anxieties. She had lost so much in life, she felt. And now she had lost her husband. Eventually, Patricia was made to realize that she had not lost everything. She still had herself. "You are a great mother, Patricia," Reverend Mother Dolores told her. "You can give life forever—if you will stop trying to keep score."[16]

Lucy, now nineteen years old and living in London, where she worked at a publishing house, flew to New York to spend the first part of 1983 with her mother. On Valentine's Day, Patricia was presented with the National Board of Review of Motion Pictures' Lifetime Achievement Award at the New York Public Library for the Performing Arts in Lincoln Center. She had to accept the award via telephone because she had broken her leg when she ran into a door at a friend's house.

Patricia continued with her speaking engagements that spring. In Houston in mid-March, she told Joe Leyden, of the *Houston Post*:

> My husband wants a divorce very badly. He's had this affair for God knows how many years. It's not the first one, I know, but I think this one's been going on for nine years. So that's a little *much*. . . .
>
> It's just really *ghastly*. I mean, our marriage was good until I became ill. And then he took over *everything*. And then, he—well I don't know. I don't know when he [had an affair] first. Maybe he did all through our married life. But it was so obvious, right in my face, you know? And I'm so stupid, I didn't even see it. And that's a little painful for me to think about.
>
> It's really agony for me, because I never wanted a divorce. Ever.

Ever. And the fact that I am about to have a divorce is really *hideous* for me. I mean, my mother and father were never divorced. And his mother and father were never divorced. And none of his brothers and sisters were ever divorced. Just him. That's the end of it all.

He's old now, 64. I just think it's a middle-aged thing that has really taken him over. It's sad. . . . I'm not sure what's going to happen. . . . It's very sad for me after 30 years to have failed at something. But we all do, I guess.[17]

In a London court in early July 1983, almost thirty years to the day after they were wed, Patricia Neal and Roald Dahl were granted a divorce based on uncontested and unspecified complaints about Roald's behavior. Neither Patricia nor Roald were present. The divorce had been bitter and drawn out. At stake were hundreds of thousands of dollars in funds, securities and bonds, plus nearly $1 million worth of collected paintings alone. Their law firms had done their best to protect assets for their respective clients.

Patricia declined to talk about the divorce or the settlement in her memoirs, but it was painful. Works of art and paintings were sold or auctioned off; moneys were transferred from fund to fund. Faxes and letters, and replies to those faxes and letters, flew from one firm to another, with Patricia and Roald evaluating each transaction and responding in kind. Patricia always maintained that she "got screwed" in the divorce.[18] In actuality she was given a suitably substantial settlement. In fairness to Dahl, he struggled to maintain sizable funds for his children.

Patricia once said, "Roald was a very important part of my life. We had known one another for thirty-one years of my life. . . . [With] Roald . . . [there] was never any affection . . . no real love . . . loyalty always. There were times when we counted on one another, we really did, and that worked divinely."[19]

After Roald married Felicity Crosland—which he did, not long after the divorce was granted—he entered into the most successful period of his literary life. Felicity possessed formidable domestic traits that Patricia did not. She created the lifestyle Roald needed to feel creative, and which he enjoyed for the rest of his life.

The children worried about their mother, now "banished" in America.[20] But their devotion to their father was unquestioned. Tessa and James and little Sophie left Boston and were living in England, Ophelia was a pre-med student in London (soon afterward she came to America and completed her studies at Wellesley), Lucy had just graduated from secondary school, and Theo was running an antiques business.

Before Christmas 1983 Patricia returned to Gipsy House and selected those items she wanted to keep from her marriage. She was accompanied by her sister-in-law Alfhild and her friend Lourdes Nicholas. She left a picture that Olivia had painted for Roald. "Leave it for him," Patricia recalled in her memoirs. "It would have killed him if I took it."[21]

The year 1984 promised to be a busy one for Patricia. For her birthday, Barry Landau threw a black-tie party at the fashionable club Regine's. Patricia wore a half-million dollars in diamonds and emeralds loaned by Tiffany's for the occasion. Guests included friends and former costars Anthony and Yolande Quinn, Swoosie Kurtz, Amanda Plummer, Shelley Winters, Maureen Stapleton, and Susan and John Weitz, to name a few.

Patricia had agreed to write her autobiography, and she began the tedious process of tape-recording her memories, collecting her scrapbooks and memorabilia, and contacting friends and family to help her remember her nearly six decades of life. She chose ghost-writer Dick DeNeut to help write it.

In the spring of 1984, New York gossip columnist Liz Smith wrote in a syndicated column: "Dear Aaron Spelling and the rest of you Hollywood producers. What are you waiting for? Patricia Neal is out and about and as one of New York's most visible social belles. Everybody loves her. Admires and praises her great body of work. . . . Neal has taken plenty of hard knocks from life . . . but the hardest knock is the one today—where everybody kisses her hand, but nobody thinks of putting her back to work."[22]

Perhaps Spelling or his people read that piece. In any event, Spelling hired Patricia for a brief role in his new pilot film for a projected series, *Glitter*, for ABC. The project required Patricia for only one day of filming, March 28, on stage one at her old studio, Warner Brothers. Directed by former child star Jackie Cooper, Patricia's segment told of Senator Jonathan McCary (Ken Howard), whose mother, Madame Lil (Neal), lies dying in a hospital, withholding from him, but possibly not the press, a secret. The cast included David Birney, Morgan Brittany, and Van Johnson. The film aired on September 13, 1984, but the series was short-lived. *Glitter* was yanked from the network within the year.

The first of April, Patricia flew to Nashville to begin her role in the Disney Channel telefilm *Love Leads the Way*, directed by Delbert Mann. The ninety-eight-minute biopic tells the story of Morris Frank (Timothy Bottoms), who is blinded in a gym accident in 1927. His parents (Arthur Hill and Neal) encourage him to begin a new program that uses seeing-eye dogs. Also in the cast were Eva Marie Saint, Ernest Borgnine, Susan Dey, and Glynnis O'Connor. Patricia's scenes again were brief; most of the story deals with

Frank's relationships with his girlfriends and his dogs. Tastefully directed and performed, *Love Leads the Way* was extremely well received when it aired on Disney's television cable channel on October 7.

Patricia told United Press International in Boston that *Glitter* and *Love Leads the Way* were "the shortest things I've done in my life. They're such tiny parts but they're good. The thing I want most is to do another great acting job. I want to be in a fabulous film. It's so sad to be an actress and I really am a good actress—and to have a stroke—but that's the way things happen. I don't know what makes me so gutsy but something does."[23]

At the end of April, Patricia went to England for three weeks, reviewing acting offers and staying with Tessa, now pregnant with her second daughter, and her husband at their London home. Back in the States in May, Patricia retired to the Vineyard for the summer.

On June 30, Lillian Hellman died in Tisbury, Massachusetts. Speaking at the memorial service on Martha's Vineyard, Patricia said Hellman was "a friend whose fibers were woven into every aspect of my life. . . . I will remember her with deep love for ever and ever. *Shalom*."[24]

Later that summer, Patricia flew to Hollywood for a small role—one close to her heart, that of a nun—in the made-for-television film *Shattered Vows*.

Shattered Vows was based on the autobiographical novel *Nun: A Memoir*, by Dr. Mary Gilligan Wong, who entered a convent in 1957 and left it in 1968. In 1984 she was a clinical psychologist in California. As a young woman Mary Gilligan (Valerie Bertinelli) enters the convent, taking the name Sister de Paul, only to find that she longs for a family. Sister Carmelita (Neal), Mary's superior, senses Sister de Paul's tormented feelings. When the two-hour film was aired on NBC on October 29, it was received with yawning indifference.

In December, Patricia's friend Kirk Douglas sent a letter of apology to her for not being able to secure the role of Hester Farrell for her in his upcoming television film *Amos*, produced for his Bryna Productions and costarring Elizabeth Montgomery. The role was given to Dorothy McGuire.

Patricia's career was slowing down. She would continue to give speeches, not on national tours now, but in selected venues. And she would continue to lend her voice, talent, and time for special events. She would remain socially active throughout the coming years, though her focus was not totally on acting.

27

Serenity

Remember me with smiles and laughter,
for that's the way I'll remember you all.
If you can only remember me with tears,
then don't remember me at all.

—Julia Sanderson,
Little House on the Prairie (1975)

From the mid-1980s to the present, Patricia Neal has been able to channel her energies into things she really cares about: the Patricia Neal Rehabilitation Center, her family, and, of course, her career. Inevitably, acting roles have been harder to come by, but she continues to lend her time and talent to worthy projects. And the many awards and honors she has received have given her ample opportunity to reflect on a long and distinguished career.

Starting in 1985, Patricia became a strong drawing card for the Theatre Guild Theatre at Sea program, in which actors perform readings from plays, sing and tell stories, and interact with cruise passengers on voyages. She has performed on Mediterranean islands, Alaskan glaciers, and even on the Amazon. She has sailed with such distinguished performers as Anne and Eli Wallach, Kitty Carlisle Hart, Helen Hayes, Lynn Redgrave, Roddy McDowall, Eartha Kitt, Cliff Robertson, Jane Powell, Jean Stapleton, Zoë Caldwell, Ben Gazzara, Gena Rowlands, Larry Kert, and Richard Kiley.

On March 8, 1986, Patricia received a Living Legacy Award at a ceremony at San Diego's famed Hotel del Coronado. The award honors the significant, lasting contributions of women in all professions. Patricia was made an honorary spokeswoman for the awards, which she continues to support. Two weeks later, on March 23, she received the Perlman Award for Human

Facing page: Patricia Neal, circa 2000. From the Patricia Neal Collection.

Achievement at the B'nai B'rith Women International Biennial Convention at the Las Vegas Hilton. That spring, she worked diligently on her memoirs, taping her recollections and accumulating materials. In June, she flew to England to help launch Valerie Eaton Griffith's National Stroke Campaign for the Chest, Heart, and Stroke Association.

Tessa and James Kelly divorced shortly after the birth of their son, Luke James Roald, on July 17, 1986. (Their first child, Clover Martha Patricia, was born September 11, 1984.) Ophelia, after graduating from Wellesley and living briefly in Haiti, eventually settled in Massachusetts. Encouraged by her father, she dedicated her life to volunteer work. In 1983 she and Dr. Paul Farmer, concerned with the prevalence of major diseases like tuberculosis and AIDS in such impoverished countries as Haiti and Peru, established an organization called Partners In Health (PIH). The two major goals of PIH are to bring the best of modern medical care to these countries and to serve as an antidote to despair.

Theo was still in England in the late 1980s, living in Great Missenden. Twenty-two-year-old Lucy had taken a Club Med cruise with her mother and enjoyed the experience so much she went to work for the company. She met Englishman Michael Faircloth and married him in Great Missenden on September 21, 1987. Patricia could not attend. The Faircloths settled in Captiva, Florida, and ran a water sports business at South Seas Plantation. They had two daughters, Phoebe Patricia Rose, born November 4, 1988, and Chloe Michaela, born September 12, 1990.

The big event of 1987 for Patricia was the October 8 fund-raiser for the tenth anniversary of the Patricia Neal Rehabilitation Center in Knoxville, including the presentation of the First Annual Patricia Neal Awards. Patricia's longtime friend and former costar Eddie Albert was her co-presenter at the black-tie event.

In April 1988, Patricia did publicity for her autobiography, *As I Am*, which was published on April 20. The book, published by Simon and Schuster, was an enormous best seller. Critics were abundant with praise. The *Los Angeles Times* said, "Neal writes with dignity and clarity about the courageousness of survival."[1] *Booklist* called the work "a unique, brutally honest work."[2] And the *Chicago Tribune* raved, "A harrowing story—Patricia Neal's quick voyage from triumph to catastrophe and her courageous recovery [is] a private hell, a life regained."[3]

The book itself is remarkably candid and written the way Patricia speaks. It covers her life sincerely and truthfully, and although several minor parts of her career are left out and there are several chronological errors, *As I Am* remains one of the most accurate and moving "movie star" autobiographies ever written.

That fall, Patricia signed for an independent film costarring Shelley Winters, *An Unremarkable Life*, produced and directed by Amin Q. Chaudhri. The picture tells the story of two sisters: Frances (Neal), retiring and lonely, and Evelyn (Winters), the dominant one. They have lived together in their family house in Pennsylvania for over fifteen years after World War II. Their lives are quiet and circumspect. They both have lost their husbands, and share a routine existence. Into Frances's life comes the Japanese-American Max Chen (Mako); he and Frances start to date. Evelyn sees Max as a threat to their existence and voices her disapproval; she is afraid of change and is prejudiced. Max makes Frances happy, and she realizes time is slipping away quickly. In the end she moves out of the house, and Evelyn is left alone.

A quiet and moody film, *An Unremarkable Life* offered Patricia a starring role. The picture was shot in part in Sharon, Pennsylvania, as well as in parts of Ohio and in Greece. Patricia used a hearing device in her ear for the first time to help her through her scenes. "The sound man on the picture told me about this great thing I could wear in my ear and have the lines fed to me so I wouldn't hold things up," she told Harry Haun of the *New York Daily News*. "It worked fabulously, and it's not noticeable in the acting. . . . It's sensational."[4] There is one scene when Frances is reading a bedtime story to a child. The selection is from Roald's *Charlie and the Chocolate Factory*. "I thought it would be fun," said Patricia to a reporter.[5]

An Unremarkable Life generally failed to excite the critics upon its release in October. Janet Maslin panned the film in the *New York Times*: "The best that can be said for 'An Unremarkable Life' . . . is that it strikes a blow against prejudice, provincialism, depression, loneliness and fear of the unknown. The worst that can be said is that the blow lands with an awful thud. . . . Ms. Neal at least manages to give Franny some foxy charm."[6] Critic Mike Cidoni, of Gannett Newspapers, liked the picture and said of Patricia, "Considering her stellar track record, it seems downright inadequate to call Neal's performance here her tour de force. But it is. She's never been better. Patricia Neal puts in the performance of her lifetime. Consider it a crime against god and country if she doesn't make more films. Are you listening, Woody Allen?"[7] Hank Gallo of the *New York Daily News* said, "Neal is a wonder to watch, turning in a truly touching performance as a woman coming to grips with what she is sure will be her last romantic hurrah."[8]

On October 5, Patricia was the guest of honor at the Bard Hall Auditorium Benefit at the College of Physicians and Surgeons of Columbia University, celebrating "A Retrospective of the American Musical." She was the recipient of the Second Bard Hall Players Theatre Award for Distinguished Achievements in the Arts. For the event Patricia talk-sang Stephen Sondheim's "Send In the Clowns" from the musical *A Little Night Music*. The audience was profoundly moved by her rendition.

Early in 1990, Patricia's agent, Clifford Stevens, secured her eight days' work in the made-for-television film *Caroline?* for the Hallmark Hall of Fame. It was broadcast over NBC on April 29. Directed by Joseph Sargent, the telefilm starred Stephanie Zimbalist as a woman named Caroline, who appears fourteen years after supposedly dying in an airplane crash. She says she never boarded the plane, and when it crashed, she realized she could use her apparent demise to escape her debutante life. Now she has come back to claim an inheritance. But is she Caroline? Patricia plays Miss Trollope, Caroline's former teacher, who is dubious about the woman's claim. *Caroline?* which aired April 29, was extremely well received and won several awards.

Roald Dahl died of leukemia on November 23, 1990. Before his death, Patricia had reconciled with both him and Felicity. She had been warmly welcomed by Roald and Felicity to Theo's thirtieth birthday party in July of that year, having told them she felt no more hatred or hurt. "Not long before he died, I went over to see him again. . . . I was accompanied by my daughter Ophelia. Before I left, Ophelia whispered out of the corner of her mouth, 'Kiss him goodbye.' I said, 'OK,' and I kissed him goodbye," Patricia recalled.[9] To this day she continues to be supportive of Felicity's efforts to preserve Roald's legacy.

"By the time Felicity came along my father was tired," said Ophelia. "He was looking after children and trying to write at the same time. It was one of those things. And I have no doubt it was the right thing. The last ten years of his life with Liccy were the happiest, no question."[10] On November 29, 1990, Roald was buried on a hillside at the Church of St. Peter and St. Paul in Great Missenden, near Gipsy House. He left an estate that generates over three million pounds annually for his family.[11]

Patricia appeared in an episode of *Murder She Wrote* that aired on December 16, 1990, and in mid-1992 she flew to Austria to portray Grandmother in another telling of the children's classic *Heidi*, this time for the Disney Channel. Starring Jason Robards Jr. as Grandfather, the film also features Jane Seymour, Sian Phillips, Lexi Randall, and Noley Thornton as Heidi. The program was nominated for a Golden Globe as Best Mini-Series or Motion Picture Made for TV.

Later in 1992 Patricia performed a role in the made-for-television film *A Mother's Right: The Elizabeth Morgan Story,* broadcast over ABC on November 29. Based on a true story, it told of Dr. Elizabeth Morgan (Bonnie Bedelia), who accuses her husband, Paul Michel (Kenneth Welch), of molesting their daughter, Hilary (Caroline Dollar). Elizabeth's parents, Antonia Morgan (Neal) and Bill Morgan (Rip Torn), assist their daughter in defying the law to protect her child. Patricia's performance is steady and focused, and her scenes with Torn and Bedelia are wonderfully underplayed.

In March 1993, Patricia flew to London to attend Tessa's marriage to merchant banker Patrick Donovan at the Church of Our Most Holy Redeemer and Saint Thomas More in Chelsea. Tessa had now become a writer herself, having written a children's book and a thinly disguised autobiography, the novel *Working for Love.* Theo gave his sister away.

Patricia still received film scripts, but most of the roles offered her were small or tasteless. She never lost her love of acting, but she was sad that she was not offered more work. To the *New York Post*'s Douglas J. Rowe she said, "I don't quite understand it, but nobody calls me and nobody wants me. But I love to act."[12] She told another reporter, "I love to work, and I wouldn't charge producers $10 million like these girls do today. Hell, I'd work for a lot less than a million—a real bargain."[13]

In honor of her seventieth birthday, Patricia's children threw their mother a magnificent birthday party in the ballroom at New York's Carlyle Hotel on January 29, 1996. Attending were such stars and celebrities as Douglas Fairbanks Jr., Lainie Kazan, Tony Randall, Elaine Stritch, Eartha Kitt, Eli Wallach, Anne Jackson, Mayor David Dinkins, Dr. Ruth Westheimer, and Maria Cooper Janis.

Patricia was an honored guest in Bristol, Virginia, on Saturday, March 2, 1996, at the Affair of the Heart–Queen of Hearts Gala. She told the press that she wanted to inspire hope for stroke survivors. "In my career and in my love for life I feel that my purpose now is to share my story. . . . I do so because there are millions of stroke survivors just like me in communities all over our nation, and notice I say survivors and not victims. Even with today's great advances in medical technology there is still that fierce determination and iron will necessary for recovery."[14]

Patricia traveled to England in late 1997 to film an interview segment for a British documentary on the life and work of Roald Dahl. Produced and directed by Donald Sturrock for the BBC, *An Awfully Big Adventure* featured interviews and stories about Dahl by Patricia; Felicity; Ophelia; his sisters

Alfhild, Else, and Asta; Dr. Edmund Goodman; Sonia Austrian; Amanda Conquy; and his grandchildren Clover and Luke. The program aired on March 7, 1998.

Patricia's granddaughter, Sophie Dahl, had begun a career as an international supermodel. After an unconventional childhood—she attended ten schools before she was thirteen and even lived briefly in an Indian ashram—the five-foot, eleven-inch Sophie gained fame as a plus-size beauty. In her personal life, she dated Griffin Dunne, son of celebrity writer Dominick Dunne, and aging rocker Mick Jagger. An intelligent woman, she has inherited both literary and acting ability. She played Juliet in a well-received British radio performance of Shakespeare's *Romeo and Juliet*, and she has appeared in several films. Now ravishingly thin, in 2003 she published her own novel, *The Man with the Dancing Eyes*.

Patricia's daughter Lucy and her husband Michael Faircloth divorced in 1991. Lucy remarried on June 30, 2002, to John LaViolette, a father of five. Tessa and Patrick Donovan had a son, Ned Dahl, on January 7, 1994, shortly before they, too, divorced. Theo married Madeleine Riley in 1996. Their first child, a baby girl named Alexa Isabella, was born June 26, 2005. Ophelia lives in Cambridge, Massachusetts, and continues her work with PIH in Boston.

Patricia traveled to Mississippi in January 1998 to appear in Robert Altman's picture *Cookie's Fortune*. The scenes would only take a couple of weeks to film. Patricia's character in *Cookie's Fortune* is the pipe-smoking Jewel Mae "Cookie" Orcutt, a dotty old woman living out her days in Holly Springs, Mississippi. Cookie wants to depart the world. Her nieces Camille Dixon (Glenn Close) and Cora Duvall (Julianne Moore) are putting on a play, *Salome,* at the local little theater and have little time to spend with their eccentric old aunt. Cookie's best friend is Willis Richland (Charles S. Dutton), a black handyman who cleans guns for her. Returning to town is Cora's daughter Emma Duvall (Liv Tyler). Before Cora can pay a visit to Cookie, the old woman takes a gun and kills herself. Camille discovers the body and a suicide note, which she quickly destroys, intent on covering up the suicide.

"She is a terrific actress," said Altman of Patricia in 2003. "We had met each other when I went to Hawaii when she was doing the Preminger film, and I worked on a project with her husband. When she had her strokes in Hollywood, we were there, working with Dahl and taking care of the kids. When I finally was able to work with her in *Cookie's Fortune*, I just remember we *really* had a lot of fun doing that film."[15]

Cookie's Fortune was released nationally in April 1999. *Village Voice* critic J. Hoberman wrote, "If diva Neal appears to be having the time of her life as a pipe-smoking kook installed in a complimentarily creaking old house, she doesn't overstay her welcome. Indeed, she rises splendidly to the occasion of her departure, effectively burying the movie's discomfiting echoes of *Driving Miss Daisy*, albeit raising the specter of *To Kill A Mockingbird* lite."[16] Rex Reed wrote in the *New York Observer*, "The best thing about Robert Altman's *Cookie's Fortune* is the return to the screen, after too long an absence, of the legendary Patricia Neal. Time and the weather have taken their toll, but quality always triumphs. As an eccentric old matriarch living in what's left of a decaying antebellum mansion in Holy Springs, Miss., with a horde of loony relatives to contend with, the Oscar-winning actress, with her spirited and indomitable inner candle and her grits-and-gravy drawl, adds a proud charm to this chicken-fried Southern Gothic comedy the rest of the film never quite equals. She retires from the movie much too early, and everything that follows rings hollow. It's a very peculiar kind of letdown."[17]

Appearances in film and television documentaries increasingly filled Patricia's calendar. She was interviewed for the *E! Celebrity Profile—Patty Duke*, broadcast over E! Entertainment Network; for *From Russia To Hollywood: The 100-Year Odyssey of Chekhov and Shdanoff*, shown on ABC; for *Inside You Only Live Twice*, produced by MGM Entertainment; and for *Conversations with Remarkable People*, detailing the life and work of the Rev. Mother Dolores Hart, produced for Wisdom Television.

In the summer of 2000, Patricia acted in a seventeen-minute short film written, produced, and directed by Mary Beth McDonough, Patricia's "daughter" in *The Homecoming*. Called *For the Love of May*, it was produced as a promotion for prospective backers of a feature film based on material in the short. The film tells the story of four generations of women and how they view womanhood. Grammy May (Neal) receives a telephone call from her long-ago beau, a World War II soldier. Grammy May has decided to meet with him, and Grammy's daughter Mary Lou (Michael Learned), granddaughters Emily (Alexandra Paul) and Kate (Annie LaRussa), and great-grandaughter Sarah (Karle Warren) discuss the issue around the dinner table. Parts of the film were shot in the home of Michael Learned. McDonough invested heavily in the production, but it was never expanded to feature-film length.

Several lifetime recognitions would be given Patricia in the coming years. On August 9, 2000, she received the Fourth Annual Lifetime Achievement Award at the Rhode Island International Film Festival held in Providence. On July 26, 2001, the American Film Institute Board of Trustees sent Patricia a letter of appreciation for her work in *The Day the Earth Stood Still*, now recognized as one of the most important films of the twentieth century. Fittingly, Patricia was seen the same year in the documentary *The Android Prophecy: A History of Robots in Film*, a British television documentary directed by Jamie Doran.

For PBS, Patricia lent her unique voice to a remarkably effective project called *The Face: Jesus in Art*. Directed and coproduced by Craig McGowan, the two-hour documentary traces the depiction of Christ in Christian art throughout history. Patricia's narration is stunning.

On May 31, 2001, she participated in the Museum of Modern Art's centennial tribute to Gary Cooper. The New York event was hosted by Peter Bogdanovich; other speakers included Fay Wray, Teresa Wright, and Maria Cooper Janis. In her remarks Patricia said, "Gary was a beautiful man and a marvelous actor. You could see in Gary's eyes not only what he was saying but, more importantly, what he was thinking and what he was feeling."[18]

In 2002 Patricia flew to New Orleans, Louisiana, to participate in the Sixteenth Annual Tennessee Williams/New Orleans Literary Festival, held March 20–24. On March 21, she performed in Williams' *Portrait of a Madonna* at the Le Petit Theatre. That year she was also asked by Paramount Pictures to be among the many stars who had worked for the studio over the years to sit for a picture to be published in the October 2002 *Vanity Fair*. Among some one hundred stars including Jessica Lange, Tom Cruise, Jane Fonda, Harrison Ford, Jon Voight, Jane Russell, Charlton Heston, Timothy Hutton, and Matthew Broderick, Patricia sat center front.

Patricia's mother, Eura Neal, died peacefully in her sleep on February 11, 2003, at a nursing home in Atlanta. She was nearly 103 years old and had been bedridden for several years. Patricia flew home for the funeral. Though they had been separated for almost 60 years, Eura Neal was finally laid to rest next to her Coot in the Highland Cemetery in Williamsburg, Kentucky.

For a *Hollywood at Home* segment, shown on the Home and Garden cable TV network on March 21, Patricia was interviewed in her tastefully appointed East Side Manhattan apartment. Show host Chantal Westerman and Patricia were filmed talking in her dining room and standing outside on her balcony.

Two documentaries released in 2003 featured interviews with Patricia: *Bright Leaves*, a highly personal exploration of the North Carolina tobacco industry produced, written, and directed by Ross McElwee; and the thirty-minute French film *Gary Cooper and Patricia Neal*, directed and written by Laurent Preyale. (Little is known about the latter film; it could have been made as far back as 1979.)

Another documentary featuring Patricia, Rick McKay's brilliant *Broadway: The Golden Age*, had made the rounds of the film festivals for several years. Written, directed, produced, and photographed by McKay, *Broadway: The Golden Age* was a heartfelt tribute to the lost golden age of Broadway. Patricia, filmed in 2002 in her apartment, speaks about her first days in New York. There are also interviews with Gwen Verdon, Carol Channing, Ben Gazzara, Elizabeth Ashley, Celeste Holm, Kitty Carlisle Hart, Hume Cronyn, Gena Rowlands, Jane Powell, Carol Lawrence, Eli Wallach, Tommy Tune, Maureen Stapleton, Carol Burnett, and Ann Miller, to name but a few. The picture was picked up by a major distributor and released to theaters, with openings throughout 2003 and 2004.

On October 11, 2003, Patricia traveled back to Great Missenden to participate with her children and grandchildren in reading selections from Roald Dahl's works. In past years, Felicity had organized these readings to raise funds for the Roald Dahl Foundation to support medical research. For this event, organized by Valerie Eaton Griffith, funds were raised for a new roof for the village church. "Pat has a huge generosity—a huge capability of opening her arms to people," Felicity said in a 2003 interview.[19]

On January 26, 2004, Patricia was inducted into the Theatre Hall of Fame in a ceremony held at the Gershwin Theatre in New York. She told the gathering that her strokes had left her "never able again to do a Broadway play, though I wouldn't rule that possibility out."[20] She read Fanny Cavendish's speech from *The Royal Family*, ending it with, "Do you suppose I could have stood these two years hobbling about on this damn cane if I didn't think I was going back [on stage]? . . . That's all that kept me alive these two years . . . my life, my work, going on!"

While on a Theatre Guild cruise in Alaska, Patricia fell and injured her shoulder. For months afterward doctors told her it was simply dislocated, but the pain became unbearable and eventually she was diagnosed with a shattered shoulder blade, requiring replacement. The seventy-eight-year-old actress underwent surgery in Boston on July 20. Her recovery and therapy took several months.

Robert Osborne hosted an hour-long tribute to Patricia on a Turner Classic Movies Channel broadcast that was shown June 28, 2004. Patricia, in interviews filmed in Atlanta in January, appeared relaxed and forthcoming. Said Hal Bodeker in the *Boston Globe*, "Patricia Neal's life has been more tumultuous than most Greek tragedies. But she doesn't want or need anyone's tears. The actress has weathered crises with grace, wit, and a refusal to see herself as a victim."[21] Marilyn Moss of the *Hollywood Reporter* wrote, "The image of Patricia Neal speeding up in an elevator at the close of 'The Fountainhead' must surely be a central metaphor for her life, personally as well as professionally. In that wonderful shot, Neal's character seems almost to ascend to the heavens to meet her lover, played by Gary Cooper (who also was her lover in real life). She ascends with exuberance, almost with abandon. . . . Neal, whom we see all too rarely these days, still exhibits an unbridled exuberance, a raw kind of female gustiness that had defined her in life and onscreen. This is a wonderful hour to share with her."[22]

In February 2005, Patricia underwent surgery again, this time to have her left knee replaced. She was hospitalized for several weeks in Boston, then transferred to New York Presbyterian Hospital, before beginning therapy in Knoxville at the Patricia Neal Rehabilitation Center. She recovered rapidly.

On May 20, prior to embarking on another Theatre Guild cruise to Alaska, Patricia was honored by the Hollywood Chamber of Commerce with her own star on the Hollywood Walk of Fame, located at 7018 Hollywood Boulevard in front of the legendary Hollywood Roosevelt Hotel. The ceremony was presided over by the unofficial mayor of Hollywood, Johnny Grant, with whom Patricia had toured in Korea in 1952. Speaking at the ceremony were Robert Osborne, Margaret O'Brien, and Cliff Robertson. Present were Eli Wallach and Anne Jackson, Kitty Carlisle Hart, Billy Gray, Randal Malone, Lee Roy Reams, Philip and Marilyn Langner, and David Stevenson. O'Brien said, "Patricia Neal's star is long overdue. After I was no longer at Metro, I entered television and theatre. I remember watching Patricia Neal on those live television anthologies, which I also did. I also remember her in her films. She has been my whole life, my most favorite actress."[23]

Patricia spoke briefly to the crowd: "In the past year I received two very good parts—a new shoulder and a new knee. They both are working beautifully. I am an actress, and I will take any good part as long as I can stand up. And when I can no longer do that, I will take them lying down."[24]

Patricia Neal spends her summers at her home in Martha's Vineyard with her beloved housekeeper Ruth Parks. There she is visited by her children and their families. In Manhattan, Patricia lives in a comfortable East Side apartment overlooking the East River. She attends the theater, makes appearances at benefits, lends her time to social causes, and supplies her talents to arts-related functions. She is still open to good roles in good productions.

At a period in life when most people have retired or withdrawn from public life, Patricia Neal continues to pursue an active lifestyle. Thanks to good investments, she doesn't need to worry about her financial future. But she does worry about inactivity. Felled by three major strokes over forty years ago, when she was thirty-nine, she is just as mentally alert and intellectually stimulated by the world around her as she ever was. Blessed with amazingly good health, Patricia Neal still lends her time, name, money, and knowledge to causes that are dear to her heart, the most important being the Patricia Neal Rehabilitation Center in Knoxville.

Her career has been remarkable. Aiming at success at an early age, Patricia was able to climb from the humble hills of Packard to the heights of stardom on Broadway and Hollywood during their last golden ages. The cost she paid, both personally and professionally, was high. She fought back from depression, the death of a child, a loveless marriage, near death, professional struggles, and divorce. And she did so with dignity, courage, and an astonishing lack of self-pity.

Never an ingénue, and never forgotten, Patricia Neal will remain forever— a star.

Appendix

CAREER

Professional Theater

The Voice of the Turtle, Morosco Theatre, New York, September 1945. Staged by John Van Druten; written by John Van Druten; settings, Stewart Chaney; musical arrangements, Alexander Haas; costumes, Bianca Stroock; presented by Alfred de Liagre Jr. *Cast*: Martha Scott (Sally Middleton), Alan Baxter (Bill Page), Vicki Cummings (Olive Lashbrooke); Patricia Neal was understudy for the roles of Sally and Olive.

The Voice of the Turtle, Selwyn Theatre, Chicago, September 1945–January 1946. *Cast*: K. T. Stevens (Sally Middleton), Hugh Marlowe (Bill Page), Vivian Vance (Olive Lashbrooke); Patricia Neal was understudy for the roles of Sally and Olive and replaced Vivian Vance as Olive in Chicago beginning December 31, 1945 for two and one-half weeks.

Bigger than Barnum, Wilbur Theatre, Boston, April 22, 1946. Staged by Edward Clarke Lilly; written and produced by Lee Sands and Fred Rath; settings, H. Gordon Bennett; Miss Williams's costume by Oberon; Miss Neal's act-two suit by Florence Lustig; produced by Lee Shubert and J. J. Shubert. *Cast*: Benny Baker (Perly Drake), Sid Melton (Chuck Jenkins), Jean Mode (Girl Attendant), Oscar Polk (Alex), Patricia Neal (Claire Walker), Chili Williams (Roberta Dixon); "Julius" as himself.

Devil Take a Whittler, Westport Country Playhouse, Westport, Connecticut, July 29, 1946. Staged by Paul Crabtree; written by Weldon Stone; settings, Lawrence Goldwasser; music by Tom Scott; special lyrics by Joy Scott; choreography, John Larson; special costume supervision, Hallye Clogg; costumes, the Theatre Guild and Brooks Costume; managers of The Westport Playhouse, Lawrence Langner, Armina Marshall, and John C. Wilson; managing director, Martin Manulis. *Cast*: Carol Stone (Myra Thompson), Paul Crabtree (Lem Skaggs), John Conte (The Devil), Patricia Neal (Kat Skaggs), Chuck Palmer and his Rustic Ramblers (themselves).

The Voice of the Turtle, Morosco Theatre, New York, August 1946–September 1946. *Cast*: Beatrice Pearson (Sally Middleton), John Beal (Bill Page), Vicki Cummings (Olive Lashbrooke); Patricia Neal replaced Vicki Cummings as Olive for two weeks beginning August 12, 1946.

Another Part of the Forest, Fulton Theatre, New York, November 20, 1946. Staged by Lillian Hellman; written by Lillian Hellman; produced by Kermit Bloomgarden; settings by Jo Mielziner; lighting by Jo Mielziner; music by Marc Blitzstein; costumes, Lucinda Ballard; assistant to Miss Ballard, Anna Hill Johnstone; Miss Dunnock's costumes and all men's costumes, Eaves Inc.; costumes of Misses Neal, Phillips, and Hagen, Brooks Costume;

stage manager, Jose Vega; assistant stage manager, Richard Beckhard; presented by Kermit Bloomgarden. *Cast*: Percy Waram (Marcus Hubbard), Mildred Dunnock (Lavinia Hubbard), Leo Genn (Benjamin Hubbard), Scott McKay (Oscar Hubbard), Margaret Phillips (Birdie Bagtry), Patricia Neal (Regina Hubbard), Bartlett Robinson (John Bagtry, Jean Hagen (Laurette Sincee), Paul Ford (Harold Penniman), Beatrice Thompson (Coralee).

Made in Heaven, Elitch Gardens Theatre, Denver, June 22, 1947. Staged by George Somnes; written by Hagar Wilde; scenic director, Joseph De Luca. *Cast*: Ellen-Cobb Hill (Nancy Tennant), Johnnye Akin (Marian Hunt), Craig Kelly (Laszlo Vertes), Joel Marston (Philip Dunlap), Patricia Neal (Elsa Meredith), Peter Cookson (Zachary Meredith), Grant Gordon (Harry Hunt), Helen Bonfils (Dorothy), Elizabeth Wetzel (Miss Crowder), Harry Mehaffey (Hank), Norman Budd (Man at Bar), Barbara Brady (Jane).

Laura, Elitch Gardens Theatre, Denver, June 29, 1947. Staged by George Somnes; written by Vera Caspary and George Sklar, based on the novel by Vera Caspary; scenic director, Joseph De Luca. *Cast*: Peter Cookson (Mark McPherson), Joel Marston (Danny Dorgan), Harry Mehaffey (Waldo Lydecker), Grant Gordon (Shelby Carpenter), Ellen-Cobb Hill (Bessie Clary), Helen Bonfils (Mrs. Dorgan), Patricia Neal (A Girl), Craig Kelly (Olsen).

Parlor Story, Elitch Gardens Theatre, Denver, July 6, 1947. Staged by George Somnes; written by William McCleery; scenic director, Joseph De Luca; assistant scenic director, Arthur Streator. *Cast*: Patricia Neal (Marian Burnett), Barbara Brady (Katy), Peter Cookson (Charles Burnett), Ellen-Cobb Hill (Christine), Joel Marston (Eddie West), Norman Budd (Lainson), Harry Mehaffey (Mike), Katharine Alexander (Mrs. Bright), Craig Kelly (Governor Sam Bright), Grant Gordon (Mel Granite).

The Trial of Mary Dugan, Elitch Gardens Theatre, Denver, July 13, 1947. Staged by George Somnes; written by Bayard Veiller; scenic director, Joseph De Luca. *Cast*: Barbara Brady (Tall Girl Reporter), Joel Marston (Court Clerk), Craig Kelly (Edward West), Patricia Neal (Mary Dugan), Grant Gordon (Judge Nash), Ellen-Cobb Hill (May Harris), Peter Cookson (Jimmy Dugan), Katharine Alexander (Mrs. Edgar Rice), Helen Bonfils (Marie Ducrot), Norman Budd (Patrick Kearney).

The State of the Union, Elitch Gardens Theatre, Denver, July 20, 1947. Staged by George Somnes; written by Howard Lindsay and Russel Crouse; scenic director, Joseph De Luca. *Cast*: Grant Gordon (James Conover), Joel Marston (Spike McManus), Katharine Alexander (Katherine "Kay" Thorndyke), Peter Cookson (Grant Matthews), Ellen-Cobb Hill (Norah), Patricia Neal (Mary Matthews), Walter Sawicki (Stevens), Norman Budd (Bellboy), Boyd Bennett (Waiter), Craig Kelly (Sam Parrish), Earl Scholl (Swenson), Harry Mehaffey (Judge Jefferson Davis Alexander), Helen Bonfils (Mrs. Lulubelle Alexander), Barbara Brady (Mrs. Grace Draper).

Candlelight, Elitch Gardens Theatre, Denver, July 27, 1947. Staged by George Somnes; written by Siegfried Geyer, adapted from the German by P. G. Wodehouse; scenic director, Karl Ramet. *Cast*: Peter Cookson (Josef), Grant Gordon (Prince Rudolf Haseldorf-Schlebitten), Patricia Neal (Marie), Ellen-Cobb Hill (Liserl), Harry Mehaffey (Baron von Reichenheim), Norman Budd (Waiter), Helen Bonfils (Baroness von Reichenheim).

Joan of Lorraine, Elitch Gardens Theatre, Denver, August 3, 1947. Staged by George Somnes; written by Maxwell Anderson; scenic director, Karl Ramet. *Cast*: Peter Cookson (Jimmy Masters, Director/The Inquisitor), Ellen-Cobb Hill (Tessie, assistant stage manager/ Aurora), Helen Bonfils (Marie, the Costumer), Harry Mehaffey (Abbey, Jacques d'Arc/ Cauchon, Bishop of Beauvais), Patricia Neal (Mary Gray/Joan), Boyd Bennett (Dollner/ Pierre d'Arc), Joel Marston (Jo Cordell/Jean d'Arc), Barbara Brady (Miss Reeves/St. Catherine), Katharine Alexander (Miss Sadler/St. Margaret), James Herrick (Noble/La Hire), Craig Kelly (Sheppard/Alain Chartier), Norman Budd (Les Ward/The Dauphin), Grant Gordon (Jefferson/Georges de Tremoille).

The Barretts of Wimpole Street, Elitch Gardens Theatre, Denver, August 10, 1947. Staged by George Somnes; written by Rudolf Besier; scenic director, Karl Ramet. *Cast:* Norman Budd (Dr. Chambers), Patricia Neal (Elizabeth Barrett Moulton-Barrett), Helen Bonfils (Wilson), Ellen-Cobb Hill (Henrietta Moulton-Barrett), Katharine Alexander (Arabel Moulton-Barrett), Joel Marston (Octavius Moulton-Barrett), Boyd Bennett (Septimus Moulton-Barrett), Harry Mehaffey (Edward Moulton-Barrett), Barbara Brady (Bella Hedley), Grant Gordon (Henry Bevan), Peter Cookson (Robert Browning), Craig Kelly (Capt. Surtees Cook), Mr. Chips (Flush).

The Two Mrs. Carrolls, Elitch Gardens Theatre, Denver, August 24, 1947. Staged by George Somnes; written by Martin Vale; scenic director, Joseph De Luca. *Cast:* Patricia Neal (Sally Carroll), Donald Woods (Geoffrey Carroll), Louise LaBat (Clemmence), Joel Marston (Pennington), Helen Bonfils (Mrs. Latham), Ellen-Cobb Hill (Cecily Harder), Harry Mehaffey (Dr. Tuttle), Katharine Alexander (Harriett Carroll).

Another Part of the Forest, tour, closed at Erlanger Theatre, Chicago, October 13, 1947. Staged by Lillian Hellman; written by Lillian Hellman; produced by Kermit Bloomgarden; settings by Jo Mielziner; lighting by Jo Mielziner; music by Marc Blitzstein; costumes, Lucinda Ballard; assistant to Miss Ballard, Anna Hill Johnstone; Miss Dunnock's costumes, Eaves Inc.; costumes of Misses Neal, Phillips, and Hagen, Brooks Costume; stage manager, Jose Vega; assistant stage manager, Richard Beckhard; presented by Kermit Bloomgarden. *Cast:* Carl Benton Reid (Marcus Hubbard), Mildred Dunnock (Lavinia Hubbard), Wesley Addy (Benjamin Hubbard), Scott McKay (Oscar Hubbard), Margaret Phillips (Birdie Bagtry), Patricia Neal (Regina Hubbard), Hugh Reilly (John Bagtry), Jean Hagen (Laurette Sincee), Harry Mehaffey (Harold Penniman), Eulabelle Moore (Coralee).

The Cocktail Party, La Jolla Playhouse, La Jolla, California, August 14, 1951. Staged by Norman Lloyd; produced by Dorothy McGuire, Mel Ferrer, and Gregory Peck; written by T. S. Eliot; settings by Robert Tyler Lee; lighting by James Nielson; costumes, Liz Calovich; stage manager, Syl Lamont. *Cast:* Vincent Price (Sir Henry Harcourt Reilly), Patricia Neal (Celia Coplestone), Reginald Denny (Alexander MacColgie Gibbs), Harry Ellerbe (Edward Chamberlayne), Rose Hobart (Lavinia Chamberlayne), Lillian Bronson (Julia Shuttlethwaite), William Schallert (Peter Quilpe).

The Children's Hour, Coronet Theatre, New York, December 18, 1952. Staged by Lillian Hellman; produced by Kermit Bloomgarden; associate producer, Peter Glenn; written by Lillian Hellman; settings by Howard Bay; costumes, Anna Hill Johnstone; stage manager, Jose Vega; assistant stage manager, Gordon Russell. *Cast:* Patricia Neal (Martha Dobie), Kim Hunter (Karen Wright), Iris Mann (Mary Tilford), Katherine Emmett (Mrs. Amelia Tilford), Robert Pastene (Dr. Joseph Cardin), Mary Finney (Mrs. Lily Mortar), Leora Thatcher (Agatha), Janet Parker (Rosalie Wells), Denise Alexander (Evelyn Munn), Sandra March (Peggy Rogers), Sandee Preston (Leslie), Gordon Russell (Grocery Boy).

The Scarecrow, Theatre de Lys, New York, June 16, 1953. Staged by Frank Corsaro; produced by Terese Hayden, Liska March; written by Percy Mackaye based on stories by Nathaniel Hawthorne; designed by William and Jean Eckart; lighting by William and Jean Eckart; music by Joseph Liebling; musical superviser, Max Marlin; costumes, Ruth Morley, Brooks Costume; production manager, Julian Bercovici; assistant director, Sherwood Arthur; art director, Robert Cato; presented by Terese Hayden. *Cast:* Douglas Watson (Lord Ravensbane), Eli Wallach (Dickon), Patricia Neal (Goody Rickby), Anne Jackson (Rachel

Merton), Milton Selzer (Justice Gilead Merton), Mary Bell (Mistress Cynthia Merton), Bradford Dillman (Richard Talbot), Albert Salmi (Captain Bugby), Alan MacAteer (Minister Dodge), Stefan Girasch (Micah), James Dean (The Scarecrow's Reflection).

The School for Scandal, Theatre de Lys, New York. June 23, 1953. Staged by Terese Hayden; produced by Terese Hayden and Liska March; written by Richard Brinsley Sheridan; designed by William and Jean Eckart; lighting by William and Jean Eckart; music by Joseph Liebling; musical supervisor, Max Marlin; costume supervisor, Frances Malek; costumes, Brooks Costume; art director, Robert Cato; presented by Terese Hayden. *Cast*: Patricia Neal (Lady Teazle), John Heldabrand (Sir Peter Teazle), David J. Stewart (Joseph Surface), Leo Penn (Charles Surface), Sara Seegar (Lady Sneerwell), Joanna Roos (Mrs. Candour), Orson Bean (Careless), Leon Janney (Sir Benjamin Backbite), Howard Caine (Sir Oliver Surface), Leo Lucker (Crabtree), Richard Poston (Rowley), William Myers (Moses), Eva Stern (Maria), Vivian Matalon (Trip).

The Children's Hour, tour, closed at Harris Theatre, Chicago, November 24, 1953. Staged by Lillian Hellman; produced by Kermit Bloomgarden; written by Lillian Hellman; settings by Howard Bay; costumes, Anna Hill Johnstone; stage manager, Jose Vega. *Cast*: Patricia Neal (Martha Dobie), Priscilla Gillette (Karen Wright), Janet Parker/Iris Mann (Mary Tilford), Fay Bainter (Mrs. Amelia Tilford), Theodore Newton (Dr. Joseph Cardin), Mary Finney (Mrs. Lily Mortar), Edna Courtleigh (Agatha), Lynn Thatcher (Rosalie Wells), Mary Lee Dearring (Evelyn Munn), June Connolly (Janet), Carol Sinclair (Lois Fisher), Sandra March (Peggy Rogers), Nancy Plehn (Catherine), Sandee Preston (Leslie), Gordon Russell (Grocery Boy), Carolyn Rosser (Helen Burton).

A Roomful of Roses, Playhouse Theatre, New York, October 17, 1955. Staged by Guthrie McClintic; produced by Guthrie McClintic and Stanley Gilkey; written by Edith Sommer; scenic design by Donald Oenslager; lighting by Donald Oenslager; costumes, Audre; Miss Neal's suit, Philip Mangone; Miss Neal's dress, Charles Galatt; Miss Frost's dresses, Charles Galatt and Vera Stewart; Miss Keim's dresses, Anne Fogarty and Rappi; Miss Keim's robe, Edward J. Macksoud; Miss Whiteside's costumes, Haymaker; hostess gown, scarves, and belts, Ben King; jewels and stockings, Sciaparelli; men's sports shirts, Izod; stage manager, Charles Forsythe. *Cast*: Patricia Neal (Nancy Fallon), Russ Conway (Jay Fallon), Alice Frost (Grace Hewitt), Warren Berlinger (Dick Hewitt), David White (Carl MacGowan), Betty Lou Keim (Bridget MacGowan), Lulu B. King (Willamay), Darryl Richard (Larry Fallon), Ann Whiteside (Jane Hewitt).

Cat on a Hot Tin Roof, Morosco Theatre, New York, March 6, 1956. Staged by Elia Kazan; produced by the Playwrights Company (Maxwell Anderson, Robert Anderson, Elmer Rice, Robert E. Sherwood, Roger L. Stevens, John F. Wharton); written by Tennessee Williams; scenic design by Jo Mielziner; lighting by Jo Mielziner; assistant designer to Mr. Mielziner, John Harvey; costumes, Lucinda Ballard; stage manager, Daniel S. Broun. *Cast*: Burl Ives (Big Daddy), Patricia Neal (Margaret "Maggie," Neal replaced Geddes for three weeks), Mildred Dunnock (Big Mama), Alex Nicol (Brick), Madeleine Sherwood (Mae, Sister Woman), Pat Hingle (Gooper, Brother Man), R. G. Armstrong (Dr. Baugh), Michele Mordana (Trixie).

Garden District, Arts Theatre Club, London, September 16, 1958. Staged by Herbert Machiz; written by Tennessee Williams; settings by Stanley Moore; costumes designed by Michael Ellis; costumes, B.J. Simmons Ltd.; incidental music, Ned Rorem; general manager, Bernard Gillman, in arrangement with Jerry Leider, John C. Wilson, and Toby Rowland Jr. *Something Outspoken* cast: Beryl Mease (Cornelia Scott), Beatrix Lehmann (Grace Lancaster). *Suddenly Last Summer* cast: Beatrix Lehmann (Mrs. Violet Venable), David

Cameron (Dr. Cukrowicz), Patricia Neal (Catharine Holly), Margo Johns (Miss Foxhill), Beryl Measor (Mrs. Holly), Philip Bond (George Holly), Gwen Nelson (Sister Felicity).

The Miracle Worker, Playhouse Theatre, New York, October 19, 1959. Staged by Arthur Penn; produced by Tamarack Productions and Hiller Productions Inc.; written by William Gibson based on his teleplay; scenic design by George Jenkins; lighting by George Jenkins; costumes designed by Ruth Morley; costumes, Brooks Costume; production stage manager, Porter Van Zandt; stage manager, Dick Via; presented by Fred Coe. *Cast:* Anne Bancroft (Annie Sullivan), Patricia Neal (Kate Keller),Torin Thatcher (Captain Keller), James Gongdon (James Keller), Kathleen Comegys (Aunt Ev), Beah Richards (Viney), Michael Constantine (Dr. Anagnos), Jack Hollander (The Doctor), Miriam Butler (Martha), Caswell Fairweather (Percy), John Marriott (John), Juanita Bethea (Mary), Candace Culkin, Dale Ellen Bethea, Rita Levy, Lynn Schoenfeld, Eileen Musumeci, Donna Pastore (Children); Patty Duke (Helen Keller).

Theatrical Events

Seven Mirrors, Blackfriars Theatre, New York, October 25, 1945. Staged by Dennis Gurney; produced by the Blackfriars Guild; written by Emmett Lavery; scenic designer, Edward Rutyna; choreographer, Patricia Newman; verse choir, Frances Mohan; women's costumes, Miss Virginia Moynahan; other costumes, Brooks Costumes; stage manager, Carol Gustafson; house manager, John McAuliffe. *Cast:* Rita Heffernan (Our Lady of Warsaw), Elizabeth Ryan (Our Lady of New York), Helen Horton (Our Lady of Berlin), Beatrice Adams (Olga/First Business Girl), Dena Desta (Janina/First Welder), Geraldine Page (Junior/First Shopper), Barclay Stevens (Civilian), Zoe Winkler (Senior), Ray L. Mahaffie (Jerry), Grace Ross (Sister Tomasco), Peggy Ann McCay (Girl), Carol Gustafson (Dissenter), Ann Rogers (Driver), Pat Neal (First Volunteer).

First Night Ball, Waldorf-Astoria Ballroom, New York, December 30, 1955. Conceived and produced by Moss Hart; staged and supervised by Ezra Stone; written and edited by Robert Downing; musical numbers staged by Joseph Santley; processional "Hail to the Theatre's Child" by Jule Styne, words and lyrics by Howard Dietz; musical direction, Milton Rosenstock; costumes, Lucinda Ballard and Bianca Stroock; the processional girls' costumes, Henri Bendel; costumes of Misses MacKenzie, Strasberg, and Neal, Henri Bendel; choreography, Peter Gennaro; lighting, Feder; Hollywood chairman, George Murphy. *Cast:* Lillian Gish (Maude Adams), George Jessel (Sam Bernard), William Warfield (Jules Bledsoe), June Havoc (Eva Tanquay), Peggy Wood (Mady Christians), Patricia Neal (Katharine Cornell), Cornelia Otis Skinner (Jane Cowl); Gwen Verdon (Marilyn Miller), Eddie Foy Jr. (Eddie Foy), George Abbott (William Gillette), Susan Strasberg (Ruth Gordon), Walter Slezak (Walter Huston), Jane Froman (Elsie Janis), Kitty Carlisle (Gertrude Lawrence), John Raitt (J. Harold Murray), Andy Griffith (Will Rogers), Michael Redgrave (Otis Skinner), Geraldine Page (Frances Starr), Helen Gallagher (Marion Sunshine), Shirley Booth (Laurette Taylor), Carol Channing (Sophie Tucker); "Stage Door Canteen" with Mary Martin.

Patchwork, South Presbyterian Church Fellowship Hall, Dobbs Ferry, New York, October 10–11, 1997. Staged by Vicki Mooney and Melora Peters; producers, Paul Golio and Vicki Mooney; a collection of monologues by Vicki Mooney; a More Light production. *Cast:* "Sparrow," Patricia Neal (Meriweather); "Jillsy and Marg," Jane K. Hamilton and Gilliam Hemstead; "Lucky," Michael Tancredi (Lucky); "Dilla Dee," Jane K. Hamilton (Dilla Dee); "72 Dorian Isn't Enough," Gillian Hemstead; "Fall Planting," Camille Wiedorn.

Love Letters, Abbey of Regina Laudi, Bethlehem, Connecticut, August 6, 1999. Staged by Melora Mennesson; produced by The Act Association; written by A. R. Gurney; set design, Melora Mennesson, Diane Egger; lighting, Kevin McElroy; stage manager, Kevin McElroy. *Cast*: Patricia Neal (Melissa), James Douglas (Andy).

Nonprofessional Theater

Twilight Alley, Park Lowery Junior High School Auditorium, Knoxville, Tennessee, May 25, 1937. Staged by Margaret McCullem; sets and scenery by the fifth and sixth graders; in charge of production, Miss Lane, Azala Newman, and Evelyn Kappes. *Cast*: Patricia Neal (Dame Needy, Mother), Helen Brown (Meg), Billy Gallagher (Jack), Nancy Buhl (Angelina), Charlcey Adcock (Meg's Sister), Billy Jones, Billy Roberts (Jack's Gang).

One Wild Night, Knoxville High School Auditorium, Knoxville, Tennessee, December 4, 1940. Staged by Mr. Sanders, Miss Ruby Bird; written by Guernsey Le Pelley; costumes, Miss Ruby Bird; stage manager, Tom Haile. *Cast*: David Lea (Rodney Dodd), Virginia Schneider (Henriette), Sarah Brier (Charlotte Allen), Patricia Neal (Nurse Trent), Kathryn Stubley (Doris Winthrope).

Penny Wise, Park Lowry Junior High School Auditorium, Knoxville, Tennessee. December 18, 1941. Staged by Oscar E. Sams; written by Jean Ferguson Black; set designers, George Sprau, Herman Straugh, Jim Penn, David Tuck, and Norman Moore; stage manager, Donald N. Edmunds; production of the Tennessee Valley Players. *Cast*: Mason Dixon (Gordon Chase), Evelyn Parks (Penny Chase), Jean Taylor (Katherine), Robert W. Teddler (Jeff), Thelma McGhee (Tina), Patricia Neal (Martha).

Hay Fever, Park Lowry Junior High School Auditorium, Knoxville, Tennessee, April 1, 1942. Staged by Mason Dixon; written by Noel Coward; lighting, Leonard Parks, Sampson Linke, John Primm; production of the Tennessee Valley Players. *Cast*: Jean Taylor (Sorel Bliss), Jules Finkelstein (Simon Bliss), Virginia Hodges (Clara), Wesley Davis (David Bliss), Patricia Neal (Myra Arundel), Mason Dixon (Richard Greatham).

Follies: Nice Going America, Lyric Theatre, Knoxville, Tennessee, April 17, 1942. Script, lyrics, music, costumes, direction by John B. Rogers Co. *Cast*: Patricia Neal.

Thunder Rock, Abingdon Civic Auditorium, Abingdon, Virginia, July 16, 1942. Staged by Alexander Ivo; produced by Robert Porterfield; written by Robert Ardrey; set design and execution by Henry May; stage manager, James Hamilton; costumes, Elinor Anton; lights and sound, Paul Wasserman; Mr. Porterfield's "Man Friday," Norman Porter; a Barter Theatre production. *Cast*: Frank Kline (Streeter), Steven Scheuer (Nonny), James Hamilton (Inspector Flanning), Lance Cunard (Briggs), Patricia Neal (Melanie), Elizabeth Wilson (Miss Kirby), Natalie Farmer (Anne Marie), Paul Wasserman (Chang).

French without Tears, Abingdon Civic Auditorium, Abingdon, Virginia, July 30, 1942. Staged by Alexander Ivo; produced by Robert Porterfield; written by Terence Rattigan; set design and execution by Henry May; stage manager, James Hamilton; costumes, Elinor Anton; lights and sound, Paul Wasserman; Mr. Porterfield's "Man Friday," Norman Porter; a Barter Theatre production. *Cast*: James Hamilton (Kenneth Lake), Melvin Miller (Brian Curtis), Philip McKenna (Hon. Alan Howard), Barbara Quel (Marianne), Lance Cunard (Monsieur Maingot), Patricia Neal (Diana Lake), Margaret Phillips (Jacqueline Maingot).

No Boys Allowed, Abingdon Civic Auditorium, Abingdon, Virginia, August 1, 1942. Staged by William Day; produced by Robert Porterfield; written by Edith Sommer; set design and execution by Henry May; production manager/coordinator, Charles Wallis; stage manager, James Hamilton; costumes, Elinor Anton; Mr. Porterfield's "Man Friday," Norman Porter; a Barter Theatre production. *Cast*: Frank Baxter (Jimmy Davis), Anne Stell (Marion), James Hamilton ("Terrible" Jones), Doris Snyder (Maggie), Elizabeth Wilson (Elizabeth), Barbara Quel (Sara), Natalie Farmer (Ellen), Margaret Phillips (Pat), Patricia Neal (Virginia), Franklin Kline (Fred Ogelsby).

Letters to Lucerne, Abingdon Civic Auditorium. Abingdon, Virginia, September 3, 1942. Staged by William Day; produced by Robert Porterfield; written by Fritz Ritter and Allen Vincent; set design and execution by Henry May; production manager/coordinator, Charles Wallis; stage manager, James Hamilton; costumes, Elinor Anton; Mr. Porterfield's "Man Friday," Norman Porter; a Barter Theatre production. *Cast*: Patricia Neal (Bingo Hill), Elizabeth Wilson (Erna Schmidt), Margaret Phillips (Olga Kirinski), Elsie Hanover (Sally Jackson). Patricia Neal replaced Juin Whipple in the role of "Bingo Hill" at the last minute.

Family Portrait, Abingdon Civic Auditorium, Abingdon, Virginia, September 4, 1942. Staged by William Day; produced by Robert Porterfield; written by Leonore Coffee, William Joyce Cowen; set design and execution by Henry May; production manager/coordinator, Charles Wallis; stage manager, James Hamilton; costumes, Elinor Anton; Mr. Porterfield's "Man Friday," Norman Porter; a Barter Theatre production. *Cast*: Patricia Neal.

And Came the Spring, Knoxville High School Auditorium Knoxville, Tennessee, June 1, 1943. Staged by M. H. Sanders; written by Marianne and Joseph Hayes; costumes, Ruby Bird; makeup, Ruby Bird; stage manager, Bill "Buddy" Smith. *Cast*: Sarah Brier (Midge Hartman), Patricia Neal (Virginia Hartman), David Lea (Elliott Hartman), Bill Robertson (Mr. Jeffrey Hartman), Don George (Clancy), Kathryn Stubley (Carollyn Webster), Betty Henson (Gabby Allen), Maurice Schwarzenberg (Freddie North).

Beggar on Horseback, Northwestern University Theatre, Evanston, Illinois, December 1, 1943. Staged by Theodore Skinner; written by George S. Kaufman and Marc Connelly; settings, McDonald Held and Ruth Bray; costumes, Charlotte Lee; lighting, Edith Bernard; choreographer, Marjorie Parks; stage managers, Barbara Ball and Nancy Hoadley; scenery, Doris Hersh; costumes, Helen Seeny; piano concerto composed by James Martyn. *Cast*: John Brooks (Dr. Albert Rice), Lydia Clarke (Cynthia Mason), James Martyn (Neil McRae), Billie Lou Watt (Mrs. Cady), Haskell Gordon (Mr. Cady), Ann Ainsworth (Miss You), Mildred Knight (Cigarette Girl), Robert Mulligan (Guide), Patricia Neal (Juror).

Twelfth Night, Northwestern University Theatre, Evanston, Illinois, February 26, 1945. Staged by Claudia Webster; written by William Shakespeare; settings, Joe Zimmermann; costumes, Grace Newell; lighting, Paul Herman; music, Nancy Kaiser; stage manager, Betty Samsel; scenery, Robert Black and Estelle Spero. *Cast*: Richard Lutton (Feste), Wesley Jones (Osino), Helen Horton (Viola), Daniel F. Hauf (Sir Toby Belch); Charlotte Lubotsky [Rae] (Maria), Hyman Liebling (Sir Andrew Aguecheck), Patricia Neal (Olivia), Robert Wright (Sebastain), Steven Meyer (Antonio).

Uncle Harry, Forest Hills Playhouse, Eagles Mere, Pennsylvania, July 11, 1945. Staged by Alvina Krause; written by Thomas Job. *Cast*: Dan Hauf (Uncle Harry), Helen Wood (Hester), Patricia Neal (Lucy), Roslyn Yastrow, Priscilla Weaver, Harold Abbey, Kelley Green.

Squaring the Circle, Forest Hills Playhouse, Eagles Mere, Pennsylvania, July 19, 1945. Staged by Alvina Krause; written by Valentine Katayev, from a translation by Charles Malamuth and Eugene Lyons. *Cast*: Erica North (Ludmilla), Vito Kosky (Rabinovitch), Harold Abbey (Abram), Dan Hauf, Mina Pendo, Steven Meyer, Patricia Neal, Dave Kaplan, Kelley Green.

The Importance of Being Earnest, Forest Hills Playhouse, Eagles Mere, Pennsylvania, July 26, 1945. Staged by Alvina Krause; written by Oscar Wilde. *Cast*: Joan Hackett, Dori Hersh, Marilynn Johnston, Erica North, Dan Hauf, Roslyn Zimmet, Mina Pendo, Steven Meyer, Patricia Neal, Priscilla Weaver, Helen Wood.

Blithe Spirit, Forest Hills Playhouse, Eagles Mere, Pennsylvania, August 22, 1945. Staged by Alvina Krause; written by Noel Coward. *Cast*: Steven Meyer (Charles), Patricia Neal (Ruth), Priscilla Weaver (Elvira), Kelley Green (Madame Arcati), Mina Pendo (Mrs. Bradman), Dan Hauf (Doctor Bradman).

Selected Radio Performances

Northwestern University Radio Playshop, "Three Strikes You're Out," WIND network, 30 minutes, April 21, 1945. Producer, Margaret Dillard; written by Vernon Delston; sound, Cottingham. *Cast*: Al Goldstone (Altar Ego), Hyman Liebling (Joe), Phylis Brodes (Mary), Patricia Neal (Mother), Bob Schneiderman (L. Brother), Les Levin (Marty), Win Douglas (Sports Announcer), Eddie Hill (Announcer/Barker).

Hollywood Family Theatre, "My Terminal Moraine," Mutual network, 30 minutes, June 20, 1949. Director, Hymie Du Weyey; based on novelette "My Terminal Moraine" by Frank R. Stockton, adapted by Sidney Marshall; music, Harry Zimmermann; music conducted by F. J. Mansfield. *Cast*: Alan Young (Walter Cuthby), Mala Powers (Agnes Havelot), Robert North (Butler), Gene Baker (Announcer), Patricia Neal (Hostess).

Camel Screen Guild Theatre, "John Loves Mary," NBC, 30 minutes, February 2, 1950. Ronald Reagan, Patricia Neal.

Lux Radio Theatre, "John Loves Mary," CBS, 60 minutes, June 19, 1950. Director, Fred MacKaye; based on the play by Norman Krasna; screenplay, Henry and Nora Ephron, adapted by Sanford Barnett; musical director, Louis Silvers; sound effects, Charlie Forsyth. *Cast*: William Keighley (Host), Ronald Reagan (John Lawrence), Patricia Neal (Mary McKinley), Dorothy Lovett (Libby), John Milton Kennedy (Announcer), Lonnie Petrie (Intermission Guest).

Hollywood Family Theatre, "The Triumphant Exile," Mutual network, 30 minutes, July 12, 1950. Written by Dale Mutant Whitney, based on a story by Robert Lewis Stevenson; music, Harry Zimmermann; music conducted by F. J. Mansfield. *Cast*: Glenn Langan (Robert Lewis Stevenson), Jeanne Cagney (Fanny Osbourne), Carleton Young (Lloyd Osborne), Gene Baker (Announcer), Patricia Neal (Hostess).

Stars over Broadway, CBS, 60 Minutes, July 22, 1950. Sponsored by Dari-Rich.

Lux Radio Show, "One Sunday Afternoon," CBS, 60 minutes, September 4, 1950. Directed by Fred MacKaye; adapted by Sanford Barnett based on the play by James Hagen; musical director, Louis Silvers. *Cast*: William Keighley (Host), John Milton Kennedy (Announcer), Dennis Morgan (Timothy L. "Biff" Grimes), Patricia Neal (Virginia Bush), Ruth Roman (Amy Lind).

Gray Matters: Aging and the Brain, Public Radio International, 60 minutes. Produced in association with The Dana Alliance for Brain Initiatives. *Cast*: Patricia Neal (Narrator), Dr. Guy McKhann, Angie Dickinson.

Feature Films

John Loves Mary, Warner Brothers, 96 minutes, released February 4, 1949. Producer, Jerry Wald; director, David Butler; screenplay, Phoebe and Henry Ephron, based on the play by

Norman Krasna; art director, Robert Haas; set director, William L. Keuhl; original music, David Buttolph; song, "Someone To Watch Over Me," words and music by George Gershwin; costumes, Milo Anderson; men's wardrobe, Henry Field; ladies' wardrobe, Martha Bunch; makeup, Perc Westmore and Bill Crosley; hair stylist, Ray Foreman; sound, Francis J. Scheid; production supervisor, Eric Stacey; cinematographer, J. Peverell Marley; editor, Irene Morra; still photographer, Eugene Richee. *Cast*: Ronald Reagan (John Lawrence), Jack Carson (Fred Taylor), Patricia Neal (Mary McKinley), Wayne Morris (Lieutenant O'Leary), Edward Arnold (Senator McKinley), Virginia Field (Lilly Herbish), Katharine Alexander (Phyllis McKinley), Paul Harvey (General Biddle), Ernest Cossart (Oscar Dugan), Irving Bacon (Beachwood).

The Fountainhead, Warner Brothers, 114 minutes, released July 2, 1949. Producer, Henry Blanke; director, King Vidor; screenplay, Ayn Rand, based on her novel; art directors Edward Carrere and John Holden; matte artist, Chesley Bonestell; illustrator, Harold Michelson; set decorator, William Keuhl; properties, Bud Friend; original music, Max Steiner; costumes, Milo Anderson, Clayton Brackett, and Martha Bunch; makeup, Perc Westmore, Johnny Wallace; hair stylist, Gertrude Wheeler; sound, Oliver S. Garretson; production manager, Eric Stacey; cinematographer, Robert Burks; camera operator, James Bell; editor, David Weisbart; still photographer, Jack Woods. *Cast*: Gary Cooper (Howard Roark), Patricia Neal (Dominique Francon), Raymond Massey (Gail Wynand), Kent Smith (Peter Keating), Robert Douglas (Ellsworth Toohey), Henry Hull (Henry Cameron), Ray Collins (Enright), Moroni Olsen (Chairman), Jerome Cowan (Alvah Scarret), Paul Harvey, Thurston Hall (Businessmen), Ann Doran (Secretary), Almira Sessions (Housekeeper), Dorothy Christy (Society Woman), Jonathan Hale (Guy Francon), Frank Wilcox (Gordon Prescott).

It's a Great Feeling, Warner Brothers, Technicolor, 85 minutes, released August 1, 1949. Producer, Alex Gottlieb; director, David Butler; story, I. A. L. Diamond; screenplay, Jack Rose and Melville Shavelson; art director, Stanley Fleischer; set director, Lyle B. Reifsnider; original music, Howard Jackson; songs, "It's a Great Feeling," "Blame It on My Absent-Minded Heart," "At the Café Rendezvous," "That's a Big Fat Lie," "There's Nothing Rougher than Love," "Give Me a Song with a Beautiful Melody," "Fiddle-Dee-Dee," music by Jule Styne and lyrics by Sammy Cahn; musical director Ray Heindorf; choreographer, LeRoy Prinz; Technicolor consultants, Natalie Kalmus and Mitchell Kovaleski; costumes, Milo Anderson; makeup, Perc Westmore and Mickey Marcellino; hair stylist, Agnes Flanagan; sound, Dolph Thomas and Charles David Forrest; production manager, Frank Mattison; cinematographer, Wilfrid M. Cline; camera operator, Al Green; editor, Irene Morra; still photographer, Pat Clark. *Cast*: Dennis Morgan (Himself), Doris Day (Judy Adams), Jack Carson (Himself), Irving Bacon (Information Clerk), Nita Talbot (Model), Sandra Gould (Upper Berth Train Passenger), Errol Flynn (Jeffrey Bushwinkle), Mel Blanc (Voice of Bugs Bunny), Frank Cady (Oculist); with Edward G. Robinson, Gary Cooper, Jane Wyman, Maureen Reagan, Joan Crawford, Danny Kaye, Sydney Greenstreet, Ronald Reagan, Patricia Neal, Eleanor Parker, Ray Heindorf, David Butler, Michael Curtiz, Raoul Walsh, King Vidor (themselves).

The Hasty Heart, Warner Brothers, 99 minutes, released December 2, 1949. Producers, Alex Boyd and Robert Clark; director, Vincent Sherman; screenplay, Ranald MacDougall, based on the play by John Patrick; art director, Terence Verity; original music, Jack Beaver; costumes, Peggy Henderson; makeup, Bob Clark; hair stylist, A. G. Scott; sound, Harold V. King; production manager, Gerry Mitchell; cinematography, Wilkie Cooper; editor, E. B. Jarvis. *Cast*: Richard Todd (Corporal Lachlan "Lachie" MacLachlan), Ronald

Reagan (Yank), Patricia Neal (Sister Margaret Parker), Anthony Nichollis (Lieutenant Colonel Dunn), Howard Marion-Crawford (Tommy), John Sherman (Digger), Ralph Michael (Kini), Alfie [Alfred] Bass (Orderly), Orlando Martins (Blossom).

Bright Leaf, Warner Brothers, 110 minutes, released June 16, 1950. Producer, Henry Blanke; director, Michael Curtiz; screenplay, Ranald MacDougall, based on the novel by Foster Fitz-Simmons; art director, Stanley Fleischer; set director, Ben Bone; original music, Victor Young and Max Steiner; costumes, Leah Rhodes and Marjorie Best; makeup, Perc Westmore, Ray Romero, and John Wallace; hair stylist, Myrl Stoltz; sound, Stanley Jones; cinematographer, Karl Freund; editor, Owen Marks; still photographer, Jack Woods. *Cast*: Gary Cooper (Brant Royle), Lauren Bacall (Sonia Kovac), Patricia Neal (Margaret Jane Singleton), Jack Carson (Chris Malley "Doctor Monaco"), Donald Crisp (Major Singleton), Gladys George (Rose), Elizabeth Patterson (Aunt Tabitha Singleton), Jeff Corey (John Barton), Taylor Holmes (Lawyer Calhoun), Thurston Hall (Phillips), Cleo Moore (Cousin Louise), Nita Talbot (Cousin Theodora), Chick Chandler (Tobacco Auctioneer), Marshall Bradford (Farmer).

The Breaking Point, Warner Brothers, 97 minutes, released October 6, 1950. Producer, Jerry Wald; director, Michael Curtiz; screenplay, Ranald MacDougall, based on the novel *To Have and Have Not* by Ernest Hemingway; art director, Edward Carrere; set decorator, George James Hopkins; original music, Ray Heindorf, Howard Jackson, and Max Steiner; costumes, Leah Rhodes; makeup, Bill Phillips; hair stylist, Myrl (as Myra) Stoltz; sound, Leslie G. Hewitt; cinematographer, Ted D. McCord; editor, Alan Crosland Jr.; still photographer, Jack Woods. *Cast*: John Garfield (Harry Morgan), Patricia Neal (Leona Charles), Phyllis Thaxter (Lucy Morgan), Juano Hernandez (Wesley Park), Wallace Ford (F. R. Duncan), Edmon Ryan (Rogers), Ralph Dumke (Hannagan), Guy Thomajan (Danny), William Campbell (Concho), Sherry Jackson (Amelia Morgan), Donna Jo Boyce (Connie Morgan), Victor Sen Young (Mr. Sing).

Three Secrets, United States Pictures–Warner Brothers, 98 minutes, released October 20, 1950. Producer, Milton Sperling; director, Robert Wise; screenplay, Martin Rankin and Gina Kaus, based on their story "Rock Bottom"; art director, Charles H. Clarke; set director, Fred M. MacLean; original music, David Buttolph; costumes, Leah Rhodes; makeup, Perc Westmore, Eddie Voight, and John Wallace; hair stylists, Myrl Stoltz and Betty Delmont; sound, Charles Lang; cinematographer, Sidney Hickox; editor, Thomas Reilly; still photographer, Eugene Richee. *Cast*: Eleanor Parker (Susan Adele Connors Chase), Patricia Neal (Phyllis Horn), Ruth Roman (Ann Lawrence), Frank Lovejoy (Bob Duffy), Leif Erickson (Bill Chase), Ted de Corsia (Del Prince), Edmon Ryan (Hardin), Larry Keating (Mark Harrison), Katherine Warren (Mrs. Connors), Arthur Franz (Paul Radin), Nana Bryant (Supervisor of The Shelter), John Dehner (Gordon Crossley), Ross Elliott (Reporter), Paul Picerni (Sergeant), Duncan Richardson (Johnnie Peterson), William Self (Sergeant), Kenneth Tobey (Officer), Frank Wilcox (Charlie), Frances E. Williams (Delia).

Operation Pacific, Warner Brothers, 111 minutes, released January 27, 1951. Producer, Louis F. Edelman; director, George Waggner; screenplay, George Waggner, based on his story; art director, Leo K. Kuter; set director, John Gilbert Kissel; original music, Max Steiner; makeup, Gordon Bau; sound, Francis J. Scheid; cinematographer, Bert Glennon; editor, Alan Crosland Jr.; technical advisor, Vice Admiral Charles A. Lockwood. *Cast*: John Wayne (Commander Duke E. Gifford), Patricia Neal (Mary Stuart), Ward Bond (Captain John T. "Pop" Perry), Scott Forbes (Larry), Philip Carey (Bob Perry), Paul Picerni (Jonesy), Bill Campbell (The Talker), Kathryn Givney (Commander Steele), Martin Milner (Caldwell), Virginia Brissac (Sister Anna), William Self (Helmsman), James Flavin

(Mick, Shore Patrol Chief), Carleton Young (Briefing Officer, USAF), Harlan Warde (Commander), Richard Loo (Japanese Flyer), Brett King (Lieutenant Ernie Stark), Milburn Stone (Ground Control Officer), Bess Flowers (dance extra), Gail Davis (bit).

Raton Pass, Warner Brothers, 84 minutes, released April 19, 1951. Producer, Saul Elkins; director, Edwin L. Marin; screenplay, Thomas W. Blackburn and James R. Webb, based on the novel by Thomas W. Blackburn; art director, Edward Carrere; set director, William Wallace; original music, Max Steiner; song "No, I Don't Wish To Tarry, It's Better To Marry," music and lyrics by Frank La Forge; costumes, Marjorie Best; sound, Charles Lang; cinematography, Wilfred M. Cline; editor, Thomas Reilly. *Cast*: Dennis Morgan (Marc Challon), Patricia Neal (Ann Challon), Steve Cochran (Cy Van Cleave), Scott Forbes (Prentice), Dorothy Hart (Lena Casamajor), Basil Ruysdael (Pierre Challon), Louis Jean Heydt (Jim Pozner), Roland Winters (Sheriff Perigord), Elvira Curci (Tia), John Crawford (Sam), Ted Mapes (Stagecoach Driver), Bob Herron (Stuntman).

The Day the Earth Stood Still, 20th Century-Fox, 92 minutes, released September 18, 1951. Producer, Julian Blaustein; director, Robert Wise; screenplay, Edmund H. North, based on the novelette "Farewell to the Master" by Harry Bates; art directors, Lyle R. Wheeler and Addison Hehr; set directors, Claude E. Carpenter and Thomas Little; original music and orchestration, Bernard Herrmann; Theremin musicians, Paul Shure and Robert Moog; costumes, Travilla, Clinton Sandeen, and Perkins Bailey (Klaatu's costume); wardrobe directors, Charles Le Maire and Sam Benson; makeup, Ben Nye; sound, Harry M. McLeonard and Arthur L. von Kirbach; special effects, Fred Sersen, L. B. Abbott, Ray Kellogg, and Emil Kosa; production manager, Gene Bryant; cinematography, Leo Tover; editor, William Reynolds; technical advisor, Dr. Samuel Herrick; executive in charge of production, Darryl F. Zanuck. *Cast*: Michael Rennie (Klaatu/Carpenter), Patricia Neal (Helen Benson), Hugh Marlowe (Tom Stevens), Sam Jaffe (Professor Jacob Barnhardt), Billy Gray (Bobby Benson), Frances Bavier (Mrs. Barley), Lock Martin (Gort), Marshall Bradford (Chief of Staff), Wheaton Chambers (Mr. Bleeker, Diamond Dealer), James Craven (Businessman), Marjorie Crossland (Hilda, Barnhardt's Secretary), Elmer Davis, Gabriel Heater, Drew Pearson, H.V. Kalterborn (themselves), Lawrence Dobkin (Medical Captain), Charles Evans, Fay Roope (Major Generals), Edith Evanson (Mrs. Crockett), Elizabeth Flourney (Jewelry Customer), Stuart Whitman (Army Sentry); Harry Harvey Sr. (Taxi Driver), Harry Lauter (Platoon Leader), House Peters Jr. (MP Captain), Olan Soule (Mr. Krull), Harlan Warde (Carson).

Week-End with Father, Universal-International, 83 minutes, released November 22, 1951. Producer, Ted Richmond; director, Douglas Sirk; screenplay, Joseph Hoffman, George W. George, and George F. Slavin based on their original story; art directors, Robert F. Boyle and Bernard Herzbrun; set decorators, Russell A. Gausman and Ruby R. Levitt; original music, Frank Skinner; costumes, Bill Thomas; gowns, Bill Daniels; makeup, Bud Westmore; hair stylist, Joan St. Oegger; sound, Glenn E. Anderson and Leslie I. Carey; production manager, Mack D'Agostino; cinematography, Clifford Stine; editor, Russell F. Schoengarth. *Cast*: Van Heflin (Brad Stubbs), Patricia Neal (Jean Bowen), Gigi Perreau (Anne Stubbs), Virginia Field (Phyllis Reynolds), Richard Denning (Don Adams), Jimmy Hunt (Gary Bowen), Janine Perreau (Patty Stubbs), Tommy Rettig (David Bowen), Gary Pagett (Eddie Lewis), Forrest Lewis (Innkeeper), Frances E. Williams (Cleo), Elvia Allman (Mrs. G.), Maudie Prickett (Maid), Martha Mears (Singing Voice of Phyllis), Carl Saxe (Eddie's Father), Dabbs Greer (bit).

Diplomatic Courier, 20th Century-Fox, 97 minutes, released June 13, 1952. Producer, Casey Robinson; director, Henry Hathaway; screenplay, Casey Robinson and Liam O'Brien, based on the novel *Sinister Errand* by Peter Cheyney; production design, John De Cuir; art directors, Lyle R. Wheeler and John De Cuir; set directors, Thomas Little and Stuart A. Reiss; original music, Sol Kaplan; musical director, Lionel Newman; costumes, Charles Le Maire, Eloise Janssen [Jensson]; makeup, Ben Nye and Linn Reynolds; sound, W. D. Flick and Roger Herman; production manager, Abe Steinberg; cinematographer, Lucien Ballard; editor, James B. Clark. *Cast*: Tyrone Power (Mike Kells), Patricia Neal (Joan Ross), Stephen McNally (Colonel Cagle), Hildegarde Neff (Janine), Karl Malden (Ernie), James Millican (Sam Carew), Stefan Schnabel (Platov), Herbert Berghof (Arnov), Arthur Blake (Max Ralli), Helene Stanley (Airline Stewardess), Michael Ansara (Ivan), Sig Arno (Chef de Train), Lee Marvin (MP in Trieste), Tyler McVey (Watch Officer), Dabbs Greer (Intelligence Clerk), Carleton Young (Brennan), Monique Chantal (French Airline Stewardess), Russ Conway (Bill), Nestor Paiva (Train Conductor), Charles Buchinski [Bronson] (The Russian), E. G. Marshall (MP Driving Jeep), Hugh Marlowe (Narrator).

Washington Story, Metro-Goldwyn-Mayer, 81 minutes, released July 1, 1952. Producer, Dore Schary; director, Robert Pirosh; screenplay, Robert Pirosh; art directors, Cedric Gibbons and Daniel B. Cathcart; set designers, Alfred E. Spencer and Edwin B. Willis; original music, Conrad Salinger; costumes, Helen Rose; sound, Conrad Kahn; production manager, Al Shenberg; cinematography, John Alton; editors, John Durant and John Dunning; technical advisors, Cecil B. Dickson and Mike Masaoka; publicist, James W. Merrick. *Cast*: Van Johnson (Joseph T. Gresham), Patricia Neal (Alice Kingsley), Louis Calhern (Charles W. Birch), Sidney Blackmer (Philip Emery), Philip Ober (Gilbert Nunnally), Patricia Collinge (Miss Galbreth), Moroni Olsen (Speaker of the House), Elizabeth Patterson (Miss Dee), Reinhold Schuntzel (Peter Kralik), Fay Roope (Caswell), Madge Blake (Woman Bystander), Hugh Beaumont (The Chaplain), Don Beddoe (Congressman Reciting Post Office History), Wheaton Chambers (Representative), Marjorie Bennett, Frank Sully (Bystanders), Philo McCullough (Businessman), Carleton Young (Congressional Clerk), Bess Flowers and Selmer Jackson (Party Guests Greeting Ambassador), William Self (Johnny), Emory Parnell (Howard, the INS Chief), Norma Varden and Elizabeth Flournoy (bits).

Something for the Birds, 20th Century-Fox, 81 minutes, released November 14, 1952. Producer, Samuel G. Engel; director, Robert Wise; screenplay, Boris Ingster and I. A .L. Diamond, based on stories by Alvin M. Josephy, Joseph Petracca, and Boris Ingster; art directors, Lyle R. Wheeler and George Patrick; set decorators, Thomas Little and Bruce MacDonald; original music, Sol Kaplan; musical director, Lionel Newman; non-original music, "Again," Lionel Newman; costumes, Eloise Jensson; wardrobe director, Charles Le Maire; makeup, Ben Nye and Gene Romer; sound, Arthur L. Kirbach and Harry M. Leonard; production supervisor, A. F. Erickson; cinematographer, Joseph LaShelle; editor, Hugh S. Fowler; technical advisor, A. F. Erickson. *Cast*: Victor Mature (Steve Bennett), Patricia Neal (Anne Richards), Edmund Gwenn (Johnnie Adams), Larry Keating (Roy Patterson), Gladys Hurlbut (Mrs. Rice), Hugh Sanders (Grady), Christian Rub (Leo), Wilton Graff (Taylor), Joan Miller (Mac), Madge Blake (Mrs. Chadwick), Norma Varden (Congressman Bates), Elizabeth Flournoy (Receptionist), Maude Prickett (Woman with Vacuum Cleaner), Marshall Bradford (Admiral), James Craven (V.I.P.), Joan Shawlee (Woman at Station), Louise Lorimer (Mrs. Winthrop).

Stranger from Venus, Princess Pictures Inc, 75 minutes, released in England August 23, 1954. Producers, Burt Balaban and Gene Martel; associate producer, Roy Rich; director, Burt Balaban; screenplay, Desmond Leslie and Hans Jacoby, based on a story by Desmond

Leslie; art director, John Elphick; original music, Eric Spear; costumes, Laura Nightingale; makeup, Nell Taylor; hair stylist, Barbara Ritchie; sound, John Cape; production supervisor, George R. Busby; cinematographer, Kenneth Talbot; editor, Peter R. Hunt. *Cast*: Patricia Neal (Susan North), Helmut Dantine (The Stranger), Derek Bond (Arthur Walker), Cyril Luckham (Dr. Meinard), Willoughby Gray (Tom Harding), Marigold Russell (Gretchen Harding).

La tua donna, Deneb Films, 105 minutes, released in Italy December 28, 1954. Producer, Mario Pitto; assistant producers, Gianachi Nazzi and Alfredo Veloccia; director, Giovanni Paolucci; screenplay, Giuseppe Berto, Giovanni Paolucci, and Paride Rombi; production designer, Virgilio Marchi; set decorator, Piero Poletto; original music, Angelo Francesco Lavagnino; costumes, Mirella Morelli Deledda; makeup, Franco Palombi; hair stylist, Lucianni Palombi; sound, Agostino Moretti; production manager, Orlando Orsini; cinematographer, Vaclav Vich; editor, Vittorio Solito. *Cast*: Massimo Girotti (Sandro Ademari), Patricia Neal (Contessa Germana de Torri), Lea Padovani (Luisa, Sua Moglie), Eduardo Cianelli, Nerio Bernardi, Alberto Sorrentino; Hilda Roberts, Pio Campa, Alan Furlan, Anna Maria Paolucci, Alex Girotti (Figlio di Sandro e Luisa).

A Face in the Crowd, Warner Brothers, 125 minutes, released May 28, 1957. Producer and director, Elia Kazan; screenplay, Budd Schulberg, based on his short story "Your Arkansas Traveler"; art directors, Richard Sylbert and Paul Sylbert; original music, Tom Glazer; songs, "Free Man In the Morning," "Vitajex Jingle," "Just Plain Folks," "Old Fashioned Marriage," "Mama Guitar," music by Tom Glazer, lyrics by Budd Schulberg; costumes, Anna Hill Johnstone and Florence Transfield; makeup, Robert E. Jiras; hair stylist, Willis Hanchett; sound, Ernest Zatorsky and Eddie Johnstone; production manager, George Justin; cinematographers, Harry Stradling Sr. and Gayne Rescher; editor, Gene Milford. *Cast*: Andy Griffith (Larry "Lonesome" Rhodes), Patricia Neal (Marcia Jeffries), Anthony Franciosa (Joey de Palma), Walter Matthau (Mel Miller), Lee Remick (Betty Lou Fleckum), Percy Waram (General Hainsworth), Paul McGrath (Macey), Rod Brasfield (Beanie), Marshall Neilan (Senator Worthington Fuller), Alexander Kirkland (Jim Collier), Charles Irving (S. J. Luffler), Kay Medford (Mrs. Rhodes), Lois Chandler (Secretary), Walter Winchell, Mike Wallace, John Cameron Swayze, Earl Wilson, Faye Emerson, Sam Levenson, Burl Ives, Virginia Graham, Bennett Cerf, Betty Furness (themselves), Charles Nelson Reilly, Diana Sands (bits), Lois Nettleton (Macey's Nurse), Rip Torn (Barry Mills).

Breakfast at Tiffany's, Paramount Pictures, Technicolor, 115 minutes, released October 5, 1961. Producers, Martin Jurow and Richard Shepherd; director, Blake Edwards; screenplay, George Axelrod, based on the novella by Truman Capote; art directors, Hal Pereira and Roland Anderson; set directors, Sam Comer and Ray Moyer; original music, Henry Mancini; song, "Moon River," words by Johnny Mercer, music by Henry Mancini, sung by Ms. Hepburn; costume supervisor, Edith Head; costumes for Ms. Hepburn, Hubert de Givenchy; costumes for Ms. Neal, Pauline Trigere; makeup, Wally Westmore; hair stylist, Nellie Manley; sound, Hugo Grenzbach and John Wilkinson; cinematography, Franz F. Planer; cat trainer, Frank Inn. *Cast*: Audrey Hepburn (Lulamae Brown, "Holly Golightly"), George Peppard (Paul Varjak, "Fred"), Patricia Neal (Mrs. Failenson, "2E"), Buddy Ebsen (Doc Golightly), Martin Balsam (O. J. Berman), Mickey Rooney (Mr. Yunioshi), José Luis de Villalonga (José da Silva Pereira), Dorothy Whitney (Mag Wildwood), Stanley Adams (Rusty Trawler), Alan Reed Sr. (Sally Tomato), John McGiver (Tiffany's Salesman), Beverly Hills (Nightclub Dancer), Elvia Allman (Librarian), Joan Staley (Girl in Low-cut Dress), Gil Lamb, Tommy Farrell, Fay McKenzie (Party Guests), Putney (Cat), Jesse Wayne (stunt double).

Hud, Paramount Pictures, Panavision, 112 minutes, released May 29, 1963. Producers, Martin Ritt and Irving Ravetch; director, Martin Ritt; screenplay, Irving Ravetch and Harriet Frank Jr., based on the novel *Horseman, Pass By* by Larry McMurtry; art directors, Hal Pereira and Tambi Larsen; set directors, Robert R. Benton and Sam Comer; original music, Elmer Bernstein; costumes, Edith Head; makeup, Wally Westmore; hair stylist, Nellie Manley; cinematography, James Wong Howe; sound, John R. Carter and John Wilkinson; editor, Frank Bracht; a Salem-Dover production. *Cast:* Paul Newman (Hud Bannon), Melvyn Douglas (Homer Bannon), Patricia Neal (Alma Brown), Brandon De Wilde (Lonnie Bannon), Whit Bissell (Burris), John Ashley (Hermy), Val Avery (Jose), Curt Conway (Truman Peters), Sharyn Hillyer (Myra), Yvette Vickers (Lily Peters), Carl Saxe (Proprietor), Monty Montana (Cowboy), Richard Deacon (Pharmacist in Restaurant).

The Third Secret, 20th Century-Fox, Cinemascope, 103 minutes, released April 28, 1964. Producers, Robert L. Joseph and Hugh Perceval; associate producer, Shirley Bernstein; director, Charles Crichton; screenplay, Robert L. Joseph; production design, Thomas N. Morahan; original music, Richard Arnell; costumes, John McCorry; makeup, Kenneth Mackay; hair stylist, Iris Tilley; sound, A.W. Lumpkin; unit manager, Rita Davison; script supervisor, Joan Davis; cinematographer, Douglas Slocombe; editor, Frederick Wilson. *Cast:* Stephen Boyd (Alex Stedman), Jack Hawkins (Sir Frederick Belline), Richard Attenborough (Alfred Price-Gorham), Diane Cilento (Anne Tanner); Pamela Franklin (Catherine Whitset), Rachel Kempson (Mildred Hoving), Peter Sallis (Lawrence Jacks), Patience Collier (Mrs. Pelton), Judi Dench (Miss Humphries), Nigel Davenport (Lew Harding), Patricia Neal (scenes deleted).

Psyche '59, Columbia Pictures, 94 minutes, released April 29, 1964. Producer, Phillip Hazelton; director, Alexander Singer; screenplay, Julian Halevy, based on a novel by Françoise des Ligneris; art director, John Stoll; set decorator, Josie MacAlvin; original music, Kenneth V. Jones; musical director, Kenneth V. Jones; costumes, Julie Harris; wardrobe supervisor, Laura Nightingale; makeup, Harold Fletcher; hair stylist, Pearl Tipaldi; sound, George Stephenson and Red Law; production manager, R. L. M. Davidson; cinematographer, Walter Lassally; editor, Max Benedict; casting, James Liggat. *Cast:* Patricia Neal (Alison Crawford), Curt Jurgens (Eric Crawford), Samantha Eggar (Robin), Ian Bannen (Paul), Beatrix Lehmann (Mrs. Crawford), Elspeth March (Mme. Valadier), Shelley Crowhurst (Jean), Sandra Leo (Susan).

In Harm's Way, Paramount Pictures, Panavision, 165 minutes, released April 6, 1965. Producer, Otto Preminger; director, Otto Preminger; screenplay, Wendall Mayes, based on the novel *Harm's Way* by James Bassett; production designer, Lyle R. Wheeler; set directors, Morris Hoffman and Richard Mansfield; original music, Jerry Goldsmith and Michael Hennagin; costume coordinator, Hope Bryce; wardrobe, Eric Seelig, Alan Levine, Gordon T. Dawson, Grace M. Harris, and Gildo Scarano; makeup, Del Armstrong, Web Overlander, and David Grayson; hair stylists, Frederic Jones and Naomi Caven; sound, Harold Lewis and Charles Grenzbach; special effects, Lawrence W. Butler; production supervisors, Eva Monley, Henry Weinberger, Stanley H. Goldsmith, and James E. Henderling; cinematographer, Loyal Griggs; second unit cinematographer, Philip H. Lathrop; special photography, Farciot Edouart; editors, George Tomasini and Hugh S. Fowler; casting, Bill Barnes; technical advisor, Colin J. Mackenzie; project officer, Blake B. Booth; title design, Saul Bass; Sigma Productions. *Cast:* John Wayne (Capt. Rockwell "Rock" Torrey), Kirk Douglas (Cdr. Paul Eddington), Patricia Neal (Lt. Maggie Haynes), Tom Tryon (Lt. William "Mac" McConnell), Paula Prentiss (Bev McConnell), Brandon De Wilde (Ensign Jeremiah "Jere" Torrey); Jill Haworth (Ensign Annalee Dorne); Dana Andrews (Adm. "Blackjack" Broderick); Stanley Holloway (Clayton Canfil); Burgess Meredith (Cdr. Egan Powell); Franchot Tone (CINCPAC I Admiral), Patrick O'Neal (Cdr. Neal Owynn), Carroll O'Connor (Lt. Cdr. Burke), Slim Pickens (CPO Culpepper), James Mitchum (Ensign Griggs), George Kennedy (Col. Gregory), Bruce Cabot (Quartermaster Quoddy), Barbara Bouchet (Liz Eddington), Hugh O'Brien (Air Force Major), Larry Hagman (Lt. JG Cline), Christopher George (Sailor), Jerry Goldsmith (Piano Player), Henry Fonda (CINCPAC II Admiral), Dick Ziker (stunts).

7 Women, Metro-Goldwyn-Mayer, Panavision, Metrocolor, 93 minutes, released November 3, 1965. Producers, Bernard Smith and John Ford; director, John Ford; screenplay, Janet Green and John McCormick, based on "I Met A Gypsy" from *Chinese Finale* by Norah Lofts; art directors, George W. Davis and Eddie Imazu; set directors, Henry Grace and Jack Mills; original music, Elmer Bernstein; costumes, Walter Plunkett; makeup, William Tuttle; hair stylist, Sydney Guilaroff; assistant director, Wingate Smith; sound, Phil Mitchell; production manager, G. Rex Bailey; cinematographer, Joseph LaShelle; editor, Otho S. Lovering. *Cast:* Anne Bancroft (Dr. D. R. Cartwright), Sue Lyon (Emma Clark), Margaret Leighton (Agatha Andrews), Flora Robson (Miss Binns), Mildred Dunnock (Jane Argent), Betty Field (Florrie Pether), Anna Lee (Mrs. Russell), Eddie Albert (Charles Pether), Mike Mazurki (Tunga Khan), Woody Strode (Lean Warrior), Irene Tsu (Chinese Girl), Patricia Neal (as Dr. D. R. Cartwright, replaced in scenes, can be seen in long shot arriving at into the outpost on donkey).

The Subject Was Roses, Metro-Goldwyn-Mayer, Metrocolor, 107 minutes, released October 13, 1968. Producer, Edgar Lansbury; associate producer, Kenneth Utt; director, Ulu Grosbard; screenplay, Frank D. Gilroy, based on his play; art director, George Jenkins; set director, John Godfrey; original music, Lee Pockriss; musical director, Lee Pockriss; song "Who Knows Where the Time Goes?" by Sandy Denny, sung by Judy Collins; song "Albatross" written and sung by Judy Collins; costumes, Anna Hill Johnstone; wardrobe, Flo Transfield and George Newman; makeup, Mike Maggi; hair stylist, Vera Caruso; sound, Jack C. Jacobsen; cinematographer, Jack Priestley; editor, Jerry Greenberg. *Cast:* Patricia Neal (Nettie Cleary), Jack Albertson (John Cleary), Martin Sheen (Timmy Cleary), Don Saxon (Nightclub MC), Elaine Williams (Woman in Club), Grant Gordon (Man in Restaurant).

The Night Digger, Metro-Goldwyn-Mayer, Metrocolor, 110 minutes, released May 10, 1971. Producers, Alan D. Courtney and Norman S. Powell; executive producer, William O. Harbach; director, Alastair Reid; screenplay, Roald Dahl, based on the novel *Nest In A Falling Tree* by Joy Cowley; art director, Anthony Pratt; original music and music director, Bernard Herrmann; musician (solo viola d'amore), Rosemary Green; musician (solo harmonica), Tommy Reilly; costumes, Gabriella Falk; makeup, Ernest Gasser; hair stylist, Joan Carpenter; sound, Gerry Humphreys and Brian Marshall; production manager, John Oldknow; cinematographer, Alex Thompson; Miss Neal's assistant, Valerie Eaton Griffith; a Yongestreet Film Production. *Cast:* Patricia Neal (Maura Prince), Pamela Brown (Mother), Nicholas Clay (Billy Jarvis), Jean Anderson (Mrs. McMurtrey), Graham Crowden (Mr. Bolton), Yootha Joyce (Mrs. Palafox), Peter Sallis (Rev. Palafox).

Baxter! National General Pictures, Technicolor, 100 minutes, released March 3, 1973. Producer, Arthur Lewis; executive producers, Howard G. Barnes and John L. Hargreaves; director, Lionel Jeffries; screenplay, Michael Audiard, based on the novel *The Boy Who Could Make Himself Disappear* by Kin Platt; art director, Anthony Pratt; original music, Michael J. Lewis; sound, John Mitchell and Gordon Everett; cinematographer, Geoffrey Unsworth; editor, Teddy Darvis; Anglo-EMI and Group W Film. *Cast:* Patricia Neal (Dr.

Roberta Clemm), Jean-Pierre Cassel (Roger Tunnell), Britt Ekland (Chris Bentley), Lynn Carlin (Mrs. Baxter), Scott Jacoby (Roger Baxter), Sally Thomsett (Nemo), Paul Eddington (Mr. Rawling), Paul Maxwell (Mr. Baxter), Valerie Eaton Griffith (Nurse).

Happy Mother's Day, Love George, Taurean Films, color, 90 minutes, released August 15, 1973. Producer, Darren McGavin; director, Darren McGavin; screenplay, Robert Clouse; production designer, Hugo Wiethrich; original music, Don Vincent; song "A Man Can Be A Very Lonely Thing" by Don Vincent, sung by Mike Martsolf; costumes, Robert Anton; Miss Browne's costumes, Anne Klein; Mr. Mascolo's costumes, Pierre Cardin; makeup, Tony Lloyd; hair stylist, Bill Jack; sound, Hal Lewis; cinematographer, Walter Lassally; editor, George Grenville; still photographer, Phil Stern. *Cast*: Patricia Neal (Cara Perry), Cloris Leachman (Rhonda Carlson), Bobby Darin (Eddie), Tessa Dahl (Celia Perry), Ron Howard (Johnny Hanson), Kathie Browne (Crystal), Joe Mascolo (Piccolo), Simon Oakland (Police Chief Roy), Gale Garnett (Yolanda).

Hay que matar a "B," Taurean Films, color, 97 minutes, released in Spain June 14, 1975. Producers, José Luis Borau and Irving Lerner; executive producer, Luis Megino; screenplay, José Luis Borau and Antonio Drove; art directors, Cristina Lopez and Luis Megino; set director, Federico G. Mas; original music, José Nieto; costumes, Maiki Martin; wardrobe, Magdalena Fernandez and Juanita Ramirez; makeup, Louis Bonnemaison and Cristobal Criado; hair stylist, Ana Criado; sound, Luis Rodriguez; unit production manager, Matias Recuenco; cinematographer, Luis Cuadrado; editor, Pablo Gonzalez del Amo; still photographer, Antonio de Benito; unit publicist, Patricia Johnson; Madrid Films. *Cast*: Darren McGavin (Pal Kovak), Stephane Audran (Susana), Patricia Neal (Julia), Burgess Meredith (Hector), Pedro Diez del Corral (Jani), Rina Ottolina (Silvana), Perla Cristal (Rosita), Vicente Roca (Commercial Traveler).

The Widow's Nest, Navarro Productions, color, 119 minutes, released December 6, 1977. Producer, Tony Navarro; associate producer, Cadeo Villalba; director, Tony Navarro; screenplay, Tony Navarro; art director, José A. de la Guerra; set director, Edda Dorini; original music, Francis Lair; song "My Sweet Dolores" by Francis Lai, lyrics by Paul Taylor; "Ave Maria" sung by Madelaine Maechler; Gregorian chant sung by members of the Saint Basil's Church Choir, directed by Paul Salamunova; dialogue coach, Warren Langton; costumes, Tony Pueo; makeup, Ella Lopatowska, José Antonio Sanchez, and Alberto Gutierrez; hair stylist, Carmen Sanchez; sound, Ivan Sharrock and Eduardo Fernandez; production supervisor, Norma Garcy; cinematographer, John Cabrera; editor, Juan Serra. *Cast*: Patricia Neal (Lupe Sotomayer), Valentina Cortese (Dolores, Dona Eduardo Scarraga), Susan Oliver (Isabel, Dona Carlos Sotomayer), Yvonne Mitchell (Elvira, Dona Luis Benitez), Jadwiga Baranska (Carmen, Dona de Leon), Jerzy Zelnick (Carlos), Lila Kedrova (Mother Dona Carlos Sotomayer), Angel del Pozo (Victor), Helen Horton (Ana).

The Passage, United Artists, Technovision, Technicolor, 99 minutes, released March 9, 1979. Producers, Maurice Binder, Lester Goldsmith, and John Quested; executive producers, John Daly and Derek Dawson; associate producer, Geoffrey Helman; director, J. Lee Thompson; screenplay, Bruce Nicolaysen, based on the novel *Perilous Passage* by Bruce Nicolaysen; art directors, Jean Forestier and Constantin Mejinsky; original music, Michael J. Lewis; wardrobe supervisor, Brian Owen-Smith; armorer, Alain Alexandre; makeup, Derrick Bosch and Neville Smallwood; hair stylist, Inge Wolf; sound, Norman Bolland; production manager, Phillip Kenny; cinematographer, Michael Reed; editor, Alan Strachan; unit publicist, Geoff Freeman. *Cast*: Anthony Quinn (The Basque), James Mason (Professor Bergson), Malcolm McDowell (Von Berkow), Patricia Neal (Ariel Bergson), Kay Lenz (Leah Bergson), Paul Clemens (Paul Bergson), Christopher Lee (Head Gypsy),

Peter Arne (French Guide), Neville Jason (Lieutenant Reincke), Rose Alba (Madame), Jim Broadbent (German Soldier).

Ghost Story, Universal Pictures, Panavision, Technicolor, 110 minutes, released December 16, 1981. Producers, Burt Weissbourd and Douglas Green; associate producer, Ronald G. Smith; director, John Irvin; screenplay, Lawrence D. Cohen, based on the novel by Peter Straub; art director, Norman Newberry; set director, Mary Ann Biddle; original music, Philippe Sarde; song "Sweethearts of the Sigma Chi" performed by Guy Lombardo & The Royal Canadians, courtesy of MCA Records Inc.; Aria "When I Am Laid In Earth" from the opera *Dido and Aeneas* by Henry Purcell; costumes, May Routh; makeup illusions, Dick Smith; makeup, Bob Jiras, Albert Jeyte, Rich Sharp, and Irving Buckman; hair stylists, Phil Leto and Lee Trent; supervising sound editor, Charles L. Campbell; cinematographer, Jack Cardiff; editor, Tom Rolf; casting, Mike Fenton and June Feinberg; London casting, Suzie Figgis; a Burt Weissbourd production. *Cast*: Fred Astaire (Ricky Hawthorne), Melvyn Douglas (Dr. John Jaffrey), Douglas Fairbanks Jr. (Edward Charles Wanderley), John Houseman (Sears James), Craig Wasson (Don/David Wanderley), Patricia Neal (Stella Hawthorne), Alice Krige (Eva Galli/Alma Mobley), Jacqueline Brooks (Milly), Tim Choate (young Ricky Hawthorne), Kurt Johnson (young Edward Charles Wanderley), Ken Olin (young Sears James), Mark Chamberlin (young John Jaffrey).

An Unremarkable Life, Continental Film Groups, Technicolor, 92 minutes, released 12 October 1989. Producer, Amin Q. Chaudhri; executive producers, Navin Desai, Watson Warriner, and Gay Mayer; associate producer, Brian Smedley-Aston; director, Amin Q. Chaudhri; screenplay, Marcia Dineen; production designer, Norman B. Didge Jr.; art department assistants, Michael Lies and Robert Garnack; original music, Avery Sharpe; costumes, Carol Helen Beule; Miss Neal's wardrobe, Breckenridge; makeup, Bella Sinego; hair stylist, Justine Conti; Miss Winters's hair and makeup, Chris Bingham; sound, Dorielle Rogers; unit manager, Russ T. Fisher; cinematographer, Alan Hall; editor, Sandi Gerling. *Cast*: Patricia Neal (Frances), Shelley Winters (Evelyn), Mako (Max Chen), Rochelle Oliver (Mary Alice), Charles Dutton (Lou), Lily Knight (Judy), Jenny Chrisinger (Jennie), Madeleine Sherwood (Louise).

Cookie's Fortune, October Films, Panavision, color, 118 minutes, released January 21, 1999. Producers, Robert Altman, Ernest Etchie Stroh, David Levy, and James McLinden; executive producer, Willie Baer; director, Robert Altman; screenplay, Anne Rapp; production design, Stephen Altman; art director, Richard L. Johnson; set director, Susan J. Emshwiller; original music, David A. Stewart; costumes, Dona Granata; makeup, Manlio Rocchetti and Gloria Belz; hair stylist, Linda Melazzo; sound, Frederick Howard; unit production manager, Barbara A. Hall; cinematographer, Toyomichi Kurita; editor, Abraham Lim; still photographer, Joyce Rudolph; *Salome* choreography, Jennifer M. Mizenko; assistant to Miss Neal, Warren Langton. *Cast*: Glenn Close (Camille Dixon), Julianne Moore (Cora Duvall), Liv Tyler (Emma Duvall), Chris O'Donnell (Jason Brown), Charles S. Sutton (Willis Richland), Patricia Neal (Jewel Mae "Cookie" Orcutt), Ned Beatty (Lester Boyle), Courtney B. Vance (Otis Tucker), Donald Moffat (Jack Palmer), Lyle Lovett (Manny Hood), Rufus Thomas (Theo Johnson), Ruby Wilson (Josie Martin).

Newsreels

A Date with the Stars, British Pathé, 90 seconds, released November 29, 1948. Alan Ladd, Sue Carol, Patricia Neal, Virginia Mayo, Joan Caulfield, Billy De Wolf, Robert Donat, Stewart Granger, Jean Simmons, Sid Fields.

The Queen Meets the Stars, British Pathé, 90 seconds, released December 2, 1948. Robert Donat, Glynis Johns, Robert Taylor, Elizabeth Taylor, Billy De Wolfe, John Mills, Queen Elizabeth and Princess Margaret, Prince Philip Mountbatton, J. Arthur Rank, Patricia Neal, Googie Withers, Myrna Loy.

The Royal Command Performance, 1948, British Pathé, 2 minutes 20 seconds, released 1948. Robert Taylor, Billy De Wolfe, Joan Caulfield, Elizabeth Taylor, Virginia Mayo, Michael O'Shea, Patricia Neal, Ronald Reagan, Vivien Leigh, Laurence Olivier, Alan Ladd, Sue Carol, Myrna Loy, John Mills, Mary Mills, Phyllis Calvert and daughter Auriol, Princess Margaret.

Stars Take To Chinchilla For Winter, British Pathé, 70 seconds, released November 7, 1949. Ruth Roman, Alexis Smith, Patricia Neal, Eleanor Parker.

Premiere of Bright Leaf in North Carolina, British Pathé, 70 seconds, released June 1950. Patricia Neal, Donald Crisp, Tommy Bartlett, James Brown, Ken Scott.

Breakthrough Has an Impressive Hollywood Premiere, British Pathé, 45 seconds, released November 1950. Joan Crawford, Frank and Joan Lovejoy, David Brown, Patricia Neal, Gordon McRae, John Agar, Ruth Roman, Jack L. Warner, Harry M. Warner.

Arrival of American Stars in Rio de Janiero, Hearst Newsreel, 5 minutes, released March 9, 1951. Ricardo and Georgiana Montalban, Joan Fontaine, June Havoc, Lizabeth Scott, John Derek, Wendell Corey, Patricia Neal, June Haver, Florence Marley.

Hollywood Stars Leave for Montevideo, Hearst Newsreel, 5 minutes, released February 22, 1952. June Haver, Patricia Neal, Evelyn Keyes.

A Show in the Rain in Korea, Warners Pathé, 7 minutes, released July 1952. Johnny Grant, Patricia Neal, Tony Lovello, Joy Windsor, Ginny Jackson, Pat Moran.

Spot the Stars—A New Parlour Game, British Pathé, 1 minute 25 seconds, released 1950–1959. Anna Neagle, Herbert Wilcox, Michael Wilding, George Raft, Cesar Romero, Vera-Ellen, Richard Todd, Valerie Hobson, Dave Clark, Richard Attenborough, Mae West, Barbara Stanwyck, Robert Taylor, Stan Laurel and Oliver Hardy, David and Hjordis Niven, Moira Shearer, Bing Crosby, Danny Kaye, Myrna Loy, Margaret Lockwood, Margaret Leighton, Alan Ladd, Patricia Neal, Virginia Mayo, Billy DeWolfe, Joan Caulfield, John Mills, David Lean, Ava Gardner, Coleen Gray, Stuart Granger, Jean Simmons, Bob Hope, Jack Dempsey, Dwight D. Eisenhower, Adolph Menjou.

Other Short Films

American Heart Association, 5 minutes, released February 1950. Director, Richard Bare. *Cast:* Gary Cooper, Patricia Neal.

Pat Neal Is Back, Metro-Goldwyn-Mayer, 9 minutes, released 1968. Director, Edward Beyer; written by Edward Beyer; assistant director, George A. Bowers; camera operators, Tom Mangravite and William Montgomery, a Beyro production. *Cast:* Patricia Neal, Jack Albertson, Ulu Grosbard, Martin Sheen, Edgar Lansbury, Frank Gilroy.

All Quiet on the Western Front, CBS promotional film, 10 minutes, released theatrically 1979. Same production credits as the made-for-television movie. *Cast:* Richard Thomas (Paul Maumer), Ernest Borgnine (Stanislaus Katcinsky), Patricia Neal (Paul's Mother), Delbert Mann (Director).

A Day at Camp Chewase, 15 minutes, released June 21, 1986. Producer, Jim Thompson; director, Jim Thompson; cinematographers, Jim and Bert Thompson; editor, Jim Thompson. *Cast:* Patsy Neal, Margaret Ann Neal, Monie Thomson, Bert Thomson, "over 300 summer campers." (Filmed the summers of 1937 and 1938.)

For the Love of May, Mary McDonough Film, Panavision, color, 17 minutes, released 2000. Producer, June Dowad; director, Mary Beth McDonough; screenplay, Mary Beth McDonough; art director, Deborah Karpinski; set directors, Isabelle Trichard and Emily O'Brien; original music, Jon Walmsley; song "Sentimental Journey" sung by Rosemary Clooney, from *For the Duration*; song "For Your Love" by Jon Walmsley and Lisa Harrison, sung by Lisa Harrison; song "Sentimental" by Jon Walmsley; costumes, David Norbury; makeup, Christalee; hair stylist, Donna Anderson; sound supervisor/mixer, Timothy J. Borquez; production supervisor, Steve Stills; cinematographer, Bojan Bazelli; editor, Dayna Cernansky; still photographers, Thom Elder and Brooks Ayola; assistant to Miss Neal, Warren Langton. *Cast*: Patricia Neal (May), Alexandra Paul (Emily), Michael Learned (Mary Lou), RuPaul Charles (Jimbo), Annie LaRussa (Kate), Alison Arngrim (Jude), Karle Warren (Sarah), Tony Becker.

Selected Documentaries

Preminger: Anatomy of a Filmmaker, Preminger Films, 123 minutes, released 1991. Producer, Valerie A. Robins; associate producer, Susan R. Block; executive producer, Hope Bryce Preminger; director, Valerie A Robins; written by Thomas J. Wiener; lighting cameraman, Paul C. Goldberg; on-line editor, Gary J. Woodruff; title design, Saul Bass; post-production supervisor, Gary Mascato, production in association with the Austrian Broadcasting Corp. *With*: Burgess Meredith (Narrator), Saul Bass, Peter Bogdanovich, Michael Caine, Ossie Davis, José Ferrer, Jack Haley Jr., Ken Howard, Deborah Kerr, Carol Lynley, Joseph L. Mankiewicz, Don Murray, Patricia Neal, Otto Preminger (archival footage), Vincent Price, George C. Scott, Frank Sinatra, James Stewart, Tom Tryon.

Theremin: An Electronic Odyssey, Orion Films, 83 minutes, released January 29, 1994. Producer, Steven A. Martin; associate producers, Kate Carty, Frank de Marco, Loretta Farb, Brian Kelly, Amy Smith, and Robert Stone; director, Steven A. Martin; written by Steven A. Martin; cinematography Los Angeles, Chris Lombardi; cinematography Moscow, Robert Stone; music, Hal Willner; gaffer, Greg Arciniega; Steadicam, Ian Nicol; sound mixer, Andy Green; editor, David Greenwald; in association with Channel 9. *With*: Leon Theremin, Clara Rockmore, Robert Moog, Brian Wilson, Todd Rundgren, Dr. Samuel Hoffman, V. I. Lenin (archival footage), Ingrid Bergman (archival footage), Bobby Burgess, Jerry Lewis (archival footage), Ray Milland (archival footage), Michael Rennie (archival footage), Patricia Neal (archival footage).

Making the Earth Stand Still, 20th Century-Fox, 70 minutes, released 1995. *With*: Patricia Neal, Billy Gray, Robert Wise, Julian Blaustein, Joe Dante, Steven C. Smith, Bob Burns, Marc Zubatkin, William Malone.

The Lives of Lillian Hellman, 55 minutes, released 1998. Director, Phillip Schopper. *With*: Warren Beatty, Maureen Stapleton, Patricia Neal, Norman Mailer, Ring Lardner Jr.

From Russia to Hollywood: The 100-Year Odyssey of Chekhov and Shdanoff, Keeve Productions, 82 minutes, released August 8, 1999. Producers, Frederick Keeve, Peter Spirer, and Chuck Block; co-producers, Lisa Dalton and Sue Mischel; director, Frederick Keeve; written by Frederick Keeve; original music, Frederick Reeve; cinematography, Peter Bonilla and R. G. Wilson; editors, Tee Bosustow (Bosustow Media Group) and Robert Gordon; sound, Margaret Duke; Keeve Productions in association with City Block Productions and Aslan Dix. *With*: Gregory Peck (Narrator), Mala Powers (Narrator), Lloyd Bridges, Leslie Caron, Jeff Corey, Sharon Gless, Hurd Hatfield, Jack Larson, Patricia Neal,

Jack Palance, Anthony Quinn, George Shdanoff, Robert Stack, Beatrice Straight, Clint Eastwood.

Inside You Only Live Twice, Metro-Goldwyn-Mayer, 31 minutes, released 2000. Producers, John Cork, David Naylor, and Bruce Scivally; producers London, Antonia de Barton-Watson and David Worrall; director, John Cork; written by John Cork; makeup and costumes, Joannel Clenete, Abigail Graves, and Lynn Jackett; music, John Barry and Monty Norman; cinematography, Geoff Greenside, Graham Minassian, Henry Nield, Steve Suggs, Steven Wacks, and John Whatton; sound, Scott Ikegami, George Ann Muller, Geoff Neate, Dave Rody, Doug Smith, and Chris White. *With*: Patrick McNee (Narrator); Ken Adams, Dana Broccoli, Patricia Neal, Roald Dahl (archival footage), Karin Dor, Diane Cilento (archival footage), Albert Broccoli (archival footage), Harry Saltzman (archival footage), Sean Connery (archival footage), George Lazenby (archival footage).

The Face: Jesus in Art, Voyager Productions Ltd., 120 minutes, released March 31, 2001. Producers, Craig McGowan and Rosemary Plum; director, Craig McGowan; original music, Chip Ellinghouse and Grant Slawson; written by Dr. James Clifton; set director, Brian Bonas; costumes, Angels & Bermans Ltd. London; cinematography, Dean Cundey; executive producer for Channel 13, WNET New York, William F. Baker. *With*: Mel Gibson, Patricia Neal, Ricardo Montalban, Edward Herrmann, Starr Herrmann, Stacy Keach, Juliet Mills, Bill Moyers (Narration).

Bright Leaves, First Run Features, 107 minutes, released October 12, 2003. Producer, Ross McElwee; associate producer, Linda Morgenstern; written by Ross McElwee; cinematography, Ross McElwee; sound, Rick Beck; editors, Ross McElwee and Mark Meatto; produced by Homemade Movies at the Film Study Center, Cambridge, Massachusetts. *With*: Ross McElwee (Narration), Marian Fitz-Simmons, Patricia Neal.

Broadway: The Golden Age, Dada Films, color, 111 minutes, released June 11, 2004. Producers, Anne L. Bernstein, Jamie De Roy, Albert Tapper, and Rick McKay; associate producers, Jack Coco, Sandi Durell, Jane Klain, and Richard Weigle; executive producer, Georgia Frontierre; director, Rick McKay; screenplay, Rick McKay; cinematography, Rick McKay; editor, Rick McKay; production manager, Nicole London; sound mixer, Tom Paul. *With*: Beatrice Arthur, Elizabeth Ashley, Alec Baldwin, John Barrowman, Betsy Blair, Marlon Brando (archival footage), Carol Burnet, Kitty Carlisle Hart, Carol Channing, Arlene Dahl, Fred Ebb, Nanette Fabray, Ben Gazzara, Robert Goulet, Farley Granger, Tammy Grimes, Uta Hagen, Julie Harris, Jerry Herman, Celeste Holm, Sally Ann Howes, Kim Hunter, Jeremy Irons, Martin Landau, Angela Lansbury, Arthur Laurents, Carol Lawrence, Shirley MacLaine, Karl Malden, Ann Miller, Patricia Neal, Jerry Orbach, Jane Powell, Harold Prince, John Raitt, Lee Roy Reams, Rex Reed, Charles Nelson Reilly, Mary Rodgers, Gena Rowlands, Eva Marie Saint, Marian Seldes, Vincent Sherman, Stephen Sondheim, Kim Stanley (archival footage), Maureen Stapleton, Elaine Stritch, Laurette Taylor (archival), Gwen Verdon, Fay Wray, and Gretchen Wyler.

Made-for-Television Films

The Homecoming: A Christmas Story, CBS, 120 minutes, December 19, 1971. Producer, Robert L. Jacks; executive producer, Lee Rich; director, Fielder Cook; assistant director, Max Stein; written by Earl Hamner Jr., based on his novel; production designer, Robert E. Smith; art director, Robert Emmet Smith; set designer, James G. Cane; original music by Jerry Goldsmith; costumes, Bob Harris Jr. and Betsy Cox; makeup, Bob Sidell; hair stylist,

Dione Taylor; cinematography, Earl Rath; editors, Marjorie Fowler and Gene Fowler Jr.; portions of the *Fibber McGee and Molly* program courtesy of NBC Radio; Lorimar Productions. *Cast*: Patricia Neal (Olivia Walton), Richard Thomas (John-Boy Walton), Edgar Bergen (Grandpa Walton), Ellen Corby (Grandma Walton), Cleavon Little (Hawthorne Dooley), Dorothy Strickney (Emily Baldwin), William Windom (Charlie Snead), Andrew Duggan (John Walton), Woodrow Parfrey (Ike Godsey), Judy Norton (Mary Ellen Walton), Mary Elizabeth McDonough (Erin Walton), Kami Colter (Erin Walton), Eric Scott (Ben Walton); David S. Harper (Jim-Bob Walton); Jon Walmsley (Jason Walton); David Huddleston (Sheriff Bridges), Sally Chamberlin (City Lady).

Things in Their Season, CBS, 90 minutes, November 27, 1974. Producer, Herbert Hirschman; executive producer, Philip Barry Jr.; director, James Goldstone; written by John Gay; art director, Ed Graves; original music, Ken Lauber; costume supervisor, Bruce Wallup; costumer, Lee Peters; makeup, Jack Petty; hair stylist, Delyte Petty; cinematography, Terry K. Meade; unit production manager, Donald Roberts; sound, Don Johnson; editor, Edward A. Biery; vice president in charge of production, Roger Gimball; Tomorrow Entertainment. *Cast*: Patricia Neal (Peg Gerlach), Ed Flanders (Carl Gerlach), Marc Singer (Andy Gerlach), Meg Foster (Judy Pines), Charles Haid (Dr. Willis McCreevy), Doreen Lang (Millie Havemeyer).

Eric, NBC, 120 minutes, November 10, 1975. Producer, Herbert Hirschman; executive producers, Lee Rich and Philip Capice; written by Nigel McKeand and Carol Evan McKeand, based on the book by Doris Lund; art director, Phil Barber; set director, Robert de Vestal; costume supervisor, Patricia Norris; makeup, Mel Berns Jr.; hair stylist, Mary Keats; music, Dave Grusin; song "Loving Somebody" written and performed by John Savage; cinematography, Terry K. Meade; editor, Edward A. Biery; production manager, Lynn Guthrie; casting, Bert Remsen & Associates; color by Movielab. *Cast*: Patricia Neal (Lois Swenson), Claude Akins (Stanley "Stan" Swenson), Sian Barbara Allen (Marilyn Porter), Mark Hamill (Paul Swenson), Nehemiah Persoff (Dr. Duchesnes), John Savage (Eric Swenson), Tom Clancy (Murphy), James G. Richardson (Tom), Eileen McDonough (Linda Swenson).

The American Woman: Portraits of Courage, ABC, 90 minutes, May 20, 1976. Producer, Gaby Monet; associate producer, Robert Barclay; director, Robert Deubel; written by Gaby Monet and Anne Grant, developed from *Our North American Foremothers* by Anne Grant; costumes, Malia; makeup, Gabriella Csorba, Dossie Donaldson, and Robert Gordon; hair stylist, Gabriella Csorba, Dossie Donaldson, and Robert Gordon; original music composed and conducted by John Randall Booth; music and lyrics by Elliott Siegel, sung by Julie Budd; song "A New Sun Shining" sung by Melba Moore; cinematography, Stephen H. Burum; editor, Arthur Ginsburg; sound, Jay Freund and Chat Gunter; still photographer, Marie Cosindas. *Cast*: Patricia Neal (Narrator), Walter Abel (Judge), Jonelle Allen (Rosa Parks), Helen Gallagher (Mary Harris Jones), Joan Hackett (Belva Lockwood), Hal Holden (The Husband at Belva Lookwood Trial), Celeste Holm (Elizabeth Cady Stanton), Frank Langella (John Adams), Claudia McNeil (Sojourner Truth), Joanna Miles (Abigail Adams), Melba Moore (Harriet Tubman), Kate Mulgrew (Deborah Sampson), Lois Nettleton (Susan B. Anthony).

Tail Gunner Joe, NBC, 180 minutes, February 6, 1977. Producer, George Eckstine; associate producer, Norman Chandler Fox; director, Jud Taylor; written by Lane Slate; art director, Lawrence G. Paull; set director, Lloyd A. Linnean; music, Billy May; music editor, Bettie Biery; costumes, Charles Waldo; cinematography, Ric Waite; editor, Bernard J. Small; sound, Don Parker; aviation technical advisor, Cliff Shirpser; production manager, Fred R. Simpson; casting, Reuben Cannon. *Cast*: Peter Boyle (Joseph McCarthy), John Forsythe (Paul Cunningham), Heather Menzies (Logan), Burgess Meredith (Joseph Welch), Patricia Neal (Senator Margaret Chase Smith), Jean Stapleton (Mrs. DeCamp), Tim O'Connor (Librarian), Philip Abbott (Senator Scott Lewis), Wesley Addy (Middleton), Ned Beatty (Sylvester), Karen Carlson (Jean Kerr), John Carradine (Wisconsin Farmer), Diana Douglas (Sarah), Andrew Duggan (President Dwight D. Eisenhower), Henry Jones (Armitage), Murray Matheson (Publisher), Andrew Prine (Farmer), William Schallert (General Zwicker), Sam Chew Jr. (Robert F. Kennedy), Richard M. Dixon (Senator Richard M. Nixon), Howard Hesseman (Lieutenant Cantwell), Shirley O'Hara (Marie), Allan Miller, Addison Powell, Alan Oppenheimer, Allan Rich, Simon Scott, Bill Quinn.

A Love Affair: The Eleanor and Lou Gehrig Story, NBC, 120 minutes, January 15, 1978. Producer, David Manson; associate producer, Thomas Fries; executive producers, Charles W. Fries and Richard Berg; director, Fielder Cook; written by Blanche Hanalis, based on the book *My Luke and I* by Eleanor Gehrig and Joseph Durso; art director, Herman Zimmerman; original music, Eddy Lawrence-Manson; costumes, Frank Novak and Toby Gardner; makeup, Frank Westmore and Michael Westmore; hair stylist, Jean Austin; cinematography, Michel Hugo; editor, David Newhouse; unit production manager, Ron Wright; sound mixer, Tom Verton; technical advisor, Joseph Dukso; casting, Melnick/Holstra; executive in charge of production, Malcolm Stuart; Charles Fries Productions Inc. *Cast*: Blythe Danner (Eleanor Gehrig), Edward Herrmann (Lou Gehrig), Patricia Neal (Mrs. Gehrig), Gerald S. O'Loughlin (Joe McCarthy), Ramon Bieri (Babe Ruth), Jane Wyatt (Eleanor's Mother), Georgia Engel (Claire Ruth), Michael Lerner (Dr. Canlan), David Ogden Stiers (Dr. Charles Mayo), Gail Strickland (Dorothy), Valerie Curtin (Kitty), Lainie Kazan (Sophie Tucker), William Wellman Jr. (Bill Dickey).

The Bastard, MCA-TV, 240 minutes, May 22 and 23, 1978. Producer, Joe Byrne; associate producer, Susan Lichtwardt; executive producer, John Wilder; director, Lee H. Katzin; written by Guerdon Trueblood, based on the novel by John Jakes; art director, Loyd S. Papez; set director, Richard Friedman; set designer, Roy Barnes; costumes, Vincent Dee and Jean-Pierre Dorleac; original music, John Addison; cinematography, Michel Hugo; unit production manager, Fred R. Simpson; sound, Andrew Gilmore; editors, Robert F. Shugrue and Michael S. Murphy; casting, Lyle Kenyon Engel; developed for television by John Wilder; a John Wilder Production in Technicolor. *Cast*: Andrew Stevens (Phillipe Chabonneau/Philip Kent), Tom Bosley (Benjamin Franklin), Kim Cattrall (Annie Ware), Buddy Ebsen (Benjamin Edes), Lorne Greene (Bishop Francis), Olivia Hussey (Alicia), Cameron Mitchell (Captain Plummer), Harry Morgan (Captain Caleb), Patricia Neal (Marie Charbonneau), Eleanor Parker (Lady Amberly), Donald Pleasence (Solomon Sholto), William Shatner (Paul Revere), Barry Sullivan (Abraham Ware), Herbert Jeffries Jr. (Lucas), Keenan Wynn (Johnny Malcolm), Raymond Burr (Narrator), Sam Chew Jr. (Major), Charles Haid (George Lumden), Russell Johnson (Colonel James Barrett), James Whitmore Jr. (Esau Sholto).

All Quiet on the Western Front, CBS, 180 minutes, November 14, 1979. Producer, Norman Rosemont; associate producer, Ron Carr; executive producer, Martin Starger; director, Delbert Mann; written by Paul Monash, based on the novel by Erich Maria Remarque; production designer, John Stoll; art director, Karel Vacek; costumes by Bermans & Nathans Ltd.; makeup chief, Yvonne Coppard; makeup artist, Jiri Simon; hair stylist, Pat McDermott; original music, Allyn Ferguson; cinematography, John Coquillon; editor, Alan Pattillo; supervising sound editor, Don Sharpe; executive in charge of production,

Richard L. O'Connor; a Norman Rosemont Production in association with Marble Arch Productions. *Cast*: Richard Thomas (Paul Baumer), Ernest Borgnine (Stanislaus Katczinsky), Ian Holm (Himmelstoss), Donald Pleasence (Kantorek), Patricia Neal (Paul's Mother), Mark Drewry (Tjaden), Paul Mark Elliott (Josef Behm), Dai Bradley (Albert Kropp), Mary Miller (Kemmerich's Mother), Michael Sheard (Paul's Father), Drahomira Fialkova (Sister Libertine).

An Act of Love: The Patricia Neal Story, CBS, 120 minutes, December 8, 1981. Producer, Don Silverman; associate producer, Michael Economou; executive producer, Lawrence Schiller; directors, Anthony Harvey and Anthony Page; written by Robert Anderson, based on the book *Pat and Roald* by Barry Farrell; original music, Laurence Rosenthal; art director, Peter Landsdowne Smith; art director London, Tony Curtis; set director, Herman N. Schoenbrun; costume supervisors, Jac McAnelly and Ann Somers Major; makeup, Bob Mills; makeup London, Wally Schneiderman; hair stylist, Carolyn Ferguson; hair stylist London, Joan Carpenter; cinematography, Mike Fash and Reynaldo Villalobos; sound mixer, Jim Cook; editors, Edward M. Abrams and Bernard Gribble; executive in charge of production, Barbara Persons; executive in charge of production London, Peter Katz. *Cast*: Glenda Jackson (Patricia Neal), Dirk Bogarde (Roald Dahl), Mildred Dunnock (Herself), Ken Kercheval (Dr. Charles Carton), Jane Merrow (Valerie Eaton Griffith), John Reilly (Barry Farrell), Sydney Penny (Tessa Dahl), Robby Kiger (Theo Dahl), Priscilla Morrill (Sarah), Gloria Stroock Stern (Herself), Newell Alexander, James Bacon, Dolores Quinton (Reporters), Brianne Strauss (Ophelia Dahl), Rock Hudson (Himself).

Glitter, ABC, 85 minutes, September 13, 1984. Executive producers, Aaron Spelling and Douglas S. Cramer; executive supervising producer, E. Duke Vincent; supervising producers, Ben Joelson and Art Baer; producer, Lynn Loring; written by Nancy Sackett, Ben Joelson, and Art Baer; director, Jackie Cooper; set director, Deborah Siegel; unit production manager, Blair Gilbert. *Cast*: David Birney (Sam Bozak), Morgan Brittany (Kate Simpson), Van Johnson (Mark Hughes), Tracy Nelson (Angela Timini), Barbara Sharma (Shelley Sealy), Teri Copley (Carol), Joan Van Ark (Dr. Martha Kendricks), Mike Connors (George Kincaid), Adrian Zmed (Tom), Barbara McNair (Marian), Juliet Prowse (Marlene Corbett), Arte Johnson (Clive Richlin), Arthur Hill (Charles Hardwick), Ken Howard (Senator Jonathan McCary), Patricia Neal (Madame Lil).

Love Leads the Way: A True Story, Walt Disney Productions, 98 minutes, October 7, 1984. Producer, Jimmy Hawkins; associate producer, Robert Charles Stroud; executive producer, David Permut; director, Delbert Mann; written by Henry Denker, based on the book *First Lady of the Seeing Eye* by Morris Frank and Blake Clark and on a story by Jimmy Hawkins and Henry Denker; original music, Fred Karlin; song "Someone to Watch Over Me," lyrics by Ira Gershwin, music by George Gershwin; art directors, Carolyn Ott/Nashville and Dumas Production Services/Washington; set director, Fred Schwoebel/Nashville; costumes, Dodie Shephard; makeup, Cheryl Buttrey; hair stylist, Linda Conroy; cinematography, Gary Graver; editor, Art Seid; sound mixer, Ronald Curfman; sound, Glen Glenn Sound; dog trainer, Ron Bledsoe; special thanks to The Seeing Eye, Morristown, New Jersey; technical advisor, Ned Myrose. *Cast*: Timothy Bottoms (Morris Frank), Eva Marie Saint (Dorothy Eustis), Arthur Hill (Mr. Frank), Patricia Neal (Mrs. Frank), Glynnis O'Connor (Lois), Susan Dey (Beth), Michael Anderson Jr. (Hank), Stephen Young (Mike McShane), Ralph Bellamy (Senator Christl), Ernest Borgnine (Senator Brighton), Pilot (Buddy).

Shattered Vows, NBC, 120 minutes, October 29, 1984. Producer, Robert Lovenheim; associate producer, Richard Sawyer; executive producers, Jack Grossbart and Marty Litke;

director, Jack Bender; written by Audrey Davis Levin based on the book *Nun: A Memoir* by Dr. Mary Gilligan Wong; art director, Shari Adagio; original music, Lee Holdridge; cinematography, Misha Suslov; production sound mixer, Mark Ulano; editor, Lori Jane Coleman; Bertinelli Inc.; River City Productions. *Cast*: Valerie Bertinelli (Mary Gilligan), David Morse (Father Tim), Caroline McWilliams (Sister Agnes), Tom Parsekian (Rick), Millie Perkins (Mrs. Gilligan), Leslie Ackerman (Bonnie), Lisa Jane Persky (Cathy), Patricia Neal (Sister Carmelita), Matt Adler (Pat), Father Joseph Battaglio (Priest).

Caroline? CBS, 120 minutes, April 29, 1990. Producer, Dorothea G. Petrie; associate producers, John Beaird, Paul A. Levin, and Paula A. Levin; executive producers, Les Alexander, Don Enright, Joseph Broido, and Barbara Hiser; director, Joseph Sargent; written by Michael De Guzman, based on the novel *Father's Arcane Daughter* by E. L. Konigsburg; production design, Jan Scott; set director, Joseph Litsch; original music, Charles Bernstein; costumes, Peter Mitchell; makeup, Lynn Barber; hair stylist, Philip Ivey; cinematography, William Wages; editor, Paul LaMastra; sound editor, G. Michael Graham; executive in charge of production, Russell Vreeland. *Cast*: Stephanie Zimbalist (Caroline), Pamela Reed (Grace Carmichael), George Grizzard (Paul Carmichael), Patricia Neal (Miss Trollope), Dorothy McGuire (Flora Atkins), John Sargent.

A Mother's Right: The Elizabeth Morgan Story, Lifetime, 120 minutes, November 29, 1992. Producer, Kay Hoffman; executive producers, Alan Lansburg and Linda Otto; director, Linda Otto; written by Lucretia Baxter and Alan Lansburg based on a story by Lucretia Baxter; production design, Norm Baron; set director, Steven K. Barrett; original music, James McVay; song "Sacrifice" by Elton John; costumes, Faye Sloan; makeup, Vincent Fauci; hair stylist, Doreen F. Schultz; cinematography, Mike Fash; editor, Robin Wilson; sound mixer, Steven R. Smith; executive in charge of production, Howard Lipstone. *Cast*: Bonnie Bedelia (Dr. Elizabeth Morgan), Terence Knox (Eric Foretich), Kenneth Welsh (Paul Michel), Nick Searcy (Rob Morgan), Pam Grier (Linda Holman), Caroline Dollar (Hilary), Patricia Neal (Antonia Morgan), Rip Torn (Bill Morgan), Jim Sharp (Himself), Stephen Michael Ayers (Richard Ducote), Catherine Shaffner (Elaine Mittleman), Tom Lankford (Himself).

Heidi, Walt Disney Productions, 193 minutes, July 18, 1993. Producers, Frank Agrama, Nick Gillott, and Daniele Lorenzano; executive producers, Bill McCutchen and Mirjana Mijojlic; director, Michael Ray Rhodes; written by Jeanne Rosenberg based on the novel by Johanna Spyri; art directors, John Blezard and Vladislav Lasic; set director, Peter Manhardt; costumes, Derek Hyde; women's costumer, Marina Skundric; men's costumer, Zoran Savic; makeup, Penny Bell; hair stylist, Stephanie Kaye; original music, Lee Holdridge; cinematography, Dennis C. Lewiston; sound mixer, Paul Le Mare; editor, Randy Jon Morgan; unit manager, Miodrag Stevanovic. *Cast*: Jason Robards Jr. (Grandfather), Jane Seymour (Fraulein Rottenmeier), Patricia Neal (Grandmother), Sian Phillips (Frau Sesmann), Lexi Randall (Klara), Noley Thornton (Heidi).

Television Performances

Goodyear TV Playhouse, NBC, "Spring Reunion," 60 minutes, April 11, 1954. Producer, Fred Coe; director, Delbert Mann; written by Robert Alan Arthur. *Cast*: Patricia Neal (Maggie Hackett), Kevin McCarthy (Harry), Kathleen Maguire (Burna), William Harrigan, May (Frances Fuller), Phillip Abbott.

Studio One, CBS, "A Handful of Diamonds," 60 minutes, April 19, 1954. Producer, Worthington Miner; director, Paul Nickell. *Cast*: Patricia Neal (Miriam Leslie), Lorne Greene

(Frank Leslie), Paula Dehelly (Marie), William Harrigan (Hansen), Gene Peterson (Joquin), John Cannon (Announcer), Betty Furness (Commercial Hostess).

Your Show of Shows, NBC, 90 minutes, May 24, 1954. Producer, Max Liebman; directors, Nat Hiken and Max Liebman; written by Woody Allen, Mel Brooks, Larry Gelbart, Lucille Kallen, Danny Somin, Neil Simon, Mel Tolken, and Sylvester "Pat" L. Weaver Jr.; set director, Frederick Fox; original music, Louis Baldwin Bergerson; conductors, Johnny Green and Irwin Kostal; camera director, Bill Hobin; costumes, Paul Dupont; created by Sylvester "Pat" L. Weaver Jr. *Cast:* Sid Caesar, Imogene Coca, Howard Morris, Carl Reiner, with Patricia Neal (Guest Hostess).

Omnibus, CBS, "Salome," 90 minutes, December 18, 1955. Producer, Robert Saudek; director, John Stix; based on the play *Salome* by Oscar Wilde, adapted for television by Ellen Violett; original music, Leonard Bernstein; set director, Henry May; lighting director, Imero Fiorentino; choral director, Merrill Staton; casting, Joe Scully. *Cast:* Eartha Kitt (Salome), Leo Genn (Herod), Patricia Neal (Herodius), Martin Landau (Jokanaan/John the Baptist), Mario Alcade (Captain of the Guards), Salvatore Mineo (Guard's brother).

Matinee Theatre, NBC, "The Good-Time Boys," 60 minutes, June 4, 1956. Producers, George Cahan, Fred Price, and Darrell Ross; executive producer, Albert McCleery; director, Arthur Hiller; written by Ira Avery; adapted for television by Nicholas E. Baehr; cinematography, Lester Shorr and Roger Sherman; casting, Lynn Stalmaster. *Cast:* Patricia Neal, Addison Richards, John Conte (Show Host).

Playhouse 90, CBS, "The Playroom," 90 minutes, October 10, 1957. Producer, Martin Margulis; executive producer, Peter Kortner; associate producer, Peter Kortner; director, Franklin Schaffner; written by Tad Mosel; story editor, Del Reisman; assistants to Mr. Margulis, Russell Stoneham and Dominick Dunne; art director, Albert Heschong; musical supervisor, Ed Dinstedter; cinematography, Joseph F. Biroc; makeup, Bus Westmore; hair stylist, Larry Germain. *Cast:* Tony Randall (Kenneth Rutherford), Nina Foch (Mrs. Dorothy Kelly), Patricia Neal (Mrs. Margaret Flood), Marilyn Erskine (Katherine "Kate" Rutherford), Charles Drake (George Rutherford), Mildred Dunnock (Mrs. Millie Rutherford), Nora Marlowe (Mrs. Beal), Lewis Martin (Toastmaster), Florida Friebus (Woman Reporter), Dennis King Jr. (Clerk), Therese Lyon (Messenger).

Suspicion, NBC, "Someone Is After Me," 60 minutes, January 6, 1958. Associate producer, Joan Harrison; executive producer, Alfred Hitchcock; director, David Greene; written by Robert Soderberg; original music, Dave Kahn; cinematography, John L. Russell and John F. Warren; editor, Edward W. Williams. *Cast:* Patricia Neal (Paula Elgin), Lee Bowman (Guy Elgin), Edward Andrews (Carl), Joanne Linville (Lois), Mary James (Miss Fenwick), Mary Perry (Mrs. Fenwick), Cec Linder (Lieutenant Green).

Playhouse 90, CBS, "The Gentleman from Seventh Avenue," 90 minutes, January 30, 1958. Producer, Martin Manulis; executive producer, Peter Kortner; associate producer, Peter Kortner; director, Alan Reisner; written by Elick Moll; story editor, Del Reisman; assistants to Mr. Margulis, Dominick Dunne and Russell Stoneham; art director, Albert Heschong; musical supervisor, Robert Drasnin; cinematography, Joseph F. Biroc; makeup, Bud Westmore; hair stylist, Larry Germain; Miss Neal's wardrobe, Women's Haberdashers; costumes, Lilli Ann; factory layout by Singer Sewing Machine Company. *Cast:* Walter Slezak (Mr. Golden), Patricia Neal (Rena Menken), Silvia Sydney (Mrs. Golden), Robert Alda (Morris Kogen), Judy Nugent (Jenny Golden), Leo Fuchs (Bianco), Lawrence Dobkin (Elbaum Golden), Joyce Jameson (Miss Cooper), Howard Dayton (Sidney), Don Washbrook (Marvin), Amanda Randolph (Gladys), Peggy Maley (Shelley), Carol Morris and Ingrid Goude "Miss Sweden" (Models), Dana Wynter (Show Hostess).

Studio One, CBS, "Tide of Corruption," 60 minutes, February 17, 1958. Producer, Worthington Miner; writer, Marc Brandel. *Cast*: Amanda Blake (Joan Roberts), Ray Danton (Callaghan), Patricia Neal (Caroline Mann), Barry Sullivan (Edward Roberts), Murvyn Vye (Mr. Antony).

Sunday-Night Theatre, BBC, "Biography," 120 minutes, June 22, 1958. Producer, John Jacobs; director, Barry Learoyd; written by S. N. Behrman; designed by Barry Learoyd. *Cast*: Vivian Matalon (Richard Kurt), Henzie Raeburn (Minnie), Ferdy Mayne (Melchior Feydak), Patricia Neal (Marion Froude), Gordon Sterne (Leander Nolan), Robert Perceval (Orrin Kinnicott), Betty McDowall (Slade Kinnicott), David Chivers (Stand-In for Mr. Perceval).

Sunday-Night Theatre, BBC, "The Royal Family of Broadway," 120 minutes, August 3, 1958. Producer, Eric Fawcett, director, Eric Fawcett; written by Edna Ferber and George S. Kaufman based on their play, *The Royal Family*; designed by Guy Sheppard; dogs supplied by Mrs. Jane Russell Darroch; duel arranger, Terry Baker; photocall artist, Derek Sidney; off-camera pianist, Winifred Taylor. *Cast*: Fay Compton (Fanny Cavendish), Patricia Neal (Julia Cavendish), Peter Wyngarde (Tony Cavendish), Clive Morton (Herbert Dean), Gareth Jones (Oscar Wolfe), Jon Farrell (Gilbert Marshall), Mario Lorenzo (Gunga), Eira Heath (Gwen Cavendish), Brenda Dunrich (Della), Sidney Keith (Jo).

Pursuit, CBS "The Silent Night," 60 minutes, December 24, 1958. Producer, Charles Russell; director, Buzz Kulik; written by Paul Monash. *Cast*: Lew Ayres (John Conrad), Patricia Neal (Mrs. Conrad), Frank Lovejoy (Dr.), Victor Jory (Cop), Eduard Franz, Steven Hill.

Clash by Night, BBC, 90 minutes, July 7, 1959. Producer and director, John Jacobs; designed by Reece Pemberton; based on the play by Clifford Odets; concertina composition, Alfred Edwards. *Cast*: Nehemiah Persoff (Jerry Wilenski), Neil McCarthy (Joe Doyle), Patricia Neal (Mae Wilenski), Suzanne Finlay (Peggy Coffee), Sam Wanamaker (Earl Pfeiffer), Sean Sullivan (Vincent Kress), Arnold Marle (Jerry's Father), Paddy Joyce (Waiter).

Play of the Week, Channel 13, "Strindberg on Love," 120 minutes, January 25, 1960. Producer, Lewis Freedman; executive producer, David Susskind; director, Henry Kaplan; adapted for television by George Tabori, based on *Miss Julie* and *The Stronger* by August Strindberg, translated by Arvid Paulson; set designer, William Bohnert; art director, Myron Bleam; costumes, Michael Travis; makeup, Inez Lopardo; music, Ronnie Noll; production supervisor, Buddy Wilds; an NTA Production in association with Talent Associates. *Miss Julie* cast: Lois Smith (Miss Julie), Robert Loggia (Jean), Madeleine Sherwood (Kristin); *The Stronger* cast: Nancy Wickwire (Mrs. X), Patricia Neal (Amelia/Miss Y), Patricia Neal (Hostess).

Play of the Week, Channel 13, "The Magic and the Loss," 120 minutes, February 20, 1961. Producer, Lewis Freedman, executive producer, David Susskind; director, Richard Dunlap; written by Julian Funt based on his play; set designer, William Bohnert; art director, Myron Bleam; costumes, Michael Travis; makeup, Inez Lopardo; music, Ronnie Noll; production supervisor, Buddy Wilds, an NTA Production in association with Talent Associates. *Cast*: Patricia Neal (Grace Wilson), Jeffrey Lynn (George Wilson), Vicki Cummings (Anita Harmon), Patrick O'Neal (Larry Graves), Frederick Clarke (Nicki Wilson).

Purex Special for Women, NBC, "Mother and Daughter," 60 minutes, March 9, 1961. Producer, George Lefferts; director, George Lefferts; written by George Lefferts. *Cast*: Patricia Neal (Ruth Evans), Lynn Loring (Jeannie Evans), Arthur Hill (Philip Evans), Pauline Frederick (Hostess-Narrator), Trude Lash.

Rendezvous, ITV, "London-New York," 30 minutes, August 23, 1961. Producer, Edwin K. Knopf; associate producer, Dennis O'Dell; director, Fletcher Markle; cinematography,

Geoffrey Faithfull and Brendon J. Stofford; a Rapallo Pictures Ltd. production. *Cast*: Charles Drake (John Burden), Patricia Neal (Kate Merlin), Peter O'Toole (John), Pamela Alan (Miss Kit), George Patterson (Elderly Man), Max Faulkner (Official), Audrey Nicholson (Miss Sloan), Virginia Bedard (Elderly Woman), Reginald Hearne (Passenger), Moira Lynd (Hysterical Woman).

Drama '62, ATV, "The Days and Nights of Beebee," 60 minutes, January 14, 1962. Director, Philip Wiseman; based on the play *The Days and Nights of Beebee Fenstermaker* by William Hartwell Snyder Jr., adapted for television by William Hartwell Snyder Jr.; designed by Vic Symonds. *Cast*: Patricia Neal (Beebee Fenstermaker), Brandon Brady (Bob Smith), Angela Browne (Nettie Jo Repult), Ronald Allen (Tommy Prince).

Checkmate, CBS, "The Yacht Club Gang" 60 minutes, January 31, 1962. Producer, Dick Berg; associate producer, Dorothy Hechtlinger; director, Alex Singer; written by Robert Shaw; original music, Pete Rugolo; "Checkmate Theme" by Johnny Williams; art director, John J. Lloyd; set directors, John McCarthy, James J. Walters; editor, Howard Epstein; cinematography, William Margulies; assistant director, Carter de Haven III; sound, Corson Jowett; costumes, Burton Miller; makeup, Leo Lotito; hair stylist, Florence Bush; casting director, Vincent Dee; created by Eric Ambler. *Cast*: Anthony George (Don Corey), Doug McClure (Jed Sills), Sebastian Cabot (Carl Hyatt), Patricia Neal (Fran Davis), John Baragrey (Mitchell Kane), Stephen Franken (Dunc Tomlinson), Lucy Prentis (Martha Kane), John Astin (Jim Poole), Paul Tripp (Dean Phillips).

The Untouchables, ABC, "The Maggie Storm Story," 60 minutes, March 29, 1962. Producer, Del Reisman; associate producer, Vincent McEveety; executive producer, Alan Armer; director, Stuart Rosenberg; "The Untouchables Theme" by Nelson Riddle; art directors, Rolland M. Brooks and Howard Hollander; set director, Harry Gordon; costumes, Frank Delmar; makeup, Kiva Hoffman; hair stylist, Lorraine Roberson; cinematographer, Charles Straumer; sound, S. G. Haughton and Glen Glenn Sound Co.; editor, Robert Watts; casting, Stalmaster-Lister Co.; executive in charge of production, Jerry Thorpe; Desilu Productions Inc. and Langford Productions Inc. *Cast*: Robert Stack (Elliot Ness), Paul Picerni (Lee Hobson), Patricia Neal (Maggie Storm), Vic Morrow (Vincent Shine), John Kellogg (Lucky Quinn), Joseph Ruskin (Lewis "Lepke" Buchalter), Frank de Kova (The Man).

Westinghouse Presents, CBS, "That's Where the Town Is Going," 60 minutes, April 17, 1962. Director, Jack Smight; written by Tad Mosel. *Cast*: Kim Stanley (Wilma Sills), Patricia Neal (Ruby Sills), Jason Robards Jr. (Hobart Cramm), Buddy Ebsen (George Prebble).

Winter Journey, BBC, 60 minutes, October 19, 1962. Producer, John Jacobs; director, John Jacobs; based on the play *The Country Girl* by Clifford Odets; designed by Barry Learoyd. *Cast*: Eddie Albert (Frank Elgin), Patricia Neal (Georgie Elgin), Sam Wanamaker (Bernie Dodd), Chuck Julian (Assistant Stage Manager), Jared Allen (Paul Unger), Alan Gifford (Phil Cook), Guy Kingsley Poynter (Larry), Sonia Fox (Nancy Stoddard).

Zero One, BBC, "Return Trip," 60 minutes, November 28, 1962. Producer, Lawrence P. Bachmann; associate producer, Aida Young; director, George Pollack; written by David T. Chandler. *Cast*: Nigel Patrick (Alan Garnett), Patricia Neal (Margo), Bill Nagy (Mike Stacey), Robert McKenzie (Steve Mailer), Robert O'Neill (Davis).

Ben Casey, ABC, "My Enemy Is a Bright Green Sparrow," 60 minutes, April 29, 1963. Producer, Matthew Rapf; associate producer, John Laird; executive producer, John E. Pommer; director, Robert Butler; assistant director, Gilbert Mandelik; written by Barry Oringer; story editor, Fred Frieberger; "Ben Casey Theme" by David Raskin; art director, Rolland R. Brooks; set director, John Sturtevant; costumes, Oscar Rodriguez; makeup, E. Thomas

Case; hair stylist, Gale McGarry; cinematography, Ted Voightlander; sound, Vic Appel; editor, Al Clark, Bruce Schoengarth; sound, Glen Glenn Co.; casting, Stalmaster-Lister Co.; a Bing Crosby Production in association with Desilu Productions Inc. *Cast*: Vincent Edwards (Dr. Ben Casey), Sam Jaffe (Dr. David Zorba), Patricia Neal (Dr. Louise Chappelle, M.D.), John Larch (Robert Anderson), Harry Landers (Dr. Ted Hoffman), Bettye Ackermann (Dr. Maggie Graham), Jeanne Bates (Miss Wells), Nick Dennis (Nick Cavanaugh), Marcel Dalio (Dr. Ernest Joffe).

Espionage, ITV, "The Weakling," 60 minutes, October 19, 1963. Producer, George Justin; executive producer, Herbert Hirschman; director, Stuart Rosenberg; written by Arnold Perl; original music, Malcolm Arnold; cinematographer, Geoffrey Faithfull. *Cast*: Dennis Hopper (Joe Ferno), Patricia Neal (Dr. Jeanne Termoille), John Gregson (Colonel Trevor Ballin), Steve Plytas (Handler), Robert Avon (Medical Officer), Robert Henderson (U.S. General).

Ghost Story, NBC, "Time of Terror," 60 minutes, December 22, 1972. Producer, Joel Rogosin; executive producer, William Castle; director, Robert Day; written by Jimmy Sangster, based on the story "Traveling Companion" by Elizabeth Walter; developed for television by Richard Matheson; music, Billy Goldberg and Robert Prince; "Ghost Story Theme" by Billy Goldberg; art directors, Ross Bellah and Carr Odell; set director, Stuart Reiss; makeup supervisor, Ben Lane; cinematography, Emmett Bergholz; editor, John Sheets; a William Castle production. *Cast*: Craig Stevens (Brett, Assistant Hotel Manager), Patricia Neal (Ellen Alexander), Alice Ghostley (Betty Carter), Elliott Montgomery (Harry Alexander), Doug Henderson (George Carter), Mark Tapscott (Security Guard), Frank Whiteman (Desk Clerk).

Kung Fu, ABC, "Blood of the Dragon: Parts One and Two," 120 minutes, September 14, 1974. Producers, Herman Miller and Alex Beaton; executive producer, Jerry Thorpe; director, Richard Lang; written by John T. Dugan; developed for television by Herman Miller; art director, Gene Lourie; set director, John D. W. Lamphear; costumes, Henry Salley; makeup, Michael A. Hanck; original music composed and conducted by Jim Helms; cinematography, Chuck Arnold; editors, Joseph T. Dervin and Gary Griffen; sound, Dean Salmon; kung fu advisor, Kam Yuen; stunt coordinator, Greg Walker; created by Ed Speilman. *Cast*: David Carradine (Kwai/Chang Caine), Keye Luke (Master Po), Philip Ahn (Master Kan), Radames Pera (Caine as a Youth), Patricia Neal (Sara Kingsley), Season Hubley (Margot Kingsley McLean), Edward Albert (Johnny Kingsley McLean), Eddie Albert (Dr. George Baxter), Tom Reese (Sheriff), Dean Jagger (Henry Raphael, Grandfather).

Little House on the Prairie, NBC, "Remember Me: Part One," 60 minutes, November 5, 1974; "Remember Me: Part Two," 60 minutes, November 12, 1974. Producer, John Hawkins; associate producer, Kent McCray; co-producer, B. W. Sandefur; executive producer, Michael Landon; director, Michael Landon; developed for television by Blanche Hanalis; based on the Little House series of books by Laura Ingalls Wilder; written by Michael Landon; art director, Walter M. Jeffries; set director, Don Webb; music director, David Rose; women's costumes, Richalene Kelsay; men's costumes, Andy Matyasi; makeup, Allan Snyder; hair stylist, Larry Germain; cinematographer, Ted Voigtlander; editor, Jerry Taylor; sound, Glen Glenn Sound; in association with Ed Friendly. *Cast*: Michael Landon (Charles Ingalls), Karen Grassle (Caroline Ingalls), Melissa Gilbert (Laura Ingalls), Melissa Sue Anderson (Mary Ingalls), Lindsay/Sidney Greenbush (Carrie Ingalls), Dabbs Greer (Reverend Robert Alden), Katherine MacGregor (Harriet Oleson), Victor French (Isaiah Edwards), Bonnie Bartlett (Grace Snider), Radames Pera (John Sanderson Jr.),

Patricia Neal (Julia Sanderson), Brian Part (Carl Sanderson), Kyle Richards (Alicia Sanderson), Jim Goodwin (Tyler), Sheldon Allman (Jason Anders).

Movin' On, NBC, "Prosperity One," 60 minutes, November 18, 1975. Producer, Ernie Frankel; executive producers, Philip D'Antoni and Barry Weitz; director, Corey Allen; written by Ron Bishop; music, Earle Hagen; "Movin' On Theme" written and performed by Merle Haggard; costumes, Ken Hanley; makeup, John Alese; cinematography, Jack Priestley; sound, Larry Hadsell and Hal Watkins; vice president in charge of production, William C. Snyder; created by Barry Weitz and Philip D'Antoni; a D'Antoni/Weitz Television production. *Cast*: Claude Akins (Sonny Pruitt), Frank Converse (Will Chandler), Patricia Neal (Mady Staton), Gary Merrill (Sampson Eubanks), Tessa Dahl (Haley Eubanks), George Murdock (Cap Delph), Lesley Wood (Mina Eubanks), William Smith (Frank Stone).

Murder, She Wrote, CBS, "Murder in F Sharp," 60 minutes, December 16, 1990. Producer, Robert Van Scoyk; supervising producer, Robert F. O'Neill; executive producer, Peter S. Fischer; associate producer, Anthony J. Magro; director, Kevin G. Cremin; written by William Bigelow; production designer, Hub Braden; costume supervisors, Robert Eli Bodeford Jr., Nick Mezzanotti, and Deborah Orrico; music, Richard Markowitz; "Murder, She Wrote Theme" by John Addison; set director, Robert Wingo; cinematographer, John Elsenbach; costumes, Sharon Day; makeup, Teresa M. Austin and Vera Yurtchuk; hair stylist, Rita Bellissimo Bordonaro; editor, John C. Horger; sound mixer, Don Sharpless; created by Peter S. Fischer, Richard Levinson, and William Link. *Cast*: Angela Lansbury (Jessica Beatrice McGill Fletcher), Ricardo Montalban (Vaaclav Maryska), Patricia Neal (Milena Maryska), Stephen Caffrey (Alex Seletz), James Sloyan (Robert Butler), Joe Dorsey (Ben Devlin), Keith Michell (Dennis Stanton), Melinda Culea (Nicole Gregory), Ken Swofford (Lieutenant Perry Catalano).

Television Documentaries and Specials

Good Company, ABC, 30 minutes, October 12, 1967. Executive Producer, David Susskind. *Cast*: F. Lee Bailey (Host), Patricia Neal, Roald Dahl.

Life, Death and the American Woman, ABC, 60 minutes, April 27, 1972. Producer, Laurence D. Salvador; executive producer, Alan Lansburg; written by Laurence D. Salvador; music, Harry Sukman; cinematographer, Jim Arnold; editor, Ken Plokin. *Cast*: Patricia Neal (Narrator).

The Hollywood Greats, "Gary Cooper," BBC, 60 minutes, August 25, 1977. Producer, Barry Brown; executive producer, Barry Norman; director, Margaret Sharp; written by Barry Norman; editor, Colin Rae. *Cast*: Barry Norman (Presenter), Patricia Neal, Maria Cooper Janis, Henry Hathaway, Helen Hayes, Howard Hawks, Delmar Daves, Princess Grace of Monaco, Joe Hyams, Stanley Kramer.

Comeback, CBS, 30 minutes, September 22, 1979. Producer, Richard Arlatt; executive producer, Lawrence Jacobson; director, Paul C. Morgan; written by Paul C. Morgan; Maramy Productions and American International Television. *Cast*: James Whitmore (Host), Patricia Neal, Roald Dahl, Valerie Eaton Griffith, Tessa Dahl.

This Other Eden, KET, 240 minutes, May 19–21, 1980. Producers, Dorothy Peterson and Tim Ward; associate producers, Jody Hein and Luralyn Lahr; director, Tim Ward; written by Steven A. Channing; art director, Skip Taylor; set directors, Tay Breen and Lynn Cooper; costume design and makeup, Jo Motsinger; original music, David Ott; videography, Marta Penticuff; sound, Mike Puckett; editor, James Walker. *Cast*: Patricia Neal (Narrator).

The Way We Were, syndicated, 120 minutes, February 1981. Producers, Bob Banner and Gerald Freedman; executive producer, Bob Banner; directors, Clark Jones and Tim Kiley; written by Marty Farrell; original music, Larry Grossman; song "In The Beginning" by Larry Grossman, lyrics, and Sheldon Harnick, music. *Cast:* Dick Tufeld (Announcer); Claude Akins, Ann-Margret, Richard Benjamin, Candice Bergen, Robert Conrad, Nancy Dussault, Penny Fuller, Charlton Heston, Ron Husmann, Carol Lawrence, Cloris Leachman, Garry Marshall, Sherrill Milnes, Patricia Neal, Jerry Orbach, Paula Prentiss, Charlotte Rae, Robert Reed, Tony Roberts, McLean Stevenson, Peter Strauss.

The Nature of Things, "Bring Back My Bonnie," CBC, 60 minutes, 1981. *Cast:* Patricia Neal (Narrator).

20/20 The Barbara Walters Special, ABC, 60 minutes, November 26, 1981. Producer, Joann Goldberg; executive producer, Don Mischer; director, Don Mischer; editors, Andy Zall and Ken Denisoff. *Cast:* Barbara Walters (Hostess); Ronald Reagan and Nancy Reagan (guests), Michael Reagan, Maureen Reagan, Ron Reagan Jr., Pat O'Brien, Patricia Neal, Ginger Rogers, George Murphy (interviewed).

How Long You Gonna Be Gone? PBS, 30 minutes, 1993. Producer, Larry Winchester; director, Bill Terry of University of Tennessee Audio Services; videography, Larry Winchester; Click and Wheel Productions. *Cast:* Patricia Neal (Narrator).

Biography, "Andy Griffith: Hollywood's Homespun Hero," A&E, 58 minutes, September 1, 1997. Producer, Torrie Rosenzweig; supervising producer, Kim Egan; A&E supervising producer, Carolanne Dolan; associate producer, Gidion Phillips; executive producer, Kevin Burns; A&E executive producer, Michael Cascio; director, Torrie Rosenzweig; written by Jerry Decker; editor, Abby Schwarzwalder; camera, Sandy Spooner, James Mulryan, Art Howard, and Keith Silverman; sound, Mark Lyons, Jay Brothers, Ben Turney, and Alex Batenko; music, Tom Jenkins and Chris Many; the theme song from "The Andy Griffith Show" by Earl Hagen, courtesy of the Harry Fox Agency; coordinating producer, Sophie Levy; Van Ness Films in association with Foxstar Productions, Twentieth Television, and A&E. *Cast:* Peter Graves (Host); Andy Griffith, Don Knotts, Patricia Neal, Roddy McDowall, Emmett Forrest, Lorraine Beasley Gilley, Ron Howard, R. G. Armstrong, Danny Thomas (archival footage), Jamie Smith Jackson (archival footage), Dan Roebuck.

Hollywood Aliens and Monsters, Sci-Fi Channel, 120 minutes, November 7–9, 1997. Producer, Kim Egan; associate producer, David A. Kleiler Jr.; director, Kevin Burns; editors, David Comtois and Peter Gust; sound rerecording mixer German Version, Heiko Muller. *Cast:* Mark Hamill (Host), interviews with Robert Wise, Patricia Neal, Robert Clarke, Gene Barry, Ann Robinson, David Hedison, Barbara Eden, Saul David, Arthur C. Clarke (archival footage), Charlton Heston, George Lucas, Veronica Cartwright, Sigourney Weaver (archival footage), David Cronenberg (archival footage), James Cameron (archival footage), Dean Devlin, Bill Pullman.

Biography, "Gary Cooper: Face of A Hero," A&E, 58 minutes, March 17, 1998. Producers, Gene Feldman, Suzette Winter; associate producer, Lisa Ann Everson; executive producer, Stephen Janson; A & E supervising producer, Carolanne Dola; A&E executive producer, Machael Cascio; director, Gene Feldman; written by Gene Feldman; music, Richard Fiocca; "Gary Cooper Theme" by Byron Janis; instrumentalist, Harvey Kay; cinematography, Matthew Ransom; editor, Matthew Ransom; sound mixer, Michael Ruschak; Wompat Productions Inc. in association with Janson Associates. *Cast:* Peter Graves (Narrator), Maria Cooper Janis, Edward Dmytryk, Jane Greer, Charlton Heston, James Hill, A. C. Lyles, Joan Leslie, Jim Mahoney, Jeffrey Meyers, Patricia Neal, Peter Mark Richman, George C. Scott, Walter Seltzer.

An Awfully Big Adventure, BBC, 50 minutes, March 7, 1998. Producer, Donald Sturrock; executive producer, Robert Warr; director, Donald Sturrock; production manager, Elizabeth Flowers; art director, Robin Rawstorme; original music, Peter Ash; rostrum camera, Ken Morse; editor, Clare Palmer; series narrator, Juliet Aubrey; sound, Brian Buffen, Dave Brabandts, and William Tzouriss; Music Link International Production for BBC & NVC Arts. *Cast*: Harriet Walker (Narrator), John Wilkinson, Roald Dahl (archival footage), Ophelia Dahl, Patricia Neal, Felicity Dahl, Clover Kelly, Luke Kelly, Else Logsdail, Asta Anderson, Alfhild Hansen, Dr. Edmund Goodman, Sonia Austrian, Amanda Conquy, Ian Maschler, Quentin Blake, Ian Holm, Ben Reuss.

E! Celebrity Profile, "Patty Duke," E! Network, 60 minutes, April 21, 1999. Producer, Edward Boyd; associate producer, Andrea Janalas; executive producer, Greg Snegaraff; executive in charge of production, John Rieber. *Cast*: John Meyer (Narrator), Patty Duke, Sean Astin, Mackenzie Astin, William Schallert, Patricia Neal, Paul O'Keefe, Eddie Applegate, Ray Duke, Sonny Fox, Bob Banner, Richard Crenna.

Conversations with Remarkable People, "Mother Dolores Hart," Wisdom Television, 50 minutes, April 14, 2000. Producers, Karen G. Cadle, Gary Bernstein, and Tito Romero; executive producer, Sheila Shayson; editor, Hamid Bayan; cinematography, Tony Pagano and Mike Giovingo; sound, Rick Juliano and Jeff Hayash; executive in charge of production, Norma Scheck; 1.4.3. Productions. *Cast*: Chantal Westerman (Hostess); Reverend Mother Dolores Hart, Patricia Neal.

The Android Prophecy: A History of Robots in Film, Atlantic Celtic Film Partnership, 60 minutes, September 22, 2001. Producer, Piers Bizony; director, Jamie Doran. *Cast*: Tom Baker (Narrator); interviews with Ridley Scott, Steven Speilberg, Brian Aldiss, Billy Mumy, Rutger Hauer, Anne Francis, Patricia Neal, Anthony Daniels, Arthur C. Clarke.

Gary Cooper and Patricia Neal, Striana Productions, 26 minutes, 2003. Producer, Antoine Disle; director, Laurent Preyale; written by Laurent Preyale. *Cast*: Gary Cooper, Patricia Neal.

The John Garfield Story, Turner Classic Movies, 60 minutes, February 3, 2003. Producers, Joan Kramer and David Heeley; executive producers, Turner Entertainment, George Feltenstein, Roger Mayer, and Tom Brown; supervising producer, Melissa Roller; coordinating producer, Lynda Sheldon; director, David Heeley; written by Joan Kramer and David Heeley; original music, Michael A. Levine and Mark Suozzo; makeup, Kara Crean Raynaud; hair stylist, Kara Crean Raynaud; cinematography, Michael Barry and Mark Zavad; sound, Michael Scott Goldbaum and Keith Winner; Top Hat Production. *Cast*: Julie Garfield (Narrator), John Garfield (archival footage), Ellen Adler, Joseph Bernard, Phoebe Brand, Michael Coppola, James Cromwell, Hume Cronym, Richard Dreyfuss, Julie Garfield, Danny Glover, Lee Grant, Harvey Keitel, Norman Lloyd, Patricia Neal, Martin Scorsese, Richard Sklar, Joanne Woodward, Richard Nixon (archival footage), Harry Cohn (archival footage), Isaac Stern (archival footage), J. Parnell Thomas (archival footage), Jack L. Warner (archival footage), Franz Waxman (archival footage).

Private Screening, "Patricia Neal," Turner Classic Movies, 41 minutes, June 28, 2004. Producer, Dena Krupinsky; executive producer, Tom Brown; director, Sean Cameron; set director, Dan Riggs; wardrobe stylist, Holly Hadesty; makeup, Pat Seegers; hair stylist, Jean Young; camera operators, Pam Ritzie, Ralph Prado, Andy Ransom, and Cybele Washington; sound designers, Kevin Sems and Brian Rio; editors, Gary Slawitschka, Myron Vasquez, Dan Monro, and Tim Garner; Turner Classic Movies, a Time Warner Company. *Cast*: Robert Osborne (Host), Patricia Neal.

Facing the Past, Warner Brothers, 29 minutes, May 10, 2005. *Cast*: Leo Braudy, Anthony Franciosa, Patricia Neal, Andy Griffith, Louis B. Mayer (archival footage), Budd Schulberg, Jeff Young.

Imagine, "The Fantastic Mr. Dahl," BBC, 50 minutes, June 22, 2005. Producer, John Birdcut; director, John Birdcut; editors, Andy Matthews and Henry Trotter (aka Franklin Franklin). *Cast*: Roald Dahl (archival footage), Quentin Blake, Felicity Dahl, Patricia Neal, Tessa Dahl, Theo Dahl, Ophelia Dahl, Lucy Dahl, Sophie Dahl, Luke Kelly, Valerie Eaton Griffith.

Award and Tribute Television Appearances

15th Annual Tony Awards, CBS, Waldorf-Astoria Hotel Ballroom, New York, 53 minutes, April 16, 1961.

36th Annual Academy Awards, ABC, Santa Monica Civic Auditorium, Santa Monica, California, 120 minutes, April 14, 1964. Patricia Neal was seen in a prerecorded film clip. She won the Best Actress Oscar for *Hud*.

37th Annual Academy Awards, ABC, Santa Monica Civic Auditorium, Santa Monica, California, 120 minutes, April 5, 1965. Patricia Neal was not seen on this telecast. She should have presented the Oscar to the Best Actor winner, Rex Harrison, that year. Bob Hope announced that she could not appear in person.

British Academy Film Awards, BBC, Grosvenor Hotel, London, England, 60 minutes, March 23, 1966. *With*: James Mason (Announcer); Leslie Caron (Presenter), Michael Crawford, Patricia Neal, Michael Scott, Julie Christie, Dirk Bogarde, Frederic Raphael, Ray Simm, Judi Dench.

38th Annual Academy Awards, ABC, Santa Monica Civic Auditorium, Santa Monica, California, 120 minutes, April 18, 1966. Patricia Neal appeared in a filmed segment recounting her Oscar win.

39th Annual Academy Awards, ABC, Santa Monica Civic Auditorium, Santa Monica, California, 120 minutes, April 10, 1967. Patricia Neal presented Claude Lalouche an Oscar for Best Foreign Film.

41st Annual Academy Awards, ABC, Dorothy Chandler Pavillion, Los Angeles, California, 180 minutes, April 14, 1969.

British Screen Awards/ Gala Night for Television and Film, BBC, London, England, 60 minutes, March 4, 1971. *With*: Richard Attenborough (Host); The Princess Royal Anne (Award Presenter), Dustin Hoffman, Peter Sellers, John Mills, Morecambe and Wise, Mia Farrow, Judy Garland, Margaret Tyzack, Barbara Murray, Sacha Distel, Patricia Neal, Young Generation (Dancers).

This Is Your Life, "Patricia Neal," BBC, 30 minutes, November 22, 1978. Producer, Jack Crawshaw; program associate, Kay Bird; directors, Royston Mayoh and Terry Yarwood; written by John Sandilands; wardrobe supervisor, Pat North; makeup supervisor, Jeannie MacKenzie; created by Ralph Edwards; researched by Debbie Grant and Maurice Leonard; Thames Television Color Production. *With*: Eamonn Andrews (Presenter); Roald Dahl, Patricia Neal, Mrs. Eura Neal, George and Margaret Ann Vande Noord, W. Pete Neal, Dame Wendy Hiller, Elaine Stritch, Patricia Medina, Joseph Cotton, Kenneth Haigh, Tessa Dahl, Theo Dahl, Ophelia Dahl, Lucy Dahl, Valerie Eaton Griffith, Emily Mahan Faust, Marius Goring, Richard Greene, Wally Saunders, Else Logsdail, Alfhild Hansen, Asta Anderson, Marjorie Clipstone, Pam Lawndes, Frankie Conquy, Brigadier Dick and Patricia Kirwan, Angela Hogg, Jae Faye, Helen Horton, Audrey Rae-Smith; Sophie Dahl, Dr. Charles Carton, John Wayne, Kirk Douglas (special taped segments).

35th Annual Tony Awards, CBS, Mark Hellinger Theatre, New York, 120 minutes, June 7, 1981. Patricia Neal was a presenter.

34th Annual Emmy Awards, ABC, Pasadena Civic Center, Pasadena, California, 118 minutes, September 19, 1982.

Your Choice for the Film Awards, syndicated, Coconut Grove, Los Angeles, California, 60 minutes, 1983. *With*: Lee Majors, Brook Shields (Hosts); Patricia Neal, Patty Duke (Presenters).

50th American Presidential Inaugural Gala, ABC, Washington, D.C., 60 minutes, January 19, 1985. Producers, Michael B. Seligman and Frank Sinatra; executive producers, Dwight Hemion, Gary Smith; director, Dwight Hemion; written by Buz Kohan; music directors, Nelson Riddle and Dr. Arthur C. Bartner; choral directors, John B. Talley and Norman Scribner; choreography, Jim Bates. *With*: Frank Sinatra (Host); Pearl Bailey, Mikhail Baryshnikov, Beach Boys, Mac David, Ray Charles, Michael Davis, Larry Gatlin and the Gatlin Brothers, Crystal Gayle, Merv Griffin, Charlton Heston, Emmanuel Lewis, Rich Little, Dean Martin, Patricia Neal, New York City Breakers, Tony Randall, Lou Rawls, Don Rickles, Tom Selleck, James Stewart, Jill St. John, Donna Summer, Mr. T., Elizabeth Taylor, Frederica Van Stade, Robert Wagner.

Seventh Annual American Cinema Awards, syndicated. Los Angeles, California, 60 minutes, January 27, 1990. Producer, David Guest. *With*: Lauren Bacall, Sophia Loren, Elizabeth Taylor (Presenters); Jane Fonda, Farley Granger, Celeste Holm, Whitney Houston, Tab Hunter, Jermaine Jackson, Van Johnson, Roddy McDowall, Patricia Neal, Maureen O'Sullivan, Ruth Warrick, Andy Williams, Shelley Winters, James Woods, Teresa Wright; Michael Jackson, Gregory Peck.

American Film Institute Tribute to Kirk Douglas, CBS, Los Angeles, California, 120 minutes, May 23, 1991. Producer, George Stevens Jr.; associate producer, Michael B. Seligman; director, Louis J. Horvitz; associate director, Allan Kartum; written by Bob Schrum and George Stevens Jr.; art director, Romaine Johnston; music, Nelson Riddle; editor, Randall MacLowry; audio, Ed Greene; gala coordinator, Jackie Frame; production of the American Film Institute. *With*: Kirk Douglas, Michael Douglas (Host); Lauren Bacall, Dana Carvey, Tom Cruise, Danny DeVito, Angie Dickinson, Richard Harris, Karl Malden, Patricia Neal, Jean Simmons, Sylvester Stallone.

50th Annual Tony Awards, CBS, Majestic Theatre, New York, 120 minutes, June 2, 1996. Producer, Walter C. Miller; executive producer, Gary Smith; supervising producer, Roy A. Somlyo; director, Walter C. Miller; written by Thomas Meehan; musical director, Elliott Lawrence; choreographer, Walter Painter. Nathan Lane (Host); Patricia Neal was a presenter.

70th Annual Academy Awards, ABC, 180 minutes, Los Angeles, March 23, 1998. Billy Crystal (Host); Patricia Neal was among the "Salute to Past Winners."

American Film Institute Tribute to Robert Wise, NBC, Los Angeles, California, 120 minutes, July 7, 1998. Producer, Michael Stevens; associate producer, Charles F. Haykel; executive producer, George Stevens Jr.; director, Louis J. Horvitz; written by Robert Shrum, Chris Henchy, and George Stevens Jr.; Miss Neal's speech written by Warren Langton; main title and theme composed by Dennis McCarthy; production designer, Rene Legler; editor, Michael Polito; audio, Doug Nelson; cameras, Ted Ashton, John Burdick, Tom Green, Larry Heider, Bill Philbin, David Plakos, Hector Ramirez, and Manny Rodriguez; New Liberty Productions. *With*: Robert Wise (Honoree); Julie Andrews (Hostess); Peter Fonda, Patricia Neal, Leonard Nimoy, Rita Moreno, Candice Bergen, Charles Durning, Theodore Bikel, Christopher Plummer, Jack Lemmon, George Chakiris, Ernst Borgnine,

Tovah Borgnine, William Shatner, James Cameron, Gregory Peck, Red Buttons, John Sayles, Marvin Hamlisch, Oliver Stone.

75th Annual Academy Awards, ABC, 210 minutes, Kodak Theatre, Los Angeles, California, March 23, 2003. Steve Martin (Host); Patricia Neal was among those in the "Salute to Past Winners."

Selected Miscellaneous Programs

Hollywood Calling (NBC)	July 1949
Association of American Artists (KNBH), Los Angeles	August 4, 1949
Twenty Questions (Dumont)	1953
Tonight Show (BBC), British	April 14, 1964
The Merv Griffin Show (syndicated)	April 1966
This Morning (ABC)	March 4, 1968
The Tonight Show with Johnny Carson (NBC)	October 1968
The Dick Cavett Show (ABC)	October 1968
The Today Show (NBC)	October 1968
The Merv Griffin Show (syndicated)	October 1968
The Irv Kupcinet Show (syndicated), Chicago	October 1968
The Merv Griffin Show (syndicated)	1972
Russell Harty Plus (LWT)	January 13, 1973
Russell Harty Plus (LWT), British	January 1973
Front Page Challenge (CBC), Canadian	1973
What's My Line (Syndicated)	February 22, 1975
Good Company (ABC)	1978
Dinah! (Syndicated)	1978
Sonya, "Tribute to Paul Newman" (WDIV Detroit)	1982
CBS Evening News with Dan Rather (CBS)	January 21, 1983
National Stroke Campaign (BBC), British	June 3, 1986
Breakfast Time (BBC), British	June 3, 1986
The Today Show (NBC)	April 6, 1988
Desert Island Discs (BBC), British	April 14, 1988
Entertainment Tonight (syndicated)	November 5, 1988
WTNH-TV Evening News, "In the Spotlight" (ABC)	January 13, 1989
The Joe Franklin Show (WWOR-TV), New York	February 10, 1989
Good Morning America (ABC)	February 14, 1989
20/20 (ABC)	February 28, 1989
Best Talk in Town (WPIX), New York	December 20, 1989
One on One with John Tesh (NBC)	May 2, 1992
Turning Point (MET)	January 11, 1993
Quiet Triumphs (ODY)	1997

Lancaster and Company	1998
Behind the Scenes (AMC)	March 22, 1998
The Rosie O'Donnell Show (ABC)	March 26, 1999
NBC News Today (NBC)	September 7, 2000
The Byron Allen Show (syndicated)	2000
The Dog Days of Summer "Crime Dogs" (TCM)	August 2002
Hollywood at Home (HGTV)	March 21, 2003

Health-Related Films

Stroke Counter Stroke, 30 minutes, 1971. Producer, Allen Hooshire; director, John Ward; assistant director, Roger Duchovny; written by Roald Dahl; art director, Don Baer; set director, John Lamphear. *With*: Roald Dahl (Narrator), Patricia Neal, Valerie Eaton Griffith.

Including Me: Children with Disabilities, PBS, 60 minutes, September 15, 1977. Released by Capitol Cities Television Productions, Eastmancolor. Patricia Neal (Narrator).

The Unfinished Child, 30 minutes, late 1970s. Patricia Neal (Narrator). Filmed in Jersey City, New Jersey.

The Healing Influence: Guidelines for Stroke Families, Danamar, 20 minutes, 1990. Produced in association with the American Heart Association. Patricia Neal (Hostess). Received award from the National Educational Film/Video Festival as "the best film/video produced for training health professionals and caregivers" in 1990.

Moving Easy: Lift-Free Patient Transfers. Danamar, 15 minutes, 1990. Patricia Neal (Hostess); introduced by Carol Bernstein Lewis, PT, Ph.D.

Brain Attack: A New Way of Looking at Stroke, NTSC, 28 minutes, 1996. *With*: Patricia Neal, Jack Lemmon (Hosts).

After Words, Flag Day Productions, 55 minutes, 2003. Executive producers, Jerome H. Kaplan, Vincent Straggas; producer and director, Vincent Straggas; graphic design, Alison Kennedy, Bruce Walker; music, APM; audio mix, Richard Bock. Funding provided by Spaulding Rehabilitation Hospital. *With*: Patricia Neal, Julie Harris, Robert McFerrin, Bobby McFerrin, Jan Curtis, David Caplan, M.D., Ph.D., Leonard Zion, Herman Roman, Dr. Martha Taylor Sarno, Nancy Helm-Estabrook, Sc.D., Jerome H. Kaplan, M.A., CCC-SLP, Joel Stein, M.D., Rich Arsenault, Gloria S. Waters, Ph.D., John Roberts, Diane Parris M.S., CCC-SLP, and Annette Berger.

Notes

In addition to the publications cited in the bibliography, I have drawn on vast numbers of clippings, reviews, and memorabilia from Ms. Neal's personal archives, scrapbooks, files, and letters. Many of these clippings lack date and publication information, and I have quoted them rather sparingly. I have also used other archives and collections; their names and abbreviations used in the notes are listed below. In addition, I have conducted a number of interviews; in some instances, several people have recounted their own versions of various events. Over the course of many years, I have had numerous conversations with Ms. Neal; these are recorded to the best of my recollection.

Abbreviations

AMPAS	Margaret Herrick Library of Motion Picture Arts & Sciences, Los Angeles
BFI	British Film Institute, London
EMFC	Emily Mahan Faust Collection (private)
MOMA	Museum of Modern Art Film Library, New York
NYPL	New York Public Library of the Performing Arts
PNC	Patricia Neal Collection (private)
USCTV	University of Southern California Warner Brothers Cinema-TV Library and Jack Warner Archives
USCWB	University of Southern California Warner Brothers Archives, Los Angeles
VEGC	Valerie Eaton Griffith Collection (private)

Chapter 1. Beginnings

1. Jo Anne Sexton, letter to author (hereafter SMS), November 23, 2003.
2. Patricia Neal (hereafter PN), *As I Am* (New York: Simon & Schuster, 1988), 24.
3. "Pat Neal's Recall of the Wild," *Life*, June 16, 1967.
4. PN, *As I Am*, 21.
5. "Pat Neal's Recall of the Wild,"
6. PN, unpublished article, 1950, PNC.
7. PN, unpublished article, 1950, PNC.
8. PN, unpublished article, 1950, PNC.
9. PN, letter to William Coot Neal, n.d., PNC.
10. PN, *As I Am*, 35.
11. PN, *As I Am*, 37.
12. John Keating, "The Second Life of Patricia Neal," *Cosmopolitan*, May 1964, 52.

13. Emily Mahan Faust, interview by SMS, Knoxville, Tenn., July 23, 2003.

14. Betsy Morris, "Among Friends, A Star Was Born," *Knoxville News-Sentinel,* October 30, 1973.

15. PN, conversation with SMS, 2004.

16. Gloria Lucas Young, telephone interview by SMS, June 23, 2003.

17. Young interview.

18. *Patricia Readings*, "Movie Stars Parade," March–August 1951, 16.

19. "Valley Players Present Comedy," n.d., PNC.

20. Untitled review, n.d., PNC.

21. Keith Runyon, "The Class of '43 Remembers 'Patsy,'" *Louisville Courier-Journal,* May 24, 1973.

22. Runyon, "Class of '43 Remembers 'Patsy.'"

23. "New Personality Rises in Knoxville," *Louisville Courier-Journal,* March 29, 1942.

Chapter 2: Progress

1. Robert Porterfield, unpublished autobiography, Barter Theatre Archives, Abingdon, Va.

2. Porterfield, unpublished autobiography.

3. Elizabeth Wilson, interview by SMS, New York City, October 31, 2003.

4. PN, letter to Maude Mahan, n.d., PNC.

5. Wilson interview.

6. Gloria Lucas Young, telephone interview by SMS, June 23, 2003.

7. Untitled review, n.d., PNC.

8. Wilson interview.

9. Untitled review, n.d., PNC.

10. PN, *As I Am,* 42.

11. PN, *As I Am,* 50.

12. PN, *As I Am*, 41.

13. PN, *As I Am*, 47.

14. Vande Noord interview.

15. Lee Davis, "Patsy Neal's Father Saw Big Future," *Louisville Courier-Journal,* April 14, 1964.

16. *And Came the Spring* program, PNC.

17. Keating, "The Second Life of Patricia Neal," 52.

18. Margaret Ann Vande Noord, telephone interview by SMS, December 17, 2003.

19. Rhea Talley, "Kentucky Girl Is a Stage Star at 21," *Louisville Courier-Journal,* February 16, 1947.

20. Edwin Howard, "Class of '43 Honors Patricia Neal," *Memphis Press-Scimitar,* May 22, 1973.

21. Hedda Hopper, "She's Looking for a Gallant Gentleman," n.d. (c.1951), NYPL.

22. PN, letter to Eura Neal, n.d., PNC.

23. Lloyd L. Sloan, "The Past Can Be Awfully Dull, Says Patricia Neal," *Hollywood Citizen-News,* June 22, 1949.

24. Vande Noord interview.

25. Charlton Heston, *In the Arena* (New York: Simon & Schuster, 1995), 48.

26. James Goode, "Biography of Alvina Krause," (www.bte.org/ak2.htm), 2003.

27. PN interview, n.d., PNC.

28. Helen Horton, interview by SMS, New York, July 17, 2003.

29. Virginia Leimert, "The American Look," *Chicago Daily News*, n.d. (c.1945), PNC.

30. PN, *As I Am*, 54.

31. PN, *As I Am*, 54.

32. PN, conversation with SMS, 2004.

33. PN, unpublished speech, PNC.

34. Neal Weaver, "Alvina Krause: Teacher," *Ballroom Dance Magazine*, March 1968, 18.

35. "Uncle Harry Scores Hit," *Eagles Mere (Pa.) Eagle*, n.d., PNC.

36. PN, *As I Am*, 56.

37. PN, conversation with SMS, 2003.

38. PN, conversation with SMS, 2004.

39. Jen Heslie, "I Saw It Happen," n.d., PNC.

40. PN, conversation with SMS, 2004.

41. PN, conversation with SMS, 2004.

Chapter 3: Broadway

1. PN, *As I Am*, 60.

2. "Good Deal For Neal," *Screenland*, January 1949, 68.

3. PN, *As I Am*, 60.

4. Keating, "The Second Life of Patricia Neal," 53.

5. Louis Sheaffer, *O'Neill: Son and Artist* (Boston: Little, Brown, 1973), 498–99.

6. PN, *As I Am*, 64.

7. PN, *As I Am*, 66. Patricia wrote home to her mother and aunt Maude after the first of the year, "I can't begin to tell you how nice they [the cast] have been to me. They have helped me every inch of the way. Oh, yes, I signed my first autograph last night—I signed *two*."

8. Sheaffer, *O'Neill: Son and Artist*, 498–99.

9. PN, *As I Am*, 61.

10. Keating, "Second Life of Patricia Neal," 53.

11. Elie, untitled review, April 24, 1946, PNC.

12. PN, *As I Am*, 67.

13. *Devil Take a Whittler* playbill, PNC.

14. *Devil Take a Whittler* playbill, PNC.

15. Fred H. Russell, untitled review, n.d., PNC.

16. Untitled review, n.d., PNC.

17. Untitled article, n.d., PNC.

18. Untitled article, n.d., PNC.

19. PN, *As I Am*, 70.

20. PN, *As I Am*, 70.

21. Untitled article, n.d., PNC.

22. Christina Kirk, "Hollywood Rediscovers Patricia Neal," *Sunday News*, March 29, 1964.

23. PN, *As I Am*, 70.

24. PN, *As I Am*, 73.

25. Rex Reed, *Conversations in the Raw* (New York: Signet, 1969), 82. The next year (1970) in a *New York Tribune* interview with Reed, Patricia informed him, "I got into so much trouble with Richard Rodgers I don't think he will ever speak to me again. . . . I sent him a dozen roses, but he never spoke to me again."

26. PN, letter to Maude Mahan, n.d., PNC.

27. Carl Rollyson, *Lillian Hellman: Her Legend, and Her Legacy* (New York: St. Martins Press, 1988), 248.

28. William Wright, *Lillian Hellman: The Image, the Woman* (New York: Simon & Schuster, 1986), 206.

29. PN, *As I Am*, 75.

30. Lillian Hellman, *Pentimento* (New York, Signet, 1973), 163.

31. C.L.J., untitled review, n.d., PNC.

32. Ruth Anne Russell, "Play Portrays Greed, Hatred," *Baltimore Journal*, n.d., PNC.

33. Gilbert Kanour, "Theatre Goers," n.d., PNC.

34. Maynard Morris, letter to PN, November 6, 1946, PNC.

35. Richard Rodgers, letter to PN, November 3, 1946, PNC.

36. Eura Neal, unpublished interview transcript, n.d. (c. 1987), PNC. "I was so fidgety and excited when the curtain rose," Eura Neal told Andrew Sparks in the March 23, 1947, *Atlanta Journal*, "that I hardly got the gist of the play." To make certain she understood the play, Mrs. Neal attended another performance before she returned home.

37. Hector Arce, *Gary Cooper: An Intimate Biography* (New York: William Morrow, 1979), 222.

38. PN, *As I Am,* 76.

39. Robert Garland, "At Fulton, 'Another Part of the Forest,'" *New York Journal-American*, November 21, 1946.

40. Howard Barnes, "At Home with the Foxes," *New York Herald Tribune*, November 21, 1946.

41. Brooks Atkinson, "The Play," *New York Times*, November 21, 1946.

42. Margaret Vande Noord, *Patricia Readings,* March–August 1951, 16.

Chapter 4: Stock

Epigraph. Myrtle Gebhart, "Success Begins at 30," *Boston Post Magazine*, August 1, 1948.

1. Keating, "The Second Life of Patricia Neal," 58.

2. Gloria Stroock Stern, telephone interview by SMS, August 17, 2003.

3. Untitled article, April 3, 1949, MOMA.

4. John Snyder, "Elitch Cast Performs Admirably in 'Laura,'" *Denver Post*, June 30, 1947.

5. Richard Detwiler, "Elitch Cast Does 'Laura' Up Brown," *Rocky Mountain News*, n.d., PNC.

6. "Mrs. Mayfield, What's Marital Status of Elitch Players?" n.d., PNC.

7. PN, conversation with SMS, June 2005.

8. PN, conversation with SMS, June 2005.

9. PN, *As I Am*, 81.

10. PN, conversation with SMS, 2004.

11. John Snyder, "Neal Shines in Current Elitch Stage Production," *Denver Post*, August 4, 1947.

12. Along with Patricia Neal and Peter Cookson, the rest of the stock company from the fifty-sixth season of the Elitch Gardens Summer Theatre of 1947 included Katharine (sometimes spelled Katherine) Alexander, the sister-in-law of Alice Brady. Alexander was in the original Broadway production of *Letter to Lucerne* in 1941 and would appear with Patricia in her film debut the following year; Grant Gordon would appear in Patricia's comeback film in 1968; Helen Bonfils, whose father, Frederick, was the founder of the *Denver Post*, and along with her husband George Somnes had produced four unsuccessful plays on Broadway in the late 1930s, would later become a respected Broadway producer in her own right, produc-

ing such hits as *Sail Away* (1962), *The Killing of Sister George* (1966), and winning a Tony Award for Best Play for *Sleuth* (1971); Harry Mehaffey was a character actor in early television and film and would appear with Patricia in the road company of *Another Part of the Forest*; Joel Marston was best known as Owen Stratton in the TV soap opera *General Hospital*; Ellen Cobb-Hill, Elitch's stock ingénue that season, starred with Helen Hayes in the 1950 Broadway hit *Wisteria Trees*, directed by Joshua Logan, and would become an original cast member of the TV soap opera *The Secret Storm* in 1954; British actor Norman Budd was in Jack Kirkland's Broadway play *Tobacco Road* (1941); Barbara Alexander Brady made her Broadway debut in 1949 as Barbara Brady in *The Velvet Glove*, which was directed by Guthrie McClintic, husband of Katharine Cornell, and won Brady the 1950 Theatre World Award; and Craig Kelly, who would have a long career in such films as Clint Eastwood's *Dirty Harry* (1971).

13. PN, *As I Am*, 81.

14. PN conversation with SMS, 2004.

15. PN, *As I Am*, 77.

16. "Knoxville's Patricia Neal, New Broadway Star, Visits," *Knoxville News-Sentinel*, n.d., (c. 1947), PNC.

17. William T. Orr, telegram to Harry Mayer, November 24, 1947, PNC.

18. Orr telegram to Mayer, December 18, 1947, PNC.

19. PN, *As I Am*, 84.

Chapter 5: Warner Brothers

Epigraph. Gregg Swem, "Patricia Neal Sees Young Players Unearth Her Roots," *Knoxville Courier-Journal*, November 22, 1979.

1. PN, conversation with SMS, 2005.

2. Eric Stacey, interoffice memo to T. C. Wright, December 31, 1947, USCWB.

3. PN, *As I Am*, 90.

4. Jerry Wald, interoffice memo to PN, January 8, 1948, PNC.

5. PN, *As I Am*, 90.

6. Jerry Wald, interoffice memo to David Butler, January 13, 1948, USCWB.

7. PN, *As I Am*, 90.

8. Budd Schulberg, "Hollywood," *Holiday*, January 1949, 35.

9. USCWB.

10. *Hollywood Reporter*, untitled, n.d., PNC.

11. Gebhart, "Success Begins at 30."

12. Untitled article, n.d., PNC.

13. PN, *As I Am*, 92.

14. Sidney Skolsky, "Hollywood Is My Beat," n.d. (c. 1948), PNC.

15. Robert Stack, telephone interview by SMS, April 11, 2003.

16. PN, conversation with SMS, 2005.

17. Jeffrey Meyers, *Gary Cooper: American Hero* (New York: William Morrow, 1998), 216.

18. Meyers, *Gary Cooper: American Hero*, 216.

19. Michael Paxton, *Ayn Rand: A Sense of Life* (Layton, Utah: Gibbs Smith, 1998), 132.

20. Barbara Brandon, *The Passion of Ayn Rand* (New York: Doubleday, 1986), 207.

21. Hector Arce, *Gary Cooper: An Intimate Biography* (New York: William Morrow, 1979), 225.

22. Brandon, *The Passion of Ayn Rand*, 208.

23. Jerry Wald, letter to PN, June 10, 1948, PNC.

24. Merrill Schleier, "Ayn Rand and King Vidor's *The Fountainhead*," *Journal of the Society of Architectural History*, September 22, 2002, 322.

25. Rudy Behlmer, *Inside Warner Brothers* (New York: Viking, 1985), 305–6.

26. Behlmer, *Inside Warner Brothers*, 306.

Chapter 6: Gary Cooper

1. Brandon, *The Passion of Ayn Rand*, 205.

2. Untitled article, n.d., PNC.

3. Howard C. Heyn, "Patsy Finds Stardom Easy—Her Real Problems Are Nags, Autos," unidentified publication, July 24, 1948, PNC.

4. Schleier, "Rand and Vidor's *The Fountainhead*," 324.

5. Meyers, *Gary Cooper: American Hero*, 218.

6. Censors bureau, interoffice memo, July 20, 1948, USCTV.

7. PN, *As I Am*, 99.

8. Meyers, *Gary Cooper: American Hero*, 35–36. Gary Cooper was born Frank James Cooper on May 7, 1901, and was educated in England.

Lupe Velez (1908–1944) was one of the great loves of Cooper's life. However, she was emotionally demonstrative on almost every level, and she suffered from epilepsy. (Throughout their volatile affair, from 1929 to 1931, Cooper always feared Lupe would have a seizure during an intimate moment and that scandal would ensue if he needed to summon medics.) Their romance was damaging to Gary's emotional equilibrium, and eventually his health deteriorated. His weight dropped during their relationship from 180 to 138 pounds. But the affair opened Cooper up emotionally. On screen it had always been hard for Cooper to relax and especially to play love scenes. Following his romance with Velez, Cooper found expressing emotions on film somewhat easier.

His next relationship was completely different. Ostensibly in Europe to recover his health, Cooper was introduced to the Countess Dorothy di Frasso (1888–1954) in Rome. Married to her second husband, the penniless Count Carlo Dentrice di Frasso, she was both enticing and witty and was known for her humor, intelligence, and style. In short order Cooper became her kept man. "The countess taught the cowboy about good food and vintage wines, enough French and Italian to read the menus in the finest restaurants. She deepened his understanding of art by guiding him through the museums and galleries of Italy, and also let him drive her collection of racing cars," wrote Jeffrey Meyers in *Gary Cooper: American Hero* (77). (The relationship was parodied by the characters Countess de Lage and Buck Winston in Claire Boothe Luce's scathing comedy *The Women*.) When Cooper and the countess returned to America in February 1932, Cooper was quite a different man than when he left Hollywood. Shortly after their return, Cooper and the countess parted ways. He was always grateful to her for his grooming, and she always remembered Gary in her own special way.

9. On the Anderson Lawler affair, see Larry Swindell, *The Last Hero: A Biography of Gary Cooper* (New York: Doubleday, 1980), 104–5; Floyd Conner, *Lupe Velez and Her Lovers* (New York: Barricade Books, 1993), 85–86; and William J. Mann, *Behind the Screen: How Gays and Lesbians Shaped Hollywood, 1910–1969* (New York: Viking, 2001), 103–10. Anderson Lawler (1902–1959) was an aspiring young film actor, recently signed by Paramount Studios, when he met Cooper in 1929. He was also a well-known homosexual and a witty bon vivant. Lawler possessed a charm, and social connections, that Cooper envied. Lawler's knowledge of music, literature, and art was not lost on Gary, and Lawler eagerly adapted to Cooper's pleasures as well. The two men enjoyed hunting and fishing, as well as attending concerts together under

the stars at the Hollywood Bowl. Lupe Velez soon felt like a third wheel. She took to unzipping Gary in private to try to smell Lawler's cologne on Cooper's genitals. Lawler frequently stayed at the Cooper home at 7511 Franklin Avenue while Cooper's parents were away. When Cooper eventually took his own apartment on Argyle Avenue, Anderson casually moved in. Cooper's star was now on the rise. Cooper's and Lawler's relationship ended almost before it had begun, though they would remain friends until 1933. Lawler had served his purpose, and Cooper effectively discarded him. PN confirmed in conversation with SMS in May 2005 that she knew of this relationship.

10. Meyers, *Gary Cooper: American Hero,* 101.

11. PN, *As I Am,* 99.

12. Brandon, *The Passion of Ayn Rand,* 209.

13. Untitled article, n.d., PNC.

14. PN, *As I Am,* 99.

15. Arce, *Gary Cooper: An Intimate Biography,* 226.

16. Paxton, *Ayn Rand,* 138.

17. PN, *As I Am,* 106. Jean Acker Valentino (1893–1978) was once the lesbian lover of the great stage and silent screen star Alla Nazimova. She met the struggling young Italian actor, and part-time gigolo, Rudolph Valentino, and they wed on November 5, 1919. On their wedding night, she locked him out of their bedroom, and their marriage was never consummated. (She would tell Patricia the true reason she locked Valentino out was that he had gonorrhea.) The couple divorced in 1923. Jean then met former Ziegfeld showgirl Lillian Chloe Carter, and the two remained lovers until Jean's death. They owned the duplex on Fox Hills Drive when they met Patricia in 1948 and remained close friends with her until their deaths. They also played extras and bit parts in such films as *San Francisco* (1936), *Vogues of 1938* (1937), *My Favorite Wife* (1940), and *Spellbound* (1945). Chloe Carter was also a beautician.

18. "Good Deal for Neal," *Screenland,* January 1949, 69.

19. Euel Ewings, *Patricia Readings,* July–October, 1950, 10.

20. PN, *As I Am,* 102.

21. Hedda Hopper, "Looking at Hollywood with Hedda Hopper," *Chicago Sunday Tribune,* June 10, 1951, 6.

22. PN, letter to Malcolm Miller, n.d., PNC.

23. PN, conversation with SMS, 2005.

24. "Hollywood Film Celebrities Hobnob with British Royalty," *Los Angeles Daily News,* November 30, 1948.

25. PN, *As I Am,* 110.

26. PN, conversation with SMS, 2005.

27. PN, letter to Jean Valentino and Chloe Carter, December 12, 1948, PNC.

28. PN to Valentino and Carter.

29. Gary Cooper, night letter to PN, December 16, 1948, PNC.

Chapter 7: London

Epigraph. "It's A Great Feeling," music by Jule Styne, lyrics by Sammy Cahn, 1949.

1. John McLain, "Must Be Love, Old Girl," *New York Journal-American,* November 7, 1955.

2. Vincent Sherman, letter to SMS, March 25, 2003.

3. Vincent Sherman, *Studio Affairs* (Lexington: University Press of Kentucky, 1996), 183–84.

4. Sherman, *Studio Affairs,* 184.

5. Richard Todd, letter to SMS, September 3, 2003.

6. PN, *As I Am,* 112.

7. PN, *As I Am,* 111.

8. PN, *As I Am,* 113.

9. PN, letter to Jean Valentino and Chloe Carter, December 17, 1948, PNC.

10. George Shdanoff, letter to PN, December 25, 1948, PNC.

11. Gary Cooper, Jean Valentino, and Chloe Carter, night letter to PN, December 31, 1948, PNC.

12. Jack M. Warner, telegram to Jack L. Warner, February 8, 1949, USCTV.

13. Jack M. Warner, telegram to Jack L. Warner, March 5, 1949, USCTV.

14. Jack M. Warner, telegram to Jack L. Warner, March 21, 1949, USCTV.

15. W. E. Oliver, "John Loves Mary Light," *Los Angeles Herald Express,* n.d., PNC.

16. Lowell E. Redelings, "'John Loves Mary' First-Rate Comedy," n.d., PNC. Patricia told columnist Eileen Creelman in an untitled article April 6, 1949, "I'm no ingénue, and I don't think I can play one very well." MOMA.

17. Barry Farrell, *Pat and Roald* (New York: Random House, 1969), 61. Patricia told Howard Thompson: "As for Hollywood, I was so young that I suffered a hideous set-back. I couldn't relax in front of the camera. I've learned though. How? Kind friends have shown me how to radiate, rather than add, and I've studied under an excellent teacher. But adverse notices are a terrible discouragement when you're young—and vulnerable. They're an incentive, but they stick" (*New York Times,* November 2, 1952).

18. Box-office gross total amounts up to 1957 for PN's Warner Brothers films per records held at USCTV-Cinema Library.

19. Lydia Lane, "Patricia Neal Discloses Secret of Intriguing, Melodious Voice," *Los Angeles Times,* November 2, 1952, C11.

20. Maude Mahan, letter to PN, February 21, 1949, PNC.

21. Eileen Creelman, untitled article, April 6, 1949, MOMA.

22. Kirk Douglas, *The Ragman's Son* (New York: Simon & Schuster, 1988), 169.

23. PN, *As I Am,* 116.

24. Brog, *Variety,* June 24, 1949, PNC.

25. Malcolm Miller, "Music and Drama," *Knoxville Journal,* August 7, 1949.

26. Eura Neal, letter to PN, n.d. (c. 1949), PNC.

27. PN, *As I Am,* 116.

28. PN, *As I Am,* 116.

Chapter 8: Hollywood

1. Meyers, *Gary Cooper: American Hero,* 226.

2. PN, *As I Am,* 124.

3. PN, conversation with SMS, 2003.

4. PN, *As I Am,* 126.

5. Arce, *Gary Cooper: An Intimate Biography,* 229–30.

6 PN, *As I Am,* 120.

7. Arce, *Gary Cooper: An Intimate Biography,* 230.

8. Sergio Leeman, *Robert Wise on His Films* (Los Angeles: Silman-James Press, 1995), 94.

9. PN, *As I Am,* 118.

10. Jane Ellen Wayne, *Cooper's Women* (New York: Prentice Hall, 1988), 120.

11. Lauren Bacall, *By Myself* (New York: Alfred A. Knopf, 1979), 177.

12. Emery Wister, "Show 'Nuf," *Charlotte News,* February 10, 1950, USCWB.

13. Bradford Dillman, *Are You Anybody?* (Santa Barbara, CA: Fithian Press, 1997), 106.

14. Jerry Wald, letter to PN, September 15, 1949, PNC.

15. Marjorie Turner, untitled article, March 12, 1950, PNC. The cinematographer for *The Hasty Heart* was Wilkie Cooper, and his sensitive work was remarkable, accentuating Patricia's unconventional beauty. Perhaps the most memorable aspect of the film is the original music by Jack Beaver, directed by Louis Levy. Patricia and Todd's "I think I've shared a moment with kings" scene is heartbreaking, and all elements of the film meld.

16. Marjorie Turner, untitled article, March 12, 1950, PNC.

17. Louella Parsons, untitled article, January 28, 1950, PNC.

18. PN letter, *Patricia Readings,* July–October 1950, 2.

19. Ezra Pound, *Los Angeles Daily News*, April 14, 1950, PNC.

20. PN, conversation with SMS, 2003.

21. Bosley Crowther, *New York Times*, June 17, 1950, PNC.

22. Louella Parsons, *Cosmopolitan*, (c. 1950), PNC.

23. Lawrence J. Quirk, *Lauren Bacall: Her Films and Career* (Secaucus, NJ: Citadel, 1986), 107.

Chapter 9: Tinseltown

1. PN, *As I Am*, 127–28.

2. Harry Mayer, telegram to Steve Trilling, July 11, 1950, USCWB.

3. Jim Ruth, "Patricia Neal: Portrait of a Survivor," *Lancaster (Pa.) Sunday News*, n.d. (c. 1984), PNC.

4. PN, *Patricia Readings,* March–August 1951, 24.

5. John Buonomo, conversation with SMS, 2003.

6. Untitled review, n.d., PNC.

7. Kay Proctor, *Los Angeles Examiner*, n.d., PNC.

8. Bosley Crowther, *New York Times*, October 7, 1950, PNC.

9. Leonard Mosley, London *Daily Express*, n.d., PNC.

10. Reg Whitley, London *Daily Mirror*, n.d., PNC.

11. "The Reel Dope," *Family Circle*, October 1950.

12. Alan W. Petrucelli, "A Survivor's Story," *Primetime*, August 1997, 9.

13. Paul Picerni, telephone interview by SMS, May 20, 2003.

Chapter 10: 20th Century-Fox

1. PN, *As I Am*, 134. When Patricia found out that Gary had told Rocky about the pregnancy, she felt betrayed. This had been their child, and Patricia felt hurt that Gary would share this very private secret with Rocky of all people.

2. PN, *As I Am*, 135.

3. PN, *Patricia Readings,* March–August 1951, 2.

4. *Variety*, January 9, 1951, AMPAS.

5. *Fortnight*, January 22, 1951, AMPAS.

6. Bosley Crowther, *New York Times*, February 3, 1951.

7. "'Operation Pacific' Top Drama of Submarine Warfare,'" *Hollywood Reporter*, January 9, 1951.

8. Ruth Waterbury, *Los Angeles Examiner*, January 10, 1951, AMPAS.

9. T.M.P., *New York Times*, April 20, 1951, NYPL.

10. Untitled, February 27, 1951, *Variety* review, AMPAS.

11. PN, *As I Am,* 129.

12. PN, *As I Am,* 129.

13. PN, *As I Am,* 129.

14. PN, *As I Am,* 129.

15. Joan Fontaine, *No Bed of Roses* (New York: William Morrow, 1978), 205.

16. PN, *As I Am,* 130.

17. PN, *As I Am,* 131.

18. Darryl F. Zanuck, memo to Julian Blaustein, August 10, 1950, USCTV.

19. Arce, *Gary Cooper: An Intimate Biography,* 232.

20. Arce, *Gary Cooper: An Intimate Biography,* 232.

21. Elsa Maxwell, untitled article, April 1951, PNC.

22. PN, *As I Am,* 138.

23. Aline Mosby, "Impertinent Interview," *Photoplay,* August 1951.

24. Mosby, "Impertinent Interview."

25. Larry Swindell, *The Last Hero: A Biography of Gary Cooper* (New York: Doubleday, 1980), 281.

26. Wayne, *Cooper's Women,* 120.

27. Hedda Hopper, "Meet the Reel Neal," *Chicago Sunday Tribune,* June 10, 1951, 6.

Chapter 11: Purgatory

1. J. Hoberman, "Back to the Summer Suburban 50s and Its Dark Secrets," *New York Times,* November 10, 2002.

2. Hoberman, "Summer Suburban 50s."

3. Jim Hunt, telephone interview by SMS, October 21, 2003.

4. Norman Lloyd, telephone interview by SMS, March 10, 2003.

5. Lloyd interview.

6. Swindell, *The Last Hero,* 281.

7. Bosley Crowther, *New York Times,* January 13, 1951.

8. Arce, *Gary Cooper: An Intimate Biography,* 235.

9. PN, *As I Am,* 140; PN, conversation with SMS, June 2005.

10. Wayne, *Cooper's Women,* 121.

11. PN, *As I Am,* 137.

12. Wayne, *Cooper's Women,* 123–24. Louella Parsons reported in her Hollywood Highlights column on October 13, 1951 that when Gary held a seventy-eighth birthday party for his mother in September at the Bel Air Hotel, it was all very sentimental. "His mother sat on Gary's right, and Pat on his left," Parsons wrote. It is unlikely that this forced understanding between the two women was comfortable.

13. Bosley Crowther, *New York Times,* September 19, 1951.

14. *American Film Institute Feature Films,* 19511960, USCTV. One of the film's biggest contributions to the science fiction genre is its use of music and sound. Composed by Bernard Herrmann, the score made maximum use of two theremins, early Moog-like instruments, played for the film by Samuel Hoffman. Herrmann had used the theremin in Alfred Hitchcock's *Spellbound* and *The Lost Weekend* (both 1945). For the recording of the score, Herrmann employed the young Robert Moog, himself a fan and designer of theremins and later the creator of the Moog synthesizer. The theremin conveys in all three of these films an unnatural, "otherworldly" sound. The score to *The Day the Earth Stood Still* is uniquely compelling and remains one of Herrmann's most memorable.

15. Untitled, n.d. article, PNC.

16. Kay Proctor, "'Week End' Lots of Fun," *Los Angeles Examiner*, January 5, 1952.

17. "'Weekend with Father' Warm and Amusing Family Comedy," *Hollywood Citizen-News*, January 5, 1952.

18. During their separation, Cooper once came over to see Rocky at their home and discovered Lawford's toothbrush and other personal items there. He did not seem to be bothered by this, but on another visit he found Lawford working on one of his beloved cars. Gary berated him, saying, "I don't mind a man tinkering with my wife, but I won't have him tinkering with my car." Meyers, *Gary Cooper: American Hero*, 230–31.

19. Wayne, *Cooper's Women*, 125.

20. PN, *As I Am*, 141.

21. Christina Kirk, "Hollywood Rediscovers Patricia Neal," *New York Sunday News*, March 29, 1964; Meyers, *Gary Cooper: American Hero*, 232; PN, *As I Am*, 141; Lloyd Shearer, "Nobody Knows the Trouble She's Seen," *Parade Magazine*, October 13, 1963.

22. PN, *As I Am*, 142.

23. PN, *As I Am*, 144.

24. PN, *As I Am*, 145.

25. Meyers, *Gary Cooper: American Hero*, 259.

26. Stuart Kaminsky, *Coop: The Life and Legend of Gary Cooper* (New York: St. Martin's Press, 1980), 168.

27. Arce, *Gary Cooper: An Intimate Biography*, 236.

Chapter 12: New York

Epigraph. "Again," music by Lionel Newman, lyrics by Dorcus Cochran, 1948.

1. PN, *Patricia Readings*, March–August, 1951, 2.

2. Sheilah Graham, *Variety*, March 6, 1952, MOMA.

3. Walter Winchell, untitled article, March 10, 1952, MOMA.

4. Meyers, *Gary Cooper: American Hero*, 233.

5. Leeman, *Robert Wise on His Films*, 111. Fox executives liked the looks of Victor Mature and Patricia together and announced to the press that they were planning another film for the two, a melodrama called *The Desert*, to begin shooting immediately after *Something for the Birds*. When *Something for the Birds* failed at the box office, the other picture was shelved. It was eventually filmed in 1952 as *Inferno*, starring Robert Ryan (his favorite film) and Rhonda Fleming.

6. Hedda Hopper, "Patricia Neal's Heartbreak," *Photoplay*, August 1951, 80.

7. PN, *As I Am*, 150.

8. *Hollywood Reporter*, n.d. (c. June 1952), MOMA.

9. Wayne, *Cooper's Women*, 126.

10. Louella Parsons, "In Hollywood," n.d., PNC.

11. Louella Parsons, "Pat Neal Weathers Emotional Crisis, Plans Trip to Korea," n.d., PNC.

12. Brog, *Variety*, June 11, 1952.

13. Otis Guernsey, "On the Screen," *New York Herald Tribune*, June 14, 1952.

14. Ruth Waterbury, "Superb Cast in Spy Thriller," *Los Angeles Examiner*, July 26, 1952.

15. Brog, *Variety*, July 2, 1952.

16. Untitled review, June 27, 1952, AMPAS.

17. Bosley Crowther, *New York Times*, July 2, 1952.

18. Louella Parsons, "In Hollywood," n.d., PNC.

19. PN, *As I Am,* 151.

20. PN, conversation with SMS, June 2005.

21. PN, conversation with SMS, June 2005.

22. PN, conversation with SMS, June 2005

23. Johnny Grant, telephone interview by SMS, March 27, 2003.

24. Bill G. Barnett, letter to PN, June 5, 2003, PNC.

25. David C. Bass and Richard L. Salhany, original song "Pat Is Our Girl" and letter to PN, July 16, 1952, PNC.

26. PN, conversation with SMS, June 2005.

27. PN, *As I Am,* 152.

28. PN, "This Is the Real Me," *Screenland,* January 1952, 58.

29. William Hawkins, "It's Ol' New York for Patricia Neal," *New York Telegram & Sun,* December 13, 1952.

30. "Wash'n Comedy Warm and Mirthful," *Hollywood Reporter,* October 8, 1952.

31. P.V.B., *New York Herald Tribune,* November 15, 1952.

32. PN, conversation with SMS, June 2005.

33. PN, *As I Am,* 154.

34. PN, *As I Am,* 154.

35. PN, *As I Am,* 154.

36. Howard Thompson, "Portrait of the Lady Named Neal," *New York Times,* November 2, 1952.

37. PN, *As I Am,* 155.

38. Barry Farrell, "The Gallant Fight for Pat Neal's Life," *Life,* October 22, 1965, 112.

39. Farrell, *Pat and Roald,* 124–25.

40. John McLain, "Must Be Love, Old Girl," *New York Journal-American,* November 7, 1955.

41. PN, *As I Am,* 156.

Chapter 13: Roald Dahl

1. Jeremy Treglown, *Roald Dahl: A Biography* (New York: Farrar, Straus Giroux, 1994), 15.

2. Treglown, *Roald Dahl,* 59.

3. Farrell, *Pat and Roald,* 125.

4. Betty Lou Keim Berlinger, telephone interview by SMS, July 22, 2003.

5. Rollyson, *Lillian Hellman,* 335, 336.

6. Rollyson, *Lillian Hellman,* 337.

7. Rollyson, *Lillian Hellman,* 338.

8. Rollyson, *Lillian Hellman,* 337.

9. Iris Mann, telephone interview by SMS, April 12, 2004.

10. PN, *As I Am,* 156.

11. Mann, interview.

12. William Hawkins, "'Children's Hour' at 18 Still Shocks," *New York World-Telegram,* December 19, 1952.

13. Richard Watts Jr., "'The Children's Hour' Scores Again," *New York Post,* December 19, 1952.

14. Brooks Atkinson, "At the Theatre," *New York Times,* December 19, 1952.

15. Farrell, *Pat and Roald,* 125.

16. Gloria Lucas Young, telephone interview by SMS, July 23, 2003.

17. Rollyson, *Lillian Hellman,* 342.

18. Louella Parsons, untitled article, June 16, 1953, MOMA.

19. Treglown, *Roald Dahl,* 109.

20. Treglown, *Roald Dahl,* 109.

21. PN, letter to Jean Valentino and Chloe Carter, March 3, 1953, PNC.

22. PN, letter to Valentino and Carter.

23. PN, *As I Am,* 166.

24. Eliza Schallert, *Los Angeles Times,* May 27, 1953.

25. PN, *As I Am,* 161.

26. PN, *As I Am,* 162.

27. PN, *As I Am,* 166.

28. PN, *As I Am,* 166.

29. PN, *As I Am,* 167.

30. PN, *As I Am,* 166.

31. Roald Dahl, letter to Eura Neal, May 26, 1953, PNC.

Chapter 14: Marriage

1. Eli Wallach, interview by SMS, March 11, 2003.

2. James Dean was still learning his craft in New York, having already been in Hollywood and having appeared in New York on live television. Director Frank Corsaro at first felt that Dean was not experienced enough but then decided he could do the role because of all the quality actors from the Actors Studio in the production. Corsaro felt that Dean reflected the inner aspects of man. Producer Terese Hayden felt Dean was beautiful as Watson's mirror image. She thought that with his physical grace he made a difference.

3. Bradford Dillman, correspondence with SMS, February 4, 2003.

4. Frank Corsaro, telephone interview by SMS, October 14, 2004.

5. Walter Kerr, "Theatre de Lys Presents Revival of 'The Scarecrow,'" *New York Herald Tribune,* June 17, 1953.

6. Brooks Atkinson, *New York Times,* June 17, 1953.

7. Terese Hayden, interview by SMS, June 12, 2003.

8. Vernon Rice, "Pat Has That Extra Tension," *New York Post,* June 22, 1953.

9. Brooks Atkinson, *New York Times,* June 24, 1953.

10. Hector Arce, *New York Post,* January 24, 1980; Radie Harris, *Radie's World* (London: W. H. Allen, 1975).

11. PN, conversation with SMS, 2003.

12. Treglown, *Roald Dahl,* 113.

13. McLain, "Must Be Love, Old Girl."

14. Farrell, *Pat and Roald,* 127.

15. Farrell, *Pat and Roald,* 127.

16. Kasper Monahan, "Show Stops," newspaper clipping, n.d., PNC.

17. Harold V. Cohen, "'Children's Hour' at Nixon Is Still a Shattering Drama," *Pittsburgh Post-Gazette,* October 14, 1953.

18. Sidney J. Harris, "'Children's Hour' Still a Hit Play," n.d., PNC.

19. PN, *As I Am,* 210.

20. Gloria Vanderbilt, *It Seemed Important at the Time: A Romance Memoir* (New York: Simon & Schuster, 2004), 141.

21. Vanderbilt, *It Seemed Important at the Time,* 141–42.

22. Untitled article, n.d., PNC.

23. *TV Guide*, April 19, 1954, A-30.

Chapter 15: England

1. In 2003 science-fiction critic Dave Sinclair wrote on his Web site "Fantastic Movie Musings and Ramblings," "It is possible to make a low budget but thought provoking science fiction movie that emphasizes ideas over action, but it helps if you have an original concept to begin with, and you're not just doing a low budget take on an established movie? I managed to keep away. . . . It just makes me miss Gort."

Hollywood still showed some interest in Patricia, according to a report by Edwin Schallert in the *Los Angeles Times*, October 9, 1954: "Patricia Neal will have a chance to resume on the screen as Nefertiti, Queen of Egypt, in a picture that will carry just that as its title, with Ricardo Montalban enacting the Pharaoh. According to Montalban, the picture was to have been produced by Venturini-Cappolino Productions and set to begin shooting in 1955. It was never made.

2. John Francis Lane, in the January 7, 2003, *Guardian*, upon the death of Girotti, wrote, "[Girotti] was the most engagingly handsome of the young actors who emerged in the Italian cinema of the last years of fascism and the early postwar period." Girotti starred in *Ossessione* in 1943, based on James Cain's novel *The Postman Always Rings Twice* and directed by Luchino Visconti. Continued Lane, "The combined sexiness of Girotti and Clara Calamai was provocative for the times—as was the daring earthiness of the story—and marked the birth of what was later known as 'neo-realism.'"

3. PN, *As I Am*, 187.

4. PN, *As I Am*, 187.

5. Hedda Hopper, untitled article, December 6, 1954, MOMA.

6. Frances Herridge, "Women Cry, Men Laugh at 'Roses,'" *New York Post*, November 14, 1955.

7. Keim Berlinger, interview.

8. Rhea Talley, "Broadway Plays Minor Role in Pat Neal's Life," *Louisville Courier-Journal*, October 25, 1955.

9. Robert Coleman, "Familiar Themes in 'A Roomful of Roses.'" *New York Daily Mirror*, October 18, 1955.

10. Walter Kerr, *New York Herald Tribune*, October 18, 1955, NYPL.

11. Brooks Atkinson, *New York Times*, October 18, 1955, NYPL.

12. PN, *As I Am*, 192.

13. Sarah Booth Conroy, "Pat Neal, Here for Visit, Misses Baby," newspaper clipping, n.d., PNC.

14. Talley, "Broadway Plays Minor Role."

15. Talley, "Broadway Plays Minor Role."

16. PN, *As I Am*, 192–93.

17. Dorothy Kilgallen, untitled newspaper article, November 20, 1955, MOMA.

18. Chan, *Variety*, December 21, 1955.

19. PN, letter to Jean Valentino and Chloe Carter, December 27, 1955, PNC.

Chapter 16: Career

1. Wallach interview. Shortly after her stint in *Cat on a Hot Tin Roof*, Patricia was offered a role opposite Pat Hingle and the young George Peppard in an upcoming Broadway produc-

tion of *The Girls of Summer,* written by N. Richard Nash, produced by Cheryl Crawford, and staged by Jack Garfein. When *A Face in the Crowd* was offered to Patricia, Shelley Winters stepped into the role of Hilda Brookman.The play opened on November 19, 1956, to less-than-brilliant reviews and ran for only fifty-six performances.

2. Treglown, *Roald Dahl,* 126.

3. Treglown, *Roald Dahl,* 126.

4. Farrell, *Pat and Roald*, 64.

5. PN, *As I Am,* 200.

6. PN, conversation with SMS, 2004.

7. PN, conversation with SMS, 2004.

8. Jeff Young, *Kazan: The Master Director Discusses His Films*, (New York: New Market Press, 1999), 23.

9. "100 of Them to Be Seen in Film," newspaper article, n.d., PNC.

10. Andy Griffith, telephone interview by SMS, August 8, 2003.

11. PN, *As I Am,* 196.

12. Anthony Franciosa, interview by SMS, August 13, 2003.

13. PN, *As I Am,* 197. When production was completed on *A Face in the Crowd*, Patricia told reporter Lydia Lane of the *Los Angeles Times* (August 11, 1957), "It was such a pleasure working for Elia Kazan. He knows exactly what he wants and how to convey his ideas to you."

14. Radie Harris, "Broadway Ballyhoo," *Hollywood Reporter,* n.d., PNC. Immediately after the filming of Kazan's picture, director-producer Tom Gries offered Patricia the starring role in his projected film of *Jenessa*, with an original screenplay based on the UCLA play production by John Green. Patricia passed on the project, and it was not filmed.

15. Untitled article, n.d., PNC.

16. PN, conversation with SMS, June 2005.

17. PN, letter to Jean Valentino and Chloe Carter, December 27, 1955, PNC.

18. David Bongard, "'Face in the Crowd' Has Evil Gleam in His Eye," *New York Mirror*, May 19, 1957.

19. William K. Zinsser, untitled review, n.d., PNC.

20. Justin Gilbert, "'Face in the Crowd' Elia Kazan at Best," *New York Daily News*, n.d., PNC.

21. Edwin Schallert, "Kazan Film Powerful and Ironic," *Los Angeles Times*, May 31, 1957.

22. "You Would Notice Her Face in Any Crowd," newspaper clipping, n.d. (c. 1957), PNC.

Chapter 17: Triumph

1. Treglown, *Roald Dahl,* 127.

2. Tony Randall, telephone interview by SMS, August 20, 2003.

3. Raus, *Variety*, n.d., PNC.

4. Untitled article, n.d., PNC.

5. PN, conversation with SMS, 2003.

6. PN, conversation with SMS, 2003.

7. R.P.M.G., "Acting Family Off-Stage Producer's Success," n.d., BFI.

8. PN, *As I Am,* 205.

9. Kenneth Tynan, "The British Stage," *Holiday*, April 1956, 128.

10. "Williams' Play Called 'Slimy', Great By Britons," newspaper clipping, September 17, 1958, PNC.

11. Cecil Wilson, "Two Tortured Women by Tennessee," *London Daily Mail*, September 17, 1958.

12. Milton Shulman, "Tennessee Puts Miss Neal on the Rack," *London Evening Standard*, n.d., PNC.

13. John Barber, "Tennessee Williams Digs Down Still Deeper," *Daily Express*, September 17, 1958.

14. Harold Conroy, untitled review, *London Daily Sketch*, September 17, 1958.

15. Weyland Young, untitled review, *London Tribune*, September 17, 1958.

16. Kenneth Tynan, "At the Theatre—In Darkest Tennessee," *London Observer*, September 17, 1958.

17. Ronald Vivian, letter to PNC, n.d. (c. 1958), PNC.

18. PN, *As I Am*, 206.

19. Hayden, interview.

20. Chan, *Variety*, December 26, 1958, NYPL.

21. PN, *As I Am*, 207.

22. Sonia Austrian, telephone interview by SMS, August 14, 2003.

23. Austrian, interview.

24. PN, conversation with SMS, 2004.

25. PN, conversation with SMS, June 2005.

26. Untitled review, *London Star*, n.d. (c. 1959), BFI.

27. A. V. Coton, *Daily Telegraph*, August 7, 1959, PNC.

28. Elizabeth Wilson, interview by SMS, October 31, 2003.
The *Los Angeles Times* reported on August 19, 1959, that producer Irving Starr had offered Patricia a role in a film to be called *L'honte des innocents*, with a screenplay by Lou Breslow and Arnold Belgarde. The picture was not made.

29. Anne Bancroft, telephone interview by SMS, August 7, 2003.

30. Patty Duke, *Call Me Anna* (New York: Bantam, 1987), 75.

31. Henry T. Murdock, "'Miracle Worker' Is Superb Drama," *Philadelphia Inquirer*, September 14, 1959.

32. Don Ross, "One Big Happy Family in a Painless Program," *New York Sunday Herald*, n.d., PNC.

33. PN, *As I Am*, 210.

34. Farrell, *Pat and Roald*, 126.

35. Hobe, *Variety*, October 21, 1959.

36. Walter Kerr, *New York Herald Tribune*, October 20, 1959.

37. Brooks Atkinson, *New York Times*, October 20, 1959.

38. Ward Morehouse, "Patricia Neal Prefers Mom's Role to Star's," *Birmingham (Ala.) News*, December 19, 1959.

Chapter 18: Tempest

1. PN, *As I Am*, 211.

2. Duke, *Call Me Anna*, 68.

3. Morehouse, "Neal Prefers Mom's Role."

4. Duke, *Call Me Anna*, 67–68.

5. Art, *Variety*, January 27, 1960, NYPL.

6. Morehouse, "Neal Prefers Mom's Role."

7. Virginia Mayo, interview by SMS, July 1, 2003.

8. Blake Edwards, telephone interview by SMS, August 15, 2003.

9. PN, conversation with SMS, 2003.

10. Edwards, interview.

11. Edwards, interview.

12. PN, *As I Am,* 214.

13. PN, *As I Am,* 215–16; PN, conversation with SMS, 2004.

14. PN, *As I Am,* 215–16; PN, conversation with SMS, 2004.

15. Treglown, *Roald Dahl,* 138.

16. PN, *As I Am,* 216; PN, conversation with SMS, June 2005.

17. PN, *As I Am,* 216; PN, conversation with SMS, June 2005.

18. Austrian, interview.

19. Austrian, interview.

20. Farrell, *Pat and Roald,* 131.

21. Dr. Edmund Goodman recalled Roald's deep curiosity with every new crisis involving Theo's health. Roald saw that everything was being done and taken care of: "Any new problem aroused this wonderful curiosity he had, as well as deep feelings. He kept things moving. Roald always did that. Nothing was ever stagnant with him. He wanted to find out if there was anything to be done and to do it or try and get someone at it" (Treglown, *Roald Dahl,* 139).

22. Walter Winchell, untitled article, April 21, 1961, MOMA.

23. PN, *As I Am,* 223.

24. PN, letter to Jean Valentino and Chloe Carter, January 12, 1962, PNC.

25. A. H. Weiler, *New York Times,* October 6, 1961.

26. Judith Crist, *TV Guide,* n.d., PNC; Jerry Vermilye, *The Complete Films of Audrey Hepburn* (New York: Citadel, 1995), 153.

27. "Can Phoebe Hold Her Tongue?" *TV Times,* n.d. (c. 1962), 12, BFI.

28. "Glory for a Solo Talker Miss. P. Neal's Skill in Impossible Role," *TV Times,* January 15, 1962.

29. William A. Burns, "Superb Phoebe," *TV Times,* February 4–10, 1962.

30. *Variety,* February 2, 1962, NYPL.

31. Stack, interview.

32. Picerni, interview.

33. Keating, "The Second Life of Patricia Neal," 56; Kirk, "Hollywood Rediscovers Patricia Neal," 11. Ritt told Kirk: "She wanted the role very much. Who wouldn't jump at the chance to play with Paul Newman? But she wouldn't sign until I agreed to let her off about two or three weeks in the middle of the production so she could nip back to England and see her family." He met her terms, he said, because, "she stuck in my mind from the time I saw her on Broadway in *Another Part of the Forest.*"

34. Three films released in 1962 were the advance guard of this movement in Westerns: *The Man Who Shot Liberty Valance* (Paramount), *Ride the High Country* (MGM), and *Lonely Are the Brave* (Paramount). The last big-scale glamorization of the West would come in 1963, the year *Hud* was released: MGM's *How the West Was Won.* After John Ford's sweeping *Cheyenne Autumn* (Warners, 1964) the genre would never be the same. Gabriel Miller, *The Films of Martin Ritt* (Jackson: University Press of Mississippi, 2000), 52–53.

35. PN, *As I Am,* 241.

36. Keating, "The Second Life of Patricia Neal," 56.

37. Keating, "The Second Life of Patricia Neal," 57. *Hud* was filmed in Texas and Hol-

lywood between May 21 and August 1, 1962. In October 1965, after Patricia's illness, Barry Farrell's *Life* magazine article hit the stands. In it he wrote, "When *Hud* was offered to her six months after Olivia died, she accepted." Thus was etched in the public mind what followed in magazine piece after magazine piece, and even in Patricia's retelling of her life—that because Olivia had just died, she had asked Ritt to split her scenes. However, in newspaper interviews before Patricia's illness, Louella Parsons wrote in her syndicated Hollywood Scene column (September 1962) that Patricia was glad Ritt was allowing her the time off in the middle of filming: "Theo is beginning to walk just a few steps at a time, but is so encouraging to Roald and me. Although our picture isn't nearly completed, I'm flying back soon to be with my darlings." In Sheilah Graham's September 1963, article, "Yep, London Is a Wild Spot, Red-Wigged Pat Agrees," she quoted Patricia as saying, "I went home after four weeks, and came back after three weeks to Hollywood for another five. You can't go away from home for long, long months when your children are tiny. They forget you." The split in filming was also mentioned in an untitled article, July 7, 1962, "Her heart is in England where her three-year-old son Theo is recuperating from his seventh major brain operation" (PNC).

    Hud was previewed in late October 1962 in Los Angeles, and again in New York in an opening on December 31. John Buonomo attended the viewing of *Hud* in California and wrote Patricia shortly after that that he was overwhelmed by it. Her response, in a letter dated November 13, 1962, said, "I only hope other people react as enthusiastically." She added, "We have measles in the house." Buonomo received the letter the day the press announced Olivia's death.

38. Untitled article, n.d., PNC.
39. Paul Newman, telephone interview by SMS, September 30, 2003.
40. Newman, interview.
41. Kirk, "Hollywood Rediscovers Patricia Neal," 11.
42. Newman, interview.
43. PN, letter to Jean Valentino and Chloe Carter, September 25, 1962, PNC.
44. C. Hardy, untitled article, *London Spectator*, October 26, 1962, BFI.
45. PN, *As I Am*, 230.
46. PN, *As I Am*, 230.
47. PN, *As I Am*, 232.

Chapter 19: Tragedy

1. Alfhild Hansen, letter to Eura Neal, November 28, 1962, PNC.
2. Frankie Conquy, interview by SMS, October 12, 2003.
3. Conquy, interview.
4. PN, *As I Am*, 234.
5. Untitled article, n.d., PNC.
6. PN, letter to Jean Valentino and Chloe Carter, November 29, 1962.
7. Tessa Dahl, *Working for Love* (New York: Delacorte, 1989), 45.
8. Untitled article, *Radio Times*, November 22, 1962, PNC.
9. Austrian, interview.
10. Conquy, interview.
11. PN, letter to Jean Valentino and Chloe Carter, January 9, 1963.
12. Untitled article, n.d., NYPL.
13. Louella Parsons, untitled article, February 19, 1963, NYPL.
14. PN, letter to Jean Valentino and Chloe Carter, March 29, 1963.

15. Stanley Kaufman, untitled review, n.d., *New Republic*; Lawrence J. Quirk, *The Films of Paul Newman* (New York: Citadel, 1971), 121.

16. Justin Gilbert, "'Hud' Has Realism and Wallop," *New York Newsday*, n.d. (c. 1963), PNC.

17. Richard L. Coe, "'Hud': Rare Probing Film," *Washington Post*, May 29, 1963.

18. Thomas Wiseman, "A Heel—But you just can't hate this man Hud," newspaper clipping, n.d. (c. 1963), PNC.

19. Bosley Crowther, *New York Times*, May 29, 1963. The *Time* magazine critic (March 20, 1964) noted: "To all her roles, good and indifferent, Patricia Neal brings a sense of quiet excitement that speeds the circulation of contemplative men. . . . Her mahogany voice manages to create an air of sex without regret. Her steady eyes look through anything they see, and she creates the impression that no detonation could make her blink."

20. Newman, interview.

21. Pauline Kael, "'Hud' Deep in the Heart of Hollywood," in *I Lost It at the Movies* (Boston: Little, Brown, 1965), 88.

22. PN, conversation with SMS, 2003.

23. Untitled article, n.d., PNC.

24. Untitled article, n.d., PNC.

25. Graham, "London Is a Wild Spot."

26. Gerard Garrett, "Hollywood Warms to Patricia Neal after Her Startling 'Hud' Success," newspaper clipping, September 11, 1963, PNC.

27. Dame Judi Dench, letter to SMS, February 11, 2003.

28. PN, letter to Jean Valentino and Chloe Carter, September 2, 1963, PNC.

29. Dahl, *Working for Love*, 35.

30. Dahl, *Working for Love*, 38–39.

31. Dennis Hopper, letter to SMS, May 5, 2003.

32. Columnist Louella Parsons announced in the *New York Journal*, November 17, 1963, that Patricia had turned down a role in Alfred Hitchcock's upcoming thriller *Marnie* (1964) because she was pregnant. Patricia was most probably offered the part of Bernice Edgar, the mother of Marnie (Tippi Hedren).

33. Lloyd Shearer, "Patricia Neal: Nobody Knows the Trouble She's Seen," *Parade Magazine*, October 13, 1963.

Chapter 20: Stardom

1. Hedda Hopper, untitled article, March 11, 1963, MOMA.

2. Louella Parsons, untitled article, March 18, 1963, MOMA.

3. Hopper, untitled article, August 29, 1964, MOMA.

4. Hopper, untitled article, n.d. (c. March 1964), PNC.

5. "The Ring of Victory," *New York Herald Tribune*, April 14, 1964.

6. Ramsden Greig, "I Couldn't Be More Excited," newspaper clipping, n.d., PNC.

7. Greig, "I Couldn't Be More Excited." When Patricia received the New York Film Critics Award for *Hud*, she told Howard Thompson of the *New York Times* (January 26, 1964), "I'd rather have this. You win an Oscar, your price goes up and nobody wants you."

8. Herbert Kretzmer, "Everybody Wants the Oscars, but Triumphant Pat Neal Has Won One," *London Daily Express*, April 15, 1964.

9. Universal International Newsreel, c. March 1964.

10. Universal International Newsreel, c. March 1964.

11. Shearer, "Nobody Knows the Trouble She's Seen."

12. Parsons, untitled article, *New York Journal-American*, April 25, 1964, MOMA.

13. Howard Thompson, *New York Times*, April 30, 1964.

14. Ed Lipton, *Film Daily,* April 28, 1964, AMPAS.

15. "New Daughter Brings Joy Again for Patricia," *London Daily Sketch*, May 13, 1964.

16. PN, *As I Am,* 249.

17. PN, letter to Jean Valentino and Chloe Carter, May 20, 1964, PNC.

18. PN, letter to Valentino and Carter.

19. PN, *As I Am,* 246.

20. Untitled article, n.d., PNC.

21. Untitled article, n.d., PNC.

22. Willi Frischauer, *Behind the Scenes of Otto Preminger* (New York: William Morrow, 1974), 216.

23. Frischauer, *Behind the Scenes,* 215.

24. Stanley Frank, "Patricia Neal: A Woman's Fight to Live," *Good Housekeeping*, August 1965, 190.

25. Frischauer, *Behind the Scenes,* 215.

26. PN, conversation with SMS, June 2005.

27. Untitled article, n.d., PNC.

28. PN, letter to Eura Neal, August 15, 1964, PNC.

29. Untitled article, August 31, 1964, MOMA.

30. Louis Sobol, untitled article, *New York Journal-American*, September 1, 1964, MOMA.

31. Treglown, *Roald Dahl,* 157.

32. Arno Johansen, "Pat Neal: Her Luck Has Changed at Last," *Parade Magazine*, October 14, 1964.

33. Johansen, "Neal: Her Luck Has Changed."

34. PN, letter to Jean Valentino and Chloe Carter, November 10, 1964, PNC.

35. Louella Parsons, "Pat Neal to Star In Ford Film," *New York Journal-American*, November 16, 1964.

36. The following sources are used for the account of the next twenty-four hours, including the beginning of chapter 21: Farrell, *Pat and Roald*, 102–4; Treglown, *Roald Dahl,* 166–67; Roald Dahl, "My Wife Patricia Neal," *Ladies Home Journal*, September 1965, 54–55, 118–20; PN, *As I Am,* 252–56; Dahl, *Working for Love,* 51–53, 58–60; Tessa Dahl, conversation with SMS, 2003; Dr. Charles and Mrs. Claire Carton, interview by SMS, 2003.

Chapter 21: Illness

1. Treglown, *Roald Dahl,* 167.

2. Anne Bancroft, telegram to Dahls, n.d. (c. February 1965), PNC.

3. Untitled article, n.d. (c. February 1965), PNC.

4. Alex March, "Patricia Neal Critical after Brain Surgery," *New York Journal-American*, February 19, 1965.

5. "Patricia Neal's Condition Grave," *Los Angeles Times*, February 19, 1965.

6. "Patricia Neal May Survive Two Strokes," *Hollywood Citizen-News*, February 19, 1965.

7. Jean Alexander, telephone interview by SMS, September 16, 2003.

8. Else Logsdail, letter to Eura Neal, February 24, 1965, PNC.

9. Barry Farrell, "The Gallant Fight for Pat Neal," *Life*, October 22, 1965, 104.

10. PN, *As I Am*, 254.

11. PN, *As I Am*, 255.

12. Else Logsdail, letter to Eura Neal, March 11, 1965, PNC.

13. Sofie Dahl, letter to Eura Neal, March 15, 1965, PNC.

14. Alexander, interview.

15. Carson Brewer, "Pat Neal Wears 'Scars' with Flair," *Knoxville News-Sentinel*, October 15, 1965.

16. Brewer, "Neal Wears 'Scars' with Flair."

17. Hedda Hopper, untitled article, March 19, 1965, PNC.

18. Art Berman, "Patricia Neal Partly Paralyzed, Five Months Pregnant, Husband Says," *Los Angeles Times*, March 19, 1965.

19. Berman, "Patricia Neal Partly Paralyzed."

20. Vernon Scott, "Bancroft Sad to Be Pat's Replacement," newspaper clipping, n.d., PNC.

21. Scott Eyman, *Print the Legend: The Life and Times of John Ford* (New York: Simon & Schuster, 1999), 522–23.

22. Eyman, *Print the Legend*, 523.

23. Alexander, interview.

24. Dr. Charles Carton, telephone interview by SMS, September 28, 2003.

25. Louella Parsons, Hollywood Snapshots, March 27, 1965, PNC.

26. Claire Carton, telephone interview by SMS, September 28, 2003.

27. Parsons, Hollywood Snapshots, n.d., PNC.

28. Else Logsdail, letter to Eura Neal, March 22, 1965, PNC.

29. Pry, *Variety*, March 31, 1965.

30. "'Harm's Way' Stunning Action Film with Big Box-Office Potential," *Hollywood Reporter*, March 31, 1965.

31. PN, *As I Am*, 262.

32. PN, *As I Am*, 262.

33. Farrell, *Pat and Roald*, 33.

34. "Pat Neal a Little Hurt at Oscar Snub," newspaper clipping, n.d. (c. 1965), PNC.

35. PN, *As I Am*, 265.

36. "Patricia Neal Will Leave for London," *Los Angeles Times*, May 15, 1965.

37. PN, *As I Am*, 269.

38. Charles Davis, "Radiant Patricia Neal Meets the Public," *Los Angeles Times*, May 18, 1965.

39. Richard L. Coe, "Patricia Neal Sightsees Here," *Ladies Home Journal*, n.d., PNC.

40. Coe, "Patricia Neal Sightsees Here."

41. Coe, "Patricia Neal Sightsees Here."

42. *Newsweek*, untitled article clipping, May 31, 1965, PNC.

43. Untitled article, n.d., PNC.

44. PN, *As I Am*, 270.

45. PN, conversation with SMS, June 2005.

46. Barry Farrell, "The Gallant Fight for Pat Neal," *Life*, October 22, 1965, 107.

47. Austrian, interview.

48. William Tusher, "Patricia Neal: Her Valiant Fight to Live," *Motion Picture*, May 1965.

49. Farrell, "Gallant Fight for Pat Neal," 108.

50. Radie Harris, untitled newspaper clipping, July 14, 1965, PNC.

51. PN, *As I Am,* 277.

52. PN, *As I Am,* 278; PN, conversation with SMS, June 2005.

53. Farrell, "Gallant Fight for Pat Neal," 110.

54. PN, letter to Eura Neal, August 17, 1965, PNC.

55. Roald Dahl, letter to Eura Neal, August 17, 1965, PNC.

56. PN, *As I Am,* 282.

57. Roald Dahl, letter to Eura Neal, November 1, 1965, PNC.

58. Alexander, interview.

Chapter 22: Comeback

Epigraph. "The Remarkable Pat Neal: From Tragedy To Triumph," magazine clipping, 1967, PNC.

1. Stanley Frank, "Suddenly I Wanted to Live," *Good Housekeeping,* July 1967, 137.

2. PN, conversation with SMS, 2003.

3. Valerie Eaton Griffith, interview by SMS, October 12, 2003.

4. Farrell, "Gallant Fight for Pat Neal," 110.

5. Eaton Griffith, interview.

6. Ed DeBlasio, "We Watched Patricia Neal Come Back to Life," *Photoplay,* June 1967, 34.

7. Valerie Eaton Griffith, conversation with SMS, October 2003.

8. Untitled article, n.d., PNC.

9. Untitled review, n.d., PNC.

10. PN, *As I Am,* 276. Roald had sold their New York apartment with most of their belongings there, including all the furniture Patricia had had custom made in California and her silver and china. (One piece was a priceless antique she had purchased in South America. Dahl didn't know its value.) The buyer was a pushy fellow, and he intimidated Dahl. Gary's letters were simply left in the apartment, and Patricia never knew what became of them. "[Cooper] was a beautiful writer," she told the author of an untitled article in her personal archives. "His letters were filled with a quiet, pervasive passion. I kept all of them for many years, until they disappeared at the time of my stroke."

11. Lee Israel, "A Miracle," *Movie Life,* July 1966, 53.

12. "Patricia Neal: There's Only Sunshine Ahead," *Screen Stories,* July 1967, 85.

13. Bob Thomas, "Pat Neal Hopes to Work," *Los Angeles Mirror-News,* January 31, 1966.

14. "A Star Returns," *Daily Express,* March 25, 1966, PNC.

15. "A Star Returns."

16. Michael Walsh, "Courageous Pat Wins Once Again," newspaper clipping, n.d., PNC.

17. "Patricia Neal Wins British Film Prize," *Los Angeles Herald-Examiner,* March 24, 1966.

18. Untitled article, *Time,* April 1, 1966, PNC.

19. Treglown, *Roald Dahl,* 170.

20. PN, unpublished interview transcript, n.d. (c. 1983), PNC. Roald wrote a close friend about his feelings toward his wife around this time: "I love her. I'll never leave her. But I have to live with her all the time, and you would go round the bend within a couple of hours" (Treglown, *Roald Dahl,* 181).

21. Patricia Davies, "The Lovely Lady Who Knew She Could," *Motion Picture,* June 1967, 73.

22. Gereon Zimmermann, "Does Everyone Love Pat Neal? Oh, Yes!" *Look,* February 18, 1969, 84.

23. PN, *As I Am,* 292.

24. Edgar Lansbury, telephone interview by SMS, August 14, 2003.

25. Roderick Mann, "A New Triumph for Pat Neal: She'll Make a Film in June," *London Express*, n.d., PNC.

26. Stanley Frank, "Suddenly I Wanted To Live," *Good Housekeeping*, July 1967.

27. Val Adams, "Pat Neal Accepts Movie Role Here," *New York Times*, n.d., PNC.

28. Adams, "Neal Accepts Movie Role."

29. Adams, "Neal Accepts Movie Role."

30. Valerie Eaton Griffith, speech, VEGC.

31. PN, speech written by Roald Dahl, VEGC.

32. Barry Farrell, "Pat Makes A Radiant Return," *Life*, April 7, 1967. Patricia was seated at a table with Valerie Eaton Griffith and Lillian Hellman, when people at the speech came round to congratulate her. Among those were Eli Wallach and Anne Jackson, Lee Strasberg, Peter Cookson and Beatrice Straight, Van Johnson, Melvyn Douglas, Rod Steiger, Mildred Dunnock and Keith Umry, Elia Kazan, Otto Preminger, Sharman Douglas, Phyllis Newman and Adolph Green, Lauren Bacall, the Cusicks, the Goodmans, the Austrians, and Joan Crawford, who brought her own photographer. (The night before, Crawford had missed the posh pre-ceremony cocktail party at the apartment of theatrical attorney L. Arnold Weissberger. Her reason, she informed the press: "I'm a mother you know, and had to cook dinner for the children." (untitled article, n.d., PNC)

After the event, Patricia wrote that then Crawford every night "would call me at some unearthly hour, dead drunk, and talk my ear off, and she would snarl, 'All right, goodbye!' and slam the phone down" (Philip Wuntch, "Pat Neal Seizes the Last Laugh," *Dallas Morning News*, October 2, 1981).

33. Sidney Skolsky, "Patricia Neal Biggest Winner at Academy Show," newspaper clipping, n.d., PNC.

34. "Only Sunshine Ahead," 86.

35. PN, *As I Am*, 299.

36. PN, conversation with SMS, June 2005; PN, *As I Am*, 299.

37. Gene Shalit, "What's Happening," *Ladies Home Journal*, December 1967.

38. Untitled article, n.d., PNC.

39. PN, *As I Am*, 301.

40. PN, *As I Am*, 301.

41. Carolyn Lewis, "LBJ and Patricia Swap Heart Stories," *Washington Post*, n.d., PNC.

42. "Johnson Gives Award to Actress for Heart Work," *Tampa Tribune*, February 2, 1968.

43. Untitled article, n.d., PNC.

Chapter 23: Roses

1. Untitled article, n.d., PNC.

2. Untitled article, March 3, 1968, PNC.

3. Untitled article, n.d., PNC.

4. Untitled article, n.d., PNC.

5. Raymond Tuers, "Star Comforts Stricken Woman," newspaper clipping, n.d., PNC.

6. Richard Lemon, "Patricia Neal: A Star Reborn," *Saturday Evening Post*, October 5, 1968, 87.

7. "On 'Roses' Set, a Bouquet for Pat Neal," *Chicago Tribune*, n.d., PNC.

8. Eaton Griffith, interview.

9. Untitled article, *New York Times*, May 18, 1969, PNC.

10. PN, letter to Jean Valentino and Chloe Carter, June 1967, PNC.

11. Harvey Orkin, telegram to PN, July 26, 1968, PNC.

12. PN, postcard to Jean Valentino and Chloe Carter, n.d., PNC.

13. John E. Fitzgerald, "Blame," newspaper clipping, September 15, 1968, PNC.

14. John Mahoney, untitled review, n.d., PNC.

15. Lemon, "Patricia Neal: A Star Reborn."

16. Cecil Smith, "Glenda Jackson to Portray Patricia Neal," *Los Angeles Times*, February 12, 1981.

17. Richard L. Coe, "Patricia Neal: Living Legend," *Washington Post*, October 8, 1968.

18. Harry MacArthur, "Patricia Neal Relishes Her Life," *Washington Evening-Star*, October 9, 1968.

19. Judith Crist, untitled article, *New York* magazine, n.d., PNC.

20. Earl Wilson, "Pat Joins Oscar Derby," *New York Post*, n.d., PNC.

21. Vincent Canby, untitled article, *New York Times*, October 14, 1968, PNC.

22. *Time*, October 18, 1968, PNC.

23. Zimmermann, "Does Everybody Love Patricia Neal?" 86.

24. Dale Munroe, "Handsomely Mounted 'Roses,'" *Los Angeles Herald-Examiner*, October 18, 1968.

25. Charles Champlin, untitled review, *Los Angeles Times*, October 18, 1968, PNC.

26. John Torzilli, untitled article, *Knoxville News-Sentinel*, May 11, 1969, PNC.

27. PN, conversation with SMS, June 2005.

28. "Tears of Joy for Pat Neal," *Chicago Daily News,* October 26, 1968.

29. William Mullen, "Patricia Neal's Visit Brings Inspiration to Stroke Victims," *Chicago Tribune*, October 26, 1968.

30. Untitled article, *Hartford Times*, December 8, 1968, PNC.

31. Zimmermann, "Does Everybody Love Patricia Neal?" 86.

32. Untitled article, n.d., PNC; PN, conversation with SMS, June 2005.

33. PN, *As I Am,* 314.

34. PN, conversation with SMS, 2004; PN, *As I Am,* 314.

35. Rex Reed, "Pat Neal's Portrait of Courage," *New York Sunday News*, November 8, 1970.

36. William Hall, untitled article, n.d., PNC.

37. PN, letter to Jean Valentino and Chloe Carter, May 21, 1971, PNC.

38. Raymond Villwock, "Patricia Neal Talks of the Romances, Triumphs, and Tragedies of Her Life," *National Enquirer*, May 9, 1971.

39. Villwock, "Romances, Triumphs, and Tragedies."

40. Untitled article, n.d. (c. 1971), PNC.

41. Gold, *Variety*, May 12, 1971.

42. Ann Gurino, reprinted in *Motion Picture Exhibitor*, May 19, 1971, PNC.

43. A. H. Weiler, reprinted in *Motion Picture Exhibitor*, May 19, 1971, PNC.

44. PN, conversation with SMS, April 2005.

45. Dick Adler, *TV Guide*, December 18, 1971, 14.

46. Phil Strassberg, "Patricia Neal Builds New Career," *Arizona Republic Entertainment*, November 7, 1971.

47. Richard Thomas, telephone interview by SMS, September 15, 2003.

48. Tone, *Variety*, December 17, 1971.

49. Morton Moss, "It's Something Real," newspaper clipping, n.d., PNC.

50. Bill Barrett, untitled article, *Cleveland Press*, December 20, 1971, PNC.

51. Ann Hodges, "'Homecoming' Should Be Classic," *Houston Chronicle*, December 20, 1971.

52. Alan Bunce, "'Homecoming' on TV: Full of Hard-Won Kind of Joy," *Christian Science Monitor*, n.d., PNC.

53. Cecil Smith, "'Homecoming': A Christmas Story to Be Remembered," *Los Angeles Times Sunday supplement*, December 19–26, 1971.

Chapter 24: Television

1. Untitled article, n.d., (c. 1971), PNC.
2. Dick Kleiner, "She Oozes Class; Pat Neal Is a Real Lady," *Corbin (Ky.) Times-Tribune*, April 23, 1972.
3. Earl Wilson, *It Happened Last Night*, n.d., PNC.
4. Wilson, *It Happened Last Night*, n.d., PNC.
5. Christine Anderson, "Tessa Has Looks, Gestures Down Pat," *Knoxville News-Sentinel*, n.d., PNC.
6. Untitled article, n.d., PNC.
7. Bob Thomas, "Patricia Neal's Subject Is Roses Now," *Chicago Daily News*, August 27, 1975.
8. Archer Winston, Rages and Outrages, *New York Post*, May 7, 1973, PNC.
9. Murf, *Variety*, January 26, 1973.
10. Vincent Canby, "Baxter! Arrives," *New York Times*, March 5, 1973.
11. *Hay que matar a "B"/B Must Die*, www.imdb.com, 2003.
12. Anderson, "Tessa Has Looks, Gestures."
13. Eve Sharbutt, "Patricia Neal and Daughter Team Up," *Los Angeles Times*, August 24, 1973.
14. Jan Hodenfield, "Patricia Neal and Tessa Dahl Entitled," *New York Post*, July 28, 1973.
15. Robe, *Variety*, August 21, 1973.
16. Roger Greenspun, untitled review, *New York Times*, August 18, 1973.
17. Nancy Mills, "Patricia Neal: The Strong Smiling Type," *Chicago Tribune*, February 10, 1974.
18. PN, *As I Am*, 328.
19. Kay Gardella, "And I Think It's Grande," *New York Sunday News*, November 24, 1974.
20. Gardella, "And I Think It's Grande."
21. Gardella, "And I Think It's Grande."
22. Gardella, "And I Think It's Grande."
23. Tom Donnelly, "A Sensitive Season," n.d. (c. 1975), PNC.
24. Vernon Scott, "Stroke Victim Active Again," *Tallahassee Democrat*, May 14, 1975.
25. Peter Douglas, telephone interview by SMS, July 2005.
26. PN, *As I Am*, 332.
27. Treglown, *Roald Dahl*, 208.
28. Thomas, "Neal's Subject Is Roses Now."
29. Joan Hanauer, untitled article, n.d., PNC.

Chapter 25: Independence

1. Untitled article, n.d., PNC.
2. Treglown, *Roald Dahl*, 210.
3. PN, letter to Jean Valentino and Chloe Carter, December 4, 1974, PNC.
4. "Old-Fashioned Pat Alarmed over Daughter," n.d., PNC.

5. Hal Erickson, *All Movie Guide*, www.allmovie.com, 2003.

6. Margaret Chase Smith, letter to PN, September 25, 1976, PNC.

7. Sandra Pesman, "Patricia Neal, Smiling Survivor," *Los Angeles Times,* December 7, 1976.

8. Pesman, "Patricia Neal, Smiling Survivor."

9. PN, conversation with SMS, 2003.

10. PN, conversation with SMS, 2003; Helen Horton, interview by SMS, April 17, 2003; Warren Langton, conversation with SMS, May 2005.

11. Michael Silverberg, "More Than Job," *Knoxville Journal,* September 9, 1977.

12. Jeff Freedman, *Hollywood Reporter*, December 7, 1977.

13. Charles Champlin, "Turgid Tale in 'Widow's Nest,'" *Los Angeles Times*, December 7, 1977.

14. Bridget Byrne, "'Widow's Nest' Pathetic Outing," *Los Angeles Herald-Tribune,* December 10, 1977.

15. Roald Dahl, letter to PN, December 14, 1978.

16. William Hall, "Tessa Dahl Talking to William Hall; Report from Cannes," n.d. (c. 1978), PNC.

17. PN, *As I Am,* 345.

18. PN, letter to Chloe Carter, August 31, 1978, PNC. When Chloe Carter died, she was laid to rest beside her longtime lover, Jean Valentino, at the Holy Cross Cemetery in Los Angeles.

19. Patricia Neal has received four honorary doctorates: from Rockford College (Illinois), February 21, 1979; Simmons College (Boston), May 12, 1984; University of Massachusetts, Dartmouth, May 31, 1992; Niagara University (Buffalo, N.Y.), May 22, 1994; and an honorary degree from Northwestern University, June 18, 1994.

20. Sege, *Variety*, February 28, 1979.

21. David Ansen, "Sourkraut," *Newsweek*, March 12, 1979.

22. Vincent Canby, *New York Times,* March 9, 1979.

23. Malcolm McDowell, telephone interview by SMS, June 14, 2003. Patricia was offered a much better film role by Martin Ritt around this time, in *Norma Rae,* to star as Sally Fields's mother. Patricia regretted turning down the role, "But there was nothing to play. I guess if you don't live in Hollywood they don't think about you." Biographical notes, PNC.

24. PN, *As I Am,* 348.

25. Thomas, interview.

26. PN, *As I Am,* 354.

27. Untitled article, n.d., PNC.

28. Treglown, *Roald Dahl,* 218.

29. Ronald Reagan, telegram to PN, November 14, 1980, PNC.

30. Barry Koltnow, "Patricia Neal Tells Truth, Whole Truth," newspaper clipping, n.d., PNC.

Chapter 26: Divorce

1. Nancy Mills, "Roald Dahl Opts for the Children's Hour," *Sunday Calendar*, March 22, 1981.

2. PN, *As I Am,* 356.

3. PN, *As I Am,* 356.

4. Nigel Dempster, "Just Don't Bring Drugs into Class," *London Daily Mail*, September 7, 1981.

5. Susan Slavetin, "At 65, Roald Dahl Is Just an Adolescent," *Boston Globe,* n.d. (c. 1981), PNC.

6. "It's Tessa Slagging Off Glenda," newspaper clipping, December 17, 1980, PNC.

7. "Patricia Neal's Advice: Don't Give Up," *New York Times*, n.d., PNC.

8. "Mrs. Neal Responds," magazine article, n.d., PNC.

9. John J. O'Conner, "TV: Patricia Neal's Victory over Crippling Stroke," *New York Times*, December 8, 1981.

10. Ed Bark, "Patricia Neal Brings Life Back to TV," *Dallas Morning News*, December 8, 1981.

11. PN, *As I Am*, 358.

12. PN, *As I Am*, 358.

13. PN, letter to Chloe Carter, May 1, 1982, PNC.

14. PN, *As I Am*, 362.

15. Alfhild Hansen, letter to PN, September 20, 1982, PNC.

16. PN, *As I Am*, 364.

17. Joe Leyden, untitled article, *Houston Post*, n.d. (c. mid-March, 1982), PNC.

18. PN, conversation with SMS, 2003.

19. Untitled article, n.d., PNC.

20. PN, conversation with SMS, 2003.

21. PN, *As I Am*, 366.

22. Liz Smith, "She's Loved and Admired . . . and Out of Work," *New York Daily News*, n.d. (c.1 984), PNC.

23. UPI, "Gutsy Lady Won't Quit," n.d. (c. 1984), PNC.

24. Peter Feibleman, *Lilly: Reminiscences of Lillian Hellman* (New York: William Morrow, 1988), 357.

Chapter 27: Serenity

Epigraph. Poem by Michael Landon, 1974.

1. Mary Dryden, "The Tragedies and Triumphs of Patricia Neal," *Los Angeles Times*, n.d., PNC.

2. Untitled review, *Booklist*, March 15, 1988, PNC.

3. Joyce Sister, "A Private Hell, a Life Regained," *Chicago Tribune*, March 3, 1988.

4. Harry Haun, "Truth in Advertising," *New York Daily News*, n.d., PNC.

5. James Mitchell, "Patricia Neal and Her Remarkable Life," February 20, 1990.

6. Janet Maslin, "Two Old Sisters and a Love Interest for One," *New York Times*, October 12, 1989.

7. Mike Cidoni, "Patricia Neal Sparks 'Unremarkable Life,'" n.d. (c. 1990), PNC.

8. Hank Gallo, "A Tale of Two Sisters," *New York Daily News*, October 12, 1989.

9. Edna Tromans, "Star Power," *Saga Magazine*, December 1997, 24.

10. Ophelia Dahl, "Ophelia's Dark Fairytale," www.theage.com, November 18, 2002.

11. Dahl's work includes numerous children's books and collections of short stories, two novels, and several screenplays. In 2004 Felicity Dahl opened the Roald Dahl Museum and Story Center in Great Missenden. It is a museum and library center close to her heart, and a living tribute to one of England's greatest children's authors. In 2005, Felicity was an executive producer of the film remake of Roald's children's classic *Charlie and the Chocolate Factory*, directed by Tim Burton and starring Johnny Depp.

12. Douglas J. Rowe, "Actress with a Disaster-Filled Life is Stubborn and Fighting All the Way," *New York Post*, April 20, 1999.

13. Cindy Pearlman, "Hollywood's Grande Dame," n.d., PNC.

14. Lisa Kereluk Shaley, "Actress Describes Struggle," *Bristol (Va.) Press*, n.d., EMFC.

15. Robert Altman, telephone interview by SMS, June 23, 2003.

16. J. Hoberman, "Spring Fever," *Village Voice*, April 6, 1999.

17. Rex Reed, "Altman Goes South, Resurrects Neal," On the Town, *New York Observer*, April 5, 1999.

18. PN, Gary Cooper memorial speech, May 31, 2001, PNC.

19. Felicity Dahl, telephone interview by SMS, September 30, 2003.

20. Christopher Rawson, "Theatre Honors Put Women in Spotlight," *Pittsburgh Post-Gazette*, January 28, 2004.

21. Hal Bodeker, "A Juicy Portrait of Actress Neal," *Boston Globe*, June 26, 2004.

22. Marilyn Moss, untitled review, *Hollywood Reporter*, June 28, 2004.

23. Margaret O'Brien, interview by SMS, May 20, 2005.

24. PN, speech May 20, 2005, PNC.

Selected Bibliography

Adams, Leith, and Keith Burns, eds. *James Dean: Behind the Scenes*. New York: Citadel Press, 1990.

Alexander, Paul. *Boulevard of Broken Dreams: The Life, Times, and Legend of James Dean*. New York: Viking Press, 1994.

Arce, Hector. *Gary Cooper: An Intimate Biography*. New York: William Morrow, 1979.

Atkins, Irene Kahn. *David Butler*. Directors Guild of America Oral History. Metuchen, N.J.: Scarecrow Press, 1993.

Bacall, Lauren. *By Myself*. New York: Alfred A. Knopf, 1979.

Bailey, Margaret J. *Those Glorious Glamour Years: Classic Hollywood Costume Design of the 1930s*. Secaucus, N.J.: Citadel Press, 1982.

Basinger, Jeanine. *A Woman's View: How Hollywood Spoke to Women, 1930-1960*. New York: Alfred A. Knopf, 1993.

Baxter, John. *King Vidor*. Monarch Film Studies. New York: Simon & Schuster, 1976.

Behlmer, Rudy. *Inside Warner Brothers (1935-1951)*. New York: Viking Press, 1985.

Belafonte, Dennis, and Alvin H. Marill. *The Films of Tyrone Power*. Secaucus, N.J.: Citadel Press, 1979.

Bergan, Ronald. *The United Artists Story*. New York: Crown Publishers, 1986.

Black, Stephen A. *Eugene O'Neill: Beyond Mourning and Tragedy*. New Haven, Conn.: Yale University Press, 1999.

Blum, Daniel. *Great Stars of the American Stage: A Pictorial Record*. New York: Greenburg Publishers, 1952.

Blum, Daniel, and John Kobal. *A New Pictorial History of the Talkies*. New York: Perigee Books, 1982.

Blum, Daniel, and John Willis. *A Pictorial History of the American Theatre, 1860-1970*. New York: Crown Publishers, 1971.

Bona, Damien, and Mason Wiley. *Inside Oscar: The Unofficial History of the Academy Awards*. New York: Ballantine Books, 1987.

Brandon, Barbara. *The Passion of Ayn Rand*. New York: Doubleday, 1986.

Brooks, Tim, and Earle Marsh. *The Complete Directory to Prime Time Network and Cable TV Shows, 1946-Present*. 7th ed. New York: Ballantine Books, 1999.

Burrows, Michael. *Patricia Neal and Margaret Sullavan*. London: Primestyle, 1971.

Cardigan, J. H. *Ronald Reagan: A Remarkable Life*. Kansas City, Mo.: Andrews & McMeel, 1995.

Castelluccio, Frank, and Alvin Walker. *The Other Side of Ethel Mertz: The Life of Vivian Vance*. Manchester, Conn.: Knowledge, Ideas & Trends, 1998.

Conner, Floyd. *Lupe Velez and Her Lovers*. New York: Barricade Books, 1993.

Dahl, Roald. *Boy: Tales of Childhood*. New York: Farrar, Straus & Giroux, 1984.

———. *Going Solo*. New York: Farrar, Straus & Giroux, 1986.

Dahl, Tessa. *Working for Love*. New York: Delacorte Press, 1989.

Davies, Ronald L. *Duke: The Life and Image of John Wayne*. Oklahoma City: University of Oklahoma Press, 1998.

Dickens, Homer. *The Films of Gary Cooper*. Secaucus, N.J.: Citadel Press, 1970.

———. *The Films of Ginger Rogers*. Secaucus, N.J.: Citadel Press, 1975.

———. *The Films of Barbara Stanwyck*. Secaucus, N.J.: Citadel Press, 1984.

Dillman, Bradford. *Are You Anybody? An Actor's Life*. Santa Barbara, Calif.: Fithian Press, 1997.

Douglas, Kirk. *The Ragman's Son*. New York: Simon & Schuster, 1988.

———. *My Stroke of Luck*. New York: William Morrow, 2002.

Druxman, Michael B. *Charlton Heston*. New York: Pyramid Publications, 1976.

Duke, Patty. *Call Me Anna*. New York: Bantam Books, 1987.

Durgnat, Raymond, and Scott Simmon. *King Vidor, American*. Berkeley and Los Angeles: University of California Press, 1988.

Eames, John Douglas. *The MGM Story*. New York: Crown Publishers, 1976.

———. *The Paramount Story*. New York: Crown Publishers, 1984.

Eaton Griffith, Valerie. *A Stroke in the Family*. New York: Penguin Handbook, 1970.

Eliot, T. S. *The Cocktail Party*. Cambridge: Cambridge University Press, 1966.

Epstein, Edward Z., and Joe Morella. *Paul and Joanne*. New York: Dell Paperback, 1988.

Eyman, Scott. *Print the Legend: The Life and Times of John Ford*. New York: Simon & Schuster, 1999.

———. *John Ford*. Los Angeles: Taschen/US, 2004.

Falk, Doris V. *Lillian Hellman*. New York: Frederick Ungar Publishing, 1978.

Farrell, Barry. *Pat and Roald*. New York: Random House, 1969.

Feibleman, Peter. *Lilly: Reminiscences of Lillian Hellman*. New York: William Morrow & Co. Inc., 1988.

Ferber, Edna, and George S. Kaufman. *The Royal Family*. New York: Doubleday, 1928.

Fontaine, Joan. *No Bed of Roses*. New York: William Morrow, 1978.

Frischauer, Willi. *Behind the Scenes of Otto Preminger: An Unauthorised Biography*. New York: William Morrow, 1974.

Frommer, Harvey, and Myrna Katz Frommer. *It Happened on Broadway*. New York: Harcourt Brace & Co., 1998.

Gallagher, Tag. *John Ford: The Man and His Films*. Berkeley and Los Angeles: University of California Press, 1988.

Gelman, Howard. *The Films of John Garfield*. Secaucus, N.J.: Citadel Press, 1975.

Gianakos, Larry James. *Television Drama Series Programming: A Comprehensive Chronicle, 1947–1959*. Metuchen, N.J.: Scarecrow Press, 1980.

Gibson, William. *The Miracle Worker*. New York: Alfred A. Knopf, 1957.

Gilroy, Frank D. *The Subject Was Roses*. New York: Dell Paperback, 1965.

Harris, Radie. *Radie's World*. London: W. H. Allen, 1975.

Hellman, Lillian. *The Children's Hour*. New York: Alfred A. Knopf, 1934.

———. *Another Part of the Forest*. New York: Dramatists Play Service, 1947.

———. *An Unfinished Woman*. New York: Bantam Books, 1969.

———. *Pentimento*. New York: Signet Paperback, 1973.

———. *Scoundrel Time*. Boston: Little, Brown, 1976.

Henabery, Joseph E. *Before, in, and after Hollywood*. Lanham, Md.: Scarecrow Press, 1997.

Heston, Charlton. *In the Arena: An Autobiography*. New York: Simon & Schuster, 1995.

Hirschhorn, Clive. *The Warner Brothers Story*. New York: Crown Publishers, 1979.

———. *The Hollywood Musical*. New York: Crown Publishers, 1981.

———. *The Universal Story*. New York: Crown Publishers, 1983.

———. *The Columbia Story*. New York: Crown Publishers, 1989.

Holden, Anthony. *Behind the Oscar: The Secret History of the Academy Awards*. New York: Simon & Schuster, 1993.

Holley, Val. *James Dean: A Biography*. New York: St. Martin's Press, 1995.

Hunter, Kim. *Loose in the Kitchen*. Los Angeles: Domina Books, 1975.

Jerome, Stuart. *Those Crazy Wonderful Years When We Ran Warner Brothers*. Secaucus, N.J.: Lyle Stuart, 1983.

Johnson, Diane. *Dashiell Hammett: Life*. New York: Random House, 1983.

Kael, Pauline. *I Lost It at the Movies*. Boston: Little, Brown, 1965.

Kaminsky, Stuart M. *Coop: The Life and Legend of Gary Cooper*. New York: St. Martin's Press, 1980.

Kazan, Elia. *Elia Kazan: A Life*. New York: Alfred A. Knopf, 1988.

Lambert, Gavin, *Nazimova: A Biography*. New York: Alfred A. Knopf, 1997.

Langner, Lawrence. *The Magic Curtain*. New York: E. P. Dutton, 1951.

Leemann, Sergio. *Robert Wise on His Films: From Editing Room to Director's Chair*. Los Angeles: Silman-James Press, 1995.

Lloyd, Norman. *Stages: Of Life in Theatre, Film, and Television*. New York: Proscenium /Limelight, 1993.

Maltin, Leonard. *2001 Movie and Video Guide*. New York: Signet Paperback, 2000.

Mandelbaum, Howard, and Eric Meyers. *Forties Screen Style: A Celebration of High Pastiche in Hollywood*. Santa Monica: Hennessey & Ingalls, 2001.

Mann, William J. *Behind the Screen: How Gays and Lesbians Shaped Hollywood, 1910–1969*. New York: Viking Press, 2001.

McBride, Joseph. *Searching for John Ford*. New York: St. Martin's Press, 2001.

McClelland, Doug. *Hollywood Talks Turkey: The Screen's Greatest Flops*. New York: Faber & Faber, 1990.

McMurtry, Larry. *Horseman, Pass By*. New York: Popular Library, 1961.

Meyers, Jeffrey. *Gary Cooper: American Hero*. New York: William Morrow, 1998.

Michael, Paul, ed. *The American Movies Reference Book: The Sound Era*. Englewood, N.J.: Prentice Hall, 1969.

Miller, Gabriel. *The Films of Martin Ritt*. Jackson: University Press of Mississippi, 2000.

Morris, Michael. *Madam Valentino: The Many Lives of Natacha Rambova*. New York: Abbeville Press, 1991.

Nadel, Norman. *A Pictorial History of the Theatre Guild*. New York: Crown Publishers, 1969.

Neal, Patricia. *As I Am*. New York: Simon & Schuster, 1988.

O'Neil, Thomas. *The Emmys*. 3rd ed. New York: Perigee Books, 1992.

Osborne, Robert. *Seventy-five Years of the Oscar: The Official History of the Academy Awards*. New York: Abbeville Press, 2003.

Parish, James Robert. *The Paramount Pretties*. New York: Arlington House, 1972.

———. *The Tough Guys*. New York: Arlington House, 1976.

———. *Actors' Television Credits*. Metuchen, N.J.: Scarecrow Press, 1978.

Parish, James Robert, and Ronald L. Bowers. *The MGM Stock Company: The Golden Era*. New York: Arlington House, 1975.

Parish, James Robert, and Gregory W. Monk. *The Hollywood Reliables*. New York: Arlington House, 1980.

Parish, James Robert, and Don E. Stanke. *The Debonairs*. New York: Arlington House, 1975.

———. *The Swashbucklers*. New York: Arlington House, 1976.

———. *The All-Americans*. New York: Arlington House, 1977.

———. *The Leading Ladies*. New York: Arlington House, 1977.

———. *The Hollywood Beauties*. New York: Arlington House, 1978.

———. *The Forties Gals*. New York: Arlington House, 1980.

Paxton, Michael. *Ayn Rand: A Sense of Life; The Companion Book*. Layton, Utah: Gibbs Smith Publishers, 1998.

Peyser, Joan. *Bernstein: A Biography*. New York: William Morrow, 1987.

Ponzi, Maurizio. *The Films of Gina Lollobrigida*. Secaucus, N.J.: Citadel Press, 1982.

Price, Victoria. *Vincent Price: A Daughter's Biography*. New York: St. Martin's Press, 1999.

Quirk, Lawrence J. *The Films of Paul Newman*. New York.: Citadel Press, 1971.

———. *Lauren Bacall: Her Films and Career*. Secaucus, N.J.: Citadel Press, 1986.

———. *The Complete Films of Joan Crawford*. Secaucus, N.J.: Citadel Press, 1988.

———. *Paul Newman*. Dallas: Taylor Publishing, 1996.

Reed, Rex. *Conversations in the Raw: Dialogues, Monologues, and Selected Short Subjects*. New York: Signet Paperback, 1969.

Riese, Randall. *The Unabridged James Dean: His Life and Legacy from A to Z*. Chicago: Contemporary Books, 1991.

Rigdon, Walter, ed. *Biographical Encyclopedia and Who's Who of American Theatre*. New York: James H. Heineman, 1966.

Ringgold, Gene, and DeWitt Bodeen. *The Films of Cecil B. DeMille*. New York: Cadillac Publishing, 1969.

Rodgers, Richard. *Musical Stages: An Autobiography*. New York: Random House, 1975.

Rollyson, Carl. *Lillian Hellman: Her Legend and Her Legacy*. New York: St. Martin's Press, 1988.

Secrest, Meryle. *Somewhere for Me: A Biography of Richard Rodgers*. New York: Alfred A. Knopf, 2001.

Sheaffer, Louis. *O'Neill: Son and Artist*. Boston: Little, Brown, 1973.

Shepherd, Donald, and Dave Grayson. *Duke: The Life and Times of John Wayne*. New York: Doubleday, 1985.

Sherman, Vincent. *Studio Affairs: My Life as a Film Director*. Lexington: University Press of Kentucky, 1996.

Shipman, David. *The Great Movie Stars: The International Years*. New York: St. Martin's Press, 1972.

Sirk, Douglas, and Jon Halliday. *Sirk on Sirk: Interviews with Jon Halliday*. New York: Viking Press, 1972.

Stack, Robert, and Mark Evans. *Straight Shooting*. New York: Macmillan, 1980.

Staggs, Sam. *When Blanche Met Brando: The Scandalous Story of "A Streetcar Named Desire."* New York: St. Martin's Press, 2005.

Stapleton, Maureen, and Jane Scovell. *A Hell of a Life: A Memoir*. New York: Simon & Schuster, 1995.

Stevenson, Isabelle, ed. *The Tony Awards: A Complete Listing with a History of the American Theatre*. New York: Crown Publishers, 1987.

Swindell, Larry. *Body and Soul: The Story of John Garfield*. New York: William Morrow, 1975.

———. *The Last Hero: A Biography of Gary Cooper*. New York: Doubleday, 1980.

Thomas, Tony. *The Films of Kirk Douglas*. Secaucus, N.J.: Citadel Press, 1972.

Thomas, Tony, and Aubrey Solomon. *The Films of 20th Century Fox*. Secaucus, N.J.: Citadel Press, 1979.

Thompson, Frank T. *Robert Wise: A Bio-Bibliography*. Westport, Conn.: Greenwood Press, 1995.

Thomson, David, *Showman: The Life of David O. Selznick*. New York: Random House, 1992.

Todd, Richard. *Caught in the Act: The Story of My Life*. London: Hutchinson, 1986.

Treglown, Jeremy. *Roald Dahl: A Biography*. New York: Farrar, Straus and Giroux, 1994.

Vanderbilt, Gloria. *It Seemed Important at the Time: A Romance Memoir*. New York: Simon & Schuster, 2004.

Van Druten, John. *The Voice of the Turtle*. New York: Dramatists Play Service, 1945.

Vermilye, Jerry. *Barbara Stanwyck*. New York: Pyramid Publications, 1975.

———. *The Complete Films of Audrey Hepburn*. New York: Citadel Press, 1995.

Walker, Alexander. *Elizabeth: The Life of Elizabeth Taylor*. New York: Grove Weidenfeld, 1990.

Walker, Joseph, and Juanita Walker. *The Light on Her Face*. Hollywood: ASC Press, 1984.

Wayne, Jane Ellen. *Cooper's Women*. New York: Prentice Hall, 1988.

Wilkerson, Tichi. *The Hollywood Reporter: The Golden Years*. New York: Coward-McCann, 1984.

Williams, Mary Alice. *Quiet Triumphs: Celebrities Share Survival Strategies for Getting through the Hard Times*. New York: HarperCollins, 1999.

Williams, Tennessee. *Cat on a Hot Tin Roof*. New York: Dramatists Play Service, 1958.

———. *Suddenly Last Summer*. New York: New Directions, 1958.

Wright, William. *Lillian Hellman: The Image, The Woman*. New York: Simon & Schuster, 1986.

Young, Jeff. *Kazan: The Master Director Discusses His Films*. New York: New Market Press, 1999.

Zmijewsky, Boris, and Steve Ricci. *The Complete Films of John Wayne*. Secaucus, N.J.: Citadel Press, 1985.

Index